UNIX and Shell Programming
A Textbook

Behrouz A. Forouzan
De Anza College

Richard F. Gilberg
De Anza College

BROOKS/COLE

THOMSON LEARNING

Australia • Canada • Mexico • Singapore • Spain • United Kingdom • United States

BROOKS/COLE
THOMSON LEARNING

Sponsoring Editor: *Kallie Swanson*
Marketing Team: *Christopher Kelly,*
  Laura Hubrich
Editorial Assistant: *Carla Vera*
Production Service: *Publication Services, Inc.*
Media Editor: *Burke Taft*
Permissions Editor: *Sue Ewing*
Manuscript Editor: *Frank Hubert*

Interior Design: *Lisa A. Devenish*
Cover Design: *Jeanne Calabrese*
Cover Illustration: *Masterfile/Guy Grenier*
Print Buyer: *Vena M. Dyer*
Typesetting: *Publication Services, Inc.*
Cover Printing, Printing and Binding:
  R.R. Donnelley & Sons Company/Crawfordsville

For more information about this or any other Brooks/Cole product, contact:
BROOKS/COLE
511 Forest Lodge Road
Pacific Grove, CA 93950 USA
www.brookscole.com
1-800-423-0563 (Thomson Learning Academic Resource Center)

All products used herein are used for identification purpose only and may be trademarks or registered trademarks of their respective owners.

Printed in the United States of America

10 9 8 7 6 5 4 3

Library of Congress Cataloging-in-Publication Data

Forouzan, Behrouz A.
  UNIX and Shell programming: a textbook / Behrouz A. Forouzan and Richard F. Gilberg.

    p.   cm.
  ISBN 0 534-95159-7 (text)
  1. UNIX (Computer file). 2. UNIX Shells. 3. Operating systems (computers) I. Gilberg, Richard F. II. Title.
QA76.76.O63 F59715 2003
005.2'82--dc21

To my niece, Lily
Behrouz Forouzan

To Bob and Barbara
Richard Gilberg

Preface

UNIX was introduced to the world by Bell Labs in the late 1970s. From the beginning it was intended to be a powerful operating system that could be ported to a variety of hardware environments. Over the years, UNIX® has gone through many editions, versions, and changes; but it never lost its main feature—power.

UNIX was designed as an operating system for programmers and scientists who work closely with the hardware; it was never intended to be "friendly." Although its cryptic interface can be intimidating to anyone not familiar with UNIX, its ability to write short, powerful code to accomplish virtually any task is praised by experienced users.

Since UNIX was originally created, several operating systems have been created and died. Meanwhile UNIX survived as a niche product, highly useful in the scientific and engineering community, large corporations, academia, and most importantly, as the operating system of choice for the Internet. Most recently, we have seen it emerge as the underlying operating system for Macintosh™ OS/X and as the highly popular freeware operating system, Linux®.

Features of This Book

Our primary focus in this text is to present the new UNIX user with a progressive introduction to UNIX starting with the basics, followed by simple scriptwriting concepts, and concluding with writing shell programs. This breadth of material supports courses for UNIX users as well as majors requiring a solid foundation in UNIX. Readers from both academia and industry will find it a handy reference for refreshing techniques on seldom used commands.

We assume no knowledge of UNIX, although the reader should be computer literate. With this focus in mind, we present the material in a simple, straightforward manner with many examples and figures. The chapter-end materials contain several summaries along with questions, exercises, and lab sessions to assist the student in becoming familiar with UNIX's operation.

Structure and Style

One of our basic educational tenets is that good habits are formed early. The corollary is that bad habits are hard to break. Therefore, we consistently emphasize good command-line and scripting styles. Our experience is that if students are shown simple examples in a clear style, they will be able to remember them more easily in daily use. On the other hand, unlearning sloppy short-cut habits is very difficult.

Visual Approach

A brief scan of the book will demonstrate that our approach is primarily visual. There are more than 300 figures, 150 tables, 400 sessions, 125 scripts, and numerous code examples. Although this amount of material tends to create a large book, these materials make it much easier for students to follow the concepts.

Pedagogical End Materials

End-of-chapter materials reinforce what the student has learned. A list of key terms recapitulates the major topics and UNIX commands covered in the chapter. A list of tips to help the student avoid common mistakes follows the key terms. A list of commands, cross-referenced to their location in the chapter, provides a synopsis of each command and an explanation of its use. The important chapter topics are summarized in a list. Following the summary are three practice sets: review questions, exercises, and lab sessions.

Review questions are multiple choice and short answer questions covering the material in the chapter. The answers to the odd numbered questions are available on the Internet at www.brookscole.com.

Exercises are short assignments that help students understand UNIX as an operating system and master its general concepts.

Lab sessions are interactive exercises that give the student hands-on experience with UNIX commands. Starting in Chapter 13, lab sessions specify shell scripts that students write and run. All lab sessions require the student to sit at a terminal and work with UNIX.

Organization and Order of Topics

We have tried to build flexibility into the text so that the material may be covered in the order that best suits the needs of a particular course. Although we use the materials in the order presented in the text, there are other possible sequences that can be used depending on the objectives of a particular course. We outline four possibilities.

Objective	Semesters (Units)	Quarters (Units)
Introduction to UNIX for Non-Majors	Chapters 1–8 (3)	Chapters 1–8 (4)
UNIX for Majors (First Course)	Chapters 1–12 (5)	A: 1–8 (4 Units) B: 9–12 (4 Units)
Shell Programming Course	Chapters 13–18 (3)	Chapters 13–18 (4)
UNIX and Shell Programming	A: Chapters 1–12 (5 Units) B: Chapters 13–18 (4 Units)	A: Chapters 1–8 (4 Units) B: Chapters 9–12 (4 Units) C: Chapters 13–18 (4 Units)

Acknowledgments

No text of this scope can be developed without the support of many people. This is especially true for this text. The basic material was field-tested by our students at De Anza College. Our first acknowledgment, therefore, has to be to the hundreds of students who, by using and commenting on the text, made a vital contribution. We thank our students, especially Jay Zipnick, who diligently worked on the solutions to the review questions and exercises, and Scott Demouth, who proofread the text.

We would also like to acknowledge the support of the De Anza staff. Their encouragement helped us launch the project and their comments contributed to its success. To name them all is impossible, but we especially thank Ira Oldham, Clare Nguyen, George Rice, Letha Jeanpiere, Judy Miner, and Martha Kanter.

To anyone who has not been through the process, the value of peer reviews cannot be fully appreciated. Writing a text becomes a myopic process quite rapidly. The important guidance of reviewers who can stand back and review the text as a whole cannot be measured. To twist an old cliche, "They are not valuable, they are priceless." We would especially like to acknowledge the contributions of the following reviewers:

Jim Ball, Indiana State University
Ronald Czik, Boston University Metropolitan College
Mark S. Hutchenreuther, California Polytechnic University
Michael Paul Reed Johnson, Oregon State University
Sami Kuri, San Jose State University
Michael Lewis, New York University
Mary Ann May-Pumphrey, De Anza College

Our thanks also go to our editors and staff at Brooks/Cole, Kallie Swanson, Carla Vera, and Kelsey McGee. We would also like to acknowledge Frank Hubert (the copy editor—who was great) and Lori Martinsek, Susan Yates, and Paul Mitchell at Publication Services.

Last, and most obviously not the least, we thank our families and friends for their support. While authors suffer through the writing process, spending numerous hours on the computer, families and friends suffer through their absence. We can only hope that as they view the final product, they feel that their sacrifices were worth it.

BEHROUZ A. FOROUZAN
RICHARD F. GILBERG

PART I

Chapter 1
Introduction 3

Chapter 2
Basic vi Editor 41

Basic Concepts and Utilities

## CHAPTER I

Introduction

Welcome to UNIX, the *open* operating system. UNIX is found on virtually all computer hardware in use today. In fact, its very pervasiveness is most likely the reason you are starting to explore its capabilities. In this text, we introduce you to the basic aspects of UNIX as it is found in most modern installations.

To the casual user, UNIX is simple and easy to use. To the experienced user, it is powerful with a certain elegance that makes it extremely popular. We start with the simple aspects, showing you the ease and simplicity of the system, and then gradually increase your knowledge and understanding until you are a UNIX power user.

This chapter introduces you to the UNIX environment. After providing a basic understanding of its environment, we show you how to access a UNIX system and present its basic structure and some common commands.

1.1 Why UNIX?

Several features of UNIX have made it very popular. Its popularity is still growing, partially due to the development of the Linux version that has been ported to many platforms. In this section, we describe some of the features that have made UNIX so popular.

Portable

UNIX is found on more hardware platforms than any other operating system ever developed. Its widespread use can be directly traced to the decision to develop it using the C language. Because C programs are easily moved from one hardware environment to another, it is relatively simple to port it to different environments. All that is needed is a standard C compiler.

Multiuser

In an environment where hundreds of users connect to the Internet daily, operating systems must be able to support multiple users. The UNIX design allows multiple users to concurrently share hardware and software. The UNIX resource-sharing algorithms allow them to share the resources while at the same time preventing any one user from locking out others. In other words, it is a very democratic operating system, and everyone gets an equal chance at the resources.

Multitasking

Multitasking is an operating system feature that allows a user to run more than one job at a time. In UNIX, a user can start a task, such as a C compilation, and then move to another task, such as editing a file, without quitting the first. In fact, more than one program can be running in the background while a user is working in the foreground.

Networking

While UNIX was originally designed to be an interactive, multiuser, multitasking system, it was not originally a networking system. Networking was added after the split between BSD UNIX and AT&T UNIX (see UNIX History in Appendix B). Both developers, however, incorporated networking into the heart of the operating system.

Networking allows users at one location to log into systems at other sites. Once access is gained to a remote system, users operate just as though they were on a system in their area. Having direct access to a remote system means that, within the permissions granted to visitors, they can execute any UNIX command. Access to another system uses a standard communications protocol known as Transmission Control Protocol/Internet Protocol (TCP/IP).

Organized File System

With the large disk capacity in computer systems today, it is not unusual to have hundreds—if not thousands—of files in a system. UNIX has a very organized file and directory system that allows users to organize and maintain files.

Device Independence

UNIX treats input/output devices like ordinary files. This means that the input to a program can come from any device or file and the output of a program can go to any device or file. The source or destination for file input and output is easily controlled through a UNIX design feature known as redirection.

Utilities

Productivity is directly proportionate to the software facilities available on a system. Over the years, software developers have developed over 100 utilities that a user can use in a UNIX system and more are being developed continuously. This rich library of utility programs provides the user with easily used productivity tools readily available with short keyboard commands.

Services

In a large user environment, specially designated administrators monitor the system and help users when necessary. Often known as system administrators, they need support utilities to work with the system resources such as disk and security access. UNIX also includes the support utilities for system administration and control.

1.2 Computer System

A **computer system** is a combination of hardware and software that lets us work with a computer. The hardware is the physical equipment. The software is a set of programs (instructions) that allows the hardware to do its job. The components of a computer system are shown in Figure 1.1.

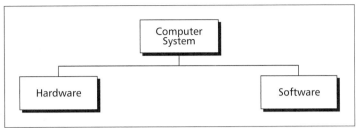

FIGURE 1.1 *Computer System*

Hardware

The **hardware** in a computer system is the combination of devices that can be seen and touched. Every computer, small or large, is made up of four basic types of devices: input devices, output devices, the central processing unit (CPU), and auxiliary or secondary storage devices. These components appear in Figure 1.2.

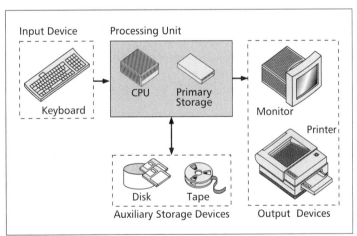

FIGURE 1.2 *Components of Computer Hardware*

Software

The **software** of a computer system is the combination of programs written to make the computer a multipurpose machine. It is divided into two different types: system software and application software. **System software** consists of the set of programs that serve the computer itself; that is, its primary purpose is to support the computer. It generally consists of an operating system and a set of support programs, such as disk copy, that provide general functionality. **Application software** consists of programs that are written to solve users' problems. They can range from everyday word processors to a specialized application that supports the operation of a dental office. Figure 1.3 shows this division.

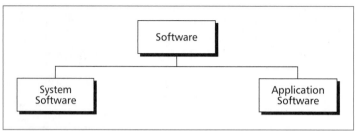

FIGURE 1.3 *Types of Software*

The Operating System

The **operating system** is a special category of system software that manages all operating facets of the computer; it gives the computer its heart and character. UNIX is an operating system. As such, it is different from other common operating systems such as DOS, Windows, and the Mac OS. Because it makes the computer what it is, an operating system is the most important part of a system's software.

Unfortunately, the term operating system is often used loosely. Sometimes operating system refers to all of the system software, which is too broad a use of the term, and sometimes it refers only to the central kernel, which is too narrow a use. In this text, operating system includes its primary tasks such as resource allocation and scheduling, data management including file input and output, and system security. Specifically excluded are the system auxiliary tasks such as text creation and editing, copying files, and sorting.

1.3 The UNIX Environment

UNIX is a multiuser, multiprocessing, portable operating system designed to facilitate programming, text processing, communication, and many other tasks that are expected from an operating system. It contains hundreds of simple, single-purpose functions that can be combined to do virtually every processing task imaginable. Its flexibility is demonstrated in that it is used in three different computing environments: stand-alone personal environment, time-sharing systems, and client/server systems.

> **UNIX is a multiuser, multiprocessing, portable operating system. It is designed to facilitate programming, text processing, and communication.**

Personal Environment

Although originally designed as a multiuser environment, many users are installing UNIX on their personal computers. This trend to personal UNIX systems accelerated in the mid-1990's with the availability of Linux, a free UNIX system. The Apple System X, released in 2001, incorporated UNIX as its kernel.

Time-Sharing Environment

Employees in large companies often work in what is known as a **time-sharing environment.** In a time-sharing environment, many users are connected to one or more computers. Their terminals are often nonprogrammable, although today we see more and more microcomputers being used to simulate terminals. Also, in a time-sharing environment, the output devices (such as printers) and auxiliary storage devices (such as disks) are shared by all of the users. A typical college lab in which a minicomputer is shared by many students is shown in Figure 1.4.

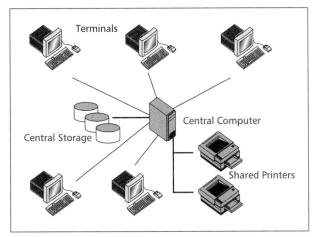

FIGURE 1.4 *The Time-Sharing Environment*

In a time-sharing environment, all of the computing must be done by the central computer. In other words, the central computer has many duties: It must control the shared resources, it must manage the shared data and printing, and it must also do the computing. All of this work tends to keep the computer busy. In fact, it is sometimes so busy that the user becomes frustrated and nonproductive because of the computer's slow responses.

Client/Server Environment

A **client/server** computing environment splits the computing function between a central computer and users' computers. The users are given personal computers or workstations so that some of the computation responsibility can be moved off the central computer and assigned to the workstations. In the client/server environment, the users' microcomputers or workstations are called the **client.** The central computer, which may be a powerful microcomputer, a minicomputer, or a central mainframe system, is known as the **server.** Because the work is now shared between the users' computers and the central computers, response time and monitor display are faster and the users are more productive. Figure 1.5 shows a typical client/server environment.

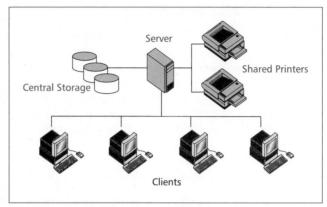

FIGURE 1.5   *The Client/Server Environment*

1.4   UNIX Structure

UNIX consists of four major components: the kernel, the shell, a standard set of utilities, and application programs. These components are shown in Figure 1.6.

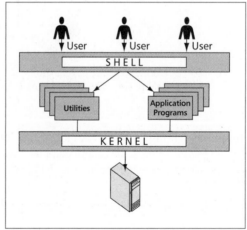

FIGURE 1.6   *Components of UNIX*

The Kernel

The **kernel** is the heart of the UNIX system. It contains the two most basic parts of the operating system: process control and resource management. All other components of the system call on the kernel to perform these services for them.

The Shell

The **shell** is the part of UNIX that is most visible to the user. It receives and interprets the commands entered by the user. In many respects, this makes it the most important component of the UNIX structure. It is certainly the part that we, as users, get to know the most. To do anything in the system, we must give the shell a command. If the command requires a utility, the shell requests that the kernel execute the utility. If the command requires an application program, the shell requests that it be run. The shells are shown in Figure 1.7.

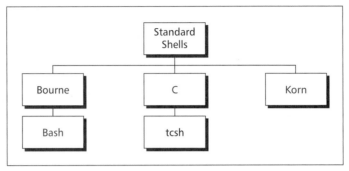

FIGURE 1.7   *Some Standard UNIX Shells*

There are two major parts of a shell. The first is the interpreter. The interpreter reads your commands and works with the kernel to execute them. The second part of the shell is a programming capability that allows you to write a shell (command) script. A **shell script** is a file that contains shell commands that perform a useful function. It is also known as a **shell program.**

There are three standard shells used in UNIX today. The Bourne shell, developed by Steve Bourne at the AT&T Labs, is the oldest. Because it is the oldest and the most primitive, it is not used on many systems today. An enhanced version of the Bourne shell, called Bash (Bourne again shell), is used in Linux.

The C shell, developed in Berkeley by Bill Joy, received its name from the fact that its commands were supposed to look like C statements. A compatible version of the C shell, tcsh,[1] is used in Linux.

The Korn shell, developed by David Korn, also of the AT&T Labs, is the newest and most powerful. Because it was developed at the AT&T Labs, it is compatible with the Bourne shell. We use the Korn shell for our examples in the first part of this text. We discuss the other shells when we discuss script programming.

Utilities

There are literally hundreds of UNIX utilities. A **utility** is a standard UNIX program that provides a support process for users. Three common utilities are text editors, search programs, and sort programs.

Many of the system utilities are actually sophisticated applications. For example, the UNIX email system is considered a utility as are the three common text editors, **vi, emacs,** and **pico.** All four of these utilities are large systems in themselves. Other utilities are short, simple functions. For example, the list (**ls**) utility displays the files that reside on a disk.

---

[1]The tcsh shell is pronounced tee-cee shell.

Applications

Applications are programs that are not a standard part of UNIX. Written by systems administrators, professional programmers, or users, they provide an extended capability to the system. In fact, many of the standard utilities started out as applications years ago and proved so useful that they are now part of the system. We discuss writing applications when we cover shell script writing in the second half of the text.

1.5 Accessing UNIX

In this section, we discuss some of the basic concepts that you use to access UNIX. To begin, you need to **log in** to the system before doing any work with UNIX. Once you are logged in, you enter commands and the system responds. When you have finished your work, you log out. The time spent working with the system is known as a **session.**

User ID

When you work with your own computer at home, you don't need to log in or be too concerned about who uses the system. When you work in a UNIX environment, however, security and user control become major concerns. Generally, you cannot access the computer until you have been given permission to do so. Permission comes in the form of an account created by the system administrator (sys admin). You and your account are identified by a special code known as a **user id.**

Passwords

To ensure that it is really you at the other end of the line, you must enter a password. A **password** is a secret code that you supply to the server and that is known only to you. UNIX encrypts passwords when it stores them in the server so that no one can figure out what they are. Not even the sys admin, who has absolute control over the server, can tell you what your password is if you forget it. All he or she can do is **reset** it so that you can create a new one.

> **Your password must be safeguarded: Never share it with anyone.**

Many systems require that your password fit a secure profile. For example, besides being easy for you to remember, a good password has at least six characters. It should contain both upper- and lowercase letters, along with at least one digit or special character. Obviously, if you follow these rules, your password will not be a word that can be found in a dictionary. You should not use your name, the name of a friend, or any other word that people who know you well might guess.

You can also expect that you will have to change your password from time to time. Depending on the system and the type of work being done on it, password changes may be required weekly, monthly, quarterly, or semiannually.

Interactive Session

The interactive session in Figure 1.8 contains three steps: login, interaction, and logout.

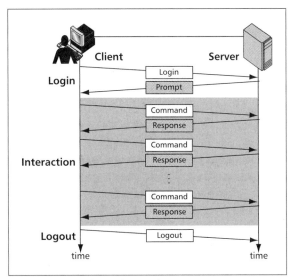

FIGURE 1.8   *Interactive Session*

Login

The details of the **login** process vary from system to system. There is a general pattern to the steps, however, as listed here.

1. You must make contact with the system.

   If you are working on a local network and are always connected to a remote server, starting the **login** process is as simple as selecting an option in a menu. On the other hand, if you are making the connection from a remote location, such as from home to work, then you will need to use special connection software, often referred to as **Telnet** software.

2. Wait for the system **login** prompt.

   Once you have connected to the server, you must wait for the server to ask you to identify yourself. Note that good security requires that the server give you only the minimum information you need to make the connection. This is usually just a **login** prompt, sometimes with the name of the system. A typical **login** prompt is:

   ```
   login:
   ```

3. Type user id.

   Once the server has responded with a request for you to identify yourself, enter your user id. Note that UNIX is a case-sensitive system. This means that the uppercase letter A is different than the lowercase letter a. Usually, your user id is all lowercase. If it contains both uppercase and lowercase, you must type it exactly as it was given to you.

UNIX is case sensitive.

---

4. Type your password.

   After you enter your user id, the system will prompt you for your password. The password prompt is almost always the word Password on a new line. As you type your password, it will not be displayed on the screen. This is another security caution—somebody may be watching over your shoulder to learn your password. In the following example, the system displays an asterisk for each letter of the password. Some systems don't even display the asterisks; they just leave the screen blank.

```
Password: ******
```

If you do everything correctly, you will see a shell prompt. If you make a mistake, the system will give you a cryptic error message, such as "login incorrect," and ask for your user id again. Don't expect a lot of help from the system. It expects you to be able to **log in** without help. Yes, this is another one of those security precautions.

The default system prompt for the bourne, bash, and korn shells is a dollar sign ($). For the C and tcsh shells, the prompt is a percentage sign (%).

The default system prompts are:
   $ bourne, bash, and korn shells
   % C and tcsh shells

Interaction

Once you connect to the server, you can enter commands that allow you to work with the computer. Typical commands allow you to work with files—edit, copy, and sort; process data and print the result; send and receive mail; and many other processing operations.

Logout

It is very important that you log out when you are through with the system. There are several reasons for this. First, it frees system resources for others who may need to use them. More important, it is a security concern to leave a terminal logged in with no one working at it. Some unauthorized person may walk up and gain access to the system, and your files, if you do not log out.

> **Never leave the computer without logging out when you are working in a time-sharing or network environment.**

Although there are variations in the logout command, it is most typically the typed command, **logout,** at the system prompt.

```
$ logout
```

A typical user session appears in Session 1.1.

SESSION 1.1   *A Typical User Session*

```
IRIX (voyager)
      This system is for the use of authorized users only.
login: gilberg
password:

UNIX BSD Release 4.0
  Welcome ...
$ ls
file1 file2 file3
$ cat file1
  Hello World!
  .
  .
  .
$ logout
```

1.6 Commands

The basis of all UNIX interaction is the command. Commands are not unique to UNIX. Many other systems, most notably MS-DOS, use commands. While they are generally a single line entered at a console, they can also be included in executable files to form scripts.

In this section, we introduce the basic concept and format of the UNIX command. Once we have covered its general format, we introduce some simple but useful commands.

Basic Concepts

A UNIX command is an action request given to the UNIX shell for execution. The simplest commands are a single line entered at the command line prompt that cause a program or shell script to be executed. Often the program is a UNIX utility; it may also be an application program.

Source and Destination of Data

All UNIX commands apply an action or a series of actions to some input data and create some output data. Although we do not need to worry about *how* the command does its job, we must understand exactly *what* it does. We must also know where to find the input and where we want the output placed. The input usually comes from the keyboard; the output is usually shown on the monitor (screen). To get from the input to the output, the data must be processed by a program.

There are a variety of sources that input data. For example, input can come from the keyboard, from files on a disk, or from a work file controlled by the shell. In a similar fashion, output data can go to the monitor, to a file residing on the disk, to a printer, or to a work file. Figure 1.9 demonstrates different source and destination points.

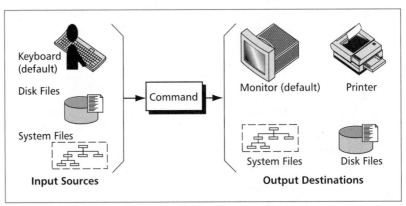

FIGURE 1.9   *Command Source and Destination*

Although most UNIX commands use the keyboard or system files as the normal sources for data, this is not always true. For each command, we must check and find out the default input source and output destination.

Command Syntax

Commands are entered at the shell prompt. You must see the prompt, such as the Korn shell $ prompt, before you can enter a command. Every command must have a verb and may also have options and arguments. The command format is:

```
$ verb [options] [arguments]
```

The brackets indicate that the options and arguments are optional. We use this notation when we describe individual commands. If an option or argument is in brackets, it is optional. If it is not in brackets, it is required.

The **verb** is the command name. The command indicates what action is to be taken. This action concept gives us the name *verb* for action.

The **option** modifies how the action is applied. For example, when we display the date, we can use an option to specify if we want the time in Greenwich Mean Time or local time. Options are usually one character preceded by a minus sign or a plus sign. Many commands, however, have multiple options available.

Finally, the **argument** provides additional information to the command. For example, when displaying the contents of a file, an argument can be used to specify the name of the file. Some commands have no arguments, some accept only one argument, and some accept multiple arguments. You must know, for each command you use, what are the options and what are the arguments. The general format or syntax of a command appears in Figure 1.10.

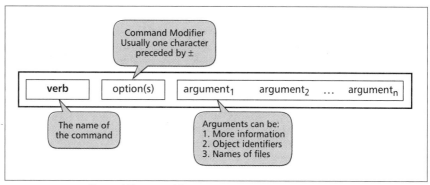

FIGURE 1.10 *General Command Format*

1.7 Common Commands

In this section, we present some of the simpler UNIX commands as an introduction to the system. You will find that many of these commands are used regularly by users. As we proceed through the text, we will introduce many more.

Date and Time (date) Command

The **date** command displays the system date and the time. If the system is local—that is, one in your own area—it is the current time. If the system is remote, such as across the country somewhere, the reply will contain the time where the system is physically located. By using an option, you can even get the current Greenwich Mean Time (GMT). Each date response indicates what time zone is being used. For example, 17:56:52 PST indicates that the time is Pacific Standard Time. The concept and the general format of the command are shown in Figure 1.11.

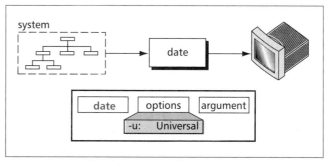

FIGURE 1.11 *The **date** Command*

The input for **date** is the system itself; the date is actually maintained in the computer as a part of the operating system. Most modern hardware also has a hardware date and time clock that is often updated automatically to ensure that it is accurate. The **date** command sends its response to the monitor.

If you enter the **date** command without any options, it displays the current date and time as shown in the following example:

```
$ date
Wed Mar 6 17:56:52 PST 2002
```

The **date** command has only one user option and one argument. If no option is used, the time is local time. If a -u option is used, the time is GMT. The following example shows the time displayed in GMT:

```
$ date -u
Wed Apr 3 08:24:19 GMT 2002
```

The **date** command argument allows you to customize the format of the date. For example, you can spell out the month and day or omit them entirely rather than use the standard abbreviations. To create your own format, you use arguments.

Command arguments are tailored to the command. Because different arguments have different requirements, each command requires a unique set of arguments. For the **date** command, the format is a plus sign (+) followed by text and a series of format codes all enclosed in double quote marks. Each code is preceded by a percentage sign (%) that identifies it as a code. Text may appear anywhere in the argument and is displayed just as it is entered. The output display follows the command on the console. For example, the following argument prints the date and text as shown:

```
$ date "+Today's date is: %D. The time is: %T"
Today's date is: 03/15/02. The time is: 15:25:16
```

Although you would seldom display a specially formatted date on the console, you will find the date arguments very useful when you are preparing a report or other output where you need to tailor the date's format. In these cases, the date command is usually included as part of a script. The date formats are shown in Table 1.1.

TABLE 1.1 **date** *Arguments*

Format Code	Explanation
a	abbreviated weekday name, such as Mon
A	full weekday name, such as Monday
b	abbreviated month name, such as Jan
B	full month name, such as January
d	day of the month with two digits (leading zeros), such as 01, 02, . . . , 31
e	day of the month with spaces replacing leading zeros, such as 1, 2, . . . , 31

Continued

TABLE 1.1 **date** *Arguments*

Format Code	Explanation
D	date in the format mm/dd/yy, such as 01/01/99
H	military time two-digit hour, such as 00, 01, . . . , 23
I	civilian time two-digit hour, such as 00, 01, . . . , 12
j	Julian date (Day of the year), such as 001, 002, . . . , 366
m	numeric two-digit month, such as 01, 02, . . . , 12
M	two-digit minute, such as 00, 01, . . . , 59
n	newline character (used to display date on multiple lines)
p	display am or pm
r	time in format hour:minute:second with am/pm, such as 01:15:33 pm
R	time in format hour:minute, such as 13:15
S	seconds as a decimal number [00–61], allows for leap seconds
t	tab character
T	time in format hour:minute:second, such as 13:15:48
U	week number of year, such as 00, 01, . . . , 53
W	week of year [00–53] with Monday being first day of week; all days preceding the first Sunday of the year are in week 0
y	year within century (offset from %C) as a decimal number [00–99]
Y	year as ccyy (4 digits)
Z	time zone name, or no characters if no time zone is determinable

The **date** command can also be used to set the date and the time, but only by a system administrator.

Calendar (cal) Command

The calendar command, **cal,** displays the calendar for a specified month or for a year. It is an example of a command that has no options but uses arguments. Its general format is in Figure 1.12.

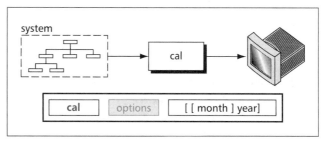

FIGURE 1.12 *The* **Calendar** *Command*

As shown in Figure 1.12, there are two arguments and no options for the calendar command. The arguments are optional: If no arguments are entered, the calendar for the current month is printed. If only one argument is entered, it is assumed to be a year, and the calendar for that year is displayed. If both a month and a year are entered, then just one month is displayed. Note that the two arguments are separate. To print the month for January 2001, you must enter 1 2001, not 1/2001. Also, a four-digit year is required. If you enter 1 01 you will get the calendar for January in the year 01, not 2001! The command to print the calendar for January 2001 is shown in Session 1.2.

SESSION 1.2 *Calendar Output*

```
$ cal 1 2001
    January 2001
 S  M Tu  W Th  F  S
    1  2  3  4  5  6
 7  8  9 10 11 12 13
14 15 16 17 18 19 20
21 22 23 24 25 26 27
28 29 30 31
```

Who's Online (who) Command

The **who** command displays all users currently logged into the system. As we will see in Chapter 7, Communications, you can send messages to other people logged into the system. Before you do, however, you should check to make sure that they are in fact logged in. The general format of the **who** command is presented in Figure 1.13.

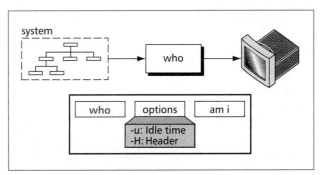

FIGURE 1.13 *The **who** Command*

The **who** command returns the user's name (id), terminal, and time he or she logged in. A basic **who** command is shown in Session 1.3.

SESSION 1.3 *Basic **who** Command*

```
$ who
nb045527     ttyq0        Mar 15 15:23
tran         ttyq1        Mar 10 12:15
```

Continued

SESSION 1.3   *Basic **who** Command*

```
gilberg      ttyq5         Mar 15 14:57
ryan         ttyq12        Mar 15 11:57
rdr59404     ttyq21        Mar 15 15:03
```

Just knowing that someone is logged in is not sufficient, however. You also want to know that he or she is active and not out getting a cup of coffee.[2] In this case, you want to use the -u **option,** which also indicates how long it has been since there was any activity on the line. This is known as **idle time.** It also returns the process id for the user. This information is of little use now. We will discuss it later. A **who** request with the -u option is shown in Session 1.4.

SESSION 1.4   *The **who** Command Option* u

```
$ who -u
nb045527     ttyq0         Mar 15 15:23   0:41   19590
tran         ttyq1         Mar 10 12:15   old     8315
gilberg      ttyq5         Mar 15 14:57    .     17737
ryan         ttyq12        Mar 15 11:57   0:01    2378
rdr59404     ttyq21        Mar 15 15:03    .     18082
```

If you look at this example carefully, you will see three different formats for idle time. The first user has had no activity for 0 hours and 41 minutes. The second user has had no activity for over 24 hours. Because there is only enough room for 24 hours in the idle time format, when a user is inactive for more than 24 hours, the system simply says "old." There are also two users whose idle time is a period. They have both done something in the last minute.

Another helpful option, especially for new UNIX users, is the header. If you add an H to the **option,** UNIX displays a header that explains each column. The header is shown in Session 1.5.

SESSION 1.5   *The **who** Command Option* H

```
$ who -uH
NAME         LINE          TIME           IDLE     PID   COMMENTS
nb045527     ttyq0         Mar 15 15:23   0:41   19590
tran         ttyq1         Mar 10 12:15   old     8315
gilberg      ttyq5         Mar 15 14:57    .     17737
ryan         ttyq12        Mar 15 11:57   0:01    2378
rdr59404     ttyq21        Mar 15 15:03    .     18082
```

If all you want to see is information about yourself, you can use an argument of am I. In this case, the *i* can be either uppercase or lowercase. There can be no options when you ask for information about yourself.

---

[2]As we mentioned before, it is a poor security practice to leave your terminal logged in when you are not present.

SESSION 1.6   **who** *with Argument* am i

```
$ who am i
gilberg     ttyq3        Mar 15 16:34
```

whoami

If you key **whoami** as the command, the system returns your user id. While you may wonder who is so forgetful that they can't even remember their own id, administrators use this command to find out who has left the terminal unguarded. It is also used to show the user id on a report.

Change Password (passwd) Command

The password command, **passwd,** is used to change your password. It has no options or attributes but rather does its work through a dialog of questions and answers. The general format is shown in Figure 1.14.

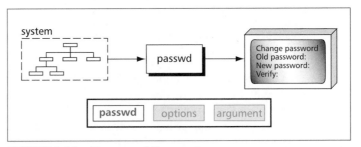

FIGURE 1.14   *The* **passwd** *Command*

It begins by asking you to enter your old password. While you might think that asking for your old password is unnecessary, it is done for security reasons; if you were to leave your area for even a minute (for example, to get a report out of the printer) someone could come in and quickly change your password. Then, they could later come back and gain access to your system. By verifying that it is actually you at the terminal, this potential security breach is prevented.

After you verify your password, the system asks you for a new password. A good security system will make sure that the password is not one you have used recently and not too close to the one you are currently using. In other words, you must make a significant change for the new password to be accepted. Your system administrator may also require that it contain at least one special character or digit.

> In general, good passwords:
> 1. are significantly different from previous passwords
> 2. have at least six characters
> 3. are not common words found in a dictionary
> 4. are not your name, user id, or a combination of them
> 5. contain special characters or digits when required by the system administrator

Of course, using good security, what you type is not displayed on the terminal. Some systems display bullets as you type; other systems don't even let an observer know how many characters are in your password—they display nothing at all. Then the system asks you to enter your password again to verify that you did not make any mistakes when you keyed it the first time. If you enter your new password exactly the same twice, the system changes it for future entries and displays a success message. A sample password dialog is shown in Session 1.7.

SESSION 1.7 **passwd** *Command*

```
$ passwd
Changing password for …
Old password:
New password:
Re-enter new password:
```

If you make a mistake and the new passwords don't agree, you will see a message like the one in Session 1.8.

SESSION 1.8 **passwd** *Change Error*

```
They don't match
Try again.
```

Print Message (echo) Command

The **echo** command copies its argument back to the terminal. In this chapter, we cover only its basic format. Its format appears in Figure 1.15.

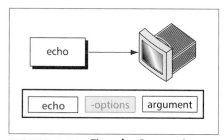

FIGURE 1.15 *The* **echo** *Command*

Let's look at a short example that prints a message back to the screen.

SESSION 1.9 *The* **echo** *Command*

```
$ echo Hello World
Hello World

$ echo "Error 105: Invalid total sales"
Error 105: Invalid total sales
```

Online Documentation (man) Command

One of the most important UNIX commands is **man.** The **man** command displays online documentation. When you can't remember exactly what the options are for a command, you can quickly check the online manual and look up the answer. There is even a manual explanation for the **man** command itself. The **man** command is shown in Figure 1.16.

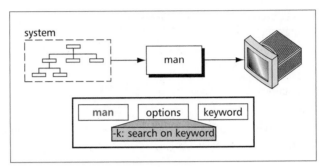

FIGURE 1.16 *The **man** Command*

Let's begin by looking at the **man** documentation for **cal.**

SESSION 1.10 **man** *Documentation*

```
$ man cal
cal(1)                                                                cal(1)
NAME
      cal - print calendar
SYNOPSIS
      cal [ [ month ] year ]
DESCRIPTION
      cal prints a calendar for the specified year. If a month is also
      specified, a calendar just for that month is printed. If neither
      is specified, a calendar for the present month is printed. The
      month is a number between 1 and 12. The year can be between 1 and
      9999. The calendar produced is that for England and the United
      States.
NOTES
      An unusual calendar is printed for September 1752. That is the
      month 11 days were skipped to make up for lack of leap year
      adjustments. To see this calendar, type: cal 9 1752
      The command cal 83 refers to the year 83, not 1983.
      The year is always considered to start in January even though
      this is historically naive.
```

After the heading, the documentation begins with the name and a short description of the command, in this case, **cal.**

Following the name is a synopsis of the different formats that can be used with the command. For the calendar, there is only one command format. Note the use of brackets after the verb. The outer set of brackets indicates that the entire attribute section is optional, in which case only the current month is printed (see description). The inner brackets around the month indicate that it can be omitted and the year requested.

The description completes the explanation of what happens when the command is used. It often clarifies the synopsis. For the calendar, the description tells us that we can use no arguments, a year, or a year and a month.[3] This was not apparent from the syntax in the synopsis shown in Session 1.10.

Finally, one or more notes may be found that elaborate on the command. In the calendar notes, we are reminded that when we switched to the Gregorian calendar in 1752, 11 days had to be dropped to put the calendar back on schedule with the solar seasons.

To learn more about the **man** command, we suggest that you experiment with it. Start with the documentation for the **man** command itself. To see it, use the following command:

```
$ man man
```

But what if you don't know the name of the command you want? All you can remember is that there is a command that does what you want, and you know that if you could just see a list of the related commands, you would recognize it. In this case, you use the **man** command with an option of -k and it will display information, including commands, about the topic. For instance, if you want to know what UNIX sort utilities are available, you can enter the following command and get a list of sort utilities:

```
$ man -k sort
```

Print (lpr) Command

The most common print utility is line printer (**lpr**). The line printer utility prints the contents of the specified files to either the default printer or to a specified printer. Multiple files can be printed with the same command. If no file is specified, the input comes from the standard input, which is usually a keyboard unless it has been redirected. Its format is presented in Figure 1.17.

To direct the output to a specified printer, we use the -P option. The name of the printer immediately follows the option with no spaces.

> One caution: Do not print a binary file using **lpr**. The output will be unreadable and it can waste much paper.

---

[3] Actually, it does, but you have to understand the syntax. Anything in brackets is optional. Therefore, the entire date is optional or we can enter either a year or both a month and a year.

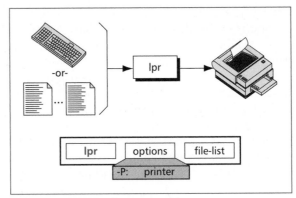

FIGURE 1.17 *The **lpr** Command*

In the following examples, the first command prints one file to the standard printer, the second command prints three files to the standard printer, and the third command prints three files to printer lp0 (note the leading −P in the option).

```
$ lpr file1
$ lpr file1 file2 file3
$ lpr -Plp0 file1 file2 file3
```

1.8 Other Useful Commands

In this section, we introduce some less frequently used but useful commands.

Terminal (tty) Command

The **tty** utility is used to show the name of the terminal you are using. Later, we will see that UNIX treats each terminal as a file, which means that the name of your terminal is actually the name of a file. The **tty** command is shown in Figure 1.18.

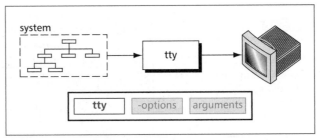

FIGURE 1.18 *The **tty** Command*

The name of the terminal file can be displayed with the **tty** command as in the following example:

```
$ tty
/dev/ttyq0
```

The output shows that the name of the terminal is /dev/ttyq0 or, more simply, ttyq0. In UNIX, the name of a terminal usually has the prefix tty.

Clear Screen (clear) Command

The **clear** command clears the screen and puts the cursor at the top. It is available in most systems. Its format appears in Figure 1.19.

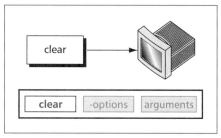

FIGURE 1.19   *The **clear** Command*

The following example demonstrates the **clear** command:

```
$ clear
```

Set Terminal (stty) Command

The set terminal (**stty**) command sets or unsets selected terminal input/output options. When the terminal is not responding properly, the set terminal command can be used to reconfigure it. Depending on the arguments, it has several uses. Its basic format is shown in Figure 1.20.

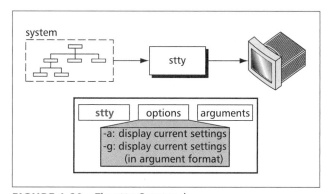

FIGURE 1.20   *The **stty** Command*

Set Terminal Without Option or Argument

If we use the **stty** without any options or arguments, it shows the current common setting for your terminal. Some of these settings are communications settings, such as the baud rate. Others are control settings such as the Delete key setting (default `ctrl-h`). The basic command is demonstrated in Session 1.11.

SESSION 1.11 *The **stty** Command*

```
$ stty
speed 9600 baud; -parity hupcl clocal
line = 1; intr = ^A; erase = DEL; old-swtch = ^@; dsusp = ^@;
brkint -inpck icrnl onlcr tab3
echo echoe echok echoke
```

Set Terminal With Options Only

The set terminal command can be used with two options (`-a` and `-g`), neither of which allows arguments. With the `-a` option, it displays the current terminal option settings. With the `-g` option, it displays selected settings in a format that can be used as an argument to another set terminal command.

Set Terminal With Arguments

Many of the terminal settings should be set only by a superuser. Examples of these arguments strip input to seven-bit characters, force all uppercase characters to lowercase, and echo characters as they are typed. One of the common user arguments sets values for the system editing control characters, such as delete. We discuss these in this section.

Set Erase and Kill (ek) The `ek` argument sets the default erase (Delete key—`ctrl+h`) and kill (`ctrl+c`) to their defaults.

Set Terminal to General Configuration (sane) The `sane` argument sets the terminal configuration to a reasonable setting that can be used with a majority of the terminals.

```
$ stty sane
```

Set Erase Key (erase) By default, the Erase key is `ctrl+h` on the terminal. It deletes the previous character typed (in modern terminals, the Delete key also deletes the previous key). We can reconfigure the keyboard to use another key as the Delete key with the `erase` argument as shown in the following example:

```
$ stty erase ^e
```

The new key follows the keyword `erase` in the argument and defines the keystroke that is to be used to erase characters. It should always be a control key + key combination, but UNIX will accept a single key. In the previous example, we set the delete to `ctrl+e` (for erase). To reset it to the default, we could simply reset it to `ctrl+h`, but it is easier to use the erase and kill argument (`ek`) or the `sane` argument.

Set Kill (kill) The Kill key deletes a whole line. By default, it is `ctrl+u`. We can change it using the set terminal command with the `kill` argument as shown in the next example.

```
$ stty kill 9
```

In this example, we set the Kill key to the digit 9. In this case, it is not a control key combination. We highly recommend that you don't use a single key because it's easy to forget and use it accidentally in typing normal commands or input.

> **We recommend that the terminal control key options not be changed. If you do change them, always use a control key combination for the new setting.**

Set Interrupt Key (intr) The interrupt key interrupts or suspends a command. By default, it is ctrl+c. It can be reset using the intr argument as shown in the following example:

```
$ stty intr ^9
```

Table 1.2 summarizes the common control key commands that can be set.

TABLE 1.2 *Common Control Keys That Can Be Set*

Command	Attribute	Default
Erase text	erase	^h
End of file key	eof	^d
Kill command	kill	^u
Interrupt command	intr	^c
Start output	start	^q
Stop output		^d
Suspend command		^z

There are many more **stty** command options and arguments. Many of them are applicable only to superusers. Others are well beyond the scope of this text.

Record Session (script) Command

The **script** command can be used to record an interactive session. When you want to start recording, key the command. To record a whole session, including the logout, make it the first command of the session. Its format is shown in Figure 1.21.

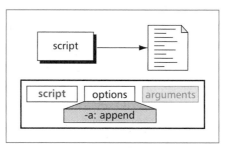

FIGURE 1.21 *The **script** Command*

To stop the recording, key **exit.** The session log is in a file named `typescript`. An example is shown in Session 1.12. Some of the lengthy output, such as for the **who** and **ls** commands, has been edited to reduce the number of lines. After keying **exit,** you can print the script output file using the **lpr** command. (A word of warning: You may have to use `ctrl+d` to log out after the **exit** command.)

SESSION 1.12   *Session Log Example*

```
$ script
Script started, file is typescript
$ date
Mon May 28 13:40:59 PDT 2001

$ who
forouzan    ttyq0        May 28 12:33   (153.18.171.128)
spk49772    ttyq3        May 28 11:27   (c296129-a.frmt1.sfba.home.com)
xf043637    ttyq4        May 28 11:25   (ACB46F15.ipt.aol.com)
$ ls -l
total 168
-rw-r--r--    1 forouzan staff           26 Apr 22 10:45 file1.dat
-rw-r--r--    1 forouzan staff           49 May 14 15:42 notes.dat
$ exit
Script done, file is typescript
```

The `typescript` filename does not have to be used. We can give it any name by passing the filename as an argument. We demonstrate using a filename in the next example.

```
$ script myfilename
```

Each **script** command execution erases the old script file output. To append to the file rather than erase it, we use the append option (`-a`) as in the next example.

```
$ script -a
```

System Name (uname) Command

Each UNIX system stores data, such as its name, about itself. To see these data, we use the **uname** command. The command format appears in Figure 1.22.

We can display all of the data using the all option (`-a`) or we can specify only the name (`-n`), operating system (default or `-s`), or software release (`-r`). There are other options that you can explore in the system documentation (**man**). Session 1.13 demonstrates the more common options. Options can be combines; for example, to display the operating system and its release, use `-sr`.

SESSION 1.13   *Demonstrate **uname** Options*

```
$ uname
IRIX64
$ uname -s
IRIX64
```

Continued

```
$ uname -r
6.5
$ uname -n
challenger
$ uname -sr
IRIX64 6.5
$ uname -a
IRIX64 challenger 6.5 04191225 IP19
```

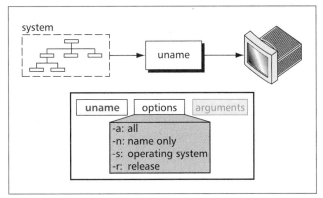

FIGURE 1.22   *The* **uname** *Command*

Calculator (bc) Command

The **bc** command is one of the most interesting commands in UNIX. It turns UNIX into a calculator. However, it is much more than just a calculator. In many respects, it is actually a language, similar to C, with a powerful math library ready at your fingertips. We could write a small book on all of the features in the calculator. Our purpose here is to introduce some of its more basic commands. The command format is shown in Figure 1.23.

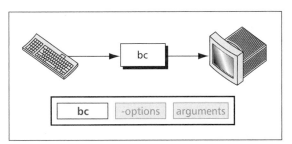

FIGURE 1.23   *The* **bc** *Command*

To start the calculator, we simply key the **bc** command. To terminate it, we key end of file (ctrl+d).

Simple Arithmetic

Simple arithmetic is done at the command line. It supports addition (+), subtraction (−), multiplication (*), division (/), modulus (%), and power (^). These features are demonstrated in Session 1.14.

SESSION 1.14   *Calculator (**bc***) Arithmetic Operations*

```
$ bc
12 + 8
20

45 - 56
-11

34 + 34 * 3
136

34 + 34 / 3
45

8%3
2

24.5 ^ 67
535952736437245636258131049114399022990229 50.4
```

As you study the output, note that the normal algebraic precedence is followed: multiplicative (* / % ^) operations before additive (+ −). Also, the divide operation results in an integer.

Floating-Point Calculations   To use floating-point arithmetic, we must specify the number of decimal points to be used. This is done with the scale expression, which sets the number of digits after the decimal in a floating-point number. Session 1.15 demonstrates the scale expression. Note, however, that **bc** does not round like C does.

SESSION 1.15   *Demonstrate Scale Expression*

```
19/3
6
scale=2
19/3
6.33
20/3
6.66
21/3
7.00
scale=8
19/3
6.33333333
20/3
6.66666666
21/3
7.00000000
scale=0
19/3
6
```

Arithmetic Base Calculations[4] The **bc** calculator can be used in decimal, binary, octal, or hexadecimal bases. The base is specified by one of two expressions: ibase (or simply base) or obase. The ibase expression specifies that input will be in the specified base. The obase expression specifies the output base. If the input or output base is not defined, it is assumed to be decimal (base 10).

You can change the base of your calculation by setting the input base (ibase) or output base (obase) to the base you want (from 2 to 16). Base 2 means binary, base 8 means octal, base 16 means hexadecimal. Session 1.16 demonstrates each input base.

SESSION 1.16 *Demonstrate Calculator Input Base*

```
$ bc
ibase=2
111
7
111*111
49
ibase=8
10
8
10*11
72
ibase = 16
1A
26
10 * 10
256
```

Session 1.16 Analysis: As you study this simple session, note that spaces can be used or omitted as desired. In each example, we first demonstrate the value of the base number and then use the number in a calculation. Make sure you understand why the result is what it is.

Session 1.17 demonstrates output bases. Note that the third example uses base 13. We can use any base up to 16; however, only bases 2, 8, 10, and 16 have any usefulness in UNIX.

SESSION 1.17 *Demonstrate Calculator Output Base*

```
obase = 2
5
101
15 / 3
101
obase = 8
9
11
99 / 10
11
```

Continued

----

[4]Before studying this section, you may find it helpful to review Appendix D, Numbering Systems.

SESSION 1.17   *Demonstrate Calculator Output Base—Continued*

```
obase = 13
13
10
130 / 10
10
obase = 16
26
1A
256
100
16 * 16
100
```

1.9 Key Terms

application	login	shell
argument	login name	shell program
bash shell	logout	shell script
Bourne shell	multiuser	software
C shell	networking	tcsh
client/server environment	operating system	time-sharing environment
command	option	UNIX
hardware	password	user id
interaction	personal environment	utilities
kernel	portable	verb
Korn shell	services	
Linux	session	

1.10 Tips

1. UNIX is case sensitive.
2. To start a session, you log into the system.
3. After finishing a session, you log out of the system.
4. Before using a command in a session, you must see the system prompt of the current shell.
5. The default prompts for the different shells are:
    a. Bourne and bash shell: $
    b. Korn shell: $
    c. C and tcsh shell: %
6. A system may have a customized system prompt.
7. A command is made of many fields such as verb, option, and argument. There must be at least one space between each of these fields when you type a command.
8. Options are normally preceded by a minus sign (occasionally a plus sign). There should be no space between the sign and the next character.
9. The **date** command gives you both date and time, not only the date.

10. Your password must be safeguarded: Never share it with anyone.

11. If you give no argument for the **cal** command, it gives you the calendar of the current month, not the current year.

12. If you give only one argument for the **cal** command, it is interpreted as the year. The command then displays the calendar for the whole year.

13. The year argument in the **cal** command should not be abbreviated; do not use 99 for 1999.

14. The **who** command with an am i argument displays a different format than the **whoami** command.

15. When you change your password, the new password must be different from the old one.

16. When you use the **passwd** command to change your password, the new password must be typed two times.

17. When you type your password, the system does not show it on the screen for security purposes.

18. When you are unsure about the syntax (synopsis) or the application of a command, use the **man** command followed by the name of the command for which you want information.

1.11 Commands

The following commands were discussed in this chapter. For more details, see Appendix F and the corresponding pages shown in the following table.

Command	Description	Options	Page
bc	*Synopsis:* bc Calculator.		29
cal	*Synopsis:* cal [[month] year] Displays the calendar for a month or a year.		17
clear	*Synopsis:* clear Clears monitor screen.		25
date	*Synopsis:* date [-options] [+format] Displays the time and date.	u	15
echo	*Synopsis:* echo [message] Displays its argument.	n	21
lpr	*Synopsis:* lpr [-options] [file-list] Prints the file list.	P	23
man	*Synopsis:* man command-name Displays online documentation for the command.		22
passwd	*Synopsis:* passwd Changes the user password.		20
script	*Synopsis:* script [filename] Records interactive session.	a	27

Continued

Command	Description	Options	Page
stty	**Synopsis:** *stty* Sets or unsets selected terminal input/output options.	a, g	25
tty	**Synopsis:** *tty* Displays name of terminal.		24
uname	**Synopsis:** *uname* Displays system data.	a, n, r, s, sr	28
who	**Synopsis:** *who [-options] [am i]* Displays all users currently logged into the system.	H, u	18
whoami	**Synopsis:** *whoami* Displays the id of the user.		20

1.12 Summary

- A computer system is a combination of hardware and software that lets users work with a computer.
- The hardware is a combination of devices that can be seen or touched.
- The software is a combination of programs written to make the computer a multi-purpose machine. The software is divided into two different types: system software and application software.
- System software is a set of programs that serves the computer itself.
- Application software is programs that are written to solve users' problems.
- The operating system is a special category of system software that manages all operating facets of the computer itself.
- UNIX is a multiuser, multiprocessing, portable operating system designed to facilitate programming, text processing, communication, and many other tasks that are expected from an operating system.
- UNIX supports three environments: personal environments, time-sharing environments, and client/server environments.
- UNIX consists of four major components: the kernel, the shell, a standard set of utilities, and application programs.
- The kernel is the heart of the UNIX system. Its primary functions are process control and resource management.
- The shell provides two services to the user. It is an interpreter that reads the user commands and interprets them. It is also a programming language that allows users to write shell programs (scripts).
- There are three standard shells used in UNIX today: Bourne shell, Korn shell, and C shell.
- There are hundreds of utilities available to users. A utility is a standard UNIX program that provides a support process for users.
- Application programs are customized programs written to provide extended capability to the system.

- To access the UNIX operating system in a shared environment, a user must have a user id and a password.
- An interactive session in UNIX consists of three different phases: login, interaction, and logout.
- The basis of all UNIX interaction is the command. A UNIX command is an action request given to the UNIX shell for execution.
- A command is made of three components: a verb, a set of options, and a set of arguments. Although the first component is always present, the options and the arguments may or may not be present in a command.
- In this chapter, we discussed 14 common commands: **bc, cal, clear, date, echo, lpr, man, passwd, script, stty, tty, uname, who,** and **whoami.**
- To direct the output from a command to the printer, use the **lpr** command.

1.13 Practice Set

Review Questions

1. Explain the meaning of the word *portable* in the phrase *portable operating system.*
2. Explain the difference between *multiuser operating system* and *multitask operating system.*
3. Explain the difference between a time-sharing and a client/server environment.
4. Explain the difference between utilities and applications.
5. Define the parts of a command.
6. What is the purpose of a shell?
7. What are the names of three common shells in UNIX?
8. What is the default prompt in each shell?
9. Describe the three phases involved in a session.
10. How many utilities were discussed in this chapter?
11. How many options are available for the **date** command? What do they do?
12. How many options are available for the **who** command? What do they do?
13. How many options are available for the **whoami** command? What do they do?
14. How many options are available for the **cal** command? What do they do?
15. How many options are available for the **passwd** command? What do they do?
16. How many options are available for the **echo** command? What do they do?
17. How many options are available for the **man** command? What do they do?
18. Answer the following questions about the **cal** command:
    a. Are both the month and the year required?
    b. Can we enter the year without the month?
    c. Can we enter the month without the year?
    d. Can we abbreviate the year, such as 00 for the year 2000?
    e. What is the difference between the year value 66 and 1966?

f. On what day of the week does the calendar start?

g. How many columns are in a calendar printout?

h. Can we print a calendar only for 1 week?

19. Answer the following questions about the **who** command:

   a. What is the meaning of the first column in the result?

   b. What is the meaning of the second column in the result?

   c. What is the meaning of the third column in the result?

20. Answer the following questions about the **passwd** command:

   a. Can you find the value of your password from the result of this command?

   b. Can you change your password using this command?

   c. Can you use an old password for the new password?

   d. When you change your password, why do you have to enter the old password?

   e. When you change your password, why do you have to enter the new password twice?

21. Answer the following questions about the **date** command:

   a. How many lines do you see in the result?

   b. How many characters are in the result (including spaces)?

   c. Is the total number of characters different if the day of the month is one digit or two?

   d. How many characters define the date (day)? Show the date format.

   e. How many characters define the time (hours and minutes)? Show the time format.

22. Answer the following questions about the **man** command:

   a. Can you get information about the **man** command itself using the **man** command?

   b. Can you change the **man** file containing information about a command?

   c. Can you get information about a file using the **man** command?

Exercises

23. Find the error (if any) in each of the following commands ($ is the prompt of the system):

   a. `$ cal`

   b. `$ cal -u`

   c. `$ cat 1944`

   d. `$ cal jan`

24. Find the error (if any) in each of the following commands ($ is the prompt of the system):

   a. `$ Date`

   b. `$ date -U`

   c. `$ date -u 1999`

   d. `$ date %D`

25. Find the error (if any) in each of the following commands ($ is the prompt of the system):

   a. `$ echo echo`

   b. `$ echo man`

   c. `$ echo -u hello`

   d. `$ echo "-u hello"`

26. Find the error (if any) in each of the following commands ($ is the prompt of the system):

   a. `$ passwd XXXYYY`

   b. `$ passwd -u XXXYYY`

   c. `$ passwd XXXXXX YYYYYY`

   d. `$ Passwd`

27. Find the error (if any) in each of the following commands ($ is the prompt of the system):
    a. `$ man password`
    b. `$ man whoami`
    c. `$ man who passwd`
    d. `$ man -i who`

28. Determine and explain the result of the following commands:
    a. `$ cal 2100`
    b. `$ cal 0`
    c. `$ cal 1`
    d. `$ cal 2000`

29. Determine and explain the result of the following commands:
    a. `$ cal 8 2000`
    b. `$ cal 08 2000`
    c. `$ cal 18 2000`
    d. `$ cal 9`

30. Determine and explain the result of the following commands:
    a. `$ date "+%D"`
    b. `$ date "+%H"`
    c. `$ date "+%I"`
    d. `$ date "+%D %H"`

31. Determine and explain the result of the following commands:
    a. `$ date "+%m %M"`
    b. `$ date "+%r %R"`
    c. `$ date "+%a %A"`
    d. `$ date "+%b %B"`

32. Determine and explain the result of the following commands:
    a. `$ echo date`
    b. `$ echo `date`            # backquotes`
    c. `$ echo date is `date``
    d. `$ echo `$$$``

33. Determine and explain the result of the following commands:
    a. `$ man cal`
    b. `$ man calendar` (It is different from part a?)
    c. `$ man date`
    d. `$ man whoami` (Is it different from who?)

34. Determine and explain the result of the following commands:
    a. `$ date ; who`   (Can you guess the effect of ";" here?)
    b. `$ date ; date "+%D"`
    c. `$ who ; whoami`
    d. `$ cal 2000 ; date`

1.14 Lab Sessions

Each of the following sessions uses one or more practical exercises. After finishing each session, write a report that explains the result of each step and answer any questions asked.

Session 1

1. Obtain your user id from the instructor, the system administrator, or the system.
2. Obtain your password from the instructor, the system administrator, or the system.
3. Log into the system using your user id and password.
4. Identify the system prompt. What is it?

Continued

Session I—*Continued*

5. Determine your logon shell. (Hint: What is your prompt?)
6. Use the **passwd** command to change your password. Use a password that you won't forget.
7. Log out of the system.

Session II

1. Log into the system using the new password.
2. Has the prompt of the system been changed? In what shell are you now?
3. Use the **man** command to find out about the **man** command itself. Write a brief report of your findings.
4. Use the **man** command to find out about the **who** command. Write a brief report of your findings.
5. Use the **man** command to find out about the **whoami** command. Write a brief report of your findings.
6. Use the **man** command to find out about the **date** command. Write a brief report of your findings.
7. Use the **man** command to find out about the **passwd** command. Write a brief report of your findings.
8. Make sure you understand the terminology and the language used in the electronic manual. If you have questions, consult with the instructor or the system administrator. Be sure that you understand the synopsis (syntax) of each command.
9. Log out of the system.

Session III

1. Log into the system.
2. Use the **who** command to find out about the users logged into the system. Make sure you see yourself.
3. Can you tell what terminal you are using by looking at the **who** command?
4. In some systems, there are some options in the **who** command that we did not discuss in this chapter (-q, -b, -s). Try to use these options (if available) and determine what they do.
5. Log out of the system.

Session IV

1. Log into the system.
2. Use the **date** command to find the local time.
3. Use the **date** command to find the universal time.

Continued

4. What is the difference between your local time and the universal time? Is your local time ahead of or behind the universal time?

5. Use all of the **date** arguments in Table 1.1 on page 16 one by one and write a brief explanation of the results.

6. What do you get if you use the following commands?
   a. `$ date       "+This is the date"`
   b. `$ date       "+This is the date: %B"`

7. Write a command to show the date using the following formats:
   a. `05/21/99`
   b. `Friday, May 21, 1999`
   c. `Friday, 05/21/1999`

8. Write a command to show the date using each of the following formats:
   a. `Day: Friday`
   b. `Month: May`
   c. `Year: 1999`

9. Write a command to show the time using each of the following formats:
   a. `08:22:24 PM`
   b. `08:22 PM`
   c. `08 AM`

10. Write a command to show the time using each of the following formats:
    a. `Hours : 08`
    b. `Hours : 08 Minutes : 22`
    c. `Hours : 08 Minutes : 22 Seconds: 24`

11. Log out of the system.

Session V

1. Log into the system.

2. Use a command to display the whole calendar for the current year. Do you need to type a value for the year?

3. Use a command to get the calendar of the current month.

4. Use a command to get the calendar for the month of July in the year 2232.

5. Use a command to find out which day of the week was the beginning of our calendar (0001). What was it?

6. Use a command to determine if the year 2000 is a leap year. A leap year has 29 days in February instead of 28.

7. Use a command to determine if the year 1900 was a leap year.

8. Compare the results of steps 6 and 7 and explain the difference.

9. Use a command to find a historical fact about the year 1752.

10. Use the **man** command to explain the result of step 9.

11. There is a "calendar" command in some UNIX systems. Try this command (if available) and find the difference between it and the **cal** command.

12. Log out of the system.

Session VI

1. Log into the system.
2. In some systems, there is a command called **learn.** Use **man** to determine the syntax of the **learn** command (if available) and then experiment with it. Do you find it useful?
3. In some systems, there is a command called **help.** Use **man** to determine the syntax of the **help** command (if available). Experiment with this command. Do you find it useful?
4. In some systems, there is a command called **finger.** Use **man** to find out about the syntax of the **finger** command (if available). Experiment with this command. Do you find it useful?
5. Log out of the system.

## CHAPTER 2

Basic vi Editor

In this chapter, we introduce a basic version of the **vi** editor. We begin with a short discussion of editor concepts and then discuss the basic **vi** commands that you will need to work with simple UNIX files. In Chapter 8, we discuss **vi**'s full capabilities.

2.1 Editor Concepts

Before we begin the discussion of **vi**, let's review some general editor concepts. Some of these concepts differ from non-UNIX systems such as word processors.

As used in UNIX, **editing** includes both creating a new file and modifying an existing text file. An **editor** is a utility that facilitates the editing task—that is, the creation and modification of text files. Because of their close association with text files, editors are often called **text editors.**

A text editor differs from a word processor in that it does not perform typographical formatting such as bolding, centering, and underlining. In other words, an editor is a basic text processor that is used to create and edit text quickly and efficiently. Editors come in two general types: line editors and screen editors.

Line Editors

In a line editor, changes are applied to a line or group of lines. To edit a line, the user must first select a line or group of lines for editing. The selection can be by line number, such as edit line 151, or through an expression that defines the line, such as edit the line beginning with "Once."

Line editors are more useful when you want to make global changes over a group of lines. For example, if you want to add an extra space at the beginning of each line, it is easier to use a line editor to change all lines at once rather than adding the space to individual lines. However, using a line editor is more complex than using a screen editor; it is necessary to know how to select the group of lines and then how to apply the change. Two common UNIX line editors are **sed** and **ex.** We will study them in future chapters.

Screen Editors

A **screen editor** presents a whole screen of text at a time. The obvious major difference between a line and screen editor is that with screen editors we can see each line of text in its context with other lines. We can move the cursor around the screen and select a part of the text (a character, a word, or a line). We can also **scroll** the screen—that is, move the view of the data up or down to see different parts of the text document.

The current position in the text is shown by a cursor. The cursor's form depends on the operating system. In some systems, it is a black square with white text. In others, it is indicated by a blinking square or an underline. In our examples, we show the cursor as a black square. The **current character** is the character at the cursor. The **current line** is the line containing the cursor.

As we search for text, the contents of the screen change. When we scroll up, the text moves down and new lines appear at the top of the screen; when we scroll down, new lines appear at the bottom of the screen. As we enter text, the text at the end of the line wraps to the next line, and the line at the bottom of the screen is pushed down below the screen and out of sight. The screen editors are more convenient and more user-friendly than line editors.

2.2 The vi Editor

The **vi** (pronounced vee-eye) editor is a screen editor available on most UNIX systems. When you invoke the **vi** editor, it copies the contents of a file to a memory space known as a **buffer.** Once the data have been loaded into the buffer, the editor presents a screen full of the buffer to the user for editing. If the file does not exist, an empty buffer is created. The **vi** editor is shown in Figure 2.1.

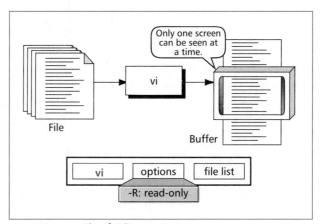

FIGURE 2.1 *The **vi** Editor*

Note that the buffer is only a temporary version of the file. When we exit **vi,** the buffer is erased. At exit time, we have two choices: We can quit **vi** without saving the file, which means that the contents of the original file remain unchanged, or we can save the file, which means that the contents of the original file are replaced by the new version.

> **vi** is a screen editor.

2.3 Modes

The **vi** editor uses two basic modes: the command mode and the text mode.

Command Mode

When the **vi** editor is in the **command mode,** any key that is pressed by the user is considered a command. Commands are used to move the cursor, to delete or change part of the text, or to perform many other operations. As soon as the command is entered, it is executed—the Return key is not required. On some systems, commands are known as *hot keys*. Of course, the key or key sequence must be a valid command. If it is not, the result is unpredictable.

There are two aspects of the **vi** editor that are frustrating to new users:

- Most of the commands are not echoed on the screen. This means that you will not see the command itself on the screen. What you will usually see is some change in the cursor position, in the current line, or in the mode. Only a few commands—those that start with a colon (:), a slash (/), or a question mark (?)—will be shown on the last line at the bottom of the screen.
- Most commands should not be followed by a Return key. The single character or the sequence of characters pressed is the command itself. Only the commands that will show at the bottom of the screen—those that start with :, /, or ?—require a Return key to finish the command.

Text Mode

When the **vi** editor is in the text mode, any key that is pressed by the user is considered text. The keyboard acts as a typewriter. In the text mode, the characters typed by the user, if they are printable characters, are inserted into the text at the cursor. This means that to add text in a document, we should first place the cursor at the desired location. To place the cursor, however, we must be in the command mode. The typical operation, therefore, is to place the cursor with a command, switch to the text mode and edit the text, then switch back to the command mode for the next operation.

Changing Modes

From the foregoing discussion, it is clear that we must switch back and forth between **vi** command and text modes. To tell **vi** to do something, it must be in the command mode; to edit text, it must be in the text mode. The relationship between these two modes is summarized in Figure 2.2.

Before discussing the different commands, let's summarize the points shown in Figure 2.2.

- To invoke **vi,** you type the following command at the UNIX prompt:

```
$ vi filename
```

The *filename* is the name of the file that already exists or the name of the file that you want to create.

- When you invoke **vi,** you are always in the command mode. During the session, you can move back and forth between the command mode and the text mode.
- To exit **vi,** you must be in the command mode.
- There are six commands that take you to the text mode (a, A, i, I, o, and O). We will discuss each of them shortly. For the moment, remember that if you are in the

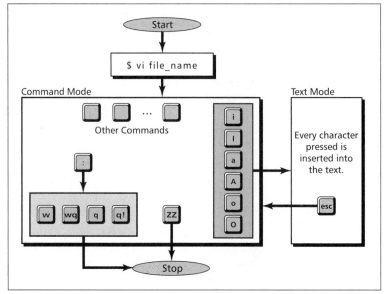

FIGURE 2.2 **vi** *Modes*

command mode and use any of these commands, **vi** switches immediately to the text mode. Anything you type will be added to the buffer.

• When you are in the text mode, you press the Escape key (esc) to go to the command mode.

> When you enter **vi**, you are in the command mode. To exit **vi**, you must be in the command mode.

2.4 Commands

The **vi** editor is the interactive part of **vi/ex.** When initially entered, the text fills the buffer and one screen is displayed. If the file is not large enough to fill the screen, the empty lines below the text on the screen will be identified with a tilde (~) at the beginning of each line. The last line on the file is a **status line;** the status line is also used to enter **ex** commands (see Figure 2.3).

Add Commands

As we said, to insert text, you need to be in the text mode. The **vi** editor contains several commands to change the mode to text. In this section, we study only six of these commands: i, I, a, A, o, and O. Table 2.1 summarizes these commands and their use.

Insert Commands (i *and* I)

We can insert text before the current position or at the beginning of the current line. The lowercase insert command (i) changes to the text mode. We can then enter text.

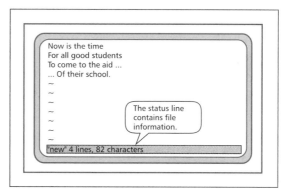

FIGURE 2.3 *A Small File in* **vi**

TABLE 2.1 *Add Text Commands*

Command	Function
i	Inserts text before the current character.
I	Inserts text at the beginning of the current line.
a	Appends text after the current character.
A	Appends text at the end of the current line.
o	Opens an empty text line for new text after the current line.
O	Opens an empty text line for new text before the current line.

The character at the cursor is pushed down the line as the new text is inserted. When we are through entering text, we return to the command mode by keying esc. The uppercase insert command (I) opens the beginning of the current line for inserting text. Figure 2.4 shows two examples of character insertion. In this and the following examples, the cursor is shown as white text on a black background.

Regardless of which command is used, once **vi** is in the insert mode, you can add as many characters or lines as needed. The difference between the two commands is where the insertion begins, not what can be inserted after the mode is changed. Figure 2.4(a) contains an example of inserting text before the cursor, and Figure 2.4(b) is an example of inserting text at the beginning of the line. As you study them, note that there is no space between the **vi** command and the text being entered. If you enter a space, there will be a space in the text because the insertion commands are immediate; they do not need a space or a return to be effective.

Append Commands (a *and* A)

The basic concept behind all append commands is to add text after a specified location. In **vi,** we can append after the current character (a) or after the current line (A). As with the insert command, we need to escape to return to the command mode. Figure 2.5 demonstrates the append command. As you study the figure, note that there is a space after the command, whereas in Figure 2.4 the space is at the end of the command. Make sure that you understand why one time the space is at the beginning and one time it is at the end.

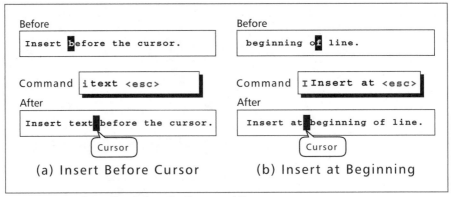

FIGURE 2.4 *Insert Text Before the Cursor and Line*

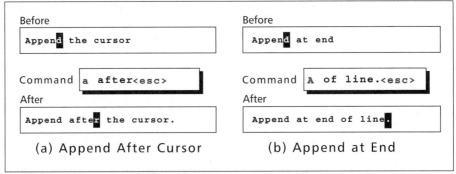

FIGURE 2.5 *Insert Text After Cursor and Line*

New Line Commands (o *or* O)

The new line commands create an open line in the text file and insert the text provided with the command. Like insert and append, after entering the text, we must use the Escape key to return to the command mode. Think of the letter O in the new line command as a window into which you can insert text.

The lowercase new line (o) command opens a new line *after* the current line so you can add text there. To add text in a new line below the current line, use the lowercase new line (o) command. If the current line spans multiple screen lines, the new line is opened after the screen line that contains the return character, not after the screen line that contains the cursor. To add the new text in a line above the current line, use the uppercase new line (O) command. Figure 2.6 shows examples of the new line commands.

Cursor Move Commands

To edit text, we need to move the cursor to the text to be edited. The cursor move commands are effective only in the command mode. After the execution of a move command, the **vi** editor is still in the command mode. There are many cursor move commands; we study eight here as shown in Table 2.2.

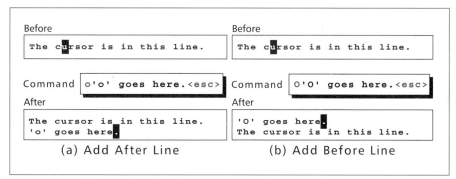

FIGURE 2.6 *Insert New Lines*

TABLE 2.2 *Cursor Move Commands*

Command	Function
Horizontal Moves	
h, ⇐ , Backspace	Moves the cursor one character to the left.
l, ⇒, Spacebar	Moves the cursor one character to the right.
0	Moves the cursor to the beginning of the current line.
$	Moves the cursor to the end of the current line.
Vertical Moves	
k,⇑	Moves the cursor one line up.
j, ⇓	Moves the cursor one line down.
–	Moves the cursor to the beginning of the previous line.
+, Return	Moves the cursor to the beginning of the next line.

Horizontal Move Commands

The horizontal move commands move the cursor one character to the left or right or to the beginning or end of the current line.

Move Left (h, ⇐, ***Backspace)*** Each of the three move left commands moves the cursor one character to the left. To move multiple characters, the key is repeated, once for each character position to be moved. Figure 2.7(a)[1] shows an example of using a horizontal move left command.

Move Right (l, ⇒, ***Spacebar)*** Like the horizontal left moves, there are three horizontal right moves. Each command moves the cursor one character to the right. Figure 2.7(b) shows an example of using a horizontal move right command.

Beginning of Line (0) or End of Line ($)

To move to the beginning of the line containing the cursor, we use the beginning of line command (0). Similarly, to move to the end of the current line, we use the end of line

---

[1]The text in these and other examples throughout the book is from Edgar Allan Poe's *The Raven*.

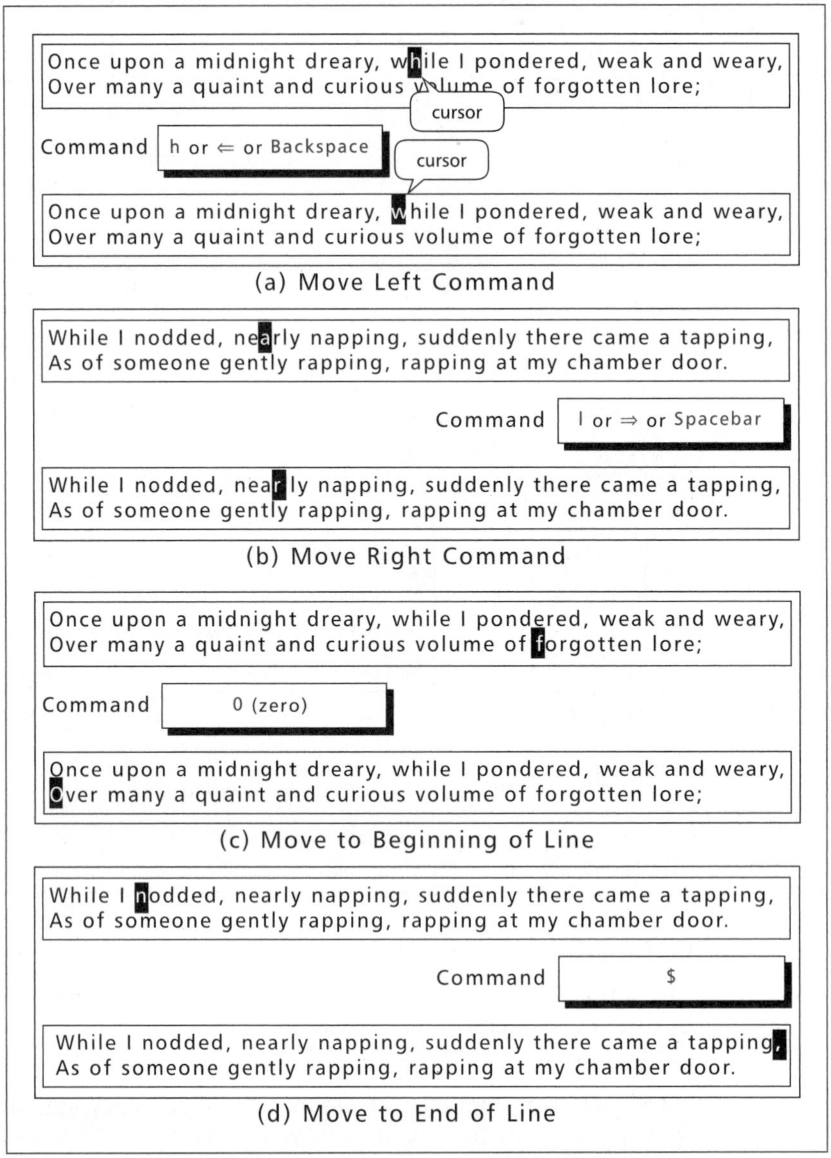

Once upon a midnight dreary, while I pondered, weak and weary,
Over many a quaint and curious volume of forgotten lore;

cursor

Command | h or ⇐ or Backspace

cursor

Once upon a midnight dreary, while I pondered, weak and weary,
Over many a quaint and curious volume of forgotten lore;

(a) Move Left Command

While I nodded, nearly napping, suddenly there came a tapping,
As of someone gently rapping, rapping at my chamber door.

Command | l or ⇒ or Spacebar

While I nodded, nearly napping, suddenly there came a tapping,
As of someone gently rapping, rapping at my chamber door.

(b) Move Right Command

Once upon a midnight dreary, while I pondered, weak and weary,
Over many a quaint and curious volume of forgotten lore;

Command | 0 (zero)

Once upon a midnight dreary, while I pondered, weak and weary,
Over many a quaint and curious volume of forgotten lore;

(c) Move to Beginning of Line

While I nodded, nearly napping, suddenly there came a tapping,
As of someone gently rapping, rapping at my chamber door.

Command | $

While I nodded, nearly napping, suddenly there came a tapping,
As of someone gently rapping, rapping at my chamber door.

(d) Move to End of Line

FIGURE 2.7   *Horizontal Moves*

command ($). These two moves are shown in Figure 2.7(c) and Figure 2.7(d), respectively.

Vertical Move Commands

The vertical move commands move the cursor up or down one line, which may be more than one screen line.

Move Up Command (k, ⇑ ***)*** The move up commands move the cursor up one line. If the upward line has at least the same number of characters as the line we are moving from, the cursor is placed in the same relative position in the upward line. However, if the upward line is shorter than the line we are moving from, the cursor is placed at the end of the upward line. Figure 2.8(a) shows an example of a move up command.

Move Down Command (j, ⇓ ***)*** The move down command moves the cursor down one line. The cursor will be positioned in the lower line in the same manner

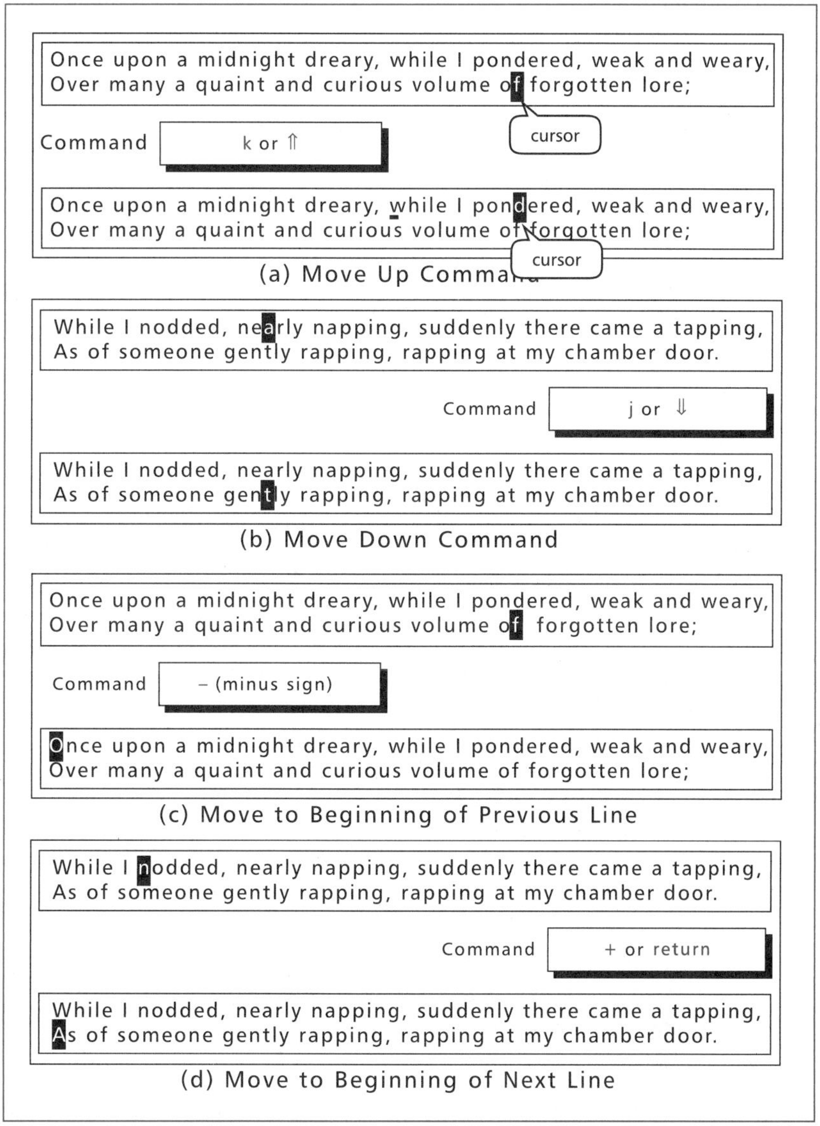

Once upon a midnight dreary, while I pondered, weak and weary,
Over many a quaint and curious volume of forgotten lore;

Command   k or ⇑   cursor

Once upon a midnight dreary, while I pondered, weak and weary,
Over many a quaint and curious volume of forgotten lore;
cursor

(a) Move Up Command

While I nodded, nearly napping, suddenly there came a tapping,
As of someone gently rapping, rapping at my chamber door.

Command   j or ⇓

While I nodded, nearly napping, suddenly there came a tapping,
As of someone gently rapping, rapping at my chamber door.

(b) Move Down Command

Once upon a midnight dreary, while I pondered, weak and weary,
Over many a quaint and curious volume of forgotten lore;

Command   – (minus sign)

Once upon a midnight dreary, while I pondered, weak and weary,
Over many a quaint and curious volume of forgotten lore;

(c) Move to Beginning of Previous Line

While I nodded, nearly napping, suddenly there came a tapping,
As of someone gently rapping, rapping at my chamber door.

Command   + or return

While I nodded, nearly napping, suddenly there came a tapping,
As of someone gently rapping, rapping at my chamber door.

(d) Move to Beginning of Next Line

FIGURE 2.8 *Vertical Moves*

as we saw for the move up command. If the lower line is shorter, the cursor is placed at the end of the line. If the lower line has the same number or more characters than the line we are moving from, the cursor is positioned at the same relative character in the lower line. Figure 2.8(b) shows an example of a move down command.

Up Line (–) or Down Line (+ or return)

The up line command moves the cursor to the beginning of the line above the current line. If there is no line above the current line, the cursor does not move. Similarly, the down line command moves the cursor to the beginning of the next line. If there is no next line, the cursor does not move. These two commands are shown in Figure 2.8(c) and Figure 2.8(d), respectively.

Deletion Commands

Although there are several deletion commands, we discuss only two here: x and dd. They are defined in Table 2.3.

TABLE 2.3   **vi** *Delete Commands*

Command	Function
x	Deletes the current character.
dd	Deletes the current line.

Delete Character (x)

The delete character command deletes the current character—that is, the character pointed to by the cursor. After the deletion, the cursor points to the character after the deleted character. When the last character on the line is deleted, however, the cursor moves to the character on the left. If the only character on a line is deleted, the cursor stays at the beginning of the line, and further deletions have no effect. The delete character command is shown in Figure 2.9(a).

Delete Line (dd)

The delete line command deletes the current line. After the deletion, the cursor is at the beginning of the next line. If the last line is deleted, the cursor is at the beginning of the line above the deleted line, which is now the last line of the file. Multiple delete line commands can be executed to delete a series of lines. Figure 2.9(b) shows the delete line operation.

Join Command

Two lines can be combined using the join command (J). The command can be used anywhere in the first line. After the two lines have been joined, the cursor will be at the end of the first line. The join command is shown in Figure 2.10.

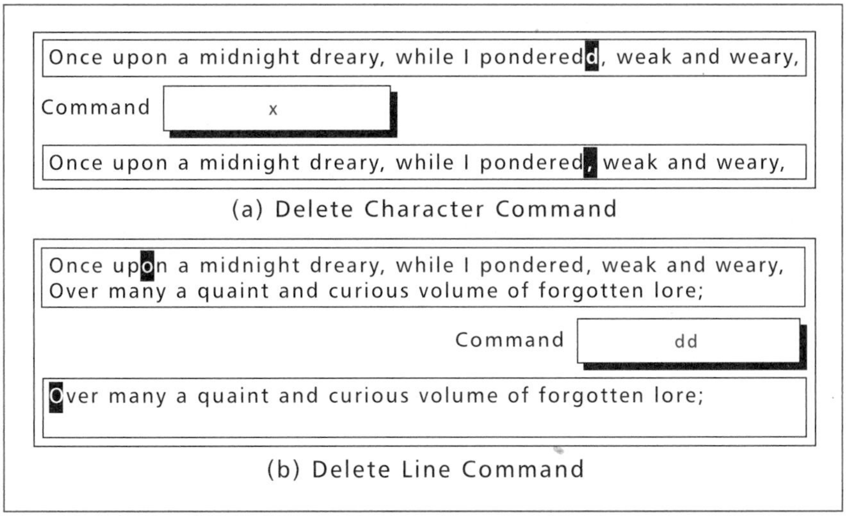

Once upon a midnight dreary, while I ponderedd, weak and weary,

Command   x

Once upon a midnight dreary, while I pondered, weak and weary,

(a) Delete Character Command

Once upon a midnight dreary, while I pondered, weak and weary,
Over many a quaint and curious volume of forgotten lore;

Command   dd

Over many a quaint and curious volume of forgotten lore;

(b) Delete Line Command

FIGURE 2.9 *Delete Commands*

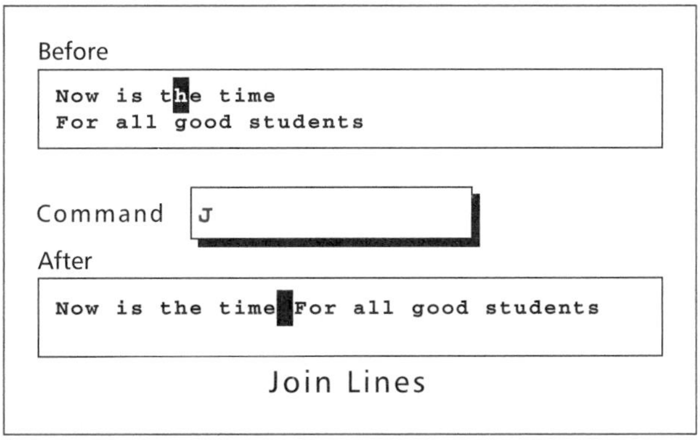

Before

Now is the time
For all good students

Command J

After

Now is the time For all good students

Join Lines

FIGURE 2.10 *The Join Command*

Scrolling Commands

The standard UNIX window is only 24 lines long.[2] When editing a document longer than 24 lines, therefore, we need to scroll through the buffer to see the text. You can scroll up and you can scroll down. The direction of the scroll is relative to the text, not to the screen. The text moves up and down. Scrolling down, therefore, means moving down in the text toward the end of the file. As you move down, lines disappear at the top of the screen and new lines are added at the bottom.

Similarly, scrolling up means moving the text up—that is, toward the beginning of the buffer. As you scroll up, lines are added at the top of the screen, and the lines at the bottom disappear. Figure 2.11 demonstrates how the text scrolls through the screen window.

---

[2]Some operating systems allow you to increase the size of the window, but the default is 24 lines.

Table 2.4 shows the six **vi** commands for scrolling up and down. All of the scrolling commands are Control key (ctrl) sequences. To execute them, you must depress and hold the Control key and then press the Command key corresponding to the desired action.

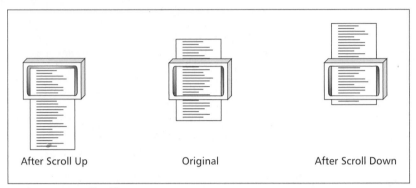

After Scroll Up   Original   After Scroll Down

FIGURE 2.11   *Scrolling*

TABLE 2.4   **vi** *Scroll Commands*

Command	Function
ctrl+y	Scrolls up one line.
ctrl+e	Scrolls down one line.
ctrl+u	Scrolls up half a screen (12 lines).
ctrl+d	Scrolls down half a screen (12 lines).
ctrl+b	Scrolls up whole screen (24 lines).
ctrl+f	Scrolls down whole screen (24 lines).

Line Scroll Commands (ctrl+y *and* ctrl+e)

There are two **vi** commands that scroll the text one line. The ctrl+y command scrolls the text up one line. When you scroll the text up, the cursor location does not change unless it is on the line at the bottom of the screen, in which case it must move up one line because the last line disappears.

To scroll down one line, use the ctrl+e command. Again, the cursor location does not move unless it is in the top line of the screen, in which case it must move down one line because the top line disappears.

Half Screen Commands (ctrl+u *and* ctrl+d)

Half screen scrolls the cursor 12 lines up or down. This is true even if you have enlarged the screen size in your software because the vi screen standard is 24 lines—half a screen is therefore 12 lines. After the scroll, the cursor is at the beginning of the target line. The text on the screen also scrolls 12 lines unless it is already at the top or the bottom, in which case only the cursor moves. If there are fewer than 12 lines to the top or the bottom, the cursor is placed at the top or bottom line as appropriate.

To scroll up half a screen, use `ctrl+u` (u for up). To scroll down half a screen, use `ctrl+d` (d for down).

Full Page Commands (`ctrl+b` *and* `ctrl+f`)

With one exception, the full screen scrolls operate like the half screen scrolls. The exception is that they will not move the cursor to the beginning or the end of the document. If the top line is already visible on the screen and you scroll up a full screen, the cursor doesn't move. (To move it to the top, use the half screen up command.)

To scroll up a full screen, use `ctrl+b` (b for beginning). To scroll down a full screen, use `ctrl+f` (f for finish).

Undo Commands

If after editing text you decide that the change was not what you really wanted, you can undo it. There are two undo commands. One reverses only the last change. Another reverses all changes to the current line. The undo commands are summarized in Table 2.5.

TABLE 2.5 *The Undo Commands*

Command	Function
u	Undoes only the last edit.
U	Undoes all changes on the current line.

Undo Last Edit (`u`)

The undo last edit command restores the text to the way it was before the last edit command. For example, assume that you have just inserted 50 characters in a line and are now in the command mode. If before you use any more edit commands you undo your editing, the inserted text is deleted. The undo works even if you have repositioned the cursor as long as you don't execute another edit command.

You need to be more careful with delete commands, however. Remember that each delete is a command. So if you delete three characters and then undo the edit, only the last character will be restored. However, if you delete an entire line with the delete line command (`dd`), then the entire line is restored.

> **The undo last edit command (`u`) undoes only one edit command.**

It is possible to undo an undo command[3]. For example, if you insert text and then undo the change, the text you inserted is removed. If you then undo the undo, the text is reinserted. If you then repeat the undo, the text is removed. There is no limit to the number of times an undo can be repeated. Figure 2.12(a) shows how the undo last edit command works.

---

[3]Some UNIX systems allow multiple undo commands.

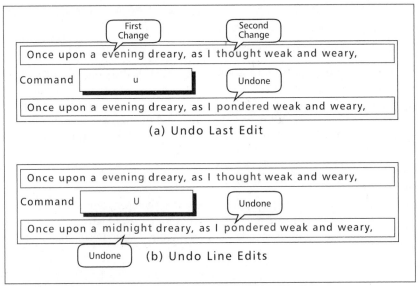

FIGURE 2.12 *Undo*

*Undo Line Edits (*u*)*

The undo line edits command removes all edits performed on a line. For example, assume that in the first line of *The Raven,* Mr. Poe was trying different wording to see the effect. He first deletes "midnight" and substitutes "evening." Then he changes "pondered" to "thought." Reflecting on the changes, he decides that he liked the original version better, so he undoes all of the changes in the line with the undo line edits command, and the original version is restored. Once again, if he wants, he can undo the changes and redo them, but to do this he must use the last edit undo command (u). The undo line edits command is shown in Figure 2.12(b).

Saving and Exit Commands

Even though UNIX is a very stable operating system, you should save your work often during a session to prevent losing it in case of a system failure. You also need to save it at the end of the session.

There are six save and exit commands. One saves your work but does not exit. There are two commands to save your work and exit. One command exits, but only if there have been no changes to the text. And there is one command to exit and discard any changes. These commands are summarized in Table 2.6. With the exception of the ZZ command, all of these commands require that you first key the colon character (:) to open a command line at the bottom of the screen. Once the command line is opened, you can key the save or quit command and key return.

Save Work and Continue (:w*)*

The save and continue command saves (writes) the contents of the buffer back into the file. The original file on the disk is changed and cannot be retrieved. After saving, you are still in **vi** and can continue editing.

TABLE 2.6 **vi** *Save and Exit Commands*

Command	Function
:w	Saves the contents of the buffer without quitting **vi.**
:w filename	Writes contents of buffer to new file and continues.
ZZ	Saves the contents of the buffer and exits.
:wq	Saves the contents of the buffer and exits.
:q	Exits the **vi** (if buffer changed will not exit).
:q!	Exits the **vi** without saving.

Save to New File (`:w filename`)

This command writes the contents of the buffer to a new file. The original file is unchanged. After the save, you are still in **vi,** but you are editing the newly saved file.

Save and Quit (`ZZ`)

The save and quit command is very handy. It allows you to save your work and exit from **vi.** Note that the ZZ command does not need the command line at the bottom of the screen; it is an immediate command and is therefore faster.

Write and Quit (`:wq`)

The write and quit command has the same effect as the ZZ command, but it requires that you open the command line at the bottom of the screen. Therefore, you must first type a colon (:) and then w followed by q. This sequence is actually two commands: first a write command to write the buffer to the file and then a quit command to exit **vi.**

Quit (`:q`)

The quit command exits **vi,** but only if the buffer is unchanged. If the buffer has been changed, **vi** displays a message and returns to the command mode. You should use it only if you have made no changes since you last saved the file.

Quit and Don't Save (`:q!`)

If you really want to discard the changes you have made, use the quit and don't save command. Note, however, that you will not be warned that your changes are being discarded. Be very careful with this command—it can be very dangerous.

> **You must be in the command mode to use any of the save or exit commands.**

2.5 Two Practice Sessions

In this section, we take you through the steps necessary to create and then edit a file. In the first session, we create a short file using a famous John Fitzgerald Kennedy quote. In the second session, we modify the quote to make it more appropriate for your college life.

Session I: Creating a File

To create a file, type **vi** and the filename as shown in Session 2.1.

SESSION 2.1 *Starting* **vi**

```
$ vi jfkQuote
~
~
~
```

When **vi** opens, you will be in the command mode with a screen containing 24 empty lines. Empty lines are designated with a tilde (~) in the first character. To begin inserting text, key the insert command (i). You will see no change in the screen. Type the text you want to enter. After you have completed entering the new text, key esc to return to the command mode. To save the file, first type a colon (:) and then w to write the file to the disk. After the editor writes the file, it displays the file status as shown on the last line in Session 2.2. This session shows the results after we have entered and saved JFK's quotation. The double underscore shows the current position of the cursor.

SESSION 2.2 *Inserting Text*

```
Ask not what your country can do for you;
Ask what you can do for your country.

John Fitzgerald Kennedy
Inaugural Address
January 1961
~
...
"jfkQuote" [New file] 6 lines, 143 characters
```

Session II: Modifying a File

Now let's modify the quote. We begin by opening the file again using the same **vi** command we used to create it. At the command line, type the following line. Be sure to use the correct case because UNIX is case sensitive.

```
$vi jfkQuote
```

We want to replace the word "country" with "college." Using the arrow or Spacebar, move the cursor to the beginning of "country" and press the delete character command (x) seven times. Now key the insert command (i) and type the word "college," ending with the esc command to return to the command mode. Now move down one line (down arrow or k) and again change "country" to "college."

Position the cursor at the beginning of JFK's name and delete line (dd) three times. Now insert your name, college, and today's date. At this point, the screen should look like Session 2.3. Close **vi** and save your work.

SESSION 2.3 *Revising Text*

```
Ask not what your college can do for you.
Ask what you can do for your college.

Ima Student
De Anza College
January 14, 2001
~
...
```

2.6 Key Terms

buffer   editing   scrolling
command mode   line editor   text editor
current character   modes   text mode
current line   screen editor

2.7 Tips

1. A line editor presents one and only one line at a time, whereas a screen editor presents a full screen at a time.
2. The **vi** editor always copies the content of the file to a buffer. The editing is done on the buffer, not on the original file. This means that if the contents of the buffer are not saved, the editing is lost.
3. The **vi** editor, as a screen editor, shows one screen of text in the buffer. To see other parts of the buffer, you need to scroll.
4. Remember to save the buffer from time to time to prevent losing the changes made during the editing session.
5. When you enter the **vi** editor, it is in the command mode.
6. To use a command, you must be in the command mode; to enter text, you must be in the text mode.
7. If you are not sure which mode you are in, press the esc key until you hear the beep.
8. There are several ways you can move the cursor in **vi.** However, remember to practice the letter commands (h, l, k, j) for moving left, right, up, and down. The arrow keys will not work in later chapters when we use **vi** for command-line editing.
9. Remember that some commands need the colon (:), which opens the command line at the bottom of the screen.

2.8 Commands

In this chapter, we covered only one command, **vi.**

Command	Description	Options	Page
vi	***Synopsis:*** *vi [-options] [file-name]* Used to create a new file or edit an existing file.	R	42

The **vi** command as an editor uses many commands (or subcommands), and several of them were introduced in this chapter. The rest will be discussed in Chapter 8.

Category	Command	Description
Adding Text	i	Inserts text before the current character.
	I	Inserts text at the beginning of the current line.
	a	Appends text after the current character.
	A	Adds text at the end of the current line.
	o	Opens an empty text line for new text after the current line.
	O	Opens an empty text line for new text before the current line.
Deleting Text	x	Deletes the current character.
	dd	Deletes the current line.
Moving Cursor	h, <=, Backspace	Moves the cursor one character to the left.
	l, =>, Spacebar	Moves the cursor one character to the right.
	0	Moves the cursor to the beginning of the current line.
	$	Moves the cursor to the end of the current line.
	k, ⇑	Moves the cursor one line up.
	j, ⇓	Moves the cursor one line down.
	−	Moves the cursor to the beginning of the previous line.
	+, return	Moves the cursor to the beginning of the next line.
Join	J	Joins two consecutive lines.
Undo	u	Undoes only the last edit.
	U	Undoes all changes on the current line.
Scrolling	ctrl+y	Scrolls up one line.
	ctrl+e	Scrolls down one line.
	ctrl+u	Scrolls up half a screen.
	ctrl+d	Scrolls down half a screen.
	ctrl+b	Scrolls up whole screen.
	ctrl+f	Scrolls down whole screen.
Saving and Quitting	:w	Saves buffer contents to original file and continues.
	:w filename	Saves buffer contents to filename and continues.
	:wq , ZZ	Saves the contents of the buffer and exits.
	:q	Quits if contents have not been changed.
	:q!	Exits **vi** without saving.

2.9 Summary

- An editor (or text editor) is a utility that facilitates editing—that is, the creation and modification of text files.

- Editors come in two general types: line editors and screen editors.
- In a line editor, changes are applied to a line or groups of lines. They are more useful when you want to make global changes over a group of lines. Two common UNIX line editors are **sed** and **ex.**
- A screen editor presents a whole screen of text at a time. Two common text editors in UNIX are **vi** and **emacs.**
- The **vi** editor is a screen editor available on most UNIX systems.
- In **vi,** the current position in the text is shown by a cursor.
- The current character is the character at the cursor; the current line is the line containing the cursor.
- When you invoke the **vi** editor, it copies the contents of a file to a memory space known as a buffer. The buffer is a temporary version of the file. When we exit **vi,** the buffer is erased.
- The **vi** editor uses two basic modes: the command mode and the text mode.
- When the **vi** editor is in the command mode, any key that is pressed by the user is considered as a command. To tell **vi** to do something, it must be in the command mode.
- When the **vi** editor is in the text mode, any key that is pressed by the user is considered as text.
- When you invoke **vi,** it is always in the command mode; when you exit **vi,** it must be in the command mode.
- There are six commands that take you from command mode to the text mode: a, A, i, I, o, and O. To move from the text mode to the command mode, you should press the esc key.
- There are six commands that are used to add text. The commands i and I are used to insert text. The commands a and A are used to append text. The commands o and O are used to open new lines and then add text.
- There are several commands that are used to move the cursor on the screen.
- The move left commands (h, <=, Backspace) move the cursor one character to the left. The move right commands (l, =>, Spacebar) move the cursor one character to the right. The beginning of line command (0) moves the cursor to the beginning of the current line. The end of line command ($) moves the cursor to the end of the current line.
- The move-up command (k, up arrow) moves the cursor up one line. The move-down command (j, down arrow) moves the cursor down one line. The up-line command (-) moves the cursor to the beginning of the previous line. The down-line command (+ or return) moves the cursor to the beginning of the next line.
- There are two delete commands: x and dd. The x command deletes the current character. The dd command deletes the current line.
- There are six commands to scroll the text. To scroll the text one line at a time, use ctrl+y (up) and ctrl+e (down). To scroll the text half a screen at a time, use ctrl+u (up) and ctrl+d (down). To scroll the text a whole screen at a time, use ctrl+b (up) and ctrl+f (down).
- There are two commands to undo editing. To undo the last command, use the u command. To undo all changes in the current line, use the U command.

- To save the content of the buffer without quitting **vi,** use the :w command. To quit without saving the contents of the buffer, use the :q! command. To save the contents of the buffer and quit, use the :wq command.

2.10 Practice Set

Review Questions

1. Define an editor and explain the differences between an editor and a word processor.
2. Explain the differences between a line editor and a screen editor.
3. Identify some line editors in UNIX.
4. Identify some screen editors in UNIX.
5. Is **vi,** as represented in this chapter, a screen editor or a line editor?
6. Define a cursor and explain the role it plays in **vi** editor.
7. What is the current character as defined in this chapter?
8. What is the current line as defined in this chapter?
9. How many modes were defined for **vi** in this chapter?
10. What is the difference between the **vi** text mode and command mode?
11. In which mode is **vi** when you invoke it?
12. In which mode are you when you are typing a word?
13. In which mode are you when you are moving the cursor?
14. How can you move from the text mode to the command mode?
15. How can you move from the command mode to the text mode?
16. What is scrolling? Explain the role it plays in **vi.**
17. Why should you frequently save your file when you are editing?
18. What is the only option defined in this chapter that you can use with **vi**? What is its purpose?
19. Can a new (nonexisting) file be created with **vi**? What command should you use?
20. Can an old (existing) file be edited with **vi**? What command should you use?

Exercises

21. Which of the following keystrokes can delete the current character?
    - a. d
    - b. x
    - c. dd
    - d. delete
22. Which of the following keystrokes can delete the current line?
    - a. d
    - b. x
    - c. dd
    - d. delete
23. Which of the following keystrokes moves you from the command mode to the text mode?
    - a. i
    - b. I
    - c. a
    - d. all of the above

24. Which of the following keystrokes moves you from the command mode to the text mode?

    a. o   c. h
    b. x   d. all of the above

25. Which of the following keystrokes moves you from the command mode to the text mode?

    a. o   c. I
    b. O   d. all of the above

26. Which of the following keystrokes moves you from the text mode to the command mode?

    a. o   c. h
    b. ESC   d. all of the above

27. If your cursor is on the eighth character on the line and you want to move to the ninth character, what is the command?

28. If your current line is line 9 and you want to move to the beginning of line 8, what is the command?

29. If your current line is line 9 and you want to move to the beginning of line 9, what is the command?

30. If your cursor is on line 12 and you want to move to the beginning of line 13, what is the command?

31. Imagine line 12 has 22 characters and line 11 has only 10 characters. If you are on line 12 and issue the following commands, one after another, where would the cursor be?

    a. 0   c. k
    b. i   d. i

32. Imagine line 12 has 22 characters and line 11 has only 10 characters. If you are on the sixth character of line 12 and issue the following commands, one after another, where would the cursor be?

    a. j
    b. h
    c. h

33. Imagine line 12 has 22 characters and line 11 has 30 characters. If you are on the sixth character of line 12 and issue the following commands, one after another, where would the cursor be?

    a. k   b. h

34. Imagine there are 70 lines in your file. What is the size of your buffer in lines?

35. Imagine there are 70 lines in your file. If the screen can hold only 24 lines, what is the line number of the last line you can see on the screen when you open **vi?**

36. Imagine there are 70 lines in your file. If the screen can hold only 24 lines, what is the line number of the last line you can see on the screen after the following events?

    a. $ vi filename   c. ctrl+b
    b. ctrl+y   d. ctrl+d

37. If you feel that all editing you have done on a file should be discarded, which of the following commands will leave your original file untouched?

    a. :w   c. :q!
    b. :q   d. :wq

38. If you want to save all of your editing and quit **vi**, which of the following commands would you use?
    a. `:w`   c. `:q!`
    b. `:q`   d. `:wq`

39. If you want to save all of your editing without quitting **vi**, which of the following commands would you use?
    a. `:w`   c. `:q!`
    b. `:q`   d. `:q`

2.11 Lab Sessions

Each of the following sessions uses one or more practical exercises. After finishing each session, write a report that explains the result of each step and answer any questions asked.

Session I

1. Log into the system.
2. Use the `vi` editor to create a file called `gtysbrg.txt` which contains the following paragraph with the same alignment and format.

```
Four score and seven years ago our fathers brought forth on this continent
a new country, conceived in liberty, and dedicated to the idea that
all men are created equal. Now we are engaged in a great war,
testing whether our nation, or any nation so conceived and so dedicated
can last. We are met on a great battlefield of that war. We have
come to dedicate a portion of that field as a final resting-place for
those who here gave their lives that that nation might live.
```

3. Correct your typing errors during creation.
4. Save the file.
5. Log out of the system.

Session II

1. Log into the system.
2. Open the file created in Session I.
3. Change the previously typed paragraph to look like the following. You should add some text, change some text, and delete some text.

```
Four score and seven years ago our fathers brought forth on this continent
a new nation, conceived in liberty, and dedicated to the proposition that
all men are created equal. Now we are engaged in a great civil war,
testing whether that nation, or any nation so conceived and so dedicated,
can long endure. We are met on a great battlefield of that war. We have
come to dedicate a portion of that field as a final resting-place for
those who here gave their lives that that nation might live.
It is very fitting and proper that we should do this. But in a
larger sense, we cannot dedicate nor consecrate nor can we hallow
this ground. The brave men, who died here, who struggled here have
```

Continued

> consecrated it far above our power to add or detract. The world will
> little note, nor long remember what we say here, but it can never forget
> what they did here.

4. Save the new file with the name `gtsybrgII.txt`.
5. Log out of the system.

Session III

1. Log into the system.
2. Open the file created in Session II.
3. Change the previously typed paragraph to look like the following. You should add some text, change some text, and delete some text.

> Four score and seven years ago our fathers brought forth on this continent
> a new nation, conceived in liberty, and dedicated to the proposition that
> all men are created equal. Now we are engaged in a great civil war,
> testing whether that nation, or any nation so conceived and so dedicated,
> can long endure. We are met on a great battlefield of that war. We have
> come to dedicate a portion of that field as a final resting-place for
> those who here gave their lives that that nation might live.
>
> It is altogether fitting and proper that we should do this. But in a
> larger sense, we cannot dedicate, we cannot consecrate, we cannot hallow,
> this ground. The brave men, living and dead, who struggled here have
> consecrated it far above our poor power to add or detract. The world will
> little note, nor long remember what we say here, but it can never forget
> what they did here.
>
> It is for us the living, rather to be dedicated here to the unfinished
> work which they who fought here have thus far so nobly advanced. It is
> rather for us, to be here dedicated to the great task remaining before
> us, that from these honored dead we take increased devotion to that cause
> for which they gave the last full measure of devotion; that we here
> highly resolve that these dead shall not have died in vain; that this
> nation, under God, shall have a new birth of freedom, and that government
> of the people, by the people, for the people, shall not perish from the
> earth.
>
> Abraham Lincoln
> Sixteenth President of the United States
> Gettysburg, Pennsylvania
> November 19, 1863

4. Save the changes in the same file.
5. Log out of the system.

## CHAPTER 3

File Systems

UNIX uses a broader interpretation of files[1] than found in most operating systems. In UNIX, a file is any source from which data can be read or any destination to which data can be written. Therefore, the keyboard, a source of input, is a file; the monitor, a destination for output, is a file; a printer, another destination for output, is a file; and a document stored on a disk, a source or destination of data, is also a file.

3.1 Filenames

There are very few restrictions on how you make up filenames in UNIX. Some implementations limit the length of a filename to 14 characters. Others have names as long as 255 characters.

A filename can be any sequence of ASCII characters. However, we recommend that you not use some characters in a filename. For example, the greater than (>) and less than (<) characters cannot be used in a filename because they are used for file redirection.[2] On the other hand, a period in UNIX does not have a special meaning as it does in other operating systems. In many operating systems, a period separates the name of a file from its extension. In UNIX, you can use the period anywhere in a filename.

To make your names as meaningful as possible, we recommend that you use the following simple rules:

1. Start your names with an alphabetic character.
2. Use dividers to separate parts of the name. Good dividers are the underscore, period, and the hyphen.
3. Use an extension at the end of the filename, even though UNIX doesn't recognize extensions. Some applications, such as compilers, require file extensions. In addition, file extensions help you classify files so that they can be easily identified. A few common extensions are .txt for text files, .dat for data files, .bin for binary files, and .c and .c++ for C and C++ files, respectively.
4. Never start a filename with a period. Filenames that start with a period are hidden files in UNIX. Generally, hidden files are created and used by the system. They will not be seen when you list your files.

A filename that starts with a period is a hidden file, generally used by a **UNIX** utility. Examples of system hidden files are .profile, .mailrc, and .cshrc.

---

[1]A named collection of related data stored on an auxiliary storage device.

[2]File redirection is studied in Chapter 5, page 147. It is used in a UNIX command to specify a filename for input or output.

Wildcards

Each filename must be unique. At the same time, we often need to work with a group of files. For example, we may want to copy or list all files belonging to a project. We can group files together using wildcards that identify portions of filenames that are different. A **wildcard** is a token that specifies that one or more different characters can be used to satisfy a specific request. In other words, wildcards are like blanks that can be filled in by any character.

There are three wildcards in UNIX: the single character (?) wildcard, the set ([...]) wildcard, and the multiple character (*) wildcard. They appear in Figure 3.1.

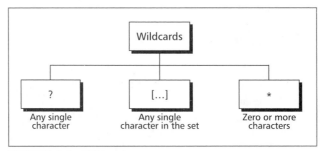

FIGURE 3.1 *Wildcards*

Matching Any Single Character

Often it is necessary to group a set of files that all have the same filename except for one or two characters. For example, three files named `red1`, `red2`, and `red3` could be grouped by their first three characters. To do this, we would use a wildcard specification of `red?` to group them.

The single-character wildcard can be used more than once in a group. You need to understand, however, that each `?` can match only one character. Table 3.1 contains several examples of single-character wildcards.

TABLE 3.1 *Examples of Matching Any Single-Character (?)*

File	Matches				Does Not Match	
c?	c1	c2	c3	ca	ac	cat
c?t	cat	cet	cit	c1t	cad	dac
c??t	caat	cabt	cact	c12t	cat	daat
?a?	bat	car	far	mar	bed	cur

Matching a Single Character from a Set

The single-character wildcard provides powerful capabilities to group files. Sometimes, however, it is too powerful and we need to narrow the grouping. In this case, we use the character set, which specifies the characters that we want to match enclosed in brackets. Like the single-character wildcard, a set matches only one character in the filename. We can, however, combine the set with fixed values, other sets, the single-character wildcard, and the asterisk. Examples of the wildcard set are in Table 3.2.

TABLE 3.2 *Examples of the Character Set [...] Wildcard*

File	Matches				Does Not Match	
f[aoei]d	fad	fed	fod	fid	fud	fab
f[a-d]t	fat	fbt	fct	fdt	fab	fet
f[A-z][0-9]	fA3	fa3	fr2	f^2	FA3	fa33

A word of caution about the third example in Table 3.2. The intent is that the second character in the filename can be any upper- or lowercase alphabetic character. However, if you examine the ASCII table in Appendix A carefully, you will see that there are six special characters[3] between Z and a. If any of these special characters are found as the second character, and the rest of the specification is met, then the filename will be included in the group. Thus, we see that f^2 matches the wildcard specification. To limit the test to only alphabetic characters, we should use [A-Za-z].

Sometimes, it is easier to specify what we don't want. For instance, if we know that the filename contains only lowercase alphabetic characters, we can specify the vowels with only 5 characters, and it takes 21 characters to specify the consonants. In this case, we can negate the set with the bang (!) character as shown here:

```
f[!aeiou]*
```

This wildcard specification matches any file whose name begins with f and that has a consonant as the second character. Thus, fc and fd match, but f and fa do not.

> A (?) and a ([...]) replace only one character in a filename.

Matching Zero or More Characters

The asterisk (*) is used to match zero or more characters in a filename. Whereas the single-character wildcard matched one and only one character, the asterisk matches everything, and everything includes nothing. Obviously, it is very powerful and you must be very careful when you use it. Table 3.3 contains several examples of the asterisk wildcard.

---

[3] [, \ ,] , ^ , _ , and ` .

TABLE 3.3 *Examples of Matching Zero or More Characters (*)*

Wildcard	Matches	Example	Does Not Match
*	every file		
f*	every file whose name begins with *f*	f5c2	afile, cat
*f	every file whose name ends in *f*	staff	f1, faF
.	every file whose name has a period	file.dat	bed, cur

Echo Command and File Wildcards

One way to check the existence of files using the wildcards is the use of echo command. As we learned before (see "Print Message (echo) Command" on page 21), the **echo** command displays its argument. However, if the argument has a wildcard in it, the shell first expands the argument using the wildcard and then it displays it. It can be used with all wildcards.

You can display all three-character filenames that start with f and end with t with the command in Session 3.1.

SESSION 3.1 *Echo Filenames Using Wildcard*

```
$ echo f?t
f-t f1t fat fbt fgt fwt
```

> Use wildcards, especially the asterisks, cautiously.

3.2 File Types

UNIX provides seven file types as shown in Figure 3.2. We provide a brief definition here and discuss two of them in detail in the following sections.

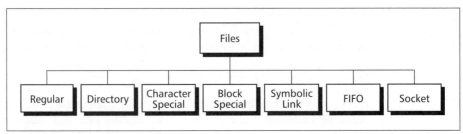

FIGURE 3.2 *Files in UNIX*

- **Regular Files:** Regular files contain user data that need to be available for future processing. Sometimes called ordinary files, regular files are the most common files found in a system. Throughout the rest of the text, whenever we use "file" without any qualification (that is, by itself), we are referring to a regular file.

- **Directory Files:** A directory is a file that contains the names and locations of all files stored on a physical device. Throughout the rest of the text, whenever we use "directory" without any qualification (that is, by itself), we are referring to a directory file.
- **Character Special Files:** A character special file represents a physical device, such as a terminal, that reads or writes one character at a time.
- **Block Special Files:** A block special file represents a physical device, such as a disk, that reads or writes data a block at a time.
- **Symbolic Link Files:** A symbolic link is a logical file that defines the location of another file somewhere else in the system.
- **FIFO Files:** A first-in, first-out file, also known as a named pipe,[4] is a file that is used for interprocess communication. We do not discuss FIFO files in this text.
- **Socket:** A socket is a special file that is used for network communication. Because we do not discuss network programming in this text, we do not discuss sockets.

A file's type can be determined by the list command discussed in List Directory (ls) Command on page 81.

3.3 Regular Files

The most common file in UNIX is the regular file. Regular files are divided by the physical format used to store the data as text or binary. The physical format is controlled by the application program or utility that processes it. UNIX views both formats as a collection of bytes and leaves the interpretation of the file format to the program that processes it.

Text Files

A text file is a file of characters drawn from the computer's character set. UNIX computers use the ASCII character set. Because the UNIX shells treat data almost universally as strings of characters, the text file is the most common UNIX file. The ASCII character set is found in Appendix A.

Binary Files

A binary file is a collection of data stored in the internal format of the computer. In general, there are two types of binary files: data files and program files. Data files contain application data. Program files contain instructions that make a program work. If you try to process a binary file with a text-processing utility, the output will look very strange because it is not in a format that can be read by people.

---

[4]Do not confuse the FIFO file with the pipe operator discussed later in the text.

3.4 Directories

Like other operating systems, UNIX has a provision for organizing files by grouping them into directories. A directory performs the same function as a folder in a filing cabinet. It organizes related files and subdirectories in one place.

In most systems, the directory hierarchy is designed as shown in Figure 3.3. At the top of the directory structure is a directory called the *root*. Although its name is root, in the commands related to directories, it is typed as one slash (/). In turn, each directory can contain subdirectories and files.

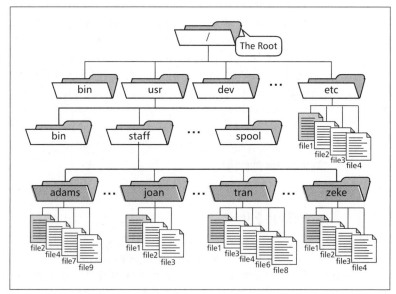

FIGURE 3.3   *A Directory Hierarchy*

Special Directories

There are four special directories that play an important role in the directory structure: root directory, home directory, working directory, and parent directory.

Root Directory

The root directory is the highest level in the hierarchy. It is the root of the whole file structure; therefore, it does not have a parent directory. In a UNIX environment, the root directory always has several levels of subdirectories. The root directory belongs to the system administrator and can be changed by only the system administrator.

Home Directory

We use the home directory when we first log into the system. It contains any files we create while in it and may contain personal system files such as our profile file and the command history.[5] Our home directory is also the beginning of our personal directory structure.

---

[5]We discuss these files in Chapter 5.

Each user has a home directory. The name of the home directory is the user login id or the user id. For example, in Figure 3.3, the colored subdirectory named `adams`, `joan`, `tran`, and `zeke` are all home directories.

Working Directory

The working, or current, directory is the one that we are in at any point in a session. When we start, the working directory is our home directory. If we have subdirectories, we will most likely move from our home directory to one or more subdirectories as needed during a session. When we change directory, our working directory changes automatically.

Parent Directory

The parent directory is immediately above the working directory. When we are in our home directory, its parent is one of the system directories. In our environment, the parent of our home directory is a directory known as `staff`. When we move from our home directory to a subdirectory, our home directory becomes the parent directory.

Paths and Pathnames

Every directory and file in the system must have a name. As we saw in Chapter 1, when we refer to files in a command, we use their filenames. If you examine Figure 3.3 carefully, however, you will note that there are some files that have the same names as files in other directories. It should be obvious, therefore, that we need more than just the filename to identify them. While you might think that the directory and the filename would be enough to uniquely identify a file, a further examination of Figure 3.3 shows that directory names can also be duplicated.

To uniquely identify a file, therefore, we need to specify the file's **path** from the root directory to the file. The file's path is specified by its **absolute pathname,** a list of all directories separated by a slash character (/). The absolute pathname for a file or a directory is like an address of a person. If you know only the person's name, you cannot easily find that person. On the other hand, if you know a person's name, street address, city, state, and country, then you can locate anyone in the world. This full or absolute pathname can get quite long. For that reason, UNIX also provides a shorter pathname under certain circumstances; this shorter pathname is known as a **relative pathname**.

Absolute Pathnames

As we have stated, an **absolute pathname** specifies the full path from the root to the desired directory or file. Table 3.4 lists the full pathname for the gray shaded files in each directory in Figure 3.3. Because directories also have absolute pathnames, we also show the path to each of their directories.

TABLE 3.4 *Absolute Pathnames for Some Files in Figure 3.3*

File	File Absolute Pathname	Directory Absolute Pathname
file1	/etc/file1	/etc
file2	/usr/staff/adams/file2	/usr/staff/adams
file1	/usr/staff/joan/file1	/usr/staff/joan

Continued

TABLE 3.4 *Absolute Pathnames for Some Files in Figure 3.3—Continued*

File	File Absolute Pathname	Directory Absolute Pathname
file1	`/usr/staff/tran/file1`	`/usr/staff/tran`
file1	`/usr/staff/zeke/file1`	`/usr/staff/zeke`

Absolute pathnames can be used all the time regardless of where we are in the directory hierarchy. Their main disadvantage is that they change as directories and their subdirectories are moved around a system by the system administrator. For that reason, we would like to be able to locate files by finding their locations relative to our current location.

Every pathname that starts with a slash is an absolute pathname.

Relative Pathname

Wherever we are working in UNIX, we are always in a directory. When we start, we are in our home directory, which is different from the root directory. Our current, or working, directory is the directory we are in. We can move from one directory to another anytime we need by changing our working directory.

If we need to reference a file in our working directory, we can use a relative rather than the absolute pathname. A **relative pathname** is the path from the working directory to the file. Therefore, when we refer to a file in the working directory, we simply use the filename with no path. This works because when a relative pathname is used, UNIX starts the search from the working directory.

Similarly, from our working directory, we can refer to a file in a subdirectory by using a relative path from the working directory to the file. For example, referring to Figure 3.3 on page 70, if we are in the `staff` directory, we can refer to `file8` in the `tran` directory as shown below. In fact, as we shall see shortly, we can refer to a directory or file anywhere in the system by using a relative pathname.

```
tran/file8
```

Relative Pathname Abbreviations

The home directory, working directory, and parent directory all have abbreviations that make it easy to refer to them, even when we don't know their names.

Home Directory (~)

The abbreviation of a user's home directory is the tilde (~). When we use the tilde, the shell uses the home directory pathname set for us by the system. When we need to refer to our own home directory, we can just use the tilde. For example, to refer to a file named `project.list` in our home directory, we would use the pathname shown in the next example.

```
~/project.list
```

This format works from any point in the directory hierarchy. Note, however, that the slash separating the directory and the file is required.

If we know that there is a file in another user's directory, and if we are permitted to look at it, we can also refer to it by using his or her user id. For example, from within gilberg, we can refer to a file in the forouzan directory as shown in the next example.

```
~forouzan/file1
```

Notice the difference between these two file references. For our own home directory, we just use the tilde. Without a user id, the tilde refers to our home directory. To refer to another user's home directory, however, we must use his or her user id. In this case, a slash does not follow the tilde. In other words, a user's home directory is the home directory abbreviation followed immediately by a user id. To refer to a specific file, the home directory is followed by a slash and the filename just as in the first example.

Working Directory (.)

The abbreviation for the working directory is a dot (.). While it may seem strange that we need an abbreviation for the current directory, some UNIX commands (such as **find,** page 108) require that the pathname for a start directory be specified even when it is the current directory. In these cases, the dot abbreviation makes constructing the relative path easy. For example, in Figure 3.3 (page 70), we see that file6 is stored in tran's home directory. It can be referred to in four ways as shown in the next example.

```
file6
./file6
~/file6
~tran/file6
```

All of these pathnames are relative to the tran's home directory, which in this case is also the current directory. We just used four different techniques to construct the relative path.

Parent Directory (..)

The parent of any directory is the directory immediately above it in the directory path from the root. This means that every directory, except the root directory, has a parent. In Figure 3.4, the parent of reports is adams. Likewise, the parent of adams is the staff directory, and the parent of the staff directory is the usr directory.

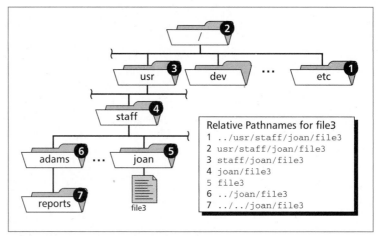

FIGURE 3.4 *Relative Pathnames for* **file3**

The abbreviation for the parent directory is two dots (..). If reports is the current directory, we can refer to its parent (adams) using two dots (..). Furthermore, we can refer to the staff directory as the parent of the parent (../..).

Creating Relative Paths

Given the directory structure shown in Figure 3.4, let's examine some possible relative pathnames for file3. As a point of reference, the absolute pathname for file3 is

/usr/staff/joan/file3

1. From /etc.

   If our working directory is /etc, the shortest pathname is actually the absolute pathname. We can use a relative pathname (../usr/staff/joan/file3), but it is not recommended because it is longer than the absolute pathname. Because UNIX will follow whatever pathname we provide, for efficiency we should use the shortest possible pathname.

2. From the root.

   If our working directory is the root, then the relative pathname is usr/staff/joan/file3. Note that the only difference between the absolute and relative pathnames is the first slash representing the root itself.

3. From /usr.

   If our working directory is /usr, then the relative pathname is staff/joan/file3.

4. From /usr/staff.

   If our working directory is /usr/staff, then the relative pathname is joan/file3. A word of caution is in order here. A common mistake is to start a relative path with a slash. In this case, that would make it /joan/file3. Remember, however, that whenever a pathname starts with a slash, it is an absolute pathname. In this case, UNIX would begin its search for the file at the root, and because there is no directory named `joan` immediately under the root, it would raise an error file not found. Relative addresses can never start with a slash.

5. From `/usr/staff/joan`.

   If our working directory is `/usr/staff/joan`, then the relative pathname is just `file3`. When the file is in the working directory, the relative pathname is just the filename.

6. From `/usr/staff/adams`.

   If our working directory is `/usr/staff/adams`, then we are out of the path from the root to the file. We must therefore find a starting point somewhere on the path from the root to the file.[6] In this case, the relative path would then be `../joan/file3`. This assumes that we know the exact directory configuration above our home directory. A safer path would be to use `joan`'s home directory, `~joan/file3`.

7. From `/usr/staff/adams/reports`.

   Once again, there are two paths. The first uses the home directory abbreviation as shown in example 6. The second uses two parent abbreviations; the first takes us to `adams` and the second to the staff directory. This choice gives us `../../joan/file3`. Again, the safer and shorter path is `~joan/file3`.

These seven examples are summarized in Table 3.5.

TABLE 3.5 *Relative Pathname Examples*

Working Directory	Relative Path to `file3`
1. `/etc`	Use absolute pathname; it's faster.
2. `/`	`usr/staff/joan/file3`
3. `/usr`	`staff/joan/file3`
4. `/usr/staff`	`joan/file3`
5. `/usr/staff/joan`	`file3`
6. `/usr/staff/adams`	`../joan/file3 or ~joan/file3`
7. `/usr/staff/adams/reports`	`../../joan/file3 or ~joan/file3`

3.5 File System Implementation

When a disk is formatted, space is divided into several sections. Some sections contain structural information about the disk itself. The last section contains the physical files. In this section, we examine the UNIX file system to better understand how these sections are related.

Disk storage can be conceived of as a continuous linear storage structure, starting with track 0 on the first track surface and moving down through track 0 of all surfaces before continuing with track 1 on the first surface.

---

[6]We could use the absolute pathname, but that is generally inefficient, and often we don't know all of the directories between the root and the directory containing the file.

File Systems

In UNIX, a **file system** has four structural sections known as blocks: the boot block, the super block, the inode block, and the data block. The boot block, super block, and inode blocks are fixed at the beginning of the disk. They occupy the same locations on the disk even when the disk is reorganized. These blocks are shown in Figure 3.5.

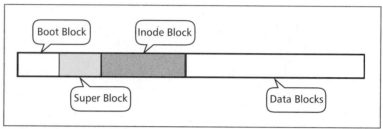

FIGURE 3.5 *A Disk File Format*

Boot Block

When an operating system is started, a small program known as the **boot program** is used to load the kernel into memory.[7] The boot program, when present, is found at the beginning of a disk in the boot block.

Super Block

The next block on the disk, the **super block,** contains information about the file system. Stored here are such items as the total size of the disk, how many blocks are empty, and the location of bad blocks on the disk.

Inode Block

Following the super block is the **inode** (information node) **block,** which contains information about each file in the data block. The file information is stored in records known as inodes. There is one inode for each file on the disk. They contain information about the file, most notably the owner of the file, its file type, permissions, and address. As shown in Figure 3.6, each inode contains the address of its corresponding file.

Data Blocks

The data block contains several types of files. First and foremost from the user's point of view, it contains all of the user files; it is where data are stored. It also contains the special files that are related to user data: regular files, directory files, symbolic link files, and FIFO files. Finally, it contains the character special, block special, and socket system files.

---

[7]Booting the system, also known as bootstrapping, is a term created by early programmers to describe their manual system initialization process. While its meaning has been lost over the years, the term continues to be used to describe the process.

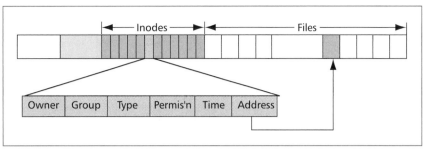

FIGURE 3.6 *Inodes*

Directory Contents

Given the concept of inodes pointing to files, the directory becomes a very simple structure. Remember that the directory is itself a file. Its contents are a set of inode-file entries containing the filename and its corresponding inode. A directory is seen in Figure 3.7. In this figure, each file is paired with an inode, which as we have seen contains the address of and other information about the file. This pairing of filename and inodes is the basis of a UNIX concept called links.

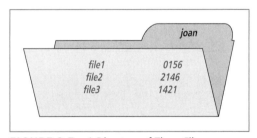

FIGURE 3.7 *A Directory of Three Files*

Links

A link is a logical relationship between an inode and a file that relates the name of a file to its physical location. UNIX defines two types of links: hard links and symbolic links.

Hard Links

In a **hard link** structure, the inode in the directory links the filename directly to the physical file. While this may sound like an extra level of structure, it provides the basis for multiple file linking, which we will see shortly. The hard link concept is shown in Figure 3.8.

Symbolic Links

A **symbolic** (or soft) **link** is a structure in which the inode is related to the physical file through a special file known as a symbolic link (page 69). This structure is shown in Figure 3.9.

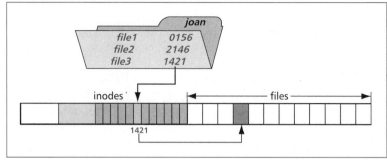

FIGURE 3.8　*A Hard Link*

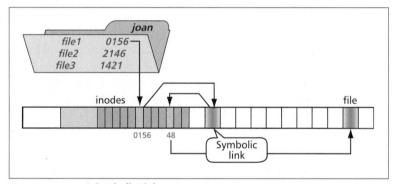

FIGURE 3.9　*A Symbolic Link*

As you study Figure 3.9, if you come to the conclusion that a symbolic link is not as efficient as a hard link, you would be correct. Soft links were designed for two specific situations: links to directories, which must be symbolic, and links to files on other file systems. Similarly, for technical reasons beyond the scope of this text, it is not possible to use a hard link to a file that is on another file system. Symbolic links work well, however. Figure 3.10 shows the structural design of a symbolic link and how it links a filename to a file in another file system.

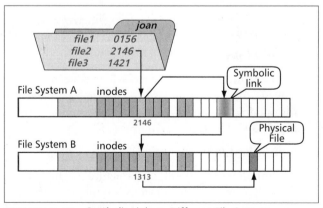

FIGURE 3.10　*Symbolic Links to Different File Systems*

Multiple Links

One of the advantages provided by the inode design is the ability to link two or more different filenames to one physical file. The filenames can be in the same directory or in different directories. This makes the multilink structure a convenient and efficient method of sharing files. Files are commonly shared among a team working on a large system. Additionally, given a user with a large file system, it may be convenient to share a highly used file among several directories. In either case, the important point to note is that although there are several different references to the file, *it exists only once.*

In UNIX, a physical file has only one inode, but it can have many names.

When a file is created, an entry containing its name and inode link is stored in its directory. To share the file, the same entry can be created in another directory. As we will see, the filename in the second directory entry can use the same or a different filename. Both entries, however, link to the same inode, which in turn points to the physical file. In Figure 3.11, we show three different files all pointing to one inode. Assuming that all permissions are properly set, both Juan and Tuan could update the file. On the other hand, the permissions could be set so that only one could update and the other could only read.

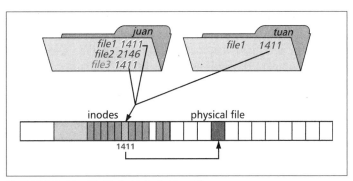

FIGURE 3.11   *Multiple Links to One File*

Hard links can be used only with files; soft links can be used with both files and directories.

Current and Parent Directories

In all of our examples so far, we have excluded two entries: one that represents the current directory (.) and one that represents the parent directory (..). These entries provide the inode entry for these two directories so that we can reference them when necessary. Session 3.2 contains an inode directory listing (for more information on the list command, see page 81). We used the options to print all entries (-a) and inode entries (-i). Because the current and parent directories start with a period, they are considered hidden files and are not normally printed. Note that in this list, the current directory is listed first and the parent directory is listed second. These two directories are generally at the top of the list.

SESSION 3.2 **inode** *List*

```
$ ls -ai
79944 .               79887 DirE          79937 file1
80925 ..              79942 backUpDir      79872 lnDir
79965 DirA            79906 backUpDir.mt   79871 mvDir
```

Session 3.2 Analysis: There are three columns, each containing an inode and filename pair. Note that the inode for the current directory is 79944, and its parent directory is inode 80925. Assuming a structure similar to the one in Figure 3.3 on page 70, if you were to move to the parent directory (see **cd** command, page 88), you would see the same inodes. The inode for current directory (staff) would be 80925, and inode 79944 would be your home directory.

3.6   Operations Unique to Directories

A careful analysis of the UNIX directory and file operations reveals that some are used only with directories, some are used only with files, and some are used with both directories and files. In this section, we discuss those operations that are used only with directories. In the next two sections, we discuss those that are used only with files and those that are used with both. The five directory operations covered in this section are shown in Figure 3.12.

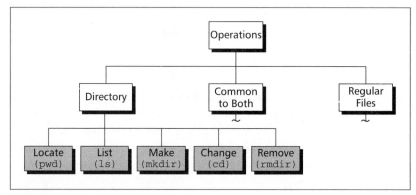

FIGURE 3.12   *Directory Operations*

Locate Directory (pwd) Command

We can determine the location of the current directory in the directory structure. This is particularly useful after we have navigated through the directory structure and we need to know where we are.

The command used to determine the current directory is print working directory (**pwd**). It has no options and no attributes. When executed, it prints the absolute path-name for the current directory. Its format is shown in Figure 3.13.

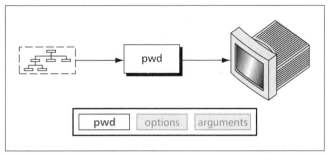

FIGURE 3.13   *The **pwd** Command*

The name print working directory is misleading because it does not actually print the working directory; it only displays it on the screen. This is one of those historical utilities. It was created when UNIX was run on teletypes. An example is in Session 3.3.

SESSION 3.3   *Print Working Directory*

```
$ pwd
/usr/~gilberg/tran
```

List Directory (ls) Command

The list (**ls**) command lists the contents in a directory. Depending on the options used, it can list files, directories, or subdirectories. If the name of a directory is not provided, it displays the contents of the working directory. Its basic format is presented in Figure 3.14. In the discussion that follows, we cover only the more common options.

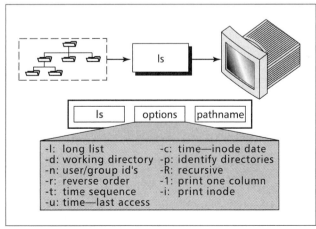

FIGURE 3.14   *The **ls** Command*

Let's begin with the simplest list, a basic list of the directories and files under the working directory. This command uses no options or pathnames. A sample is in Session 3.4.

SESSION 3.4 *Basic List Directory*

```
$ ls
BST.c       aFile       file1       memo509     saturn      zFile
BST.h       binSrch.c   gnuFile     note311     statusRpt
```

The basic list command formats the directories and files alphabetically in columns. If you know the ASCII collating sequence well, you will recognize that the files in Session 3.4 are listed down the columns, BST.c, BST.h, aFile, and so forth. This list excludes hidden files. To see all of the files, including hidden files, you need to include the all option (-a).

Long List

The simple list command is good for a quick review of the files in a directory, but much more information is available with the long list. Let's look carefully at the attributes shown in Figure 3.15. We examine each in turn.

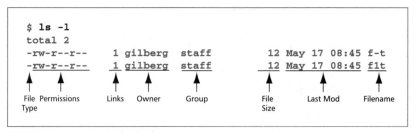

FIGURE 3.15 *Long List Option*

File Type As we discussed at the beginning of this chapter, there are seven file types in UNIX. Table 3.6 contains the file type designation, which is the first character of each line in Figure 3.15.

TABLE 3.6 *File Type Designators*

File Designation	File Type
–	Regular file
d	Directory
c	Character special
b	Block special
l	Symbolic link
p	FIFO
s	Socket

Permissions Permissions are discussed in Chapter 4, page 123. There are three sets of permissions: owner, group, and other. Each group has three possible permissions: read (r), write (w), and execute (x) in that order. If a permission is granted, the appropriate letter is shown. If it is not permitted, a dash is shown.

Links Links is a count of the number of files that are linked to this directory or file. We will study links later.

Owner Owner is the user name for that account that owns the file. It is usually the same as the login name.

Group If the owner of the file is a member of a group, such as staff in Figure 3.15, the group name is shown here.

File Size The file size in bytes.

Last Modification The date and time of the last modification. If the file is more than a year old, the time is replaced by the year.

Filename The name of the file. Normally, filename is just that, the name the owner used when the file was created. Sometimes, however, you will see some additional characters in a filename. Text editors often create a work file. When the editor is not terminated correctly, these working versions can be left hanging around. Working files begin and/or end with a pound sign (#). Hidden files are identified with a leading period. Occasionally you will see a system file with a tilde (~) at the end of the name.

List Options

List All Hidden files are normally not displayed in a file list. That's why they are called "hidden" files. To display all files, including the hidden ones, use option -a as shown in Session 3.5.

SESSION 3.5   *List All Option*

```
$ ls -a ~
.                    .mailrc            file2
..                   .profile           mail
.forward             .sh_history        mail.instr
.desktop-cis-b12     C-Programs         mail.staff.ids
.history             f-files            manVi
.login               file.c             status
.lsignature          file.bin
```

Working Directory The directory option (-d) displays only the working directory name. If used with the long list, it displays the working directory attributes. Session 3.6 shows the list directory option results.

SESSION 3.6   *List Directory Option*

```
$ ls -ld
drwxr-xr-x    14 gilberg   staff         3584 May 17 15:17 .
```

List User and Group ID The list user and group id option (-n) is the same as a long list except that the user and group ids are displayed rather than the user and group names. Session 3.7 shows a sample output. Notice that the user's name, gilberg, has been replaced by his user id, 3988, and his group name, staff, has been replaced with the group id, 24.

SESSION 3.7 *List User and Group IDs*

```
$ ls -nd
drwxr-xr-x    2 3988      24           512 May 17 08:53 .
```

Reverse Order The reverse order option (-r) sorts the display in descending (reverse) order. This causes the file names starting with 'z' to be displayed before files names starting with 'a'. Session 3.8 shows the file list output in reverse order.

SESSION 3.8 *List Directory in Reverse Order*

```
$ ls -r
zFile       saturn      memo509      file1        aFile        BST.c
statusRpt   note311     gnuFile      binSrch.c    BST.h
```

Time Sorts There are three time sorts. They should all be used with the long list option. The basic time sort (-lt) sorts by the time stamp with the latest file first. The second time sequence is by last access (-lu). The third time sequence lists the files by the inode date change (-lc); this is basically the file creation date, although some other changes, such as permission changes, affect it. Session 3.9 shows the basic time sequence output.

SESSION 3.9 *List Directory in Basic Time Sequence*

```
$ ls -lt
total 12
-rw-r--r--    1 gilberg   staff          14 May 19 13:33 file1
drwxr-xr-x    2 gilberg   staff         512 May 19 13:29 memos
-rw-r--r--    1 gilberg   staff          15 May 18 18:17 zFile
-rw-r--r--    1 gilberg   staff          15 May 18 18:16 aFile.tmp
```

Identify Directories We can identify directories in a long list by the file type, which is the first character of each line. If the file type is d, the file is a directory. On a short list, however, there is no way to identify which files are directories and which are ordinary. The -p option appends each directory name with a slash (/) as shown in Session 3.10. Note that both memos and unix7.1 are directories.

SESSION 3.10 *List Directory—Identify Directories*

```
$ ls -p
BST.c        binSrch.c    memo509      saturn       zFile
BST.h        file1        memos/       statusRpt
aFile.tmp    gnuFile      note311      unix7.1/
```

Recursive List Recursive means reentering over and over again. In a list structure command, recursive means to list the directory, and then list another directory, and then another one. Specifically, when we list a directory recursively, option -R, we want to list not only the contents of the directory itself but also the contents of all of its subdirectories. The recursive directory list is used primarily to study the structure of a directory. This needs to be done whenever we are considering reorganizing a directory. To demonstrate how a recursive list works, let's list all directories shown in Figure 3.16.

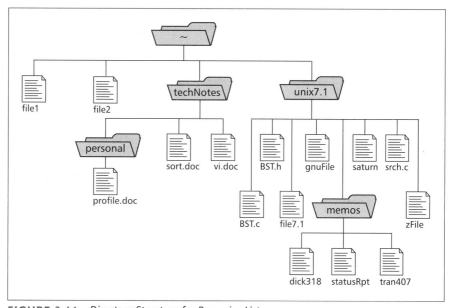

FIGURE 3.16   *Directory Structure for Recursive List*

To see the complete structure, we need two options. First, we need the option R for the recursion. However, if we just use the recursive option, we won't be able to tell the directories from the files. Therefore, we also used the p option, which tells UNIX that we want the directories identified with a slash. The output is shown in Session 3.11.

SESSION 3.11   *Recursive List*

```
$ ls -Rp
file1       file2       techNotes/  unix7.1/

./techNotes:
personal/  sort.doc   vi.doc

./techNotes/personal:
profile.doc
```

Continued

SESSION 3.11   *Recursive List—Continued*

```
./unix7.1/
BST.c          file7.1       memos/        srch.c
BST.h          gnuFile       saturn        zFile

./unix7.1/memos:
dick318        statusRpt     tran407
```

Session 3.11 Analysis: Compare the output in Session 3.11 with Figure 3.16. The first thing to note is that the listing starts with the current working directory. It then lists the contents of the first subdirectory under the working directory and its subdirectory, per-sonal. Finally, it lists the contents of the subdirectory to unix7.1 and its subdirectory, memos.[8]

Each directory list starts with the pathname on the first line. Between directories is a blank line. Within each directory, the contents are listed alphabetically. When multiple columns are needed, the sequencing runs down the columns first, just like in a telephone book.

Print One Column   There will be situations in which you want the filenames printed as a column rather than several files in one line (multicolumn). The print option for print one column is -1. Note that this is a numeric one, not the character ell. A sample is shown in Session 3.12. We have abbreviated Session 3.12 in the interest of space.

SESSION 3.12   *Print One Column*

```
$ ls -1
BST.c
BST.h
aFile.tmp

zFile
```

Print inode Number   Occasionally, you will need to see the inode numbers for a file. The print inode number option is -i. If you want to see all of the inodes for all files, you simply use the list command, either short or long, with no file list. If you want to see it for one or more files, you can list the filenames as shown in Session 3.13. Note that the inode number is printed as the first column, and the filename becomes the last column.

SESSION 3.13   *Print **inode** Number*

```
$ ls -li file1 zFile
37585 -rw-r--r--    1 gilberg   staff        14 May 17 16:32 file1
33809 -rw-r--r--    1 gilberg   staff        15 May 18 18:17 zFile
```

Make Directory (mkdir) Command

To create a new directory, you use the make directory (**mkdir**) command. It has two options: permission mode and parent directories. Its format appears in Figure 3.17.

---

[8]If you have studied data structures, you will recognize this as a *depth-first traversal* of the directories in the structure.

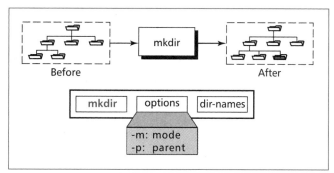

FIGURE 3.17 *The **mkdir** Command*

You can control the permissions for the new directory with the mode (-m) option. If the mode is not specified, the directory will typically have a mode that includes read and execute for all three sets (owner, group, other) and write only for the owner. In Session 3.14, we create a directory for the saturn group files and then list its attributes with the list directory command. In Chapter 4, you will learn how to use and change them to make your files secure.

SESSION 3.14 *Make Directory*

```
$ mkdir saturnGp
$ ls -ld saturnGp
drwxr-xr-x    2 gilberg   staff          512 May 19 14:03 saturnGp
```

The second make directory option, parent (-p), creates a parent directory in the path specified by the directory name. For example, if we need to create a memos directory for the saturn project, and within memos we want to create a schedule directory, we could create both with the options in Session 3.15.

SESSION 3.15 *Make Directory in Path*

```
$ mkdir -p saturnGp/memos/schedule
$ ls -lR saturnGp
total 1
drwxrwxr-x    3 gilberg   staff          512 May 19 14:17 memos

saturnGp/memos:
total 1
drwxrwxr-x    2 gilberg   staff          512 May 19 14:17 schedule

saturnGp/memos/schedule:
total 0
```

Session 3.15 Analysis: Let's look at the make directory command a little closer. Before it was executed, the saturnGp was empty; after the command was executed, it has one file, the memos directory. At the same time we created the memos directory, we also created its subdirectory, schedule. The list command that verifies the creation of our directories specifies a long list option with recursion (-lR). This allows us to verify that the directories were created as desired.

Change Directory (cd) Command

Now that we have multiple directories, we need some way to move among them—that is, to change our working directory. The change directory (**cd**) command does exactly that. Its format is shown in Figure 3.18.

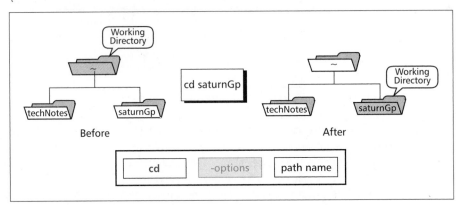

FIGURE 3.18   *The **cd** Command*

There are no options for the change directory command. The pathname can be relative or absolute; generally, it is relative. If there is no pathname argument, the target is the home directory. The home directory can also be targeted by using the home abbreviation (cd ~). To move from our home directory in Figure 3.18 to the saturnGp directory, we use the command in Session 3.16.

SESSION 3.16   *Change Directory*

```
$ pwd
/usr/~gilberg
$ cd saturnGp
$ pwd
/usr/~gilberg/saturnGp
```

Assume that below saturnGp we created a directory memos and within memos we created a schedule directory. Using the home abbreviation, we can move to the schedule directory from anywhere in our account using the command in Session 3.17.

SESSION 3.17   *Change Directory with Home Reference*

```
$ cd ~/saturnGp/memos/schedule
$ pwd
/usr/~gilberg/saturnGp/memos/schedule
```

> To move directly to the home directory, use the change directory command with no argument.

Remove Directory (rmdir) Command

When a directory is no longer needed, it should be removed. The remove directory (**rmdir**) command deletes directories. Its format is shown in Figure 3.19.

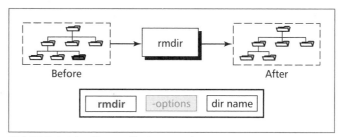

FIGURE 3.19   *The **rmdir** Command*

The **rmdir** command cannot delete a directory unless it is empty. If it contains any files, UNIX will return an error message, "Directory not empty." Session 3.18 shows both a successful and an unsuccessful remove directory. Note that when the command is executed successfully, the only response is the shell prompt.

SESSION 3.18   *Remove Directory*

```
$ rmdir memos
memos: Directory not empty
$ rmdir memo
```

On page 108, we show how to remove a directory even if it's not empty; however, the **rmdir** command is preferred because it does not delete a nonempty directory and is therefore much safer.

3.7   Operations Unique to Regular Files

In this section, we discuss the four operations that are unique to regular files: create file, edit file, display file, and print file. These utilities are highlighted in Figure 3.20.

Create File

The most common tool to create a text file is a text editor such as **vi** (see Chapter 2). Other utilities, such as **cat,** that are useful to create small files are discussed in future chapters. Binary files are created by application programs written for a specific application and utilities such as the C compiler.

Edit File

UNIX provides several utilities to edit text files. The most common is a basic text editor such as **vi.** In addition, there are others that we discuss in future chapters, such as **sed,** that provide powerful search and edit tools. All of the basic edit utilities can create a file, but only some can edit one.

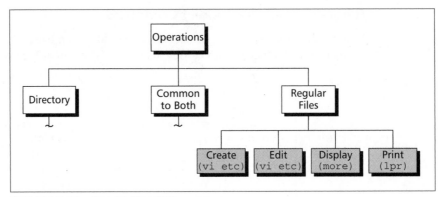

FIGURE 3.20   *Regular File Utilities*

Display File (more) Command

Although many utilities write their output to standard output (the monitor), the most useful one to display a file is **more.** It allows us to set the output page size and pauses at the end of each page to allow us to read the file. After each page, we may request one or more lines, a new page, or quit. The **more** command is shown in Figure 3.21.

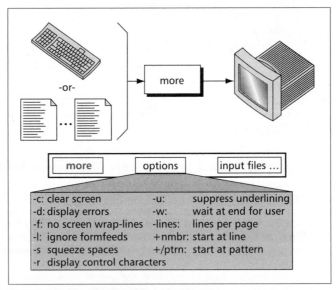

FIGURE 3.21   *The **more** Command*

The basic **more** options are summarized in Table 3.7. There are others that we leave for you to discover as you work with UNIX. For a complete list of the **more** options, we suggest you check **man** (see Chapter 1).

The most basic use of **more** uses no options. In this basic form, **more** starts at the beginning of the file. If the file is small (that is, less than one screen's worth of lines), it prints all of the data and an "end" message. To return to the command line, key enter.

TABLE 3.7   *Display Options for the **more** Command*

Option	Explanation
-c	Clears screen before displaying.
-d	Displays error messages.
-f	Does not screen wrap long lines.
-l	Ignores formfeed characters.
-r	Displays control characters in format ^C.
-s	Squeezes multiple blank lines (leaving only one blank line in output).
-u	Suppresses text underlining.
-w	Waits at end of output for user to enter any key to continue.
-lines	Sets the number of lines in a screen (default is screen size – 2).
+nmbr	Starts output at the indicated line number (nmbr).
+/ptrn	Locates first occurrence of pattern (ptrn) and starts output two lines before it.

If there is more than one screen of data, **more** displays one screen, less two lines. At the bottom of the screen, it displays the message "`--more--(dd%)`". This message indicates that there are more lines in the file and how much has been displayed so far. To display the next screen, key the Spacebar. The basic **more** command is shown in the next example.

```
$ more TheRaven
```

We can control the size of the output with the lines option. For practical reasons, this option should not be set larger than the screen size unless the screen is scrollable. We can also set the starting line in the file with the number option. In Session 3.19, which you may recognize as the middle of Edgar Allan Poe's "The Raven," we set the page size to six lines and start printing at line 49.

SESSION 3.19   *Sample **more** Output*

```
$ more -ds -6 +49 TheRaven
Then this ebony bird beguiling my sad fancy into smiling,
By the grave and stern decorum of the countenance it wore,
"Though thy crest be shorn and shaven, thou," I said, "art sure no craven,
Ghastly grim and ancient Raven wandering from the Nightly shore--
Tell me what thy lordly name is on the Night's Plutonian shore!"
Quoth the Raven, "Nevermore."
--More--(46%)
```

Session 3.19 Analysis: Some points worth noting: First, the options are separated into three groups. This apparent exception to the rules occurs because the last three options are treated as though they were attributes; however, they must follow the basic options and precede the filename attribute, although either one can be listed first. We also requested that error messages be listed (-d option) and that duplicate blank lines be squeezed out (-s option). These two options were grouped together.

The last **more** example, Session 3.20, demonstrates how you can start the output two lines before specified text appears in the file. In this case, we selected the text "crest be shorn" so that the display would match the previous example. Note that the **more** display begins two lines before the matching text.

SESSION 3.20   *Specifying Start Line in* **more**

```
$ more -df -7 +/"crest be shorn" TheRaven
Then this ebony bird beguiling my sad fancy into smiling,
By the grave and stern decorum of the countenance it wore,
"Though thy crest be shorn and shaven, thou," I said, "art sure no craven,
Ghastly grim and ancient Raven wandering from the Nightly shore--
Tell me what thy lordly name is on the Night's Plutonian shore!"
Quoth the Raven, "Nevermore."
TheRaven (44%)
```

After the text has been displayed, we must enter a command to get **more** going again. The two most common commands are space to display the next screen of output and return to display one more line. If we are done and don't need to see any more output, we enter the quit (q) command. The common **more** continue options are shown in Table 3.8.

TABLE 3.8   **more** *Continue Options*

Command	Explanation
space	Displays next screen of output.
n+space	Displays next screen of output and sets screen size to n lines.
return	Advances one line.
d	Displays half a screen.
nf	Skips n screens and displays a screen.
nb	Moves back n screens and displays a screen.
q	Quits **more**.
Q	Quits **more**.
=	Displays current line number.
:f	Displays the current filename and line number.
v	Transfers to vi editor at the current line.
h	Displays a list of **more**'s commands.
.	Repeats the previous command.

Print File

The most common print utility is line printer (**lpr**). The line printer utility prints the contents of the specified files to either the default printer or to a specified printer. Multiple files can be printed with the same command. If no file is specified, the input comes from the standard input, which is usually a keyboard unless it has been redirected. For a complete discussion, refer to Print (lpr) Command on page 23.

3.8 Operations Common to Both

In this section, we discuss the operations that are common to both directories and regular files: copy, move, rename, link, delete, and find. They are shown in Figure 3.22.

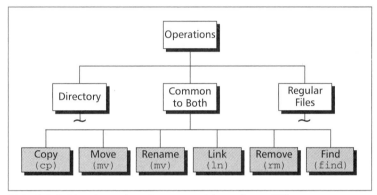

FIGURE 3.22 *Operations Common to Directories and Files*

Copy (cp) Command

The copy (**cp**) utility creates a duplicate of a file, a set of files, or a directory. If the source is a file, the new file contains an exact copy of the data in the source file. If the source is a directory, all of the files in the directory are copied to the destination, which must be a directory. If the destination file already exists, its contents are replaced by the source file contents. The **cp** command copies both text and binary files. Its format is presented in Figure 3.23.

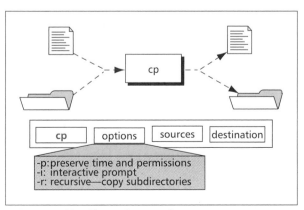

FIGURE 3.23 *The* **cp** *Command*

The first argument lists one or more files, or one directory, to be copied. The destination identifies the filename for the new file or, when multiple files are being copied, the directory for the new files. Multiple files cannot be copied into the same directory as the source files.

To copy a file successfully, several rules must be followed:

- The source must exist. Otherwise, UNIX prints the following error message:

<source> - No such file or directory

- If no destination path is specified, UNIX assumes the destination is the current directory.
- If the destination file does not exist, it is created; if it does exist, it is replaced.
- If the source is multiple files or a directory, the destination must be a directory.
- If the destination is the same directory as the source, the destination filename must be different.
- To prevent an automatic replacement of the destination file, use the interactive (-i) option. When interactive is specified, UNIX issues a warning message and waits for a reply. Any reply other than yes will cancel the copy of the specific file. Note, however, that if the file/destination directory is write protected, you cannot use this option to write to the directory.
- To preserve the modification times and file access permissions, use the preserve option (-p). In the absence of the preserve options, the time will be the time the file was copied, and the file access permissions will be the defaults.

Using the cp Command

Let's look at some simple copy command examples.

1. Copy one file in the working directory to the same directory. In Figure 3.24, the working directory is DirA. Because we are copying a file and placing it in the same directory, we must provide the source and destination files individually.

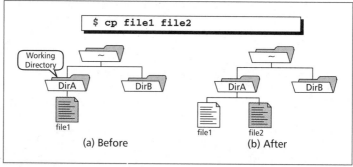

FIGURE 3.24 *Simple File Copy*

After copying file1, we have two files with identical permissions, owner, and groups. A simple copy preserves these file attributes. On the other hand, the last modification date of the target and the last access date of the source are changed to the current time. These effects are shown in Session 3.21.

SESSION 3.21   *Copy File to Same Directory*

```
$ ls -l f*
-rw-r--r--    1 gilberg  staff          120 May 25 15:10 file1

$ cp file1 file2
$ ls -l f*
-rw-r--r--    1 gilberg  staff          120 May 25 15:10 file1
-rw-r--r--    1 gilberg  staff          120 May 25 17:02 file2
```

If the file already exists, it is replaced. In this case, the permissions, owner, and group are not changed. To prove this, in Session 3.22, we change the permissions of file2 and recopy file1 to file2. Note, however, that the time still changes.

SESSION 3.22   *Copy and Replace File*

```
$ ls -l f*
-rw-r--r--    1 gilberg  staff          120 May 25 15:10 file1
-rw-------    1 gilberg  staff          120 May 25 17:02 file2

$ cp file1 file2
$ ls -l f*
-rw-r--r--    1 gilberg  staff          120 May 25 15:10 file1
-rw-------    1 gilberg  staff          120 May 25 17:08 file2
```

2. In the previous example, we assumed that the working directory contained the file to be copied. If we are in another directory, for example, our home directory (~), we simply include the path as shown in the next example. Note that the path must be included in the destination entry also. If we omit the path from the destination, the file will be copied to the working directory.

```
$ cp DirA/file1 DirA/file2
```

3. In this example, we need to copy a file in one directory to another directory from our home directory. This copy requires that we specify the path to the file to be copied and the path to the destination directory. The concept is shown in Figure 3.25.

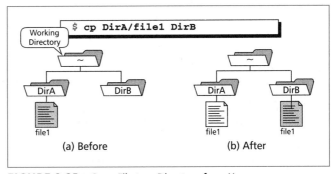

FIGURE 3.25   *Copy File to a Directory from Home*

Because we are keeping the filename the same, all we need to specify for the destination is the directory. The command with before and after directory listings is shown in Session 3.23.

SESSION 3.23 *Copy File to a Directory from Home*

```
$ ls -l DirB
total 0
$ cp DirA/file1 DirB
$ ls -l DirB
total 1
-rw-r--r--    1 gilberg  staff           120 May 27 10:38 file1
```

4. Now let's copy the file and rename it. In the example in Figure 3.26, the working directory is DirA.

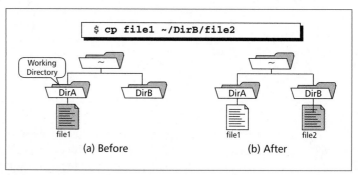

FIGURE 3.26 *Copy and Rename File*

In Session 3.24, we need to specify the destination path, starting at our home directory.

SESSION 3.24 *Copy File to Different Directory*

```
$ ls -l ~/DirB
total 0

$ cp file1 ~/DirB/file2

$ ls -l ~/DirB
total 1
-rw-r--r--    1 gilberg  staff           120 May 27 10:46 file2
```

cp Command Options

The copy command has three options: preserve attributes, interactive, and recursion.

Preserve Attributes Option   As stated in the Copy (cp) Command section, when the destination file exists, its permissions, owner, and group are used rather than the source file attributes. We can force the permissions, owner, and group to be changed, however, by using the preserve (-p) option. This is demonstrated in Session 3.25. Note how the permissions of `file2` have been changed to match those of the source file, `file1`.

SESSION 3.25   *Preserve Attributes Option*

```
$ ls -l
total 2
-rw-r--r--    1 gilberg    staff          120 May 25 15:46 file1
-rw-------    1 gilberg    staff          120 May 27 11:03 file2

$ cp -p file1 file2

$ ls -l
total 2
-rw-r--r--    1 gilberg    staff          120 May 25 15:46 file1
-rw-r--r--    1 gilberg    staff          120 May 25 15:46 file2
```

Interactive Option   We can guard against a file being accidentally deleted by a copy command by using the interactive (-i) option. When the interactive option is specified, copy asks if we want to delete an existing file. If we reply y or yes, the file is replaced. If we reply n or no, the copy is cancelled. Session 3.26 demonstrates the interactive option. Note that the reply of yep was not accepted. It must be y or yes. Likewise, to cancel the copy, the response must be n or no.

SESSION 3.26   *Interactive Option*

```
$ cp -i file1 file2
UX:cp: overwrite file2? (yes/no)[no] : yep
UX:cp: overwrite file2? (yes/no)[no] : y
```

The interactive option is especially useful and highly recommended when you are copying multiple files as shown in the next section.

Recursive Copy   Another way we can copy a collection of files is with the recursive (-r) copy. While the wildcard copy copies the matching files in a directory, the recursive copy copies the whole directory and all of its subdirectories to a new directory. The recursive copy is shown in Figure 3.27.

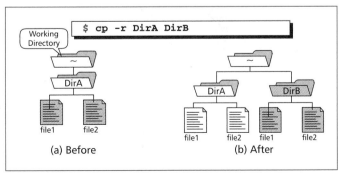

FIGURE 3.27   *Recursive Copy*

In this basic example, the source directory has no subdirectories, and the destination directory does not exist. As you can see in Figure 3.27, both the source directory and its files were copied. When the destination directory does not exist, UNIX first creates it and then copies the necessary files. If the directory already exists, only the files are copied. The recursive copy code is shown in Session 3.27.

SESSION 3.27   *Example of Recursive Copy*

```
$ ls
DirA
$ ls DirB
Cannot access DirB: No such file or directory
$ cp -r DirA DirB

$ ls
DirA    DirB

$ ls DirB
file1  file2
```

Special care must be taken to make sure the new directory is not a subdirectory of the directory being copied. This condition creates a never-ending copy that terminates only when the disk space is exhausted or some other condition, such as a name that exceeds the maximum name length (255 characters), occurs.

In the next example, we demonstrate how the recursive copy also copies subdirectories. In Figure 3.28, DirC is copied to DirD. Because the source has two subdirectories, each with one file, the entire subdirectory structure is copied, and DirC becomes a subdirectory to DirD.

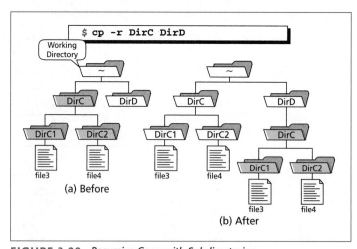

FIGURE 3.28   *Recursive Copy with Subdirectories*

The code for this copy is shown in Session 3.28.

SESSION 3.28   *Recursive Copy with Subdirectories*

```
$ ls -R DirC
DirC1   DirC2

DirC/DirC1:
file3

DirC/DirC2:
file4

$ ls -R DirD

$

$ cp -r DirC DirD

$ ls -R DirD
DirD

DirD/DirC:
DirC1   DirC2

DirD/DirC/DirC1:
file3

DirD/DirC/DirC2:
file4
```

Wildcard Copies

Wildcards can be used to copy files as long as the destination is another directory. You cannot use wildcards if you are copying to and from the same directory. Figure 3.29 shows a simple example in which we copy all files beginning with the letter f from DirA to DirB.

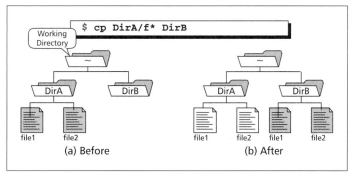

FIGURE 3.29   *Wildcard Copy*

In the code demonstration for the wildcard copy in Figure 3.29, we begin with a list command to demonstrate that the destination directory is empty. We then copy the files from DirA to DirB. After the files are copied, we list the directory to show that both files were indeed copied. The code is shown in Session 3.29.

```
$ ls DirB
$
$ cp DirA/f* DirB
$ ls DirB
file1  file2
```

Move (mv) Command

The move (**mv**) command is used to move either an individual file, a list of files, or a directory. After a move, the old file name is gone and the new file name is found at the destination. This is the difference between a move and a copy. After a copy, the file is physically duplicated; it exists in two places. The move format appears in Figure 3.30. The first argument is the name of the file to be moved. The second argument is its destination or, in the case of a rename, its new name.

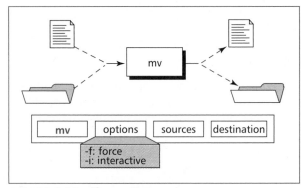

FIGURE 3.30   *The **mv** Command*

To demonstrate a file move, let's move a file from one directory to another as shown in Figure 3.31.

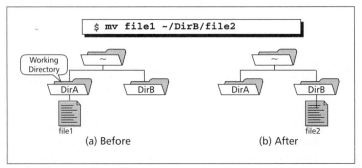

FIGURE 3.31   *Move File*

In Session 3.30, we move a file from `DirA` to another directory (`DirB`). Notice that the file name is the same before and after the move; after the move, the file in `DirA` has been deleted.

SESSION 3.30 *Move File*

```
$ ls -i DirA/file1
79915 DirA/file1
$ ls -i DirB
$
$ mv DirA/file1 DirB
$ ls -i DirA
$
$ ls -i DirB
79915 file1
```

Session 3.30 Analysis: We begin by listing the contents of both directories, showing that there is only one file in the source directory and none in the destination directory. Then we move the file. After the move, we repeat the lists, showing that the source directory is now empty and that the file has indeed been moved to the destination. Note that we have shown the inodes in the directory lists (option -i) to prove that the file is exactly the same physical file.

mv Options

Move has only two options: interactive (-i) and force (-f). They are described here.

Interactive If the destination file already exists, its contents are destroyed unless we use the interactive flag (-i) to request that **move** warn us. When the interactive flag is on, move asks if we want to destroy the existing file.

Session 3.31 contains an example of how we can prevent accidental deletions by using the interactive flag. Note that the options are (yes/no) [no]. The fact that no is in brackets indicates that it's the default: If you key Enter or Return without an option, no is assumed. We respond n to prevent the move that would delete the file.

SESSION 3.31 *Using the Interactive Flag to Prevent Move Errors*

```
$ ls mvDir
file1   gilbergfile3

$ mv -i file1 mvDir
overwrite mvDir/file1? (yes/no)[no] : n
```

Force As demonstrated earlier, when we are not allowed to write a file, we are asked if we want to destroy the file or not. If we are sure that we want to write it, even if it already exists, we can skip the interactive message with the force (-f) option. We repeat Session 3.31 using a new filename to demonstrate the force option.

SESSION 3.32   *Force Replacement with Move Command*

```
$ ls -l mvDir
total 2
-rw-r--r--     1 gilberg   staff          120 Sep 19 11:40 file1
-rw-r--r--     1 gilberg   staff          120 Sep 19 11:40 file3
$ mv -f file1 mvDir

$ ls -l mvDir
total 2
-rw-r--r--     1 gilberg   staff          120 Oct 28 16:06 file1
-rw-r--r--     1 gilberg   staff          120 Sep 19 11:40 file3
```

Session 3.32 Analysis: As you study this example, note that the creation date and time have changed indicating that a copy of file1 created on Oct 28 has replaced the copy created on Sep 19.

Rename (mv) Command

UNIX does not have a specific rename command. Recall that the move (**mv**) command (see page 100) with a new name (second argument) renames the file. If the destination file is in the same directory as the source file, the effect is a renaming of the file.

Let's look at a simple rename. In Session 3.33, file1 is renamed file0. We list the inode numbers before and after the rename to prove that the rename worked correctly.

SESSION 3.33   *A Simple Move (Rename)*

```
$ ls -i file*
79914 file1   79937 file2

$ mv file1 file0

$ ls -i file*
79914 file0   79937 file2
```

Link (ln) Command

The link command is presented in Figure 3.32. It receives either a file or directory as input, and its output is an updated directory.

ln Options

Link has three options: symbolic, interactive, and force.

Symbolic   The default link type is hard. To create a symbolic link, the symbolic option (-s) is used. We demonstrate symbolic links in Symbolic Links starting on page 77.

Interactive   If the destination file already exists, its contents are destroyed unless we request to be warned by using the interactive flag (-i). When the interactive flag is on, link asks if we want to destroy the existing file. This is similar to the message we get when the permissions don't allow us to write the file. Session 3.34 contains an example

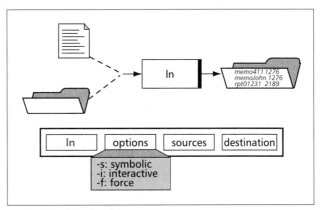

FIGURE 3.32 *The **ln** Command*

of how we can prevent accidental deletions by using the interactive flag. Note that we respond n to prevent the link that would delete the file.

SESSION 3.34 *Using the Interactive Flag to Prevent Errors*

```
$ ls lnDir
file2        linkedFile

$ ln -i file2 lnDir
overwrite lnDir/file2? (yes/no)[no] : n
```

Force As demonstrated earlier, when we are about to overwrite a file, we are asked if we want to destroy the file or not. If we are sure that we want to write it, even if it already exists, we can skip the interactive message with the force (-f) option. In Session 3.35, we repeat Session 3.34 using a new filename to demonstrate the force option.

SESSION 3.35 *Force Write*

```
$ ls -l lnDir
total 2
lrwxr-xr-x    1 gilberg   staff            5 May 28 15:39 file2 -> file2
-rw-r--r--    2 gilberg   staff          120 May 25 15:10 linkedFile

$ ln -f file2 lnDir

$ ls -l lnDir
total 2
-r--r--r--    2 gilberg   staff          120 May 25 17:08 file2
-rw-r--r--    2 gilberg   staff          120 May 25 15:10 linkedFile
```

Session 3.35 Analysis: As you study this example, compare the listings for file2 carefully. First note that, in the first listing, it is a symbolic link as indicated by the file type and pathname. After the link command, it is an ordinary file (-), and there is no path in the filename. Also, the creation date and time have changed.

Hard Links

Hard Links to Files To create a hard link to a file, we specify the source file and the destination file. If the destination file doesn't exist, it is created. If it exists, it is first removed and then re-created as a linked file. Session 3.36 demonstrates creating a new file with a link.

SESSION 3.36 *Create Hard Link Demonstration*

```
$ ls lnDir
$
$ ln file1 lnDir/linkedFile
$

$ ls -i file1
79914 file1
$ ls -i lnDir/linkedFile
79914 lnDir/linkedFile
```

Session 3.36 Analysis: We begin by listing the contents of the target directory, `lnDir`, which is empty. We then link `file1` in the working directory to `linkedFile` in `lnDir`, giving it a new name. We could have used the source filename but chose to rename it for clarity. Because the file doesn't exist in `lnDir`, UNIX creates an entry for it in the directory and then links it to the inode for `file1`. This is verified by listing both the source and destination files with the display inode number option (`-i`). They are the same, indicating that both `file1` and `linkedFile` are the same physical file.

As has been stated, if the file already exists, it is destroyed and the new link file takes its place. We demonstrate this in Session 3.37 by repeating the link in Session 3.36 with a new file, linking another file from the working directory, and showing the changed contents.

SESSION 3.37 *Link to Existing File*

```
$ ln file2 lnDir/linkedFile
May not unlink existing lnDir/linkedFile   - Error 0

$ ln -f file2 lnDir/linkedFile

$ ls -i file2
79937 file2
$ ls -i lnDir/linkedFile
79937 lnDir/linkedFile
```

Session 3.37 Analysis: This session verifies our previous statement that a link is a remove and a link. When we try to link to the existing file (`linkedFile`) in the first command, UNIX rejects the command with a message that we can't unlink it. We therefore repeat the command with the force option (`-f`: page 107) and display the inode for both the source and destination files. They are both the same, and the `linkedFile` number has been changed from 79914 (Session 3.36).

Hard Links to Directories UNIX does not allow hard links to directories.

Symbolic Links

When the link (**ln**) command is executed with no options, the result is a hard link. If we try to create a hard link to a different file system, however, it is rejected because hard links must be made within the current directory structure. To link to a different file system, therefore, we must use symbolic links. We must also use symbolic links when we are linking to directories.

There is a danger with symbolic links because, although they behave like files and directories, they do not physically exist. They only point to the real directory or file. If the physical file is deleted, the file will no longer appear on a listing under its original name. It will still be available under its symbolic link name, but it is not accessible.

If a physical directory is deleted, the symbolic link to the directory still exists. If we try to list the symbolic directory, it lists with no files. If we try to move to it, however, we receive a message that it doesn't exist. Furthermore, to delete it, we must use the delete file command (**rm**—see page 106), not the delete directory command (**rmdir**).

Symbolic Link to Files For all purposes, a symbolic link functions exactly the same as a hard link, albeit not as efficiently. To demonstrate a symbolic link, in Session 3.38 we repeat Session 3.36, this time with symbolic links.

SESSION 3.38   *Symbolic Link Demonstration*

```
$ ls lnDir
linkedFile

$ ln -s file2 lnDir
$ ls -i file2
79937 file2

$ ls -il lnDir
total 2
79898 lrwxr-xr-x    1 gilberg   ...      5 May 28 15:39 file2 -> file2
79914 -rw-r--r--    2 gilberg   ...    120 May 25 15:10 linkedFile
```

Session 3.38 Analysis: This time we did not change the name of the file when we linked to it. There are two differences in the directory list between a hard linked file and a symbolically linked file. First, in a symbolically linked file, the file type (first character of the line) is `l`. Second, the name of the file includes the path to the physical file. Both of these differences are shown in Session 3.38.

Symbolic Link to Directory The code to create a symbolic link to a directory is the same as the code to link files. In Session 3.39, we demonstrate the right and wrong way to create a link to a directory.

SESSION 3.39   *Symbolic Link to Directory*

```
$ ls -il DirC                    # From parent, List DirC
total 2
```

Continued

SESSION 3.39   *Symbolic Link to Directory—Continued*

```
79917 drwxr-xr-x    2 gilberg  staff     512 Aug 29 12:03 DirC1
79961 drwxr-xr-x    2 gilberg  staff     512 May 27 11:40 DirC2
$ ln DirC1 hardDir              # Try to create a hard link to directory
Cannot link directory DirC1    # Fails--Cannot create hard link
$ ls symDir                    # Verify that there's no symDir
Cannot access symDir: No such file or directory
$ ln -s DirC symDir            # Create symbolic link for symDir
$ # We have now created a symbolic directory as verified by inodes
$ ls -il symDir                # Show symDir is symbolic link to DirC
79914 lrwxr-xr-x    1 gilberg  staff       4 Sep 18 21:53 symDir -> DirC
$ cd symDir                    # Move to newly created symDir
$ ls -il                       # Verify its contents same as DirC
total 2
79917 drwxr-xr-x    2 gilberg  staff     512 Aug 29 12:03 DirC1
79961 drwxr-xr-x    2 gilberg  staff     512 May 27 11:40 DirC2
```

Session 3.39 Analysis: We begin by listing the inodes of directory DirC, a subdirectory in the working directory. It contains two subdirectories, DirC1 and DirC2. The next command verifies that we can't create a hard link to a directory. We then demonstrate that there is no symbolic directory (symDir). The next command creates a symbolic link to the new symbolic directory. Note that this time there is a symbolic (-s) link option in the link command. At this point, we have successfully created a symbolic link.

To verify that the symbolic directory has been created, we first list its inode. Then we move to it and display its contents, which are the same as DirC's contents as verified by the inodes. We have now verified that the symbolically linked directory is valid.

Remove (rm) Command

The remove (**rm**) utility deletes an entry from a directory by destroying its link to the file. Remember, however, that there can be multiple links to a physical file. This means that a remove does not always physically delete a file. The file is deleted only if, after the remove, there are no more links to it. The remove command is shown in Figure 3.33.

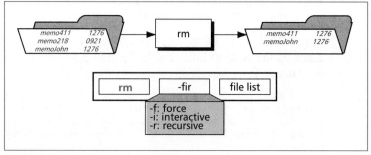

FIGURE 3.33   *The **rm** Command*

To delete a file, we must have write permission. If we try to remove a file that does not have its write flag set, UNIX asks for confirmation. In Session 3.40, we begin by listing `file2`, which can only be read as indicated by the permissions. Because we don't have write permission, when we try to remove it, UNIX asks for a confirmation. After completing the remove, we try to list the file to prove that it is in fact gone.

SESSION 3.40   *Remove (Delete)*

```
$ ls -l file2
-r--r--r--    2 gilberg  staff          120 May 25 17:08 file2

$ rm file2
file2: 444 mode. Remove ? (yes/no)[no] : y

$ ls -l file2
Cannot access file2: No such file or directory
```

Remove Options

There are three options for the remove command: force, recursive, and interactive.

Force Removal   Force removal (`-f`) works just like the forced move. The file will be removed even it is write protected as long as we have write permission in the directory. If the directory is write protected, no files are removed and no warning messages are issued.

Recursive Removal   The recursive removal (`-r`) removes all files and empty directories in the path from the source directory. Files are deleted first, then the directory, so a directory can have files before the remove command. A directory is considered empty if all files are deleted. If a write-protected file is found in the path, remove asks for a confirmation before completing the remove. If the response is no, the file is not deleted, but the recursive remove command continues with other files and directories.

Session 3.41 recursively removes `delRecDir`. It contains one empty directory (`emptyDir`) and one file without write permissions (`file1`). After the remove command has been executed, we list it to prove that it is completely deleted.

SESSION 3.41   *Recursive Removal*

```
$ ls -Rl delRecDir
total 4
drwxr-xr-x    2 gilberg  staff          512 May 29 11:44 DirA
drwxr-xr-x    2 gilberg  staff          512 May 29 11:44 DirB
drwxr-xr-x    2 gilberg  staff          512 May 29 11:44 emptyDir
-r--r--r--    1 gilberg  staff          120 May 29 11:44 file1

delRecDir/DirA:
total 2
-rw-r--r--    1 gilberg  staff          120 May 29 11:44 file2
```

Continued

SESSION 3.41   *Recursive Removal—Continued*

```
-rw-r--r--     1 gilberg   staff          120 May 29 11:44 file3

delRecDir/DirB:
total 2
-rw-r--r--     1 gilberg   staff          120 May 29 11:44 file4
-rw-r--r--     1 gilberg   staff          120 May 29 11:44 file5
delRecDir/emptyDir:

delRecDir/emptyDir:
total 0

$ rm -r delRecDir
delRecDir/file1: 444 mode. Remove ? (yes/no)[no] : y

$ ls delRecDir
Cannot access delRecDir: No such file or directory
```

Wildcard Remove

Remove can be used with wildcards. This option is highly dangerous, however, and should be used with caution. It is generally considered a good idea to use the echo command to test the effect before actually executing a remove. Session 3.42 demonstrates how echo can be used to preview what will be removed.

SESSION 3.42   *Using* echo *to Preview Effects of Remove*

```
$ echo rm -r f*
rm -r file1 file2 file2.bak file2.sym

$ rm -r file2.bak file2.sym
```

Find File (find) Command

Given a large file environment, it can quickly become difficult to find a given file. It is not surprising, therefore, that almost all operating systems provide a file search command. In UNIX, it is **find**. Find has no options. Its first argument is the path that we want to search, usually from our home directory. The second argument is the criterion that find needs to complete its search. The find format is seen in Figure 3.34. Table 3.9 (page 111) contains a complete list of the criteria.

We start with a simple example. Let's find and print the absolute pathname of a file. We show how to do this in Session 3.43.

SESSION 3.43   **find** *Address of File*

```
$ find DirC -name file3 -print
DirC/DirC1/file3
```

Now assume that we are doing our monthly file backup and want to know all files that were changed in the last 30 days. We can use the find command to list all files whose modification date (mtime) is within the last 30 days. Session 3.44 demonstrates this command.

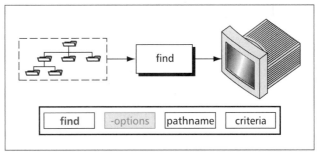

FIGURE 3.34 *The **find** Command*

SESSION 3.44 **find** *Command*

```
$ find DirC -type f -mtime -30
DirC/file1
DirC/DirC1/file2
DirC/DirC2/file3
```

Let's look at how this command works. Starting with the directory specified in the command, it looks at each file in the directory one at a time. If the file matches the criteria, the requested action is taken. In this case, no action was requested, so the file and its path are printed. After all of the files in the current directory have been evaluated, find moves to the first subdirectory and repeats the evaluations file by file. It stops only after all files in all subdirectories have been evaluated.

Finding and printing our modified files were not our objectives; however, we want to copy them to a backup file. We can execute other UNIX commands, in this case to copy the changed files. How to execute other commands based on the find results is discussed in the following sections. Remember, however, that the actions are taken only when the evaluation criteria are true.

Execute Action

The execute action (-exec) attribute invokes another UNIX command. Its format is shown in Session 3.45.

```
-exec   command   {}   \;
```

The two braces in the action command are replaced by the pathname of each file that matches the evaluation criteria. The command must end with a semicolon (;). In the preceding example, we escaped the semicolon. It can also be put into quotes. To automatically copy each file to a backup directory, we could use the following find command. Session 3.45 demonstrates two find criteria: execute action and type. Type allows us to specify the file type. In this session, we specify regular files.

SESSION 3.45 *Find and Backup*

```
$ ls backUpDir
$
```

Continued

SESSION 3.45   *Find and Backup—Continued*

```
$ find DirC -type f -mtime -30
DirC/file1
DirC/DirC1/file2
DirC/DirC2/file3
$ find DirC -type f -mtime -30 -exec cp {} backUpDir ;
$ ls backUpDir
file1   file2   file3
```

Session 3.45 Analysis: The criteria are the same as in Session 3.44. The execute criteria use the copy command (cp) followed by braces, which are replaced by the pathname as files are located that match the criteria. Recall that copy requires a second attribute, the destination directory. We must therefore specify the destination directory (backUpDir) after the braces.

Okay Criterion The okay (-ok) criterion works just like execute action, but it prompts for an "ok" before it competes the action. In our copy example, it asks for a yes or no response before executing the copy. As you would expect, if the action is yes, it completes the copy. If it is no, it skips the copy. Except for the output directory, Session 3.45 is repeated using the okay criterion in Session 3.46.

SESSION 3.46   *Find and Backup with Okay*

```
$ ls mvDir
$
$ find DirC -type f -mtime -30 -ok cp {} mvDir \;
< cp ... DirC/file1 >?    y
< cp ... DirC/DirC1/file2 >?    n
< cp ... DirC/DirC2/file3 >?    y
$ ls mvDir
file1   file3
```

Session 3.46 Analysis: We first demonstrate that the target directory is empty. The find command locates three files to be copied and asks for an ok to copy them. We respond yes to the first and third and no to the second. Another directory list shows that in fact the first and third files were copied, but the second one was not.

Combining Criteria

In the **find** command, we can combine criteria as needed. If multiple criteria are listed, they must all be true for the action to be executed. This is known as an **and** expression. If any of the criteria are not satisfied, the find skips the file and moves on. We can also combine two criteria so that if either of them is true the criteria are satisfied. This is known as an **or** expression. An **or** condition is specified by -o.

Let's list all files that can be read but not written by anyone. There are two sets of permissions that meet this criterion: 444 and 555. We therefore need to combine the two using the **or** (-o) condition so that any file whose permissions are either 444 or 555 will be listed. When combining criteria using the **or** condition, they need to be enclosed in parentheses. To specify parentheses, we must enclose them in quotes or escape them. To demonstrate the different ways to identify control characters in a command, the following example uses an escape for the opening parentheses, single quotes for the closing parentheses, and double quotes for the semicolon. This code is shown in Session 3.47.

SESSION 3.47 *Find Permissions—Or Criteria Example*

```
$ ls -l DirE
total 4
-rw-r--r--      1 gilberg   staff          120 May 29 13:47 file1
-r-xr-xr-x      1 gilberg   staff          120 May 29 13:47 file2
-r--r--r--      1 gilberg   staff          120 May 29 13:47 file3
-rw-rw-rw-      1 gilberg   staff          120 May 29 13:47 file4
$ find DirE \( -perm -444 -o -perm -555 ')'  -exec ls -l {} ";"
-r-xr-xr-x      1 gilberg   staff          120 May 29 13:47 DirE/file2
-r--r--r--      1 gilberg   staff          120 May 29 13:47 DirE/file3
```

Newest File

As our last example, let's search our directories for the latest version of a file. This is done with the newer criterion. We give it a copy of the file, and it looks for any copy that has been modified more recently. If we simply ask for newer, however, we will find all files that are newer. We only want files with the same filename. Therefore, we use the filename and newer as shown in Session 3.48.

SESSION 3.48 *Find Newer—And Criteria Example*

```
$ ls -l file1
-rw-r--r--      2 gilberg   staff          120 May 25 15:10 file1

$ find . -name file1 -newer file1 -exec ls -l {} \;
-rw-r--r--      1 gilberg   staff          120 May 25 15:46 ./DirA/file1
-rw-r--r--      1 gilberg   staff          120 May 27 15:49 ./DirB/file1
-rw-r--r--      1 gilberg   staff          120 May 29 13:15 ./DirC/file1
```

Session 3.48 Analysis: In this case, we see that there are three files that are newer than our file. To verify this, compare the dates.

Complete List of Find Criteria

Table 3.9 contains a complete list of find criteria.

TABLE 3.9 *Find Criteria*

Criteria	Matches ...
-name file	filename
-perm nnn	permissions to nnn. nnn must be an octal number.
-perm -nnn	permissions to bit mask, nnn. If bit mask contains 1, permission matches if it is on.
-type c	file type. Valid file types are: block (b), character (c), directory (d), link (l), pipe (p), file (f), socket (s)

Continued

TABLE 3.9 *Find Criteria—Continued*

Criteria	Matches ...
-link n	number of links for a file
-user uname	user name. Numeric user id can also be used.
-nouser	no name in the /etc/passwd file
-group gname	group name
-nogroup	no group name in the /etc/group file
-size n | nc	exactly file size in blocks (n) or characters (nc)
-inum n	the inode number
-atime +n | -n	file that has been accessed n or more days ago (+n) or in the last n days (-n). Note that find changes the access time.
-mtime +n | -n	file that has been modified n or more days ago (+n) or in the last n days (-n).
-ctime +n | -n	file that has been changed n or more days ago (+n) or in the last n days (-n).
-newer file	file's modification date is later than file's date
-anewer file	file's access date is later than file's date
-cnewer file	file's change date is later than file's date
-print	Displays absolute pathname on standard output
-exec	Executes specified command
-ok	Same as execute except asks for yes/no confirmation on action
-depth	Processes files in a directory before the file directory itself
-prune	Terminates the examination of files in the current directory and its subdirectories once a matching file is found.
-follow	When a matching file is symbolically linked, uses linked file to match criteria.

3.9 Key Terms

absolute pathname	hard link	root directory
binary file	home directory	socket
block special file	inode	super block
boot block	inode blocks	symbolic link
character special file	parent directory	symbolic link file
current directory	pathname	text file
data blocks	regular file	wildcards
directories	relative pathname	working directory
FIFO file		

3.10 Tips

1. Use wildcards, especially the asterisks (*), cautiously.
2. A (?) and a ([...]) replace only one character in a filename.
3. The terms *current directory* and *working directory* are used interchangeably in this text.
4. Your home directory may or may not be the same as your current (working) directory.
5. If a pathname starts with a slash (/), it is an absolute pathname.

6. A file can have one and only one inode, but it can have several names.

7. Use hard links to link files in the same file system; use soft links to link files in different file systems.

8. A user can edit the contents of a regular file; the contents of a directory are edited by the system.

9. Hard links can be used only with files; soft links can be used with both files and directories.

10. A filename that starts with a period is a hidden file, generally used by a UNIX utility. Examples of system hidden files are .profile, .mailrc, and .cshrc.

3.11 Commands

The following commands were discussed in this chapter. For more details, see Appendix F and the corresponding pages shown in the following table.

Command	Description	Options	Page
cd	*Synopsis:* cd [directory] Changes the current directory to the directory defined by the pathname. If the pathname is missing, the home directory becomes the working directory.		88
cp	*Synopsis:* cp [-options] source destination Copies files or directories from source to the destination.	p, i, r	93
find	*Synopsis:* find pathname criteria Finds a file or a directory based on the criteria.		108
ls	*Synopsis:* ls [-options] [pathname] Lists the contents of a directory.	l, d, n, r, t, u, c, p, R, 1, i	81
ln	*Synopsis:* ln [-options] source link Links the source to the destination.	s, i, f	102
lpr	*Synopsis:* lpr [-options] [file-list] Prints the file list.	P	92
mkdir	*Synopsis:* mkdir [-options] directory-list Creates one or more directories.	p, m	86
more	*Synopsis:* more [-options] [file-list] Displays the contents of a file one screenful at a time.	c, d, f, l, r, s, u, w, lines, +nmbr, +/ptrn	90
mv	*Synopsis:* mv [-options] source destination Moves a file or directory from source to destination or renames a file or directory.	f, i	100
pwd	*Synopsis:* pwd Displays the absolute pathname of the current (working) directory.		80

Continued

Command	Description	Options	Page
rm	*Synopsis: rm [-options] list* Removes (deletes) files or directories.	f, i, r	106
rmdir	*Synopsis: rmdir directory-list* Removes (deletes) directories.		89

3.12 Summary

- In UNIX, a file is any source from which data can be read or any destination to which data can be written.
- Some implementations of UNIX limit the length of a filename to 14 characters; others have names as long as 255 characters.
- A filename can be any sequence of ASCII characters. However, we recommend that you use only a subset of ASCII characters that does not contain characters that have special meaning, such as wildcards, in UNIX.
- A filename that starts with a period is a hidden file.
- We can group filenames using wildcards that identify a portion of filenames that are different.
- There are three wildcards in UNIX: single character (?), one character from a set ([...]), and multiple characters (*).
- One way to check the existence of files using wildcards is the use of the echo command.
- UNIX recognizes seven file types: regular, directory, character special, block special, symbolic link, FIFO, and socket.
- Regular files can be either text files or binary files.
- A directory is a type of file that is used to organize other files into groups.
- The directory hierarchy is designed as an upside down tree with a special directory, called the root, at the highest level.
- There are four special directories with abbreviated labels: root (/), home (~), working or current (.), and parent (..).
- To uniquely identify a file in the directory hierarchy, we use the pathname of the file.
- There are two ways we can use the pathnames: absolute and relative. The absolute pathname starts from the root directory. The relative pathname starts from the working directory.
- File systems in UNIX are normally implemented on a hard disk. However, from the user point of view, a file system in UNIX is a continuous linear storage structure.
- A file system in UNIX is divided into four areas: boot block, super block, inodes block, and data block.
- An inode (information node) is a file identifier; it uniquely defines a file. It contains all information about a file, including the address of the file on the disk.
- The concept of inode is directly related to the concept of links. The name of a file in a directory is linked to the physical file through the inode structure.
- UNIX defines two types of links: hard and symbolic. A hard link is a direct link. A symbolic (or soft) link is an indirect link.
- In UNIX, a file has only one inode, but it can have several names.

- We discussed five operations that are used uniquely with directories: locate (**pwd**), list (**ls**), make (**mkdir**), navigate (**cd**), and delete (**rmdir**).
- We discussed four operations that are used uniquely with files: create (**vi** etc.), edit (**vi** etc.), display (**more**), and print (**lpr**).
- We discussed six operations that are used with both files and directories: copy (**cp**), move (**mv**), rename (**mv**), delete (**rm**), link (**ln**), and find (**find**).

3.13 Practice Set

Review Questions

1. List some rules that should be followed when naming a file (regular or directory).
2. Define a wildcard. Why do we use wildcards? When do we use wildcards?
3. Name three wildcards used in UNIX to name files.
4. What is a single-character wildcard?
5. What is the set-of-character wildcard? How many characters can be matched by this wildcard?
6. What is the zero-or-more-character wildcard?
7. Name the seven types of files recognized by UNIX.
8. What is a regular file? Give an example.
9. What is a directory file? Give an example.
10. What is a character special file? Give an example.
11. What is a block special file? Give an example.
12. What is a symbolic link file? Give an example.
13. What is a FIFO?
14. What is a socket?
15. Name two categories of regular files. Does UNIX recognize the difference between these two categories? Explain your answer.
16. What is the difference between a text file and a binary file?
17. What is the directory hierarchy?
18. What is a root directory? What is the token to define the root directory?
19. What is a current (working) directory? What is the token to define the current directory?
20. What is a home directory? What is the token to define the home directory?
21. What is a parent directory? What is the token to define the parent directory?
22. Are the working directory and home directory always the same? Explain your answer.
23. What is an absolute pathname? What is a relative pathname? Is there any quick rule to distinguish an absolute pathname from a relative pathname?
24. Which pathname (absolute or relative) starts from the root?
25. Which pathname (absolute or relative) starts from the working directory?
26. Which pathname (absolute or relative) starts with a forward slash (/)?
27. Can we say that an absolute pathname is always longer than the corresponding relative pathname? Explain your answer with an example.
28. What is an inode?

29. What is the relationship of a file name to its inode? Is the relationship one-to-one, one-to-many, or many-to-one? Explain your answer with an example.

30. What is the relationship of an inode to the physical file stored on the disk? Is the relation-ship one-to-one, one-to-many, or many-to-one? Explain your answer with an example.

31. Name the areas of a file system designed for UNIX.

32. Define boot block, super block, inodes block, and data block.

33. Name different fields in an inode.

34. Define a hard link. Can we use hard links to link files? Can we use hard links to link directories?

35. Define a symbolic (soft) link. Can we use soft links to link files? Can we use soft links to link directories?

36. Can we use hard links to link files in different file systems? Can we use soft links to link files or directories in different systems? Which link form(s) may be used to link files in the same file system? In different file systems?

37. A directory has three subdirectories and two files. How many entries are found in this directory with a basic list command? With `ls -a`?

38. Name five operations we can use uniquely with directories.

39. Name four operations we can use uniquely with regular files.

40. Name six operations we can use with both files and directories.

41. What is the difference between copying a file and moving a file?

42. What is the difference between copying a file and linking a file?

43. What is the command for each of the following tasks?
    a. list the contents of a directory
    b. link a file to another
    c. copy a file
    d. display the absolute pathname of the current directory

44. What is the command for each of the following tasks?
    a. print a document
    b. edit a file
    c. create a file
    d. delete a directory

45. What is the command for each of the following tasks?
    a. delete a file or directory
    b. copy a directory
    c. change the directory
    d. create a directory

46. What is the command for each of the following tasks?
    a. rename a file
    b. rename a directory
    c. find a file
    d. find a directory

Exercises

47. Which of the following would be a good file (or directory) name in UNIX?
    a. foo
    b. .125
    c. <name>
    d. passwd

48. Which of the following would be a good file (or directory) name in UNIX?
    a. b.forouzan
    b. *hello*
    c. how?
    d. /letter

49. Write a pattern for each line that refers to all files in the line.
    a. file1, file2, ..., file9
    b. file1, file2, ..., file25
    c. file20, file21, ..., file29
    d. all files ending with ".c"
    e. all files starting with "f"
    f. all files starting with a lowercase letter
    g. all files starting with a letter
    h. all files starting with a digit
    i. all files ending with two digits
    j. all files in the current directory
    k. all files in the parent directory
    l. all files not starting with a digit

50. You have the following files in your home directory:

file1	file2	file33	file4	f5	f6	f7
NFile1	Nfile2	Nfile441	file1a	file2a	file2b	

    Which of them would be selected by each of the following patterns?
    a. file?
    b. file??
    c. file*
    d. Nfile?
    e. ?file?
    f. ?file*
    g. file[a-z]
    h. file[0-9][0-9]
    i. *

51. Which of the following is an absolute pathname?
    a. /
    b. /bin
    c. jack
    d. ./bin?
    e. ..
    f. ~
    g. /bin/c

52. Which of the following is a relative pathname?
    a. ../bin
    b. /bin
    c. jack/letter
    d. /dev/jack/lett

53. Show how to use the relative pathname to refer to your home directory.

54. Show how to use the relative pathname to refer to the home directory of john (user name is john).

55. Draw the directory tree for the pathname /usr/user/john.

56. If a directory is five levels below the root directory, how many "/" should be in its absolute pathname? Draw a picture to explain your answer.

57. In Figure 3.35, what would be the absolute pathname for the following directories?
    a. root
    b. bin
    c. jack
    d. letter
    e. report

58. In Figure 3.35, what would be the relative pathname for the following directories if the current directory is bin?
    a. root
    b. bin
    c. john
    d. letter
    e. report

59. In Figure 3.35, what would be the relative pathname for the following directories if the current directory is john?
    a. root
    b. bin
    c. john
    d. letter
    e. report

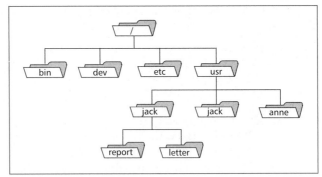

FIGURE 3.35 *Exercises*

60. In Figure 3.35, what would be the relative pathname for the following directories if the current directory is `letter`?
    a. root
    b. bin
    c. john
    d. letter
    e. report

61. In Figure 3.35, write the following pathnames as the absolute pathnames.
    a. current directory: root; pathname: /
    b. current directory: bin; pathname: .
    c. current directory: jack; pathname: report
    d. current directory: report; pathname: ../../john

62. Imagine you have two directories A and B under your home directory and two directories B1 and B2 under the directory B. You log into the system and issue the following commands one after another. What is the working directory after each command? Do you get any error message? Draw the directory structure to show the movements.
    a. cd B
    b. cd B1
    c. cd A
    d. cd
    e. cd A
    f. cd ./B1
    g. cd ../B1
    h. cd ../B/B1
    i. cd B2
    j. cd ../A

63. Find the error (if any) in each of the following commands.
    a. cd /bin hello
    b. cp file1
    c. cp file1 file2 file3
    d. cp -s file1 file2
    e. cp file1 -r file2
    f. find -name file1 -print
    g. ls

64. Find the error (if any) in each of the following commands.
    a. ln / report
    b. ln -s / report
    c. mkdir A   A/B
    d. mkdir -p   A   A/B
    e. mv file1 file2 file3 file4
    f. rm /
    g. rm *
    h. pwd ~
    i. ls -file1 file2

3.14 Lab Sessions

Each of the following sessions uses one or more practical exercises. After finishing each session, write a report that explains the result of each step and answer any questions asked.

Session I

1. Log into the system.
2. Create three directories named `letters`, `reports`, and `assignments` under your home directory.
3. Move to directory `letters`.
4. Create two directories named `friendly` and `formal` under the `letters` directory.
5. Move to directory `reports` using only one command (directly from `letters`).
6. Create three directories called `personal`, `business`, and `school` under the directory `reports` (use only one command).
7. Create a directory called `UNIX` under the `assignments` directory without moving from the `reports` directory.
8. Create two directories called `HWs` and `Projects` under directory `UNIX`. The directories in this step should be created without moving from the `reports` directory.
9. Move to your home directory.
10. Recursively list all of the directories you created and draw the directory structure on paper.
11. Log out of the system.

Session II

1. Log into the system.
2. Recursively list the directories under your home directory (the ones created in Session I).
3. Move to the `UNIX` directory.
4. Check your current directory.
5. Using **vi,** create a file named `hw4` that contains short answers to at least five review questions in this chapter.
6. Save the file (it should be saved under the `UNIX` directory).
7. Move to your home directory.
8. Print the content of `hw4` from your home directory.
9. Make a copy of `hw4` and call it `hw4.bk`. Store it under the same directory where `hw4` is stored.
10. From your home directory, check to see if both files (`hw4` and `hw4.bk`) exist.
11. Move to the `UNIX` directory.
12. Check your current working directory.
13. Make a hard link to the `hw4` file. The link should be under the `UNIX` subdirectory and be called `hw4HL`.
14. Make a soft link to `hw4` called `hw4SL` and store it under the `UNIX` directory.
15. Check the inode of `hw4`, `hw4.bk`, `hw4HL`, and `hw4SL`. Are all the same? Are all different? Explain how you determined the answer.
16. Use the **ls** command to find the file types of `hw4`, `hw4.bk`, `hw4HL`, and `hw4SL`. Explain your observation.
17. Log out of the system.

Session III

1. Log into the system.
2. Create a backup directory in your home directory called `backups`.
3. Use the find command to find the pathnames of all of the files (`hw4`, `hw4.bk`, `hw4HL`, and `hw4SL`) that you created in Session II. All of them should be found using only one find command. The command must also copy all of them to the `backups` directory.
4. Check the number of links and inode number of `hw4`, `hw4.bk`, `hw3HL`, and `hw4SL`. Make note of the results.
5. Delete the original `hw4` file without moving from your home directory.
6. Check the existence of `hw4`, `hw4.bk`, `hw4HL`, and `hw4SL`.
7. Check the contents of `hw4`, `hw4.bk`, `hw4HL`, and `hw4SL`.
8. Restore the file `hw4` by making a copy of `hw4.bk`.
9. You may have noticed that your soft link (`hw4SL`) contains garbage. Delete this file.
10. Make a new soft link to `hw4` and store it as `hw4SL` under the same directory as it was.
11. List recursively all of your files and directories to confirm all operations.
12. Draw the file and directory structure of your home directory.
13. Log out of the system.

Session IV

1. Log into the system.
2. Use wildcards to display all of the files you have created under the `HWs` directory without moving from your home directory.
3. Rename `hw4.bk` to `hw4.bak`.
4. Create a short friendly letter, called `friend.1`, using **vi** and store it under the `friendly` directory.
5. Create a short formal letter, called `formal.1`, using **vi** and store it under the `formal` directory. Give a title to `formal.1` letter.
6. Copy the file `formal.1` and call the new copy `formal.2`.
7. Change only the title of `formal.2` (using **vi**) and store it.
8. Using wildcards, print the contents of `formal.1` and `formal.2`.
9. Make a directory called `busLetters` under your home directory.
10. Move the `formal` directory (with all of its contents) under the `busLetters` directory.
11. Make a recursive list of your directory structure.
12. Draw the new directory structure on paper.
13. Log out of the system.

## CHAPTER 4

Security and File Permission

In this chapter, we will discuss security in UNIX. The security system in UNIX, like any other operating system, is designed to control the access to resources. First we introduce the users and how they are grouped together. Then we present different levels of security. Finally, we discuss commands used to change the permissions of files and directories.

4.1 Users and Groups

In UNIX, everyone who logs on to the system is called a **user.** Users are known to the system by their user-ids. In UNIX, however, not every user is created equal. Some users have more capabilities than others. These users are known as **superusers.** Also known as system administrators, superusers have the maximum set of capabilities in the system; they can even change the system itself. As you might well imagine, superusers need to have a lot of experience and a lot of training.

Users can be organized into groups. A team working on a project, for example, needs to share many of the same files. By creating a project group, the team members can have easy access to each other's files while still protecting the files from users outside the group. Users can belong to multiple groups. Figure 4.1 demonstrates the concepts of the superuser, groups, and users. Note that one user is in both groups.

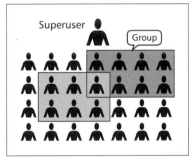

FIGURE 4.1   *Users*

Group (groups) Command

UNIX provides a command, **groups**, to determine a user's group. It is shown in Figure 4.2.

You can check your group or any other user's group. If you enter the command with no user id, the system responds with your group. If you enter the command with a user id, it returns the user's group. If a user belongs to multiple user groups, all of them will be listed. Session 4.1 shows a typical **groups** response.

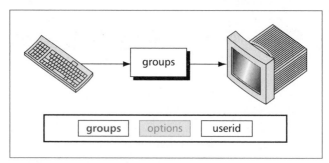

FIGURE 4.2   *The **groups** Command*

SESSION 4.1   *Determining a User's Group*

```
$ groups
staff
$ groups forouzan
instructor
```

> The name of the command that displays or sets the group or groups that a user is associated with is **groups**, not *group*.

4.2 Security Levels

There are three levels of security in UNIX: system, directory, and file. The system security is controlled by the system administrator,[1] a superuser. The directory and file securities are controlled by the users who own them. The security levels and the people who use the system are presented in Figure 4.3.

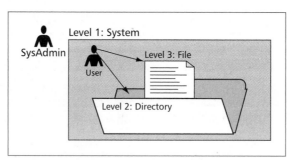

FIGURE 4.3   *Security Levels*

System Security

System security controls who is allowed to access the system. It begins with your login id and password. When the system administrator opens an account for you, he or

---

[1]System administrator is often abbreviated as sysadmin.

she creates an entry in the system password file. This file, named /etc/passwd, is located in the etc directory and contains several important pieces of information about you. You can look at this file, but unless you are a superuser, you can't change it. The contents of an entry in our password file are shown in Figure 4.4.

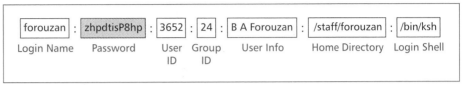

FIGURE 4.4   *A Typical Password File Entry*

You might be surprised to find the password in such a public file. Before you get too concerned, however, let us assure you that you can't use the password you see in Figure 4.4 which is not readable when you look at the file. Passwords are encrypted, meaning that they have been converted from the entry you use on the keyboard to a coded value that only the system understands. Password encryption only works when you start with your password at the keyboard. There is no way to start with the encrypted code and work back to a password. What you see when you look at a password in the file is simply the encrypted value that represents the password.

Let's examine each of these fields in turn.

- **Login Name:** the name you are known by to all of the other users in the system. It uniquely identifies you as one of the users in the system.
- **Password:** the one-way encrypted password that identifies you to the system.
- **User id:** your internal user id. It is a unique number between 0 and 65,535. If you know the binary system, you will recognize 65,535 as the maximum unsigned number that can be represented in 16 bits. It also means that one UNIX system can have a maximum of only 65,535 users. User id zero is reserved for the superuser. Although there may be several superusers in the system, there is only one superuser id, zero.
- **Group id:** similarly, group id is a unique number between 100 and 65,535 that identifies users who have common access.
- **User Information:** is used to store data about the user. Traditionally, it is the user's given name. Another common use is an accounting number for systems that need to bill usage back to a user.
- **Home Directory:** the login or home directory when you first log into the system. It is represented as the absolute pathname for your home directory.
- **Login Shell:** identifies the shell that is loaded when you login. It is also an absolute pathname. In Figure 4.4, forouzan is in the **korn** shell when he logs in.

Permission Codes

Both the directory and file security levels use a set of **permission codes** to determine who can access and manipulate a directory or file. The permission codes are divided into three sets of codes. The first set contains the permissions of the owner of the directory or file. The second set contains the group permissions for members in a group as identified by the group id. The third set contains the permissions for everyone else—that is, the general public.

The code for each set is a triplet representing read (r), write (w), and execute (x). Read indicates that a person in that category may read a file or directory. Likewise, a write permission indicates that the user can change the file or directory. The last permission, execute, has different meanings for directories and files. For a file, it indicates that the file is a program or script that can be executed. When it is a directory, an execute permission allows access to the directory.

The permission codes are presented in Figure 4.5.

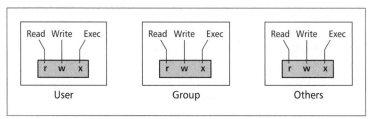

FIGURE 4.5   *Directory and File Permissions*

Table 4.1 summarizes the permission rules.

TABLE 4.1   *Summary of Permission Rules*

Permission	read (r)	write (w)	execute (x)
Directory	Read contents of directory	Add or delete entries (files) in directory using commands	Reference or move to directory
File Level	Read or copy files in directory	Change or delete files	Run executable files

Directory Level Permissions

Read Permission   When users have **read permission** for a directory, they can read the directory, which contains the names of the files and subdirectories and all of their attributes. They can then display the names and attributes with the list command. As a general rule, everyone is given read permissions for directories. However, if for some reason you don't want other users to see what files you have in a directory, you can set its permission to remove the read permission.

Write Permission   When users have **write permission,** they can add or delete entries in a directory. This means that they can copy a file from another directory, move a file to or from the directory, or remove (delete) a file. Obviously, this is a much more dangerous level of permissions. If you grant others permission to write to your directory, they can change its contents. Since its contents are your files, this means that they can delete any or all of your files. For security reasons, therefore, you generally don't grant others write permission to your directories. On the other hand, if you are maintaining a group directory within your account, it is reasonable to give group members write permission. Others are very seldom given write permission.

Execute Permission   **Execute permission**, sometimes called search permission, at the directory level allows you to reference a directory, as in a pathname or file read, or move to a directory using the **cd** command. To reference, in any way, a subdirectory or file under a directory, you must have execute permissions to all directories in the absolute pathname of that subdirectory or file. The user permissions for directories, therefore, generally include both read and execute. To grant read without execute permission is a contradiction because without execute no one, including the owner, may access the directory for any reason.

> Directory read permission allows you to read files in a directory, but only if you also have execute permission. Without execute permission, no access is allowed to a directory or any of its subdirectories.

The execute rule for directory is absolute. For example, if execute permission is not on, nobody can access a directory in any way, including using it in a path. This rule is demonstrated in Session 4.2.

SESSION 4.2   *Demonstrate Directory Execute Permission*

```
$ ls -R permissionTest
file1     ptSubDir

permissionTest/ptSubDir:
file2

#Permission changed to rw- (no x) for user (see page 132)
$ ls -R permissionTest
Cannot access permissionTest/file1: Permission denied
Cannot access permissionTest/ptSubDir: Permission denied

$ more permissionTest/file1
Cannot open permissionTest/file1: Permission denied

#Permission changed to rwx for user (see page 132)
$ ls -Rl permissionTest
total 2
-rw-r--r--    1 gilberg  staff          120 Aug 30 08:28 file1
drwxr-xr-x    2 gilberg  staff          512 Aug 30 08:50 ptSubDir

permissionTest/ptSubDir:
total 1
-rw-r--r--    1 gilberg  staff          120 Aug 30 08:40 file2
```

Session 4.2 Analysis: We begin by demonstrating that we can reference the `permission-Test` directory with a list command. We then change its permissions to read and write only (666) and try to execute the same list command, only to be denied for both the `permission-Test` directory and its subdirectory, `ptSubDir`. Because the execute permission was the only one not set, this demonstrates that we cannot even reference the directory. To further demonstrate the point, we tried to **more** its only file, which has read access. This time we were told we could not open the file. After changing the permissions back to read and execute, we were able to list the contents of the directory.

File Level Permissions

File permissions are similar to directory permissions, except that they pertain to a file rather than a directory.

Read Permission Users who have file **read permission** can read or copy a file. Files that contain public information generally have read permission. Private files, however, should be read only by the user (owner). Of course, group files should be readable by anyone in the group.

Write Permission Files with **write permission** can be changed. They can also be deleted. As with directories, you generally restrict write permissions to yourself (user) and other users in your group.

Execute Permission With files, **execute permission** means that you can execute (run) programs, utilities, and scripts. Whether or not you grant execute permissions to others depends on what the program does. If it is benign and can't destroy anything or give out private information, execute permission is often granted. For example, if you have a program in a Web page, it needs to have its execute permission set for all levels. If it doesn't, visitors to your Web site cannot execute your Web program. On the other hand, even if you have execute permission, you cannot run a file unless it is a program. Executing a text file, for example, can cause funny things to happen. We have seen the system font changed by executing a text file; the only way to correct this situation is to log out and log in again.

Checking Permissions

To check the permissions of a file or directory, we use the long list command, (`ls -l`). As discussed in Operations Unique To Directories in Chapter 3 (page 87), the permissions appear at the beginning of the line right after the file type. Session 4.3 shows the permissions displayed by a long list command.

SESSION 4.3 *Typical Permissions*

```
$ ls -l
total 487
drwxr-xr-x   11 gilberg   staff       1024 Aug  3  1999 C-Programs
-rw-------    1 gilberg   staff       5782 May 16 14:55 TheRaven
-rw-r--r--    1 gilberg   staff      10857 Apr  5  1999 adt3.c++
drwxr-xr-x    2 gilberg   staff        512 May 29 13:08 backUpDir
drwxr-xr-x    2 gilberg   staff        512 Apr 25 16:10 dump.scr
```

4.3 Changing Permissions

When a directory or a file is created, the system automatically assigns default permissions. The owner of the directory or file can change them. To change the permissions, we use the **chmod**[2] command shown in Figure 4.6.

---

[2]Pronounced cha-mod.

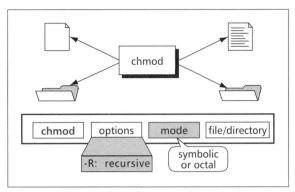

FIGURE 4.6 *The **chmod** Command*

As shown in Figure 4.7, there are two ways to change the permissions: symbolic or octal. Both use the format shown in Figure 4.6.

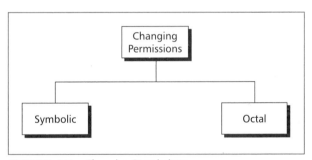

FIGURE 4.7 *Changing Permissions*

Symbolic Codes

When we use symbolic codes, we tell UNIX what permissions we want to set, and it does all of the work for us.

As we discussed earlier, there are three sets of permissions: user, group, and other. Each set uses its first letter as a mnemonic identifier. Thus, u represents user, g represents group, and o represents others. If we want to set all three groups at the same time, we use a set of a for all. No groups also defaults to all, but it is better to use a when we want all. It's a good habit that prevents errors.

There are three sets of operators. To assign absolute permissions to a set, we use the assignment operator (=). In this case, the current permissions for a set are replaced by the new permissions. To change only one or two of the permissions in a set and leave the others as they are currently set, we use a plus sign (+) to add permissions. To remove one or two permissions and leave the others alone, we use a minus sign (–).

Finally, the permissions are represented by their symbolic letters: r represents read, w represents write, and x represents execute. One, two, or three symbolic letters can be used in each command. Each set of symbolic codes must be separated by commas, and there can be no spaces. Figure 4.8 shows how these symbolic modes are used.

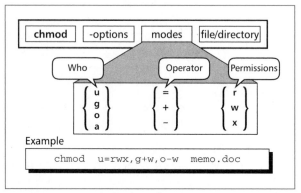

FIGURE 4.8 *Symbolic* **chmod** *Codes*

Note that we can specify up to three symbolic modes in one **chmod** command. We could also specify multiple files or files with wildcards. Table 4.2 contains examples of the more common symbolic **chmod** commands.

TABLE 4.2 *Common Symbolic* **chmod** *Commands*

Command	Interpretation
chmod u=rwx file	Sets read (**r**), write (**w**), execute (**x**) for user.
chmod g=rx file	Sets only read (**r**) and execute (**x**) for group; write (**w**) denied.
chmod g+x file	Adds execute (**x**) permission for group; read and write unchanged.
chmod a+r file	Adds read (**r**) to all users; write and execute unchanged.
chmod o-w file	Removes others' write (**w**) permission; read and execute unchanged.

> The use of symbolic code in the **chmod** command allows a user to set, add, or remove individual permissions.

Octal Codes

A faster way to enter permissions is to use the octal equivalent of the codes. You must realize, however, that when using the octal codes, all the permission codes are changed. It is not like the symbolic modes where you need to specify only what you want to change. With octal codes, you must completely represent all of the user codes each time.

In an octal digit, there are three bit positions.[3] The three different permissions for each set of codes correspond to the three different bit positions in an octal digit. The first bit represents the read permission, the second bit represents the write permission, and the third bit represents the execute permission. This relationship of octal bit positions to the permissions is seen in Figure 4.9. Note that the total of all three binary positions is seven, which is the maximum value that can be stored in one octal digit.

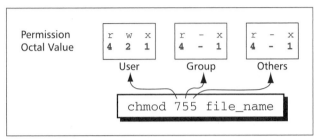

FIGURE 4.9 *Octal **chmod** Commands*

From Figure 4.9, we see that we can use one digit to set each set of permissions. The digit value is determined by which permissions we want to turn on. When the read permission is to be set on, its value is 4. To set it off, its value is 0. Similarly, to set the write permission on, its value is 2; to set it off, its value is again 0. Finally, to set the execute permission on, its value is 1; to set it off, its value is 0.

Normally, we want the permissions to be different for each set of permissions (user, group, and others). This requires that we specifically state the octal digit for each of the three sets. For example, to set the user permissions to read/write/execute, the group permissions to read/write, and the others permissions to read only, we would use the following command:

```
chmod  764  file1
```

There is one major difference between the symbolic mode commands and the octal commands. The octal commands set every permission. We cannot set just one or two, leaving the others unchanged, as we can with the symbolic + operator. When you use octal commands, therefore, you should first check the settings with a long list command (`ls`) to determine the current settings.

Table 4.3 shows some of the more common permission commands.

> **The use of octal code in the `chmod` command requires that all permissions be completely reset; a user cannot set, add, or remove individual settings.**

---

[3]If you are not familiar with octal, it is discussed in Appendix D, Numbering Systems.

TABLE 4.3 *Common Symbolic* **chmod** *Commands*

Command	Description
chmod 777 file	All permissions on for all three settings
chmod 754 directory	User all, group read + execute; others read only
chmod 664 file	User and group read + write, others read only
chmod 644 file	User read + write, group and others read only
chmod 711 program	User all, group and others execute only

Option

There is only one option, recursion (-R). The **chmod** recursion works just as in other commands. Starting with the current working directory, it changes the permissions of all files and directories in the directory. It then moves to the subdirectories and recursively changes all of their permissions. We recommend, however, that you use it only with symbolic changes because both directories and files are changed. Using the octal codes would change everything to the same permissions. With the symbolic settings, we can selectively make changes and, more important, leave the execute permissions unchanged. Session 4.4 demonstrates recursion by using symbolic codes to remove read from the others' permissions.

SESSION 4.4 *Demonstrate Recursive Use of* **chmod**

```
$ ls -lR unix4sec
total 4
-rw-r--r--    1 gilberg   staff        120 Aug 30 10:36 file1
-rw-r--r--    1 gilberg   staff        120 Aug 30 10:38 file2
drwxr-xr--    2 gilberg   staff        512 Aug 30 10:39 subDirA
drwxr-xr--    2 gilberg   staff        512 Aug 30 10:39 subDirB

unix4sec/subDirA:
total 1
-rw-r--r--    1 gilberg   staff        120 Aug 30 10:39 file1A

unix4sec/subDirB:
total 1
-rw-r--r--    1 gilberg   staff        120 Aug 30 10:39 file1B

$ chmod -R o-r unix4sec

$ ls -Rl unix4sec
total 4
-rw-r-----    1 gilberg   staff        120 Aug 30 10:36 file1
-rw-r-----    1 gilberg   staff        120 Aug 30 10:38 file2
drwxr-x---    2 gilberg   staff        512 Aug 30 10:39 subDirA
drwxr-x---    2 gilberg   staff        512 Aug 30 10:39 subDirB

unix4sec/subDirA:
total 1
-rw-r-----    1 gilberg   staff        120 Aug 30 10:39 file1A

unix4sec/subDirB:
total 1
-rw-r-----    1 gilberg   staff        120 Aug 30 10:39 file1B
```

4.4 User Masks

In this section, we discuss how default permissions are defined when a new directory or file is created.

Basic Concept

The permissions are initially set for a directory or file using a three-digit octal system variable, the user mask (mask). Defined initially by the system administrator when your account is created, the mask contains the octal settings for the permissions that are to be *removed* from the default when a directory or file is created. You can change the settings by creating a mask entry in your login file (see Chapter 5).

When a new directory or file is created, the number in the mask is used to set the default permissions. The default permissions are 777 for a directory and 666 for a file. Table 4.4 shows how the mask is used to create the default permissions.

TABLE 4.4 *User Mask Results*

mask	Directory Permission (Default 777)	File Permission (Default 666)[a]
0	7 (read/write/execute)	6 (read/write)
1	6 (read/write)	6 (read/write)
2	5 (read/execute)	4 (read)
3	4 (read)	4 (read)
4	3 (write/execute)	2 (write)
5	2 (write)	2 (write)
6	1 (execute)	0 (none)
7	0 (none)	0 (none)

[a]File default assumes file is data file. Executable file must be manually set.

Each mask digit means remove the corresponding digits from the default permission. For example, mask digit 1 means remove 1 from directory and file permission. For directories, the default permission is 7 (4 + 2 + 1), so we remove the 1 and the result is 6 (4 + 2). The default for a file, on the other hand, is 6 (4 + 2) so there is no 1 to be removed. The result is, therefore, also 6 (4 + 2).

Table 4.5 shows the results of some of the more common settings.

TABLE 4.5 *Examples of Default Calculations for Permissions*

Mask	Directory Permissions (Default 777)	File Permissions (Default 666)
000 (Public)	777 (rwx rwx rwx)	666 (rw– rw– rw-)
011 (Public)	766 (rwx rw– rw–)	666 (rw– rw– rw–)
022 (Write Protected)	755 (rwx r–x r–x)	644 (rw- r-- r--)

Continued

TABLE 4.5   *Examples of Default Calculations for Permissions—Continued*

Mask	Directory Permissions (Default 777)	File Permissions (Default 666)
007 (Project Private)	770 (rwx rwx ---)	660 (rw– rw– ---)
077 (Private)	700 (rwx --- ---)	600 (rw- --- ---)

User Mask (umask) Command

The user mask is displayed and set with the **umask** command as shown in Figure 4.10.

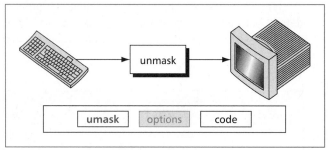

FIGURE 4.10   *The* **umask** *Command*

To display the current user mask setting, use the **umask** command with no arguments. To set it, use the command with the new mask setting.

Session 4.5 has examples to display the current user mask settings and to change them. After we change the user mask, we display the setting again to verify that it was in fact changed.

SESSION 4.5   *Displaying and Setting* **umask**

```
$ umask
000
$ umask 022
$ umask
022
```

When you set the user mask in a session, it is temporary only for that session. When you log out the settings, revert to the default. To make it permanent, you must add it to the user login file as explained in Chapter 5.

4.5 Changing Ownership and Group

Every directory and file has an owner and a group. When you create a directory or file, you are the owner and your group is the group. There are two commands that allow the owner and group to be changed. The change ownership (**chown**) command can change the owner or the owner and the group. The change group (**chgrp**) command can change only the group.

Change Ownership (chown) Command

The owner and optionally the group are changed with the change ownership (**chown**) command. The new owner may be a login name or a user id (UID). The group is optional. When it is used, it is separated from the owner by a colon or a period. The group may be a group name or a group id (GID), and the new owner must be a member of the group. The group does not have to be changed when the owner is changed unless the new owner is not a member of the current group.

Only the current owner or superuser may change the ownership or group. This means that once the ownership is changed, the original owner cannot claim it back. Either the new owner or the system administrator must change it back. You change the file ownership and its associated group by using the change ownership (**chown**) command shown in Figure 4.11.

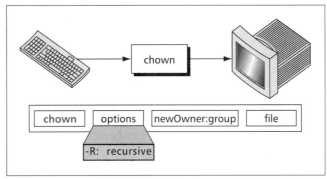

FIGURE 4.11 *The **chown** Command*

When the recursive option (-R) is used with a directory, all files in the directory and all subdirectories and their files are changed recursively. Session 4.6 demonstrates the use of the **chown** command. Note that after the owner is changed, it no longer displays in the directory list.

SESSION 4.6 *The **chown** Command*

```
$ ls -l
total 2
-rw-r--r--    1 rfg3988   staff          120 Aug 30   2002 file1
-rw-r-----    1 rfg3988   staff          120 Aug 30   2002 file2
$ chown forouzan file1
$ ls -l
total 1
-rw-r-----    1 rfg3988   staff          120 Aug 30   2002 file2
```

Change Group (chgrp) Command

To change the group without changing the owner, you use the change group (**chgrp**) command. This command, shown in Figure 4.12, operates the same as the change owner command.

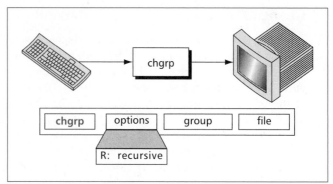

FIGURE 4.12 *The* **chgrp** *Command*

Session 4.7 demonstrates the use of the **chgrp** command.

SESSION 4.7 *The* **chgrp** *Command*

```
$ ls -l
total 1
-rw-r-----    1 gilberg  staff        120 Aug 30  2002 file2
$ chgrp proj15 file2
$ ls -l
total 1
-rw-r-----    1 gilberg  proj15       120 Aug 30  2002 file2
```

4.6 Key Terms

directory level security
execute security
file level permission
group
group id (GID)
home directory
login name

login shell
octal code
password
password file
permission code
read permission
superuser

symbolic code
system level security
user
user mask
user id (UID)
user information
write permission

4.7 Commands

The following commands were discussed in this chapter. For more details, see Appendix F and the corresponding pages shown in the following table.

Command	Description	Options	Page
chgrp	**Synopsis:** *chgrp [-option] group list* Changes a group associated with a list of files or directories.	R	133
chmod	**Synopsis:** *chmod [-option] mode list* Sets or changes the permission of a list of files or directories.	R	126

Continued

Command	Description	Options	Page
chown	**Synopsis:** *chown [-option] owner [:group] list* Changes the owner (and the group associated to) a list of files or directories.	R	133
groups	**Synopsis:** *groups [user id]* Displays the user's group.		121
umask	**Synopsis:** *umask [mask]* Displays or sets the default permission for newly created files or directories.		132

4.8 Tips

1. The name of the command that displays or sets the group or groups that a user is associated with is **groups,** not *group*.

2. To read or copy a file, the user must have read permission for that file and execute permission for all directories that define the absolute pathname of the file.

3. To modify a file, the user must have write permission for that file and execute permission for all directories that define the absolute pathname of the file.

4. To execute an executable file, the user must have execute permission for that file and execute permission for all directories that define the absolute pathname of the file.

5. To look at the contents of a directory (using the **ls** command), the user must have read permission for that directory and execute permission for all directories (including that directory itself) that define the absolute pathname of the directory.

6. To change the contents of a directory (adding or deleting files or subdirectories), the user must have write permission for that directory and execute permission for all directories (including the directory itself) that form the absolute pathname of the directory.

7. Note that having only execute permission for a directory allows the user to move to that directory (if the user also has execute permission for all directories forming the absolute pathname). Once there, however, the user can do nothing without read or write permission for the directory.

8. The system default permission for a file is 666 (which means no execute permissions), and the system default permission for a directory is 777 (a directory must have execute permission).

9. The use of symbolic code in the **chmod** command allows a user to set, add, or remove individual permissions.

10. The use of octal code in the **chmod** command requires that all permissions be completely reset; a user cannot set, add, or remove individual settings.

4.9 Summary

- In UNIX, everyone who logs into the system is called a user.
- A superuser is the system administrator in the UNIX environment.

- Users can be organized into groups.
- There are three levels of security in UNIX: system level, directory level, and file level.
- Access to the system is controlled by the superuser who controls the entries in the /etc/passwd file.
- The directory and file level use permission codes to control the access to the directories and files.
- The permission defines the access of the user (owner), group, and others.
- A directory or a file can have read (r), write (w), and execute (x) permissions.
- In a directory, read permission allows the use of the **ls** command to see the contents of a directory; the write permission allows entries to be added and deleted to a directory; execute permission allows navigating to and through a directory using the **cd** command.
- In a regular file, read permission allows a file to be read or copied; write permission allows a file's contents to be changed; execute permission allows a file to be executed (run).
- The `ls -l` command can be used to check the permission of a file or directory.
- The owner of a directory or regular file can change the permissions using the **chmod** command.
- Permission can be changed using either the symbolic or octal mode. In the symbolic mode, changing can be absolute (reset) or relative (add or delete); in the octal mode, it can only be absolute (reset).
- The default permission for a directory or file is determined by the user mask. The user mask is a value that is set by the system administrator, a user login file, or the user.
- To check the value of the user mask, we use the **umask** command with no argument. To change the value of the user mask, we use the **umask** command with one value, the mask.
- The owner of a file or a directory can pass the ownership to another user with the **chown** command.
- The **groups** command shows the group or groups a user belongs to. To change the default group membership of a file or directory, the **chgrp** command is used.

4.10 Practice Sets

Review Questions

1. Define a user in UNIX.
2. Define a group in UNIX.
3. Can a user belong to more than one group? Give an example.
4. Define the superuser.
5. Where is the home directory of the superuser?
6. Can the superuser delete a file or directory of a user no matter how the permissions are set by the user?

7. What are the three levels of security in UNIX?

8. Define system security.

9. What methods are available to the system administrator to control system security? Explain each one.

10. What is the purpose of the /etc/passwd file?

11. How many fields are in each entry of the /etc/passwd file? Name them.

12. In the /etc/passwd file, what character separates the fields in an entry?

13. In the /etc/passwd file, should the length of each field be predetermined? Why?

14. What is the directory that holds the /etc/passwd file?

15. Draw a directory structure to show the location of the /etc/passwd file.

16. Explain the meaning of each of the following fields in an entry of /etc/passwd file:
    a. Login Name
    b. Password
    c. User id
    d. Group id
    e. User Information
    f. Home Directory
    g. Login Shell

17. How many triplets are in each permission code?

18. What does the first triplet (rwx) define in a permission code?

19. What does the second triplet (rwx) define in a permission code?

20. What does the third triplet (rwx) define in a permission code?

21. Define the directory level permission.

22. What is the meaning of r for a directory? Elaborate on your answer.

23. What is the meaning of w for a directory? Elaborate on your answer.

24. What is the meaning of x for a directory? Elaborate on your answer.

25. Define the file level permissions.

26. What is the meaning of r for a file? Elaborate on your answer.

27. What is the meaning of w for a file? Elaborate on your answer.

28. What is the meaning of x for a file? Elaborate on your answer.

29. What is the command to change a directory or file permission?

30. Define the symbolic codes for changing permissions.

31. Can we use symbolic codes to totally reset the permissions for user, group, and other? Elaborate on your answer.

32. Can we use symbolic codes to partially change the permissions for user, group, and other? Elaborate on your answer.

33. Can we use symbolic codes to partially change the permission only for user but keep the permission for group and other? Elaborate on your answer.

34. Define the octal code for changing permissions.

35. Can we use the octal code to totally reset the permissions for user, group, and other? Elaborate on your answer.

36. Can we use the octal code to partially change the permissions for user, group, and other? Elaborate on your answer.

37. Can we use the octal code to partially change the permission only for user, but keep the permission for group and other? Elaborate on your answer.

38. What permission is needed in a directory so that everybody can list the contents of the directory?

39. What permission is needed in a directory so that everybody can copy the contents of the directory?

40. What permission is needed in a directory so that the owner of the directory can copy a file into the directory?

41. What permission is needed in a directory so that everybody can execute programs under that directory? What permission is needed for the program itself?

42. What is a user mask (file creation mask)?

43. What is the system default permission for a newly created directory?

44. What is the system default permission for a newly created file?

45. How is the actual permission setting for a newly created directory determined?

46. How is the actual permission setting for a newly created file determined?

47. What is the command to set the user mask (file creation mask)?

48. What is the command to check membership of a user to a group or groups?

49. What is the command to change the ownership of a file?

50. What is the command to check or change the group associated with a file?

51. Is it possible to have multiple permission sets for a file or directory? Explain your answer.

52. What type of permission is needed to delete a file from a directory?

53. What permission do you use in a directory to prevent anyone but yourself from deleting a file?

54. How do you explain that we have read, write, and execute permissions for a file, but do not have a delete permission?

55. If a person cannot delete a file, can he or she destroy it? Explain your answer.

Exercises

56. Translate the following permissions to octal code:
    a. `--x--x--x`   c. `--xrwx--x`
    b. `rwx--x--x`   d. `r-xr-xrwx`

57. Repeat Exercise 56 using symbolic code.

58. Translate the following permissions into rwx triplets:
    a. Only read for the owner
    b. Read/write for the owner; nothing for others
    c. Read for owner; execute only for others
    d. All for the owner; read for the group; execute for others

59. Repeat Exercise 58 using symbolic code.

60. Repeat Exercise 58 using octal code.

61. Translate the following permissions to octal. Which one(s) cannot be done?

    a. `u=rwx,g=x,o=x`   c. `u=rwx,g+x,o-x`

    b. `u=rw`   d. `g=rwx`

62. Change the following octal permissions to rwx triplets:

    a. 110   c. 505

    b. 777   d. 111

63. Repeat Exercise 62 using symbolic code.

64. A file has 000 (in octal) permission. How can an owner access this file?

65. George needs to copy the `/usr/john/report` (under the john home directory) to his directory. What type of permissions should the file have? What type of permission should the root directory have? What type of permission should the `/usr/john` directory have?

66. A file has a 000 (in octal) access permission. How can an owner read this file? How can the owner write to this file? How can the owner execute this file?

67. George needs to copy a file named `report` with an absolute pathname of `/usr/john/report` to his directory. What permission type is required for each of the following?

    a. `report`   d. `/usr/john`

    b. `root`   e. `~george`

    c. `/usr`

68. Joan needs to edit a file with an absolute pathname of `/usr/joan/ personal/ letter`. What type of permission is required for each of the following?

    a. `letter`   d. `/usr/joan`

    b. `root`   e. `/usr/joan/personal`

    c. `/usr`

69. Anne needs to copy a file with an absolute pathname of `/usr/anne/sales` to John's directory (`/usr/john`). What type of permission is required for each of the following?

    a. `sales`   d. `/usr/john`

    b. `/`   e. `/usr/anne`

    c. `/usr`

70. What is the permission of file `sample` after the following command?

```
chmod 555 sample
```

  Define the different permissions for the user, group, and others.

71. What is the permission of file `sample` after the following command?

```
chmod 111 sample
```

Define the different permissions for the user, group, and others.

72. What is the permission of file `sample` after the following command?

```
chmod 444 sample
```

Define the different permissions for the user, group, and others.

73. The file `sample` has the permission `rwxr-xr-x`. What are the permissions after the following command?

```
chmod u-x,g+w,o-x sample
```

74. The file `sample` has the permission `rwx--x--x`. What are the permissions after the following command?

    ```
    chmod u-x,g=w,o=r sample
    ```

75. A user issues the following command:
    ```
    umask 022
    ```
    a. What are the default permissions for all files created after this command?

    b. What are the default permissions for all directories created after this command?

76. A user issues the following command:
    ```
    umask 111
    ```
    a. What are the default permissions for all files created after this command?

    b. What are the default permissions for all directories created after this command?

4.11 Lab Sessions

Each of the following sessions uses one or more practical exercises. After finishing each session, write a report that explains the result of each step and answer any questions asked.

Session I

1. Log into the system.
2. Check which group or groups you belong to.
3. Use the **umask** command to set the default permission to be 700 for directories. What is the default permission for files after this command?
4. Create a directory named `chapter_4` under your home directory.
5. Check the default permission of this directory. Is it 700?
6. Create a directory under the `chapter_4` directory (without moving from your home directory) and name it `session_I`.
7. Check the permission of this directory. Is it 700?
8. Move to the `session_I` directory.
9. Create a file named `hw_4_1` under this directory and type the answers to the first five exercises in Section 4.10 on page 136.
10. Save this file.
11. Check the permission of this file. Is it 700 or 600? Why? Explain the difference between the permissions for files and directories.
12. Do users in your group have any access to this file? Do other users (outside of your group) have any access to this file?
13. Change the permissions to allow users in your group only to copy this file to their own directories. Is there a need to change the permission of any directories? If yes, make the necessary change(s).

Continued

14. Ask a user in your group to copy this file into his or her home directory. Was the copy successful? If not, find the reason and take the appropriate action(s) to correct it. Then have your user-group friend try again.
15. Log out of the system.

Session II

1. Log into the system.
2. Check which group or groups you belong to.
3. Check your default mask.
4. Create a directory called `garbage` under your home directory.
5. Check the permission of this directory. Make a note of it.
6. Change your default mask so that the default permission is 664. What is the default permission for directories after you make this change?
7. Check the permission for the `garbage` directory. Has it been changed after setting the default mask? Why or why not?
8. Delete this directory.
9. Create a directory called `session_II` under the `chapter_4` directory.
10. Check the permission of this directory and make a note of it.
11. Remove the `x` permission for the user from this directory.
12. Move to the `session_II` directory. You should have a problem. Do you know what the problem is? Fix the problem.
13. Create a file named `hw_4_2` under this directory and type the answers to the second five exercises in Section 4.10 on pages 136–137.
14. Save this file.
15. Check the permissions of this file. Can users in your group copy this file? Can they change this file? Can users outside your group copy this file? Can they change this file? Is this file executable?
16. Change the permissions of this file so that every user can read, modify, but not execute this file.
17. Print this file.
18. Log out of the system.

## CHAPTER 5

Introduction to Shells

As we discussed in Chapter 1, the UNIX operating system contains four distinct parts: the kernel, the shell, utilities, and applications. To refresh your memory, you may want to look at Figure 1.6 on page 8. We discuss the shell in this chapter.

The **shell** is the part of UNIX that is most visible to the user. It receives and interprets the commands entered by the user. In many respects, this makes it the most important component of the UNIX structure. It is certainly the part that we, as users, get to know the most. To do anything in the system, we must give the shell a command. If the command requires a utility, the shell requests that the kernel execute the utility. If the command requires an application program, the shell requests that it be run. The shells are shown in Figure 5.1.

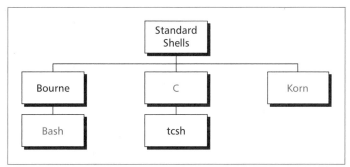

FIGURE 5.1 *Five Standard UNIX Shells*

There are two major parts to a shell. The first is the interpreter. The interpreter reads your commands and works with the kernel to execute them. The second part of the shell is a programming capability that allows you to write a shell (command) script. A **shell script** is a file that contains shell commands that perform a useful function. It is also known as a **shell program.**

Three traditional shells are used in UNIX today. The Bourne shell, developed by Steve Bourne at the AT&T Labs, is the oldest. Because it is the oldest and most primitive, it is not used on many systems today. An enhanced version of the Bourne shell, called Bash (Bourne again shell), is used in Linux.

The C shell, developed in Berkeley by Bill Joy, received its name from the fact that its commands were supposed to look like C statements. A compatible version of the C shell, tcsh,[1] is used in Linux.

---

[1]The tcsh shell is pronounced tee-cee shell.

The Korn shell, developed by David Korn, also of the AT&T Labs, is the newest and most powerful. Because it was developed at the AT&T Labs, it is compatible with the Bourne shell.

In this chapter, we concentrate on the Korn shell. In those areas, however, where there are differences between the Korn shell and the Bash and C shells, we point out the differences.

5.1 UNIX Session

A UNIX session consists of logging into the system and then executing commands to accomplish our work. When our work is done, we log out of the system. This workflow is shown in the flowchart in Figure 5.2.

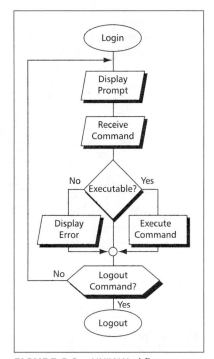

FIGURE 5.2 *UNIX Workflow*

As previously stated, when you log in, you are in one of five shells. The system administrator determines which shell you start in by an entry in the password file (/etc/passwd).

Even though your start up shell is determined by the system administrator, you can always switch to another shell. The following example shows how to move to other shells:

```
$ bash            # Move to Bash shell
$ ksh             # Move to Korn shell
$ csh             # Move to C shell
```

Login Shell Verification

UNIX contains a system variable, SHELL, that identifies the path to your login shell. You can check it with the command in Session 5.1.

SESSION 5.1 *Verify Login Shell*

```
$ echo $SHELL
/bin/ksh
```

Note that the variable name is all uppercase. We discussed the basic use of the **echo** command in Chapter 1.

Current Shell Verification

Your current shell may or may not be your login shell. To determine what your current shell is, you can use the following command. Note, however, that this command works only with the Korn and Bash shells; it does not work with the C shell.

SESSION 5.2 *Verify Current Shell*

```
$ echo $0
ksh
```

Shell Relationships

When you move from one shell to another, UNIX remembers the path you followed by creating a parent-child relationship. Your login shell is always the most senior shell in the relationship—the parent or grandparent depending on how many shells you have used.

Let's assume that your login shell is the Korn shell. If you then move to the Bash shell, the Korn shell is the parent and the Bash shell is the child. If later in the session you move to the C shell, the C shell is the child of the Bash shell and the Bash shell is the child of the Korn shell. Looking at the relationship from the top, the Korn shell is the parent of the Bash shell, and the Bash shell is the parent of the C shell. Although it is technically possible to move to the Korn shell at this point, it is not advisable. Figure 5.3 diagrams the shell relationships.

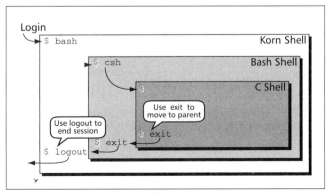

FIGURE 5.3 *Shell Relationships*

To move from a child shell to a parent, we use the **exit** command. Each **exit** moves up one shell in the hierarchy; that is, it moves up one shell in the parent-child relationship.

```
$ exit
```

When you move up to the parent shell, the child shell is destroyed—it no longer exists. Should you create a child again, an entirely new shell is created. All of the previous shell's history—that is, all the commands you executed earlier—is gone, and even though they may both be the same shell type, there is no connection between the old child and the new one.

Logout

To quit the session—that is, to log out of the system—you must be at the original login shell. You cannot log out from a child. If you try to log out from a child, you will get an error message. The Korn shell and the Bash shell both display a not-found message such as "logout not found." The C shell is more specific: It reports that you are not in the login shell.

The reason for this rule is to ensure that everything is done neatly. For example, there may be a job running in the background of a parent that needs to be properly terminated. If a child could terminate the session, the parent's job would be terminated abruptly and its processing would not be valid.

The correct command to end the session at the login shell is **logout,** but the **exit** command also terminates the session.

5.2 Standard Streams

UNIX defines three standard streams that are used by commands. Each command takes its input from a stream known as **standard input.** Commands that create output send it to a stream known as **standard output.** If an executing command encounters an error, the error message is sent to **standard error.** The standard streams are presented in Figure 5.4.

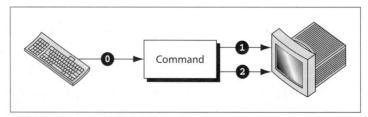

FIGURE 5.4   *Standard Streams*

So that we can reference them, UNIX assigns a descriptor to each stream. As seen in Figure 5.4, the descriptor for standard input is 0 (zero), for standard output is 1, and for standard error is 2. Also shown in Figure 5.4 is the default physical file associated with each stream: Standard input is associated with the keyboard; standard output is associated with the monitor; and standard error is also associated with the monitor. We can change the default file association using pipes or redirection.

Not every command gets its input from standard input. For example, in Chapter 1 on page 18, we discussed the **who** command. It gets its input from a system file. Other commands require an input disk file.

> **Not all commands use the standard input file for their input.**

Likewise, not every command sends its output to standard output. For example, the **lpr** command sends its output directly to the printer.

5.3 Redirection

As we learned earlier in the chapter, each command may use standard input stream, standard output stream, and standard error stream. These streams are preassigned to the keyboard and the monitor. Whenever necessary, we can change these default assignments temporarily using redirection. **Redirection** is the process by which we specify that a file is to be used in place of one of the standard files. With input files, we call it input redirection; with output files, we call it output redirection; and with the error file, we call it error redirection.

In the examples in this section, we use the stream descriptors for the standard files: 0 for standard input, 1 for standard output, and 2 for standard error.

Redirecting Input

We can redirect the standard input from the keyboard to any text file. The input redirection operator is the less than character (<). Think of it as an arrow pointing to a command, meaning that the command is to get its input from the designated file. Figure 5.5 shows how a file can be redirected to replace the keyboard. In this figure, the standard output and error files remain at the default.

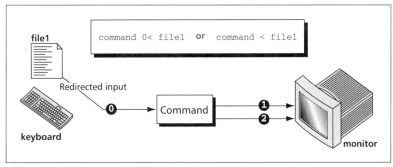

FIGURE 5.5 *Redirecting Standard Input*

Figure 5.5 shows two ways to express the redirection. The first method explicitly specifies that the redirection is applied to standard input by coding the 0 descriptor. The second method omits the descriptor. Because there is only one standard input, we can omit it. Also note that there is no space between the descriptor and the redirection symbol.

Redirecting Output

When we redirect standard output, the command's output is copied to a file rather than displayed on the monitor. The concept of redirected output appears in Figure 5.6.

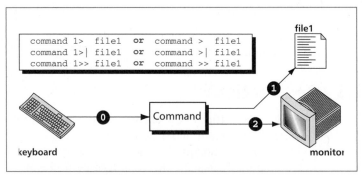

```
command 1>  file1  or  command >  file1
command 1>| file1  or  command >| file1
command 1>> file1  or  command >> file1
```

FIGURE 5.6   *Redirecting Standard Output*

There are two basic redirection operators for standard output. Both start with a greater than character (>). Think of the greater than character as an arrow pointing away from the command and to the file that is to receive the output. Which of the operators you use depends on how you want the output file handled. If you want the file to contain only the output from this execution of the command, you use one greater than token (>) . In this case, when you redirect the output to a file that doesn't exist, UNIX creates it and writes the output. If the file already exists, the action depends on the setting of a UNIX option known as **noclobber.** When the noclobber option is turned on (see page 183), it prevents redirected output from destroying an existing file. In this case, you get an error message. Session 5.3 shows the error message when the noclobber option is on.

SESSION 5.3   *Output Redirection Error*

```
$ who > whoOct2
ksh: whoOct2: file already exists
```

If you want to override the option and replace the current file's contents with new output, you must use the redirection override operator, greater than bar (>|). In this case, UNIX first empties the file and then writes the new output to the file. The redirection override output is shown in Session 5.4.

SESSION 5.4   *Output Redirection Error Override*

```
$ who >| whoOct2
$ more whoOct2
ab052408    ttyq3          Oct  2 15:24  (atc2west-171.atc.fhda.edu)
```

On the other hand, if you want to append the output to the file, the redirection token is two greater than characters (>>). Think of the first greater than as saying you want to redirect the output and the second one as saying that you want to go to the end of the file before you start outputting.

When you append output, if the file doesn't exist, UNIX creates it and writes the output. If it already exists, however, UNIX moves to the end of the file before writing any new output.

Redirecting Errors

One of the difficulties with the standard error stream is that it is, by default, combined with standard output stream on the monitor. In the following example, we use the long list (**ls**) command to display the permissions of two files. If both are valid, one displays after the other. If only one is valid, it is displayed, but **ls** displays an error message for the other one on the same monitor.

SESSION 5.5   *Standard Output and Error on Monitor*

```
$ ls -l file1 noFile
Cannot access noFile: No such file or directory
-rw-r--r--    1 gilberg  staff        1234 Oct  2 18:16 file1
```

We can redirect the standard output to a file and leave the standard error file assigned to the monitor. To demonstrate this capability, we repeat Session 5.5, this time with standard output directed to a file. Note that the output from the valid file is written to the output file. This is true regardless of which filename is wrong; that is, all valid files are written to the output file, and all error messages are written to standard error.

SESSION 5.6   *Standard Output to File; Errors on Monitor*

```
$ ls -l file1 noFile 1>fileList
Cannot access noFile: No such file or directory
$ more fileList
-rw-r--r--    1 gilberg  staff        1234 Oct  2 18:16 file1
```

First note that the only output we see is the error message. It makes sense to have the error message sent to the monitor so that we immediately know that there was a problem. After the error message, we display the contents of the redirected output to prove that everything worked as planned.

But what if you want both output and errors sent to a file? In this case, we must specify that both are to be written to files. The files can be the same, or they can be different. Let's look at the case where they are different files first.

Redirecting to Different Files

To redirect to different files, we must use the stream descriptors. Actually, when we use only the greater than sign, the system assumes that we are redirecting the output (descriptor 1). To redirect them both, therefore, we specify the descriptor (0, 1, or 2) and then the redirection operator as in Session 5.7.

SESSION 5.7   *Standard Output and Errors to Different Files*

```
$ ls -l file1 noFile 1> myStdOut 2> myStdErr
$ more myStdOut
-rw-r--r--    1 gilberg   staff        1234 Oct  2 18:16 file1
$ more myStdErr
Cannot open noFile: No such file or directory
```

The descriptor and the redirection operator must be written as consecutive characters; there can be no space between them. It makes no difference which one you specify first. The **ls** command in Session 5.7 could just as easily have been written as shown in the line of code that follows. However, from a human-engineering point of view, it makes a little more sense to do the good output first (descriptor 1) and then the errors (descriptor 2) as we did in Session 5.7.

```
$ ls file1 noFile 2> myStdErr 1> myStdOut
```

Redirecting to One File

If we want both outputs to be written to the same file, we cannot simply specify the file name twice. If we do, the command fails because the file is already open. This is the case in Session 5.8.

SESSION 5.8   *Standard Output and Errors to Same File*

```
$ ls -l file1 noFile 1> myStdOut 2> myStdOut
ksh: myStdOut: file already exists
```

If we use the redirection override operator, the output file contains only the results of the last command output as in Session 5.9.

SESSION 5.9   *Standard Output to Files with Redirection Override*

```
$ ls -l file1 noFile 1>| myStdOut 2>| myStdOut
$ ls myStdOut
Cannot open noFile: No such file or directory
```

To write all output to the same file, we must tell UNIX that the second file is really the same as the first. We do this with another operator, the **and** operator (&). An example of the substitution operator is shown in Session 5.10.

SESSION 5.10   *Redirecting Output and Errors to One File*

```
$ ls -l file1 noFile 1> myStdOut 2>& 1
$ more myStdOut
Cannot access noFile: No such file or directory
-rw-r--r--    1 gilberg   staff        1234 Oct  2 18:16 file1
```

Let's look at this code a little more closely. First, we specify that standard output is to be written to a file called myStdOut. Then, we specify that standard error is to be written to file descriptor 1. In this case, the **redirection substitution operator** (>&) says that what follows is a file number, in this case, 1 or the file descriptor for standard output.

The Korn and Bash shells use the same redirection methods, but the C shell is different. It doesn't support the use of stream directors. This means that we can redirect only standard input and standard output; standard error cannot be redirected. The differences are presented in Table 5.1.

TABLE 5.1 *Redirection Differences between Shells*

Type	Korn and Bash Shells		C Shell
Input	`0 < file1`	or `< file1`	`< file1`
Output	`1 > file1`	or `> file1`	`> file1`
	`1 >| file1`	or `>| file1`	`>! file1`
	`1 >> file1`	or `>> file1`	`>> file1`
Error	`2 > file2`		Not supported
	`2 >| file2`		Not supported
	`2 >> file2`		Not supported
Output & Error (different files)	`1 > file1` `2 > file2`		Not supported
	`> file1` `2 > file2`		Not supported
Output & Error (same file)	`1 > file1` `2>&1`		`>& file1`
	`> file1` `2>&1`		`>& file1`
	`1 >| file1` `2>&1`		`>&! file1`

5.4 Pipes

We often need to use a series of commands to complete a task. For example, if we need to see a list of users logged into the system, we use the **who** command. However, if we need a hard copy of the list, we need two commands. First, we use **who** to get the list and store the result in a file using redirection. We then use the **lpr** command to print the file. This sequence of commands is shown in Figure 5.7.

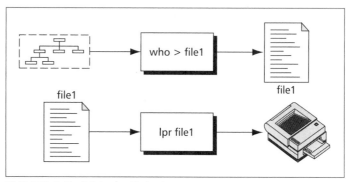

FIGURE 5.7 *Print **who** Output*

We can avoid the creation of the intermediate file by using a pipe. Pipe is an operator that temporarily saves the output of one command in a buffer that is being used at the same time as the input of the next command. The first command must be able to send its output to standard output; the second command must be able to read its input from standard input. This command sequence appears in Figure 5.8.

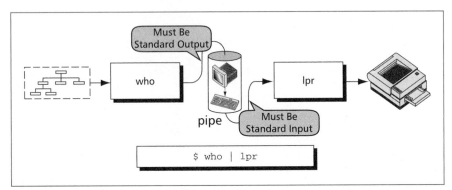

FIGURE 5.8   *Piping Output to Next Command*

Think of the pipe as a combination of a monitor and a keyboard. The input to the pipe operator must come from standard output. This means that the command on the left that sends output to the pipe must write its output to standard output. In Figure 5.8, for example, we use the **who** command because it reads the system and sends the list of users to standard output. The pipe command uses a buffer to send the piped data to the next command. The receiving command must receive its data from standard input. If it can't, it cannot receive the piped output.

> **A pipe operator receives its input from standard output and sends it to the next command through standard input. This means that the left command must be able to send data to standard output and the right command must be able to receive data from standard input.**

The token for a pipe is the vertical bar (|). There is no standard location on the keyboard for the bar. Usually, you will find it somewhere on the right side, often above the Return key. The code for Figure 5.8 is shown in the next example:

```
$ who | lpr
```

As a second example, often when you list who is logged into the system, there is more than one screen of output, and the list scrolls off the top of the screen. If you need to see the complete list, you have to stop it temporarily while you look at the first screen and then scroll to the next screen. The **more** command scrolls a list in just this fashion. To see the complete user list one screen at a time, simply pipe the output of the **who** command to **more** as shown here:

```
$ who | more
```

New UNIX users often have a difficult time recognizing which operations are commands and which are operators. They often have a very similar syntax and usage. The pipe is one of those situations. The pipe is not a command; it is an operator. It must be placed between two commands, the first of which must direct its output to standard output and the second of which must receive its input from standard input. The pipe tells the system that these two commands need to share the output of the first command and to pass it directly to the second command.

> Pipe is an operator, not a command. It tells the shell to immediately take the output of the first command, which must be sent to standard output, and turn it into input for the second command, which must get its input from standard input.

5.5 tee Command

The **tee** command copies standard input to standard output and at the same time copies it to one or more files. The first copy goes to standard output, which is usually the monitor. At the same time, the output is sent to the optional files specified in the argument list. The concept is presented in Figure 5.9.

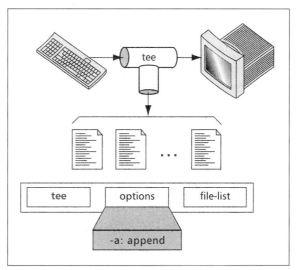

FIGURE 5.9 *The* **tee** *Command*

The **tee** command creates the output files if they do not exist and overwrites them if they already exist. To prevent the files from being overwritten, we can use the option -a, which tells **tee** to append the output to existing files rather than deleting their current content. Note, however, that the append option does not apply to standard output because standard output is always automatically appended. Session 5.11 demonstrates a simple **tee** command in which the input is from the keyboard. To verify the output to the file, we use **more** to copy it to the screen.

SESSION 5.11   *Demonstrate Simple* **tee** *Command*

```
$ tee teeOut
This is a sample of the tee command. You see each line repeated
This is a sample of the tee command. You see each line repeated
on the standard output as soon as I key enter. Each line is also
on the standard output as soon as I key enter. Each line is also
written to teeOut.
written to teeOut.

$ more teeOut
This is a sample of the tee command. You see each line repeated
on the standard output as soon as I key enter. Each line is also
written to teeOut.
```

Instead of using the keyboard, we can feed the **tee** command through a pipe. This is a commonly used sequence. For example, in Session 5.12, we use the **who** command and copy the results to whoOct2. Again, to verify the output, we display the contents of whoOct2 with a **more** command. In the interest of space, we have abbreviated the output.

SESSION 5.12   *Demonstrate* **tee** *to Two Files*

```
$ who | tee whoOct2
ab052408    ttyq3          Oct  2 15:24   (atc2-321.atc.fhda.edu)
rrp58061    ttyq4          Oct  2 13:17   (351.18.203.129)
bachlan     ttyq5          Oct  2 07:48   (mystic.atc.fhda.edu)
cpt46698    ttyq8          Oct  2 15:54   (402.247.190.5)
gilberg     ttyq14         Oct  2 15:04   (adsl-36-202-180-43..pacbell.net)
gdt43614    ttyq15         Oct  2 16:00   (atc2-99.atc.fhda.edu)
rn031017    ttyq16         Oct  2 15:51   (c036-a.stcla1.home.com)

$ more whoOct2
ab052408    ttyq3          Oct  2 15:24   (atc2-171.atc.fhda.edu)
rrp58061    ttyq4          Oct  2 13:17   (351.18.203.129)
bachlan     ttyq5          Oct  2 07:48   (genii.atc.fhda.edu)
cpt46698    ttyq8          Oct  2 15:54   (402.247.190.5)
gilberg     ttyq14         Oct  2 15:04   (adsl-36-202-180-43..pacbell.net)
gdt43614    ttyq15         Oct  2 16:00   (atc2-99.atc.fhda.edu)
rn031017    ttyq16         Oct  2 15:51   (c036-a.stcla1.home.com)
```

5.6   Command Execution

Nothing happens in a UNIX shell until a command is executed. When a user enters a command on the command line, the interpreter analyzes the command and directs its execution to a utility or other program.

Some commands are short and can be entered as a single line at the command prompt. We have seen several simple commands, such as **cal** and **date,** already. At other times, we need to combine several commands. There are four syntactical formats for combining commands into one line: sequenced, grouped, chained, and conditional.

Sequenced Commands

A sequence of commands can be entered on one line.. Each command must be separated from its predecessor by a semicolon. There is no direct relationship between the commands; that is, one command does not communicate with the other. They are simply combined into one line and executed. As an example of a command sequence, assume that we want to create a calendar with a descriptive title. This is easily done with a sequence as shown in Session 5.13.

SESSION 5.13   *Sequenced Command*

```
$ echo "\n Goblins & Ghosts\n        Month" > Oct2000; cal 10 2000 >> Oct2000
$ more Oct2000

   Goblins & Ghosts
        Month
    October 2000
 S  M Tu  W Th  F  S
 1  2  3  4  5  6  7
 8  9 10 11 12 13 14
15 16 17 18 19 20 21
22 23 24 25 26 27 28
29 30 31
```

Session 5.13 Analysis: Study the technique used in this example carefully. First, we redirect **echo**'s output to a file. To center the caption over the calendar, we used newlines ($\backslash$n) and spaces. Then we used **cal** to generate the calendar month and appended it to the file that contains the date. To verify the results, we used **more** to print the file.

Grouped Commands

In Session 5.13, we redirected the output of two commands to the same file. This technique gives us the intended results, but we can do it more easily by grouping the commands. When we group commands, we apply the same operation to the group. Commands are grouped by placing them in parentheses. Session 5.14 repeats the file created in Session 5.13 by grouping the command sequence and then applying the redirection. Again, we **more** the results to verify that the commands worked as planned.

SESSION 5.14   *Grouped Commands*

```
$ (echo "\n Goblins & Ghosts\n        Month"; cal 10 2000) > Oct2000
$ more Oct2000

   Goblins & Ghosts
        Month
    October 2000
 S  M Tu  W Th  F  S
 1  2  3  4  5  6  7
 8  9 10 11 12 13 14
```

Continued

SESSION 5.14   *Grouped Commands—Continued*

```
15 16 17 18 19 20 21
22 23 24 25 26 27 28
29 30 31
```

Session 5.14 Analysis: There is a very subtle difference between Session 5.13 and Session 5.14. In Session 5.13, we used two commands. The first created the file and the second appended to it. In Session 5.14, we concatenated the results of two commands and redirected the concatenated data to the file.

Chained Commands

In the previous two methods of combining commands into one line, there was no relationship between the commands. Each command operated independently of the other and only shared a need to have their output in one file. The third method of combining commands is to pipe them. In this case, however, there is a direct relationship between the commands. The output of the first becomes the input of the second. We discussed pipes in Section 5.4 (page 151). You may want to review the pipe operator from a viewpoint of combined commands.

Conditional Commands

We can combine two or more commands using conditional relationships. There are two shell logical operators, *and* (&&) and *or* (| |). In general, when two commands are combined with a logical *and,* the second executes only if the first command is successful. Conversely, if two commands are combined using the logical *or,* the second command executes only if the first fails. These commands are demonstrated with two simple examples in Session 5.15.

SESSION 5.15   *Demonstrate and/or Commands*

```
$ cp file1 tempfile && echo "Copy successful"
Copy successful
$ cp noFile tempfile || echo "Copy failed"
noFile - No such file or directory
Copy failed
```

5.7   Command-Line Editing

The phrase "to err is human" applies with a harsh reality to all forms of computing. As we enter commands in the UNIX command line, it is very easy to err. As long as we haven't keyed Return and we notice the mistake, we can correct it. But what if we have keyed Return? There are two ways we can edit previous commands in the Korn and Bash shells and one way in the C shell.

In the Korn and Bash shells, we can use the history file or we can use command-line editing. The history file is a special UNIX file that contains a list of commands used during a session. In the C shell, we can use only the history file. Table 5.2 summarizes the command-line editing options available. In Chapter 13 and Chapter 16, we discuss editing using the history file. Korn and Bash command-line editing is discussed in the following section.

TABLE 5.2 *Command-Line Editing Options*

Method	Korn Shell	Bash Shell	C Shell
Command Line	✓	✓	
History File	✓	✓	✓

Command-Line Editing Concept

As each command is entered on the command line, the Korn shell copies it to a special file. With command-line editing, we can edit the commands using either **vi** or **emacs** (see Appendix C) without opening the file. It's as though the shell keeps the file in a buffer that provides instant access to our commands. Whenever a command completes, the shell moves to the next command line and waits for the next command. This concept is shown in Figure 5.10.

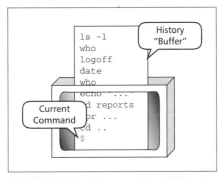

FIGURE 5.10 *Command-Line Editing Concept*

Editor Selection

The system administrator may set the default command-line editor, most likely in /etc/profile (see "System Profile File:" on page 186). You can switch it, however, by setting it yourself. If you set it at the command line, it is set for only the current session. If you add it to your login file, it will be changed every time you log in. During the session, you can also change it from one to another and back whenever you like.

To set the editor, we use the **set** command with the editor as shown in the next example. Obviously, you would use only one of the two commands.

```
$ set -o vi        # Turn on vi editor
$ set -o emacs     # Turn on emacs editor
```

vi Command-Line Editor

We cannot tell which editor we are using at the command line simply by examining the prompt. Both editors return to the shell command line and wait for a response. It quickly becomes obvious, however, by the behavior of the command line. The **vi** command-line editor opens in the insert mode. This allows us to enter commands easily. When we key Return, the command is executed and we return to the **vi** insert mode waiting for input.

vi Edit Mode

Remember that the **vi** editor treats the history file as though it is always open and available. Because **vi** starts in the insert mode, however, to move to the **vi** command mode we must use the Escape key. Once in the **vi** command mode, we can use several of the standard **vi** commands. The most obvious commands that are not available are the read, write, and quit commands. The basic commands that are available are listed in Table 5.3.

TABLE 5.3   *Basic **vi** Commands*

Category	Command	Description
Adding Text	i	Inserts text before the current character.
	I	Inserts text at the beginning of the current line.
	a	Appends text after the current character.
	A	Adds text at the end of the current line.
Deleting Text	x	Deletes the current character.
	dd	Deletes the command line.
Moving Cursor	h	Moves the cursor one character to the left.
	l	Moves the cursor one character to the right.
	0	Moves the cursor to the beginning of the current line.
	$	Moves the cursor to the end of the current line.
	k	Moves the cursor one line up.
	j	Moves the cursor one line down.
	–	Moves the cursor to the beginning of the previous line.
	+	Moves the cursor to the beginning of the next line.
Undo	u	Undoes only the last edit.
	U	Undoes all changes on the current line.
Mode	\<esc\>	Enters command mode.
	i, I, a, A	Enters insert mode.

Only one line is displayed at any time. Any changes made to a line do not change the previous line in the file. However, when the edited line is executed, it is appended to the end of the file.

Move Commands

When we move from the insert mode to the command mode, we are always at the bottom of the history file. This means that all of the line history is above us. To move up the list to an older line, we use the k key. Once we have moved up the file, we can move down using the j key. On any given history line, we can move left using the h key or move right using the l key. These are the standard **vi** directional keys. Note, however, that the arrow keys do not work with **vi** command-line edits. Figure 5.11 summarizes these directional key moves.

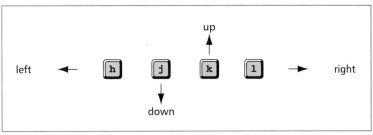

FIGURE 5.11 **vi** *Directional Keys*

Using the Command-Line Editor

In this section, we demonstrate several techniques for using the command-line editor.

Execute a Previous Line

To execute a previous line, we must move up the history file until we find the line. This requires the following steps.

1. Move to the command mode by keying Escape (esc).
2. Move up the list using the Move-up key (k).
3. When command has been located, key Return to execute it.

After the command has been executed, we are back at the bottom of the history file in the insert mode.

Edit and Execute a Previous Command

Assume that we have just executed the **more** command with a misspelled filename. In the next example, we left off the last character of the filename, such as "file" rather than "file1."

1. Move to the command mode by keying Escape (esc).
2. Using the Move-up key (k), recall the previous line.
3. Use the append-at-end command (A) to move the cursor to the end of the line in the insert mode.
4. Key the missing character and Return.

After executing the line, we are in the insert mode.

5.8 Quotes

The shells use a selected set of metacharacters in commands. **Metacharacters** are characters that have a special interpretation. We have already seen some of them, for example, the pipe (|). Appendix G contains a complete metacharacter list. Some of them are discussed in this section. Others are developed as we continue through the text.

In addition to being used to communicate with the shell, metacharacters are commonly used as text. We therefore need some way to tell the shell interpreter when we want to use them as metacharacters and when we want to use them as text. Three of the metacharacters known collectively as quotes serve this purpose: backslash, double quotes, and single quotes (Figure 5.12).

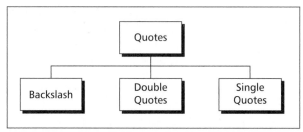

FIGURE 5.12   *Quotes*

Backslash

The backslash metacharacter (\) changes the interpretation of the character that follows—it converts literal characters into special characters and special characters into literal characters. Literal characters are interpreted in the normal, noncomputer meaning; special characters are interpreted as shell command characters. For example, the less than (<) character is interpreted as "less than" in its literal meaning and as "input redirection" when used in a command.

If the character is interpreted as a literal character by the shell, such as the character n, then to turn it into the newline character, we use the backslash (\n). On the other hand, if the character is interpreted as a special character by the shell, such as redirection (<), then to turn it into a literal character, we must escape it (\<).

For example, if we display a quoted comment with the **echo** command, the shell will interpret the quotes as special characters and strip them from the output. To turn the quotes into literal characters, we can use a backslash as in Session 5.16.

SESSION 5.16   *Using Backslashes to Print Quotes*

```
$ echo Dick said "Hello World!"
Dick said Hello World!

$ echo Dick said \"Hello World!\"
Dick said "Hello World!"
```

As another example, let's display the metacharacters as we would in an error message to the user. The first example in Session 5.17 doesn't work. The second example displays the characters correctly because they have all been escaped. Note that to display the escape character, it must be keyed twice; that is, we must escape the escape character.

SESSION 5.17 *Displaying Special Characters as Literal Text*

```
$ echo < > " ' \ $
ksh: syntax error: '>' unexpected
$ echo \< \> \"  \' \\  \$
< > " ' \ $
```

There are times when a command requires more than one line. At the same time, all commands entered on the command line must be only one line. This apparent dilemma is solved by the last use of the backslash character, canceling the end of line.

The backslash character changes only one character—the one immediately following it.

The Return key has two effects on a UNIX shell: It is a command separator (end of command) and it is a line separator (end of line). When we use the escape character immediately before the return, we cancel the first effect while keeping the second one. The cursor goes to the next line, but the shell does not interpret the command until it finds an unguarded end of command. Session 5.18 contains an interesting, albeit not very practical, use of canceling the return. Later in the text, we will present more practical examples.

SESSION 5.18 *Using Escape to Cancel Return*

```
$ (date; \
> echo ;\
> more TheRavenV1) \
> > tempFile
$ more tempFile
Sun Sep 10 16:31:39 PDT 2000

Once upon a midnight dreary, while I pondered, weak and weary,
...
Perched, and sat, and nothing more.
```

Session 5.18 Analysis: We begin the command using an open parenthesis. The matching close parenthesis is found at the end of the third line of the command. You should recognize this as a group command. Within the group, we generate the date output followed by an **echo** command to generate a blank line and then a **more** command to generate the first verse of "The Raven" file. These three outputs are then redirected to a file. To verify the results, we then **more** `tempFile`. In the interest of space, we have abbreviated the output.

Double Quotes

When we need to change the meaning of several characters, we can use double quotes. Double quotes remove the special interpretation of most metacharacters. The exceptions are the dollar sign in front of a variable name ("Accessing a Variable" on page 178), and single quotes. In Session 5.19, we create a variable x and assign it the value `hello`. We then use the **echo** command to display several metacharacters. Study the output carefully. Note that the value of x is displayed rather than $x.

SESSION 5.19 *Using Double Quotes to Guard Metacharacters*

```
$ x=hello
$ echo "< > $x 'y' ? &"
< > hello 'y' ? &
```

When a text line is enclosed in double quotes, we cannot use a double quote in the string because the shell interprets the second quote as the end quote. Therefore, to include quotes inside of quotes, we must turn them back into literal quotes by using a backslash with them. The concept is shown in Session 5.20.

SESSION 5.20 *Quotes Inside Quotes*

```
$ echo "Quoth the Raven, "Nevermore."
> "
Quoth the Raven, Nevermore.
$ echo "Quoth the Raven, \"Nevermore.\""
Quoth the Raven, "Nevermore."
```

Session 5.20 Analysis: We made a common mistake in the first line. Quotes must always be entered in pairs; the beginning quote must have an ending quote. Because we didn't have an ending quote when we keyed Return on the first line, the shell went to the next line with a continue prompt. . . (the greater than). We then entered the ending quote to complete the command.

> **Single quotes and double quotes must always be used in pairs.**

In the first example, we placed quotes around the entire text line and also around the word "Nevermore." The **echo** command displays the text correctly, but there are no quotes around Nevermore. The reason is that **echo** looks at this line as three text strings. The first is "Quoth the Raven," and the second string is the unquoted text Nevermore. The third string is the null string created by consecutive double quotes (" ").

A simpler solution uses a combination of single quotes and double quotes. We show this solution in the next section.

Double quotes also preserve whitespace characters in the text. Whitespace characters are the tab, newline, and the blank or space character. In Session 5.21, we demonstrate that the quotes do indeed preserve whitespace.

SESSION 5.21 *Quotes Preserve Whitespace*

```
$ echo "Now       is       the       time
> For   all   good   students
> To    come   to    the    aid
> Of    their   college!"
```

Continued

SESSION 5.21   *Quotes Preserve Whitespace*

```
Now      is      the      time
For   all   good   students
To    come   to   the   aid
Of     their     college!
```

Session 5.21 Analysis: In the first line, we use tabs between words; in the second line, we use two spaces; in the third line, three spaces; and the fourth line, four spaces. At the end of each line, there is a newline. The output shows the keyboard input exactly as we input it, minus the quotes.

> **Double quotes preserve whitespace characters such as space, tab, and newline.**

Single Quotes

Single quotes operate like double quotes, but their effect is stronger. They preserve only the meaning of single quotes. Any enclosed metacharacters are treated as literal characters. To demonstrate this, Session 5.22 repeats Session 5.19 using single quotes.

SESSION 5.22   *Using Single Quotes to Change Meaning of Special Characters*

```
$ x=hello
$ echo '< > $x "y" ? &'
< > $x "y" ? &
```

Session 5.22 Analysis: The output to look at in this session is $x. In Session 5.19, the value of the variable x (hello) was displayed. In this session, $x itself was displayed.

Like double quotes, the shell expects to find single quotes in matching pairs, start and end. Four single quotes are therefore two single quoted text strings. Consider the code in Session 5.23. This is very similar to Session 5.22, but the $x is not quoted.

SESSION 5.23   *Matching Single Quotes*

```
$ x=hello
$ echo '< > '$x' "y" ? &'
< > hello "y" ? &
```

Session 5.23 Analysis: This time, the value of $x is displayed. When **echo** parses the text to be displayed, it first finds the single quoted string, '< > ' followed by the variable reference operator ($) with the variable x, and then the single quoted text string ' "y" ? &' at the end of the line. Because the variable reference ($x) is not quoted, its value is displayed.

Also demonstrated in this script is the fact that double quotes lose their special character properties when placed inside single quotes. Note that the double quotes are displayed as double quotes around the "y."

As a final example, we repeat Session 5.20 using single quotes as the outside quotes and double quotes around "Nevermore." When it's necessary to print double quotes, it's easier to put them into a set of single quotes.

SESSION 5.24 *Quotes inside Quotes*

```
$ echo 'Quoth the Raven, "Nevermore."'
Quoth the Raven, "Nevermore."
```

5.9 Command Substitution

When a shell executes a command, the output is directed to standard output. Most of the time, standard output is associated with the monitor. There are times, however, such as when we write complex commands or scripts, that we need to change the output to a string that we can store in another string or a variable. **Command substitution** provides the capability to convert the result of a command to a string. The command substitution operator that converts the output of a command to a string is a dollar sign and a set of parentheses (Figure 5.13).

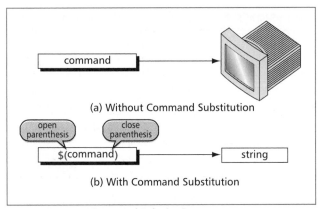

FIGURE 5.13 *Command Substitution*

As shown in Figure 5.13, to invoke command substitution, we enclose the command in a set of parentheses preceded by a dollar sign ($). When we use command substitution, the command is executed, and its output is created and then converted to a string of characters.

Session 5.25 contains a simple demonstration of command substitution. We begin by using the **date** command within an **echo** command. This doesn't work, however, because the **date** command is interpreted as text to be displayed.

To execute the **date** command and convert its output to a string we can display in the **echo** command, we need to use command substitution. In the second example, the

date command is enclosed in parentheses preceded by a dollar sign making it command substitution. The result is that the **date** output is converted to a string and then included in the **echo** output.

SESSION 5.25 *Using Command Substitution with* **date**

```
$ echo Hello! The date and time are: date
Hello! The date and time are: date

$ echo Hello! The date and time are: $(date)
Hello! The date and time are: Mon Sep 11 09:48:04 PDT 2000
```

Command Substitution in the C Shell

The C shell does not support the dollar sign-parentheses format for command substitution. Rather, it encloses the command in a set of backquotes (grave accents) as shown in the following example:

```
% echo The date and time are: `date`
The date and time are: Mon Sep 11 18:27:25 PDT 2000
```

5.10 Job Control

One of the important features of a shell is job control. In this section, we first discuss the job concept and then how jobs are run.

Jobs

In general, a job is a user task run on the computer. Editing, sorting, and reading mail are all examples of jobs. However, UNIX has a specific definition of a job: A job is a command or set of commands entered on one command line. For example,

```
$ ls
$ ls | lpr
```

are both jobs.

Foreground and Background Jobs

Because UNIX is a multitasking operating system, we can run more than one job at a time. However, when we start a job in the foreground, the standard input and output are locked. They are available exclusively to the current job until it completes. This means only one job that needs these files can run at a time. To allow multiple jobs, therefore, UNIX defines two types of jobs: foreground and background.

Foreground Jobs

A **foreground** job is any job run under the active supervision of the user. It is started by the user and may interact with the user through standard input and output. While it is running, no other jobs may be started. To start a foreground job, we simply enter a command and key Return. Keying Return at the end of the command starts it in the foreground. As you may have realized from this description, all commands we have run so far have been run as foreground jobs.

Suspending a Foreground Job While a foreground job is running, it can be suspended. For example, while you are running a long sort in the foreground, you get a notice that you have mail. To read and respond to your mail, you must suspend the job. After you are through with the mail, you can then restart the sort.

To suspend a foreground job, key `ctrl+z`. To resume it, use the foreground **fg** command. In Session 5.26, we start a long running job, then suspend it so that we can check the time using the **date** command, and then restart it. While a job is suspended, any command, even the one that has been suspended, can be used.

SESSION 5.26 *Suspending and Restarting a Foreground Job*

```
$ fgLoop.scr
^z                                           #foreground job suspended
[2] + Stopped (SIGTSTP)        fgLoop.scr

$ date
Tue Sep 12 12:43:44 PDT 2000

$ fg                                         #resume job
fgLoop.scr
```

Terminating a Foreground Job If for any reason we want to terminate (kill) a running foreground job, we use the cancel metacharacter, `ctrl+c`. After the job is terminated, we key Return to activate the command-line prompt. If the job has been suspended, it must first be resumed using the foreground command. Session 5.27 demonstrates stopping a foreground process.

SESSION 5.27 *Terminating a Foreground Job*

```
$ fgLoop.scr
^z                                           # Suspend job
[2] + Stopped (SIGTSTP)        fgLoop.scr

$ fg                                         # Restart job
fgLoop.scr
^c                                           # Cancel job
<return>
$
```

Background Jobs

When we know a job will take a long time, we may want to run it in the background. Jobs run in the background free the keyboard and monitor so that we may use them for other tasks like editing files and sending mail. Note, however, that foreground and background jobs share the keyboard and monitor. Any messages sent to the monitor by the background job will therefore be mingled with the messages from foreground job.

This can quickly become very confusing. If a background job requests user input, the job must be brought to the foreground to receive the response.

> Monitor output from background jobs can be very confusing. Background jobs cannot receive input from the keyboard while they are running in the background. For these reasons, we highly recommend that input and output for background jobs be redirected.

Session 5.28 starts a job in the background. If the job requires an argument, such as the name of a file, then the ampersand (&) goes immediately after the last argument. There can be no space between the end of the command and the ampersand.

SESSION 5.28   *Starting a Background Job*

```
$ longJob.scr&
[1]      1728406
```

Session 5.28 Analysis: Note the output. The number in the brackets ([1]) is the **job number.** The number on the right is the **process identifier (PID)**, which we discuss in the next section.

Suspending, Restarting, and Terminating Background Jobs To suspend a background job, we use the **stop** command. To restart it, we use the **bg** command. To terminate it, we use the **kill** command. All three commands require the job number, prefaced with a percent sign (%).[2] In Session 5.29, we start a background job, then stop and restart it, and finally terminate it. Bringing the job to the foreground also restarts it. We discuss this in the next section.

SESSION 5.29   *Suspending, Restarting, and Terminating a Background Job*

```
$ longJob.scr&
[1]      1795841
$ stop %1
[1] + 1795841 Stopped (SIGSTOP)         longJob.scr&
$ bg %1
[1]      longJob.scr&
$ kill %1
[1] + Terminated                 longJob.scr
```

Session 5.29 Analysis: Study the output from these three commands. All repeat the job number in brackets. When we start and **stop** the job, we also see the PID number.

---

[2]When there is only one job, the **fg** and **bg** commands do not require a job number.

The **stop, bg,** and **kill** commands display the program name on the right. Finally, the **kill** command displays a terminate message.

Moving Between Background and Foreground To move a job between the foreground and background, the job must be suspended. Once the job is suspended, we can move it from the suspended state to the background with the **bg** command. Because the job is in the foreground, no job number is required. To move a background job to the foreground, we use the **fg** command. In Session 5.30, we start a long running job in the foreground, suspend it so that we can move it to the background, and then bring it back to the foreground.

SESSION 5.30   *Moving a Job Between Foreground and Background*

```
$ longJob.scr                             # Start long running job in fg
                                          # Job is running in foreground.
^z                                        # Suspend job
[1] + Stopped (SIGTSTP) longJob.scr
$ bg                                      # Move job to background.
[1]      longJob.scr&
$ fg %1                                   # Bring active job to foreground
longJob.scr                               # Job running in fg
```

Multiple Background Jobs

In the discussion so far, we have had only one job running in the background at a time. When multiple jobs are running in the background, the job number is required on commands to identify which job we want to affect.

jobs Command

To list the current jobs and their status, we use the **jobs** command. This command lists all jobs whether or not they are running or stopped. For each job, it shows the job number, currency, and status, running or stopped. A typical **jobs** output is shown in Session 5.31.

SESSION 5.31   **jobs** *Status Report*

```
$ jobs
[4] + Stopped (SIGTSTP)        longJob.scr
[3] -  Running                 bgCount200.scr&
[2]    Running                 bgCount200.scr&
[1]    Running                 bgCount200.scr&
$ bgCount200.scr: 2000              # Message from job [1]
bgCount200.scr: 800                 # Message from job [3]
bgCount200.scr: 1600                # Message from job [2]
bgCount200.scr: 2200                # Message from job [1]
bgCount200.scr: 1000                # Message from job [3]
bgCount200.scr: 1800                # Message from job [2]
bgCount200.scr: 2400                # Message from job [1]
```

Session 5.31 Analysis: The **jobs** report indicates that there are four jobs running. Job 4 is a stopped foreground job. Jobs 1, 2, and 3 are background jobs that display a count every 200 loops. The lines following the **jobs** report are output from the background jobs. By analyzing the counts, we can determine which job is which. What is important about this output is that it shows the jobs are taking turns executing. Job 3 executes, then job 2, and then job 1.

Currency Flag

Note that job 4 in Session 5.31 has a plus (+) in the second column. Job 3 has a minus (−) in the second column. These tokens are known as the **currency flags**. In the previous section, we were able to use the job commands without a job number. The plus indicates which job is the default if a command is entered without a job number. The minus indicates which job will be the default if the first job were to complete. Suspended (ctrl+z) jobs are automatically given the default currency plus. If two jobs are suspended, then the most recently suspended job is plus and the older job is minus. If there are no suspended jobs, the plus is assigned to the most recently started job and the minus to the second most recent job.[3]

Using Job Numbers

As previously noted, the **stop** and **kill** commands always require a job number, and the **fg** and **bg** commands require one only if there is more than one job. The job number is preceded by a percent sign (%) and is separated from the command by one space. In addition to the job number, the default job (+) can be referred to as %+ or %%. The job with minus currency can be referred to as %−. All of the following job references are valid:

```
fg %3   bg %+   stop %%   kill %−
```

Job numbers are unique to a user session. This means that if a user is logged into two different sessions at the same time, his or her jobs may have the same number. This is also true if you have running jobs in one shell and then switch to another shell. The jobs in the two shells will both start with 1 and may be duplicated.

Job States

At any time, a job may be in one of three states: foreground, background, or stopped. When a job starts, it runs in the foreground. While it is running, the user can stop it, terminate it, or let it run to completion. The user can restart a stopped job by moving it to either the foreground or the background state. The user can also terminate a job. A terminated job no longer exists. To be terminated, a job must be running. Figure 5.14 summarizes the job states.

While a job is running, it may complete or it may exit. A job that completes has successfully finished its assigned tasks. A job that exits has determined that it cannot complete its assigned tasks but also cannot continue running because some internal status has made completion impossible. When a job terminates, either because it is done or it must exit, it sets a status code that can be checked by the user.

---

[3]This is the general rule. It can be changed by moving jobs to and from the foreground and suspending jobs.

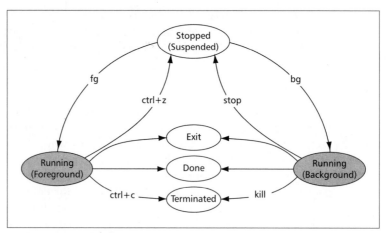

FIGURE 5.14   *Job States*

> To move a foreground job to the background or to move a background job to the foreground, the job must first be stopped.

Process ID

Job numbers are related to the user session and the terminal; they are not global. UNIX assigns another identification, which is global in scope, to jobs or processes. It is called the process identifier, or PID. Although process commands are beyond the scope of this text, we discuss one here. The **ps** command displays the current PIDs associated with the terminal from which it is entered. The output in Session 5.32 contains a listing of the process IDs, terminal identifiers, cumulative execution time for each PID process, and the command name.

SESSION 5.32   *PID Command Output*

```
$ ps
        PID TTY       TIME CMD
    2229478 ttyq0     9:44 sh
    2229618 ttyq0     9:27 sh
    2247678 ttyq0    10:55 sh
    2209680 ttyq0     9:42 sh
```

5.11 Aliases

An alias provides a means of creating customized commands by assigning a name to a command. Aliases are handled differently in each shell. We discuss them separately.

Aliases in the Korn and Bash Shells

In the Korn and Bash shells, an alias is created by using the **alias** command. Its format is

$$\texttt{alias name=command-definition}$$

where **alias** is the command keyword, name is the name of the alias being created, and command-definition is the code. As we have seen before, there can be no spaces before or after the assignment operator (=). Let's look at four examples.

Example 1: Renaming Commands One of the common uses of aliases is to create a more intuitive name for a command. For example, instead of using **ls** for the list command, we can use the DOS name, **dir.** We demonstrate this use in Session 5.33.

SESSION 5.33 *Using Alias to Rename the List Command*

```
$ alias dir=ls
$ dir
TheRaven           file1             longJob.scr       tee2
TheRavenV1         fileOut           loop.scr          tee3
bgCount200.scr     goodStudents.dat  man.jobs          teeOut
blankLine.dat      linkDir           newStudents.dat   teeOut1
fgLoop.scr         lnDir             tee1              teeOut2
```

Example 2: Alias of Command with Options An even better example is the definition of a command with options. In Session 5.34, we define a directory command with the long list option. (In the interest of space, we have omitted some of the output.)

SESSION 5.34 *Alias of Command with Options*

```
$ alias dir='ls -l'
$ dir
total 30
-rw-------    1 gilberg   staff          5782 Sep 10 16:19 TheRaven
-rw-------    1 gilberg   staff           366 Sep  9 19:56 TheRavenV1
...
-rw-r--r--    1 gilberg   staff           149 Apr 18  2000 teeOut1
-rw-r--r--    1 gilberg   staff           149 Apr 18  2000 teeOut2
```

Session 5.34 Analysis: Because options require at least one space between the command and the first option, the command must always be quoted. In this session, we used single quotes. Double quotes are also valid.

Example 3: Alias of Multiple Command Lines Often a process requires more than one command. As long as the commands are considered one line in UNIX, they can be assigned an alias. Because some list output can be larger than one screen of output, it is a good idea to pipe the output to **more.** We incorporate this change in Session 5.35. Once again, we condense the output.

SESSION 5.35 *Using Alias with Multiple-Command Lines*

```
$ alias dir="ls -l | more"
$ dir
total 30
-rw-------    1 gilberg   staff        5782 Sep 10 16:19 TheRaven
-rw-------    1 gilberg   staff         366 Sep  9 19:56 TheRavenV1
...
-rw-r--r--    1 gilberg   staff         149 Apr 18  2000 teeOut1
-rw-r--r--    1 gilberg   staff         149 Apr 18  2000 teeOut2
```

Example 4: Using an Alias in an Alias Definition It is possible to create an alias definition using a definition. There is one danger in this usage, however; if a definition uses multiple aliases and one of them refers to another one, the definition may become recursive and it will bring down the shell. For this reason, we recommend that only one definition be used in defining a new alias definition. Session 5.36 contains a simple definition within a definition.

SESSION 5.36 *Using Alias in an Alias Definition*

```
$ alias dir=ls
$ alias lndir='dir -l | more'
$ lndir
total 30
-rw-------    1 gilberg   staff        5782 Sep 10 16:19 TheRaven
-rw-------    1 gilberg   staff         366 Sep  9 19:56 TheRavenV1
...
-rw-r--r--    1 gilberg   staff         149 Apr 18  2000 teeOut1
-rw-r--r--    1 gilberg   staff         149 Apr 18  2000 teeOut2
```

Arguments to Alias Commands

An argument may be passed to an alias as long as it is not ambiguous. Arguments are added after the command. The arguments may contain wildcards as appropriate. For example, we can pass a file to the **list** command so that it lists only the file(s) requested as shown in Session 5.37.

SESSION 5.37 *Passing Arguments to Alias Commands*

```
$ alias fl="ls -l"
$ fl f*
+ ls -l fgLoop.scr file1 fileOut
-rwx------    1 gilberg   staff         175 Sep 13 10:38 fgLoop.scr
-rw-r--r--    1 gilberg   staff          15 May 17  2000 file1
-rw-r--r--    1 gilberg   staff         395 Sep  9 20:00 fileOut
```

Session 5.37 Analysis: We named this alias file list (fl). To see exactly what's happening with this command, we turned on the expanded command option xtrace (page 184).

Expanded commands are displayed starting with a plus followed by the command with its arguments filled in.

Sometimes arguments can be ambiguous. This usually happens when multiple commands are included in one alias. In Session 5.38, we use the wrong alias, lndir (see Session 5.36), so that it is ambiguous. The output is condensed.

SESSION 5.38 *Ambiguous Alias Command*

```
$ lndir TheRavenV1
+ ls -l
+ more TheRavenV1
Once upon a midnight dreary, while I pondered, weak and weary,
...
Perched, and sat, and nothing more.
```

Session 5.38 Analysis: What we wanted was a long list of "The RavenV1" file. What we got instead was its contents. From the expanded commands, we note that the shell adds the argument to the last command, in this case the **more.** Rather than a long listing of the file, therefore, we ended up with a listing of its contents.

Listing Aliases

The Korn and Bash shells provide a method to list all aliases and to list a specific alias. Both use the **alias** command. To list all aliases, we use the **alias** command with no arguments. To list a specific command, we use the **alias** command with one argument, the name of the **alias** command. These variations are demonstrated in Session 5.39.

SESSION 5.39 *Alias Command Lists*

```
$ alias
autoload='typeset -fu'
cat=/sbin/cat
dir='echo '\''Listing for Gilberg'\''; ls -l | more'
fl='ls -l | more'
...
stop='kill -STOP'
suspend='kill -STOP $$'
$ alias dir
dir='echo '\''Listing for Gilberg'\''; ls -l | more'
```

Session 5.39 Analysis: The first execution lists all aliases in a condensed format. A quick glance reveals that there are many shell aliases already defined. Our two are the third and fourth. The second execution shows the results for a specified alias, "dir."

Removing Aliases

Aliases are removed by using the **unalias** command. It has one argument, a list of aliases to be removed. When it is used with the all option (-a), it deletes all aliases. You should be very careful, however, with this option: It deletes all aliases, even those defined by the system administrator. For this reason, some system administrators disable this option. Session 5.40 demonstrates only the remove name argument.

SESSION 5.40 *Removing Alias Names*

```
$ alias dir
dir='echo '\''Listing for Gilberg'\''; ls -l | more'
$ unalias dir
$ alias dir
dir: alias not found
```

Aliases in the C Shell

C shell aliases differ from Korn shell aliases in format but not in function. They also have a more powerful set of features, especially for argument definition.

The syntax for defining a C shell alias differs slightly in that there is no assignment operator. The basic format is:

> **alias name definition**

In Session 5.41, we redefine our directory list option for the C shell.

SESSION 5.41 *Alias Definition in C Shell*

```
% alias dir "echo Gilbergs Directory List; ls -l | more"
% dir
Gilbergs Directory List
total 30
-rw-------    1 gilberg   staff        5782 Sep 10 16:19 TheRaven
...
-rw-r--r--    1 gilberg   staff         149 Apr 18   2000 teeOut1
-rw-r--r--    1 gilberg   staff         149 Apr 18   2000 teeOut2
```

Arguments to Alias Commands Whereas the Korn shell positions arguments at the end of the generated command, the C shell allows us to control the positioning. Table 5.4 contains the position designators used for alias arguments.

TABLE 5.4 *C Shell Argument Designators*

Designator	Meaning
\!*	Position of the only argument.
\!^	Position of the first argument.
\!$	Position of the last argument.
\!:n	Position of the nth argument.

When we wrote the file list alias in the Korn shell, the argument was positioned at the end, where it caused a problem. In Session 5.42, we rewrite it using the only argument position indicator.

SESSION 5.42   *Only Argument Position Example*

```
% alias fl 'ls -l \!* | more'
% fl TheRavenV1
-rw-------    1 gilberg  staff        366 Sep  9 19:56 TheRavenV1

% fl
total 30
-rw-------    1 gilberg  staff       5782 Sep 10 16:19 TheRaven
...
-rw-r--r--    1 gilberg  staff        149 Apr 18  2000 teeOut2
```

Session 5.42 Analysis: Note that the quotes are placed around the **alias** command, including the only argument designator (\ ! *), which placed it in the middle of the command exactly where it belongs. We ran the command twice: once with an argument and once with no argument. The no-argument output is abbreviated.

For a more complex example, let's write a command that copies one file and renames it. We need two parameters: one for the original filename and one for the copy name. The code is in Session 5.43.

SESSION 5.43   *Alias Command with Two Arguments*

```
% ls ~/delete.me
No such file or directory

% alias cpto 'cp \!:1 \!:$'
% cpto file1 ~/delete.me
% ls ~/delete.me
/mnt/diska/staff/gilberg/delete.me
```

Session 5.43 Analysis: We start this script with a **list** command to prove that the file doesn't exist. We then create the copy-to command and execute it copying a file from the current directory to the home directory (~/). After the copy, we list it again to prove that it was copied.

Listing Aliases   Just like the Korn shell, we can list a specific alias or all aliases. The syntax for the two shells is identical. Session 5.44 contains an alias list.

SESSION 5.44   *List Alias Example*

```
% alias
cpto    cp \!:1 \!:$
dir     echo Gilbergs Directory List; ls -l | more
fl      ls -l \!* | more
```

Removing Aliases As we saw in the Korn shell, the C shell uses the **unalias** command to remove one or all aliases. Session 5.45 demonstrates the **unalias** command in the C shell.

SESSION 5.45 *Removing Aliases in C Shell*

```
% unalias f1
% alias
cpto      cp \!:1 \!:$
dir       echo Gilbergs Directory List; ls -1 | more
```

Alias Summary

Table 5.5 summarizes the use of aliases in the three shells.

TABLE 5.5 *Alias Summary*

Feature	Korn and Bash	C
Define	`$ alias x=command`	`% alias x command`
Argument	Only at end	Anywhere
List	`$ alias`	`% alias`
Remove	`$ unalias x y z`	`% unalias x y z`
Remove All	`$ unalias -a`	`% unalias *`

5.12 Variables

A variable is a location in memory where values can be stored. Each shell allows us to create, store, and access values in variables. Each shell variable must have a name. The name of a variable must start with an alphabetic or underscore (_) character. It then can be followed by zero or more alphanumeric or underscore characters. There are two broad classifications of variables: user-defined and predefined.

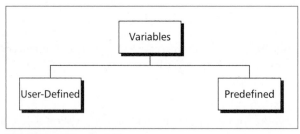

FIGURE 5.15 *Variables*

User-Defined Variables

User variables are not separately defined in UNIX. The first reference to a variable establishes it. When we discuss shells later in the book, we will elaborate on them. The syntax for storing values in variables is the same for the Korn and Bash shells, but it is different for the C shell.

Predefined Variables

Predefined variables are used to configure a user's shell environment. For example, a system variable determines which editor is used to edit the command history. Other systems variables store information about the environment. For example, a system variable contains the pathname to the home directory. We discuss these variables in detail in the next section.

Storing Data in Variables

All three shells provide a means to store values in variables. Unfortunately, the C shell's method is different. The basic commands for each shell are presented in Table 5.6.

TABLE 5.6 *Variable Shell Commands*

Action	Korn and Bash	C Shell
Assignment	`variable=value`	`set variable = value`
Reference	`$variable`	`$variable`

Storing Data in the Korn and Bash Shells

The Korn and Bash shells use the assignment operator, =, to store values in a variable. Much like an algebraic expression, the variable is coded first, on the left, followed by the assignment operator and then the value to be stored. There can be no spaces before and after the assignment operator; the variable, the operator, and the value must be coded in sequence immediately next to each other as in the following example:

```
varA=7
```

In this example, `varA` is the variable that receives the data and 7 is the value being stored in it. While the receiving field must always be a variable, the value may be a constant, the contents of another variable, or, as we will see later, any expression that reduces to a single value. Session 5.46 shows some examples of storing values in variables.

SESSION 5.46 *Assignment in Korn and Bash Shells*

```
$ x=23
$ echo $x
23
$ x=hello
$ echo $x
hello
$ x="Go Don's"
$ echo $x
Go Don's
```

Session 5.46 Analysis: Note that although the first example in Session 5.46 contains a number, it is stored as a string of two digits. The third example shows how we store a character string. We did not use quotes in the assignment for the second example, but we did in the third example. The difference is that the third example contains spaces and special characters. Whenever a string contains spaces or special characters, it must be quoted.

Storing Data in the C Shell

To store data in a variable in the C shell, we use the **set** command. While there can be no spaces before and after the assignment operator in the Korn and Bash shells, C needs them. C also accepts the assignment without spaces before and after the assignment operator. In Session 5.47, we repeat the assignments in Session 5.46.

SESSION 5.47 *Assignments in C Shell*

```
% set x = 23
% echo $x
23

% set x = hello
% echo $x
hello

% set x = "Go Don's"
% echo $x
Go Don's
```

Accessing a Variable

To access the value of a variable, the name of the variable must be preceded by a dollar sign. In Session 5.48, we use the **echo** command to display the values created in Session 5.46.

SESSION 5.48 *Using Values*

```
$ x=23
$ echo The variable x contains $x
The variable x contains 23

$ x=hello
$ echo The variable x contains $x
The variable x contains hello

$ x="Go Don's!"
$ echo The variable x contains $x
The variable x contains Go Don's!
```

5.13 Predefined Variables

Predefined variables can be divided into two categories: shell variables and environmental variables. The shell variables are used to customized the shell itself. The environmental variables control the user environment and can be exported to subshells.

Table 5.7 lists the common predefined variables that we discuss in this section. The complete list of predefined variables is in Appendix E. In the C shell, the shell variables are in lowercase letters, and the corresponding environmental variables are in uppercase letters (some variables do not have the corresponding shell counterpart).

TABLE 5.7 *Predefined Variables*

Korn and Bash	C[a]	Explanation
CDPATH	cdpath	Contains the search path for **cd** command when the directory argument is a relative pathname.
EDITOR[b]	EDITOR	Pathname of the command-line editor.
ENV		Pathname of the environment file.
HOME[b]	home (HOME)	Pathname for the home directory.
PATH[b]	path (PATH)	Search path for commands.
PS1	prompt	Primary prompt, such as $ and %.
SHELL[b]	shell (SHELL)	Pathname of the login shell.
TERM[b]	term (TERM)	Terminal type.
TMOUT	autologout	Defines idle time, in seconds, before shell automatically logs you off.
VISUAL[b]	VISUAL	Pathname of the editor for command-line editing. See EDITOR table entry.

[a]Shell variables are in lowercase; environmental variables are in uppercase.

[b]Both a shell and an environmental variable.

CDPATH

The CDPATH variable contains a list of pathnames separated by colons (:) as shown in the next example:

```
:$HOME:/bin/usr/files
```

There are three paths in the preceding example. Because the path starts with a colon, the first directory is the current working directory. The second directory is our home directory. The third directory is an absolute pathname to a directory of files.

The contents of CDPATH are used by the **cd** command using the following rules:

1. If CDPATH is not defined, the **cd** command searches the working directory to locate the requested directory. If the requested directory is found, **cd** moves to it. If it is not found, **cd** displays an error message.

2. If CDPATH is defined as shown in the previous example, the actions listed below are taken when the following command is executed:

```
$ cd reports
```

    a. The **cd** command searches the current directory for the `reports` directory. If it is found, the current directory is changed to `reports`.

    b. If the `reports` directory is not found in the current directory, **cd** tries to find it in the home directory, which is the second entry in CDPATH. Note that the home directory may be the current directory.

    Again, if the `reports` directory is found in the home directory, it becomes the current directory.

    c. If the `reports` directory is not found in the home directory, **cd** tries to find it in `/bin/usr/files`, which is the third entry in CDPATH. If the `reports` directory is found in `/bin/usr/files`, it becomes the current directory.

    d. If the `reports` directory is not found in `/bin/usr/files`, **cd** displays an error message and terminates.

In Session 5.49, we set CDPATH to the PATH shown in the previous example and then **echo** the path. Note that it begins with a colon, but HOME is replaced by its absolute PATH because we used $HOME.

SESSION 5.49 *Set* **CDPATH**

```
$ echo $CDPATH
$ CDPATH=:$HOME:/bin/usr/files

$ echo $CDPATH
:/mnt/diska/staff/gilberg:/bin/usr/files
```

HOME

The HOME variable contains the PATH to your home directory. The default is your login directory. Some commands use the value of this variable when they need the PATH to your home directory. For example, when you use the **cd** command without any argument, the command uses the value of the HOME variable as the argument. You can change its value, but we do not recommend you change it because it will affect all the commands and scripts that use it. In Session 5.50, we demonstrate how it can be changed to the current working directory. Note that because **pwd** is a command, it must be enclosed in backquotes.

SESSION 5.50 *Demonstrate Change Home Directory*

```
$ echo $HOME
/mnt/diska/staff/gilberg
$ oldHOME=$HOME
$ echo $oldHOME
/mnt/diska/staff/gilberg

$ HOME=$(pwd)
$ echo $HOME
/mnt/diska/staff/gilberg/unix13bash

$ HOME=$oldHOME
$ echo $HOME
/mnt/diska/staff/gilberg
```

PATH

The PATH variable is used to search for a command directory. The entries in the PATH variable must be separated by colons.

PATH works just like CDPATH. When the SHELL encounters a command, it uses the entries in the PATH variable to search for the command under each directory in the PATH variable. The major difference is that for security reasons, such as a Trojan horse virus, we should have the current directory last.

If we were to set the PATH variable as shown in the next example,

```
$ PATH=/bin:/usr/bin::
```

the shell would look for the **date** command by first searching the /bin directory, followed by the /usr/bin directory, and finally the current working directory.

Primary Prompt (PS1 Prompt)

The primary prompt is set in the variable PS1 for the Korn and Bash shells and prompt for the C shell. The shell uses the primary prompt when it expects a command. The default is the dollar sign ($) for the Korn and Bash shells and the percent sign (%) for the C shell.

We can change the value of the prompt as shown in Session 5.51. We begin by changing the primary prompt to reflect the shell we are working in, the Korn shell. Because we have a blank at the end of the prompt, we must use quotes to set it. As soon as it is set, the new prompt is displayed. At the end, we change it back to the default.

SESSION 5.51   *Change the Primary Prompt*

```
$ PS1="KSH> "
KSH> echo $PS1
KSH>
KSH> PS1="$ "
$
```

SHELL

The SHELL variable holds the path of your login shell.

TERM

The TERM variable holds the description for the terminal you are using. The value of this variable can be used by interactive commands such as **vi** or **emacs.** You can test the value of this variable or reset it.

Handling Variables

We need to set, unset, and display the variables. Table 5.8 shows how this can be done for each shell.

TABLE 5.8   *Set and Unset Variables*

Operation	Korn and Bash	C Shell
Set	var=value	set var = value (setenv var value)
Unset	unset var	unset var (unsetenv var)
Display One	echo $var	echo $var
Display All	set	set (setenv)

Korn and Bash Shells

Setting and Unsetting   In the Korn and Bash shells, variables are set using the assignment operator as shown in the next example:

```
$ TERM=vt100
```

To unset a variable, we use the **unset** command. The following example shows how we can unset the TERM variable:

```
$ unset TERM
```

Displaying Variables   To display the value of an individual variable, we use the **echo** command:

```
$ echo $TERM
```

To display the variables that are currently set, we use the **set** command with no arguments:

```
$ set
```

C Shell

The C shell uses a different syntax for changing its shell and environmental variables.

Setting and Unsetting   To set a shell variable, it uses the **set** command; to set an environmental variable, it uses the **setenv** command. These two commands are demonstrated in the next example. Note that in the **setenv** command, there is no assignment operator.

```
% set prompt = 'CSH % '
CSH % setenv HOME /mnt/diska/staff/gilberg
```

To unset a C shell variable, we use the **unset** command. To unset an environmental variable, we use the **unsetenv** command. These commands are shown in the next example. Note that after we unset the prompt, the next line has no prompt: The cursor is at the beginning of a blank line. Obviously, this is not a good idea.

```
CSH % unset prompt
unsetenv EDITOR
```

Displaying Variables To display the value of the individual variable (both shell and environmental), we use the **echo** command. To list the variables that are currently set, we use the **set** command without an argument for the shell variables and the **setenv** command without an argument for the environmental variables. These commands are shown in the next example:

```
% echo $variable-name      # display one variable
% set                      # display all shell variables
% setenv                   # display all environmental variables
```

5.14 Options

Table 5.9 shows the common options used for three shells. The complete list is in Appendix E, Predefined Variables, which also shows the definition of each option in more detail. Note that the options in C are actually set/unset variables (that take only set/unset values); we classify them as options because they behave like options.

TABLE 5.9 *Shell Options*

Korn and Bash	C	Explanation
noglob	noglob	Disables wildcard expansion.
verbose	verbose	Prints commands before executing them.
xtrace		Prints commands and arguments before executing them.
emacs		Uses **emacs** for command-line editing.
ignoreeof	ignoreeof	Disallows ctrl+d to exit the shell.
noclobber	noclobber	Does not allow redirection to clobber existing file.
vi		Uses **vi** for command-line editing.

Global (noglob***)*** The global option controls the expansion of wildcard tokens in a command. For example, when the global option is off, the list file (**ls**) command uses wildcards to match the files in a directory. Thus, the following command lists all files that start with 'file' followed by one character:

```
$ ls file?
```

On the other hand, when the global option is on, wildcards become text characters and are not expanded. In this case, only the file named file? would be listed.

Print Commands (verbose **and** xtrace**)** There are two print options, verbose and xtrace, that are used to print commands before they are executed. The verbose option prints the command before it is executed. The xtrace option expands the command arguments before it prints the command. We set the xtrace option before in Session 5.37 and Session 5.38 (page 173). The print command options are very handy when we need to understand how a command is expanded.

Command-Line Editor (emacs **and** vi**)** To specify that the **emacs** editor is to be used in the Korn shell, we turn on the emacs option. To specify that the **vi** editor is to be used in the Korn shell, we turn on the vi option. Note that these options are valid only in the Korn shell.

Ignore End of File (ignoreeof**)** Normally, if end of file (ctrl+d) is entered at the command line, the shell terminates. To disable this action, we can turn on the ignore end of file option, ignoreeof. With this option, end of file generates an error message rather than terminating the shell.

No Clobber Redirection (noclobber**)** When output or errors are directed to a file that already exists, the current file is deleted and replaced by a new file. To prevent this action, we set the noclobber option.

Handling Options

To customize our shell environment, we need to set, unset, and display options. Table 5.10 shows the appropriate commands for each shell. They are discussed in the sections that follow.

TABLE 5.10 *Commands Used to Display, Set, and Unset Options*

Operation	Korn and Bash	C
Set	set -o option	set option
Unset	set +o option	unset option
Display All	set -o	set

Korn and Bash Shell Options

Setting and Unsetting Options To set and unset an option, we use the **set** command with −o and +o followed by the option identifier. Using the Korn shell format, we would set and unset the verbose option as shown in the following example:

```
$ set -o verbose          # Turn print commands option on
$ set +o verbose          # Turn print commands option off
```

Displaying Options To show all of the options (set or unset), we use the **set** command with an argument of −o. This option requests a list of all option names with their state, on or off.

```
$ set  -o                 # Korn shell format: lists all options
```

C Shell Options

Setting and Unsetting Options In C shell, options are set with the **set** command and unset with the **unset** command, but without the minus sign in both cases. They are both shown in the following example:

```
$ set    verbose        # Turn print commands option on
$ unset verbose         # Turn print commands option off
```

Displaying Options To display which options are set, we use the **set** command without an argument. However, the C shell displays the setting of all variables including the options that are variables. The options are recognized because there is no value assigned to them: Only their names are listed. The next example shows the display options format:

```
% set                   # C shell format: lists all variables
```

5.15 Shell/Environment Customization

UNIX allows us to customize the shells and the environment we use. When we customize the environment, we can extend it to include subshells and programs that we create.

There are four elements to customizing the shell and the environment. Depending on how we establish them, they can be temporary or permanent. Temporary customization lasts only for the current session. When a new session is started, the original settings are reestablished.

Temporary Customization

Temporary customization can be used to change the shell environment and configuration for the complete current session or for only part of a session. Normally, we customize our environment for only a part of the session, such as when we are working on something special. For example, if we are writing a script, it is handy to see the expanded commands as they are executed. We would do this by turning on the verbose option. When we are through writing the script, we would turn off the verbose option. Any option changed during the session is automatically reset to its default when we log on the next time.

Permanent Customization

Permanent customization is achieved through startup and shutdown files. Startup files are system files that are used to customize the environment when a shell begins. We can add customization commands and set customization variables by adding commands to the startup file. Shutdown files are executed at logout time. Just like the startup files, we can add commands to clean up the environment when we log out.

Korn Shell

The Korn shell uses the three profile files as described next.

- **System Profile File:** There is one system-level `profile` file, which is stored in the `/etc` directory. Maintained by the system administrator, it contains general commands and variable settings that are applied to every user of the system at login time. The system profile file is generally quite large and contains many advanced commands.

  The system `profile` is a read-only file; its permissions are set so that only the system administrator can change it. We suggest that you locate and read it so that you will have an idea of what it contains.

- **Personal Profile File:** The personal profile, `~/.profile`, contains commands that are used to customize the startup shell. It is an optional file that is run immediately after the system profile file. Although it is a user file, it is often created by the system administrator to customize a new user's shell. If you make changes to it, we highly recommend that you make a backup copy first so that it may be restored easily if necessary.

- **Environmental File:** In addition, the Korn shell has an environmental file that is run whenever a new shell is started. It contains environmental variables that are to be exported to subshells and programs that run under the shell. Because it is executed each time a new shell is started, we recommend that it be kept short.

The environmental file does not have a predetermined name. We can give it any name we desire. It must be stored in the home directory or in a subdirectory below the home directory. We recommend that it be stored in the home directory.

To locate the environmental file, Korn requires that its absolute or relative pathname be stored in the predefined variable, ENV. Figure 5.16 demonstrates three different techniques for storing it.

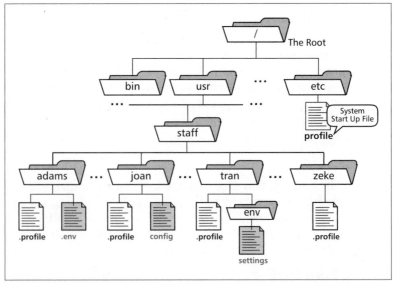

FIGURE 5.16 *Korn's Environmental File*

As you study Figure 5.16, note the different techniques. Adams created his environmental file (.env) as a hidden file in his root directory. Joan named hers config and has it as a standard file in her home directory. Tran chose to store her file, named settings, in a directory under the home directory. Finally, Zeke doesn't have an environmental file. The commands to set the predefined variable for each of these files are in the following example:

```
$  ENV=~/.env
$  ENV=$HOME/config
$  ENV=~/env/settings
```

Bash Shell

For the system profile file, the Bash shell uses the same file as the Korn shell (/etc/profile). However, for the personal profile file, it uses one of three files. First, it looks for a Bash profile file (~/.bash_profile). If it doesn't find a profile file, it looks for a login file (~/.bash_login). If it doesn't find a login file, it looks for a generic profile file (~/.profile). Whichever file the Bash shell finds, if any, it executes it and ignores the rest.

The Bash environmental file uses the same concept as the Korn shell, except that the filename is stored in the BASH_ENV variable.

The Korn shell does not have a logout file, but the Bash shell does. When the shell terminates, it looks for the logout file (~/.bash_logout) and executes it.

C Shell

The C Shell uses both startup and shutdown files: It has two startup files, ~/.login and ~/.cshrc, and one shutdown file, ~/.logout.

- **Login File:** The C shell login file (~/.login) is the equivalent of the Korn and Bash user profile file. It contains commands and variables that are executed when the user logs in. It is not exported to other shells nor is it executed if the C shell is started from another shell as a subshell.

- **Environmental File:** The C shell equivalent of the environmental file is the ~/.cshrc file. It contains the environmental settings that are to be exported to subshells. As an environmental file, it is executed whenever a new subshell is invoked.

- **Logout File:** The C shell logout file, ~/.logout, is run when we log out of the C shell. It contains commands and programs that are to be run at logout time. For example, it is the ideal place to store a script that automatically backs up critical files.

- **Other C Shell Files:** The C shell may have other system files that are executed at login and logout time. They are found in the /etc directory as /etc/csh.cshrc, /etc/csh.login, and /etc/csh.logout.

Summary

Table 5.11 contains a summary of the UNIX startup and shutdown files.

TABLE 5.11 *Summary of Startup and Shutdown Files*

Files			Korn	Bash	C
Startup	Systemwide	Shell	`/etc/profile`	`/etc/profile`	`/etc/` `csh.login`
		Env			`/etc/` `csh.cshrc`

	Personal	Shell	`~/.profile`	`~/.bash_profile`
				`~/.bash_login`
				`~/.profile`
					`~/.login`

		Env	Environmental File	Environmental File	`~/.cshrc`
Shutdown	Systemwide	Shell			`/etc/` `csh.logout`
		Env			
	Personal	Shell		`~/.bash_logout`	`~/.logout`
		Env			

5.16 Key Terms

alias	job control	sequenced commands
background job	job number	shell
Bash shell	kernel	shell program
C shell	Korn shell	shell script
chained commands	login	shell variable
command substitution	login shell	shutdown files
command-line editing	logout	standard error
conditional commands	option	standard input
duplicating output	pipe	standard output
environment	predefined variable	standard streams
environment customization	process id	startup files
foreground job	quoting	user-defined variables
group commands	redirecting	value
history file	redirecting error	variable
interpreter	redirecting input	
job	redirecting output	

5.17 Tips

1. Distinguish between your login shell and the current shell; they may be different.
2. To find your login shell, use `echo $SHELL`; to find your current shell, use `echo $0` (not available in C shell).
3. You log out of the system if you are in your login shell; you use exit if you are in a subshell.

4. You can omit the file descriptor in input and output redirection, but not in error redirection.

5. UNIX opens a redirected file before executing a command that uses redirection.

6. The pipe is an operator, not a command. It can only be used between two commands.

7. A pipe can receive its input only from a command that is able to send output data to the standard output.

8. A pipe can send its output only to a command that is able to receive its input from standard input.

9. When you use the **vi** editor for command-line editing, **vi** always starts in the text mode.

10. The token that can be used for command substitution in the Korn and Bash shells is $(...). The C shell uses backquotes.

11. A job cannot be moved from background to foreground, or vice versa, unless it has been stopped.

12. When you run a command in the background, you should normally redirect the input, output, and error to files.

13. A job number is different from a process id.

14. You need different commands to set and unset variables (user-defined or predefined) in different shells.

15. You need different commands to set and unset options in different shells.

16. Aliases are used to give new names to commands; you cannot use an alias to rename a file.

17. The Korn and Bash shell format for **alias** and **unalias** commands is different from the C shell.

18. The Bash and C shells have shutdown files.

5.18 Commands

The following commands were discussed in this chapter. For more details, see Appendix F and the corresponding pages shown in the following table.

Command	Description	Options	Page
ctrl+z	Stops (suspends) a foreground job.		166
ctrl+c	Terminates (aborts) a foreground job.		166
alias	***Synopsis:*** *alias [name=defintion]*　　　#Korn and Bash *alias [name definition]*　　　#C shell Lists exiting aliases or creates a new alias for a command.		170

Continued

Command	Description	Options	Page
bash	*Synopsis: bash* Creates a new Bash shell.		144
bg	*Synopsis:* bg *[job_number]* Moves a suspended job to the background.		168
csh	*Synopsis: csh* Creates a new C shell.		144
exit	*Synopsis: exit* Moves the user from a subshell to the parent shell.		146
fg	*Synopsis: fg [job_number]* Moves a suspended job to the foreground.		165
jobs	*Synopsis: jobs* Displays the list of active jobs.		168
kill	*Synopsis: kill [job_number]* Kills a job.		166
ksh	*Synopsis: ksh* Creates a new Korn shell.		144
ps	*Synopsis: ps* Displays information about the active processes.		170
set	*Synopsis:* *set var=value* #C shell *set -o option* #Korn and Bash *set +o option* #Korn and Bash Sets a value for a variable or sets an option. Also unsets an option in the Korn shell when used with plus option.		178
setenv	*Synopsis: setenv var = value* In C shell, sets a value for an environmental variable.		182
stop	*Synopsis: stop [job_number]* Stops (suspends) a background job.		167
tee	*Synopsis: tee [-option] file-list* Copies standard input to standard output and at the same time copies to one or more files.	a	153
unalias	*Synopsis: unalias alias-list* Removes some or all aliases.	a (Korn and Bash)	173
unset	*Synopsis:* *unset variable* *unset option* #C shell Unsets the value of a variable or unsets an option.		182
unsetenv	*Synopsis: unsetenv variable* In C shell, unsets the value of an environmental variable.		182

5.19 Summary

- There are three traditional shells in UNIX: Bourne, Korn, and C. The Bash shell is a new version of the Bourne shell. The tcsh shell is a new version of the C shell.
- When a user logs into the system, one of the three shells is active. This shell is known as the login shell.
- The system administrator determines the login shell by inserting it in the /etc/passwd file.
- You can always switch to other shells or even another copy of your login shell.
- You can always determine your login shell, but you determine your current shell only if you are in Korn or Bash.
- If you want to log out of the system, you should be in your login shell. If you are in other shells, you should move to the login shell and then log out.
- UNIX defines three standard streams: standard input (0), standard output (1), and standard error (2).
- A pipe is an operator that allows the standard output of a command to be connected to the standard input of another command.
- The **tee** command copies the standard input to the standard output and, at the same time, copies it to one or more files.
- The standard input stream can be redirected from the keyboard to a file.
- The standard output stream can be redirected from the monitor to a file.
- The standard error stream can be redirected from the monitor to a file.
- A sequence of commands can be entered on one line separated by semicolons (;).
- Commands can be grouped together using parentheses.
- Commands can be chained together using pipes.
- Commands can be conditionally executed using *and* (&&) or *or* (| |) operators.
- Command-line editing is a Korn and Bash shell facility that permits the user to edit commands using one of the screen editors (**vi** or **emacs**).
- Quotes are used to change the predefined meanings of characters. Three types of quotes are used for this purpose: backslash (\ ), a pair of double quotes (" … "), and a pair of single quotes ('…').
- Command substitution changes the output of a command to a string.
- A job is a command or a set of commands entered on one line.
- UNIX distinguishes two kinds of jobs: foreground and background.
- A foreground job is any job running under the supervision of the user.
- A background job is any job running in the background without the direct supervision of the user.
- A job can be suspended or aborted. However, the commands to suspend or abort are different for foreground and background jobs.
- To move a job from background to foreground, or vice versa, the job should first be stopped (suspended).
- A job has a job number. A process has a process id.

- A job in UNIX can be in one of six states: running in the foreground, running in the background, suspended (stopped), aborted (terminated), exit, or done.
- A variable is a location in memory where values can be stored.
- There are two kinds of variables: predefined and user-defined.
- Predefined variables are either shell variables or environmental variables.
- Options are on/off switches that are used to control the shell.
- The shell and the environment can be temporarily or permanently customized for a user.
- Customization is done using shell variables, environmental variables, options, and aliases.
- Korn shell uses three startup files: `/etc/profile`, `~/.profile`, and an environmental file whose name is stored in the ENV variable. There is no shutdown file in Korn shell.
- The Bash shell uses `/etc/profile`, one of the three files (`~/.bash_profile`, `~/.bash_login`, or `~/.profile`), and an environmental file whose name is stored in the BASH_ENV variable. It also uses a shutdown file called `~/.bash_logout`.
- C shell uses up to four startup files: `/etc/csh.login`, `/etc/csh.cshrc`, `~/.login`, and `~/.cshrc`. There may be two shutdown files: `/etc/csh.logout` and `~/.logout`.

5.20 Practice Set

Review Questions

1. Explain the two different duties of a shell.
2. Define the login shell.
3. How can you verify your login shell?
4. How can you identify your current shell?
5. Is the login shell always the same as the current shell?
6. How can you create a subshell? How can you move to the parent shell after creating a subshell?
7. If your login shell is the Korn shell, can you create another Korn shell as the child shell? Explain your answer.
8. What are the standard streams?
9. What file descriptor designates the standard input stream? The standard output stream? The standard error stream?
10. The standard input stream is normally associated with the _____.
11. The standard output stream is normally associated with the _____.
12. The standard error stream is normally associated with the _____.
13. What is redirection?
14. How can you redirect the standard input stream to a file?
15. How can you redirect the standard output stream to a file?
16. How can you redirect the standard error stream to a file?

17. What is piping? What is the pipe operator?
18. How can we make duplicates of standard output and send them to different files?
19. Distinguish between a sequence of commands, a group of commands, and a chain of commands.
20. What are the two operators that make the execution of commands conditional?
21. What is command-line editing?
22. Which shell(s) support command-line editing?
23. Which editors are normally used for command-line editing?
24. What is quoting? What are the three quote tokens?
25. What is the difference between a backslash, a pair of double quotes, and a pair of single quotes?
26. What is command substitution? What is the token used with command substitution?
27. What is a job? Distinguish between a foreground and a background job.
28. Show how you can move a job from background to foreground, and vice versa.
29. Identify and explain the six different states of a job.
30. Define a process id and distinguish between a process id and a job number.
31. Define an alias. Which shell(s) support aliases? Can an alias be used to rename a file? If it can, how?
32. Define a variable and distinguish between a variable and a value.
33. Distinguish between a user-defined variable and a predefined variable.
34. Identify at least five predefined variables and their use.
35. What is an option? Mention at least three options and their use.
36. List the ways that you can use to customize your shell environment in each shell.
37. What are the startup files for each shell?
38. What are the shutdown files for each shell?

Exercises

39. Which of the following commands displays your login shell?
    a. $SHELL
    b. echo $SHELL
    c. $0
    d. echo $0

40. Which of the following commands show your current shell?
    a. $SHELL
    b. echo $SHELL
    c. $0
    d. echo $0

41. Which of the following commands creates a Bash subshell?
    a. bash
    b. bsh
    c. csh
    d. none of the above

42. Which of the following commands creates a Korn subshell?
    a. sh
    b. ksh
    c. csh
    d. none of the above

43. Which of the following commands creates a C subshell?
    a. sh
    b. ksh
    c. csh
    d. none of the above

44. Which of the following is the descriptor of the standard input stream?
    a. 0
    b. 1
    c. 2
    d. 3

45. Which of the following is the descriptor of the standard output stream?
    a. 0
    b. 1
    c. 2
    d. 3

46. Which of the following is the descriptor of the standard error stream?
    a. 0
    b. 1
    c. 2
    d. 3

47. Explain why we cannot use input redirection with **cal, date, man, who,** or **whoami** commands.

48. Explain why we cannot use input redirection with the **echo** command.

49. Can you use input redirection with any commands we learned in Chapter 1? Which ones?

50. Can we use input redirection with the **vi** command? If your answer is no, explain why not.

51. What is the difference between the following four commands?
    a. `lpr`
    b. `lpr < file1`
    c. `lpr 0< file1`
    d. `lpr file1`

52. What is the difference between the following four commands?
    a. `more`
    b. `more < file1`
    c. `more 0< file1`
    d. `more file1`

53. What is the error in each of the following commands?
    a. `cp < file1`
    b. `ls < file1`
    c. `mkdir 0< file1`
    d. `rm 0< file1`

54. In general terms, why can't input redirection be used with the following commands?
    a. `cp`
    b. `ls`
    c. `mkdir`
    d. `rm`
    e. `rmdir`

55. Can the following commands take input redirection? Explain your answer.
    a. `lpr`
    b. `ln`
    c. `cd`
    d. `more`

56. Which of the following commands are correct? If there is an error, identify it and provide the correct code.
    a. `lpr < file1`
    b. `lpr 0< file1`
    c. `lpr 1< file1`
    d. `lpr 2< file1`

57. Which of the following commands can (or cannot) be used with output redirection? Explain the rationale for your answer.
    a. `cal`
    b. `date`
    c. `echo`
    d. `man`
    e. `passwd`
    f. `who`
    g. `whoami`

58. Which of the following commands can (or cannot) be used with error redirection? Explain the rationale for your answer.

   a. `cal`
   b. `date`
   c. `echo`
   d. `man`
   e. `passwd`
   f. `who`
   g. `whoami`

59. Explain the difference between each of the following commands.

   a. `cal`
   b. `cal > Outfile`
   c. `cal 1 > Outfile`
   d. `cal 2 > Outfile`

60. Simplify the following commands by omitting the file descriptors. If the file descriptor is required, explain why.

   a. `command 0< file1`
   b. `command 1> file2`
   c. `command 0< file1 1> file2`
   d. `command 0< file1 1> file2 2>&1`

61. What is the difference between the following commands?

   a. `date > file1`
   b. `date >| file1`
   c. `date >> file1`
   d. `date >>| file1`

62. What is the error (if any) in each of the following commands?

   a. `date > more`
   b. `more >> cal`
   c. `more < lpr`
   d. `lpr << date`

63. What is the error (if any) in each of the following commands?

   a. `date | more`
   b. `more | date`
   c. `more | lpr`
   d. `who | man`

64. Assuming `file1` is a text file, what is the error (if any) in each of the following commands?

   a. `date | file1`
   b. `file1 | date`
   c. `command1 | command2 | command3`
   d. `command1 | command2 | file1`

65. If we use the following chained command:

   `command1 | command2`

   a. What is the necessary requirement for command1?
   b. What is the necessary requirement for command2?

66. What would be the necessary requirement for a command that could be used on both sides of the pipe operator?

67. One of the following commands works and the other doesn't. Which one works and what is wrong with the other one?

   a. `date | more`
   b. `more | date`

68. If we use the following command:

   `tee file1 file2 file3`

   a. Where does the input file come from?
   b. How many output files are created?

69. If we use the following command:

   `ls -l | tee`

a. Where does the input file to the **tee** command come from?

b. How many output files are created?

70. Is the following command correct?

```
tee
```

a. Where does the input file to the tee come from?

b. Where does the output go to?

71. Can we use the **tee** command to create a file? Explain how.

72. Can we use the **tee** command to simulate the **cp** command? Explain how.

73. If we use the following command:

```
ls -l | tee > file1
```

a. Where does the result of the command go?

b. How many output files will be created?

74. If your current shell is Korn or Bash, what is the error (if any) of the following commands?

a. `a = 24` c. `a=$b`
b. `set a=24` d. `set a=$b`

75. If your current shell is C, what is the error (if any) of the following commands?

a. `a = 24` c. `set a = $b`
b. `set a = 24` d. `set $a = 34`

76. If your current shell is Korn or Bash, what would be displayed from each of the following commands?

a. `a=44; echo a` c. `a=44; echo "$a"`
b. `a=44; echo $a` d. `a=44; echo'$a'`

77. What will be displayed from the following commands?

a. `echo " Hello to the user of the "UNIX" operating system"`
b. `echo " Hello to the user of the \"UNIX\" operating system"`
c. `echo " Hello to the user of the 'UNIX' operating system"`
d. `echo ' Hello to the user of the "UNIX" operating system'`

78. What are the general rules (requirements) for a command used in command substitution? Can every command be used in command substitution? If not, give an example of one that can't.

79. What is the error in each of the following commands?

a. `$a=`cp file1 file2``  c. `$a=`ls -l``
b. `echo `lpr file1``  d. `echo `cal``

80. What is the error (if any) in each of the following commands?

a. `$a=`hello date``  c. `$a=`date``
b. `echo `this is date``  d. `echo `date; cal``

81. Assuming file1 is a text file, what is the error (if any) in each of the following commands?

a. `$a=`date > file1``  c. `$a=`file1``
b. `echo `cal | lpr``  d. `echo `date; cal &``

5.21 Lab Sessions

Session I

1. Log into the system.
2. Use the appropriate command to determine your login shell.
3. Use the /etc/passwd file to verify the result of step 2.
4. Use the appropriate command to determine your current shell. Is it the same as your login shell?
5. Create a subshell shell that is not the same shell as your login shell. For example, if your login shell is Korn, create a Bash or C shell.
6. Check the current shell again. Does it match with your login shell?
7. Create another shell which is the same type as your login shell.
8. Check the current shell again. Does it match with previous one?
9. Exit from the subshell shell and move to your login shell.
10. Check the current shell again. Is it the same as the login shell?
11. Log out of the system.

Session II

1. Log into the system.
2. Use the **who** command and redirect the result to a file called file1. Use the **more** command to see the contents of file1.
3. Use the **date** and **who** commands in sequence (in one line) such that the output of **date** will display on the screen and the output of **who** will be redirected to a file called file2. Use the **more** command to check the contents of file2. It should be the same as file1 unless someone logged in or logged off between the who commands.
4. If your login shell is not the Korn shell, create a Korn subshell.
5. Set **vi** to be your command-line editor.
6. Use your command-line editor to recall the line you typed in step 3 Edit the line so that the output of both commands (**date** and **who**) are redirected to a file called file3. Use the **more** command to display the result.
7. Use the command-line editor to recall the line you typed in step 3 Edit the line so that the output of the first command (**date**) is redirected to a file called file4, while the result of the **who** command displays on the monitor without changing the relative positions of the **date** and **who** commands. Use the **more** command to verify the result.
8. Make a duplicate of file3 and call it file3.bak
9. Use the command-line editor to recall the line created at step 6 Edit the line so that the word "date" will be misspelled as "bate". Execute the edited command and append the result to file3. Use **more** to compare file3 and file3.bak.
10. Using command-line editing, recall the line created in step 9 Edit it so that the errors also go to file3 without replacing the files contents. Check the contents of file3 for verification.

Continued

Session II—*Continued*

11. Using command-line editing, recall the line created in step 10 Edit it so that the output goes to `file4` and errors go to `file5`.
12. Log out of the system.

Session III

1. Log into the system.
2. Create a Korn subshell.
3. Set your command-line editor to **vi**.
4. Create a long list of the current directory and pipe the output to the printer.
5. Edit the line in step 4 so that the result goes to the printer and at the same time is saved as a file called `file1` with no output on the monitor (use tee, pipe, and redirection).
6. Edit the line in step 5 so that the result of `ls -l` command be sent to two files `file2` and `file3`.
7. Set the `noclobber` option.
8. Repeat the command line in step 5. Do you get any error message? If so, write down the error message.
9. Edit the command line in step 8 to force clobbering of `file1`.
10. Unset the `noclobber`.
11. Use the `ls -l` command and try to send the result to two files, `file3` and `file4`, using the pipe and the **cp** command. What message do you get? Write it down. What are the contents `file3` and `file4`? Why can't **cp** accept its input from a pipe?
12. Repeat the step 11 but use the **tee** command to solve the problem.
13. Log out of the system.

Session IV

1. Log into the system.
2. Without using an editor, create a one-line file, called `file1`, using the **echo** command (use output redirection). This is one of the way we can create a short file quickly.
3. Check the contents of `file1` using the **more** command.
4. Now, without using an editor, create a two-line file, `file2`, using the **echo** command. Use double quotes for the argument of the **echo** command. Put the opening quote in the first line and the closing quotes in the second line, but do not close it until the end of the second line. In your own words, explain what you just did and why it works.
5. Check the contents of `file2` using the **more** command.
6. Store "UNIX vs. Others" in a variable called `facts`.
7. Now use the following command:
   ```
   echo "This is a fact $facts in our life."
   ```
   What is printed and why?

Continued

8. Now use the following command:
   ```
   echo "This is a fact '$facts' in our life"
   ```
   What is printed and why?
9. Now use the following command:
   ```
   echo "This is a fact \$facts in our life"
   ```
   What would be printed and why?
10. Try to use a command to print the following message (including the quotes) using the value of the variable facts:
    ```
    "This is a fact "UNIX vs. Others" in our life"
    ```
11. Log out of the system.

Session V

1. Log into the system.
2. Store the word "PARENT" in a variable called `first`.
3. Print the value of the variable `first` (using **echo** command).
4. Create a subshell shell using the same type of shell as your login shell (Korn or Bash or C).
5. Print the value of the variable `first` in this subshell. What was printed? If "PARENT" was not printed, explain why. Hint: What did the parent export to the subshell when the subshell was created?
6. Store the word "SUBSHELL" in a variable called `second`.
7. Print the value of the variable `second`.
8. Exit from the subshell shell and move to your login shell.
9. Print the value of `first`. What was printed? How do you explain this result?
10. Print the value of `second`. What was printed? How do you explain this result?
11. Log out of the system.

Session VI

1. Log into the system.
2. Display the contents of the system startup file (the file name is different in different shells).
3. Try to change some entries in this file.
4. Display the contents of your personal startup file (the file name is different in different shells).
5. Try to change some entries in this file.
6. Display the contents of system-wide shut-down files (if there is one).
7. Display the contents of your personal shut-down files (if there is one).
8. Log out of the system.

## CHAPTER 6

Filters

In UNIX, a **filter** is any command that gets its input from the standard input stream, manipulates the input, and then sends the result to the standard output stream. Some filters can receive data directly from a file. The basic filter concept is shown in Figure 6.1.

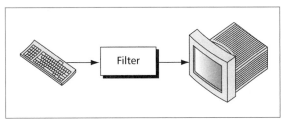

FIGURE 6.1   *Concept of a Filter*

We have already seen one filter, the **more** command. In this chapter, we study 12 more simple filters. Three filters—**grep, sed,** and **awk**—are so powerful that we devote future chapters to each of them. Table 6.1 summarizes the common filters discussed in this text.

TABLE 6.1   *Common Filters*

Filter	Action
Already Studied	
more	Passes all data from input to output, with pauses at the end of each screen of data.
Studied in This Chapter	
cat	Passes all data from input to output.
cmp	Compares two files.
comm	Identifies common lines in two files.
cut	Passes only specified columns.
diff	Identifies differences between two files or between common files in two directories.
head	Passes the number of specified lines at the beginning of the data.
paste	Combines columns.
sort	Arranges the data in sequence.
tail	Passes the number of specified lines at the end of the data.
tr	Translates one or more characters as specified.

Continued

TABLE 6.1 *Common Filters—Continued*

Filter	Action
Studied in This Chapter	
uniq	Deletes duplicate (repeated) lines.
wc	Counts characters, words, or lines.
Studied In Future Chapters	
grep	Passes only specified lines.
sed	Passes edited lines.
awk	Passes edited lines—parses lines.

6.1 Filters and Pipes

Filters work naturally with pipes. Because a filter can send its output to the monitor, it can be used on the left of a pipe; because a filter can receive its input from the keyboard, it can be used on the right of a pipe. In other words, a filter can be used on the left of a pipe, between two pipes, and on the right of a pipe. These relationships are presented in Figure 6.2.

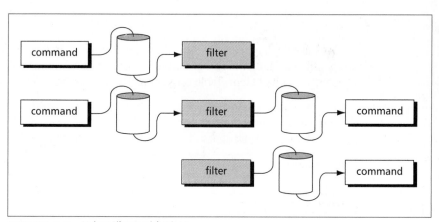

FIGURE 6.2 *Using Filters with Pipes*

6.2 Concatenating Files

UNIX provides a powerful utility to concatenate commands. It is known as the catenate command, or **cat** for short. It combines one or more files by appending them in the order they are listed in the command. The input can come from the keyboard; the output goes to the monitor. The basic concept is shown in Figure 6.3.

Catenate (cat) Command

Given one or more input files, the **cat** command writes them one after another to standard output. The result is that all of the input files are combined and become one

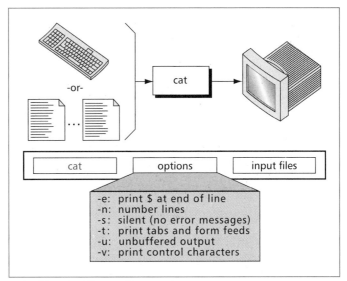

FIGURE 6.3 *The **cat** Command*

output. If the output file is to be saved, standard output can be redirected to a specified output file. The basic **cat** command appears in Figure 6.4.

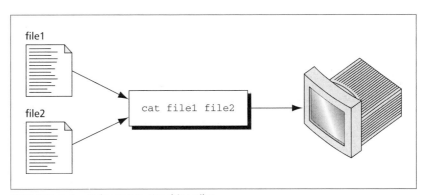

FIGURE 6.4 *Using **cat** to Combine Files*

Session 6.1 demonstrates the simplest use of the **cat** command: displaying file contents. We display the contents of three files, each of which has only one line. As you can see, the files are written one after the other and could easily be saved as one file.

SESSION 6.1 *The Basic **cat** Command*

```
$ cat file1 file2 file3
This is file1.
This is file2.
This is file3.
```

Using cat to Display a File

Its basic design makes **cat** a useful tool to display a file. When only one input file is provided, the file is catenated with a null file. The result is that the input file is displayed on the monitor. Figure 6.5 demonstrates the use of **cat** to display a file. Two points need to be noted, however. First, there are no automatic pauses at the end of the screen like we saw with the **more** command. Second, because the primary use is to combine files and not to display them, there is no check to verify that the file contains text. If we accidentally **cat** a binary file to the monitor, all sorts of strange characters and sounds result. It is our job to make sure that the file is actually a text file.

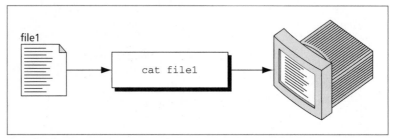

FIGURE 6.5   *Displaying a File with* **cat**

Session 6.2 demonstrates the use of **cat** to display a file. The file, TheRavenV1, contains the first six lines of "The Raven."

SESSION 6.2   *Displaying a File with* **cat**

```
$ cat TheRavenV1
Once upon a midnight dreary, while I pondered, weak and weary,
Over many a quaint and curious volume of forgotten lore
While I nodded, nearly napping, suddenly there came a tapping,
As of someone gently rapping, rapping at my chamber door.
"'Tis some visitor," I muttered, "tapping at my chamber door
Only this and nothing more."
```

Using cat to Create a File

The second special application uses **cat** to create a file. Again, there is only one input; this time, however, the input comes from the keyboard. Because we want to save the file, we redirect standard output to a file rather than to the monitor. Figure 6.6 demonstrates the use of **cat** to create a file.

Before we can demonstrate this use of **cat,** we need to tell you one more thing. Because all of the input is coming from the keyboard, we need some way to tell **cat** that we have finished inputting data. In other words, we need to tell the system that we have input all of the data and are at the end of the file. In UNIX, the keyboard command for **end of file** is the ctrl+d keys, usually abbreviated ^d. Session 6.3 creates a file named goodStudents.

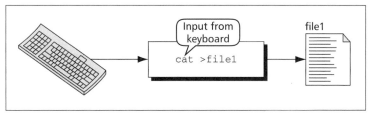

FIGURE 6.6 *Creating a File with* **cat**

SESSION 6.3 *Creating a File with* **cat**

```
$ cat > goodStudents
Now is the time
for all good students
to come to the aid
of their college.
```

Session 6.3 Analysis: The end of file token (^d) is not shown in Session 6.3 because you never see it. As soon as **cat** detects end of file, it quits and returns control to UNIX. Note, however, that it must be the first character of the line. If it is not the first character, it becomes part of the output.

cat Options

There are six options available with **cat.** They can be grouped into four categories: visual characters, buffered output, missing files, and numbered lines. We explore them next.

Visual Characters Sometimes when we display output, we need to see all of the characters. If the file contains unprintable characters, such as the ASCII control characters, we can't see them. Another problem arises if there are space characters at the end of a line—we can't see them because they have no visual graphic. The **visual option,** -v, allows us to see control characters, with the exception of the tab, newline, and form feed characters. Unfortunately, the way they are printed is not intuitive and is beyond the scope of this text.

We can easily see tabs and trailing spaces, however. If we use the option -ve, a dollar sign ($) is printed at the end of each line. If we use the option -vt, the tabs appear as ^I. With both options, nonprintable characters are prefixed with a caret (^). These two options can be combined as in Session 6.4.

SESSION 6.4 *Displaying Nonprintable Characters*

```
$ cat -vet catExample
There is a tab between the numbers on the next line$
1^I2^I3^I4^I5$
$
There are spaces at the end of the next line$
One two buckle my shoe                          $
The last character in this line is the bell^G$
```

You should study several points in this example. (1) There is a dollar sign at the end of each line. Since the third line has only a dollar sign, it must be a blank line in the file. (2) The tabs in the second line are shown as ^I. (3) In the fifth line, there are several spaces after the last word. And (4) the bell in the last line is printed as ^G because G is the seventh letter of the alphabet and the bell character has an ASCII value of seven. Session 6.5 shows what happens when we **cat** the file with no options.

SESSION 6.5 **catExample** *with No Options*

```
$ cat catExample
There is a tab between the numbers on the next line
1       2       3       4       5

There are spaces at the end of the next line
One two buckle my shoe
The last character in this line is the bell
```

If you were to **cat** this file at your terminal, you would hear the bell at the end of the last line.

Buffered Output

When output is **buffered,** it is kept in the computer until the system has time to write it to a file. Normally, **cat** output is buffered. You can force output to be written to the file immediately by specifying the option -u for unbuffered. We do not recommend this option, however, because it slows down the system.

Missing Files

When you catenate several files together, if one of them is missing, the system displays a message such as:

```
Cannot open x.dat: No such file or directory
```

If you don't want to have this message in your output, you can specify that **cat** is to be **silent** when it can't find a file. This option is -s.

Numbered Lines

The numbered lines option (-n) numbers each line in each file as the line is written to standard output. If more than one file is being written, the numbering restarts with each file. Session 6.6 demonstrates the use of the numbered lines option.

SESSION 6.6 *Numbered Lines*

```
$ cat -n goodStudents catExample
     1: Now is the time
     2: for all good students
     3: to come to the aid
     4: of their college.
```

Continued

SESSION 6.6   *Numbered Lines*

```
1: There is a tab between the numbers on the next line
2: 1       2       3       4       5
3:
4: There are spaces at the end of the next line
5: One two buckle my shoe
6:
7: The last character in this line is the bell
```

6.3 Display Beginning and End of Files

UNIX provides two commands, **head** and **tail,** to display portions of files.

head Command

While the **cat** command copies entire files, the **head** command copies a specified number of lines from the beginning of one or more files to the standard output stream. If no files are specified, it gets the lines from standard input. The basic format appears in Figure 6.7.

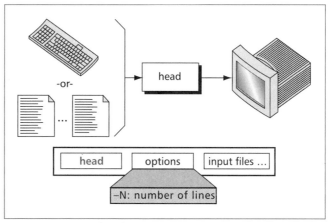

FIGURE 6.7   *The **head** Command*

The option is used to specify the number of lines. If the number of lines is omitted, **head** assumes 10 lines. If the number of lines is larger than the total number of lines in the file, the total file is used. Session 6.7 demonstrates the command with an option of 2.

SESSION 6.7   *The **head** Command*

```
$ head -2 goodStudents
Now is the time
for all good students
```

When multiple files are included in one **head** command, **head** displays the name of the file before its output. Session 6.8 contains the first two lines of goodStudents and TheRaven.

SESSION 6.8   *Multiple Files with* **head** *Command*

```
$ head -2 goodStudents TheRaven
==> goodStudents <==
Now is the time
for all good students

==> TheRaven <==
Once upon a midnight dreary, while I pondered, weak and weary,
Over many a quaint and curious volume of forgotten lore
```

tail Command

The **tail** command also outputs data, only this time from the end of the file. The general format of the **tail** command is presented in Figure 6.8.

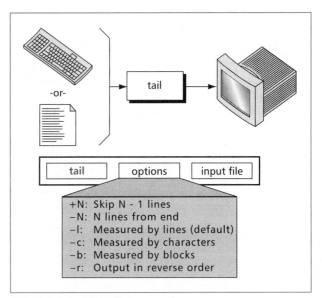

FIGURE 6.8   *The* **tail** *Command*

Although only one file can be referenced (in most systems), it has several options. If the option starts with a plus sign, **tail** skips N - 1 lines before it begins to output lines from the file and continues until it gets to the end of the file. If it starts with a minus, such as -25, it outputs the last number of lines specified in the option. If there are no line options, the default is the last 10 lines.

You can also specify the display count unit, with lines being the default. To copy the last *N* characters, use the option c. To output file blocks, use the option b.[1] One final option, r, is used to output the data in reverse order. These options are summarized in Table 6.2.

TABLE 6.2 *Options Available in* **tail**

Option	Code	Description
Count from beginning	+N	Skips $N - 1$ lines; copies rest to end of file.
Count from end	−N	Copies last *N* lines.
Count by lines	−l	Counts by line (default).
Count by characters	−c	Counts by character.
Count by blocks	−b	Counts by disk block.
Reverse order	−r	Outputs in reverse order (from bottom to top).

Session 6.9 outputs the last two lines of the goodStudents file in reverse order. Note that the number options must be first, followed by the other options if any.

SESSION 6.9 *Using the* **tail** *Option*

```
$ tail -2r goodStudents
of their college.
to come to the aid
```

We can combine the **head** and **tail** commands to extract lines from the center of a file. For example, if we want to extract the second verse (lines 8 to 13—each verse is six lines plus one line between verses) from "The Raven," we could use the **head** command to extract the first 13 lines and then the **tail** command to copy lines 8 to 13 (Session 6.10).

SESSION 6.10 *Extract Lines from Center of File*

```
$ head -13 TheRaven | tail +8
Ah, distinctly I remember it was in the bleak December;
And each separate dying ember wrought its ghost upon the floor.
Eagerly I wished the morrow, -- vainly I had sought to borrow
From my books surcease of sorrow -- sorrow for the lost Lenore
For the rare and radiant maiden whom the angels name Lenore
Nameless here for evermore.
```

---

[1] Data in files are organized in blocks. On a small disk, a block could be 512 bytes.

6.4 Cut and Paste

While they should not be confused with text editor cut and paste operations, the UNIX **cut** and **paste** commands perform similar operations on files. **cut** removes columns of data from a file, and **paste** combines columns of data.

Because the **cut** and **paste** commands work on columns, text files don't work well. Rather, we need a data file that organizes data with several related elements on each line. To demonstrate the commands, we created a file that contains selected data on the largest five cities in the United States according to the 1990 census (Table 6.3). For each city, we include the state, 1990 census, 1980 census, and number of non-government workers.

TABLE 6.3   *Data for the Five Largest Cities in the United States (1990 Census)*

```
Chicago         IL 2783726 3005072 1434029
Houston         TX 1630553 1595138 1049300
Los Angeles     CA 3485398 2968528 1791011
New York        NY 7322564 7071639 3314000
Philadelphia    PA 1585577 1688210 1736895
```

cut Command

The basic purpose of the **cut** command is to extract one or more columns of data from either standard input or from one or more files. The format of the **cut** command appears in Figure 6.9

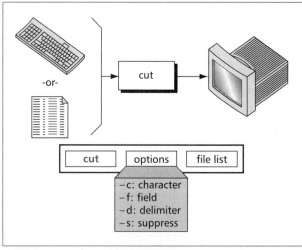

FIGURE 6.9   *The **cut** Command*

Since **cut** looks for columns, we must have some way to specify where the columns are located. This is done with one of two command options. We can specify what we want to extract based on character positions within a line or by a field number.

Specifying Character Positions

Character positions work well when the data are aligned in fixed columns. The data in Table 6.3 are organized this way. City is a string of 15 characters, state is 3 characters (including the trailing space), 1990 population is 8 characters, 1980 population is 8 characters, and work force is 8 characters. This is a conventional table format.

To specify that the file is formatted with fixed columns, we use the **character** option, -c, followed by one or more column specifications. A **column specification** can be one column or a range of columns in the format N-M, where N is the start column and M is the end column, inclusively. Multiple columns are separated by commas. For example, to extract the cities and their 1990 population data, we would specify columns 1-14 and 19-25 as in Session 6.11.

SESSION 6.11   *Example of **cut** Command*

```
$ cut -c1-14,19-25 censusFixed
Chicago        2783726
Houston        1630553
Los Angeles    3485398
New York       7322564
Philadelphia   1585577
```

In specifying the columns, we were careful to include the space that separates the city from the population figures.

Note that there is no space after the comma and before the next column specification. If you put a space in an option, the option is terminated. In this case, **cut** would think that the second column specification was a filename.

This example cut the columns from a file. If the data are already in the input stream from a previous operation, then the file is not specified. For example, assume that you need a list of your files and their size. These data are available through the extended list command (ls -l), but with other unwanted data. To see just the filenames and the file size, we can **pipe** the extended list command and **cut** the filenames and sizes (Session 6.12).

SESSION 6.12   *Cutting Piped Input*

```
$ ls -l | cut -c56-70,36-42
  5781 TheRaven
   721 census
   824 censusFixed
   512 mail
   868 yanks
```

When we coded the **cut** command, we listed the columns for the name first followed by the columns for the size. Note that they are displayed in the order they are found in the file. You can specify the columns in any order; they are always cut in the order they are found in the file. If you overlap the columns, **cut** simply combines them into one column; no data are duplicated. Thus, Session 6.13 simply displays everything from the file size to the end of the line.

SESSION 6.13 *Overlapped **cut** Ranges*

```
$ ls -l | cut -c56-70,36-60
  5781 Apr  5 12:53 TheRaven
   698 May 14 13:18 census
   823 May 13 18:39 censusFixed
   512 Apr 10 21:25 mail
   868 Mar 27 14:30 yanks
```

On the other hand, if you make a mistake, such as the end column smaller than the start column, **cut** displays an error message as shown in Session 6.14. If you don't see it immediately, the error is in the second **cut** range; the end column is less than the start column.

SESSION 6.14 *Error in **cut** Ranges*

```
$ ls -l | cut -c56-70,36-6
Bad list for c/f option
```

Field Specification

While the column specification works well when the data are organized around fixed columns, it doesn't work in other situations. In Table 6.4, the city name ranges between columns 1–7 and columns 1–12. Our only choice, therefore, is to use delimited fields. We have indicated the locations of the tabs with the notation <tab> and have spaced the data to show how it would be displayed.

TABLE 6.4 *Data for Five Largest Cities in the United States (with Tabs)*

Chicago<tab>	IL<tab>	2783726<tab>	3005072<tab>	1434029
Houston<tab>	TX<tab>	1630553<tab>	1595138<tab>	1049300
Los Angeles<tab>	CA<tab>	3485398<tab>	2968528<tab>	1791011
New York<tab>	NY<tab>	7322564<tab>	7071639<tab>	3314000
Philadelphia<tab>	PA<tab>	1585577<tab>	1688210<tab>	736895

When the data are separated by tabs, it is easier to use fields to extract the data from the file. Fields are separated from each other by a terminating character known as a **delimiter.** Any character may be a delimiter; however, if no delimiter is specified, **cut** assumes that it is a tab character.

To specify a field, we use the **field** option (-f). Fields are numbered from the beginning of the line with the first field being field number one. Like the character option, multiple fields are separated by commas with no space after the comma. Consecutive fields may be specified as a range.

The **cut** command assumes that the delimiter is a tab. If it is not, we must specify it in the delimiter option. When the delimiter has special meaning to UNIX, it must be enclosed in quotes. Because the space terminates an option, therefore, we must enclose it in quotes.

In Session 6.15, we extract the cities from the census file.

SESSION 6.15 *Extract Field 1*

```
$ cut -f1 censusTab
Chicago
Houston
Los Angeles
New York
Philadelphia
```

To **cut** the city and the three population fields, we would use the command shown in Session 6.16. Note that it demonstrates an inherent problem with the field **cut** commands: Even though there are tabs, they do not necessarily line up. In the example, the different city name lengths do not correspond with the default UNIX tab settings.

SESSION 6.16 *Extract City and Population Fields*

```
$ cut -f1,3-5 censusTab
Chicago 2783726 3005072 1434029
Houston 1630553 1595138 1049300
Los Angeles     3485398 2968528 1791011
New York        7322564 7071639 3314000
Philadelphia    1585577 1688210 736895
```

As a final example of the fields option, consider our census file with slashes used as delimiters. The file in Session 6.17 uses a slash between the fields. To cut the city, 1990 population, and working population, we use the **cut** command with the delimiter as shown in the second half of Session 6.17.

SESSION 6.17 *Using Slash for Field Separator*

```
$ cat censusSlash
Chicago/IL/2783726/3005072/1434029
Houston/TX/1630553/1595138/1049300
Los Angeles/CA/3485398/2968528/1791011
New York/NY/7322564/7071639/3314000
Philadelphia/PA/1585577/1688210/736895

$ cut -f1,3,5 -d"/" censusSlash
Chicago/2783726/1434029
Houston/1630553/1049300
```

Continued

SESSION 6.17 *Using Slash for Field Separator—Continued*

```
Los Angeles/3485398/1791011
New York/7322564/3314000
Philadelphia/1585577/736895
```

What is readily apparent from this example is that the delimiters are also copied. This was true for the examples with tab delimiters; you just couldn't see the tabs, but you could see their effect as they aligned the data.

> The **cut** command is similar to the **head** and **tail** commands: The **cut** command cuts files vertically (columns), whereas the **head** and **tail** commands cut files horizontally (lines).

Two other points about the **cut** command need to be noted. First, we must specify each option separately. Each option starts with a minus to identify it as an option. Second, the delimiter may be enclosed in either double or single quotes. Thus, the following two delimiter options are equally effective:

```
-d'/'          -d"/"
```

There is one more **cut** option of interest, the **suppress** option (-s). This option tells **cut** not to display any line that does not have a delimiter. If you don't use it, **cut** copies all of the data in a line when there is no delimiter. As a general rule, you should use the suppress option. Table 6.5 summarizes the **cut** options.

TABLE 6.5 *cut Command Options*

Option	Code	Results
Character	-c	Extracts fixed columns specified by column number.
Field	-f	Extracts delimited columns.
Delimiter	-d	Specifies delimiter if not tab (default).
Suppress	-s	Suppresses output if no delimiter in line.

paste Command

The **paste** command combines lines together. It gets its input from two or more files. To specify that the input is coming from the standard input stream, you use a hyphen (-) instead of a filename. The **paste** command is shown in Figure 6.10.

Given two files as in Figure 6.10, **paste** combines the first line of the first file with the first line of the second file and writes the combined line to the standard output stream. Between the columns, it writes a tab. At the end of the last column, it writes a newline character. It then combines the next two lines and writes them, continuing until all lines have been written. In other words, **paste** treats each line of

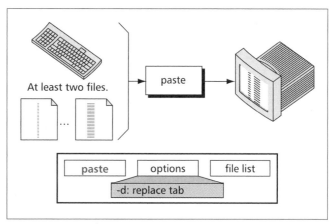

FIGURE 6.10 *The* **paste** *Command*

each file as a column. If there are more than two files, the corresponding lines from each file, separated by tabs, are written to the output stream. Session 6.18 combines two files. The first file has three columns of odd numbers. The second file has two columns of even numbers. Note that the tab is inserted after the last column of the first file.

SESSION 6.18 *Pasting Two Files*

```
$ paste fileOdd fileEven
1 11 111       2 38
3 33 333       4  8
5 55 555       6 48
7 77 777       8 22
9 99 999       0 10
```

As you can see, in this example, the lines from the two files, separated by a tab, are written to the standard output stream.

> The **cat** and **paste** commands are similar: The **cat** command combines files vertically (by lines). The **paste** command combines files horizontally (by columns).

If the file lengths are uneven—that is, if they contain a different number of lines—then all data are still written to the output. If the first file is longer than the second file, **paste** writes the extra data from the first file a separation delimiter, such as the tab, and the newline until all data have been output. If the first file is shorter than the second file, **paste** writes a delimiter followed by the extra data from the second file to the output stream. We demonstrate both situations in Session 6.19. In these examples, fileEven2 has only three entries.

SESSION 6.19   *Pasting Files of Different Lengths*

```
$ paste fileOdd fileEven2
1 11 111        2 38
3 33 333        4  8
5 55 555        6 48
7 77 777
9 99 999
$ paste fileEven2 fileOdd
2 38     1 11 111
4  8     3 33 333
6 48     5 55 555
         7 77 777
         9 99 999
```

Today, there is only one option for **paste.**[2] You can specify that one or more delimiters (-d) be used to separate the data. If there are two files, you can specify one delimiter. If there are three files, you can specify two delimiters. The first delimiter is used between the first and second file, while the second delimiter is used between the second and third files. The delimiter after the last file is always a newline. Session 6.20 pastes three files using two delimiters. The first delimiter is a tab (\t), and the second delimiter is a pound sign (#). They are enclosed in double quotes on the command line.

SESSION 6.20   *Using* **paste** *with Three Files*

```
$ paste -d"\t#" fileOddEven fileOdd fileEven
1        1#2
2        3#4
3        5#6
4        7#
5        9#
```

This example clearly demonstrates that a delimiter is written to the output even when the last column is empty. Study the delimiters carefully. The first delimiter is a tab. The second delimiter is a pound sign. Note that for the last two lines, there are no data from the even number file. Therefore, we see that the data from the odd file are immediately followed by the pound sign.

If the number of files is N, the number of delimiters should be $N - 1$. If there are fewer than $N - 1$ delimiters, then they are rotated. For example, if you paste five files with only two delimiters, the first delimiter is used between files one and two, the second delimiter is used between files two and three, the first delimiter is used again between files three and four, and so forth. Session 6.21 pastes our files five times. However, there are only two delimiters, the tab and the pound sign. As you study the output, note that the delimiter between the first two columns is always a tab; between the second and third columns, it is always a pound sign; between the third and fourth columns, it is again a tab; and between the fourth and fifth columns, it is again a pound sign. The last delimiter, after the fifth column, is always a newline regardless of the other delimiters.

---

[2]The second **paste** option is archaic and does not pertain to **paste.**

SESSION 6.21   *Pasting Files with Rotating Delimiters*

```
$ paste -d"\t#" fileOddEven fileOdd fileEven fileOddEven fileOdd
1          1#2      1#1
2          3#4      2#3
3          5#6      3#5
4          7#       4#7
5          9#       5#9
```

6.5 Sorting

When dealing with data, especially a lot of data, we need to organize them for analysis and efficient processing. One of the simplest and most powerful organizing techniques is sorting. When we **sort** data, we arrange them in sequence. Usually, we use **ascending sequence,** an arrangement in which each piece of data is larger than its predecessor. We can also sort in **descending sequence,** in which each piece of data is smaller than its predecessor.

Not all of the data in a file need to participate in the sort ordering. For example, consider our file of cities (see Table 6.3, page 210), which is sorted on city. We could also sort it on state or on any of the population figures. Which way we sort it depends on how we want to use the data. If we want to know the largest cities in 1990, we would sort it on 1990 population. While we could sort the data in ascending population sequence, that would place the largest city at the bottom. It makes more sense, if we are looking for the largest cities, to sort the data in descending sequence. That places the largest cities at the top of the list.

sort Command

The **sort** utility uses options, field specifiers, and input files. The **field specifiers** tell it which fields to use for the sort. The **sort** command format is shown in Figure 6.11.

Sort by Lines

The easiest **sort** arranges data by lines. Starting at the beginning of the line, it compares the first character in one line with the first character in another line. If they are the same (equal), it moves to the second character and compares them. This character-by-character comparison continues until either all characters in both lines have compared equal or until two unequal characters are found. If the lines are not equal, the comparison stops and **sort** determines which line should be first based on the two unequal characters.

In comparing characters, **sort** uses the ASCII value of each character. Appendix A contains a complete list of the ASCII characters arranged in order from the smallest (first) to the largest (last). The first column in the table is the decimal value of the character (symbol) in column four. As you study the ASCII character set, you should look for the following general ordering of items:

1. Uppercase letters have lower values than lowercase letters. For example, the value of A is 65, and the value of a is 96.
2. Digits (the characters zero through nine) have character values that are not equivalent to their numeric values. Specifically, the value of zero is 48, the value

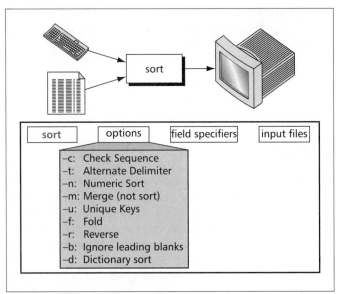

FIGURE 6.11   *The **sort** Command*

of one is 49, and so forth through nine, which is 57. They are ordered below the uppercase characters.

3. Control characters, which are characters that are used by the system, consist of the first 32 characters and the last character (value 127).

4. Special characters, such as punctuation, financial symbols, and the asterisk, are spread throughout the character set. Some appear before the digits, some between the digits and the uppercase letters, some between the uppercase and lowercase letters, and some between the lowercase letters and the last ASCII control character.

5. The space or blank character is found at decimal 32, just above the last control characters and below the first special character.

When **sort** compares two characters, therefore, it is actually comparing the values that correspond to them. This means that when A is compared to B, the values 65 and 66 are used. This makes the letter A less than the letter B, which is exactly what we expect. Similarly, when it compares A with a it uses 65 and 97, which makes corresponding uppercase letters come before their matching lowercase letters.

A problem occurs when digits are compared that are meant to be numeric (algebraic) values. While we recognize that 12 is greater than 6, **sort** compares the 1 in 12 with the 6 and decides that the 12 is less than 6 (49 is less than 54). We will see later how this problem is solved by using a **sort** option.

Let's look at an example. The first column in Table 6.6 contains a set of unsorted data. The second column contains the same data after they have been sorted. Note that `gilberg` starts with a space.

TABLE 6.6 *Line Sort Demonstration*

Unsorted Data	Sorted Data
forouzan	gilberg
gilberg	!
8	27
27	8
!	Paula
~	Paulo
Paulo	forouzan
Paula	~

As you study Table 6.6, note the following points:

1. gilberg comes first because it starts with a space.
2. The bang (!) is second. It is the first special character and therefore will always immediately follow a space character in the ordering sequence.
3. The number 27 is listed before the number 8 because the value of 2 is less than the value of 8.
4. Paula comes before Paulo because the first four characters of each are equal, but the fifth letter (a) in Paula is less than the fifth letter (o) in Paulo.
5. forouzan comes after Paulo because Paulo's first character (P) is less than the first letter in forouzan (f).
6. The tilde (~) is last because it has a value of 126. It is the highest valued printable character.

Sort by Fields

Sorting by lines is very easy, but it works only when the data at the beginning of the line control the sort sequence. When the data that control the data sequence are not at the beginning of the line, we need to use a field sort.

Fields

In general, a field is the smallest unit of data that has meaning in describing information. For example, a student file would contain name, address, major, and other fields that contain data about a student.

The UNIX **sort** defines a field as a set of characters delimited by a single blank or a tab. The first field of a line is delimited by the space or tab after it. The second field is delimited by a space or tab before it and one after it. The last field in a line is delimited only by the space or tab before it. In addition, **sort** numbers the fields in a line. The first field is number 1, the second is number 2, and so forth until the last field. Figure 6.12 shows how a line is viewed by UNIX.

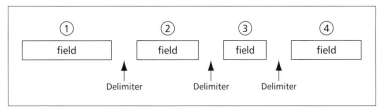

FIGURE 6.12 *Fields within a Line*

Delimiters

You may notice an inconsistency with the default delimiters among the different utilities. The cut and paste delimiters use the tab as the default delimiter. Sort uses both tab and space as its delimiter. Different definitions arose over time as different programmers contributed to the UNIX system as we know it today. Unfortunately, it's just something we have to live with.

Field Specifiers

When a field sort is required, we need to define which field or fields are to be used for the sort. Field specifiers are a set of two numbers that together identify the first and last field in a sort key. They have the following format:

$$\texttt{+number}_1 \texttt{ -number}_2$$

$\texttt{number}_1$ specifies the number of fields to be skipped to get to the beginning of the sort field, whereas $\texttt{number}_2$ specifies the number of fields to be skipped, *relative to the beginning of the line,* to get to the end of the sort key. Figure 6.13 contains several examples to study.

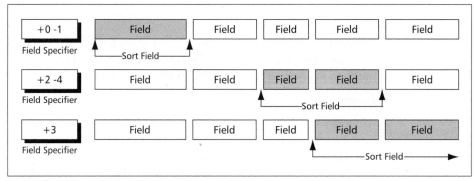

FIGURE 6.13 *Field Specifier Examples*

In Figure 6.13, we see three different situations. In the first sort, the key field is at the left end of the line. Because the key consists of the first field in the line, 0 fields are skipped; because it is the only field in the key, the end is one field away. For this sort, we could have used a line sort, and the data would still be ordered on the first field.[3]

In the second example, the sort field consists of fields three and four. We must therefore skip two fields to get to the start of the sort field. Because it is two fields, we skip four fields to get to the end of the sort field. Remember, the second number is relative to the beginning of the *line,* not the beginning of the sort field.

---

[3] If there are duplicate keys, a line sort could result in minor variations among the lines with duplicate keys.

In the last example, the sort field is at the end of the line. If no end field is specified, the end of the line is assumed. Also, the end field must be at least one larger than the start field. If an invalid field specification is specified, such as a start number greater than the number of fields on a line, the field specification is ignored and **sort** uses the beginning of the line for the sort.

As we mentioned earlier, **sort** defines a field as a word delimited by one space or tab. This means that each line in the file must be carefully formatted. If two spaces are found between two fields, then by **sort**'s definition, there is a null field between the two spaces. An extra space or tab changes the number of fields on a line and can cause the sort to give strange-looking results (Figure 6.14). Fortunately, there is a **sort** option that ignores duplicate blanks.

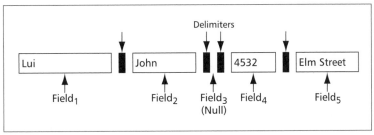

FIGURE 6.14   *Null Field Impact*

Let's look at two simple sorts. In Session 6.22, we sort the cities file (see Table 6.3 on page 210) on city, which is the first field in the file.

SESSION 6.22   *Sort by City*

```
$ sort +0 -1 censusSpace
Chicago IL 2783726 3005072 1434029
Houston TX 1630553 1595138 1049300
Los_Angeles CA 3485398 2968528 1791011
New_York NY 7322564 7071639 3314000
Philadelphia PA 1585577 1688210 736895
```

In Session 6.23, we sort the same file by the second field, state. Because the states are not aligned, we have made them underlined.

SESSION 6.23   *Sort by State*

```
$ sort +1 -2 censusSpace
Los_Angeles CA 3485398 2968528 1791011
Chicago IL 2783726 3005072 1434029
New_York NY 7322564 7071639 3314000
Philadelphia PA 1585577 1688210 736895
Houston TX 1630553 1595138 1049300
```

Options

Options can be used globally, in which case they apply to all field specifiers, or locally, in which case they apply to only the current field specifier. Global options are specified before all field specifiers. Local options are after the start field in the field specification. Figure 6.15 demonstrates the use of global and local options. At this point, don't worry about what these options do; we explain them in the following sections.

FIGURE 6.15 *Global and Local Options*

Check Sort Sequence

The check sort option (–c) verifies that the file is sorted. If it is not sorted, the first out-of-sequence line is displayed. In Session 6.24, we first check to see if the census file is ordered on city (it is) and then test to see if it is ordered on state (it is not).

SESSION 6.24 *Check Sort Sequence*

```
$ sort -c +0 -1 census
$ sort -c +1 -2 census
disorder: Los_Angeles   CA      3485398 2968528 1791011
```

Delimiter

The delimiter option (–t) specifies an alternate delimiter. Like delimiter specifications in **cut,** it can and should be placed in quotes. To demonstrate this option, we created a special version of our census file in which the delimiter is an ampersand (&). We left the tabs in the file for readability; normally, you would not use two delimiters. Session 6.25 sorts our ampersand-delimited file on the second field, state.

SESSION 6.25 *Change Sort Delimiter*

```
$ sort -t'&' +1 -2 censusAmp
Los Angeles    &CA      &3485398      &2968528      &1791011
Chicago        &IL      &2783726      &3005072      &1434029
New York       &NY      &7322564      &7071639      &3314000
Philadelphia   &PA      &1585577      &1688210      &736895
Houston        &TX      &1630553      &1595138      &1049300
```

Numeric Sort Fields

Sort assumes an ASCII value to the data to be sorted. In other words, it sorts data as though they are strings of characters. Numeric data create problems. In Session 6.26, we sort our census file by the last field, civilian work force. Note that Philadelphia is sorted after New_York because its first digit (7) is greater than New_York's first digit (3). It is obvious to us, however, that New_York's population is more than four times larger than Philadelphia's.

SESSION 6.26   *Invalid Numeric Sort*

```
$ sort +4 census
Houston         TX       1630553 1595138 1049300
Chicago         IL       2783726 3005072 1434029
Los_Angeles     CA       3485398 2968528 1791011
New_York        NY       7322564 7071639 3314000
Philadelphia    PA       1585577 1688210 736895
```

In Session 6.26, because the civilian work force is the last field, we did not specify an end field. When the end field is not specified, the sort is automatically from the start field to the end of the line.

To sort the data correctly, we need to tell **sort** to use a numeric comparison (-n). Session 6.27 re-sorts the civilian work force correctly. With a numeric sort option, the data come out correctly with Philadelphia first.

SESSION 6.27   *Sort on Numeric Fields*

```
$ sort -n +4 census
Philadelphia    PA       1585577 1688210 736895
Houston         TX       1630553 1595138 1049300
Chicago         IL       2783726 3005072 1434029
Los_Angeles     CA       3485398 2968528 1791011
New_York        NY       7322564 7071639 3314000
```

Merge Files

A **merge** combines multiple ordered files into one file that is ordered. If you know that the files are already ordered, you can save time by using the merge option (-m). Note, however, that if the files are not ordered, **sort** will not give you an error message. Rather, it will do its best to sort the data, and the output will not be ordered. In Session 6.28, we merge a file of males' names with a file of females' names. Both files are ordered.

SESSION 6.28   *Merge Two Files*

```
$ sort -m males females
Andre
Betty
Diana
George
Mai
Phan
```

Unique Sort Fields

The unique option (-u) eliminates all but one line when the sort fields are identical. Thus, if we wanted to know a large city in each state, we could sort the data by state and drop lines that were duplicated on state.[4]

To demonstrate this sort, we created a new file that contains the ten largest cities in the 1990 census. We also made it a slash (/) delimited file. Because the file is now slash delimited, we don't have to worry about the spaces in cities with two words, like New York. In some of our previous examples, we replaced the space in the middle of a city name with an underscore. Session 6.29 sorts this file by state.

SESSION 6.29 *Sort Census Data by State*

```
$ sort -t'/' +1 -2 census10
Phoenix         /AZ/1881/ 983403/ 789704/ 591142/17705
Los Angeles     /CA/1850/3485398/2968528/1791011/19906
San Diego       /CA/1850/1110549/ 875538/ 553612/18651
Chicago         /IL/1837/2783726/3005072/1434029/20349
Detroit         /MI/1815/1027974/1203368/ 441736/19660
New York        /NY/1898/7322564/7071639/3314000/22645
Philadelphia    /PA/1701/1585577/1688210/ 736895/19750
Dallas          /TX/1856/1006877/ 904599/ 649527/19485
Houston         /TX/1837/1630553/1595138/1049300/17598
San Antonio     /TX/1837/ 935933/ 785940/ 446701/14144
```

Session 6.30 repeats the sort, this time adding a unique option.

SESSION 6.30 *Eliminate Duplicate Sort Fields in Sort*

```
$ sort -t'/' -u +1 -2 census10
Phoenix         /AZ/1881/ 983403/ 789704/ 591142/17705
San Diego       /CA/1850/1110549/ 875538/ 553612/18651
Chicago         /IL/1837/2783726/3005072/1434029/20349
Detroit         /MI/1815/1027974/1203368/ 441736/19660
New York        /NY/1898/7322564/7071639/3314000/22645
Philadelphia    /PA/1701/1585577/1688210/ 736895/19750
San Antonio     /TX/1837/ 935933/ 785940/ 446701/14144
```

We place it after the delimiter option, but it can go before it just as well. We could also combine the two options with only one dash. Both of these options are shown here:

```
$ sort -u -t'/' +1 -2 census10
$ sort -ut'/' +1 -2 census10
```

---

[4]To find the largest city in a state, we need to use a multiple-pass sort. We will repeat this example shortly finding the largest city in each state.

A logical question is: Which of the lines with duplicate sort fields is kept? If you study the two examples carefully, paying special attention to California and Texas, you will note that it keeps the last duplicate.

Reverse (Descending) Order

To order the data from largest to smallest, we specify **reverse order** (-r). Session 6.31 sorts our census data in reverse (descending) order on 1990 population. Note that we need to use both the numeric and reverse options to get the correct results.

SESSION 6.31   *Sort in Descending Sequence*

```
$ sort -nr +2 -3 census
New_York        NY      7322564 7071639 3314000
Los_Angeles     CA      3485398 2968528 1791011
Chicago         IL      2783726 3005072 1434029
Houston         TX      1630553 1595138 1049300
Philadelphia    PA      1585577 1688210 736895
```

Note that the same results are obtained in Session 6.32 when we specify the reverse, numeric sort as a part of the field specification.

SESSION 6.32   *Sort Descending—Method 2*

```
$ sort +2nr -3 census
New_York        NY      7322564 7071639 3314000
Los_Angeles     CA      3485398 2968528 1791011
Chicago         IL      2783726 3005072 1434029
Houston         TX      1630553 1595138 1049300
Philadelphia    PA      1585577 1688210 7368950
```

Ignore Leading Blanks

The **blanks** option (-b) is mandatory in fixed formatted fields. If we do not ignore leading blanks, then each blank is considered a separate [null] field. When this option is used, fields can have no embedded spaces. The file in Session 6.33 has several spaces between each field so that they all align. There are no tabs in the file. Note that in this session, as in several of the others, we have placed an underscore between Los Angeles and between New York so that they are one, rather than two, fields.

SESSION 6.33   *Sort Ignoring Leading Blanks*

```
$ sort -b +1 -2 censusBlanks
Los_Angeles     CA      3485398     2968528     1791011
Chicago         IL      2783726     3005072     1434029
New_York        NY      7322564     7071639     3314000
Philadelphia    PA      1585577     1688210      736895
Houston         TX      1630553     1595138     1049300
```

Dictionary Sorting

If you look at the index in a book, you will see that it begins with special characters. Special characters are found intermixed with the digits and alphabetic characters in ASCII. If we sort the index using the default ASCII sort, therefore, they will not be at the beginning of the index like we want them. An ASCII sort of a small portion of the index is shown in Session 6.34.

SESSION 6.34   *Sort Special Characters—The Wrong Way*

```
$ sort sortGlossary
!       not
ASCII   American Standard Code for Information Interchange
\       see escape
append  To add at the end of a file
bit     Binary digit; 0 or 1
escape  The backslash character used to indicate a special code
file    A collection of related data
man     UNIX command for documentation (Manual)
sort    To arrange data in a specified order
```

To sort the index correctly, we use the dictionary option (-d). Session 6.34 is repeated using dictionary sorting. Note, however, that Session 6.35 doesn't completely do the job. The special characters are all moved to the beginning of the index, but the uppercase text still sorts before the lowercase text. We solve this problem in the next session.

SESSION 6.35   *Sort Special Characters—The Right Way*

```
$ sort -d sortGlossary
!       not
\       see escape
ASCII   American Standard Code for Information Interchange
append  To add at the end of a file
bit     Binary digit; 0 or 1
escape  The backslash character used to indicate a special code
file    A collection of related data
man     UNIX command for documentation (Manual)
sort    To arrange data in a specified order
```

Fold Lowercase

As we pointed out in the previous example, the index term *ASCII* is sorted before the term *append* when it should be after *append*. The reason is that ASCII is all uppercase, which comes first using the ASCII collating sequence. To make our sort ignore the difference between upper- and lowercase, we use the fold option (-f). In the fold option, the uppercase characters are folded into lowercase so that they all sort the same. In Session 6.36, we repeat our index sort, this time using both dictionary and fold.

SESSION 6.36 *Fold Upper- and Lowercase in Sort*

```
$ sort -df sortGlossary
!       not
\       see escape
append  To add at the end of a file
ASCII   American Standard Code for Information Interchange
bit     Binary digit; 0 or 1
escape  The backslash character used to indicate a special code
file    A collection of related data
man     UNIX command for documentation (Manual)
sort    To arrange data in a specified order
```

Multiple-Pass Sorting

We now address the problem posed earlier: How do we sort population and city to get the largest city in each state set? If the two fields are adjacent to each other, such as state and 1990 population, we can just sort on the two fields. This concept is shown in Figure 6.16. The sort in this figure uses the top 20 population states.

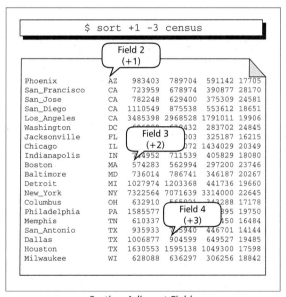

FIGURE 6.16 *Sorting Adjacent Fields*

To sort on state (field 2) and 1990 population (field 3), we specify that the start field is +1 and the end field is -3.

In Session 6.37, we sort our 10-city census file using state and population. But a careful examination quickly tells us that this is not what we want. While the population field has been sorted (look at Texas), it is sorted as text, not as numeric data; San Antonio comes after Dallas and Houston even though its population is the smallest.

SESSION 6.37 *Multiple-Pass Sort*

```
$ sort -t'/' +1 -3 census10
Phoenix         /AZ/983403/789704/591142/17705
San Diego       /CA/1110549/875538/553612/18651
Los Angeles     /CA/3485398/2968528/1791011/19906
Chicago         /IL/2783726/3005072/1434029/20349
Detroit         /MI/1027974/1203368/441736/19660
New York        /NY/7322564/7071639/3314000/22645
Philadelphia    /PA/1585577/1688210/736895/19750
Dallas          /TX/1006877/904599/649527/19485
Houston         /TX/1630553/1595138/1049300/17598
San Antonio     /TX/935933/785940/446701/14144
```

What we need to do, therefore, is define two different fields for the sort. The first is state, which we want to be sorted as text. The second is 1990 population, for which we need a numeric sort. To specify two sort fields, we just list them one after the other as shown in Session 6.38. Note that we used a numeric flag (n) with the second sort field. The numeric field tells the sort that it is to be sorted numerically while using text for the state sort. This sort is shown in Session 6.38.

SESSION 6.38 *Multiple-Pass Sort—ASCII and Numeric*

```
$ sort -t'/' +1 -2 +2n -3 census10
Phoenix         /AZ/983403/789704/591142/17705
San Diego       /CA/1110549/875538/553612/18651
Los Angeles     /CA/3485398/2968528/1791011/19906
Chicago         /IL/2783726/3005072/1434029/20349
Detroit         /MI/1027974/1203368/441736/19660
New York        /NY/7322564/7071639/3314000/22645
Philadelphia    /PA/1585577/1688210/736895/19750
San Antonio     /TX/935933/785940/446701/14144
Dallas          /TX/1006877/904599/649527/19485
Houston         /TX/1630553/1595138/1049300/17598
```

We need only one more refinement. We would like the population figures to be descending. In the following example, we add the reverse (descending) flag as a part of the second sort field. We now have our desired results.

SESSION 6.39 *Sort State Ascending, Population Descending*

```
$ sort -t'/' +1 -2 +2nr -3 census10
Phoenix         /AZ/983403/789704/591142/17705
Los Angeles     /CA/3485398/2968528/1791011/19906
San Diego       /CA/1110549/875538/553612/18651
Chicago         /IL/2783726/3005072/1434029/20349
Detroit         /MI/1027974/1203368/441736/19660
New York        /NY/7322564/7071639/3314000/22645
Philadelphia    /PA/1585577/1688210/736895/19750
Houston         /TX/1630553/1595138/1049300/17598
Dallas          /TX/1006877/904599/649527/19485
San Antonio     /TX/935933/785940/446701/14144
```

We are now ready to complete our goal of finding the largest city in each state. To do this, we need to sort twice. We first sort by state and then by population. Because we know that unique field sorts keep the last in a series, we want the largest population to be at the end of the duplicates. Therefore, we use an ascending sort for population.

> In multiple-pass sorting, when the criterion for each field is different, use separate field specifiers.

The second sort, which receives its input through a pipe from the first sort, uses the unique option while it orders the data by state. Since the data are already ordered by state, however, all it has to do is drop the duplicates, keeping the last one. We now have our list of the largest cities in each of our states. This sort is shown in Session 6.40, with the data for 20 states. Note that the skip leading blanks is required for both sorts.

SESSION 6.40 *Find Largest City in Each State*

```
$ sort -b +1 -2 +2n -3 census20 | sort -bu +1 -2
Phoenix         AZ    983403  789704   591142 17705
Los_Angeles     CA   3485398 2968528 1791011 19906
Washington      DC    606900  638432   283702 24845
Jacksonville    FL    672971  571003   325187 16215
Chicago         IL   2783726 3005072 1434029 20349
Indianapolis    IN    744952  711539   405829 18080
Boston          MA    574283  562994   297200 23746
Baltimore       MD    736014  786741   346187 20267
Detroit         MI   1027974 1203368   441736 19660
New_York        NY   7322564 7071639 3314000 22645
Columbus        OH    632910  565021   343288 17178
Philadelphia    PA   1585577 1688210   736895 19750
Memphis         TN    610337  646174   337450 16484
Houston         TX   1630553 1595138 1049300 17598
Milwaukee       WI    628088  636297   306256 18842
```

Table 6.7 summarizes the sort options discussed in this section.

TABLE 6.7 *Sort Command Options*

Option	Code	Results
Check sequence	-c	Verifies that data are correctly sorted.
Alternate delimiter	-t	Specifies alternate delimiter. Default: tab and space.
Numeric sort	-n	Data are numeric, not string. Default: string data.
Merge	-m	Input files are sorted. Merges them.
Unique sort fields	-u	Deletes duplicate sort fields, keeping last one.
Reverse order	-r	Sorts data in descending sequence.
Ignore leading blanks	-b	Considers leading blanks as one blank for field separation.
Dictionary sort	-d	Sorts special characters first.
Fold lowercase	-f	Sorts upper- and lowercase together.

6.6 Translating Characters

There are many reasons for translating characters from one set to another. One of the most common is to convert lowercase characters to uppercase, or vice versa. UNIX provides a translate utility making conversions from one set to another.

tr Command

The **tr** command replaces each character in a user-specified set of characters with a corresponding character in a second specified set. Each set is specified as a string. The first character in the first set is replaced by the first character in the second set, the second character in the first set is replaced by the second character in the second set, and so forth until all matching characters have been replaced. The strings are specified using quotes. The format for the translate filter is shown in Figure 6.17. Note that only the keyboard is specified. Translate will not accept data from a file. To translate a file, therefore, we must redirect the file into the translate command.

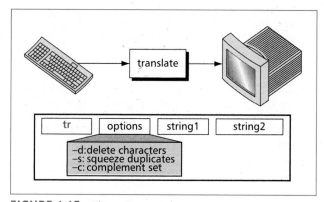

FIGURE 6.17 *The **tr** Command*

Simple Translate

Translate receives its input from standard input and writes its output to standard output. If no options are specified, the text is matched against the `string1` set, and any matching characters are replaced with the corresponding characters in the `string2` set. Unmatched characters are unchanged.

For example, Session 6.41 converts all lowercase vowels to uppercase. As you study the output, note that the uppercase vowels in the input are not changed.

SESSION 6.41 *Translate Vowels to Uppercase*

```
$ tr "aeiou" "AEIOU"
It is very easy to use TRANSLATE.          #input
It Is vEry EAs y tO UsE TRANSLATE.         #output
```

Because the input is coming from the keyboard, we must key an end of file (^d) at the end of the data. UNIX translates each line, one line at a time, changing the specified characters until it finds the end of file.

Nonmatching Translate Strings

When the translate strings are of different length, the result depends on which string is shorter. If string2 is shorter, the unmatched characters will all be changed to the last character in string2. On the other hand, if string1 is shorter, the extra characters in string2 are ignored. These cases appear in Session 6.42.

SESSION 6.42   *Translate Strings Don't Match*

```
$ tr "aeiou" "AE?"            # Case 1: string2 is shorter than string1
It is very easy to use translate.
It ?s vEry EAsy t? ?sE trAnslAtE.
$ tr "aei" "AEIOU"            # Case 2: string1 is shorter than string2
It is very easy to use translate.
It Is vEry EAsy to usE trAnslAtE.
```

Session 6.42 Analysis: First, study case 1. The translate source characters ae are correctly converted to uppercase. Likewise, the i is correctly converted to a question mark. The source characters ou, however, are both converted to question marks because there were no corresponding translation characters for them.

In case 2, there are no translation source characters for OU. Therefore, they are ignored in the translation.

Delete Characters

To delete matching characters in the translation, we use the delete option (-d). In Session 6.43, we delete all vowels, both upper- and lowercase. Note that the delete option does not use string2. Again, the session is ended with an end of file control character.

SESSION 6.43   *Delete Characters Using Translate*

```
$ tr -d "aeiouAEIOU"
It is very easy to use TRANSLATE
t s vry sy t s TRNSLT
```

Squeeze Output

The squeeze option deletes consecutive occurrences of the same character in the output. For example, if after the translation of ie to the letter "d" the output contains a string of "d's," all but one would be deleted. Session 6.44 demonstrates the squeeze option.

SESSION 6.44   *Squeeze Output with Translate*

```
$ tr -s "ie" "dd"
The fiend did dastardly deeds
Thd fdnd d dastardly ds
```

Complement

The complement option reverses the meaning of the first string. Rather than specifying what characters are to be changed, it says what characters are not to be changed. For example, Session 6.45 changes everything but vowels to asterisks.

SESSION 6.45 *Using Translate's Complement Option*

```
$ tr -c "aeiou" "*"
It is very easy to use TRANSLATE.
***i***e***ea****o*u*e**********
```

Session 6.45 Analysis: The complement indicates that we want to change everything but vowels to asterisk characters. The second string indicates that the character a is *not* to be converted. But what about the rest of the first string, the characters eiou? They are not converted to asterisks because of the rules for unmatched translation characters (see page 231).

A more interesting, and useful, example is to build a list of all of the words used in a document. For this session, we created a small file with the following contents:

```
The dastardly fiend did 101 dastardly deeds.
He was truly dastardly.
```

Each word in the output file is to be on a separate line. Let's begin by creating the list of words. Our definition of a word is one or more characters in a string. Punctuation, special characters, and control characters are not part of a word. The easiest way to identify all of the words in a string is to complement all upper- and lowercase characters. The option and translate strings for finding words are in the following example:

```
-c "A-Za-z"
```

The question is: What do we translate them to? The answer is that we translate all nonalphabetic characters to a newline (\n). Because we may get several blank lines in the output (such as numbers will convert to newlines), we also use squeeze to eliminate the empty lines. This gives us the translate command shown in Session 6.46. Note that the file is redirected into the **tr** command.

SESSION 6.46 *Using Translate to Parse Words*

```
$ tr -cs "A-Za-z" "\n" <dastardly.txt
The
dastardly
fiend
did
dastardly
deeds
He
was
truly
dastardly
```

Now that we have our list, however, we note that there are some duplicates in it. The suppress duplicates only deleted the duplicate newlines. To delete the duplicate words, and to make the list more readable, we pipe the output to sort as shown in Session 6.47.

SESSION 6.47 *Using Translate to Parse Words—Part 2*

```
$ tr -cs "A-Za-z" "\012" <dastardly.txt | sort -uf
dastardly
deeds
did
fiend
He
The
truly
was
```

Session 6.47 Analysis: In this example, we have two lines of input. For the sort, we use the unique and fold options. We do not need the dictionary command because we know there are nothing but characters in the output.

Table 6.8 summarizes the translate options discussed in this section.

TABLE 6.8 *Translate Options*

Option	Code	Results
Delete characters	-d	Deletes matching characters.
Squeeze duplicates	-s	After translation, deletes consecutive duplicate characters.
Complement set	-c	Uses complement of matching set.

> **tr** cannot accept a filename as an argument; to translate a file, use input redirection or pipe the lines from another command.

6.7 Files with Duplicate Lines

In Session 6.47, we used a sort to delete duplicate lines (words). If the lines are already adjacent to each other, we can use the unique utility.

uniq Command

The **uniq** command deletes duplicate lines, keeping the first and deleting the others. To be deleted, the lines must be adjacent. Duplicate lines that are not adjacent are not deleted. To delete nonadjacent lines, the file must be sorted.

Unless otherwise specified, the whole line can be used for comparison. Options provide for the compare to start with a specified field or character. The compare, whether line, field, or character, is to the end of the line. It is not possible to compare one field in the middle of the line. The unique command is shown in Figure 6.18.

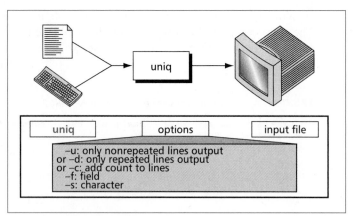

FIGURE 6.18 *The **uniq** Command*

All of the sessions in this section use a file with three sets of duplicate lines. The complete file is shown in Table 6.9.

TABLE 6.9 *Test File for the Unique Command*

```
5 completely duplicate lines
5 completely duplicate lines
5 completely duplicate lines
5 completely duplicate lines
5 completely duplicate lines
Not a duplicate--next duplicates first 5
5 completely duplicate lines
Last 3 fields duplicate: one two three
Last 3 fields duplicate: one two three
Last 3 fields duplicate: one two three
The next 3 lines are duplicate after char 5
abcde Duplicate to end
fghij Duplicate to end
klmno Duplicate to end
```

There are three options: output format, skip leading fields, and skip leading characters. They are discussed in turn in the following sections.

Output Format

There are four output formats: nonduplicated lines and the first line of each duplicate series (default), only unique lines (-u), only duplicated lines (-d), and show count of duplicated lines (-c).

Default Output Format

In Session 6.48, we use the unique command without any options. It writes all of the nonduplicated lines and the *first of a series* of duplicated lines. This is the default result.

SESSION 6.48   *Basic Unique Command*

```
$ uniq uniqFile
5 completely duplicate lines
Not a duplicate--next duplicates first 5
5 completely duplicate lines
Last 3 fields duplicate: one two three
The next 3 lines are duplicate after char 5
abcde Duplicate to end
fghij Duplicate to end
klmno Duplicate to end
```

Nonduplicated Lines (-u)

The nonduplicated lines option is -u. It suppresses the output of the duplicated lines and lists only the *unique lines in the file*. Its output is shown in Session 6.49. Compare it to the original file in Table 6.9.

SESSION 6.49   *Nonduplicated Lines*

```
$ uniq -u uniqFile
Not a duplicate--next duplicates first 5
5 completely duplicate lines
The next 3 lines are duplicate after char 5
abcde Duplicate to end
fghij Duplicate to end
klmno Duplicate to end
```

Only Duplicated Lines (-d)

The opposite of nonduplicated lines is to write only the duplicated lines. This option is –d. Its output is shown in Session 6.50.

SESSION 6.50   *Only Duplicated Lines*

```
$ uniq -d uniqFile
5 completely duplicate lines
Last 3 fields duplicate: one two three
```

Count Duplicate Lines (-c)

The count duplicates option (-c) writes all of the lines, suppressing the duplicates, with a count of the number of duplicates at the beginning of the line (Session 6.51).

SESSION 6.51   *Count Duplicated Lines*

```
$ uniq -c uniqFile
   5 5 completely duplicate lines
   1 Not a duplicate--next duplicates first 5
   1 5 completely duplicate lines
   3 Last 3 fields duplicate: one two three
   1 The next 3 lines are duplicate after char 5
```

Continued

SESSION 6.51 *Count Duplicated Lines—Continued*

```
1 abcde Duplicate to end
1 fghij Duplicate to end
1 klmno Duplicate to end
```

Skip Leading Fields

While the default compares the whole line to determine if two lines are duplicate, we can also specify where the compare is to begin. The skip duplicate fields option (-f) skips the number of fields specified starting at the beginning of the line and any spaces between them. Remember that a field is defined as a series of ASCII characters separated by either a space or by a tab. Two consecutive spaces would be two fields; that's the reason **uniq** skips leading spaces between fields.

In Session 6.52, we skip the first four fields. We combine it with the write-only duplicates option.

SESSION 6.52 *Skip Leading Fields*

```
$ uniq -d -f 4 uniqFile
5 completely duplicate lines
Last 3 fields duplicate: one two three
abcde Duplicate to end
```

Session 6.52 Analysis: The first duplicated line has only four fields. This example shows us that if only the newline is tested, then the line is automatically duplicated. In the second example, there are seven fields. The first four take us through the colon (:). The last three words are duplicated in each line. Finally, the last three lines again have only four fields and are printed because only the newline is compared.

Note that we code the duplicates only option and the skip leading fields option separately. That is, they are separated by a space, and each is prefaced with a minus. This is the correct way to code the statement.[5]

Skip Leading Characters

We can also specify the number of characters that are to be skipped before starting the compare. In the following example, note that the number of leading characters to be skipped is separated from the option (-s). This option is shown in Session 6.53.

SESSION 6.53 *Skip Leading Characters*

```
$ uniq -d -s 5 uniqFile
5 completely duplicate lines
Last 3 fields duplicate: one two three
abcde Duplicate to end
```

Table 6.10 summarizes the unique options discussed in this section.

---

[5]We can also code them with only one minus, but in this case, some UNIX versions require that the options and field count be run together, such as -df4.

TABLE 6.10 *Unique Options*

Option[a]	Code	Results
Unique	-u	Only unique lines are output.
Duplicate	-d	Only duplicate lines are output.
Count	-c	Outputs all lines with duplicate count.
Skip field	-f	Skips leading fields before duplicate test.
Skip characters	-s	Skips leading characters before duplicate test.

[a]Unique, duplicate, and count cannot be combined.

6.8 Count Characters, Words, or Lines

Many situations arise in which we need to know how many words or lines are in a file. Although not as common, there are also situations in which we need to know a character count. The UNIX word count utility handles these situations easily.

wc Command

The **wc** command counts the number of characters, words, and lines in one or more documents. The character count includes newlines (/n). Options can be used to limit the output to only one or two of the counts. The word count format is shown in Figure 6.19.

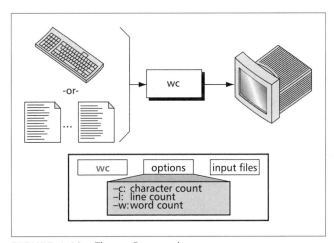

FIGURE 6.19 *The **wc** Command*

Session 6.54 demonstrates several common count combinations. The default is all three options (`clw`). If one option is specified, the other counts are not displayed. If two are specified, the third count is not displayed.

SESSION 6.54 *Common **wc** Combinations*

```
$ wc TheRaven
          116              994           5782 TheRaven
```
Continued

SESSION 6.54   *Common* **wc** *Combinations—Continued*

```
$ wc TheRaven uniqFile
          116             994           5782 TheRaven
           14              72            445 uniqFile
          130            1066           6227 total
$ wc -c TheRaven
         5782 TheRaven
$ wc -l TheRaven
          116 TheRaven
$ wc -cl TheRaven
          116            5782 TheRaven
```

Table 6.11 summarizes the **wc** options discussed in this section.

TABLE 6.11   *Word Count Options*

Option	Code	Results
Character count	-c	Counts characters in each file.
Line count	-l	Counts number of lines in each file.
Word count	-w	Counts number of words in each file.

6.9   Comparing Files

There are three UNIX commands that can be used to compare the contents of two files: compare (**cmp**), difference (**diff**), and common (**comm**).

Compare (cmp) Command

The **cmp** command examines two files byte by byte. The action it takes depends on the option code used. Its operation is shown in Figure 6.20.

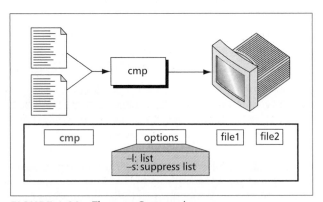

FIGURE 6.20   *The* **cmp** *Command*

cmp *without Options*

When the **cmp** command is executed without any options, it stops at the first byte that is different. The byte number of the first difference is reported. Session 6.55

demonstrates the basic operation, first with two identical files and then with different files.

SESSION 6.55 *The **cmp** Command without Options*

```
$ cat cmpFile1
123456
7890
$ cat cmpFile1.cpy
123456
7890
$ cmp cmpFile1 cmpFile1.cpy
$ cat cmpFile2
123456
as9u
$ cmp cmpFile1 cmpFile2
cmpFile1 cmpFile2 differ: char 8, line 2
```

Session 6.55 Analysis: We begin by displaying the contents of the files using the **cat** command so that you can verify the results. Note that when the files are identical, no message is displayed. When they are different, however, the location of the first difference is displayed. This message is shown on the last line of the session.

cmp *with List Option (*-l*)*

The list option displays all of the differences found in the files, byte by byte. A sample output is in Session 6.56. The file contents are displayed in Session 6.55.

SESSION 6.56 *The **cmp** Command with the List Option (*-l*)*

```
$ cmp -l cmpFile1 cmpFile2
    8   67 141
    9   70 163
   11   60 165
```

Session 6.56 Analysis: First, study the file displays in Session 6.55. The only differences are in byte 8 (7 versus a), byte 9 (8 versus s), and byte 11 (0 versus u). Each difference is displayed on a separate line followed by the octal value of the two characters. The character from the first file is listed first. Looking at the first line of output, the 8 indicates the eighth character. Remember that a newline is a character; therefore, the seventh character is the newline at the end of the first line, and the eighth character is the first character on the second line. The 67 is the octal value for the digit 7, and the 141 is the octal value for the character a.

cmp *with Suppress List Option (*-s*)*

The suppress list option (-s) is similar to the default except that no output is displayed. It is generally used when writing scripts.

   When no output is displayed, the results can be determined by testing the exit status. If the exit status is 0, the two files are identical. If it is 1, there is at least one byte that is different. We show both conditions in Session 6.57. To show the exit status, we use the **echo** command.

SESSION 6.57 *The **cmp** Command with the Suppress List Option (−s)*

```
$ cmp cmpFile1 cmpFile1.cpy
$ echo $?
0
$ cmp cmpFile1 cmpFile2
$ echo $?
1
```

Difference (diff) Command

The **diff** command shows the line-by-line differences between two files. The first file is compared to the second file. The differences are identified such that the first file could be modified to make it match the second file. The command format is presented in Figure 6.21.

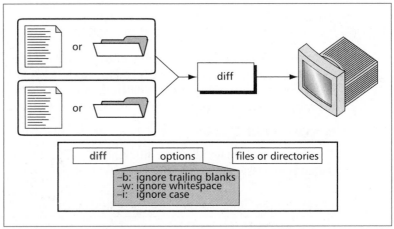

FIGURE 6.21 *The **diff** Command*

The **diff** command always works on files. The arguments can be two files, a file and a directory, or two directories. When one file and one directory are specified, the utility looks for a file with the same name in the specified directory. If two directories are provided, all files with matching names in each directory are used. Each difference is displayed using the following format:

```
range1 action range2
< text from file1
---
> text from file2
```

The first line defines what should be done at `range1` in `file1` (the file identified by the first argument) to make it match the lines at `range2` in `file2` (the file identified by the second argument). If the range spans multiple lines, there will be a text entry for each line in the specified range. The action can be change (`c`), append (`a`), or delete (`d`).

- Change (`c`) indicates what action should be taken to make `file1` the same as `file2`. Note that a change is a delete and replace. The line(s) in `range1` are replaced by the line(s) in `range2`.

- Append (a) indicates what lines need to be added to file1 to make it the same as file2. Appends can take place only at the end of file1; they occur only when file1 is shorter than file2.
- Delete (d) indicates what lines must be deleted from file1 to make it the same as file2. Deletes can occur only if file1 is longer than file2.

Table 6.12 contains an example of each action type.

TABLE 6.12 **diff** *Command Report Interpretation*

Example	Interpretation
6c6 < hello --- > greeting	Change: Replace line 6 in file1 with line 6 in file2. "Hello" in file1 should be changed to "Greeting."
25a26,27 > bye bye. > good bye.	Append: At the end of file1 (after line 25), insert lines 26 and 27 from file2. Note that for append, there is no separator (dash) line and no file1 (<) lines.
78,79d77 < line 78 text < line 79 text	Delete: The extra lines at the end of file1 should be deleted. The text of the lines to be deleted is shown. Note again that there is no separator line and, in this case, no file2 (>) lines.

Let's create three sessions to demonstrate each action. All three sessions use the files in Table 6.13.

TABLE 6.13 *Files (*diff1 *and* diff2*) for* **diff** *Command*

diff1	diff2
1 one same 2 two same 3 x and y 4 same 5 same 6 x 7 y 8 same	1 one same 2 two same 3 y and x 4 same 5 same 6 not x 7 not y 8 same 9 extra line 1 A extra line 2

The first session demonstrates the change action in the file. Remember that all changes are relative to file1 (diff1). That is, how must file1 be changed to make it match file2 (diff2)? The changes are demonstrated by lines 1 through 8 of the files. The output for the first eight lines is shown in Session 6.58.

SESSION 6.58 *Demonstration of the Change (c) and Append (a) Actions*

```
$ diff diff1 diff2
3c3
< 3 x and y
---
> 3 y and x
6,7c6,7
< 6 x
< 7 y
---
> 6 not x
> 7 not y
8a9,10
> 9 extra line 1
> A extra line 2
```

Session 6.58 Analysis: The first two lines of each file are identical, so no differences are indicated. The first difference noted (3c3) indicates that line 3 must be changed. The next line (< 3 x and y) displays the contents of line 3 on the first file. The three dashes on the next line indicate the end of the change range. The line following the dashes (> 3 y and x) displays the contents of file2. To change file1 to match file2, therefore, we would replace the contents of file1's third line (3 x and y) with the contents of file2's third line (3 y and x).

The second difference is found in lines 6 and 7. In this case, because multiple lines are different, the range is specified as a start and end position (6,7). After the range and action code, the lines for file1 are listed. Following the dash separation, the lines for file2 are listed.

There are two more lines in the second file than there are in the first file. They demonstrate the append action code. When the **diff** utility reaches the end of file1, all of the remaining lines in file2 are shown as lines that must be appended to file1 to make it the same as file2. This output is shown in the last three lines of Session 6.58. The insert position in file1 (after line 8) is specified as well as the contents of lines 9 and 10 in file2.

To demonstrate the delete action, we run the **diff** command again with the files reversed. Again, changes are noted for lines 3, 6, and 7, but this time the actions are reversed. When the second file (diff1) reaches the end of file, the remaining lines in the first file (diff2) are identified to be deleted. The results are in Session 6.59.

SESSION 6.59 *Demonstration of the Delete (d) Actions*

```
$ diff diff2 diff1
3c3
< 3 y and x
---
> 3 x and y
6,7c6,7
< 6 not x
< 7 not y
---
```

Continued

SESSION 6.59   *Demonstration of the Delete (d) Actions*

```
> 6 x
> 7 y
9,10d8
< 9 extra line 1
< A extra line 2
```

As a final example, we demonstrate the results when both arguments are directories. In this case, the differences between files with the same names in both directories are displayed (Session 6.60).

SESSION 6.60   *Directory Differences*

```
$ diff dir1 dir2
diff dir1/file1 dir2/file1
2c2
< 2
---
> 2 different
diff dir1/file2 dir2/file2
3a4
> D Extra line
```

Session 6.60 Analysis: The major difference between a directory and a file run is that the **diff** utility generates and displays a **diff** command for each set of matching filenames. In Session 6.60, there were two matching filenames.

Following the generated commands are the actions that must be taken. In our little test, only one action was required for each file. You should be able to interpret the action from our previous discussion.

Common (comm) Command

The **comm** command finds lines that are identical in two files. It compares the files line by line and displays the results in three columns. The left column contains unique lines in file 1; the center column contains unique lines in file 2; and the right column contains lines found in both files. The command format is shown in Figure 6.22.

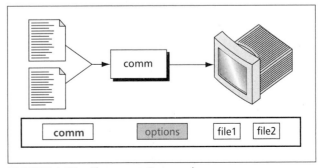

FIGURE 6.22   *The **comm** Command*

The files we use to demonstrate the **comm** command are in Table 6.14.

TABLE 6.14 *Files (*comm1 *and* comm2*) for* **comm** *Command*

comm1	comm2
`one same`	`one same`
`two same`	`two same`
`different comm1`	`different comm2`
`same at line 4`	`same at line 4`
`same at line 5`	`same at line 5`
`not in comm2`	
`same at line 7`	`same at line 7`
`same at line 8`	`same at line 8`
	`not in comm1`
`last line same`	`last line same`

The output from the **comm** utility for these two files is shown in Session 6.61.

SESSION 6.61 *The* **comm** *Command*

```
$ comm comm1 comm2
                one same
                two same
different comm1
        different comm2
                same at line 4
                same at line 5
not in comm2
                same at line 7
                same at line 8
        not in comm1
                last line same
```

6.10 Key Terms

catenate	filter	source string
destination string	leading characters	squeeze
fields	leading fields	translate

6.11 Tips

1. A filter can always receive its input from a keyboard.
2. A filter can always send its output to the monitor.
3. The input of a filter can be redirected from a file.
4. The output of a filter can be redirected to a file.
5. The **cat** command may be used to display a short text file.

6. The **cat** command may be used to create a short file.

7. Although the **head** and **tail** commands also can be used to create a file, **cat** is more commonly used.

8. When you use the **cat** (or **head** or **tail**) command to create a file, you must type ctrl+d at the end to terminate the file. It is typed as the only token at the beginning of the last line.

9. The **head** and the **tail** commands "cut" the file horizontally. The **cut** command "cuts" the file vertically—that is, in columns.

10. The **cat** command combines files vertically. The **paste** command combines files horizontally.

11. The default delimiter for the **cut** command is the tab; the default delimiter for the **sort** command is a space or a tab.

12. If you do not use the field specifier for the **sort** command, the whole line is sorted.

13. In **sort**, the field specifier defines how many fields should be skipped to get to the beginning or end of sort fields.

14. Multiple-field sorting sorts on adjacent fields; multiple-pass sorting sorts on two or more separated fields.

15. The **tr** command is unique among filters: It accepts input only from the keyboard (standard input). The only ways to translate a file are to use input redirection or a pipe:

```
tr …  file1           # wrong
tr … <file1           # correct: redirection
command | tr …        # correct: pipe
```

16. The **tr** command translation is character by character. You cannot change one word to another word.

17. The **wc** command includes the newline (\n) at the end of each line as a character. To exclude the newlines from the character count, you must subtract the number of lines from the character count.

6.12 Commands

The following commands were discussed in this chapter. For more details, see Appendix F and the corresponding pages shown in the following table.

Command	Description	Options	Page
cat	*Synopsis: cat [-options] [file-list]* Concatenates files. It may also be used to display files or create new files.	e, n, s, t, u, v	202
cmp	*Synopsis: cmp [-options] file1 file2* Determines if files are identical.	l, s	238
comm	*Synopsis: comm file1 file2* Displays common lines in two files.		243
cut	*Synopsis: cut [-options] [file-list]* Splits files into columns.	c, d, f, s	210

Continued

Command	Description	Options	Page
diff	*Synopsis:* *diff [-options] file1 file2* *diff [-options] file1 dir* *diff [-options] dir file2* *diff [-options] dir1 dir2* *Identifies differences between two files.*	`b, w, i`	240
head	*Synopsis:* *head [-options] [file-list]* Displays lines at the beginning of a file (default is 10 lines).	`-N`	207
paste	*Synopsis:* *paste [-options] [file-list]* Combines lines of files into one single line.	`d`	214

sort	*Synopsis:* *sort [-options] [field-specifiers] [file-list]*
	Sorts or merges files.
		`b, c,`
		`d, f,`
		`m, n,`
		`r, t,`
		`u`
			217

tail	*Synopsis:* *tail [-options] [file]*
	Displays lines at the end of a file (default is 10 lines).
		`-N, +N,`
		`b, c,`
		`l, r`
			208

tr	*Synopsis:* *tr [-options] [string1] [string2]* Translates (replaces) a set of characters (`string1`) with another set (`string2`).	`c, d, s`	230
uniq	*Synopsis:* *unique [-options] [input_file]* Displays the unique lines in a file.	`u, c, d`	233
wc	*Synopsis:* *wc [-options] [file-list]* Displays the number of lines, words, and characters in a file.	`c, l, w`	237

6.13 Summary

- A filter is any command that gets its input from standard input, manipulates the lines, and then sends them to standard output.
- In this chapter, we discuss the following filters: **cat, cmp, comm, cut, diff, head, paste, sort, tail, tr, uniq,** and **wc.**
- The **cat** command is used to concatenate multiple files into one file. It also can be used to display the contents of a file on the screen. With redirection, we can use the **cat** command to create a file, but it doesn't allow editing and should be used only when the file is small.
- The **head** command extracts a specified number of lines from the beginning of a file. The default is 10 lines.
- The **tail** command extracts a specified number of lines from the end of a file. The default is 10 lines.
- The **cut** command extracts one or more columns from a file.

- The **paste** command combines several files into one, where each file becomes a column in the new file.
- The **sort** command arranges data in ascending or descending order. It can sort data based on character-to-character comparison, numerically, and lexicographically (based on the dictionary). It can sort data on multiple (adjacent) fields or on separate (multiple-pass) fields.
- The **tr** command replaces each occurrence of a character with another character. After replacement, it can also eliminate (squeeze) duplicate adjacent characters.
- The **uniq** command deletes lines.
- The **wc** command counts the number of characters, words, and lines in a file.
- The **cmp** command determines if two files have identical contents.
- The **comm** command displays common lines in two files.
- The **diff** command identifies differences between two files.

6.14 Practice Set

Review Questions

1. Define a filter.
2. The input of a filter normally comes from _____. The output from a filter normally goes to _____.
3. List the filter utilities mentioned in this chapter.
4. Define the **cat** command. What is its general application? Can the input from the **cat** command come from the keyboard? From a file? From several files? Can the output of the **cat** command go to the monitor? To a file? To more than one file?
5. Define the **head** command. What is its general application? Can the input from the **head** command come from the keyboard? From a file? From several files? Can the output of the **head** command go to the monitor? To a file? To more than one file?
6. Define the **tail** command. What is its general application? Can the input from the **tail** command come from the keyboard? From a file? From several files? Can the output of the **tail** command go to the monitor? To a file? To more than one file?
7. Define the **cut** command. What is its general application? Can the input from the **cut** command come from the keyboard? From a file? From several files? Can the output of the **cut** command go to the monitor? To a file? To more than one file?
8. Define the **paste** command. What is its general application? Can the input from the **paste** command come from the keyboard? From a file? From several files? Can the output of the **paste** command go to the monitor? To a file? To more than one file?
9. Define the **sort** command. What is its general application? Can the input from the **sort** command come from the keyboard? From a file? From several files? Can the output of the **sort** command go to the monitor? To a file? To more than one file?
10. Define the **tr** command. What is its general application? Can the input from the **tr** command come from the keyboard? From a file? From several files? Can the output of the **tr** command go to the monitor? To a file? To more than one file?

11. Define the **uniq** command. What is its general application? Can the input from the **uniq** command come from the keyboard? From a file? From several files? Can the output of the **uniq** command go to the monitor? To a file? To more than one file?

12. Define the **wc** command. What is its general application? Can the input from the **wc** command come from the keyboard? From a file? From several files? Can the output of the **wc** command go to the monitor? To a file? To more than one file?

13. Compare and contrast the **paste** command and the **cat** command. That is, identify the similarities and the differences.

14. Compare and contrast the **head** and **tail** command and the **cut** command.

15. Compare and contrast the **cmp** command and the **comm** command.

16. Compare and contrast the **cmp** command and the **diff** command.

17. Compare and contrast the **comm** command and the **diff** command.

Exercises

18. Which of the following creates a file named `file1`?
    a. `cat file1`   c. `cat <file1`
    b. `cat > file1`   d. `cat >> file1`

19. Which of the following displays the contents of `file1`?
    a. `cat file1`   c. `cat <file1`
    b. `cat > file1`   d. `cat >> file1`

20. Which of the following copies `file1` to `file2`?
    a. `cat file1 file2`   c. `cat file1 > file2`
    b. `cat < file1 file2`   d. `cat 0<file1 2> file2`

21. In each of the following, what is the source of the input?
    a. `cat file1`   c. `cat > file1`
    b. `cat`   d. `cat 0<file1`

22. In each of the following, what is the destination of the output?
    a. `cat file1`   c. `cat < file1 file2`
    b. `cat`   d. `cat file1 file2`

23. Which of the following pair of commands are equivalent? If they are not equivalent, explain the difference.
    a. `cat file1; cat < file`
    b. `cat > file1 : cat file1`
    c. `cat > file1; cat >| file1`
    d. `cat > file2; cat < file1 > file2`

24. Explain the operation of each of the following commands. What is the source of its input? What is the destination of output?
    a. `cat`   c. `cat | more`
    b. `cat | lpr`   d. `cat | tee file1`

25. Find the error (if any) in each of the following commands (`file1` is a text file).
    a. `cat | date`   c. `cat | file1`
    b. `date | cat`   d. `date | cat | file1`

26. What is done by the following command?
    `date | cat file1 > file2`

27. What is done by the following command?
```
echo "Title: Report" | cat file1 > file2
```

28. What is done by the following command?
```
cat file1 - file2 > file3
```

29. What is the difference between the following three commands?
```
echo "Header"; cat file1 > file2
(echo "Header"; cat file1) > file2
echo "Header" | cat file1 > file2
```

30. If file1 has 100 lines, file2 has 50 lines, and file3 has 80 lines, how many lines will file3 have after each of the following commands (each command is independent)?
```
a. head -20 file1 > file3
b. tail +20 file1 > file3
c. tail -20 file1 >> file3
d. head -21 file1 | head -50 > file3
e. tail -20 file2 | head -40 > file3
```

31. Which of the following commands copies file1 to file2?
```
a. head -1 file1 > file2        c. tail -1 file1 > file2
b. head +1 file1 > file2        d. tail +1 file1 > file2
```

32. What is the result of each of the following commands?
```
a. head -1 file1                b. tail -1 file1
```

33. Using the **cat** command, write a single command to copy file1 to file2 (do not use the **cp** command).

34. Using the **head** command, write a single command to copy lines 1 to 20 of file1 to file2 (do not use the **cp** command).

35. If possible, using the **head** command, write a single command to copy lines 31 to 50 of file1 to file2 (do not use the **cp** command).

36. If possible, using the **tail** command, write a single command to copy lines 1 to 50 of file1 to file2 (do not use the **cp** command).

37. If possible, using the **tail** command, write a single command to copy lines 50 to last of file1 to file2 (do not use the **cp** command).

38. Using the **head** and **tail** commands, write a single command to copy lines 20 to 60 of file1 to file2.

39. Write a command to copy the first line of file1 to file2.

40. Write a command to copy the last line of file1 to file2.

41. Write a minimum number of commands to append lines 20 to 60 of file2 to lines 30 to 50 of file1. The result should be stored in file3.

42. Find the error (if any) in each of the following commands.
```
a. wc -c                        c. wc -n > file1
b. wc -f                        d. wc <file1 > file2
```

43. What is the difference between two commands in each pair?
```
a. wc file1; wc < file1
b. wc file1 file2; wc file2 file1
c. wc < file1 file2; wc file1 file2
```

44. What is the result of each command if `file1` has more than 20 lines?
    a. `head -20 file1 | tail +20 | wc -l`
    b. `head -20 file1 | tail +20 | wc -c`

45. Write a command to count the number of characters in the first line of a file.

46. Write a command to count the number of characters in the last line of a file.

47. Find the error (if any) in each of the following commands.
    a. `uniq -l`   c. `uniq -uc`
    b. `uniq -ud`   d. `uniq -s`

48. Find the error (if any) in each of the following commands.
    a. `uniq -d -f4`   c. `uniq -df4`
    b. `uniq -d4 -f`   d. `uniq -d4f`

49. Write a command to change all lowercase letters in a file to uppercase.

50. Write a command to change all uppercase letters in a file to lowercase.

51. A user wrote the following command to change every A to B and every B to A in a file.

    `tr "AB" "BA" < file1`

    Does it work? Explain why you believe it works or doesn't work.

52. What does the following command do?

    `tr "AB" "*?" < file1 | tr "*?" "BA"`

53. Can we use one single command to change all lowercase letters to uppercase and all uppercase to lowercase? If yes, what is it?

54. What does the following command do?

    `tr -s "[A-Za-z]" "[A-Za-z]" < file1`

55. What does the following command do?

    `tr -s "AB" "X"   < file1   |   tr "X"   "B"`

56. How can you create a file of 10 lines using the **head** command?

57. How can you create a file using the **tail** command?

58. Can you create a file using a **cut** command? If so, code an example.

59. Can you create a file using a **paste** command? If so, code an example.

60. Can you create a file using a **sort** command? If you can, is the file sorted?

61. Can we use a **sort** command to copy a file without actually sorting? If yes, code an example.

62. Prove that the **cat** utility is a filter (see Figure 6.2 on page 202) by using it in the following command. Then explain why the results demonstrate that it is a filter.

    ```
    cat file1 | cat | cat
    ```

63. Prove that the **head** utility is a filter (see Figure 6.2) by using it in the following command. Then explain why the results demonstrate that it is a filter.

    ```
    head -5 file1 | head -3 | head -2
    ```

64. Prove that the **tail** utility is a filter (see Figure 6.2) by using it in the following command. Then explain why the results demonstrate that it is a filter.

    ```
    tail -10 file1 | tail -5 | tail -3
    ```

65. Prove that the **cut** utility is a filter (see Figure 6.2) by using it in the following command. Then explain why the results demonstrate that it is a filter.

```
cut -f1,3 file1 | cut -f1,2 | cut  -f1
```

66. Prove that the **sort** utility is a filter (see Figure 6.2) by using it in the following command. Then explain why the results demonstrate that it is a filter.

```
sort -n +0 -1 file1 | sort -n +1 -2 | sort  -n +2 -3
```

67. Prove that the translate utility is a filter (see Figure 6.2) by using it in the following command. Then explain why the results demonstrate that it is a filter.

```
tr "l" "L" file1 | tr "i" "I" | tr "n" "N"
```

68. Prove that the **uniq** utility is a filter (see Figure 6.2) by using it in the following command. Then explain why the results demonstrate that it is a filter.

```
uniq file1 | uniq | uniq
```

69. Prove that the **wc** utility is a filter (see Figure 6.2) by using it in the following command. Then explain why the results demonstrate that it is a filter. Also explain why the result is always 1.

```
wc -l file1 | wc -l | wc -l
```

70. Compare the following three **cmp** commands and explain what they do.
    a. cmp file1 file2
    b. cmp - file2
    c. cmp file1 -

71. Which of the following commands is correct?
    a. cmp file1 file2 | file3
    b. cat file1 | cmp file2
    c. cat file1 | cmp -

72. Compare the following three **comm** commands and explain what they do.
    a. comm file1 file2
    b. comm - file2
    c. comm file1 -

73. Which of the following commands is correct?
    a. comm file1 file2 | file3
    b. comm file1 | cmp file2
    c. comm file1 | cmp -

74. Compare the following three **diff** commands and explain what they do.
    a. diff file1 file2
    b. diff - file2
    c. diff file1 -

75. Which of the following commands is correct?
    a. `diff file1 file2 | file3`
    b. `diff file1 | cmp file2`
    c. `diff file1 | cmp -`

6.15 Lab Sessions

Session I

1. Log into the system.
2. Use the **cat** command to create a file containing the following data. Call it `Ch6S1F1`. Use tabs to separate the fields.

1425	Juan	14.25
4321	George	21.11
6781	Anna	16.77
1451	Ben	21.77
2277	Tuan	18.77

3. Use the **cat** command to display the file and check for accuracy.
4. Use the **vi** command to correct any errors in the file.
5. Use the **sort** command to sort the file `Ch6S1F1` according to the first field. Call the sorted file `Ch6S1F1` (same name).
6. Print the file `Ch6S1F1`.
7. Use the **cut** and **paste** commands to swap fields 2 and 3 of `Ch6S1F1`. Call it `Ch6S1F1` (same name).
8. Print the new file `Ch6S1F1`.
9. Log out of the system.

Session II

1. Log into the system.
2. Use the **tail** command (you can do it, think about it) to create and save the following file. Call it `Ch6S2F1`.

```
PASSES ALL DATA FROM INPUT TO OUTPUT
PASSES ONLY SPECIFIED COLUMNS
PASSES NUMBER OF SPECIFIED LINES AT BEGINNING
COMBINES COLUMNS
ARRANGES DATA IN SEQUENCE
PASSES NUMBER OF SPECIFIED LINES AT THE END OF DATA
TRANSLATES ONE OR MORE CHARACTERS
DELETES DUPLICATE LINES
COUNTS CHARACTERS, WORDS, OR LINES
ABCDEFGHIJKLMNOPQRSTUVWXYZ
```

Continued

3. Use the **cat** command to view its contents.
4. Use **vi** to correct any errors.
5. Encrypt this file using the following steps:
   a. Reverse the file line by line (the last line becomes the first, the line before the last line becomes the second, and so on).
   b. Call the file `Ch6S2F1Encr`.
6. Use the **cat** command to view its contents.
7. Print the file.
8. Decrypt the file (reverse the encryption steps). Call it `Ch6S2F1` (original name).
9. Log out of the system.

Session III

1. Log into the system.
2. Use the **cat** command to create and save the following file. Call it `Ch6S3F1`.

```
ALPHABETICAL FACTS.
THE FIRST THREE LETTERS ARE ABC.
THE MEDIAN LETTERS ARE MN.
THE LAST THREE LETTERS ARE XYZ.
THE FIRST WORD IN MY DICTIONARY IS AAL.
THE LAST WORD IN MY DICTIONARY IS ZYTHUM.
THE QUICK BROWN FOX JUMPED OVER THE LAZY DOG.
THE LAST LETTER MAY BE PRONOUNCED ZEE OR ZED.
THE FIRST GREEK LETTER IS ALPHA.
THE LAST GREEK LETTER IS OMEGA.
```

3. Use the **cat** command to check the contents.
4. Use **vi** to correct any errors.
5. Print the file.
6. Using the translate command, encrypt this file by shifting each letter five characters to the end of the character set. For example, A becomes F, B becomes G, and so on. The end of the alphabet will wrap around. For example, Y becomes D and Z becomes E. Spaces and newlines would be preserved. This is called *Caesarian encryption* because it was invented by Julius Caesar. Call the encrypted file `Ch6S3F1Encr`.
7. Use the **cat** command to check the contents of the encrypted file.
8. Print the file.
9. Now use decryption (reverse strategy) to decrypt the file. Call the new file `Ch6S3F1` (original name).
10. Use the **cat** command to look at the contents of the file. Is it the same as the original file?
11. Print the file.
12. Log out of the system.

Session IV

1. Log into the system.
2. Use the **cat** command to create and save the following file. Do not type the headings. Call it Ch6S4F1.

ID	Hourly Rate	Hours Worked
1420	12.56	45
3456	14.56	22
2341	45.12	34
1122	23.56	28
1443	23.23	19
2351	67.90	56
8001	7.00	14

3. Use the **cat** command to check its contents.
4. Use **vi** to correct any errors.
5. Print the file.
6. Use a command to show the number of workers.
7. Use a command to sort the file based on id.
8. Use one single command to show the worker who is paid the highest hourly rate.
9. Use one single command to show the worker who worked more than anybody else. The command should show only the id of the worker.
10. Log out of the system.

Session V

1. Log into the system.
2. Use the **cat** command to copy file Ch6S4F1 and name it Ch6S5F1.
3. Use the **cat** command to create and save the following file. Do not type the headings. Call it Ch6S5F2.

ID	Hourly Rate	Hours Worked
1420	12.56	45
2456	14.56	22
2341	45.12	34
1322	23.56	28
1443	23.23	19
2351	67.90	56
3467	56.90	14

4. Use the **cat** command to check the contents of both files.
5. Use **vi** to correct any errors.
6. Print both files.
7. Sort each file using the file id as the sort key. Save the sorted files as separate files.

Continued

8. Use a command to merge two files created in step 7 on the id field. Call the new file Ch6S5F3.

9. Use a command to remove the duplicate from the file and save it without renaming it.

10. Print the file.

11. Log out of the system.

Session VI

1. Log into the system.

2. Use the **cat** command to create and save the following file. Do not type the headings. Call it Ch6S6F1.

Department	Course	Session	Enrollment
CIS	15	1	45
CIS	54	1	20
BUS	34	2	20
ENG	11	2	89
CIS	45	1	38
MTH	35	1	56
MTH	35	2	41
PE	17	2	25
CIS	54	2	67

3. Use the **cat** command to check the contents of the file.

4. Use **vi** to correct any errors.

5. Print the file.

6. Use one command to sort the file on department, course, and session. The resulting file should be ordered first by department; within equal departments, it should be ordered on course; and within equal courses, it should be ordered by session. Hint: use three field specifiers: department, course, and session.

7. Print the file.

8. Log out of the system.

Session VII

1. Log into the system.

2. Make a copy of /etc/passwd file and save it in a file called Ch6S7F1.

3. Use a command to count the number of users in this file. Make a note of it.

4. Cut the file so that each line has only two columns: login name (column 1) and user id (column 3). Call the new file Ch6S7F2.

5. Sort the file (Ch6S7F2) on login name without renaming it. Save the file.

6. Use the commands you have learned so far to reorganize the file Ch6S7F2 into six columns using the following format:

Name	id	Name	id	Name	id

Continued

Session VII —*Continued*

Note that you should divide the number of users by three to find out the number of lines in this new format. You should create three files and then paste them together vertically. Save the file under the name Ch6S7F3.

7. Print Ch6S7F3.

8. Log out of the system.

## CHAPTER 7

Communications

No company can exist today without quick and accurate communication among people working together. In this chapter, we discuss how UNIX can help facilitate communication among people.

UNIX provides a rather rich set of communications tools. We make no effort to cover all of them in this chapter. Rather, we provide a basic set and leave the exploration of its less used capabilities to you. Remember, there is a rich documentation facility at your fingertips that you can explore.

Even with all of its capabilities, if you use email extensively, you will most likely want to use a commercial product to handle your mail. The UNIX mail system is quite old; modern systems provide many support facilities such as filters to automatically sort your mail into directories or folders. Nonetheless, you could create much of the same capabilities using UNIX if you were to spend the time and energy writing the necessary scripts.

The utilities we discuss in this chapter are shown in Figure 7.1.

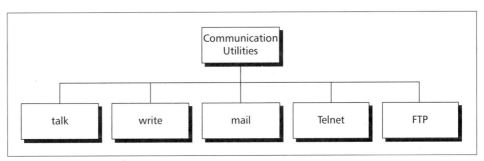

FIGURE 7.1 *Communication Utilities in UNIX*

7.1 User Communication

The first two communication utilities, **talk** and **write,** deal with communications between two users at different terminals.

talk Command

The **talk** command allows two UNIX users to chat with each other just like you might do on the phone except that you type rather than talk. When one user wants to talk to another, he or she simply types the command **talk** and the other person's login id. The command format is shown in Figure 7.2.

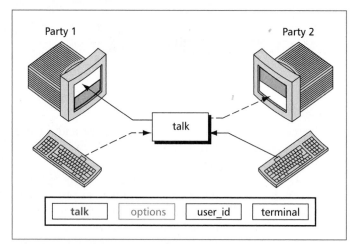

FIGURE 7.2   *The **talk** Command*

The conversation doesn't begin, however, until the called user answers. When you send a request to talk, the user you are calling gets a message saying that you want to talk. The message is shown here:

```
Message from Talk_Daemon@challenger at 18:07 ...
talk: connection requested by gilberg@challenger.atc.fhda.edu.
talk: respond with:  talk gilberg@challenger.atc.fhda.edu
```

If your friend doesn't want to talk, he or she can ignore the message, much like you don't have to answer the phone when it rings. However, UNIX is persistent. It will keep repeating the message so that the person you are calling has to respond. There are two possible responses. The first, which agrees to accept the call, is a corresponding **talk** command to connect to you. This response is seen in the third line of the preceding example. Note that all that is needed is the user id. The address, starting with the at sign (@) is not required if the person calling is on the same system.

To refuse to talk, the person being called must turn messages off. This is done with a message (**mesg**) command as shown here:

```
                              mesg n
```

The message command has one argument, either y, yes I want to receive messages, or n, no I don't want to receive messages. It is normally set to receive messages when you log into the system. Once you turn it off, it remains off until you turn it back on or restart. To turn it on, set it to yes as follows:

```
                              mesg y
```

To determine the current message status, key **mesg** with no parameters as in the next example. The response is either yes (y) or no (n).

```
$ mesg
is n
```

When you try to talk with someone who has messages turned off, you get the following message:

```
                    [Your party is refusing messages]
```

After you enter the talk response, the screen is split into two portions. In the upper portion, which represents your half of the conversation, you will see a message that the person you are calling is being notified that you want to talk. This message is:

```
                  [Waiting for your party to respond]
```

Once the connection has been made, you both see a message saying that the connection has been established. You can then begin talking. What you type is shown on the top half of your screen. Whatever you type is immediately shown in the bottom half of your friend's screen. Like the telephone, you can both talk (type) at the same time, but this is not a good idea. A complete talk session is shown in Figure 7.3.

Let's look at this session carefully. Tran's monitor display is on the left. Joan's is on the right. The figure starts just after Joan has acknowledged Tran's request for a talk session, and Tran begins typing his first message. As he types, each letter is immediately displayed in the lower portion of Joan's monitor display. If you look carefully, you will note that Tran is just typing a continuous stream of characters. Because **talk** does not wordwrap, the words at the end of the line are split. This makes them a little difficult to read. When using **talk,** you should treat your text like a typewriter and manually put breaks at the end of the line. Once UNIX moves to the next line, you cannot back up. The Delete key only works back to the beginning of a line. So you need to be careful and make sure that your line is okay before you key Enter, or UNIX automatically ends the line for you.

When Tran completes his message, Joan begins typing. Her reply is shown in the middle panel. Again, as she types, each letter is displayed in the lower half of Tran's monitor. Note that Joan does not allow a word to be split at the end of a line. She inserts breaks when she gets near the end of the line.

Now look at the third panel carefully. As Tran starts to type, there is not enough room left for his message. Therefore, the text wraps vertically, moving to the top of the monitor and deleting the text found there. You need to keep your current typing to 12 lines or fewer. Otherwise, you will be deleting the beginning of your message.

To complete the **talk** session, either party can enter the cancel command, ctrl+c. When you end the session, the text remains on the monitor, but you are no longer talking. You can recognize this because you see the command prompt token.

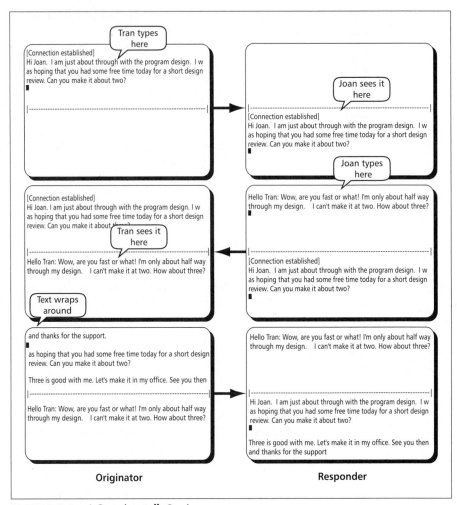

FIGURE 7.3 *A Complete **talk** Session*

> To refuse talk connections, use the **mesg** n command.
> To receive talk connections, use the **mesg** y command.

write Command

The **write** command is used to send a message to another terminal. Like **talk,** it requires that the receiving party be logged on. The major difference between **write** and **talk** is that **write** is a one-way transmission. There is no split screen, and the person you are communicating with does not see the message as it is being typed. Rather, it is sent one line at a time; that is, the text is collected until you key Enter, and then it is all sent at once. You can type as many lines as you need to complete your message. You terminate the message with either an end of file (`ctrl+d`) or a cancel command (ctrl+c). When you terminate the message, the recipient receives the last line and end of transmission (<EOT>) to indicate that the transmission is complete. The format for the **write** command appears in Figure 7.4.

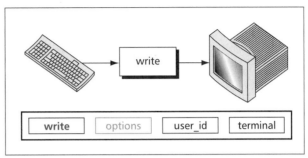

FIGURE 7.4 *The* **write** *Command*

When you write to another user, a message is sent telling him or her that you are about to send a message. A typical message follows. It shows the name of the sender, the system the message is coming from, the sender's terminal id, and the date and time.

```
Message from Joan on sys (ttyq1) [ Thu Apr  9 21:21:25 ]
```

Unless you are very quick, the user can quickly turn your message off by keying mesg n. When this happens, you get the following error when you try to send your message:

```
Can no longer write to /dev/ttyq2
```

If you try to write to a user who is not logged on, you get the following error message:

```
dick is not logged on.
```

Sometimes a user is logged on to more than one session. In this case, UNIX warns you that he or she is logged on multiple times and shows you all of the alternate sessions. A sample of this message is:

```
Joan is logged on more than one place.
You are connected to "ttyq1".
Other locations are:
        ttyq2
```

At this point, you should check to make sure that the person you are trying to send the message to is active on the terminal you are connected to. But you are in the middle of a message. If you try to do a **who** command, the command is sent to the other person rather than being recognized by UNIX. Fortunately, there is a way around this dilemma. If you start a line with a bang, such as !who, then **write** interprets it as a system command and passes it through to UNIX for execution. If you find that your friend is not active on the system you are connected to, you can then cancel the **write** and reissue it using the user id and terminal as shown here:

```
write Joan ttyq2
```

> To allow write messages, use the **mesg y** command.
> To prevent write messages, use the **mesg n** command.

7.2 Electronic Mail

Although **talk** and **write** are the fastest ways to communicate with someone who's online, it doesn't work if they're not logged on. Similarly, if you need to send a message to someone who's on a different operating system, they don't work.

There are many different email systems in use today. While UNIX does not have all of the capabilities of many of the shareware and commercial products, it does offer a good basic system. In this section, we discuss how to receive and send mail in UNIX.

A mail message is composed of two parts: the header and the body. The **body** contains the text of the message. The **header** consists of the subject, the addressees (To:), sender (From:), a list of open copy recipients (Cc:), and a list of blind copy recipients (Bcc:).

In addition to the four basic header entries, there are seven extended fields: (1) **Reply-To:** If you don't specify a reply-to address, your UNIX address will automatically be used. (2) **Return-Receipt-To:** If the addressee's mail system supports return receipts, a message will be sent to the address in return-receipt-to when the message is delivered to the addressee. (3) **In-Reply-To:** This is a text string that you may use to tell the user you are replying to a specific note. Only one line is allowed. It is displayed as header data when the addressee opens the mail. (4) **References:** When you want to put a reference, such as to a previous memo sent by the recipient, you can include a references field. (5) **Keywords:** Provides a list of keywords to the context of the message. (6) **Comments:** Allows you to place a comment at the beginning of the message. (7) **Encrypted:** Message is encrypted. All of these data print as a part of the header information at the top of the message.

A final word of caution on extended header information: Not all email systems support all of them. Generally, you can expect a UNIX system to at least print them out when the addressee opens the mail. Other systems may not.

Mail Addresses

Just as with snail mail, to send email to someone, you must know his or her address. When you send mail to people on your own system, their address is their user id. So,

Joan can send mail to Tran using his id, `tran`. This is possible because `tran` is a local user name, or alias, and UNIX knows the address for everyone on it.

To send mail to people on other systems, however, you need to know not only their local address (user id) but also their domain address. The local address and domain address are separated by an at sign (@) as shown in Figure 7.5.

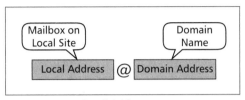

FIGURE 7.5 *Email Address*

Local Address

The local address identifies a specific user in a local mail system. It can be the user id, a login name, or an alias. All of them refer to the user mailbox in the directory system. The local address is created by the system administrator or the postmaster.[1]

Domain Address

The domain address is a hierarchical path with the highest level on the right and the lowest level on the left. There must be at least two levels in the domain address. The parts of the address are separated by dots (periods). The highest level is an Internet label.

When an organization or other entity joins the Internet, it selects its Internet label from one of two label designations: generic domain labels or country domain labels. Below the domain label, the organization (system administrator) controls the hierarchical breakdown, with each level referring to a physical or logical organization of computers or services under its control.

Generic Domains Most Internet domains are drawn from the generic domain levels, also known as top-level domains. These generic names represent the basic classification structure for the organizations in the grouping (Table 7.1).

TABLE 7.1 *Generic Internet Domain Labels (1989)*

Label	Description
com	Commercial (business) profit organizations
edu	Educational institutions (college or university)
gov	Government organizations at any level (such as federal, state, county, city)
int	International organizations

Continued

---

[1]In a large system, a separate administrator may be assigned to maintain the mail system. In this case, he or she is usually referred to as the postmaster.

TABLE 7.1   *Generic Internet Domain Labels (1989)—Continued*

Label	Description
mil	Military organizations
net	Network support organizations, such as Internet service providers (ISPs)
org	Nonprofit organizations

To better understand the hierarchical nature of the domain address, let's look at two addresses. At the time this text was written, they were valid addresses. Because systems (and their addresses) are constantly evolving within an organization, however, they may not be valid now.

1. saturn.deanza.fhda.edu

   From the domain label (edu), we determine that this address belongs to an educational institution. The second level (fhda) is an identifier for the specific educational institution, in this case the Foothill-De Anza College District. There are two colleges in the district. The third level (deanza) controls the routing for all systems and services for De Anza College. The lowest level in the address (saturn) identifies a specific computer or service. In this case, it is one of several post office systems on the campus.

2. www.whitehouse.gov

   This domain address is for the United States White House and all of its staff, including the president and the first lady. We know that it is a government organization from its domain label (gov). The second level of the address, created by a systems administrator with the federal government, is whitehouse. The lowest level of the address is a common designation for the World Wide Web and indicates that this site is primarily for Web pages, although you can send mail to the president from within it.

Because the Internet labels in Table 7.1 are becoming very crowded, an additional set of labels were approved by the Internet Corporation for Assigned Names and Numbers (ICANN) in November 2000. At the time this text was written, the implementation date was not set. We list them in Table 7.2.

TABLE 7.2   *New Generic Domain Levels (2001)*

Label	Description
aero	Airlines and aerospace companies
biz	Businesses or firms (similar to "com")
coop	Cooperative business organizations
info	Information service providers
museum	Museum and other nonprofit organizations
name	Personal names (individuals)
pro	Professional individuals and organizations

Country Domain In the country domain, the domain label is a two-character designation that identifies the country in which the organization resides. While the rest of the domain address varies, it often uses a governmental breakdown such as state and city. A typical country domain address might look like the following fictional address for an Internet provider in California:

```
yourInternet.ca.us
```

Mail Mode

When you enter the mail system, you are either in the send mode or the read mode. When you are in the send mode, you can switch to the read mode to process your incoming mail; likewise, when you are in the read mode, you can switch to the send mode to answer someone's mail. You can switch back and forward as often as necessary, but you can be in only one mode at a time. The basic mail system operation appears in Figure 7.6.

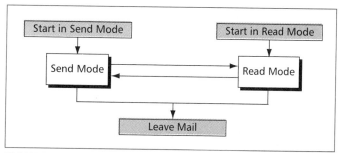

FIGURE 7.6 *The* **mail** *System*

mail Command

The **mail** command is used to both read and send mail. It contains a limited text editor for composing mail notes.

Send Mail

To send mail from the system prompt, you use the **mail** command with one or more addresses (Figure 7.7). When your message is complete, it is placed in the mail system spool where the email system can process it. If you are sending the message to more than one person, their names may be separated by commas or simply by spaces. Remember, if the person you are sending mail to is not on your system, you need to include the full email address. The last addressee in Figure 7.7 is a person on a different system.

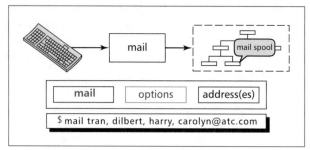

FIGURE 7.7 *The **mail** Command (Sending Mail)*

When you send mail, the system replies with a prompt that asks for a subject.[2] After you enter the subject, you can begin typing your message. An example of a send mail session is in Session 7.1.

SESSION 7.1 *Typical Send Mail Session*

```
$ mail tran, dilbert, harry, carolyn@atc.com
Subject: Project Review
There will be a project review in the blue conference room next
Wednesday at 10:00. We will discuss the system test plan.
Joan
```

The mail system provides a very limited text editor for you to write your note. It does not text wrap, and once you have gone to the next line, you cannot correct previous lines without invoking a text editor. If you are going to write a long message, therefore, you should use an editor. To invoke the editor, use the edit message command (~e). This will place you in your standard editor, such as **vi.** Once in the editor, you can use any of its features. When you are through composing or correcting your message, the standard save and exit command will take you back to your send mail session.

Send Mail Commands

The **mail** utility program allows you to enter mail commands as well as text. It assumes that you are entering text. To enter a **mail** command, you must be at the beginning of the line; a mail command in the middle of a line is considered text. When the first character you enter on the line is a tilde (~), the mail utility interprets the line as a command. This concept is presented in Figure 7.8.

In Figure 7.8, Joan makes a typing mistake and doesn't notice it until she is ready to send the message. Fortunately, there is a **mail** command to change the subject line. So she simply types ~s Lunch at the beginning of a line, and when Tran receives the message, it has a correct subject line. The complete list of send mail commands is seen in Table 7.3.

---

[2]There are many variations of UNIX mail. Your system may respond differently and may not have all the options discussed here. On the other hand, it may have more options because we are covering only the more common options.

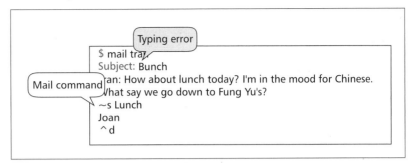

FIGURE 7.8 **mail** *Command Example*

TABLE 7.3 *Send Mail Commands*

Command	Action
~~	Quotes a single tilde.
~b users	Appends users to Bcc ("blind" cc) header field.
~c users	Appends users to Cc header field.
~cm text	Puts text in Comments header field.
~d	Reads in dead.letter.
~E or ~eh	Edits the entire message.
~e	Edits the message body.
~en text	Puts text in Encrypted header field.
~f messages	Reads in messages.
~H	Prompts for all possible header fields.
~h	Prompts for important header fields.
~irt text	Appends text to In-Response-To header field.
~k text	Appends text to Keywords header field.
~m messages	Reads in messages, right shifted by a tab.
~p	Prints the message buffer.
~q	Quits: Do not send.
~r file	Reads a file into the message buffer.
~rf text	Appends text to References header field.
~rr	Toggles Return-Receipt-To header field.
~rt users	Appends users to Reply-To header field.
~s text	Puts text in Subject header field.
~t users	Appends users to To header field.
~V or ~vh	Invokes display editor on the entire message.
~v	Invokes display editor on the message body.
~w file	Writes message onto file.

Continued

TABLE 7.3 *Send Mail Commands—Continued*

Command	Action
~?	Displays send mail commands.
~:command	Escapes to mail command line.
~!command	Invokes the shell.
~|command	Pipes the message through the command

Quit Mail and the Write Command

To quit the mail utility, you enter `ctrl+d`. If you are creating a message, it is automatically sent when you enter `ctrl+d`. If you are not ready to send the message and must still quit, you can save it in a file. To write the message to a file, you use the **write** command (~w). The name of the file follows the command, and once the file has been written, you exit the system using the **quit** command (~q) as shown in the next example:

```
~w noteToTran
q
```

To quit without saving the file, you use the quit command. In truth, the quit command saves your mail in a special dead-letter file known as `dead.letter`. You can retrieve[3] this file and continue working on it at a later date just like any other piece of mail you may have saved. Because the dead-letter file holds only one letter, however, you should always save a message you plan to finish to a specific file so you don't lose it accidentally.

Reloading Files: The Read File Command

There are two basic reasons for reading a file into a message. First, if you have saved a file and want to continue working on it, you must reload it to the send mail buffer. The second reason is to include a standard message or a copy of a note you received from someone else.

To copy a file into a note, open mail in the send mode as normal and then load the saved file using the read file command (~r). When you load the file, however, the file is not immediately loaded. Rather, the mail utility simply makes a note that the file is to be included. A typical example is in Session 7.2.

SESSION 7.2 *Copy File into Mail Buffer*

```
$ mail tran
Subject: Lunch
~r note-to-tran
"note-to-tran" 3/52
```

---

[3]Ask your system administrator for the exact location of your dead-letter file. The typical address is `~/dead.letter`.

To see the note and continue working on it, you use the print command (~p). This command reprints the mail buffer, expanding any files so that you can read their contents. If the first part of the message is okay, you can simply continue entering the text. If you want to revise any of your previous work, then you need to use an editor. To start an editor, use either the start editor (~e) or start **vi**[4] command (~v). The start editor command starts the editor designated for mail. You can ask the system administrator to designate your favorite editor for mail. If none is specified, **vi** is automatically used. When you close the editor, you are automatically back in the mail utility and can then send the message or continue entering more text.

Distribution Lists

Distribution lists are special mail files that can contain aliases for one or more mail addresses. For example, you can create a mail alias for a friend using only his or her first name. Then you don't need to key a long address that may contain a cryptic user id rather than a given name. Similarly, if you are working on a project with 15 others, you can create a mail distribution list and use it rather than typing everyone's address separately.

Distribution lists are kept in a special mail file known as .mailrc. Each entry in the distribution list file begins with "alias" and designates one or more mail addresses. Because all entries start with the word alias, they are known as alias entries. To add an alias entry to the distribution list, you must edit it and insert the alias line in the following format:

```
alias project joan jxc5936 tran bill@testing.atc.com
```

In this example, the alias name is "project." Within project, we have included four mail addresses. The first three are for people on our system as indicated by their local names. The last is for a person on a different system. Once an alias is set up, you use the alias name, and mail substitutes all of the addressees when the mail is sent. Be sure to test the alias with a test message before you rely on it. To test it, send a message with the alias and ask everyone to acknowledge that they received it. Session 7.3 demonstrates how to test an alias entry.

SESSION 7.3 *Testing an Alias List*

```
$ mail project
Subject: This is a test
Hi Everyone: I'm testing a project mail list. Please reply (r)
so that I know you received this test.
Thanks
```

If you have a long list that requires more than a single line to enter, it is a good idea to put each person on a separate line. When you create a multiple-line alias list, each line after the first must be a continuation of the previous line. To continue a line, use a

---

[4]**vi** is the standard UNIX editor. It is described in Chapters 2 and 8.

backslash (\) at the end of the line. Our project list is repeated with each person on a separate line. Note that all lines except the last end in a backslash.

```
alias project joan\
               jxc5936\
               tran\
               bill@testing.atc.com
```

Read Mode

The read mode is used to read your mail. Its operation is presented in Figure 7.9. Although the mail system is a standard utility, its implementation is anything but standard. For example, the **man** documentation indicates that messages are automatically read, starting with the latest message (last in, first out, or LIFO), when the mail is started. Many system administrators, however, prefer to present the user with a list of all messages at the start of the system. When you receive an account for a new system, therefore, you should ask the system administrator for documentation concerning the system's mail implementation.

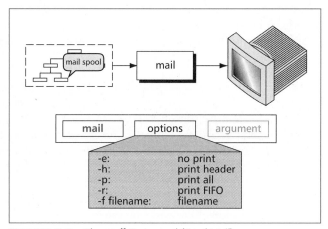

FIGURE 7.9   *The **mail** Command (Read Mail)*

You enter **mail** in the read mode by simply keying `mail` at the command line without any parameters (addresses). If you don't have any mail, a no-mail message is printed and you stay at the command line. A typical no-mail response is shown in Session 7.4.[5]

SESSION 7.4   *No-Mail Response*

```
$ mail
No mail for tran
```

---

[5]Once again, there are many variations on how the mail utility is implemented. Some implementations automatically print the first message. Our system automatically prints the header list.

Assuming you have mail, you will see a list of all mail currently in your system. A typical mail list is shown in Session 7.5.

SESSION 7.5 *Start of Read Mail Session*

```
$ mail
Mail version SGI.950426.  Type ? for help.
"/usr/mail/gilberg": 3 messages 1 new 1 unread
    1 <Joan>              Fri Jul 23 11:41   Project Review
 U  2 <tran>              Fri Jul 23 11:41   lunch
>N  3 <forouzan@fhda.edu> Fri Jul 23 11:44   Status Report
&
```

Let's look at the mail list a little more closely. The first line is a summary. It identifies the mail directory being used. It also indicates that there are currently three messages in the directory.

The list of mail follows. The first character of each line gives its status. A U indicates that the message is old (unopened) and has not been read. If the status is blank, the message has been read. The N on the third message indicates that it is the new message. Notice also that there is a greater than character before the N. This means that the mail pointer is at the third message. If you key Enter, message 3 will be displayed.

The last line starts with an ampersand (&). The ampersand is the read mail prompt. It indicates that you are reading mail and that you may enter any of the mail commands described in this section. For example, as we stated earlier, if you key Return, the next message in the mail list will be displayed.

You can also specify a specific message to be read. To read message 1, even though it had been read before, you would simply key 1 and Return. The following example shows message 1 as it is displayed:

```
& 1
Message 1:
From joan  Mon Jul 23 18:56:52 2001
Date: Mon, 23 Jul 2001 18:57:42 -0700 (PDT)
From: Joan Richardson <joan@project.atc.com>
To: gilberg@project.atc.com
Subject: Project Review
There will be a project review in the blue conference room next Wednesday
at 10:00. We will discuss the system test plan.
Joan
```

Reading New Mail

If you receive notice that mail has arrived while you are in the read mail mode, you will not be able to read it until you redisplay the mail list. If you use the headers command to reprint the list, you will still not see the new mail. To reprint the list with the new header, you must use the folder command (folder %) at the mail prompt. The folder command may be abbreviated `fo %`. Note, however, that this command has the same effect as quitting mail and reentering. For example, if you had deleted any mail, you will not be able to undelete it.

Replying to and Forwarding Mail

After you have read a piece of mail, you can reply to it. There are two reply commands. The first (R) replies only to the sender. The second (r) replies to the sender and all of the addressees. Since these two commands are so close, you want to get into the habit of reading the To list when you use reply.

When you use reply, you will see the header information for the To and Subject fields. If you want to add other header information, you must use the tilde commands described in Send Mail. (When you key Reply, you are immediately placed in the send mode.) A sample reply command is shown in Session 7.6.

SESSION 7.6 *Using the Mail Reply Command*

```
& r
To: joan
Subject: re: Project Review
```

There are a couple of points to note in Session 7.6. First, since we used the reply to sender only command, only joan is in the To field. You can add more addressees by using the append addressee list (~t) or the edit header list (~h) commands in Table 7.3 on page 267. Second, the subject is the subject of the mail you are replying to, prefixed by `re:`. If you want to change it, you can use the change subject (~s) or again the edit header list command. Finally, the cursor is on the first message line, ready for you to begin typing your message. When you are through, simply key `ctrl+d` to send the message.

Sometimes you need to forward mail to someone else for their information or action. There is no forward command in UNIX. However, we can achieve the same effect by using the send mail command (m) from the read mail prompt. To forward mail, you need to know the message number. You then enter the send mail command and load the message as in Session 7.7.

SESSION 7.7 *Forwarding a Message*

```
& m bill@testing.atc.com
Subject: Note from Tran
Bill: Here is a note from Tran with directions to his house.
==========
~m2
Interpolating: 2
(continue)
==========
Hope to see you there.
```

The send mail (~m) command reads a specified message into your new message. Once again, you note that it does not display the message in the buffer. If you need to read or change the message, you must use an editor as previously described. When the message is sent, the forwarded text will be indented one tab from the left margin. Nevertheless, we suggest that you adopt a clear style when forwarding messages. For example, first insert some text explaining why you are forwarding the message. Separate your text from the forwarded text with a double line (equal signs) or some other separation symbol. Then, copy the message using the ~m command. Finally, provide another separator so that the forwarded text is clearly set apart from adjacent text.

Quitting

Quit terminates mail. There are three ways to quit. From the read mail prompt, you can enter the quit command (q), the quit and do not delete command (x), or the end of transmission command (ctrl+d). All undeleted messages are saved in your mailbox file. Deleted messages, provided they weren't undeleted, are removed when you use quit (q) and end (ctrl+d); they are not deleted when you use do not delete (x). If new mail has arrived while you were in mail, an appropriate message is displayed. A summary message is also displayed listing how many messages are still in your mailbox. A typical end of mail message is:

```
New mail has arrived.
Held 6 messages in /var/spool/mail/tran
```

The held count does not include any new mail received while you were in mail. If three mail messages were received, there are nine messages in your mailbox.

Saving Messages

To keep your mail organized, you can save messages in different files. For example, all project messages can be saved in a project file, and all status reports can be kept in another file.

To save a message, use the save command (s or s#). The simple save command saves the current message in the designated file as in the following example:

```
s project
```

If the file, project in this example, doesn't exist, it will be created. If it does exist, the current message is appended to the end of the file.

An alternative to saving the message is to write it to a file. This is done with the write command (w), which also requires a file. The only difference between a save and a write is that the first header line in the mail is not written; the message body of each written message is appended to the specified file.

To read messages in a saved file, start mail with the file option on the command prompt as shown next. Note that there is no space between the option and the filename.

```
$ mail -fproject
```

Deleting and Undeleting Mail

Mail remains in your mailbox until you delete it.[6] There are three ways to delete mail. After you have read mail, you may simply key d at the mail prompt, and it is deleted. Actually, anytime you key d at the mail prompt, the current mail entry is deleted. After you read mail, the mail you just read remains the current mail entry until you move to another message.

If you are sure of the message number, you can use it with the delete command. For example, to delete message 5, simply key d5 at the mail prompt. You can also delete a range of messages by keying a range after the delete command. All three of these delete formats are shown here:

```
& d                        # Deletes current mail entry
& d5                       # Deletes entry 5 only
& d5..17                   # Deletes entries 5 through 17
```

You can **undelete** a message as long as you do it before you exit mail or use the folder command. To undelete a message, you use the undelete command (u) and the message number. To undelete message 5, key u5. You cannot undelete multiple messages with one command.

Read Mail Commands

The complete list of read mail commands is presented in Table 7.4.

TABLE 7.4 *Read Mail Commands*

Mail Command	Explanation
t <message list>	Types messages.
n	Goes to and types next message.
e <message list>	Edits messages.
d <message list>	Deletes messages.
folder % or fo %	Reprints mail list including any mail that arrived after start of read mail session. Has the effect of quitting read mail and reentering.
s <message list> file	Appends messages to file.
u <message list>	Undeletes messages.
R <message list>	Replies to message senders.
r <message list>	Replies to message senders and all recipients.
pre <message list>	Makes messages go back to incoming mail file.
m <user list>	Mails to specific users.
h <message list>	Prints out active message headers.

Continued

---

[6]Some systems delete mail as it is read, but keeping it is a safer practice.

TABLE 7.4 *Read Mail Commands*

Mail Command	Explanation
q	Quits, saving unresolved messages in mailbox.
x	Quits, do not remove from incoming mail file.
w <number> filename	Appends body of specified message number to filename.
!	Shell escape.
cd [directory]	Changes to directory or home if none given.

Read Mail Options

There are five read mail options of interest. They are shown in Figure 7.9 (page 270) and in Table 7.5.

TABLE 7.5 *Read Mail Command-Line Options*

Option	Usage
-e	Does not print messages when mail starts.
-h	Displays message header list and prompt for response on start.
-p	Prints all messages on start.
-r	Prints messages in first in, first out (FIFO) order.
-f file_name	Opens alternate mail file (file_name).

Mail Files

UNIX defines two sets of files for storing mail: arriving mail and read mail.

Arriving Mail Files

The system stores mail in a designated file when it arrives. The absolute path to the user's mail file is stored in the MAIL variable. As it arrives, incoming mail is appended to this file. A typical mail path is in the next example:

```
$ echo $MAIL
/usr/mail/forouzan
```

The mail utility checks the incoming mail file periodically. When it detects that new mail has arrived, it informs the user. The time between mail checks is determined by a system variable, MAILCHECK. The default period is 600 seconds (10 minutes). To change the time between mail checks, we assign a new value, in seconds, to MAILCHECK as follows:

```
$ MAILCHECK = 300                       # Check mail every five minutes
```

Read Mail File

When mail has been read, but not deleted, it is stored in the mbox file. As mail is read, it is deleted from the incoming mail file and moved to the mbox file. This file is normally stored in the user's home directory.

7.3 Remote Access

When you sit at your personal computer, you are working in your local environment. If from your personal computer you log into a computer located at another site, you are connecting remotely. UNIX uses the **telnet** utility for remote login.

The telnet Concept

The **telnet** utility is a TCP/IP[7] standard for the exchange of data between computer systems. The main task of **telnet** is to provide remote services for users. For example, we need to be able to run different application programs at a remote site and create results that can be transferred to our local site. One way to satisfy these demands is to create different client/server application programs for each desired service. Programs such as file transfer programs and email are already available. But it would be impossible to write a specific client/server program for each requirement.

The better solution is a general-purpose client/server program that lets a user access any application program on a remote computer; in other words, it allows the user to log into a remote computer. After logging on, a user can use the services available on the remote computer and transfer the results back to the local computer.

In this section, we discuss **telnet,** an abbreviation for **te**rminal **net**work. It is the standard Internet protocol and enables connection to a remote system so that the local terminal appears to be a terminal at the remote system site.

Time-Sharing Environment

Designed at a time when most operating systems, such as UNIX, were operating in a time-sharing environment, **telnet** is the standard under which Internet systems interconnect. In a time-sharing environment, a large computer supports multiple users. The interaction between a user and the computer occurs through a terminal, which is usually a combination of keyboard, monitor, and mouse. Our personal computer can simulate a terminal with a terminal emulator program.

Login

In a time-sharing environment, users are part of the system with some right to access resources. Each authorized user has an identification and probably a password. The user identification defines the user as part of the system. To access the system, the user logs into the system with a user id or login name. The system also facilitates password checking to prevent an unauthorized user from accessing the resources.

Local Login When we log into a local time-sharing system, it is called *local login.* As we type at a terminal or a workstation running a terminal emulator, the keystrokes

---

[7]Transmission Control Protocol and Internet Protocol (TCP/IP) are the standard protocols for the Internet.

are accepted by the terminal driver. The terminal driver passes the characters to the operating system. The operating system in turn interprets the combination of characters and invokes the desired application program or utility (Figure 7.10).

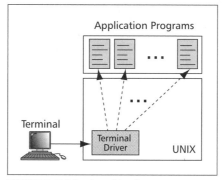

FIGURE 7.10 *Local Login*

Remote Login When we access an application program or utility located on a remote machine, we must still login, only this time it is a remote login. Here the telnet client and server programs come into use. We send the keystrokes to the terminal driver where the local (client) operating system accepts the characters but does not interpret them. The characters are sent to the client telnet interface, which transforms the characters to a universal character set called *network virtual terminal (NVT)* characters and then sends them to the server using the networking protocol's software (Figure 7.11).

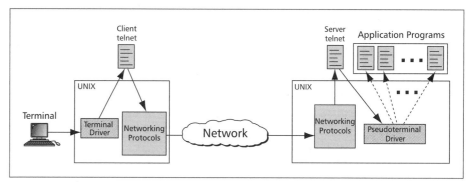

FIGURE 7.11 *Remote Login*

The commands or text, in NVT form, travel through the Internet and arrive at the remote system. Here the characters are delivered to the operating system and passed to the telnet server, which changes the characters to the corresponding characters understandable by the remote computer. However, the characters cannot be passed directly to the operating system because the remote operating system is not designed to receive characters from a telnet server: It is designed to receive characters from a terminal driver. The solution is to add a piece of software called a *pseudo-terminal driver,* which pretends that the characters are coming from a terminal. The operating system then passes the characters to the appropriate application program.

Connecting to the Remote Host

To connect to a remote system, we enter the **telnet** command at the command line. Once the command has been entered, we are in the **telnet** system as indicated by the **telnet** prompt. To connect to a remote system, we enter the domain address for the system. When the connection is made, the remote system presents its login message. After we log in, we can use the remote system as though it were in the same room. When we complete our processing, we log out and are returned to our local system. This process is shown in Session 7.8.

SESSION 7.8   *Using **telnet** to Connect to a Remote System*

```
$ telnet
telnet> open voyager.fhda.edu
Trying 255.27.191.3...

Connected to voyager.fhda.edu.
Escape character is '^]'.
•••
logout
Connection closed by foreign host.
$
```

There are several **telnet** subcommands available. The more common ones are listed in Table 7.6. To see the full set of commands, you can enter the help command (?) and **telnet** displays them.

TABLE 7.6   *Example of **telnet** Interface Commands*

Command	Meaning
open	Connects to a remote computer.
close	Closes the connection.
display	Shows the operating parameters.
mode	Changes to line mode or character mode.
set	Sets the operating parameters.
status	Displays the status information.
send	Sends special characters.
quit	Exits **telnet**
?	The help command. **telnet** displays its command list.

7.4 File Transfer

Whenever a file is transferred from a client to a server, a server to a client, or between two servers, a transfer utility is used. In UNIX, the ftp utility is used to transfer files.

The ftp Command

File Transfer Protocol (ftp) is a TCP/IP standard for copying a file from one computer to another. Transferring files from one computer to another is one of the most common tasks expected from a networking or internetworking environment.

The ftp protocol differs from other client-server applications in that it establishes two connections between the hosts. One connection is used for data transfer, the other for control information (commands and responses). Separation of commands and data transfer makes ftp more efficient. The control connection uses very simple rules of communication. We need to transfer only a line of command or a line of response at a time. The data connection, on the other hand, needs more complex rules due to the variety of data types transferred.

Figure 7.12 shows the basic ftp mode. The client has three components: user interface, client control process, and the client data transfer process. The server has two components: the server control process and the server data transfer process. The control connection is made between the control processes. The data connection is made between the data transfer processes.

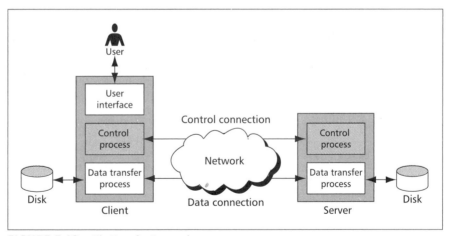

FIGURE 7.12   *File Transfer Protocol*

The control connection remains connected during the entire interactive ftp session. The data connection is opened and then closed for each file transferred. It opens each time a file transfer command is used, and it closes when the file has been transferred. In other words, when a user starts an ftp session, the control connection opens. While the control connection is open, the data connection can be opened and closed multiple times if several files are transferred.

Establishing ftp Connection

To establish an ftp connection, we enter the **ftp** command with the remote system domain name on the prompt line as shown in Session 7.9. The ellipsis on the third line represents login messages displayed by the remote system. After the connection has been made, the local system displays the ftp prompt and waits for a command.

SESSION 7.9 *Typical Connection Dialog*

```
$ ftp voyager.fhda.edu
Connected to voyager.fhda.edu.
...
220 voyager.fhda.edu FTP server ready.
Name (voyager:gilberg): gilberg
331 Password required for gilberg.
Password:
230 User gilberg logged in.
Remote system type is UNIX.
Using binary mode to transfer files.
ftp>
```

As an alternative, we can start the ftp session without naming the remote system. In this case, we must open the remote system to establish a connection. Within ftp, the open command requires the remote system domain name to make the connection. The same dialog as shown in Session 7.9 is displayed as the connection is made.

Closing an ftp Connection

At the end of the session, we must close the connection. The connection can be closed in two ways; to close the connection and terminate ftp, we use quit (Session 7.10). After the connection is terminated, we are in the command-line mode as indicated by the command prompt ($).

SESSION 7.10 *Terminate ftp Session*

```
ftp> quit
221 Goodbye.
$
```

To close the connection and leave ftp active so that we can connect to another system, we use close (Session 7.11). We verify that we are still in an ftp session by the ftp prompt. At this point, we could open a new connection.

SESSION 7.11 *Close ftp Session*

```
ftp> close
221 Goodbye.
ftp>
```

Transferring Files

Typically, files may be transferred from the local system to the remote system or from the remote system to the local system. Some systems only allow files to be copied from them; for security reasons, they do not allow files to be written to them.

There are two commands to transfer files: **get** and **put.** Both of these commands are made in reference to the local system. Therefore, **get** copies a file from the remote system to the local system, whereas **put** writes a file from the local system to the remote system. These commands are diagrammed in Figure 7.13.

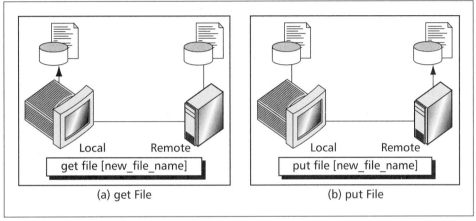

FIGURE 7.13 **get** *and* **put** *Commands*

When we ftp a file, we must either be in the correct directories or use a file path to locate and place the file. The directory can be changed on the remote system by using the change directory (**cd**) command within ftp.

There are several commands that let us change the remote file directory. For example, we can change a directory, create a directory, and remove a directory. We can also list the remote directory. These commands work just like their counterparts in UNIX. A complete list of ftp commands is shown in Table 7.7.

TABLE 7.7 *Complete* **ftp** *Command List*

!	debug	mdir	pwd	size
$	dir	mget	quit	status
account	direct	mkdir	quote	struct
append	disconnect	mls	recv	sunique
ascii	form	mode	reget	system
bell	get	modtime	rename	tenex
binary	glob	mput	reset	trace
bye	hash	newer	restart	type

Continued

TABLE 7.7 *Complete **ftp** Command List—Continued*

case	help	nlist	rhelp	umask
cd	idle	nmap	rmdir	user
cdup	image	ntrans	rstatus	verbose
chmod	lcd	open	runique	win
close	ls	prompt	send	?
cr	macdef	proxy	sendport	
delete	mdelete	put	site	

To display the **ftp** commands, use help (?). For a brief explanation of each command, use the help command followed by the command name. The **ftp** help command is demonstrated in Session 7.12. It shows the command with the first two lines and the next line of the display. It also shows the results for two individual commands.

SESSION 7.12 **ftp** *Help System*

```
ftp> ?
Commands may be abbreviated.  Commands are:
!            debug          mdir          put         size
$            dir            mget          pwd         status

...
delete       mdelete        sendport      site
ftp> ? ls
ls               list contents of remote directory
ftp> ? rmdir
rmdir            remove directory on the remote machine
```

When a file is transferred, its filename is unchanged unless a new filename is specified. To specify a new filename, we use the second command argument, new_file_name in Figure 7.13. If the filename already exists, it is overwritten with no warning.

CAUTION

If a file already exists, it is overwritten without a warning message.

7.5 Key Terms

alias mail list
country domain address
domain address
forwarding mail
generic domain address
local address

local host
local login
mail mode
pseudoterminal driver
read mail

remote host
remote login
replying to mail
send mail
terminal driver

7.6 Commands

The following commands were discussed in this chapter. For more details, see Appendix F and the corresponding pages shown in the following table.

Command	Description	Options	Page
ftp	*Synopsis:* *ftp domain_name* Transfers files to and from the remote computer defined by the argument (domain_name).		279
talk	*Synopsis:* *talk user-id [terminal]* Used to create a chatting environment between two users that are logged into the same or a different system.		257
telnet	*Synopsis:* *telnet* Connects the user to the remote computer defined by the argument (domain_name).		276
mail	*Synopsis:* *mail [receiver-list]* Used to read or send email. When it is used without argument, it is in the read mode. When an argument is used, it is in the send mode.		265
write	*Synopsis:* *write user-id [terminal]* Used to send a message to a receiver logged into the same or a different system from the sender.		260

7.7 Tips

1. Use **talk** and **write** commands if you are sure the other party has logged into the same system as you. You can always check the situation using the **who** command.
2. The **mesg** command is used to allow or disallow work interruptions by either **talk** or **write.**
3. The **mesg** command is a yes (y) or no (n) toggle switch. When it is set, it remains set until it is changed. Its default is yes (y).
4. You can set the **mesg** command in your login file to ensure that it is always set to your preference, either yes or no.
5. Incoming mail is automatically stored in your system mailbox.
6. Read mail is transferred to your private mailbox (mbox) when you quit the mail utility.
7. When you use the mail utility, you are in one of two modes: send or read.
8. In the send mode, every character you type becomes part of your message unless you precede the character with a tilde (~). If you want the tilde character to be part of the message, use two of them.
9. When you are in the read mode, every character you type is considered as a command.

10. When you are in the read mode, the reply commands (r and R) and the send mail command (m) move you to the send mode.

11. When you are in the send mode, the read messages command (~m) allows you to access mail you have received.

12. To include the contents of a file in your mail, you use the file read command (~r) or input redirection (<) to send the contents of a file to somebody.

13. To include the contents of another mail message in your outgoing mail, you use one of the read mail commands: read dead letter (~d), read message (~f), or read and shift to right (~m).

14. There is a standard reply command in mail (r). However, there is not a standard forward command. To forward mail, you must copy it into a new mail message.

15. When a message is not read, it is retained in the incoming mail file; when it is read (if not deleted), it is stored in the mbox file.

7.8 Summary

- UNIX provides a rich set of communication utilities. In this chapter, we discussed five of them: **talk, write, mail, telnet,** and **ftp.**

- The **talk** command allows two users to chat with each other just like on the phone except that they type rather than talk. The **talk** command is a two-way communication utility. Both parties can send and receive messages at the same time.

- When two users communicate with each other using the **talk** command, their monitor screens are divided into two halves. One half shows the message received; the other half shows the echo of the message sent.

- The **write** command is used to create one-way communication between two users that are logged into the same system.

- The **mail** command is used to send a message to another user. The mail utility operates in "store and forward" mode, which means that the receiver does not need to be logged in at the time the message arrives. The mail is stored in the receiver's mailbox and can be retrieved whenever the receiver is ready.

- The **mail** command uses one single command to send and read mail. However, to send mail, the user must be in the send mode; to read mail, the user must be in the read mode. A user can start in either mode and can move back and forth as necessary.

- There is no prompt in the send mode. Every character typed by the user is interpreted as part of the message. In the send mode, several subcommands are available. The send mode commands always start with a tilde (~) to tell the mail utility that the character typed is a command and not part of the message.

- The prompt in the read mode is the ampersand (&). Several subcommands can be used in the read mode. These commands are typed at the prompt and are interpreted only as commands because when reading mail we are not supposed to type messages.

- A mail address has two parts: a local part and a domain name separated by the at sign (@). The local part defines the receiver's mailbox. The domain name uniquely defines the destination mail server anywhere in the world.
- A domain name, which is made of two or more labels separated by dots, can either be generic domain or country domain.
- A generic domain uses one of the generic labels as the last entry. This label identifies the general area of the recipient's organizational activity or describes the recipient as an individual.
- A country domain uses a two-character label as the last label in the domain. This label defines the country in which the recipient's organization is located or registered.
- **telnet** (terminal network) is a utility that allows a user to log into a remote computer. Once logged in, the user has access to the remote host and can use all of the UNIX commands. However, the telnet command does not allow the user to transfer files between the local and remote computers.
- The **ftp** (File Transfer Protocol) is another utility that allows a user to access a remote host. However, unlike telnet, ftp allows the user to transfer files between the local and remote computers.

7.9 Practice Set

Review Questions

1. Name the five communication utilities discussed in this chapter.
2. Define the **talk** utility and describe its application.
3. Can **talk** be used between two users having accounts on different systems?
4. Can **talk** be used between two users if one of them is not logged onto the system?
5. How do you prevent **talk** sessions?
6. If you compare the talk utility with a telephone conversation between two parties, what is the simulation of dialing, ringing, conversing, and hanging up?
7. Is **talk** a two-way or one-way (at a time) communication utility?
8. Define the **write** utility and describe its application.
9. Can **write** be used between two users on different systems?
10. Can **write** be used to send a message to a user even if he or she is not logged onto the system?
11. Is **write** a one-way or two-way (at a time) communication utility?
12. What are the differences between **talk** and **write**?
13. Mention the main differences between **mail,** on one hand, and **talk** and **write,** on the other hand.
14. What are the parts of a mail message?
15. Define the header and the body of a mail message.

16. What is a **mail** (email) address?
17. A **mail** address is made of two parts: _____ and _____ separated by an _____ character.
18. What is a local address?
19. What is a domain address?
20. A domain address can be either _____ or _____.
21. List the original seven standard labels in a generic domain. List the labels approved in November 2000.
22. When the **mail** utility is used to read mail, does it need an argument? If yes, what is the argument?
23. When the **mail** utility is used to send mail, does it need an argument? If yes, what is the argument?
24. In **mail,** when we use a command in the _____ mode, the command must start with a _____.
25. In **mail,** when we are in the _____ mode, we can type a command without using a tilde (~) character.
26. Why do we need to precede a command with the tilde in the send mode, but we do not need to do so in the read mode?
27. Compare the read and send modes in **mail** with the text mode and command mode in **vi.** What are the similarities? What are the differences?
28. What is a distribution list and in which file is it kept?
29. How do you use the term "alias" in a distribution list?
30. How do you reply to mail in UNIX?
31. How do you forward mail in UNIX?
32. Define the **telnet** utility. What does **telnet** stand for? What is its application?
33. Why is **telnet** called a general-purpose client/server utility?
34. What is the difference between a local login and a remote login?
35. What is a terminal driver? What is a pseudoterminal driver?
36. What is an NVT character?
37. Define the **ftp** utility. What does **ftp** stand for? What is its application?
38. How many connections are established between two computers using the **ftp** utility?
39. The **ftp** utility uses two connections: _____ and _____.
40. When do we use each of the following utilities?

    a. **talk**   d. **telnet**
    b. **write**   e. **ftp**
    c. **mail**

Exercises

41. What is the **mail** utility's prompt in the send mode?
42. What is the **mail** utility's prompt in the read mode?
43. The **mail** utility tells you that you have 10 messages. If you want to read message 7, what is the command?

44. You have finished reading message 7 in the read mode. What is the command to go quickly to message 11?

45. You are in the read mode. You want to check the header of all messages. What is the command?

46. In the read mode, what is the command to delete messages 3 to 7?

47. You and seven other people have received a message. You want to send a reply only to the sender, but not to the other seven recipients. What is the command?

48. You and seven other people have received a message. You want to send a reply to the sender and to all seven people who received the original message. What is the command?

49. You have received a message that you would like to forward to a friend. What is the command?

50. What command or commands in the read mode take you to the send mode?

51. You are in the send mode and want to include the contents of a file in your message. What is the command?

52. You are in the send mode and want to add another recipient to your message. What is the command?

53. You have finished typing a message in the send mode. However, before sending, you want to save it in a file. What is the command?

54. Can you use the **vi** command when you are connected remotely to a computer using **telnet**?

55. Can you use the **vi** command when you are connected remotely to a computer using **ftp**?

7.10 Lab Sessions

Session 1

For this session, you should get permission from another student in your group to send him or her messages.

1. Log into the system.
2. Use the **mesg** command to allow receiving messages.
3. Ask a friend to use the **mesg** command to allow receiving messages.
4. Use the **talk** command to exchange messages.
5. Politely close the connection.
6. Use the **write** command to send a message to your friend. In the message, ask your friend to respond to you using the **write** command.
7. Do you need to close the connection in this case? Why or why not?
8. Log out of the system.

Session II

1. Log into the system.
2. Create a directory called `Ch7S2OutGoMail`.
3. Create a directory called `Ch7S2InComMail`.
4. Create a short email to yourself, but before sending it, save it in `Ch7S2OutGoMail`. The file should be called `OutMail1`.
5. Check to see if you have mail.
6. Read the mail that you sent to yourself and save it in `Ch7S2IncomMail`. Call it `InMail1`.
7. Exit **mail** using the `x` command.
8. Find the path of your mail file using the `MAIL` variable.
9. Display the content of your mail file using the **more** command. Do you see the mail you received?
10. Use the **mail** command to read your mail again.
11. Read the mail you sent to yourself.
12. Quit **mail** using the `q` command.
13. Display the contents of your **mail** file. Do you see the mail you received from yourself? If not, why not?
14. Find the path of your `mbox` file.
15. Check the contents of your `mbox` file. Do you see the mail you sent to yourself?
16. Print the contents of the following files and compare them.
    a. `OutMail1`
    b. `InMail1`
    c. The mail file (defined by the `MAIL` variable)
    d. `mbox`
17. Log out of the system.

Session III

In this session, assume that you are accessing your account on a remote computer.

1. Log into the system.
2. Use the **telnet** command to open a connection to your account.
3. Display the status information.
4. Check your working directory. You should be in your home directory.
5. Create a directory under your home directory and call it `MadeFromRemote`.
6. Use the **vi** editor to create a small file under this directory. Call the file `RemoteFile`.
7. Close the **telnet** connection.
8. Check your working directory. Are you in your home directory?
9. Check the existence of the directory `MadeFromRemote` and the file `RemoteFile`.

Continued

10. Was everything exactly the same as you would have done if you were not in **telnet**? What does this exercise demonstrate about the use of **telnet**?

11. Log out of the system.

Session IV

In this session, assume that you are accessing your account on a remote computer.

1. Log into the system.
2. Use a **cat** command to create a five-line file under your home directory. Call it LocalFile.
3. Establish an **ftp** connection to your account.
4. Use the **put** command to copy LocalFile from your local home directory to your remote home directory (it is the same as your local home directory, but we are pretending it's different). Call the file RemoteFile.
5. Use the **get** command to copy the RemoteFile from your remote home directory to your local home directory. Call it RemoteFileCopy.
6. Now use the appropriate command to delete the RemoteFile in your remote home directory. Remember, you are pretending that you have two home directories.
7. Close the **ftp** connection.
8. Check your current directory.
9. Verify the existence of RemoteFile, LocalFile, and RemoteFileCopy. Which ones actually exist? Explain why they exist or don't exist.
10. Explain what you have done by drawing two directory structures (one local and one remote) and show the movement of files between these two directories.
11. Log out of the system.

vi and ex

In Chapter 2, we introduced the basic elements of the **vi** editor. Because of its power, **vi** is the editor of choice among experienced UNIX users. Incorporated within **vi** as one integrated editor is the **ex** editor. The two are so tightly integrated that **vi** users switch back and forth between them within a session. Because of their seamless integration, many users don't realize they are separate utilities. Figure 8.1 presents the integration of **vi** and **ex** into one utility.

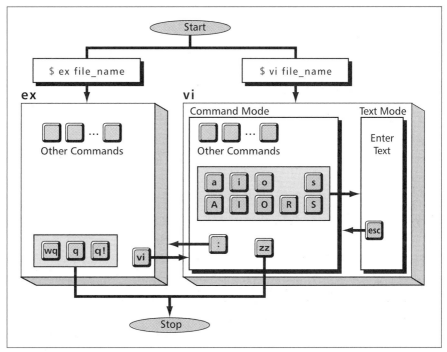

FIGURE 8.1   *The **vi** and **ex** Editors*

It is now time to expand the discussion.[1] We can enter either **ex** or **vi** directly from the shell. If we start in **ex,** we can switch to **vi.** Once in **vi,** however, we are always in a full screen editor. Whenever we need an **ex** command, we can switch back to **ex**'s command line without losing the full screen view of the text. To move from **vi** to **ex,** we use a colon. This **vi** command brings up the command line at the bottom of the

---

[1]Before you study this chapter, you may find it helpful to review Chapter 2.

screen. To return to **vi,** we use the Escape key. It switches us back to the **vi** command mode. When we are done, we can quit either from the **ex** command line or directly from **vi.**

There are three operating modes in **vi:** command, text, and **ex.** In the **command** mode, a powerful set of **vi** commands is available to move and make changes. In the **text** mode, the keyboard becomes the input through which we enter new text. Finally, the **ex** mode can be used to enter **ex** commands. The UNIX **man** documentation calls **ex** the **last line** mode; some texts call it the **external** mode. We use **ex** mode when we are entering commands because it is the most descriptive.

8.1   vi Editor

The **vi** editor is the interactive part of **vi/ex.** When initially entered, the text fills the buffer, and one screen is displayed. If the file is not large enough to fill the screen, the empty lines below text on the screen will be identified with a tilde (~) at the beginning of each line. The last line on the file is a **status line;** the status line is also used to enter **ex** commands (Figure 8.2).

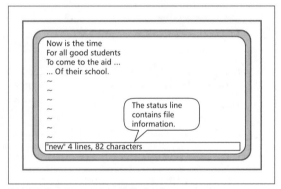

FIGURE 8.2   *A Small File in* **vi**

Commands

Commands are the basic editing tools in **vi.** In this section, we discuss some of their basic concepts.

As a general rule, commands are case sensitive. This means that a lowercase command and its corresponding uppercase command are different, although usually related. For example, the lowercase insert command (i) inserts before the cursor, whereas the uppercase insert command (I) inserts at the beginning of the line.

One of the things that most bothers new **vi** users is that the command is not seen. When we key the insert command, we are automatically in the insert mode, but there is no indication on the screen that anything has changed.[2] We simply know that the mode has changed, and we can now begin inserting text.

---

[2]We can customize **vi** to indicate the mode at the end of the status line.

Another problem for new users is that commands do not require a Return to operate. Generally, command keys are what are known as *hot keys,* which means that they are effective as soon as they are pressed. For example, if you key the insert command followed immediately by a Return, you will be in the insert mode, and a Return has been inserted into the document at the current cursor position.

Commands are case-sensitive hot keys that do not require a Return.

Command Categories

The commands in **vi** are divided into three separate categories: local commands, range commands, and global commands as shown in Figure 8.3. **Local commands** are applied to the text at the current cursor location. The **range commands** applied to blocks of text are known as text objects. **Global commands** are applied to all of the text in the whole buffer, as contrasted to the current window.

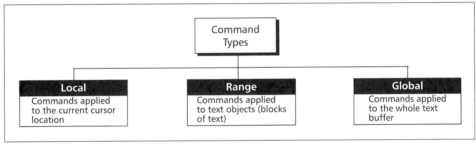

FIGURE 8.3   **vi** *Commands*

8.2 Local Commands in vi

Local commands are commands that are applied to the text relative to the cursor's current position. We call the character at the cursor the current character, and the line that contains the cursor is the current line. We discussed most of the local commands in Chapter 2 and review them here.

Insert Text Commands (i, I)

We can insert text before the current position or at the beginning of the current line. The lowercase insert command (i) changes to the text mode. We can then enter text. The character at the cursor is pushed down the line as the new text is inserted. When we are through entering text, we return to the command mode by keying esc. The uppercase insert command (I) opens the beginning of the current line for inserting text. Figure 8.4 shows two examples of character insertion. In this and the following examples, the cursor is shown as white text on a black background.

Append Text Commands (a, A)

The basic concept behind all append commands is to add text after a specified location. In **vi,** we can append after the current character (a) or after the current line (A). As with the

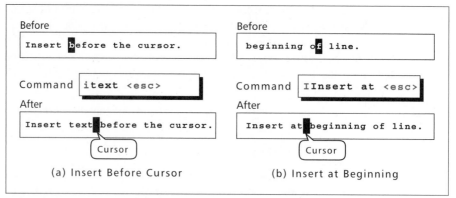

FIGURE 8.4   *Insert Text at Current Character/Line*

insert command, we need to key Escape to return to the command mode. Figure 8.5 demonstrates the append command. As you study the figure, note that there is a space after the command, whereas in Figure 8.4, the space is at the end of the command. Make sure that you understand why one time the space is at the beginning and one time it is at the end.

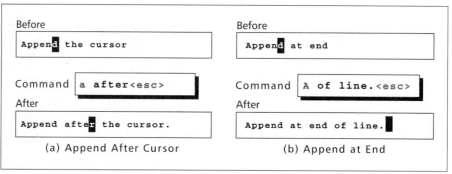

FIGURE 8.5   *Append Text after Current Character/Line*

Newline Commands (o, O)

The newline command creates an open line in the text file and inserts the text provided with the command. Like insert and append, after entering the text, we must use the Escape key to return to the command mode. To add text in a new line below the current line, use the lowercase newline command (o) . To add the new text in a line above the current line, use the uppercase newline command (O). Figure 8.6 demonstrates these commands.

Replace Text Commands (r, R)

When we replace text, we can only change text in the document. We cannot insert new text nor can we delete old text. The lowercase replace command (r) replaces a single character with another character and immediately returns to the command mode. It is not necessary to use the Escape key. With the uppercase replace command (R), on the other hand, we can replace as many characters as necessary. Every keystroke will

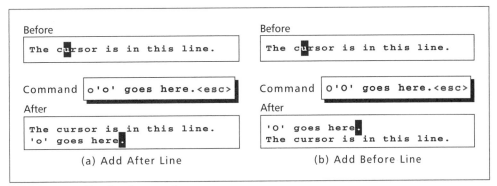

FIGURE 8.6 *Newline Commands*

replace one character in the file. To return to the command mode in this case, we need to use the Escape key. At the end of both commands, the cursor is on the last character replaced. Figure 8.7 demonstrates the replace commands.

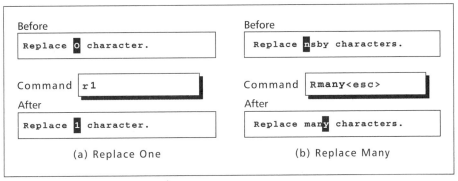

FIGURE 8.7 *Replace Commands*

Substitute Text Commands (s, S)

Whereas the replace text command is limited to the current characters in the file, the lowercase substitute command (s) replaces one character with one or more characters. It is especially useful to correct spelling errors. The uppercase substitute command (S) replaces the entire current line with new text. Both substitute commands require an Escape to return to the command mode. Figure 8.8 demonstrates the substitute commands.

Delete Character Commands (x, X)

The delete character command deletes the current character or the character before the current character. To delete the current character, use the lowercase delete command (x). To delete the character before the cursor, use the uppercase delete command (X). After the character has been deleted, we are still in the command mode, so no Escape is necessary. The delete character commands are shown in Figure 8.9. In these examples, we use four commands to delete four characters.

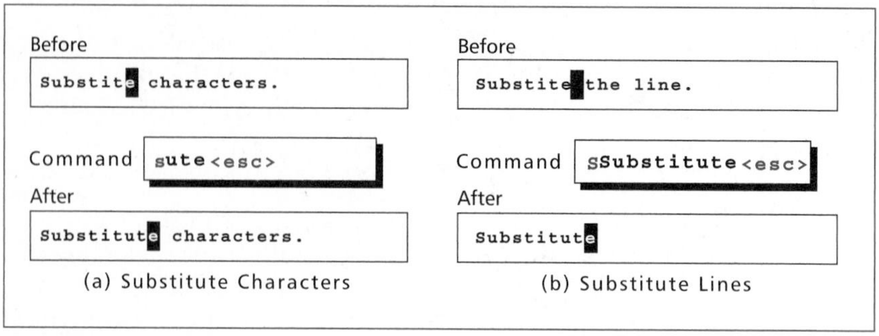

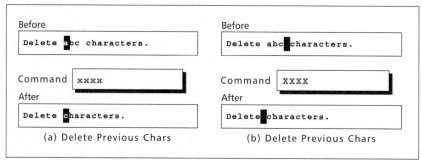

FIGURE 8.8 *Substitute Commands*

FIGURE 8.9 *Delete Character Commands*

Mark Text Command (m)

Marking text places an electronic "finger" in the text so that we can return to it whenever we need to. It is used primarily to mark a position to be used later with a range command. The mark command (m) requires a letter that becomes the name of the marked location. The letter is invisible and can be seen only by **vi.** Marked locations in the file are erased when the file is closed; they are valid only for the current session and are not permanent locations. In Figure 8.10, the location of the s mark is shown.

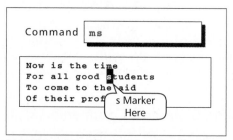

FIGURE 8.10 *The Mark Location Command*

Change Case Command (~)

The change case command is the tilde (~). It changes the current character from upper- to lowercase or from lower- to uppercase. Only one character can be changed at a time, but the cursor location is advanced so that multiple characters can easily be changed. It can also be used with the repeat modifier to change the case of multiple characters as shown in Figure 8.11(b). Nonalphabetic characters are unaffected by the command. Figure 8.11 demonstrates the change case command.

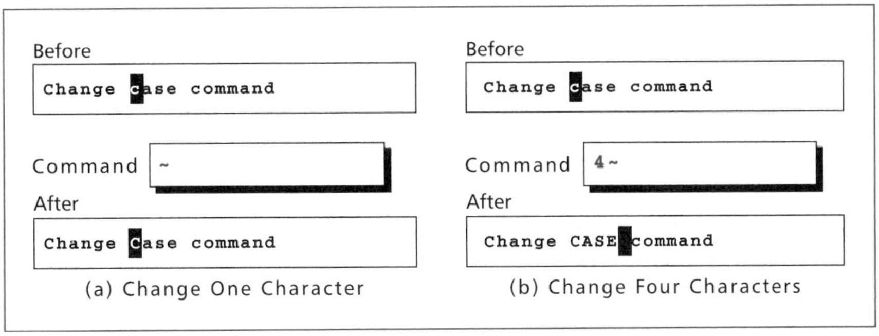

FIGURE 8.11   *The Change Case Command*

This is the first time that we have used the repeat modifier. In Figure 8.11(b), note that there is a numeric 4 before the command. It is a repeat modifier and simply indicates that the command is to be repeated four times.

Put Commands (p, P)

In a word processor, the put command would be called "paste." As with many other commands, there are two versions, a lowercase p and an uppercase P. The lowercase put copies the contents of the temporary buffer after the cursor position. The uppercase put copies the buffer before the cursor.

The exact placement of the text depends on the type of data in the buffer. If the buffer contains a character or a word, the buffer contents are placed before or after the cursor in the current line. If the buffer contains a line, sentence, or paragraph, it is placed on the previous line or the next line. The put command operation is shown in Figure 8.12.

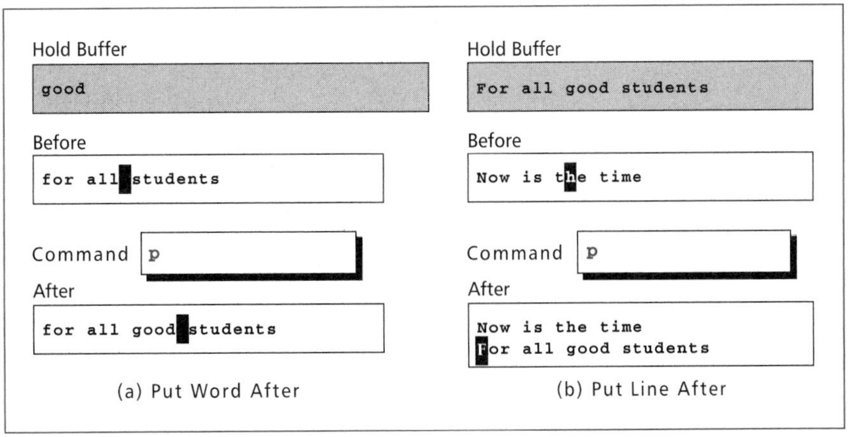

FIGURE 8.12   *Put Commands*

Join Command (J)

Two lines can be combined using the join command (J). The command can be used anywhere in the first line. After the two lines have been joined, the cursor will be at the end of the first line. The join command is shown in Figure 8.13.

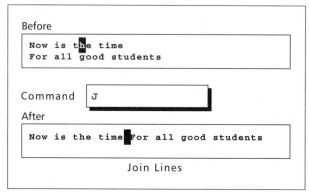

FIGURE 8.13   *The Join Command*

Local Command Summary

A summary of the local commands is shown in Table 8.1.

TABLE 8.1   *Local Command Summary*

Command	Explanation
i I	Inserts text before the current character. Inserts text at the beginning of the current line.
a A	Appends text after the current character. Appends text at the end of the current line.
o O	Opens (inserts) a line under the current line and inserts supplied text in it. Opens (inserts) a line above the current line and inserts supplied text in it.
r R	Replaces the current character at the cursor with the new one. Replaces a set of characters with the new set of characters.
s S	Substitutes the current character with the supplied text. Substitutes the current line with the supplied text.
p P	Puts the deleted (or yanked) text after the current character. Puts the deleted (or yanked) text before the current character.
x X	Deletes the current character. Deletes the character before the cursor.
m ~ J	Marks the current character with an invisible character. Changes the case of the current character (alphabetic characters only). Joins two lines.

8.3 Range Commands in vi

A **range command** operates on a text object. The **vi** editor considers the whole buffer as a long stream of characters of which only a portion may be visible in the screen window (see Figure 8.2 on page 292). Because range commands can have targets that are above or below the current window, they can affect unseen text and must be used with great care.

There are four range commands in **vi**: move cursor, delete, change, and yank. The object of each command is a text object and defines the scope of the command. Because the range commands operate on text objects, we begin our discussion of range commands with text objects.

Text Object

A **text object** is a section of text between two points: the cursor and a target. The object can extend from the cursor back toward the beginning of the document or forward toward the end of the document. The target is a designator that identifies the end of the object being defined. We discuss the targets for each command later in this chapter. The concept is presented in Figure 8.14.

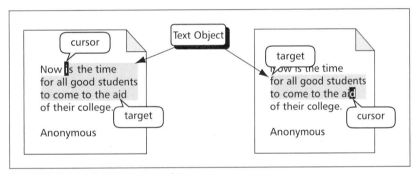

FIGURE 8.14   *Range Command Scope*

The object definitions follow a general pattern. When the object is defined before the cursor, it starts with the character to the left of the cursor and extends to the beginning of the object. When the object is defined after the cursor, it begins with the cursor character and extends to the end of the object.

Object Ranges
- To left: Starts with character on left of cursor to the beginning of the range.
- To right: Starts with cursor character to the end of range.

There are seven general classes of objects: character, word, sentence, line, paragraph, block, and file. All text objects start with the cursor.

Character Object

A character object consists of only one character. This means that the beginning and end of the object are the same. To target the character immediately before the cursor, we use the designator h. To target the current character, we use the designator 1. Figure 8.15 shows the two character objects. The cursor is on the character r.

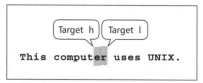

FIGURE 8.15 *Character Objects*

Word Object

A word is defined as a series of nonwhitespace characters terminated by a whitespace character.[3] A word object may be a whole word or a part of a word depending on the current character location (cursor) and the object designator. There are three word designators: The designator b means to go backward to the beginning of the current word; if the cursor is at the beginning of the current word, it moves to the beginning of the previous word. The designator w means to go forward to the beginning of the next word, including the space between the words if any. And the designator e means to go forward to the end of the current word; it does not include the space. These three designations appear in Figure 8.16.

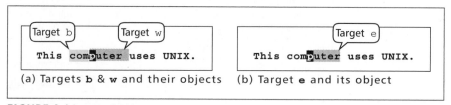

FIGURE 8.16 *Word Objects*

Line Object

A line is all of the text beginning with the first character after a newline to the next newline. A line object may consist of one or more lines. There are six line designators: To target the beginning of the current line, use 0 (zero). To target the end of the line, use $. To target the beginning of the line above the current line, use – (minus). To target the beginning of the next line, use +. To target the character immediately above the current character, use k.[4] To target the character immediately below the current character, use j. The line designators are presented in Figure 8.17.

---

[3]**vi** defines two word types: big word and small word. At this level, it is more confusing than helpful. Suffice it to say that our definition is consistent with the definition of big word.

[4]Note, however, that if a line operator is used with the j and k designators, the operation is performed on the whole line.

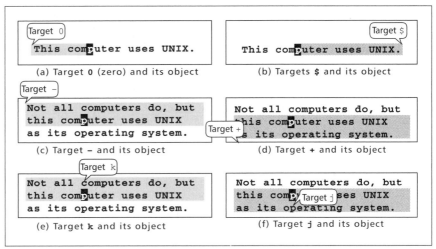

FIGURE 8.17 *Line Objects*

Target 0 (Zero) Target **0**'s range is from the current character to the beginning of the current line (Figure 8.17a).

***Target $*** Target **$**'s range is from the current cursor to the end of the line (Figure 8.17b).

Target – Target **–**'s range is from the current character to the beginning of the line above the current line (Figure 8.17c). As a move command, it moves the cursor to the beginning of the line above the current line. For all other commands, it selects the current line and the line above the current line.

Target + Target **+**'s range is from the current character to the end of the line below the current line (Figure 8.17d). As a move command, it moves the cursor to the beginning of the line below the current line. For all other commands, it selects the current line and the line below the current line.

Target k Target k's range is from the current character to the beginning of the line above the current line (Figure 8.17e). As a move command, it moves the cursor to the character immediately above it. For all other commands, it selects the current line and the line above the current line.

Target j Target j's range is from the current character to the end of the line below the current line (Figure 8.17f). As a move command, it moves the cursor to the character immediately below it. For all other commands, it selects the current line and the line below the current line.

Sentence Object

A sentence is a range of text that ends in a period or a question mark followed by two spaces or a newline. This means that there can be many lines in one sentence or, conversely, that there can be many English sentences in one UNIX sentence if they have only one space after the period. A sentence designator defines a sentence or a part of a sentence as an object. The two sentence designators appear in Figure 8.18.

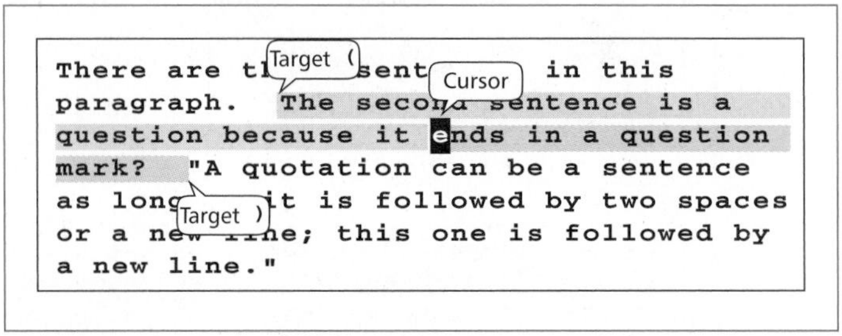

FIGURE 8.18   *Sentence Objects*

To remember the sentence targets, just think of a sentence enclosed in parentheses. The open parenthesis is found at the beginning of the sentence; it selects the text from the character immediately before the cursor to the beginning of the sentence. The close parenthesis selects the text beginning from and including the cursor to the end of the sentence, which includes the two spaces that delimit it. Both sentence objects work consistently with all operations.

Paragraph Object

A paragraph is a range of text starting with the first character in the file buffer or the first character after a blank line (a line consisting only of a newline) to the next blank line or the end of the buffer. Paragraphs may contain one or more sentences. The two designators in Figure 8.19 define a paragraph or a part of a paragraph as objects.

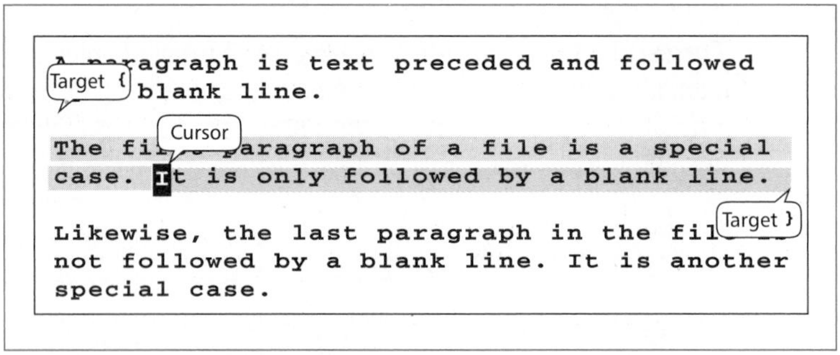

FIGURE 8.19   *Paragraph Objects*

To remember the paragraph targets, think of them as enclosed in braces, which are bigger than parentheses. The left brace targets the beginning of the paragraph, including the blank line above it. The right brace targets the end of the paragraph but does not include the blank line.

Block Object

A block is a range of text identified by a marker. It is the largest range object and can span multiple sentences and paragraphs. In fact, it can be used to span the entire file.

The two block designators in Figure 8.20 define block objects. To review setting markers, refer to Mark Text (page 296).

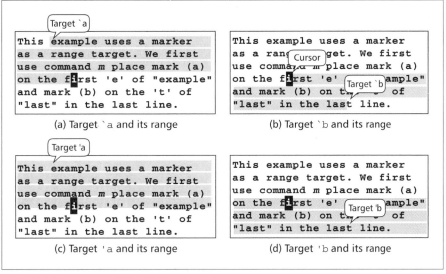

FIGURE 8.20   *Block Objects*

Screen Objects

We can define part of the text or the whole screen as a screen object. There are three simple screen cursor moves:

> H: Moves the cursor to the beginning of the text line at the top of the screen.
> L: Moves the cursor to the beginning of the text line at the bottom of the screen.
> M: Moves the cursor to the beginning of the line at the middle of the screen.

File Object

There is one more target, the file. To move to the beginning of the last line in the file object, or to create a range using it, use the designator G.

Summary

An analysis of the operations using objects discloses some general rules that help us remember how they work.

1. When a text object is from the current character forward to the target:
   a. The current character is included in the text object.
   b. The target is included if it defines the end of the object; the whole line is included for targets +, j, G, and marker.
2. When a text object is from the current character backward to the target:
   a. The current character is not included in the text object.
   b. The target is included if it defines the beginning of the object; the whole line is included for targets −, k, G, and marker.

Table 8.2 summarizes the range commands.

TABLE 8.2   *Range Object Summary*

Object	Designator	Description
Character	h l	Character before cursor Character after cursor
Line	0, $ -, + k, j	Beginning and end of current line, respectively Beginning of line above or line below, respectively Line above and line below, respectively
Word	b w e	Beginning of word backward Beginning of next word forward End of word forward
Sentence	(,)	Beginning and end of sentence, respectively
Paragraph	{ , }	Beginning and end of paragraph, respectively
Block	`x 'x	Character designated by marker x Beginning of line designated by marker x
Screen	H, L, M	Beginning of top, bottom, or middle line, respectively
File	G	Beginning of last line in file

Text Object Commands

Four **vi** commands are used with text objects: move cursor, delete, change, and yank (Figure 8.21).

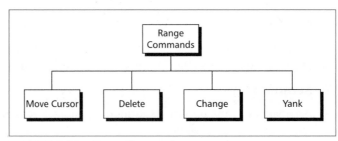

FIGURE 8.21   *Range Commands*

The range commands share a common syntactical format that includes the command and three modifiers. The format is shown in Figure 8.22.

The only required element is the text object. The repeat commands are option and modify the command and text objects, respectively. We discuss them individually as we discuss the following commands. When no command is entered, the cursor is moved as indicated by the text object.

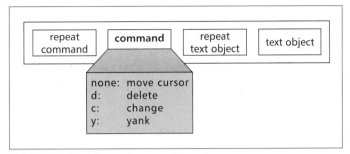

FIGURE 8.22 *Range Command Format*

Move Cursor

As we have indicated, the move command is nothing. This means that when we only enter an object, we want to move the cursor. This is a very convenient format that allows us to use the objects as seen in the previous section as move commands. Because the move command is nothing, only repeat text object can be used.

The effect of the move command with different objects is shown in Session 8.1. You may find it helpful to refer to figures in the previous section if necessary.

SESSION 8.1 *Move Cursor Examples*

```
h                       # move to previous character
4h                      # move to fourth character backward
l                       # move to next character (forward)
2l                      # move two characters forward
w                       # move one word forward
j                       # move down one line
2{                      # move backward two paragraphs
```

Delete Text

In Delete Character on page 295, we discussed how to delete one character at a time. In this section, we learn how to delete text objects and text lines. While lines are a part of text objects, deleting lines is so common that special commands are included just to delete a line or a part of a line.

> A special delete command (dd) deletes the whole line.

Session 8.2 contains examples of the delete operations.

SESSION 8.2 *Delete Examples*

```
dh                      # delete previous character
4dh                     # delete previous 4 characters
4d2h                    # delete previous 8 characters (2 * 4)
d2j                     # delete current line and next 2 lines
```
Continued

SESSION 8.2   *Delete Examples—Continued*

```
dw                          # delete from current character to next word
d)                          # delete from cursor to beginning of next sentence
d{                          # delete backward to beginning of paragraph
dd                          # delete current line
```

Change Text

To change text, we use the change command (c). It works similar to the delete commands; the range to a target is deleted, and we are switched to the text mode, where we can enter the replacement text. If the replacement text is larger than the original text, the text after the target is pushed down to make room. If necessary, the additional text flows to the next screen line. When the change is complete, we press Escape to return to the command mode.

A special change command (cc) changes the whole line.

Session 8.3 contains examples of the delete operations.

SESSION 8.3   *Change Examples*

```
ch                          # change previous character
4ch                         # change previous 4 characters
4c2h                        # change previous 8 characters (2 * 4)
c2j                         # change current line and next 2 lines
cw                          # change from current character to next word
c)                          # change from cursor to beginning of next sentence
c{                          # change backward to beginning of paragraph
cc                          # change current line
```

Yank Command

The yank command copies the current text object and places it in a temporary buffer. It parallels the delete command except that the text is left in the current position. The typical use of the yank command is the first step in a copy and paste operation. After the text has been placed in the temporary buffer, we move to an insert location and then use the put command (see page 297) to copy the text from the buffer to the file buffer.

A special yank command (yy) yanks the current line.

Session 8.4 contains examples of the yank operations.

SESSION 8.4   *Yank Examples*

```
yh                          # yank previous character
4yh                         # yank previous 4 characters
4y2h                        # yank previous 8 characters (2 * 4)
y2j                         # yank current line and next 2 lines
```

Continued

SESSION 8.4 *Yank Examples*

```
yw                          # yank from current character to next word
y)                          # yank from cursor to beginning of next sentence
y{                          # yank backward to beginning of paragraph
yy                          # yank current line
```

Range Command Summary

A summary of the range commands is shown in Table 8.3.

TABLE 8.3 *Range Command Summary*

Command	Description
nothing	Moves the cursor.
d	Deletes a text object.
c	Replaces a text object with new text.
y	Yanks a text object.

8.4 Global Commands in vi

Global commands are applied to the edit buffer without reference to the current position. We covered them in Chapter 2. In this section, we repeat the commands for your reference. To see the details, refer to the appropriate sections in Chapter 2.

Scroll Commands

Scroll commands affect the part of the edit buffer (file) that is currently in the window. They are summarized in Table 8.4.

TABLE 8.4 **vi** *Scroll Commands*

Command	Function
ctrl + y	Scrolls up one line.
ctrl + e	Scrolls down one line.
ctrl + u	Scrolls up half a screen.
ctrl + d	Scrolls down half a screen.
ctrl + b	Scrolls up whole screen.
ctrl + f	Scrolls down whole screen.

Undo Commands

The **vi** editor provides a limited undo facility consisting of two undo commands: undo the most recent change (u) and restore all changes to the current line (U). We covered these commands in Chapter 2. The undo commands are summarized in Table 8.5.

TABLE 8.5 *Undo Commands*

Command	Function
u	Undoes only the last edit.
U	Undoes all the changes on the current line.

Repeat Command

We can use the dot command (.) to repeat the previous command. For example, instead of using the delete line (dd) several times, we can use it once and then use the dot command to delete the remaining lines. The dot command can be used with all three types of **vi** commands: local, range, and global.

Screen Regeneration Commands

There are times when the screen buffer can become cluttered and unreadable. For example, if in the middle of an edit session someone sends you a message, the message replaces some of the text on the screen but not in the file buffer. At other times, we simply want to reposition the text. Four **vi** commands are used to regenerate or refresh the screen.

The first regeneration command (z return) refreshes the screen and positions the current line at the top of the screen. The second command (z.) positions the current line at the middle of the screen. The third command (z-) repositions the current line at the bottom of the screen. The fourth command simply refreshes the screen without moving the cursor. These four commands are summarized in Table 8.6.

TABLE 8.6 **vi** *Regenerate Screen Commands*

Command	Function
z return	Regenerates screen and positions current line at top.
z.	Regenerates screen and positions current line at middle.
z-	Regenerates screen and positions current line at bottom.
ctrl+L	Regenerates screen without moving cursor.

Display Document Status Line

To display the current document status in the status line at the bottom of the screen, we use the status command (ctrl+G). For example, if we are at line 36 in our file, TheRaven, we would see the following status when we enter ctrl+G:

```
"TheRaven" [Modified] line 36 of 109 --33%--
```

The status fields across the line are the filename, a flag indicating if the file has been modified or not, the position of the cursor in the file buffer, and the current line position as a percentage of the lines in the file buffer.

Save and Exit Commands

When we are done with the edit session, we quit **vi.** To quit and save the file, we use the **vi** ZZ command. If we don't want to save the file, we must use **ex**'s quit and don't save command, q! (see Quit on page 319).

8.5 Rearrange Text in vi

There are no new commands in this section. Rather, we show how we can use the commands we have learned to rearrange the text in a document. Most word processors have cut, copy, and paste commands. **vi**'s equivalents use delete and yank commands to insert the text into a buffer and then a put command to paste it back to the file buffer. In this section, we explain how to use these commands to move and copy text.

Move Text

When we move text, it is deleted from its original location in the file buffer and then put into its new location. This is the classic cut and paste operation in a word processor. There are three steps required to move text:

1. Delete text using the appropriate delete command, such as delete paragraph.
2. Move the cursor to the position where the text is to be placed.
3. Use the appropriate put command (p or P) to copy the text from the buffer to the file buffer.

In the following example, we move three lines starting with the current line to the end of the file buffer. To delete the lines, we use the delete line command with a repeat object modifier. We then position the cursor at the end of the file buffer and copy the text from the buffer.

```
3dd     # Delete three lines to buffer
G       # Move to end of file buffer
p       # put after current line
```

Copy Text

When we copy text, the original text is left in the file buffer and also put (pasted) in a different location in the buffer. There are two ways to copy text. The preferred method is to yank the text. Yank leaves the original text in place. We then move the cursor to the copy location and put the text. The steps are as follows:

1. Yank text using yank block, y.
2. Move cursor to copy location.
3. Put text using p or P.

The second method is to delete the text to be copied, followed immediately with a put. Because the put does not empty the buffer, the text is still available. Then move to the copy location and put again. The following code yanks a text block and then puts it in a new location:

```
Move cursor to the beginning of the block
ma        # set mark 'a'
          # Manually move cursor to the end of the block
y`a       # yank block 'a' leaving it in place
          # Manually move cursor to copy location
p         # put text in new location
```

Named Buffers

The **vi** editor uses one temporary buffer and 35 named buffers. The text in all buffers can be retrieved using the put command. However, the data in the temporary buffer are lost whenever a command other than a position command is used. This means that a delete followed by an insert empties the temporary buffer.

The named buffers are available until their contents are replaced. The first nine named buffers are known as the numeric buffers because they are identified by the digits 1 through 9. The remaining 26 named buffers are known as the alphabetic buffers; they are identified by the lowercase letters a through z.

To retrieve data in the temporary buffer, we use the basic put command. To retrieve the text in a named buffer, we preface the put command with a double quote, and the buffer name as shown in the following command syntax. Note that there is no space between the double quote, the buffer name, and the put command.

```
"buffer-namep
```

Using this syntax, the following three examples would retrieve the text in the temporary buffer, buffer 5, and buffer k.

```
P              "5p              "kP
```

Numeric Named Buffers

The numeric buffers are used automatically whenever sentence, line, paragraph, screen, or file text is deleted.[5] The deleted text is automatically copied to the first buffer (1) and is available for later reference. The deleted text for the previous delete can be retrieved by using either the put command or by retrieving numeric buffer 1.

Each delete is automatically copied to buffer 1. Before it is copied, buffer 8 is copied to buffer 9, buffer 7 is copied to buffer 8, and so forth until buffer 1 has been copied to buffer 2. The current delete is then placed in buffer 1. This means that at any time, the last nine deletes are available for retrieval.

---

[5]Text deletion of less than a line is only available from the temporary buffer.

If a repeat modifier (see next section) is used, then all of the text for the delete is placed in buffer 1. In the following example, the next three lines are considered one delete and are placed in buffer 1:

```
3dd
```

Alphabetic Named Buffers

The alphabetic named buffers are to save up to 26 text entities. Whereas the numeric buffers can only store text objects that are at least a sentence long, we can store any size object in an alphabetic buffer. Any of the delete or yank commands can be used to copy data to an alphabetic buffer.

To use the alphabetic buffers, we must specify the buffer name in the delete or yank command. As previously stated, the buffer names are the alphabetic characters a through z. The buffer name is specified with a double quote followed immediately by the buffer name and the yank command as shown in the next example:

```
"ad          # Delete and store line in 'a' buffer
"my          # Yank and store line in 'm' buffer
```

Once the text has been stored, it is retrieved in the same way we retrieved data from the numeric buffers. To retrieve the two text objects created in the previous example, we would enter:

```
"mp          # Retrieve line in 'm' buffer after current cursor
"aP          # Retrieve line in 'a' buffer before current cursor
```

8.6 ex Editor

The **ex** editor is a line editor. When we start **ex,** we are given its colon prompt at the bottom of the screen. Each **ex** instruction operates on one specific line. As we said earlier in the chapter, the **ex** editor is an integral part of the **vi** editor. We can start in either of these editors, and from each, we can move to the other. Figure 8.1 (page 291) depicts the interrelationships between **vi** and **ex.**

ex Instruction Format

An **ex** instruction is identified by its token, the colon (:). Following the token is an address and a command. The **ex** instruction format is shown in Figure 8.23.

FIGURE 8.23   **ex** *Instruction Format*

Addresses

Every line in the file has a specific address starting with one for the first line in the file. An **ex** address can be either a single line or a range of lines (Figure 8.24).

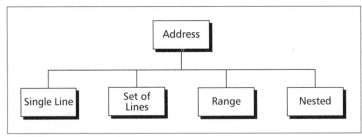

FIGURE 8.24 **ex** *Addresses*

Single Line

A single-line address defines the address for one line. The five single-line address formats are shown in Table 8.7 and discussed below.

TABLE 8.7 **ex** *Single-Line Addresses*

Address	Description
(nothing)	Current line
. (period)	
0 (zero)	Top of file (before first line)
N	Line number (*N*th line)
$	Last line in the file

Current Line The current line, represented by a period (.), is the last line processed by the previous operation. When the file is opened, the last line read into the buffer (that is, the last line in the file) is the current line. In addition to the period, if no address is specified, the current line is used.

Top of Buffer The top of the buffer, represented by zero (0), is a special line designation that sets the current line to the line before the first line in the buffer. It is used to insert lines before the first line in the buffer.

Last Line The last line of the buffer is represented by the dollar sign token ($).

Line Number Any number within the line range of the buffer (1 to $) is the address of that line.

Single-Line Examples In Session 8.5, we demonstrate one example of each single-line address. Because **ex** doesn't have a comment capability, we have added comments to the session (starting with a pound sign, #). If you use the script for practice, don't key the comments.

SESSION 8.5 *Demonstrate Single-Line Addresses*

```
:%p                         # Print entire buffer
1
2
3
Once upon a midnight dreary, while I pondered, weak and weary,
Over many a quaint and curious volume of forgotten lore
While I nodded, nearly napping, suddenly there came a tapping,
As of someone gently rapping, rapping at my chamber door.
"'Tis some visitor," I muttered, "tapping at my chamber door.
Only this and nothing more."
4
5
6
:p                          # Print current line
6
:1                          # Move to line 1 and print
1
```

Set-of-Line Addresses

There are two pattern formats that can be used to search for a single line. If the pattern search is to start with the current line and search forward in the buffer—that is, toward the end of the buffer—the pattern is enclosed in slashes (/.../). If the search is to start with the current line and move backward—that is, toward the beginning of the buffer (1)—the pattern is enclosed in question marks (?). Note, however, in both searches, if the pattern is not found, the search wraps around to completely search the buffer. If we start a forward search at line 5, and the only matching line is in line **4**, the search will proceed from line 5 through line $ and then restart at line 1 and search until it finds the match at line 4. Table 8.8 summarizes these two addresses.

TABLE 8.8 *Set-of-Line Addresses*

Address	Search Direction
/pattern/	Forward
?pattern?	Backward

Session 8.6 demonstrates some set addresses.

SESSION 8.6 *Demonstrate Set-of-Line Addresses*

```
:%p                         # Print entire buffer
1
2
3
Once upon a midnight dreary, while I pondered, weak and weary,
Over many a quaint and curious volume of forgotten lore
While I nodded, nearly napping, suddenly there came a tapping,
As of someone gently rapping, rapping at my chamber door.
```

Continued

SESSION 8.6   *Demonstrate Set-of-Line Addresses—Continued*

```
"'Tis some visitor," I muttered, "tapping at my chamber door
Only this and nothing more."
4
5
6
:/Once/                  # Search forward for 'Once'. It is a search wrap.
Once upon a midnight dreary, while I pondered, weak and weary,
:/3/                     # Search forward for 3 (search wraps)
3
:?Only?                  # Search backward for Only (search wraps)
Only this and nothing more."
```

Range Addresses

A range address is used to define a block of consecutive lines. It has three formats as shown in Table 8.9.

TABLE 8.9   *Set-of-Line Addresses*

Address	Range
%	Whole file
address1,address2	From address1 to address2 (inclusive)
address1;address2	From address1 to address2 relative to address1 (inclusive)

The last two addresses are similar; the only difference is one uses a comma separator and one uses a semicolon. To see the differences, therefore, we need to understand the syntactical meaning of the comma and the semicolon separators. The first example is a shorthand notation for the address range 1, $. All three formats are inclusive; that is, all include the end line in the address.

Comma Separator   When the comma is used, the current address is unchanged until the complete instruction has been executed. Any address relative to the current line is therefore relative to the current line when the instruction is given. To understand this, study the example in Session 8.7.

SESSION 8.7   *Demonstrate Range Comma Separator*

```
:1                            # set current address to 1
Once upon a midnight dreary, while I pondered, weak and weary,

:/While/,+3p                  # plus sign means relative to first address
While I nodded, nearly napping, suddenly there came a tapping,
As of someone gently rapping, rapping at my chamber door.

:.p                           # print current line
As of someone gently rapping, rapping at my chamber door.
```

Session 8.7 Analysis: We begin by setting the current address to 1, which also prints it. The next command sets the start line to the first line containing "While" and the end line to the third line after the current line (+3). The start address becomes line 3. Because we used the comma separator, the second address becomes the current line (that is, line 1) plus three lines, resulting in an ending address of 4. The command therefore prints only line 3 (the line containing "While") through line 4, the ending address relative to the current line (1).

Semicolon Separator When we use a semicolon, the first address is determined before the second address is calculated. It sets the current address to the address determined by the first address. The second address, therefore, is now relative to the first address. Session 8.8 repeats Session 8.7; the only difference is that we use a semicolon separator. The resulting addresses are 3, 6—which print the last four lines of the verse.

SESSION 8.8   *Demonstrate Range Semicolon Separator*

```
:1
Once upon a midnight dreary, while I pondered, weak and weary,
```
```
:/While/;+3p
While I nodded, nearly napping, suddenly there came a tapping,
As of someone gently rapping, rapping at my chamber door.
"'Tis some visitor," I muttered, "tapping at my chamber door
Only this and nothing more."
```
```
:.p
Only this and nothing more."
```

Complete Range The third format, which we use in Session 8.9, is a shorthand notation for the whole file. It is the equivalent of the range 1;$. Note that even though we set the current line to 5, the complete file is printed.

SESSION 8.9   *Demonstrate Complete Range Address*

```
:5
"'Tis some visitor," I muttered, "tapping at my chamber door
```
```
:%p
Once upon a midnight dreary, while I pondered, weak and weary,
Over many a quaint and curious volume of forgotten lore
While I nodded, nearly napping, suddenly there came a tapping,
As of someone gently rapping, rapping at my chamber door.
"'Tis some visitor," I muttered, "tapping at my chamber door
Only this and nothing more.":
```

Nested Addresses We can also use a nested address in **ex.** A nested address is an address that defines a set of lines inside a range. The nested address format is shown in Figure 8.25.

It should be noted that nested addresses are not ranges but rather a pattern that can match different lines within the range. The global flag (g) defines a set of lines that match the pattern. The invert flag (v) defines a set of lines that do not match the pattern.

Let's look at two examples to understand how the nested ranges are determined. To make it easy to identify the matches, we use the **print-line-number** flag (#). This flag prints the line number before each line.

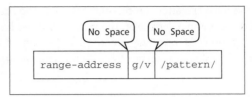

FIGURE 8.25 *Nested Addresses*

In the first example, we want to print any lines in the buffer that contain an upper-case I. This requires the global flag. We use the range 4 through 9. In the second example, we use the reverse flag to print those lines that do not have an uppercase I. Both examples are shown in Session 8.10. We print the complete range first and then the nested address examples.

SESSION 8.10 *Demonstrate Nested Addresses*

```
:4,9p
Once upon a midnight dreary, while I pondered, weak and weary,
Over many a quaint and curious volume of forgotten lore
While I nodded, nearly napping, suddenly there came a tapping,
As of someone gently rapping, rapping at my chamber door.
"'Tis some visitor," I muttered, "tapping at my chamber door
Only this and nothing more."
:4,9g/I/#p
    4  Once upon a midnight dreary, while I pondered, weak and weary,
    6  While I nodded, nearly napping, suddenly there came a tapping,
    8  "'Tis some visitor," I muttered, "tapping at my chamber door
:4,9v/I/#p
    5  Over many a quaint and curious volume of forgotten lore
    7  As of someone gently rapping, rapping at my chamber door.
    9  Only this and nothing more."
```

Commands

There are many **ex** commands. In this section, we discuss the basic commands that are commonly used. You saw some of them earlier when we discussed **vi** and in the address examples. These commands are listed in Table 8.10.

TABLE 8.10 **ex** *Commands*

Command	Description
d	Delete
co	Copy
m	Move
r	Read
w	Write to file
y	Yank

Continued

TABLE 8.10 **ex** *Commands*

Command	Description
p	Print (display)
pu	Put
vi	Move to **vi**
w filename	Write file and continue editing
s	Substitute
q	Quit
q!	Quit and do not save
wq	Write and quit
x	Write file and exit

Delete Command (d)

The delete command (d) can be used to delete a line or a range of lines. The following example deletes lines 13 through 15:

```
:13,15d
```

Copy Command (co)

The copy command (co) can be used to copy a single line or a range of lines after a specified line in the file. The original text is left in place. The following examples copy lines 10 through 20 to the beginning of the file (0), the end of the file ($), and after line 50:

```
:10,20co 0
:10,20co $
:10,20co 50
```

Move Command (m)

The format of the move command (m) is the same as the copy command. In a move, however, the original text is deleted.

Read and Write Commands (r, w)

The read command (r) transfers lines from a file to the editor's buffer. Lines are read after a single line or a set of lines identified by a pattern. The write command (w file_name), on the other hand, can write the whole buffer or a range within the buffer to a file. All address ranges (except nested range) are valid.

In Session 8.11, we first read a file after line 3 and then write the whole file to a new file.

SESSION 8.11 *Read and Write a File in* **ex**

```
$ ex file1
"file1" 5 lines, 10 characters
```
Continued

SESSION 8.11   *Read and Write a File in* **ex**—*Continued*

```
:r file2
"file2" 6 lines, 330 characters
:w TempFile
"TempFile" [New file] 11 lines, 340 characters
:q
$ ls -l TempFile
-rw-r--r--    1 gilberg    staff          340 Oct 18 18:16 TempFile
```

Session 8.11 Analysis: When we enter **ex**, it displays a file status line and a prompt (:). We then told it to read a file named `file2` after the current line. Again, **ex** displays a status line that tells us how many lines and characters it read. We then write the file to a new file named `TempFile`. Because we used the quit option, `file1` was unchanged. If we had not written the contents to a file, **ex** would have reminded us that we had not yet saved the changed buffer contents. Finally, we displayed the new file. We can see that it contains 340 characters, which are the total characters in both files. You can verify this by checking the **ex** status displays in Session 8.11.

It is not necessary to write the complete file as we did in Session 8.11. We can specify a range of the file to be written. In Session 8.12, we use a range to write only the second verse of "The Raven" to a new file.

SESSION 8.12   *Write Part of a File*

```
:8,13p
Ah, distinctly I remember it was in the bleak December;
And each separate dying ember wrought its ghost upon the floor.
Eagerly I wished the morrow; -- vainly I had sought to borrow
From my books surcease of sorrow -- sorrow for the lost Lenore
For the rare and radiant maiden whom the angels name Lenore
Nameless here for evermore.
```
```
:8,13w TheRavenV2
"TheRavenV2" [New file] 6 lines, 330 characters
```
```
$ cat TheRavenV2
Ah, distinctly I remember it was in the bleak December;
And each separate dying ember wrought its ghost upon the floor.
Eagerly I wished the morrow; -- vainly I had sought to borrow
From my books surcease of sorrow -- sorrow for the lost Lenore
For the rare and radiant maiden whom the angels name Lenore
Nameless here for evermore.
```

Yank and Put Commands (y, pu)

Yank (y) and put (pu) work as we described earlier (see yank on page 306 and put on page 297). In Session 8.13, we copy lines 20 through 30 to the yank buffer and then put them after markers a, b, c, and d.

SESSION 8.13   *Demonstrate Yank and Put*

```
:  20,30y
:  `apu
:  `bpu
:  `cpu
:  `dpu
```

Session 8.13 Analysis: We set the markers before we yanked the text. We then moved to each of the markers in turn and put the yank buffer.

Print Command (p)

The print command (p) displays the current line or a range of lines on the monitor. It was used extensively in the address sessions earlier.

Move to vi Command (vi)

The move to **vi** command (vi) switches the editor to **vi.** The cursor is placed at the current line, which will be at the top of the monitor. Once in **vi,** however, you will remain in it as though you had started it. You will be able to execute **ex** commands, but after each command, you will automatically return to **vi.**

Substitute Command (s)

Perhaps the most used command in **ex,** the substitute command (s), allows us to modify a part of a line or a range of lines. Using substitute, we can add text to a line, delete text, or change text. The format of the substitute command is:

```
addresss/pattern/replacement-string/flag
```

For example, to change every occurrence of DOS in a file to UNIX, we would use the following command. Note the global flag (g) at the end of the command. Without it, **ex** would change only the first instance of DOS on each line.

```
0,$s/DOS/UNIX/g
```

Quit Command (q, q!, wq)

The quit command was briefly covered under **vi.** It needs a little more discussion, however.

The **ex** quit command (q) exits the editor and returns to the UNIX command line. If the file has been changed, however, it presents an error message and returns to the **ex** prompt. This situation is shown in Session 8.14. At this point, we have two choices. We can write the file and quit (wq), or we can tell **ex** to discard the changes (q!). Both of these commands are also in Session 8.14.

SESSION 8.14   *Quitting* **ex**

```
:q
No write since last change (":quit!" overrides)
:wq
```

Continued

SESSION 8.14   *Quitting* **ex**—*Continued*

```
"file" 13 lines, 344 characters
...
:q
No write since last change (":quit!" overrides)
:q!
$
```

Exit Command (x)

The exit command (x) also terminates the editor. If the file has been modified, it is automatically written and the editor terminated. If for any reason, such as write permission is not set, the file cannot be written, the exit fails and the **ex** prompt is displayed.

8.7 Key Terms

buffer	line editor	scrolling
command mode	modes	set-of-line address
current character	nested address	single-line address
current line	range address	text editor
editing	screen editor	text mode
ex mode		

8.8 Tips

1. In the **vi/ex** editor, you are in the **ex** mode only when you can see a colon (:) on the status (last) line.

2. In **vi,** there is no way to tell whether you are in the command mode or the text mode unless you customize it. When in doubt, key Escape to put yourself in the command mode.

3. Remember to position the cursor at the appropriate character or line before applying a local command.

4. Remember to define a text object after a range command.

5. Moving the cursor is a range command; however, the move command is "nothing," which means that to move the cursor, you only need to define a target.

6. Marking a block is a local command; however, moving a cursor and deleting, changing, and yanking a block of text are range commands.

7. You can directly exit from **vi** using the ZZ command; however, you can also move to the **ex** mode (using :) and then exit using any of the **ex** commands.

8. The **vi** ZZ command and the **ex** exit command (x) automatically save the file.

9. The definition of a sentence in **vi** is different from the common English definition.

10. The definition of a paragraph in **vi** is different from the common English definition.

11. You can use a command multiplier, object multiplier, or both in a range command.

12. To move text in **vi,** you need first to delete the text (using a range command) and then paste it using the local put command (p).

13. To copy text in **vi,** you need to yank the text (using a range command) and then paste it using the local put command (p).

14. When you enter **ex** from the shell, the current line is the last line in the text.

15. After applying a command in **ex,** the current line is the last line to which the command was applied.

8.9 Commands

In this chapter, we covered only two commands: **vi** and **ex.** Table 8.11 shows the **vi** commands.

TABLE 8.11   **vi** *Commands*

Command	Description	Options	Page
vi	*Synopsis: vi [-options] [file-name]* Creates a new file or edits an existing file.	R	292
ex	*Synopsis: ex [-option] [file-name]* Creates a new file or edits an existing file.	R	311

The **vi** command as an editor uses three categories of commands: local, range, and global. The local commands are shown in Table 8.12.

TABLE 8.12   **vi** *Local Commands*

Command	Description
i, I	Inserts text before the current character (i) or line (I).
a, A	Appends text after the current character (a) or line (A).
o, O	Opens an empty line in the text mode after (o) or before (O) the current line.
r, R	Replaces one (r) or many (R) character(s).
s, S	Substitutes characters (s) or lines (S).
x, X	Deletes a character.
m	Inserts an invisible mark.
~	Changes the case of the current character.
p, P	Puts the contents of the buffer after (p) or before (P) current character.
J	Joins the consecutive two lines.

The range commands are shown in Table 8.13.

TABLE 8.13   **vi** *Range Commands*

Command	Description
nothing	Moves the cursor.
d	Deletes a text object.
c	Replaces a text object with new text.
y	Yanks a text object.

The global commands are shown in Table 8.14.

TABLE 8.14 **vi** *Global Commands*

Command	Description
ctrl+y, ctrl+e	Scrolls up (ctrl+y) or down (ctrl+e) one line.
ctrl+u, ctrl+d	Scrolls up (ctrl+u) or down (ctrl+d) half a screen.
ctrl+b, ctrl+f	Scrolls up (ctrl+b) or down (ctrl+f) a whole screen.
u, U	Undoes effect of last command (u) or all commands on a line (U).
z, z., z-, ctrl+L	Regenerates the screen.
. (dot)	Repeats the previous command.
ctrl+G	Shows the status line.
ZZ	Saves the buffer and exits **vi.**

Text objects used by the range commands are shown in Table 8.15.

TABLE 8.15 **vi** *Range Command Objects*

Object	Targets	Text Object
Character	h and l	A character
Word	w, b, e	A whole or part of a word
Line	0 and $ + − j k	A line or part of a line Text Text Text Text
Sentence	(and)	A whole or part of a sentence
Paragraph	{ and }	A whole or part of a paragraph
Block	`x and 'x	A whole or part of a block
Screen	H, L, and M	A whole or part of the screen
File	G and nG	A whole or part of the file

The **ex** commands are shown in Table 8.16.

TABLE 8.16 **ex** *Command Summary*

Command	Description
d	Deletes a line or a range of lines.
co	Copies a line or a range of lines after a specified line.
m	Moves a line or a range of lines after a specified line.

Continued

TABLE 8.16 **ex** *Command Summary*

Command	Description
r	Writes the contents of a file after a specified line.
w	Writes a line or a range of lines to a file.
y	Yanks a line or a range of lines.
p	Prints a line or a range of lines.
pu	Copies (put) contents of buffer to file buffer.
vi	Moves to the **vi** editor.
w filename	Writes file and continues editing.
s	Substitutes a pattern with a string.
q	Quits.
q!	Quits and does not save.
wq	Writes and quits.
x	Writes file and exits.

8.10 Summary

- Commands in **vi** are divided into three categories: local commands, range commands, and global commands.
- A local command is a command that is applied to the text containing the current cursor position.
- We have defined several local commands in **vi:** insert (i and I), append (a and A), insert line (o and O), replace (r and R), substitute (s and S), delete (x), mark (m), change case (~), put (p and P), and join (J).
- A range command is a command that operates on a text object.
- We have defined four range commands in **vi:** move cursor (nothing), delete (d), change (c), and yank (y).
- A global command is applied to the buffer without any reference to the cursor position.
- We have defined several global commands in **vi:** scroll line (ctrl+y and ctrl+e), scroll half a screen (ctrl+u and ctrl+d), scroll a full screen (ctrl+b and ctrl+f), undo (u and U), regenerate screen (z, z., z-, and ctrl+L), repeat (.), show status line (ctrl+G), and save and exit (ZZ).
- We can divide the addresses in the **ex** editor into four categories: a single-line address, a set-of-line address, a range address, and a nested address.
- A single-line address in **ex** defines one line for processing. There are four single-line addresses in **ex:**
    - current line (nothing or dot)
    - specific line (N)
    - last line ($)
    - imaginary line before the first line (0)

- A set-of-line address in **ex** defines one or more lines that are not necessarily consecutive. The lines are chosen, not based on their relative positions, but based on their contents. There are two set-of-line addresses in **ex:**
  - forward search (/ . . ./)
  - backward search (?. . .?)
- A range address in **ex** defines one or more consecutive lines. There are three range addresses in **ex:**
  - two single-line addresses separated by a comma (address,address)
  - two single-line addresses separated by a semicolon (address;address)
  - the whole file (%)
- A nested address defines a set-of-line address inside a range.
- We have defined several **ex** commands in this chapter: delete (d), copy (co), move (m), write to a file (w), read from a file (r), yank (y), put (pu), quit (q), exit (x), print (p), move to **vi** (vi), and substitute (s).

8.11 Practice Set

Review Questions

1. How many modes were defined for **vi/ex** in this chapter?
2. Can we enter **vi** directly from the shell? How?
3. Can we enter **ex** directly from the shell? How?
4. Can we enter **ex** from **vi**? How?
5. Can we enter **vi** from **ex**? How?
6. Can we exit from **vi** directly? How?
7. Can we exit from **ex** directly? How?
8. Define the text mode.
9. Define the command mode.
10. Define the **ex** mode.
11. How can we go from the command mode to the text mode?
12. How can we go from the text mode to the command mode?
13. Can we go from the command mode to the **ex** mode directly? If yes, how?
14. Can we go from the **ex** mode to the command mode directly? If yes, how?
15. Can we go from the text mode to the **ex** mode directly? If yes, how?
16. Can we go from the **ex** mode to the text mode directly? If yes, how?
17. Does the text mode have a prompt? If yes, what is it?
18. Does the command mode have a prompt? If yes, what is it?
19. Does the **ex** mode have a prompt? If yes, what is it?
20. When you see the colon prompt at the bottom of the screen, you are in the _____ mode.
21. Define local command in **vi.**
22. Define range command in **vi.**

23. Define global command in **vi.**
24. A _____ command is applied on the position of the cursor.
25. A _____ command is applied on a text object.
26. A _____ command is applied on the whole buffer.
27. How many local commands in **vi** were defined in this chapter?
28. List and define the effect of five local commands.
29. How many range commands in **vi** were defined in this chapter?
30. List and define the effect of four range commands.
31. How many global commands were defined in this chapter?
32. List and define the effect of five global commands.
33. Define a single-line address in **ex.**
34. List and define the effect of all single-line addresses in **ex.**
35. Define a set-of-line address in **ex.**
36. Explain how you create a set-of-line address.
37. Define a range address in **ex.**
38. List and define the effect of two different formats for a range address.
39. Define a nested address.
40. What is a named buffer?
41. What is an alphabetic named buffer?
42. What is a numeric named buffer?

Exercises

43. How many lines are deleted by each of the following commands in **vi**?
    a. dd
    b. 4dd
    c. 4dd2
    d. dd5
44. Which of the following commands in **vi** need a text object?
    a. u
    b. r
    c. ZZ
    d. c
45. Which of the following commands in **vi** need a text object?
    a. i
    b. d
    c. s
    d. J
46. Which of the following commands in **vi** need a text object?
    a. y
    b. z.
    c. ctrl+y
    d. m
47. Define the type of each of the following **ex** addresses.
    a. 5
    b. 20,30
    c. $
    d. /pattern/
48. Define the type of each of the following **ex** addresses.
    a. %
    b. ?pattern?
    c. /pattern/,/pattern/
    d. /pattern/;56
49. Define the type of each of the following **ex** addresses.
    a. 20,60g/pattern/
    b. ?pattern?;?pattern?
    c. /pattern/,?pattern?
    d. 45,80v?pattern?

50. Find the error (if any) in each of the following **ex** addresses.
    a. `20,60/pattern/`
    b. `?pattern?;?pattern?;45`
    c. `/pattern/,?pattern?,/pattern`
    d. `45g/pattern/`

51. Write an address in **ex** to define a block of lines containing lines 30 to 50.

52. Write an address in **ex** to define a block of lines.

53. What is the difference between the following two commands in **ex**?
    a. `%g/UNIX/d`
    b. `/UNIX/d`

54. What is the difference between the following two commands in **ex**?
    a. `%v/UNIX/d`
    b. `/UNIX/d`

55. What is the difference between the following two commands in **ex**?
    a. `20,50co1`
    b. `20,50co0`

56. What is the difference between the following two commands in **ex**?
    a. `20,50co0`
    b. `20,50m0`

57. How many lines are deleted by each of the following commands in **ex**? Which ones?
    a. `20d`
    b. `20,30d`
    c. `20;30d`
    d. `20;+30d`

8.12 Lab Sessions

Session I

1. Log into the system.
2. Use the **vi** editor to create a file called `Ch8S1F1` that contains the following paragraph with the same alignment and format.

> People naturally fear misfortune and hope for good
> fortune. But if the distinction is carefully studied,
> misfortune often turns out to be good fortune and good
> fortune to be misfortune. The wise person learns
> to meet life's changing circumstances with an equitable
> spirit, being neither elated by success nor depressed
> by failure.
>
> Buddha

3. Correct any typing errors made during creation.
4. Use the move cursor commands to move the cursor to the first "g" in the third line (the character "g" of the word "good").

Continued

5. Insert an invisible mark there.
6. Use the G command to move to the end of the file.
7. Place the cursor at the last character of the last line using the $ command.
8. Using a block object, yank the block between the cursor position and the marked point.
9. Move the cursor to the beginning of the file.
10. Use the put command to insert the yank buffer at the current position.
11. Quit **vi** without saving the file (you should move to **ex** mode first).
12. Log out of the system.

Session II

1. Log into the system.
2. Use **ex** to open the file created in Session I.
3. Check the line number of the current line using the p command.
4. Change the current line to the first line.
5. Move the last two lines to the beginning of the file.
6. Move the first two lines (the ones you moved in step 5) to the end of the file.
7. Check the line number of the current line using the p command.
8. Change the current line to be the first line.
9. Use the copy command to copy the line starting with "spirit" and the next two lines to the end of the file (using the range command with the semicolon separator).
10. Check the line number of the current line.
11. Use backward search to find the line starting with "spirit."
12. Delete the text from this line down to the end.
13. Move to the **vi** editor.
14. Save the file in the **vi** editor.
15. Log out of the system.

Session III

In this session, we learn how to customize the **vi/ex** editor. This editor uses options and variables to customize its environment. The option is an on/off switch that can be set or unset. A variable can hold a numeric or string value for use during the editing process. In this session, we show you how to check these settings and how to change them.

1. Log into the system.
2. Use the **vi** editor to create a file called Ch8S3F1.
3. At the command mode, use the command :set all to find which options are set and which variables have values. Make a list of them.

Continued

Session III—*Continued*

4. Is the *autoindent* option set? If not, use the command `:set autoindent` to set this option.
5. Now move to the **vi** text mode.
6. Use a tab to indent the first line in the file.
7. Type a line of your choice.
8. Type a second line. What do you see? Is the second line inserted and indented automatically? Is it aligned with the first line? This feature can be used when we want to create lines that need alignment (such as lines in a programming language).
9. Move to the command mode. Use the command `:set noautoindent` to unset the autoindent feature.
10. Now move the cursor to the last line of the file and type another line. What do you see? Is the line indented?
11. Log out of the system.

Session IV

In this session, we learn more about **vi/ex** customization.

1. Log into the system.
2. Use the **vi** editor to create a file called `Ch8S4F1`.
3. Use the manual and other sources to find about the following options and variables:

   `ignorecase, magic, number, scroll,`
   `shiftwidth, showmode, wrapmargin`

4. Use each of the following options or variables in the `Ch8S4F1`.
5. Save the file.
6. Log out of the system.

Session V

In this session, we learn more about **vi/ex** customization by using abbreviations.

1. Log into the system.
2. Use the **vi** editor to create a file called `Ch8S5F1`.
3. Use the manual and other sources to find out about the abbreviation command. This command allows you to use abbreviations for commonly used words. The operator can be used as follows:

   `:ab x y`   (x is abbreviation for y)

Continued

4. Use the following abbreviations:

```
cost     for      college student
cis      for      computer information system
fq       for      fall quarter
sq       for      spring quarter
jan      for      January
feb      for      February
and so on for the rest of the months
```

5. Test each of the following abbreviations in the file.
6. Use the `:unab cis` to cancel the abbreviation for cis.
7. Try to use the cis abbreviation again.
8. Save the file.
9. Log out of the system.

Session VI

In this session, we learn more about **vi/ex** customization by using macros.

1. Log into the system.
2. Use the **vi** editor to create a file called Ch8S6F1.
3. Use the manual and other sources to find about the *macros* and *map* operators. This command allows the definition of a key for a complex command. The format of the command is:

    :map key command

4. Create and test each of the following abbreviations in the file:

    :map d0 1

    :map d$ 2

    :map dd 3

5. Save the file.
6. Log out of the system.

## CHAPTER 9

Regular Expressions

A **regular expression** is a pattern consisting of a sequence of characters that is matched against text. UNIX evaluates text against the pattern to determine if the text and the pattern match. If they match, the expression is true and a command is executed. If they don't, the expression is false and a command is not executed.

Some of the most powerful UNIX utilities, such as **grep** and **sed,** use regular expressions. We must therefore understand how to use regular expressions to effectively use these utilities. In this chapter, we study the basic concepts of regular expressions including searching for and replacement of text. Then, in the following chapters, we see how they are implemented in the common UNIX utilities.

A regular expression is like a mathematical expression. A mathematical expression is made of operands (data) and operators. Similarly, a regular expression is made of atoms and operators. The **atom** specifies what we are looking for and where in the text the match is to be made. The **operator,** which is not required in all expressions, combines atoms into complex expressions. The concept of a regular expression is shown in Figure 9.1.

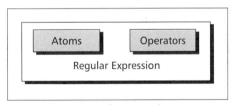

FIGURE 9.1   *Regular Expression*

9.1 Atoms

As mentioned, an atom specifies what text is to be matched and where it is to be found. An atom in a regular expression can be one of five types: a single character, a dot, a class, an anchor, or a back reference (Figure 9.2).

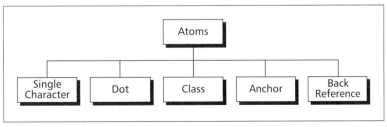

FIGURE 9.2   *Atoms*

Single Character

The simplest atom is a single character. When a single character appears in a regular expression, it matches itself. In other words, if a regular expression is made of one single character, that character must be somewhere in the text to make the pattern match successful. Conversely, if the character does not appear in the text, the pattern match is unsuccessful. An example of a successful and unsuccessful single-character pattern match is presented in Figure 9.3.

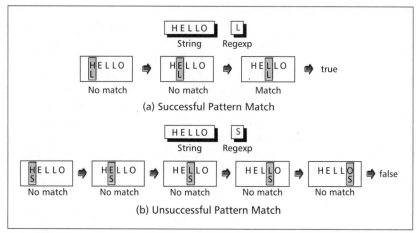

FIGURE 9.3 *Single-Character Pattern Examples*

In Figure 9.3(a), we begin the pattern match by matching L with the H on the left; it does not match. We therefore move to the E and find that it does not match. When we move to the third character, L, we find a match and return true. In Figure 9.3(b), the pattern matching begins again on the left. It tests each position in turn, all without a match. After trying to match the O, we are at the end of the text, so false is returned.

Dot

A **dot** matches any single character except the newline character (\n). This universal matching capability makes it a very powerful element in the operation of regular expressions. By itself, however, it can do nothing because it matches everything. Its power in regular expressions comes from its ability to work with other atoms to create an expression. For example, consider the regular expression

```
a.
```

This expression combines the single-character atom, a, with the dot atom. It matches any *pair* of characters where the first character is a. Therefore, it matches aa, ab, aX, and a5, but it does not match Aa, because UNIX is case sensitive, or a\n. The full power of the dot operator will be better understood when we use operators, such as repetition, that combine it with other atoms. Figure 9.4 shows three examples of the dot atom.

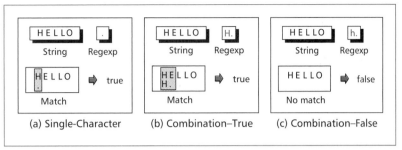

FIGURE 9.4   *Dot Atom Examples*

Class

The dot matches any single character. This is often too general. The **class** atom defines a set of ASCII[1] characters, any one of which may match any of the characters in the text. The character set to be used in the matching process is enclosed in brackets. Figure 9.5 contains an example of a class regular expression. As you study this figure, note that the class matches only one single character that can be any of the characters in the set. In other words, the class [ABC] can match either A or B or C.

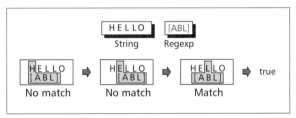

FIGURE 9.5   *Class Atom Example*

The class set is a very powerful expression component. Its power is extended with three additional tokens: ranges, exclusion, and escape characters. A **range** of text characters is indicated by a dash (-). Thus, the expression [a-d] indicates that the characters a and b and c and d are all included in the set.

Sometimes it is easier to specify which characters are to be excluded from the set— that is, to specify its complement. This can be done using **exclusion,** which is the UNIX *not* operator (^). For example, to specify any character other than a vowel, we would use [^aeiou]. The *not* operator can also be used with ranges. To specify any character other than a digit, we would use [^0-9].

> A ^ inside a class atom bracket set is a complement; it is interpreted as any **ASCII** character except those identified in the set.

---

[1]The ASCII character set is in Appendix A, *ASCII Tables*.

The third additional token is the **escape character** (\). It is used when the matching character is one of the other two tokens. For example, to match a vowel or a dash, we would use the escape character to indicate that the dash is a character and not a range token. This example is coded `[aeiou\-]`. Figure 9.6 contains several examples of the class atom.

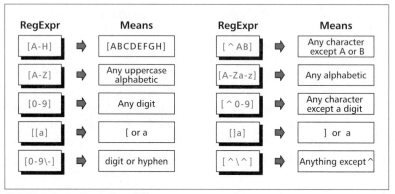

FIGURE 9.6 *Examples of Classes*

Anchors

Anchors are atoms that are used to line up the pattern with a particular part of a string. In other words, anchors are not matched to the text, but define where the next character in the pattern must be located in the text. There are four types of anchors: beginning of line (^), end of line ($), beginning of word (\<), and end of word (\>). The anchor atoms are shown in Figure 9.7.

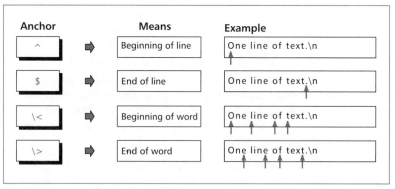

FIGURE 9.7 *Anchors*

Anchors are another atom that are often used in combinations. For example, to locate a string that begins with the letter Q, we would code the expression ^Q. Similarly, to find a word that ends in g, we would code the expression g\>.

A ^ character at the beginning of a regular expression is an anchor and means beginning of the current line. Anywhere else, it matches itself as a text character.

A $ character at the end of a regular expression is an anchor and means end of the current line. Anywhere else, it matches itself as a text character.

Back References

We can temporarily save text in one of nine save buffers (page 342). When we do, we refer to the text in a saved buffer using a **back reference.** A back reference is coded using the escape character and a digit in the range of 1 to 9 as shown here:

$$\backslash 1 \quad \backslash 2 \quad \dots \quad \backslash 9$$

A back reference is used to match text in the current or designated buffer with text that has been saved in one of the system's nine buffers. Back references and their use will become clearer after we discuss the save operator (page 342).

9.2 Operators

To make the regular expressions more powerful, we can combine atoms with operators. The regular expression operators play the same role as mathematical operators. Mathematical expression operators combine mathematical atoms (data); regular expression operators combine regular expression atoms.

We can group the regular expressions into five different categories: sequence operators, alternation operators, repetition operators, group operators, and save operators. The operator breakdown is shown in Figure 9.8.

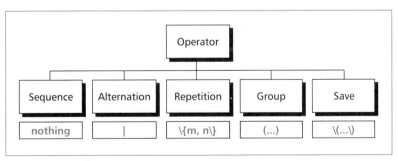

FIGURE 9.8 *Operators*

Sequence

The **sequence** operator is *nothing*. This means that if a series of atoms, such as a series of characters, are shown in a regular expression, it is implied that there is an invisible sequence operator between them. Examples of sequence operators are shown in Figure 9.9.

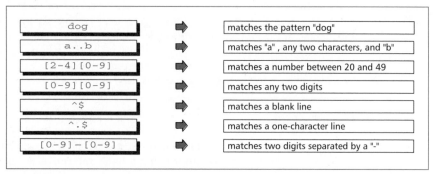

FIGURE 9.9 *Examples of Sequence Operators*

Now let's see how sequence works in a regular expression. Given a string containing the value CHARACTER, we match it with the regular expression sequence ACT. Figure 9.10 contains a step-by-step description of the matching process.

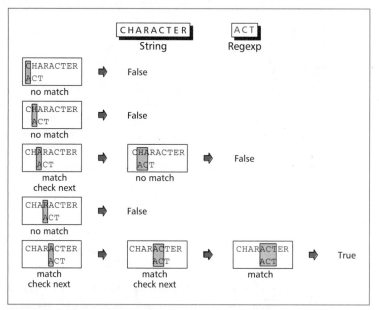

FIGURE 9.10 *Evaluation of a String Using the Sequence Operator*

The comparison begins by checking the first letter of the string, C, with the first letter of the expression, A. They are not equal, so there is no match. But the string has not been fully evaluated, so the evaluation continues by comparing the H in CHARACTER with the first letter of the expression, A. Again, there is no match. When the third character is matched against the pattern, the result appears to be true—the A in CHARACTER matches the A in ACT. Because the expression has three characters, however, the match is not complete. All three characters in the patterns must match a sequence in the string. Matching the next character in the string (R) with the second character in the expression (C) results in a nonmatch.

Again, when the matching reaches the fifth character in the string, a match is found; A appears in both the string and the pattern. This time, the next two characters also match the expression values, so there is a complete match and true is returned.

Alternation

The alternation operator (|) is used to define one or more alternatives. For example, if we want to select between A or B, we would code the regular expression as A | B. Alternation can be used with single atoms, as in the previous example, but it is usually used for selecting between two or more sequences of characters or groups of characters. That is, the atoms are usually sequences. For single alternation, we suggest that you use the class operator.

An example of alternation among sequences is presented in Figure 9.11. In the first example in the figure, we are looking for either UNIX or unix. This example locates UNIX whether it is lowercase or uppercase. In the second example, we are looking for any of the female designations, Miss, Ms, or Mrs.

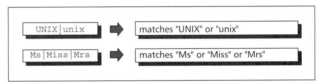

FIGURE 9.11 *Alternation Operator*

Figure 9.12 shows how text is matched. It is a descriptive example and may not be the way the UNIX programmer implemented it. The match begins by matching the expression pattern to the text. When the H doesn't match, it moves to the next character, E. Again, no match. The matching continues until the string is exhausted. At that point, UNIX repeats the matching with the second alternative, EL. This time, it finds a match in the second and third characters and returns true.

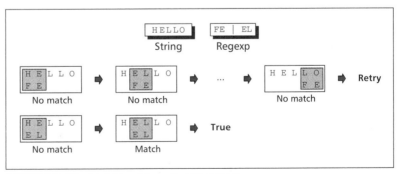

FIGURE 9.12 *Matching Alternation Operators*

Repetition

The **repetition** operator is a set of escaped braces (\{...\}) that contains two numbers separated by a comma (Figure 9.13). It specifies that the atom or expression immediately before the repetition may be repeated. The first number (m) indicates the minimum required times the previous atom must appear in the text; the second number (n) indicates the maximum number of times it may appear. For example, repetition operator \{2, 5\} indicates that the previous atom may be repeated two to five times. One is not enough, and six are too many; both result in no match.

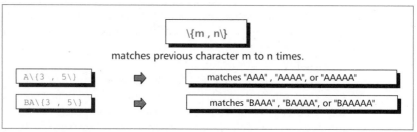

FIGURE 9.13   *Repetition Operator*

Basic Repetition Forms

The m and n values are optional, although at least one must be present. That is, either may appear without the other. If only one repetition value (m) is enclosed in the braces, the previous atom must be repeated exactly m times—no more, no less. This code follows. In this example, the previous atom must be repeated exactly three times.

\{3 \}

If the minimum value (m) is followed by a comma without a maximum value, the previous atom must be present at least m times, but it may appear more than m times. In the following example, the previous atom may be repeated three or more times but no less than three times. Note that the only difference between these two examples is the comma after the 3.

\{3, \}

If the maximum value (n) is preceded by a comma without a minimum, the previous atom may appear up to n times and no more. In the following example, the previous atom may appear zero to three times, but no more.

\{ , 3\}

These variations are shown in Figure 9.14.

Short Form Operators

Three forms of repetition are so common that UNIX has special shortcut operators for them. The asterisk (*) may be used to repeat an atom zero or more times. (It is the same as \{0,\}.) The plus (+) is used to specify that the atom must appear one or more times. (It is the same as \{1,\}.) The question mark (?) is used to repeat the

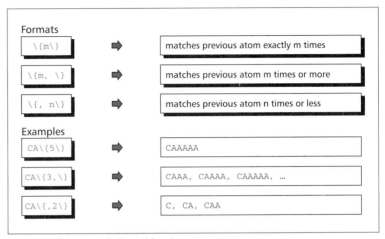

FIGURE 9.14 *Basic Repetition Forms*

pattern zero or one time only. (It is the same as \{0,1\}.) These short forms are shown in Figure 9.15, along with examples of the basic format. Study them carefully to make sure you understand what patterns they match. In the first example (BA*), any text string starting with B followed by zero or more As matches the pattern. It makes no difference how many As there are.

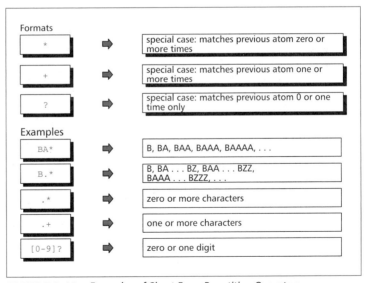

FIGURE 9.15 *Examples of Short Form Repetition Operators*

Now look at the second example (B.*). In this example, the first character must be B. The characters that follow can be anything (note the dot operator). We have shown the patterns using only uppercase alphabetic characters, but special characters, digits, and lowercase alphabetic characters all would match the pattern. The rest of the examples are relatively straightforward.

The asterisk operator (*) has a meaning in a regular expression that is different from its meaning as a wildcard. In a regular expression, it means repeat the previous character or group of characters zero or more times. As a wildcard in a filename, it means zero or more characters. The regular expression usage means that it cannot be used by itself; it must be preceded by an atom or a group of atoms.

The question mark operator (?) also has a meaning in a regular expression that is different from its meaning as a wildcard. In a regular expression, it means repeat the previous character or group of characters zero or one time. As a wildcard in a filename, it means one character. The regular expression usage means that it cannot be used by itself; it must be preceded by an atom or a group of atoms.

If the plus operator (+) is not available in a system or implementation, we can always use the asterisk (*) operator, which is supposed to be available everywhere. For example, the regular expression (a+) is the same as (aa*).

Figure 9.16 shows how a regular expression using a repeating operator matches text in a line. It begins by searching the string for a matching B, which it finds in the second position. It then looks for zero or more Cs. When it finds the first non-C in position 8, it looks for and finds a matching D, which completes the required pattern. The regular expression is therefore true.

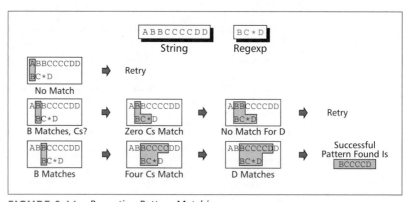

FIGURE 9.16   *Repeating Pattern Matching*

Greedy Pattern Matching

Repeating operators in UNIX are part of a general class of algorithm known as **greedy** algorithms. Greedy algorithms are designed to maximize their operation. In pattern matching, greedy means that the longest possible string of characters that matches a pattern should be used.

When a regular expression involving repeating operators is used, the repeating part tries to consume as much matching text as it can. To understand the concept, examine

Figure 9.17. In this example, the expression requires a string that starts with an A and ends with FOO, with zero or more characters between them. Note that there are two FOO character patterns in the string.

The pattern match begins by locating the A in the second position as shown in Figure 9.17(b). It then greedily consumes the rest of the string to the newline. This is the position in Figure 9.17(c). Having found the maximum string, it then backs up until it finds a matching FOO in Figure 9.17(d). Note that this approach finds the longest possible matching pattern, which is the one ending with the second FOO.

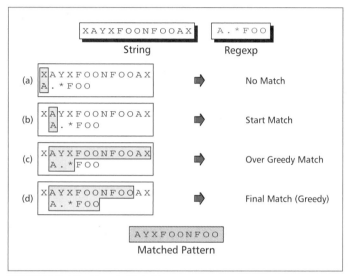

FIGURE 9.17 *Greedy Matching*

Group Operator

The **group operator** is a pair of opening and closing parentheses. When a group of characters is enclosed in parentheses, the next operator applies to the whole group, not only to the previous character. In the first example in Figure 9.18, the group (BC) must be repeated exactly three times.

FIGURE 9.18 *Group Operator*

The second example in Figure 9.18 is more complex because there are two repeating groups. The first group, BC, must be repeated twice. This inner group is combined with a leading F and a trailing G to form the second group, FBCBCG, which is then repeated twice. Study the figure carefully to make sure you understand how the group operator works.

Save

The **save operator,** which is a set of escaped parentheses, \ (...\) , copies a matched text string to one of nine buffers for later reference. Within an expression, the first saved text is copied to buffer 1, the second saved text is copied to buffer 2, and so forth for up to nine buffers. Once text has been saved, it can be referred to by using a back reference (page 335).

As a typical example of the save command, let's create a pattern that matches text beginning and ending with the same letter. The problem is that we don't know what the letters will be. The solution is to save the first letter of a text string in a buffer and then use the buffer to match with the last character in the string. This expression is shown in Figure 9.19.

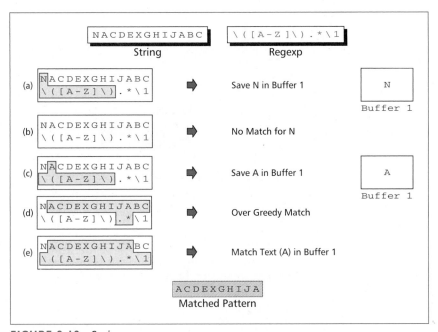

FIGURE 9.19 *Saving*

Let's break this expression down into three parts. In Figure 9.19(a), we save the first character of the string in buffer 1. Figure 9.19(b) tries to find a match for the character, N, somewhere else in the line. Because there is none, the pattern restarts at the second character in the line, A, as shown in Figure 9.19(c). This time there is a match. Figure 9.19(d) shows that the greedy expression, looking for the largest possible string, goes to the end of the line. Finally, in Figure 9.19(e), we back off the greedy match until we find a character that matches the character saved in buffer 1.

9.3 Key Terms

alternation operator	exclusion	range
anchor atom	greedy pattern matching	regular expression
atom	group operator	repetition operator
back-reference atom	operand	save operator
class atom	operator	sequence operator
dot atom	pattern	single-character atom

9.4 Tips

1. A class atom defines only one single character (length one).

2. A dot atom defines only one single character (length one).

3. An anchor atom defines no character (length zero).

4. If you want to match a special character—such as asterisk (*), dot (.), question mark (?), and so forth—literally in the text, you must use a backslash character (\) before the character. To match a dot (.), you use (\.).

5. The special character caret (^) has two different uses in a regular expressions. If it is inside set brackets ([^. . .]), it means "not" or "complement." If it is at the beginning of a regular expression (outside of the brackets), it is an anchor that matches the beginning of the line.

6. A range in a class atom means a range of characters based on the ASCII characters; it does not mean a range of numbers. For example, [30-39] does not mean the range of numbers between 30 and 39. It means character 3, or the set character 0 to character 3, or the character 9. In other words, it defines one of the characters in the set 0, 1, 2, 3, and 9.

7. If you want to define a range of numbers between 30 and 39, you should remember that you need a regular expression with a sequence of two atoms. It should be 3[0-9].

8. The back-reference atoms (\1, \2, . . ., \9) can be used in a regular expression if you have already used the save operator earlier in the same regular expression.

9. The sequence operator is nothing. Although it may be there, it is invisible. Whenever you use two or more atoms one after another in a regular expression, you have one sequence operator between each of them.

10. Repeating operators cannot be used after atoms that do not match text. For example, none of the repeating operators can be used after anchors.

11. The asterisk operator (*) has a meaning in a regular expression that is different from its meaning as a wildcard. In a regular expression, it means repeat the previous character or group of characters zero or more times. As a wildcard in a filename, it means zero or more characters. The regular expression usage means that it cannot be used by itself; it must be preceded by an atom or a group of atoms.

12. The question mark operator (?) has a meaning in a regular expression that is different from its meaning as a wildcard. In a regular expression, it means repeat the previous character or group of characters zero or one time. As a wildcard in a

filename, it means one character. The regular expression usage means that it cannot be used by itself; it must be preceded by an atom or a group of atoms.

13. The repeating operators always act greedily (try to find the maximum size string) when they specify an undefined number of characters.

14. When the dot atom (.) is repeated, it matches any character. It does not require that the repeated text characters be the same. For example, four dot operators (.... or .\{4\}) match aaaa, bbbb, aabb, abbb, abcd, and so on.

15. If the plus operator (+) is not available in a system or implementation, we can always use the asterisk (*) operator, which is supposed to be available everywhere. For example, the regular expression (a+) is the same as (aa*).

9.5 Summary

- A regular expression is a character pattern that is matched against text.
- A regular expression consists of atoms and operators.
- An atom specifies what we are looking for and where in the text the match is to be made.
- An atom can be one of five types: a single character, a dot, a class, an anchor, or a back reference.
- A single character matches itself. Its length is one.
- A dot matches any single character except the newline (\n). Its length is one.
- A class defines a set of characters, any one of which may match the corresponding character in text. Its length is one.
- An anchor is a zero-length atom that defines where the pattern must be located in the text. There are four types of anchors: ^, $, \<, and \>.
- A back reference is used to match one or more text characters to text previously saved in a buffer. We can use up to nine buffers; therefore, we can reference them using nine back references (\1, \2, . . . , \9).
- Operators are used to combine atoms into more complex regular expressions. There are five types of operators: sequence, alternation, repetition, group, and save.
- The sequence operator is nothing. It is used to concatenate a series of atoms.
- The alternation operator is used to define one or more alternatives.
- The repetition operator specifies that the atoms or expressions may be repeated. There are several short forms for the repetition operator.
- The group operator is a pair of opening and closing parentheses that allow the next operator to be applied to the whole group instead of just the previous atom.
- The save operator saves one or more characters in a buffer to be matched later with its corresponding back-reference atom.

9.6 Practice Set

Review Questions

1. Define a regular expression; compare and contrast it with a mathematical expression.
2. Name the components of a regular expression.

3. Define an atom. What is the equivalent of an atom in a mathematical expression?
4. How many types of atoms are defined in a regular expression?
5. Define a single-character atom. What is the length of text that is matched by a single-character atom?
6. Define a dot atom. What is the length of text that is matched by a dot atom?
7. Define a class atom. What is the length of text that is matched by a class atom?
8. Define an anchor atom. What is the length of text that is matched by an anchor atom?
9. How many anchors are defined in UNIX?
10. Define a back-reference atom. What is the length of text that is matched by a back-reference atom?
11. Define an operator. Compare and contrast operators in a regular expression and operators in a mathematical expression.
12. How many operators are defined for regular expressions? List them.
13. Define the sequence operator. What is the symbol for this operator?
14. Define the alternation operator. What is the symbol for this operator?
15. Define the repetition operator. What is the symbol for this operator?
16. Define the group operator. What is the symbol for this operator?
17. Define the save operator. What is the symbol for this operator?
18. What are some short forms of repetition operators?
19. Define the ? operator using the \{. . .\} format.
20. Define the * operator using the \{. . .\} format.
21. Define the + operator using the \{. . .\} format.
22. Can we use the asterisk operator (*) instead of the plus operator (+)? Show an example.

Exercises

23. How many characters can be matched by each of the following regular expressions?
    a. [ABC]
    b. .
    c. \2
    d. ABC

24. Simplify the following regular expressions.
    a. [ABCDE]
    b. [ABCDEnmopq]
    c. [0123456]
    d. [ABCDEa-q]

25. What is the minimum length of the line to be matched by each of the following regular expressions?
    a. [ABC][0-9][N-M]
    b. ^$
    c. ^...$
    d. ^.*$

26. What operators are used in each of the following regular expressions? How many?
    a. [ABC][0-9][N-M]
    b. ^$
    c. ^A\{4, 7\}$
    d. A|B*|C*

27. How many characters are matched by the following regular expressions?
    a. `A\{4\}`
    b. `A\{4, 7\}`
    c. `A\{,7\}`
    d. `A\{8, \}`

28. If possible, rewrite the following regular expressions using other operators:
    a. `A\{0, \}`
    b. `A\{1, \}`
    c. `A\{0, 1\}`
    d. `A\{2, 3\}`

29. If possible, rewrite the following regular expressions using other operators:
    a. `AAAAA`
    b. `AA|AAA|AAAA`
    c. `AA|AAAAA|AAAAAAAA`
    d. `A`

30. If possible, rewrite the following regular expressions using only the asterisk operator:
    a. `A\{0, \}`
    b. `A\{1, \}`
    c. `A+`
    d. `A`

31. If possible, rewrite the following regular expressions using only the plus operator:
    a. `A\{0, \}`
    b. `A\{1, \}`
    c. `A*`
    d. `A`

32. What is the difference between the following two regular expressions?

    `AB\{4\}` and `(AB)\{4\}`

33. Given the following regular expression

    `[ABC]`

    which of the following lines are matched by this regular expression? For those that match, identify which characters are matched.

    ```
    A
    AB
    ADBC
    D
    ```

34. Given the following regular expression

    `[^ABC]`

    which of the following lines are matched by this regular expression? For those that match, identify which characters are matched.

    ```
    A
    AB
    ADBC
    D
    ```

35. Given the following regular expression

    `[A-G]`

    which of the following lines are matched by this regular expression? For those that match, identify which characters are matched.

    ```
    A
    AB
    MBC
    D
    ```

36. Given the following regular expression

    `[^A-G]`

    which of the following lines are matched by this regular expression? For those that match, identify which characters are matched.

    ```
    A
    AB
    MBC
    D
    ```

37. Given the following regular expression

    `[ABC][AB]`

    which of the following lines are matched by this regular expression? How many characters are matched in each case? Which characters are matched in each case?

    ```
    A
    AB
    ADBC
    D
    ```

38. Given the following regular expression

    `[ABC][^AB]`

    which of the following lines are matched by this regular expression? For those that match, identify which characters are matched.

    ```
    A
    AB
    ADBC
    D
    ```

39. Given the following regular expression

    `^[ABC][AB]$`

    which of the following lines are matched by this regular expression?

    ```
    A
    AB
    ADBC
    D
    ```

40. Given the following regular expression

    `^[ABC][^AB]$`

    which of the following lines are matched by this regular expression?

    ```
    A
    AB
    ADBC
    D
    ```

41. Given the following regular expression

    ```
    bc.*
    ```

    which of the following lines are matched by this regular expression? For those that match, identify which characters are matched.

    > aaabbbcccddd
    > aaaabcsssss
    > aaaaabc
    > aabbss

42. Given the following regular expression

    ```
    bc*.
    ```

    which of the following lines are matched by this regular expression?

    > aaabbbcccddd
    > aaaabcsssss
    > aaaaabc
    > aabbss

43. Given the following regular expression

    ```
    ^[a-z]...
    ```

    which of the following lines are matched by this regular expression? For those that match, identify which characters are matched.

    > abcdefg
    > a:237efg
    > AbcDefg
    > afe

44. Given the following regular expression

    ```
    \..\{3\}$
    ```

    which of the following lines are matched by this regular expression? For those that match, identify which characters are matched.

    > rs.ef$tt
    > abc.ab
    > abc.$$$$
    > abc

45. Given the following regular expression

    ```
    s:?s*
    ```

    which of the following lines are matched by this regular expression? For those that match, identify which characters are matched.

    > efgs:sgfe
    > sssssssss
    > rsts
    > abc

46. Given the following regular expression

    `:?.?`

    which of the following lines are matched by this regular expression? For those that match, identify which characters are matched.

    :a?????????
    eeeeeefffff?hhhh
    aaa::??????
    :?.\?

47. Given the following regular expression

    `[^\$]$`

    which of the following lines are matched by this regular expression? For those that match, identify which characters are matched.

    $$$$$$aaaaaa
    bcdef$
    $
    abc

48. Given the following regular expression

    `^[^\$]*$`

    which of the following lines are matched by this regular expression? For those that match, identify which characters are matched.

    $$$$$$aaaaaa
    bcdef$
    $
    abc

49. Given the following regular expression

    `^[^\$]$`

    which of the following lines are matched by this regular expression? For those that match, identify which characters are matched.

    $$$$$$aaaaaa
    bcdef$
    $
    abc

50. Given the following regular expression

    `\$[0-9]$`

    which of the following lines are matched by this regular expression? For those that match, identify which characters are matched.

    $$$$$$
    $10
    abc$
    $

51. Given the following regular expression

    ```
    ^\$[0-9][0-9]$
    ```

    which of the following lines are matched by this regular expression? For those that match, identify which characters are matched.

    $$$$$$$
    $10
    abc$
    $

52. Given the following regular expression

    ```
    ^\$[0-9]*[^0-9]$
    ```

    which of the following lines are matched by this regular expression? For those that match, identify which characters are matched.

    $$$$$$$
    $10
    abc$
    $

53. Write a regular expression that matches a blank line.

54. Write a regular expression that matches a nonblank line.

55. Write a regular expression that matches every line.

56. Write a regular expression that matches a line with exactly three characters.

57. Write a regular expression that matches a line of at least three characters.

58. Write a regular expression that matches a line of at most three characters.

59. Write a regular expression that matches a date in the following format:

    Month dd, yy

    For example, it should match January 20, 99 or May 31, 97 and so on.

60. Write a regular expression that matches a date in the following format:

    mm/dd/yy

    For example, it should match 01/20/99 or 11/08/89 and so on.

61. Write a regular expression that matches a social security number pattern (ddd-dd-dddd).

62. Write a regular expression that matches a seven-digit telephone number (ddd-dddd).

63. Write a regular expression that matches a digit.

64. Write a regular expression that matches a nondigit character.

65. Write a regular expression that matches a five-digit zip code.

66. Write a regular expression that matches a number between 20 and 29.

67. Write a regular expression that matches an HTML tag (< . . . >).

grep

grep stands for **g**lobal **r**egular **e**xpression **p**rint. It is a family of programs that is used to search the input file for all lines that match a specified regular expression and write them to the standard output file (monitor). The concept is shown in Figure 10.1.

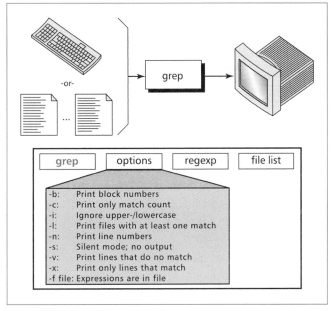

FIGURE 10.1 **grep**

10.1 Operation

To write scripts that operate correctly, you must understand how the **grep** utilities work. We begin, therefore, with a short explanation of how they work (Figure 10.2).

For each line in the standard input (input file or keyboard), **grep** performs the following operations:

1. Copies the next input line into the pattern space. The pattern space is a buffer that can hold only one text line.
2. Applies the regular expression to the pattern space.
3. If there is a match, the line is copied from the pattern space to the standard output.

The **grep** utilities repeat these three operations on each line in the input.

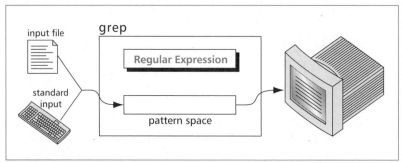

FIGURE 10.2 **grep** *Operation*

grep Flowchart

Another way to look at how **grep** works is to study a flowchart of its operation. Two points about the **grep** flowchart in Figure 10.3 need to be noted. First, the flowchart assumes that no options were specified. Selecting one or more options will change the flowchart. Second, although grep keeps a current line counter so that it always knows which line is being processed, the current line number is not reflected in the flowchart.

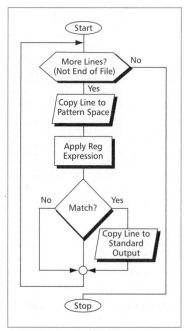

FIGURE 10.3 **grep** *Flowchart*

grep Operation Example

Let's walk through a simple example. The flow shown in Figure 10.4 displays any line in a file that contains UNIX. There are only four lines in the file and only three match the **grep** expression. As you walk through the flow, look for how **grep** handles the following situations:

1. **grep** is a search utility; it can search only for the existence of a line that matches a regular expression.
2. The only action that **grep** can perform on a line is to send it to standard output. If the line does not match the regular expression, it is not printed.
3. The line selection is based only on the regular expression. The line number or other criteria cannot be used to select the line.
4. **grep** is a filter. It can be used at the left- or right-hand side of a pipe.

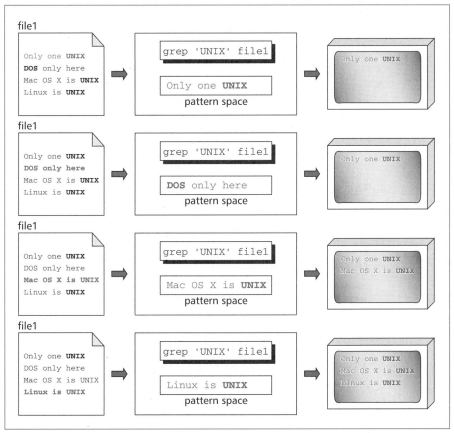

FIGURE 10.4 **grep** *Example*

In addition to the points just listed, the following **grep** limitations must be kept in mind at all times:

1. **grep** cannot be used to add, delete, or change a line.
2. **grep** cannot be used to print only part of a line.

3. **grep** cannot read only part of a file.

4. **grep** cannot select a line based on the contents of the previous or the next line. There is only one buffer, and it holds only the current line.

Many of these limitations can be overcome by combining **grep** with other utilities.

10.2 grep Family

There are three utilities in the **grep** family: **grep**, **egrep**, and **fgrep**. All three search one or more files and output lines that contain text that matches criteria specified as a regular expression. The whole line does not have to match the criteria; any matching text in the line is sufficient for it to be output. It examines each line in the file, one by one. When a line contains a matching pattern, the line is output. Although this is a powerful capability that quickly reduces a large amount of data to a meaningful set of information, it cannot be used to process only a portion of the data. The **grep** family appears in Figure 10.5.

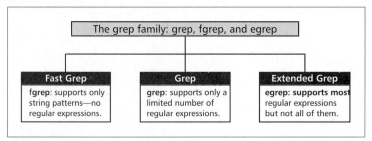

FIGURE 10.5 *The **grep** Family*

grep *Family Options*

There are several options available to the **grep** family. A summary is found in Table 10.1.

TABLE 10.1   **grep** *Options*

Option	Explanation
-b	Precedes each line by the file block number in which it is found.
-c	Prints only a count of the number of lines matching the pattern.
-i	Ignores upper- /lowercase in matching text.
-l	Prints a list of files that contain at least one line matching the pattern.
-n	Shows line number of each line before the line.
-s	Silent mode. Executes utility but suppresses all output.
-v	Inverse output. Prints lines that do not match pattern.
-x	Prints only lines that entirely match pattern.
-f file	List of strings to be matched are in file.

grep *Family Expressions*

As stated in Figure 10.5, fast grep (**fgrep**) uses only sequence operators in a pattern; it does not support any of the other regular expression operators. Basic **grep** and extended grep (**egrep**) both accept regular expressions as shown in Table 10.2. As you can see from the table, not all expressions are available.

TABLE 10.2   *Regular Expressions in the* **grep** *Family*

Atoms	grep	fgrep	egrep	Operators	grep	fgrep	egrep
Character	✓	✓	✓	Sequence	✓	✓	✓
Dot	✓		✓	Repetition	all but ?		* ? +
Class	✓		✓	Alternation			✓
Anchors	✓		^ $	Group			✓
Back Reference	✓			Save	✓		

Expressions in the **grep** utilities can become quite complex, often combining several atoms and/or operators into one large expression. When operators and atoms are combined, they are generally enclosed in either single quotes or double quotes. Technically, the quotes are needed only when there is a blank or other character that has a special meaning to the **grep** utilities. As a good technique, we recommend that you always use them. The combined expression format is shown below.

```
$grep 'Forouzan, *Behrouz' file1
```

grep

The original of the file-matching utilities, **grep** handles most of the regular expressions.[1] The middle road between the other two members of the family, **grep** allows regular expressions but is generally slower than **egrep**. Use it unless you need to group expressions or use repetition to match one or more occurrences of a pattern. It is the only member of the **grep** family that allows saving the results of a match for later use. In Session 10.1, we use **grep** to find all the lines that end in a semicolon (;) and then pipe the results to **head** and print the first five.

SESSION 10.1   **grep** *Example*

```
$ grep -n ";$" TheRaven | head -5
8:Ah, distinctly I remember it was in the bleak December;
16:Thrilled me--filled me with fantastic terrors never felt before;
18:"'Tis some visitor entreating entrance at my chamber door;
22:"Sir," said I, "or Madam, truly your forgiveness I implore;
29:Doubting, dreaming dreams no mortals ever dared to dream before;
```

---

[1]For an interesting discussion of the history of **grep,** see Jeffrey E. F. Friedl, *Mastering Regular Expressions* (Sebastopol, CA: O'Reilly & Associates, Inc., 1997).

Session 10.1 Analysis: From Table 10.1, we see that the −n option requests that the line numbers from the original file be included in the output. They are seen at the beginning of each line. The regular expression

```
;$
```

looks for a semicolon (;) at the end of the line ($). The filename is "TheRaven," and the output of the **grep** execution is piped to the head utility where only the first five lines are printed (−5).

Fast grep

If your search criteria require only sequence expressions, fast grep (**fgrep**) is the best utility. Because its expressions consist of only sequence operators, it is also easiest to use if you are searching for text characters that are the same as regular expression operators, such as the escape, parentheses, or quotes. For example, to extract all lines of "The Raven" that contain an apostrophe, we could use **fgrep** as shown in Session 10.2.

SESSION 10.2 *Fast **grep** Example*

```
$ fgrep -n "'" TheRaven
5:"'Tis some visitor," I muttered, "tapping at my chamber door
18:"'Tis some visitor entreating entrance at my chamber door;
40:'Tis the wind and nothing more!"
```

Session 10.2 Analysis: Once again we have requested that the line numbers be printed at the beginning of each line (option −n). The regular expression, enclosed in quote marks, is an apostrophe. The file is TheRaven. Three lines in the file matched the search criterion.

Extended grep

Extended grep (**egrep**) is the most powerful of the three **grep** utilities. While it doesn't have the save option (see Table 10.2), it does allow more complex patterns. Consider the case where we want to extract all lines that start with a capital letter and end in an exclamation point (!). Our first attempt at this command is shown in Session 10.3.

SESSION 10.3 *Extended **grep** Example*

```
$ egrep -n '^[A-Z].*!$' TheRaven
82:She shall press, ah, nevermore!
107:Leave no black plume as a token of that lie thy soul hath spoken!
116:Shall be lifted nevermore!
```

Session 10.3 Analysis: This is a relatively complex expression; we have actually coded three expressions in one. Let's break it down.

The first expression starts at the beginning of the line (^) and looks at the first character only. It uses a set that consists of only uppercase letters ([A-Z]). If the first character does not match the set, the line is skipped and the next line is examined.

If the first character is a match, the second expression (.*) matches the rest of the line until the last character, which must be an exclamation mark.

The third expression examines the character at the end of the line ($). It must be an explanation point (a bang). The complete expression therefore matches any line starting with an uppercase letter, that is followed by zero or more characters, and that ends in a bang.

Finally, note that we have coded the entire expression in a set of single quotes even though this expression does not require it.

While our expression appears to satisfy our request, we really wanted to find all lines that have the emphasis of a bang at the end. Some of the lines end in a quote mark, which puts the bang in the second character from the end. Also, some end in a bang followed by two hyphens. We therefore have three conditions that we need to consider.

Let's develop each pattern separately and then we'll combine all of them into one expression. We begin with the pattern to select the lines beginning with an uppercase character and ending with !". The only difference between this pattern and the one in Session 10.3 is that we must provide for the possibility of a character following the bang at the end of the line. The expression and its results are in Session 10.4. Note that the third expression is \!.$´.

SESSION 10.4 *Find Lines in "The Raven" (Part 1)*

```
$ egrep '^[A-Z].*\!.$' TheRaven
And the only word there spoken was the whispered word, "Lenore!"
This I whispered, and an echo murmured back the word, "Lenore!"
Tell me what thy lordly name is on the Night's Plutonian shore!"
Quaff, oh quaff this kind nepenthe and forget this lost Lenore!"
Is there--is there balm in Gilead? --tell me--tell me I implore!"
Clasp a rare and radiant maiden, whom the angels name Lenore!"
Take thy beak from out my heart, and take thy form from off my door!"
```

Now let's combine the first two patterns into one. This is easily done with the alternation operator (|). It is placed between the two patterns as shown in Session 10.5.

(pattern) | (pattern)

Note that when we combine patterns with the alternation operator, we group each expression by placing parentheses around it. The complete pattern and its results are shown in Session 10.5. Examine the patterns carefully. Study the results to find the lines that match each pattern.

SESSION 10.5 *Find Lines in "The Raven" (Part 2)*

```
$ egrep '(^[A-Z].*\!$)|(^[A-Z].*\!.$)' TheRaven
And the only word there spoken was the whispered word, "Lenore!"
This I whispered, and an echo murmured back the word "Lenore!"
```
Continued

SESSION 10.5 *Find Lines in "The Raven" (Part 2)—Continued*

```
Tell me what thy lordly name is on the Night's Plutonian shore!"
She shall press, ah, nevermore!
Quaff, oh quaff this kind nepenthe and forget this lost Lenore!"
Is there--is there balm in Gilead? --tell me--tell me I implore!"
Clasp a rare and radiant maiden, whom the angels name Lenore!"
Leave no black plume as a token of that lie thy soul hath spoken!
...
Take thy beak from out my heart, and take thy form from off my door!"
Shall be lifted nevermore!
```

We are now ready to add the third pattern. It specifies that there may be two characters after the bang at the end of the line. We have placed it at the end of the expression in Session 10.6. Compare the output from this expression with the previous output and note the differences.

SESSION 10.6 *Find Lines in "The Raven" (Part 3)*

```
$ egrep '(^[A-Z].*!$)|(^[A-Z].*!.$)|(^[A-Z].*!..$)' TheRaven
And the only word there spoken was the whispered word, "Lenore!"
This I whispered, and an echo murmured back the word "Lenore!"
Tell me what thy lordly name is on the Night's Plutonian shore!"
She shall press, ah, nevermore!
Quaff, oh quaff this kind nepenthe and forget this lost Lenore!"
Is there--is there balm in Gilead? --tell me--tell me I implore!"
It shall clasp a sainted maiden, whom the angels name Lenore!--
Clasp a rare and radiant maiden, whom the angels name Lenore!"
Leave no black plume as a token of that lie thy soul hath spoken!
...
Take thy beak from out my heart, and take thy form from off my door!"
Shall be lifted nevermore!
```

Session 10.6 Analysis: Let's review this pattern carefully.

It consists of three group patterns separated by the alternation operator:

```
(^[A-Z].*\!$)
(^[A-Z].*\!.$)
(^[A-Z].*\!..$)
```

Each pattern requires that the first character on the line (^) be a capital letter (^[A-Z]) followed by zero or more characters (.*). This eliminates any line that starts with anything other than a capital letter.

The last expression in each pattern specifies that at the end of the line ($) there must be:

- a bang (!$), as in "Shall be lifted nevermore!"
- a bang and one character (!.$), as in "... from off my door!"
- or a bang and two characters (!..$), as in "the angels name Lenore!--"

10.3 Examples

In this section, we demonstrate several **grep** family expressions. Each example, except the last, is run against the following test file.

```
A
AB
ABC
ABCDEFGHIJKLMNOPQRSTUVWXYZ

1A.             #one space at end
12AB.           #two spaces at end
123ABC.         #three spaces at end
1234ABCD.       #four spaces at end

    .DCBA4321
   .CBA321
  .BA21
 .A1

Now is the time,
For all good students,
To come to the aid,
Of their college.

"Quoth the Raven, 'Nevermore'"

Able was I ere I saw Elba
Madam, I am Adam

UNIX is an operating system.
My favorite operating system is UNIX
UNIX is UNIX
```

1. Select the lines from the file that have exactly three characters.

```
$ egrep '^...$' testFile
ABC
```

2. Select the lines from the file that have at least three characters.

```
$ egrep '...' testFile
ABC
ABCDEFGHIJKLMNOPQRSTUVWXYZ
1A.             #one space at end
12AB.           #two spaces at end
123ABC.         #three spaces at end
1234ABCD.       #four spaces at end
    .DCBA4321
   .CBA321
  .BA21
 .A1
```

```
Now is the time,
For all good students,
To come to the aid,
Of their college.
"Quoth the Raven, 'Nevermore'"
Able was I ere I saw Elba
Madam, I am Adam
UNIX is an operating system.
My favorite operating system is UNIX
UNIX is UNIX
```

3. Select the lines from the file that have three or fewer characters.

```
$ egrep -vn '....'   testFile
1:A
2:AB
3:ABC
5:
10:
15:
20:
22:
25:
```

Analysis: The pattern in this example is four dot operators. It matches all lines with at least four characters. But we want lines with three or fewer characters; that is, we want the inverse of the patterns—all lines that don't match the pattern. This is done by using the $-v$ option in the UNIX command. Because some of the lines are blank, we also include the option to show the line numbers in the output (n).

4. Count the number of blank lines in the file.

```
$ egrep -c '^$' testFile
6
```

Analysis: The pattern contains only begin and end of line anchors; it contains no matching characters. Therefore, the only lines that match it are lines that contain no text (that is, blank lines). To get the count, we use the count option ($-c$). Verify the results by counting the blank lines in example 3.

5. Count the number of nonblank lines in the file.

```
$ egrep -c '.' testFile
22
```

Analysis: First we select all nonblank lines ($.$) by matching lines with at least one character. Then we use the count option ($-c$).

6. Select the lines from the file that have the string UNIX.

```
$ fgrep 'UNIX' testFile
UNIX is an operating system.
My favorite operating system is UNIX
UNIX is UNIX
```

7. Select the lines from the file that have only the string UNIX.

```
$ egrep '^UNIX$' testFile
$
```

Analysis: There are no lines that contain only UNIX.

8. Select the lines from the file that have the pattern UNIX at least two times.

```
$ egrep 'UNIX.*UNIX' testFile
UNIX is UNIX
```

9. Copy the file to the monitor, but delete the blank lines.

```
$ egrep -v '^$' testFile
A
AB
ABC
ABCDEFGHIJKLMNOPQRSTUVWXYZ
1A.                #one space at end
12AB.              #two spaces at end
123ABC.            #three spaces at end
1234ABCD.          #four spaces at end
    .DCBA4321
   .CBA321
  .BA21
 .A1
Now is the time,
For all good students,
To come to the aid,
Of their college.
"Quoth the Raven, 'Nevermore'"
Able was I ere I saw Elba
Madam, I am Adam
UNIX is an operating system.
My favorite operating system is UNIX
UNIX is UNIX
```

Analysis: This is another inversion example. First we select all blank lines with a pattern that contains only the start and end line operators (^$). Then we display the file with the inversion option (-v).

10. Select the lines from the file that have at least two digits without any other characters in between.

```
$ egrep '[0-9][0-9]' testFile
12AB.              #two spaces at end
123ABC.            #three spaces at end
1234ABCD.          #four spaces at end
    .DCBA4321
   .CBA321
  .BA21
```

11. Select the lines from the file whose first nonblank character is A.

```
$ egrep '^ *A' testFile
A
AB
```

```
ABC
ABCDEFGHIJKLMNOPQRSTUVWXYZ
Able was I ere I saw Elba
$ egrep -n '^ *A' testFile
1:A
2:AB
3:ABC
4:ABCDEFGHIJKLMNOPQRSTUVWXYZ
23:Able was I ere I saw Elba
```

Analysis: This example starts at the beginning of the line (^) and looks for zero or more spaces (*). This skips any leading space characters. If there are none, it does nothing. The next character in the expression is the letter A. If the current character is an A, it matches; if it is not, the line does not match the expression and it is skipped.

12. Select the lines from the file that do not start with A to G.

```
$ egrep -n '^[^A-G]' testFile
6:1A.            #one space at end
7:12AB.          #two spaces at end
8:123ABC.        #three spaces at end
9:1234ABCD.      #four spaces at end
11:    .DCBA4321
12:   .CBA321
13:  .BA21
14: .A1
16:Now is the time,
18:To come to the aid,
19:Of their college.
21:"Quoth the Raven, 'Nevermore'"
24:Madam, I am Adam
26:UNIX is an operating system.
27:My favorite operating system is UNIX
28:UNIX is UNIX
```

Analysis: In this example, we use the complement operator (^) in a class atom that specifies a range of A to G. Sixteen of the twenty-eight lines in the file match this pattern.

13. Find out if John is currently logged into the system.

```
$ who |  grep  'John'
```

10.4 Searching for File Content

Some modern operating systems allow us to search for a file based on a phrase contained in it. This is especially handy when we've forgotten the filename but know that it contains a specific expression or set of words. Although UNIX doesn't have this capability, we can use the **grep** family to accomplish the same thing. The following sections demonstrate this search.

Search a Specific Directory

When we know the directory that contains the file, we can simply use **grep** by itself. For example, to find a list of all files in the current directory that contain "Raven," we would use the search in Session 10.7. The option 1 prints out the filename of any file that has at least one line that matches the **grep** expression.

SESSION 10.7   *Search for Text in Current Directory*

```
$ ls
RavenII      TheRaven      man.ed        regexp.dat
$ grep -l 'Raven' *
RavenII
TheRaven
```

Search All Directories in a Path

When we don't know where the file is located, we must use the **find** command[2] with the execute criterion. The **find** command begins by executing the specified command, in this case a **grep** search, using each file in the current directory. It then moves through the subdirectories of the current file applying the **grep** command. After each directory, it processes its subdirectories until all directories have been processed. In Session 10.8, we start with our home directory (~).

SESSION 10.8   *Using **find** and **grep** to Search All Directories*

```
$ find ~ -type f -exec grep -l "Raven" {} \;
/mnt/staff/gilberg/unix10grep/RavenII
/mnt/staff/gilberg/unix10grep/TheRaven
/mnt/staff/gilberg/unix6filters/TheRaven
/mnt/staff/gilberg/unix7comm/TheRaven
/mnt/staff/gilberg/unix11sed/TheRaven
/mnt/staff/gilberg/unix11sed/readScript
/mnt/staff/gilberg/unix11sed/change.sed
/mnt/staff/gilberg/unix11sed/raven.txt
/mnt/staff/gilberg/unix8vi/TheRaven
/mnt/staff/gilberg/unix5shells/TheRaven
/mnt/staff/gilberg/unix13/TheRaven
/mnt/staff/gilberg/unix3/TheRaven
/mnt/staff/gilberg/TheRaven
/mnt/staff/gilberg/unix9filters/TheRaven
/mnt/staff/gilberg/TheRavenV1
/mnt/staff/gilberg/unix12awk/TheRaven
/mnt/staff/gilberg/unix3files/TheRaven
/mnt/staff/gilberg/unix3files/TheRavenV1
/mnt/staff/gilberg/unix13bourne/TheRaven
/mnt/staff/gilberg/unix13bourne/midRaven.scr
/mnt/staff/gilberg/unix13bourne/midRaven.txt
$
```

---

[2]For a discussion of the find file command, see Find (find) File Command on page 119.

10.5 Key Terms

extended global regular expression print (**egrep**)
fast global regular expression print (**fgrep**)
global regular expression print (**grep**)

10.6 Tips

1. The **grep** family consists of three commands: **grep**, **egrep**, and **fgrep**.

2. Always enclose the regular expression in **grep** and **egrep** and the string in **fgrep** inside two double quotes or single quotes. This prevents the shell from interpreting some characters in the regular expression or the string. The whole regular expression or the string is passed to the corresponding **grep** command untouched.

3. One of the **grep** family commands can be used to search for a line in a file that matches the regular expression or a string. However, none of the **grep** family commands can change anything in the line.

4. A **grep** family command reads a file, line by line, and checks if the line matches the command's regular expression or the string. If a match is found, the line is selected. However, none of the **grep** family commands has a memory structure (or buffer) to remember anything about the previous line or lines.

5. Pay particular attention to the fact that none of the **grep** family commands can extract part of a line. Either the whole line is selected or none of the line is selected.

6. Each of the **grep** family commands is a filter (see Chapter 6), not an editor. When you use any of them, the original file remains unchanged.

7. Only the **grep** and **egrep** commands accept a regular expression. The **fgrep** accepts a string of characters, which means everything included in the string is interpreted literally.

8. Not all types of atoms are supported by either **grep** or **egrep**.

9. The word-anchor atoms (\\< and \\>) are supported by **grep** or **egrep**.

10. The back-reference atoms (\\1, \\2, . . . \\9) are supported by **grep** but not by **egrep**.

11. Not all types of operators are supported by either **grep** or **egrep**.

12. The general repetition operator (\\{. . .\\}) is not supported by **grep** or **egrep**.

13. The plus operator (+) is supported by **egrep** but not by **grep**. If you want to use this operator in **grep**, simulate it with the asterisk operator (*). For example, instead of using the regular expression "a+", use the regular expression "aa*". They have the same effect.

14. The group operator (…) is supported by **egrep** but not by **grep**.

15. The save operator is supported by **grep** but not by **egrep**.

16. Sometimes it is easier to define the regular expression that is the complement of the given criterion instead of the criterion itself and then use the -v option. For

example, if the criterion is to find the lines that have three or fewer characters, it is easier to find the lines that have four or more characters. Thus, the command would be grep -v "...." file_name.

10.7 Commands

We introduced only three commands in this chapter. For more details, see Appendix F and the corresponding pages shown in the following table.

Command	Description	Options	Page
egrep	*Synopsis:* *egrep [-options] 'regexpr' [file-list]* Selects lines that match the regular expression.	b, c, i, l, n, s, v, x, f	356
fgrep	*Synopsis:* *fgrep [-options] 'string' [file-list]* Selects lines that match the string.	b, c, i, l, n, s, v, x, f	356
grep	*Synopsis:* *grep [-options] 'regexpr' [file-list]* Selects lines that match the regular expression.	b, c, i, l, n, s, v, x, f	355

10.8 Summary

- **grep** stands for **g**lobal **r**egular **e**xpression **p**rint.
- There are three members in the **grep** family.
- The **grep** utility is the oldest member of the family. It supports standard regular expressions.
- The **fgrep** utility is the fastest member of the family. However, it supports only a string as the matching pattern. (It supports only sequence operator.)
- The **egrep** utility is the newest member of the family. It supports more regular expression operators than the other two.
- **grep** is a search utility. It searches for the existence of a line that matches a regular expression.
- **grep** is also a filter: It can be used on the left or the right of a pipe.
- **grep** cannot be used to add, delete, or change a line.
- The only action **grep** performs on a line is to send (or not to send) the line to the standard output.
- **grep** cannot be used to print only part of the line.
- There is no way to force **grep** to read only part of the file. It stops only when the end of file is reached.
- The line selection is based only on regular expression matching. The line number cannot be used as a criterion.
- There is no way to tell **grep** to print a line based on the contents of the previous or next lines. At each moment, **grep** holds only one line in its buffer.

10.9 Practice Set

Review Questions

1. What does **grep** stand for? What does **egrep** stand for? What does **fgrep** stand for?
2. Define the **grep** family.
3. How many members does the **grep** family have? Name them.
4. Mention the primary difference between **fgrep** and the other two members of the family.
5. Which of the **grep** commands cannot accept a regular expression?
6. Are all atoms supported by both **grep** and **egrep**?
7. Which atoms are not supported by **grep**?
8. Which atoms are not supported by **egrep**?
9. Are all operators supported by both **grep** and **egrep**?
10. Which operators are not supported by **grep**?
11. Which operators are not supported by **egrep**?
12. Why is it better to enclose the regular expression (in **grep** and **egrep**) and the string (in **fgrep**) in quotes?

Exercises

13. Write a **grep** (or **egrep**) command that selects the lines from `file1` that have exactly three characters.
14. Write a **grep** (or **egrep**) command that selects the lines from `file1` that have at least three characters.
15. Write a **grep** (or **egrep**) command that selects the lines from `file1` that have three or fewer characters.
16. Write a **grep** (or **egrep**) command that selects the nonblank lines from `file1`.
17. Write a **grep** (or **egrep**) command that counts the number of blank lines in `file1`.
18. Write a **grep** (or **egrep**) command that counts the number of nonblank lines in `file1`.
19. Write a **grep** (or **egrep**) command that selects the lines from `file1` that start with a capital letter.
20. Write a **grep** (or **egrep**) command that selects the lines from `file1` that end with a period.
21. Write a **grep** (or **egrep**) command that selects the lines from `file1` that contain the string "UNIX" or "unix" or "Unix".
22. Write a **grep** (or **egrep**) command that selects the lines from `file1` that start with the string "UNIX".
23. Write a **grep** (or **egrep**) command that selects the lines from `file1` that end with the string "UNIX".
24. Write a **grep** (or **egrep**) command that selects the lines from `file1` that have only the string "UNIX".
25. Write a **grep** (or **egrep**) command that selects the lines from `file1` that have the pattern "UNIX" at least twice.

26. Write a **grep** (or **egrep**) command that selects the lines from file1 that start with the string "UNIX" and end with the string "UNIX".

27. Write a **grep** (or **egrep**) command that copies file1 to file2 (use **grep** to simulate the **cp** command).

28. Write a **grep** (or **egrep**) command that copies nonblank lines from file1 to file2; that is, it deletes the blank lines.

29. Write a **grep** (or **egrep**) command that selects the lines from file1 that start with one or more blank spaces.

30. Write a **grep** (or **egrep**) command that selects the lines from file1 that end with one or more blank spaces.

31. Write a **grep** (or **egrep**) command that selects the lines from file1 that start with one or more blank spaces and end with one or more blank spaces.

32. Write a **grep** (or **egrep**) command that selects the lines from file1 that start with a capital letter after zero or more leading spaces.

33. Write a **grep** (or **egrep**) command that selects the lines from file1 that end with a capital letter and zero or more trailing spaces.

34. Write a **grep** (or **egrep**) command that selects the lines from file1 that contain a digit.

35. Write a **grep** (or **egrep**) command that selects the lines from file1 that have at least two digits without any other characters in between.

36. Write a **grep** (or **egrep**) command that selects the lines from file1 that have at least two digits.

37. Write a **grep** (or **egrep**) command that selects the lines from file1 whose first nonblank character is A.

38. Write a **grep** (or **egrep**) command that selects the lines from file1 whose last nonblank character is A.

39. Write a **grep** (or **egrep**) command that selects the lines from file1 that do not start with A.

40. Write a **grep** (or **egrep**) command that selects the lines from file1 that do not start with a digit.

41. Write a **grep** (or **egrep**) command that selects the lines from file1 that start with A, B, or C.

42. Write a **grep** (or **egrep**) command that selects the lines from file1 that start with A to E or M to P, inclusive.

43. Write a **grep** (or **egrep**) command that selects the lines from file1 that start with any letter (upper- or lowercase).

44. Write a command that selects the lines that have only one integer (not a floating-point) number. The line should not have any other characters.

45. Write a command that selects the lines that have only one floating-point (not an integer) number. The line should not have any other characters.

46. Write a command that selects the lines that have only one octal number (the octal number should start with 0). The line should not have any other characters.

47. Write a command that selects the lines that have only one hexadecimal number (the hexadecimal number should start with 0X). The line should not have any other characters.

48. Write a command that, using an input file, creates an output file that contains only lines with no alphabetic characters (no upper- and lowercase letters).

49. Write a command that, using an input file, creates an output file that contains only lines that have at least four digits. The digits can be consecutive (next to each other) or separated by other characters.

50. Write a command that, using an input file, creates an output file. The output file is the same as the input file except it contains only the lines without leading or trailing zeros.

51. Write a command that, using an input file, creates an output file. The output file is the same as the input file, but it contains only the lines that are a five-character palindrome. (A palindrome is a string that reads the same both forward and backward.)

52. Use **grep** to simulate each of the following commands (if possible):
    a. `cp file1 file2`   c. `tail +30 file1`
    b. `head -20 file1`   d. `cat file1`

53. Use **grep** to simulate each of the following commands (if possible):
    a. `cat > file1`   c. `paste file1 file2`
    b. `cut -c20-30 file1`   d. `cat file1 file2`

54. Use **grep** to simulate each of the following commands (if possible):
    a. `uniq file1`   c. `tr "ABC" "***" file1`
    b. `wc -1`   d. `sort file1`

10.10 Lab Sessions

Session 1

1. Log into the system.
2. Use a command to create a file containing the following data. Call it `Ch10S1F1`. Use tabs to separate the fields. Do not type the headings.

ID	Name	Hours Worked	Hourly Pay
1425	Juan	18	14.25
4321	George	22	21.11
6781	Anne	44	16.77
1451	Ben	36	21.77
2277	Tuan	16	18.77

3. Use a one-line command to display the hourly pay of Anne (only the last field).
4. Use a one-line command to find the name of the employee with ID 1451.

Continued

5. Use a one-line command to find the names of employees who worked more than 20 hours. Hint: You may first want to extract the second and third fields before applying one of the **grep** commands.

6. Use a one-line command to find the id and hours worked for employees who earn more than $20 per hour.

7. Use a one-line command to find the id, name, and hourly pay for employees who worked fewer than 10 hours.

8. Log out of the system.

Session II

1. Log into the system.

2. Create the following file. Call it `Ch10S2F1`.

```
                The Wisdom of Aesop
    It is one thing to say that something should be done.
      It is quite a different matter to do it.
          "Belling the Cat"

  Liars are not believed even when they tell the truth.
          "The Shepherd Boy and the Wolf"

  Flattery is not a proof of true admiration.
          "The Owl and the Grasshopper"

  Those who work the hardest do not always get the profit.
          "The Lion, the Bear, and the Fox"

  Familiarity breeds contempt.
          "The Fox and the Lion"

  Take care of little things and
      the big things will take care of themselves.
          "The Astrologer"

  Two blacks do not make a white.
          "The Stag, the Sheep, and the Wolf"

  However unfortunate we may think we are,
      there is always someone worse off than ourselves.
          "The Hares and the Frogs"

  One lie leads to another.
          "The Monkey and the Dolphin"

  One swallow does not make a summer.
          "The Spendthrift and the Swallow"
```

Continued

Session II—*Continued*

3. Use a one-line command to copy the file Ch10S2F1 without the blank lines (copy nonblank lines). Call the new file Ch10S2F2.

4. Use appropriate commands to create two new files out of Ch10S2F2. The first file, called Ch10S2F3, contains only the lines that are indented. The second file, called Ch10S2F4, contains the lines that are not indented.

5. Use a one-line command to create a new file out of Ch10S2F3. This file, which is called Ch10S2F5, contains the lines that are centered (equal leading and trailing spaces in each line).

6. Print all files created in this session.

7. Log out of the system.

Session III

1. Log into the system.

2. Create and save the following file. Do not type the headings. Call it Ch10S3F1.

Department	Course	Session	Enrollment
CIS	15	1	45
CIS	54	1	20
BUS	34	2	20
ENG	11	2	89
CIS	45	1	38
MTH	35	1	56
MTH	35	2	41
PhE	17	2	25
CIS	54	2	67

3. Use a command to create a file of courses that have only one session. Call the file Ch10S3F2.

4. Use a command to create a file of courses offered in the CIS department. Call the file Ch10S3F3.

5. Use a command to create a file of courses that have fewer than 25 students. Call the file Ch10S3F4.

6. Use a command to create a file of courses that have between 25 and 30 students. Call the file Ch10S3F5.

7. Log out of the system.

Session IV

1. Log into the system.
2. Create and save the following file. Call it Ch10S4F1.

```
This is a file that should be checked carefully.
Some lines in this file have duplicated or triplicated words.
If a word appears in the line twice, the word is duplicated.
If it is repeated thrice, it is triplicated (thrice is three).
For example, the following line has duplicated words.
The duplicated words are hard to find, but grep can find them for you.
However, you need to write the regular expression very carefully.
```

3. Use appropriate commands to create two files out of this file. The first one, Ch10S4F2, contains lines with no duplicated words. The second one, Ch10S4F3, has triplicated words.
4. Print all files created in this session and verify that they are correct.
5. Log out of the system.

Session V

1. Log into the system.
2. Create and save the following file. Call it Ch10S5F1.

```
* This is a line with only one asterisk.
* This is a line that starts with an asterisk, *but* has more.*
*** This is a line with three asterisks in a row.
This line has no asterisk.
* This is another line with only one asterisk.
This line has two asterisks * separated by other characters. *
*** The start and end have three asterisks. ***
This line has two asterisks with *a* character between them.
*** The start has three, but the end has four asterisks. ****
*The start and end have one asterisk.*
```

3. Write a command that finds the lines that start with one and only one asterisk. The line may contain more asterisks, but it must start with one asterisk followed by a nonasterisk character.
4. Write a command that finds the lines that contain two asterisks separated by another single character.
5. Write a command that finds lines with six or fewer asterisks.
6. Write a command that has an equal number of asterisks at the beginning and the end.
7. Log out of the system.

sed

sed is an acronym for stream **ed**itor. Although the name implies editing, it is not a true editor; it does not change anything in the original file. Rather sed scans the input file, line by line, and applies a list of instructions (called a **sed script**) to each line in the input file. The script, which is usually a separate file, can be included in the sed command line if it is a one-line command. The concept is shown in Figure 11.1.

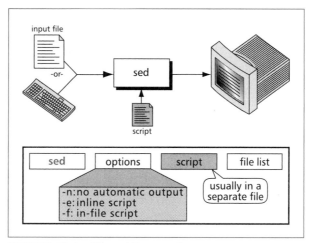

FIGURE 11.1   *The **sed** Command*

The **sed** utility has three useful options. Option -n suppresses the automatic output. It allows us to write scripts in which we control the printing. Option -f indicates that there is a script file, which immediately follows on the command line. The third option, -e, is the default. It indicates that the script is on the command line, not in a file. Because it is the default, it is not required.

11.1 Scripts

The **sed** utility is called like any other utility. In addition to input data, **sed** also requires one or more instructions that provide editing criteria. When there is only one command, it may be entered from the keyboard. Most of the time, however, instructions are placed in a file known as a **sed** script (program). Each instruction in a **sed** script contains an address and a command. The instruction format is fully developed throughout the chapter.

Script Formats

When the script fits in a few lines, its instructions can be included in the command line as shown in Figure 11.2(a). Note that in this case, the script must be enclosed in quotes.

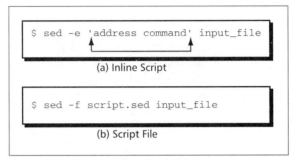

(a) Inline Script

(b) Script File

FIGURE 11.2 *Examples of sed Scripts*

For longer scripts, or for scripts that are going to be executed repeatedly over time, a separate script file is preferred. The file is created with a text editor and saved. In this book, we suffix the script filename with .sed to indicate that it is a **sed** script. This is not a requirement, but it does make it easier to identify executable scripts. Figure 11.2(b) is an example of executing a **sed** script.

Instruction Format

As previously stated, each instruction consists of an address and a command (Figure 11.3).

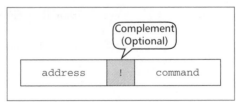

FIGURE 11.3 *Instruction Format*

The address selects the line to be processed (or not processed) by the command. The exclamation point (!) is an optional address complement. When it is not present, the address must exactly match a line to select the line. When the complement operator is present, any line that does not match the address is selected; lines that match the address are skipped. The command indicates the action that **sed** is to apply to each input line that matches the address.

Comments

A **comment** is a script line that documents or explains one or more instructions in a script. It is provided to assist the reader and is ignored by **sed.** Comment lines begin with a comment token, which is the pound sign (#). If the comment requires more than one line, each line must start with the comment token.

Session 11.1 contains an example of a **sed** script. The first line is a comment. The rest of the lines are instructions. In this example, the addresses are line numbers and the commands are one or more characters following the addresses.

SESSION 11.1 *A Sample Script*

```
# This line is a comment
2,14 s/A/B
30d
42d
```

11.2 Operation

Each line in the input file is given a **line number** by **sed.** This number can be used to address lines in the text. For each line, **sed** performs the following operations:

1. Copies an input line to the **pattern space.** The pattern space is a special buffer capable of holding one or more text lines for processing.
2. Applies all the instructions in the script, one by one, to all pattern space lines that match the specified addresses in the instruction.
3. Copies the contents of the pattern space to the output file unless directed not to by the -n option flag.

> **sed** does not change the input file. All modified output is written to standard output and to be saved must be redirected to a file.

When all of the commands have been processed, **sed** repeats the cycle starting with 1. When you examine this process carefully, you will note that there are two loops in this processing cycle. One loop processes all of the instructions against the current line (operation 2 in the list). The second loop processes all lines. This flow is presented in Figure 11.4.

A second buffer, the **hold space,** is available to temporarily store one or more lines as directed by the **sed** instructions. The **sed** operation is shown in Figure 11.5.

To fully understand how **sed** interacts with the input file, let's look at the example in Figure 11.6. This script uses range addresses with the substitution command. In the first line, "Greetings" is substituted for "Hello" in the range address 1 to 3 (1,3). The second instruction substitutes "buddies" for "friends" in lines 2 and 3. Note that the two range address overlap.

As the script is executed, the following actions are taken:

1. The first line ("Hello friends") is copied to the pattern space. The script is applied, instruction by instruction, to the contents of the pattern space.
   a. Script line 1: The address (1–3) matches the input line (1), so the instruction is applied. The pattern space now contains "Greetings friends."
   b. Script line 2: The address (2 or 3) does not match, so this instruction is not applied.
   c. End of script: The pattern space, "Greetings friends," is sent to the monitor.

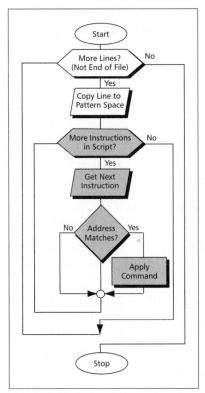

FIGURE 11.4 **sed**'s *Processing Flow*

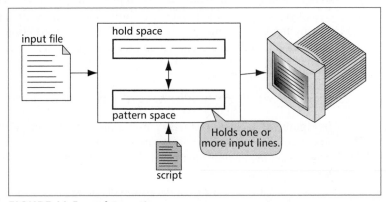

FIGURE 11.5 **sed** *Operation*

2. The second line ("Hello guests") is copied to the pattern space, replacing its contents. The script is applied, instruction by instruction, to the contents of the pattern space.

   a. Script line 1: The address (1–3) matches the input line (2), so the instruction is applied. The pattern space now contains "Greetings guests."

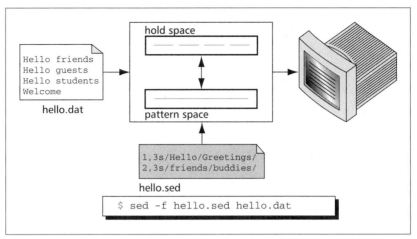

FIGURE 11.6 *Script Execution*

   b. Script line 2: The address (2 or 3) matches the input line (2), so this instruction is applied. However, because there is no "friends" in the line, the pattern space is unchanged; it still contains "Greetings guests."

   c. End of script: The pattern space is sent to the monitor.

3. The third line ("Hello students") is copied to the pattern space, replacing its contents. The script is applied, instruction by instruction, to the contents of the pattern space.

   a. Script line 1: The address (1–3) matches the input line (3), so the instruction is applied. The pattern space now contains "Greetings students."

   b. Script line 2: The address (2 or 3) matches the input line (3), so this instruction is applied. However, because there is no "friends" in the line, the pattern space is unchanged; it still contains "Greetings students."

   c. End of script: The pattern space is sent to the monitor.

4. The fourth line ("Welcome") is copied to the pattern space. The script is applied, instruction by instruction, to the contents of the pattern space.

   a. Script line 1: The address (1–3) does not match the input line (4), so the instruction is not applied.

   b. Script line 2: The address (2 or 3) does not match the input line (4), so this instruction is not applied.

   c. End of script. The unchanged pattern space is printed.

Figure 11.7 shows the script execution instruction by instruction.

11.3 Addresses

The address in an instruction determines which lines in the input file are to be processed by the commands in the instruction. Addresses in **sed** can be one of four types: single line, set of lines, range of lines, nested addresses (Figure 11.8).

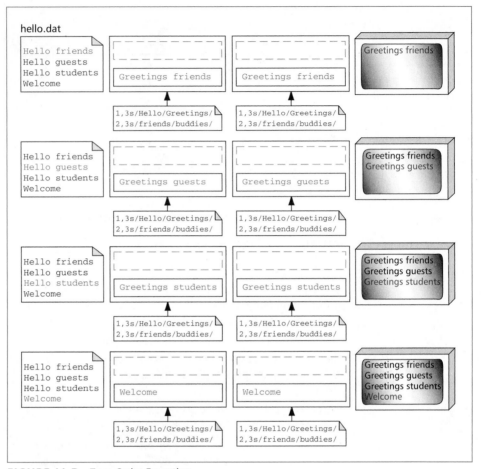

FIGURE 11.7   *Trace Script Execution*

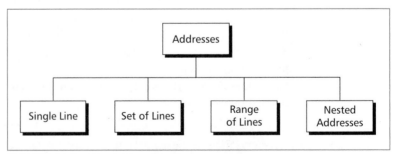

FIGURE 11.8   *Line Address in* **sed**

Single-Line Addresses

A single-line address specifies one and only one line in the input file. There are two single-line formats: a line number or a dollar sign ($), which specifies the last line in the input file.

In Figure 11.9, command$_1$ in the first instruction applies only to line 4. In the second instruction, command$_2$ applies only to line 16, and in the last instruction, command$_3$ applies only to the last line.

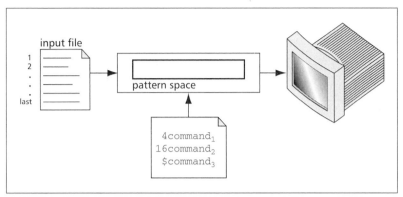

FIGURE 11.9   *Single-Line Addresses*

Set-of-Line Addresses

A set-of-line address is a regular expression that may match zero or more lines, not necessarily consecutive, in the input file. The regular expression is written between two slashes. Any line in the input file that matches the regular expression is processed by the instruction command. Two important points need to be noted: First, the regular expression may match several lines that may or may not be consecutive. Second, even if a line matches, the instruction may not affect the line. For example, a substitute command in a matching line may not find the data to be replaced.

Figure 11.10 contains two instructions with address sets. The first matches all lines that start with "A," and the second matches all lines that end with "B." For example, in Figure 11.10, line 2 matches both instructions addresses. A special case of a set-of-line

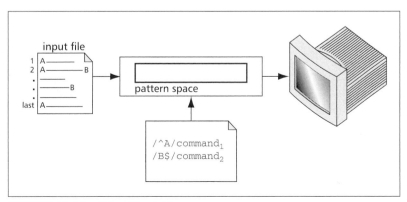

FIGURE 11.10   *Set-of-Line Addresses*

address is the every-line address. When the regular expression is missing, every line is selected. In other words, when there is no address, every line matches.

> **When no address is specified, every line is a match.**

Range Addresses

An address range defines a set of consecutive lines. Its format is start address, comma with no space, and end address:

> **start-address,end-address**

The start and end address can be a **sed** line number or a regular expression as in the next example:

```
line-number,line-number
line-number,/regexp/
/regexp/,line-number
/regexp/,/regexp/
```

When a line that is in the pattern space matches a start range, it is selected for processing. At this point, **sed** notes that the instruction is in a range. Each input line is processed by the instruction's command until the stop address matches a line. The line that matches the stop address is also processed by the command, but at that point, the range is no longer active. If at some future line the start range again matches, the range is again active until a stop address is found. Two important points need to be noted: First, while a range is active, all other instructions are also checked to determine if any of them also match an address. Second, more than one range may be active at a time. Figure 11.11 demonstrates two ranges. Note that in both, a range is terminated by reaching the end of the input file without finding an end address.

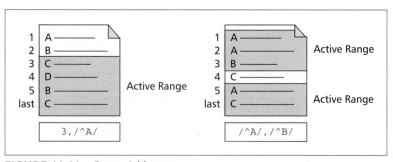

FIGURE 11.11 *Range Addresses*

A special case of range address is 1,$, which defines every line from the first line (1) to the last line ($). However, this special case address is not the same as the set-of-lines special case address, which is no address. Given the following two addresses:

```
(1) command                                    (2) 1,$command
```

sed interprets the first as a set-of-line address and the second as a range address. Some commands, such as insert (i) and append (a), can be used only with a set-of-line address. These commands accept no address but do not accept 1, $ addresses.

Nested Addresses

A **nested address** is an address that is contained within another address. While the outer (first) address range, by definition, must be either a set of lines or an address range, the nested addresses may be either a single line, a set of lines, or another range.

Let's look at two examples. In the first example, we want to delete all blank lines between lines 20 and 30. The first command specifies the line range; it is the outer command. The second command, which is enclosed in braces, contains the regular expression for a blank line. It contains the nested address.

```
20,30{
     /^$/d
     }
```

In the second example, we want to delete all lines that contain the word Raven, but only if the line also contains the word Quoth. In this case, the outer address searches for lines containing Raven, while the inner address looks for lines containing Quoth. What is especially interesting about this example is that the outer address is not a block of lines but a set of lines spread throughout the file.

```
/Raven/{
          /Quoth/d
       }
```

11.4 Commands

There are 25 commands that can be used in an instruction. We group them into nine categories based on how they perform their task. Figure 11.12 summarizes the command categories.

Line Number Command

The line number command (=) writes the current line number at the beginning of the line when it writes the line to the output without affecting the pattern space. It is similar to the **grep** -n option. The only difference is that the line number is written on a separate line. In Session 11.2, we use the **sed** utility with the line number command to print a file consisting only of the first verse of the poem. Note that this session uses the special case of the set-of-line address—there is no address, so the command applies to every line.

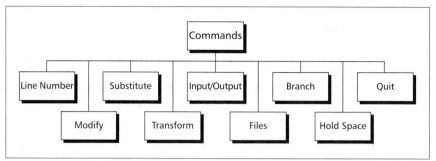

FIGURE 11.12   **sed** *Commands*

SESSION 11.2   *Display Line Numbers*

```
$ sed '=' TheRavenV1
Output:
1
Once upon a midnight dreary, while I pondered, weak and weary,
2
Over many a quaint and curious volume of forgotten lore
3
While I nodded, nearly napping, suddenly there came a tapping,
4
As of someone gently rapping, rapping at my chamber door.
5
"'Tis some visitor," I muttered, "tapping at my chamber door
6
Only this and nothing more."
```

In Session 11.3, we print only the line number of lines beginning with an upper-case O. To do this, we must use the -n option, which turns off the automatic printing. We use the regular expression /^O/ to select only lines that start with "O."

SESSION 11.3   *Print Line Numbers of Lines Beginning with "O"*

```
$ sed -n '/^O/=' TheRavenV1
Output:
1
6
```

Session 11.3 Analysis: First, refer to the previous example to verify that the only lines beginning with "O" are lines 1 and 6. Then study the **sed** command carefully. As specified, the -n option is used so that the pattern space containing the text is not to be printed; only the line numbers are printed. This option immediately follows the **sed** command.

Modify Commands

Modify commands are used to insert, append, change, or delete one or more whole lines. The modify commands require that any text associated with them be placed on the next line in the script. Therefore, the script must be in a file; it cannot be coded on the shell command line.

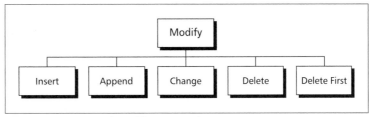

FIGURE 11.13   **sed** *Modify Commands*

In addition, the modify commands operate on the whole line. In other words, they are line replacement commands. This means that we can't use these **sed** commands to insert text into the middle of a line. Whatever text you supply will completely replace any lines that match the address.

> **All modify commands apply to the whole line. You cannot modify just part of a line.**

Insert Command (i)

Insert adds one or more lines directly to the output *before* the address. This command can only be used with the single line and a set of lines; it cannot be used with a range. In Session 11.4, we insert a title at the beginning of Poe's "The Raven."

SESSION 11.4   *Insert Title Line in "The Raven"*

```
$ sed -f insertTitle.sed TheRavenV1 | cat -n
```
```
# Script Name: insertTitle.sed
# Adds a title to file
1i\
                        The Raven\
                           by\
                  Edgar Allan Poe\
```
```
Output:
 1:                        The Raven
 2:                           by
 3:                  Edgar Allan Poe
 4:
 5: Once upon a midnight dreary, while I pondered, weak and weary,
 6: Over many a quaint and curious volume of forgotten lore
 7: While I nodded, nearly napping, suddenly there came a tapping,
 8: As of someone gently rapping, rapping at my chamber door.
 9: "'Tis some visitor," I muttered, "tapping at my chamber door
10: Only this and nothing more."
```

Session 11.4 Analysis: Study the use of the escape characters carefully in this script. A **sed** command is terminated by a return (newline). Because we want to insert four lines, each line must also have a return. This presents us with a dilemma: How do we end the line without ending the command? The answer is the escape character. By placing an escape character at the end of lines 3 through 6, we indicate that it is really not the end of the line. This keeps the newline for the end of the line but cancels the return that terminates the command. In line 7, we have an immediate return without a slash. This line therefore is both a blank line to separate the title from the body of the poem and a return to end the command.

> The escape character (\) must be immediately followed by a return. If any other character, including a space, follows it, the escape character modifies that character and sed will return an error rather than processing your commands.

If you use the insert command with the all lines address, the lines are inserted before every line in the file. This is an easy way to quickly double space a file. In Session 11.5, we demonstrate this technique with the first verse of "The Raven." Note that there is no address for the insert command.

SESSION 11.5   *Double Space File*

```
$ sed -f insertBlankLines.sed TheRavenV1
```

```
# Script Name: insertBlankLines.sed
# This script inserts a blank line before all lines in a file.
i\

# End of Script
```

```
Output:

Once upon a midnight dreary, while I pondered, weak and weary,

Over many a quaint and curious volume of forgotten lore

While I nodded, nearly napping, suddenly there came a tapping,

As of someone gently rapping, rapping at my chamber door.

"'Tis some visitor," I muttered, "tapping at my chamber door

Only this and nothing more."
```

Session 11.5 Analysis: There is only one problem with this little script. It inserts a line before the first line resulting in an empty line at the beginning of the file. With a little thought, you should be able to modify it so that the blank line appears after every line but the first. It would also be interesting to combine it with Session 11.4 to get a titled, double-spaced file.

Append Command (a)

Append is similar to the insert command except that it writes the text directly to the output *after* the specified line. Like insert, append cannot be used with a range address.

Inserted and appended text never appear in **sed**'s pattern space. They are written to the output before the specified line (insert) or after the specified line (append), even if the pattern space is not itself written. Because they are not inserted into the pattern space, they cannot match a regular expression, nor do they affect **sed**'s internal line counter.

> Inserted and appended text never appear in the pattern space; therefore, they cannot match a regular expression, nor do they affect sed's internal line counter.

Session 11.6 demonstrates the append command by appending a dashed line separator after every line and "The End" after the last line of "The Raven."

SESSION 11.6 *Append Command*

```
$ sed -f appendLineSep.sed TheRavenV1
# Script Name: appendLineSep.sed
#
# This script appends dashed dividers after each line
 a\
-----------------------------
$a\
\
                              The End
```

```
Output:
Once upon a midnight dreary, while I pondered, weak and weary,
-----------------------------
Over many a quaint and curious volume of forgotten lore
-----------------------------
While I nodded, nearly napping, suddenly there came a tapping,
-----------------------------
As of someone gently rapping, rapping at my chamber door.
-----------------------------
"'Tis some visitor," I muttered, "tapping at my chamber door
-----------------------------
Only this and nothing more."
-----------------------------

                              The End
```

Change Command (c)

Change replaces a matched line with new text. Unlike insert and append, it accepts all four address types. In Session 11.7, we replace the second line of Poe's classic with a common thought expressed by many a weary calculus student.

SESSION 11.7 *Change Script*

```
$ sed -f change.sed TheRavenV1
# Script Name: change.sed
# Replace second line of The Raven
```

Continued

SESSION 11.7 *Change Script—Continued*

```
2c\
Over many an obscure and meaningless problem of calculus bore
```
```
Output:
Once upon a midnight dreary, while I pondered, weak and weary,
Over many an obscure and meaningless problem of calculus bore
While I nodded, nearly napping, suddenly there came a tapping,
As of someone gently rapping, rapping at my chamber door.
"'Tis some visitor," I muttered, "tapping at my chamber door
Only this and nothing more."
```

Delete Pattern Space Command (d)

The **delete** command comes in two versions. When a lowercase delete command (d) is used, it deletes the entire pattern space. Any script commands following the delete command that also pertain to the deleted text are ignored because the text is no longer in the pattern space.

In Session 11.8, we delete all lines in the pattern space that begin with uppercase "O." Because this script is only one line, we code it on the shell command line.

SESSION 11.8 *Delete Entire Pattern Space*

```
$ sed '/^O/d' TheRavenV1
```
```
Output:
Over many a quaint and curious volume of forgotten lore
While I nodded, nearly napping, suddenly there came a tapping,
As of someone gently rapping, rapping at my chamber door.
"'Tis some visitor," I muttered, "tapping at my chamber door
```

Delete Only First Line Command (D)

When an uppercase delete command (D) is used, only the first line of the pattern space is deleted. Of course, if the only line in the pattern space, the effect is the same as the lowercase delete.

Recall that the basic **sed** operation (see page 375) copies one line from the file to the pattern space in each cycle. Generally, there is only one line in the pattern space at a time. We have not yet shown how to get multiple lines in the pattern space; we will see how when we discuss the hold and get commands starting on page 404. At that time, we will demonstrate the delete only first line command.

Substitute Command (s)

Pattern substitution is one of the most powerful commands in **sed.** In general, **substitute** replaces text that is selected by a regular expression with a replacement string. Thus, it is similar to the search and replace found in text editors. With it, we can add, delete, or change text in one or more lines. The format of the substitute command is shown in Figure 11.14.

Search Pattern

The **sed** search pattern uses only a subset of the regular expression atoms and patterns. The allowable atoms and operators are listed in Table 11.1.

FIGURE 11.14 *The Substitute Command*

TABLE 11.1 **sed**'s *Regular Expressions*

Atoms	Allowed	Operators	Allowed
Character	✓	Sequence	✓
Dot	✓	Repetition	* ? \{...\}
Class	✓	Alternation	✓
Anchors	^ $	Group	
Back Reference	✓	Save	✓

When a text line is selected, its text is matched to the pattern. If matching text is found, it is replaced by the replacement string. The pattern and replacement strings are separated by a triplet of identical delimiters, slashes (/) in the preceding example. Any character can be used as the delimiters, although the slash is the most common.

Pattern Matches Address

Before looking at the substitute operation further, let's look at a special case in which the address contains a regular expression that is the same as the pattern we want to match. In this case, we don't need to repeat the regular expression in the substitute command. We do need to show that it is omitted, however, by coding two slashes at the beginning of the pattern.

In Session 11.9, we replace the word "love" in the first three lines of Browning's poem, "How Do I Love Thee?"[1] with the word "adore." The search pattern in this case is the same as the address pattern, so we don't need to repeat it. Note the two slashes after the substitute command indicating that there is no pattern.

SESSION 11.9 *Address Matches Search Pattern*

```
$ sed '/love/s//adore/' browning.txt
```

Input:	Output:
How do I love thee? Let me count the ways.	How do I adore thee? Let me count the ways.
I love thee to the depth and breadth and height	I adore thee to the depth and breadth and height
My soul can reach, when feeling out of sight	My soul can reach, when feeling out of sight
For the ends of being and ideal grace.	For the ends of being and ideal grace.
I love thee to the level of everyday's	I adore thee to the level of everyday's
Most quiet need, by sun and candle-light.	Most quiet need, by sun and candle-light.

---

[1]Elizabeth Barrett Browning, "How Do I Love Thee? Let Me Count the Ways" from *Sonnets from the Portuguese.*

Replace String

The replacement text is a string. Only one atom and two metacharacters can be used in the replacement string. The allowed replacement atom is the back reference (see page 389). The two metacharacter tokens are the ampersand (&) and the backslash (\). The ampersand is used to place the pattern in the replacement string; the backslash is used to escape an ampersand when it needs to be included in the substitute text (if it's not quoted, it will be replaced by the pattern). The following example shows how the metacharacters are used. In the first example, the replacement string becomes *** UNIX ***. In the second example, the replacement string is now & forever.

```
$ sed 's/UNIX/*** & ***/' file1
$ sed '/now/s//now \& forever/' file1
```

Substitute Operation

Now that you've seen the substitute command's basic operation, let's look at the details. As shown in Figure 11.15, when the pattern matches the text, **sed** first deletes the text and then inserts the replacement text. This means that we can use the substitute command to add, delete, or replace part of a line.

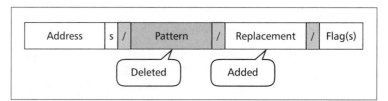

FIGURE II.15   *Substitute Operation*

Delete Part of a Line: To delete part of a line, we leave the replacement text empty. In other words, partial line deletes are a special substitution case in which the replacement is null. For example, Session 11.10 deletes all digits in the input from standard input (if no file is specified, **sed** looks for input from standard input).

SESSION II.10   *Delete Digits*

```
$ sed 's/[0-9]//g'
```
```
Input:
123abc456
321cba654
```
```
Output:
abc
cba
```

Session II.10 Analysis: An often forgotten point is that **sed** commands operate only on the first occurrence of a pattern in a line. In this session, we wanted to delete all digits.

Therefore, we used the global flag (g) at the end of the pattern. If we did not use it, only the first digit on each line would be deleted.

Change Part of a Line: To change only part of a line, we create a pattern that matches the part to be changed and then place the new text in the replacement expression. Session 11.11 changes every space in the file to a tab. Because the tab is not a printable character, you can't see it in Session 11.11, but it's there. Again, note the use of the global flag.

SESSION 11.11 *Change Part of a Line*

```
$ sed 's/ /    /g'

Input:
Now is the time
For all good students
To come to the aid
Of their college.

Output:
Now     is      the     time
For     all     good    students
To      come    to      the      aid
Of      their   college.
```

Add to Part of a Line: To add text to a line requires both a pattern to locate the text and the text that is to be added. Because the pattern deletes the text, we must include it in the new text. This can quickly become a very complex instruction. We cover complex instructions in the next section.

As a simple example, let's add two spaces at the beginning of each line and two dashes at the end of each line. This script is demonstrated in Session 11.12.

SESSION 11.12 *Add to a Line*

```
$ sed -f addPart.sed

#!/bin/ksh
#   Script Name: addPart.sed
#   This script adds two spaces to the beginning and
#   -- to the end of each line.
s/^/  /
s/$/--/
```

Input:	Output:
Now is the time	Now is the time--
For all good students	For all good students--
To come to the aid	To come to the aid--
Of their college.	Of their college.--

Back References

The examples in the previous section were all very simple and straightforward. More often, we find that we must restore the data that we deleted in the search. This problem is solved with the regular expression tools as demonstrated.

We first studied back references in Chapter 9. The **sed** utility uses two different back references in the substitution replacement string: whole pattern (&) and numbered buffer (\d). The whole pattern substitutes the deleted text into the replacement string. In numbered buffer replacement, whenever a regular expression matches text, the text is placed sequentially in one of the nine buffers. Numbered buffer replacement (\d), in which the d is a number between 1 and 9, substitutes the numbered buffer contents in the replacement string. This concept is diagramed in Figure 11.16.

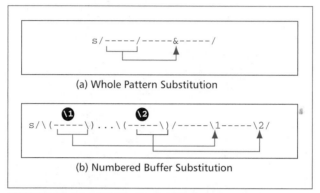

FIGURE 11.16 *Substitution Back References*

Whole Pattern Substitution: When a pattern substitution command matches text in the pattern space, the matched text is automatically saved in a buffer (&). We can then retrieve its contents and insert it anywhere, and as many times as needed, into the replacement string. Using the & buffer therefore allows us to match text, which automatically deletes it, and then restore it so that it is not lost.

As an example, let's return to Session 11.12 in which we added two spaces to the beginning of each line and two dashes to the end of each line. This script worked well, but it required two commands. We can do it in one command, as in Session 11.13, if we use command substitution.

SESSION 11.13 *Back Reference to Whole Pattern*

```
$ sed 's/^.*$/  &--/'
```

Input:	Output:
Now is the time	Now is the time--
For all good students	For all good students--
To come to the aid	To come to the aid--
Of their college.	Of their college.--

As another example, given a price list such as a restaurant menu, we can add dollar signs before prices using whole pattern substitution. The **sed** command for this problem is shown in Session 11.14.

SESSION 11.14   *Add $ to Prices*

```
$ sed 's/[0-9]/$&/' priceFile
```

Input:	Output:
Bargain Meals	**Bargain Meals**
All you can eat	*All you can eat*
Breakfast 3.99	Breakfast $3.99
Lunch 6.49	Lunch $6.49
Dinner 14.29	Dinner $14.29

Session 11.14 Analysis: A common question regarding this script is: How does the script know where to put the new data? While it doesn't look like we gave it a location, remember that we are substituting the text in the replacement string for the text that we matched and deleted with the search pattern. In the replacement pattern, we specify that the new text is a dollar sign and whatever digit we deleted in the search. Replacing only one digit works just like a replacement of the whole line.

Numbered Buffer Substitution: Numbered buffer substitution uses one or more of the regular expression numbered buffers. We use it when the pattern matches part of the input text but not all of it. For more information on its operation, refer to Chapter 9, Back References, on page 365.

As a last substitution script, let's write a script that reformats a social security number with dashes. In this example, we assume that all nine-digit numbers are social security numbers.

There are three parts to a social security number: three digits–two digits–four digits. This problem requires that we find and reformat them. Our script uses a search pattern that uses the numbered buffers to save three constitutive digits followed by two digits and then four digits. Once a complete match is found, the numbered buffers are used to reformat the numbers. Session 11.15 contains the **sed** script to reformat a file containing social security numbers.

SESSION 11.15   *Reformat Social Security Numbers*

```
$ sed 's/\([0-9]\{3\}\)\([0-9]\{2\}\)\([0-9]\{4\}\)/\1-\2-\3/' empFile
```

Input:		Output:	
George Washington	001010001	George Washington	001-01-0001
John Adams	002020002	John Adams	002-02-0002
Thomas Jefferson	003030003	Thomas Jefferson	003-03-0003
James Madison	123456789	James Madison	123-45-6789

Session 11.15 Analysis: The only new regular expression format in this expression is repeat. Each segment of the social security number is identified as a repeated digit. The number of times a digit is to be repeated is contained in the escaped braces following the digit range pattern.

Substitute Flags

There are four flags that can be added at the end of the substitute command to modify its behavior: global substitution (g), specific occurrence substitution (digit), print (p), and write file (w file-name).

Global Flag

The substitute command only replaces the first occurrence of a pattern. If there are multiple occurrences, none after the first are changed. For example, the first command in Session 11.16 replaces only the first "cat" with "dog." However, when we repeat the same command with the global flag at the end of the command, both occurrences of "cat" are changed to "dog."

SESSION 11.16 *Demonstrate Global Substitution*

$ sed '1 s/cat/dog/'	# without global flag
Input: Mary had a black cat and a white cat.	Output: Mary had a black dog and a white cat.
$ sed '1 s/cat/dog/g'	# with global flag
Input: Mary had a black cat and a white cat.	Output: Mary had a black dog and a white dog.

Specific Occurrence Flag

We now know how to change the first occurrence and all of the occurrences of a text pattern. Specific occurrence substitution (digit) changes any single occurrence of text that matches the pattern. The digit indicates which one to change. To change the second occurrence of a pattern, we use 2; to change the fifth, we use 5. Session 11.17 demonstrates the use of specific occurrence substitution.

SESSION 11.17 *Specific Occurrence Substitution*

$ sed '1 s/cat/dog/2'	
Input: Mary had a black cat, a yellow cat, and a white cat.	Output: Mary had a black cat, a yellow dog, and a white cat.

Only one specific occurrence can be changed in one command. To change the second and third occurrences requires two commands, one for the second and one for the third.

Print Flag

There are occasions when we do not want to print all of the output. For example, when developing a script, it helps to view only the lines that have been changed. To control the printing from within a script, we must first turn off the automatic printing. This is done with the -n option. Once the automatic printing has been turned off, we can add a print flag to the substitution command.

To demonstrate script controlled printing, let's look at an example that creates a list of regular files[2] and their permissions but nothing else. For this problem, we begin with the UNIX list command (ls -l). Because we want to limit the output to files, we

---

[2]Regular files are identified by a dash at the beginning of a long list.

turn off the automatic output with **sed**'s -n option. Using **sed,** we select only lines that start with a dash because we are interested only in files. To make it easier to follow the patterns, refer to the following long list output:

```
-rw-------    1 gilberg  staff       5782 Apr 27 16:22 TheRaven
```

The first regular expression in the substitute command saves the permissions. We identify the permissions as starting with a dash followed by zero or more non-blank space characters, which stops it at the first space. Then, to skip the rest of the line up to the filename, we create a pattern that includes zero or more characters and that ends with a colon (:) followed by two characters (the second digits in the time field). We then save the filename, which begins with the space character after the last time digit and ends with the end of line. This gives us the expression in Session 11.18.

SESSION 11.18 *List Permissions and Filenames*

```
$ ls -l | sed -n "/^-/s/\(-[^ ]*\).*:..\(.*\)/\1\2/p"

Output:
-rw-------  TheRaven
-rw-------  TheRavenV1
-rwxr-xr-x  appendLineSep.sed
```

Session 11.18 Analysis: This script has three parts. First, there is the long list command in which the output is piped to the second command. The second part is the **sed** command. The third part is the instruction, which is contained in double quotes. The instruction address is any line in which the first character is a dash (/^-/). The instruction's command is a replacement that saves the permissions in buffer 1 and the filename in buffer 2. The replacement pattern uses buffer 1 and buffer 2 followed by a print command because we used the no print option when we executed the **sed** command.

Write File Flag

The write file command is similar to the print flag. The only difference is that rather than a print command we use the write command. One caution: There can be only one space between the command and the filename. To write the files in Session 11.18 to a file, we would change the code as shown in the next example:

```
$ ls -l | sed -n "/^-/ s/\(-[^ ]*\).*:..\(.*\)/\1\2/w fileList.dat"
```

There can be more than one file written by a script. For example, we could write a script to write files from the long list to one file and directories to another.

Transform Command (y)

It is sometimes necessary to transform one set of characters to another. For example, IBM mainframe text files are written in a coding system known as Extended Binary Coded Decimal Interchange Code (EBCDIC). In EBCDIC, the binary codes for characters are different from ASCII. To read an EBCDIC file, therefore, all characters must be transformed to their ASCII equivalents as the file is read.

The transform command (y) requires two parallel sets of characters. Each character in the first string represents a value to be changed to its corresponding character in the second string. This concept is presented in Figure 11.17.

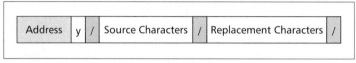

| Address | y | / | Source Characters | / | Replacement Characters | / |

FIGURE II.I7 *Transform Format*

As an example, to transform lowercase alphabetic characters to their matching uppercase characters, we would make the source set all of the lowercase characters and the replacement set their corresponding uppercase letters. These two sets would transform lowercase alphabetic characters to their uppercase form. Characters that do not match a source character are left unchanged. Session 11.19 demonstrates the transform command by translating lowercase vowels to their uppercase forms.

SESSION II.I9 *Transform Characters*

```
$ sed 'y/aeiou/EAIOU/'
```

Input:	Output:
A good time was had by all	A gOOd tImE wAs hAd by All
Under the Harvest Moon last Septem-	UndEr thE HArvEst MOOn lAst SEptEm-
ber.	bEr.

Input and Output Commands

The **sed** utility automatically reads text from the input file and writes data to the output file, usually standard output. In this section, we discuss commands that allow us to control the input and output more fully. There are five input/output commands: next (n), append next (N), print (p), print first line (P), and list (l).

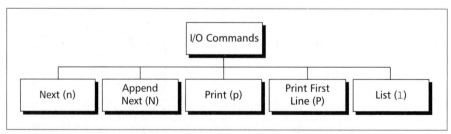

I/O Commands

| Next (n) | Append Next (N) | Print (p) | Print First Line (P) | List (l) |

FIGURE II.I8 **sed** *Input/Output Commands*

Next Command (n)

The **next** command (n) forces **sed** to read the next text line from the input file. Before reading the next line, however, it copies the current contents of the pattern space to the output, deletes the current text in the pattern space, and then refills it with the next input line. After reading the input line, it continues processing through the script.

In Session 11.20, we use the next command to force data to be read. Whenever a line that starts with a digit is immediately followed by a blank line, we delete the blank line.

SESSION 11.20 *Delete Blank Lines*

```
$ sed -f deleteBlankLines.sed deleteBlankLines.dat
```

```
# Script Name: deleteBlankLines.sed
# This script deletes blank lines only if
# the preceding line starts with a number.

/^[0-9]/{
        n
        /^$/d
      }
```

Input:	Output:
Second Line: Line 1 & line 3 blank	Second Line: Line 1 & line 3 blank
4th line-followed by non-blank line This is line 5 6th line followed by blank line	4th line-followed by non-blank line This is line 5 6th line followed by blank line Last line (#8)
Last line (#8)	

Session 11.20 Analysis: In our solution, we first locate a line that begins with a digit. We then use braces to create a set of nested commands. To see if the next line is blank, we first read it using the next command. This command forces the current line to be written. We then check the new line. If it is blank, we delete it.

This script works for this simple problem. However, it would not work if we had other commands that applied to the current line following in the script. Because the next command forces a line starting with a digit to the output, any command that follows would not see lines starting with digits.

Append Next Command (N)

Whereas the next command clears the pattern space before inputting the next line, the **append next** command (N) does not. Rather, it adds the next input line to the current contents of the pattern space. This is especially useful when we need to apply patterns to two or more lines at the same time.

To demonstrate the append next command, we create a script that appends the second line to the first, the fourth to the third, and so on until the end of the file. Note, however, that if we simply append the lines, when they are printed they will revert to two separate lines because there is a newline at the end of the first line. After we append the lines, therefore, we search for the newline and replace it with a space. The file consists of lines filled with the line number; line one is all 1s, line two is all 2s, and so forth throughout the file. Our solution is in Session 11.21.

SESSION 11.21 *Append Two Lines Together*

```
$ sed -f appendLines.sed appendLines.dat
```

```
# Script Name: appendLines.sed
# This script appends every two lines
# so that the output is Line1 Line2,
# Line3 Line4, etc.


N
s/\n/ /
```

Input:	Output:
1111first1111	1111first1111 2222second222
2222second222	3333third3333 4444fourth444
3333third3333	5555last55555
4444fourth444	
5555last55555	

Session 11.21 Analysis: This script really needs no analysis. However, we do want to comment on the test case. Note that we used an odd number of lines. Sometimes even very simple scripts fail when the test data only test the obvious. Actually, the script should be tested against two files: one with an even number of lines and one with an odd number of lines. In this script, if the last line is an odd numbered line and does not end in a newline character, it will be lost.

Another interesting, and much more useful, script replaces multiple blank lines with only one. This script is in Session 11.22.

SESSION 11.22 *Delete Extra Blank Lines*

```
$ sed -f appendBlkLines.sed appendBlkLines.dat
```

```
# Script Name: appendBlkLines.sed
# This script deletes extra blank lines

/^$/{
    $!N
    /^\n$/D
    }
```

Input:	Output:
First Line	Last Line
Second Line-One Blank Line	Second Line-One Blank Line
Third Line-Two Blank Lines	Third Line-Two Blank Lines
	Fourth Line-Three Blank Lines
Fourth Line-Three Blank Lines	
	Last Line
Last Line	

Session 11.22 Analysis: The first line of the script uses an address pattern to locate a blank line. When one is found, the first pattern in the inner command set tests to see if there is another line in the file ($!) and, if there is, uses the append next command (N), which appends it to the current line. If there are then two blank lines in the current line buffer, it deletes the first one (see page 386).

The $!N pattern is interpreted as "if the line is not the last line." Remember that $N and $!N are complements of each other.

Print Command (p)

The **print** command (p) copies the current contents of the pattern space to the standard output file. If there are multiple lines in the pattern space, they are all copied. The contents of the pattern space are not deleted by the print command. In Session 11.23's output, note that each line is repeated: The first time it was written by the print command; the second time, **sed** automatically wrote it at the end of the script.

SESSION 11.23 *Demonstrate Print Command*

```
$ sed 'p' linesOfNums.dat
```

Input:	Output:
11111111111	11111111111
22222222222	11111111111
33333333333	22222222222
44444444444	22222222222
5555Last555	33333333333
	33333333333
	44444444444
	44444444444
	5555Last555
	5555Last555

Obviously, there are very few occasions when we want to print lines twice. The real use of this command is to let the script control the printing. To do so, we must turn off the automatic printing. This is done with the -n option (see page 373). The following example copies lines 101 to 200 from file1 to file2:

```
$ sed -n '101,200p' file1 >file2
```

Print First Line Command (P)

Whereas the print command prints the entire contents of the pattern space, the **print first line** command (P) prints only the first line. That is, it prints the contents of the pattern space up to and including a newline character. Any text following the first newline is not printed.

To demonstrate print first line, let's write a script that prints a line only if it is followed by a line that begins with a tab. This problem requires that we first append two lines in the pattern space. We then search the pattern space for a newline immediately followed by a tab. If we find this combination, we print only the first line. We then delete the first line only (see Delete Only First Line Command (D) on page 429). Our solution is in Session 11.24.

SESSION II.24 *Print Line Followed by a Tab*

```
$ sed -nf printFirstLine.sed printFirstLine.dat
# Script Name: printFirstLine.sed
# Prints lines followed by a tab
$!N
# pattern in next command is newline & tab.
/\n      /P
D
```

Input:	Output:
This is line 1.	This is line 2.
This is line 2.	Line 3 starts with a tab.
Line 3 starts with a tab.	
Line 4 starts with a tab.	
This is line 5. It's the last line.	

Session 11.24 Analysis: Note the use of the append to pattern space (N) command, print first line command (P), and delete first line command (D). As the script starts, **sed** automatically loads the first line into the pattern space. When we append to the pattern space, therefore, we end up with two lines separated by a newline in the pattern space. The script then uses a newline-tab pattern[3] to determine if the appended line starts with a tab. If it does, we print the first line in the pattern space. Finally, the script deletes the first line in the pattern space, *leaving the second line*. Then, because we are at the end of the script, we loop to append the next line to the current line in the pattern space.

List Command (l)

Depending on the definition of ASCII, there are either 128 (standard ASCII) or 256 (extended ASCII) characters in the character set. Many of these are control characters with no associated graphics. Some, like the tab, are control characters that are understood and are actually used for formatting but have no graphic. Others print as spaces because a terminal doesn't support the extended ASCII characters.

The list command (l) converts the unprintable characters to their octal code. In the following example, we used C to create a file that contains five characters that are not printable in UNIX. The first is the nil character. In this case, **sed** does no conversion; the nil character is nothing and it recognizes that. The second character is a tab. Here **sed** recognizes the tab and prints the UNIX tab code (\t). In the other three cases, the octal code is printed. Note that we have suppressed the automatic output so that all we see is the list format output.

---

[3]The **sed** utility does not support the use of \t for the tab. Therefore, we must use an actual tab in the script. The only way to recognize it is by the long space. To make the script readable, we add a comment.

SESSION 11.25 *Print Nonprintable Characters*

```
$ sed -n 'l' listFile.dat
```

Input:		Output:	
Octal 0:	||	Octal 0:	||
Octal 9:	||	Octal 9:	|\t|
Octal 21:	||	Octal 21:	|\21|
Octal 22:	||	Octal 22:	|\22|
Octal 23:	||	Octal 23:	|\23|

File Commands

There are two file commands that can be used to read and write files. The basic format for the read and write commands is shown in Figure 11.19. Note that there must be exactly one space between the read or write command and the filename. This is one of those **sed** syntax rules that must be followed exactly.

FIGURE 11.19   *Read and Write Command Formats*

Read File Command (r)

The **read file** command (r) reads a file and places its contents in the output before moving to the next command. It is useful when you need to insert one or more common lines after text in a file. The contents of the file appear after the current line (pattern space) in the output.

Session 11.26 is an example of a read file application. We have prepared a standard letterhead and signature block for all letters to be sent. Using a standard text editor, we then prepare a letter. When we are satisfied with the letter, we use the script to insert the standard text. Note that because the read command inserts data after the first line of the file, the letter must start with at least one blank line.

SESSION 11.26   *Read File*

```
$ sed -f readFile.sed readFile.dat
# Script Name: readFile.sed
# This script inserts a letterhead and signature
# block in a file.
1 r letterHead.dat
$ r signature.dat
```

Continued

SESSION 11.26 *Read File—Continued*

Input:	Output:
letterHead.dat	
UNIX Consultants Inc	UNIX Consultants Inc
P.O. Box 555	P.O. Box 555
Silicon Valley, CA 94555	Silicon Valley, CA 94555
readFile.dat	April 1, 2001
April 1, 2001	John Doe
	Smart.com Inc.
John Doe	1234 Success Way
Smart.com Inc.	Userville, CA 95555
1234 Success Way	.
Userville, CA 95555	.
.	.
.	Sincerely yours,
.	
signature.dat	
Sincerely yours,	Richard F. Gilberg
	UNIX Consultants Inc
Richard F. Gilberg	
UNIX Consultants Inc	

Write File Command

The write file command (w) writes (actually appends) the contents of the pattern space to a file. It is useful for saving selected data to a file. For example, let's create an activity log in which entries are grouped by days of the week. The end of each day is identified by a blank line. The first group of entries represents Monday's activity, the second group represents Tuesday, and so forth, with the last group representing Sunday. The first word in each activity line is the day of the week: Monday, Tuesday, . . . , Sunday. We can divide this file into seven files using Session 11.27.

SESSION 11.27 *Write Files*

```
$ sed -nf aptFile.sed aptFile.dat
```

```
# Script Name: writeFile.sed
# This script creates seven activity log files, one for
# each day of the week.

/Monday/,/^$/w Monday.dat
/Tuesday/,/^$/w Tuesday.dat
/Wednesday/,/^$/w Wednesday.dat
/Thursday/,/^$/w Thursday.dat
/Friday/,/^$/w Friday.dat
/Saturday/,/^$/w Saturday.dat
/Sunday/,/^$/w Sunday.dat
```

Input:	Output: (cat -n *.dat)
Monday 10:00 Dr. Jones	1: Friday
Monday 1:30 Board meeting	2:
	1: Monday 10:00 Dr. Jones

Continued

SESSION 11.27   *Write Files*

```
Tuesday 8:30 Staff meeting          2: Monday   1:30 Board meeting
Tuesday 2:15 Scheduling             3:
Tuesday 3:00 Design review          1: Saturday
                                    2:
Wednesday                           1: Sunday

Thursday 11:30 Lunch with boss      1: Thursday 11:30 Lunch with boss
Thursday  2:00 Project              2: Thursday  2:00 Project
                                    3:
                                    1: Tuesday 8:30 Staff meeting
Friday                              2: Tuesday 2:15 Scheduling
                                    3: Tuesday 3:00 Design Review
Saturday                            4:
                                    1: Wednesday
Sunday                              2:
```

Session 11.27 Analysis: Because the only output is written to files, we ran the script using the no automatic print option (−n). The file output from this type of script is generally read by other scripts that process the daily activity. We show the file output using the **cat** command. We used the number option to indicate the different files. Note that the output comes out in filename order (by first character of day of the week).

Branch Commands

The branch commands change the regular flow of the commands in the script file. Recall that for every line in the file, sed runs through the script file applying commands that match the current pattern space text. At the end of the script file, the text in the pattern space is copied to the output file, and the next text line is read into the pattern space replacing the old text. Occasionally, we want to skip the application of the commands. The branch commands allow us to do just that, skip one or more commands in the script file. There are two branch commands: branch (b) and branch on substitution (t).

Branch Label

Each branch command must have a target, which is either a label or the last instruction in the script (a blank label). A **label** consists of a line that begins with a colon (:) and is followed by up to seven characters that constitute the **label name.** There can be no other commands or text on the script-label line other than the colon and the label name. The label name must immediately follow the colon; there can be no space between the colon and the name, and the name cannot have embedded spaces. An example of a label is:

```
:comHere
```

Branch Command

The branch command (b) follows the normal instruction format consisting of an address, the command (b), and an attribute (target) that can be used to branch to the end of the script or to a specific location within the script.

The target must be blank or match a script label in the script. If no label is provided, the branch is to the end of the script (after the last line), at which point the current contents of the pattern space are copied to the output file and the script is repeated for the next input line.

Session 11.28 demonstrates the basic branch command. It prints lines in a file once, twice, or three times depending on a print control at the beginning of the file. The format of the print control is a set of parentheses containing a digit. If the print control is (2), it prints the line twice; if it is (3), it prints the line three times. If there is no print control, it prints the line only once.

SESSION 11.28   *Using Branch to Print Lines*

```
$ sed -f branch.sed branch.dat
```

```
# Script Name: branch.sed
# This script prints a line multiple times (up to 3)
# depending on the first characters of the line.

/(1)/ b
/(2)/ b print2
/(3)/ b print3




# Branch to end of script
b

# print three
:print3
p
p
b

# print two
:print2
p
```

Input:	Output:
Print me once.	Print me once.
(2)Print me twice.	(2)Print me twice.
(3)Print me thrice.	(2)Print me twice.
(4)Print me once.	(3)Print me thrice.
	(3)Print me thrice.
	(3)Print me thrice.
	(4)Print me once.

Session 11.28 Analysis: Because **sed** automatically prints each line once at the end of the script, we need to print only the extra lines. Therefore, print2 prints once and print3 prints twice.

As you look at the output, there is one obvious problem. The print controls print also. We will take care of this problem with Session 11.29 in the next section.

A very common error in branching scripts is to forget the branch to end of script. In this script, we need it twice: once after the branch tests and once after the first label. If the branch after `print3` is missing, then the script will fall into `script2`. There are no automatic branches after a script label.

If a script requires other commands, they would be put first, followed by the branching commands. The script labels are generally placed at the end of the script.

Branch on Substitution Command

Rather than branch unconditionally, we may need to branch only if a substitution has been made. In this case, we use the **branch on substitution** or, as it is also known, the **test** command (t). Its format is the same as the basic branch command.

Let's rework Session 11.28 using branch on substitution to remove the print controls as we print. As you study Session 11.29, note that the substitution command is immediately followed by the branch. If a substitution was made, the branch is taken. If the substitution pattern was not found, the branch is ignored. There can be other commands between the substitution and the branch, but obviously, they can't be another substitution.

SESSION 11.29   *Printing with Branch on Substitution*

```
$ sed -f branchSub.sed branchSub.dat
```

```
# Script Name: branchSub.sed
# This script prints a line multiple times (up to 3)
# depending on the first characters of the line.

s/(1)//
t
s/(2)//
t print2
s/(3)//
t print3

# Branch to end of script
b

# print three
:print3
p
p
b

# print two
:print2
p
```

Input:	Output:
(1)Print me once.	Print me once.
(2)Print me twice.	Print me twice.
(3)Print me thrice.	Print me twice.
Default: print once.	Print me thrice.
	Print me thrice.
	Print me thrice.
	Default: print once.

Session 11.29 Analysis: We now have the output we wanted; the print controls have been removed except for the last one, which is a user input error. Compare this script with Session 11.28. They are very similar. Basically, all we did was change the addresses in Session 11.28, to substitutions followed by a branch on substitution.

Hold Space Commands

If you refer back to Figure 11.5 on page 376, you will note that there is a hold buffer that we have not used so far. It is used to save the pattern space. There are five commands that are used to move text back and forth between the pattern space and the hold space: hold and destroy (h), hold and append (H), get and destroy (g), get and append (G), and exchange (x). Their operation is shown in Figure 11.20.

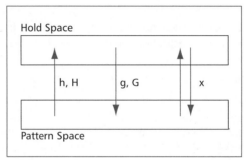

FIGURE 11.20   *Hold Space Operations*

Hold and Destroy Command

The **hold and destroy** command (h) copies the current contents of the pattern space to the hold space and destroys any text currently in the hold space.

Hold and Append Command

The **hold and append** command (H) appends the current contents of the pattern space to the hold space.

Get and Destroy Command

The **get and destroy** command (g) copies the text in the hold space to the pattern space and destroys any text currently in the pattern space.

Get and Append Command

The **get and append** command (G) appends the current contents of the hold space to the pattern space.

Exchange Command

The **exchange** command (x) swaps the text in the pattern and hold spaces. That is, the text in the pattern space is moved to the hold space, and the data that were in the hold space are moved to the pattern space.

To demonstrate the use of the hold commands, let's write a script that exchanges every two lines in a file. In other words, lines 1 and 2 are exchanged, lines 3 and 4 are exchanged, and so forth. The commands are shown in Session 11.30. Note that this script must be run with print off (option -n).

SESSION 11.30 *Exchange Lines in a File*

```
$ sed -nf exchange.sed exchange.dat
```

```
# Script Name: exchange.sed
# This script exchanges pairs of lines in a file.

# copy pattern to hold
h
# read next line
n
# retrieve hold area
G
p
```

Input:	Output:
line 1	line 2
line 2	line 1
line 3	line 4
line 4	line 3
line 5	line 6
line 6	line 5

Session 11.30 Analysis: The execution of this script is rather straightforward, especially with the comments. What is not apparent, however, is that this script has a serious limitation. Although it works well when there are an even number of lines, it does not work with an odd number of lines. In that case, the last line is printed twice. There is no simple **sed** solution to this problem. The easiest solution is to run a **sed** script to delete the last line.

Quit

The **quit** command (q) terminates the **sed** utility. For example, in Session 11.31, we write a **sed** command that prints only the first verse of "The Raven." Our script searches the file for the first blank line, printing each line as it executes. When it finds a blank line, it executes the command, in this case, quit. Note that the blank line is printed before **sed** terminates.

SESSION 11.31 *The Quit Command*

```
$ sed '/^$/q' TheRaven
```

```
Output:
Once upon a midnight dreary, while I pondered, weak and weary,
Over many a quaint and curious volume of forgotten lore
While I nodded, nearly napping, suddenly there came a tapping,
As of someone gently rapping, rapping at my chamber door.
"'Tis some visitor," I muttered, "tapping at my chamber door
Only this and nothing more."
```

A more complex script can be used to print the first verse without the blank line. In this script, we control the printing in the script itself so the no print option (-n) is turned on. When the blank line is found, we branch to the quit label, which terminates the program. As long as a blank line has not been found, we print a line and then branch to the end of the script to get the next line and process it. The revised code is in Session 11.32.

SESSION 11.32   *Demonstrate Quit Command*

```
$ sed -nf quit.sed TheRavenV1
```
```
# Script Name: quit.sed
# Prints until first blank line, then quits.
/^$/b quit
p
b

:quit
q
```
```
Output:
Once upon a midnight dreary, while I pondered, weak and weary,
Over many a quaint and curious volume of forgotten lore
While I nodded, nearly napping, suddenly there came a tapping,
As of someone gently rapping, rapping at my chamber door.
"'Tis some visitor," I muttered, "tapping at my chamber door
Only this and nothing more."
```

Session 11.32 Analysis: Note that without the branch to the end of the script, we would print one line and quit because we would enter the quit label code after printing. Even though the quit label is in the path of the code, it doesn't prevent the command sequence from flowing through it.

An interesting variation on the quit command is to use it with a line number. In this case, it acts like a head command. For example, Session 11.33 prints the first four lines of the file and then quits.

SESSION 11.33   *Print to a Specified Line*

```
$ sed '4q' TheRaven
```
```
Output:
Once upon a midnight dreary, while I pondered, weak and weary,
Over many a quaint and curious volume of forgotten lore
While I nodded, nearly napping, suddenly there came a tapping,
As of someone gently rapping, rapping at my chamber door.
```

11.5 Applications

In this section, we show some interesting applications of the **sed** utility.

Delete Lines

1. Delete lines that contain both BEGIN and END.

SESSION 11.34 *Delete BEGIN and END Lines*

```
$ sed '/BEGIN.*END/d' beginEnd.dat
```

Input:	Output:
1 This is the first line.	1 This is the first line.
2 This is the BEGINning of begin.	2 This is the BEGINning of begin.
3 It has several lines.	3 It has several lines.
4 This line has begin but not END.	4 This line has begin but not END.
5 This is just another line.	5 This is just another line.
6 This line has END in it.	6 This line has END in it.
7 But it is not the end.	7 But it is not the end.
8 This line has BEGIN and END in it.	9 This is the end--at last!
9 This is the end--at last!	

2. Delete lines that contain BEGIN but not END.

SESSION 11.35 *Delete BEGIN Not END*

```
$ sed -f beginEnd2.sed beginEnd.dat
```

```
# Delete lines that contain BEGIN but not END
/BEGIN/{
        /END/!d
        }
```

Input:	Output:
1 This is the first line.	1 This is the first line.
2 This is the BEGINning of begin.	3 It has several lines.
3 It has several lines.	4 This line has begin but not END
4 This line has begin but not END.	5 This is just another line.
5 This is just another line.	6 This line has END in it.
6 This line has END in it.	7 But it is not the end.
7 But it is not the end.	8 This line has BEGIN and END in it.
8 This line has BEGIN and END in it.	9 This is the end--at last!
9 This is the end--at last!	

3. Delete a block that starts with a line containing BEGIN and ends with a line containing END.

SESSION 11.36 *Delete BEGIN through END*

```
$ sed '/BEGIN/,/END/d' beginEnd.dat
```

Input:	Output:
1 This is the first line.	1 This is the first line.
2 This is the BEGINning of begin.	5 This is just another line.
3 It has several lines.	6 This line has END in it.
4 This line has begin but not END.	7 But it is not the end.
5 This is just another line.	
6 This line has END in it.	
7 But it is not the end.	
8 This line has BEGIN and END in it.	
9 This is the end--at last!	

Session 11.36 Analysis: The first thing to notice about this session is that **sed** does not use a greedy search. Rather than trying to find the largest block (lines 2 through 8), it finds and deletes lines 2–4 and 8–9.

There is another interesting aspect of this script. Notice that line 9 is deleted, even though it doesn't have either BEGIN or END. Can you figure out why? Think about it before you read the explanation.

When sed matches the text BEGIN in line 8, it starts looking for a matching END. It cannot find the match in the same line because the comma is a range with a start line and an end line. (Compare this code with the code in Session 11.34.) The end of the list automatically matches a block that has been started but not ended. Therefore, both lines 8 and 9 are deleted.

Delete Text

1. Delete the text string in one line that starts with BEGIN and ends with END (inclusive).

SESSION 11.37 *Delete Text between BEGIN and END*

```
$ sed 's/BEGIN.*END//' beginEnd.dat
```

Input:	Output:
1 This is the first line.	1 This is the first line.
2 This is the BEGINning of begin.	2 This is the BEGINning of begin.
3 It has several lines.	3 It has several lines.
4 This line has begin but not END.	4 This line has begin but not END.
5 This is just another line.	5 This is just another line.
6 This line has END in it.	6 This line has END in it.
7 But it is not the end.	7 But it is not the end.
8 This line has BEGIN and END in it.	8 This line has in it.
9 This is the end--at last!	9 This is the end--at last!

Session 11.37 Analysis: You will need to look closely to find the deletion in this script. It deletes only the text from the start of the text BEGIN to the end of the word END. If you still can't find the deleted text, look in line 8.

2. Delete the text between two words, BEGIN and END. The beginning and ending text can be on one line or can span many lines.

SESSION 11.38 *Delete BEGIN through END 2*

```
$ sed -f beginEnd5.sed beginEnd.dat
```

```
#   script name: beginEnd5.sed
#   Deletes the text between two words, BEGIN and END.
 /BEGIN.*END/s///
 /BEGIN/,/END/{
               # Put BEGIN line in hold space
               /BEGIN/{
                       h
                       d
                       }
               # lines between BEGIN & END in hold space
```

Continued

SESSION 11.38 *Delete BEGIN through END 2*

```
/END/!{
        H
        d
        }
# Exchange hold space and pattern space
/END/{
        x
        # Append hold (END line) to pattern space
        G
        }
# pattern space now contains all lines
s/BEGIN.*END//
}
```

Input:	Output:
1 This is the first line.	1 This is the first line.
2 This is the BEGINning of begin.	2 This is the .
3 It has several lines.	5 This is just another line.
4 This line has begin but not END.	6 This line has END in it.
5 This is just another line.	7 But it is not the end.
6 This line has END in it.	8 This line has in it.
7 But it is not the end.	9 This is the end--at last!
8 This line has BEGIN and END in it.	
9 This is the end--at last!	

Session 11.38 Analysis: This is a long script that you will need to study carefully if you want to understand it fully. Remember, it deletes the range starting with BEGIN and ending with END, regardless if they are on one line or several lines. The big question is: Where does the period in line 2 of the output line come from? The answer is the end of line 4, which was deleted except for the period.

11.6 grep and sed

As we saw in Chapter 10, the **grep** (or **egrep**) utility can be used to find (and print) the lines in a file that match (or do not match) a regular expression. The question that comes in mind is: If the **grep** utility is not available, can we use the **sed** utility to do the same job? The answer is "yes." The **sed** utility is much more powerful than **grep.** Everything we can do in **grep,** we can do in **sed;** the reverse is not true. However, we should not use **sed** instead of **grep** all of the time; **grep** is a much faster and more efficient utility.

To demonstrate how we can use **sed** in place of **grep,** we look at two general situations: (1) search for lines that match a regular expression and (2) search for lines that do not match a regular expression.

Lines That Match a Regular Expression

If we need to use **sed** instead of **grep** to find a line that matches a regular expression, we use the print (p) command in **sed** and turn off the automatic output option (−n). In other words, a **grep** regular expression command can be simulated using the regular expression in a **sed** command. The two commands are shown in the following example:

```
grep      'regular expression'    file1
sed  -n  '/regular expression/p' file1
```

To demonstrate, the Session 11.39 shows how to find lines that start and end with an uppercase letter using either **grep** or **sed.**

SESSION 11.39   *Using **grep** or **sed***

grep:
```
$ grep '^[A-Z].*[A-Z]$' file1.dat
```

Input:	Output:
abcdefghijklm	NopqrstuvwxY
NopqrstuvwxY	UVwxyz AbcdeF
Z abcdefghijk	
1MnopqrstursT	
UVwxyz AbcdeF	

sed:
```
$ sed -n '/^[A-Z].*[A-Z]$/p' file1.dat
```

Input:	Output:
abcdefghijklm	NopqrstuvwxY
NopqrstuvwxY	UVwxyz AbcdeF
Z abcdefghijk	
1MnopqrstursT	
UVwxyz AbcdeF	

Lines That Do Not Match a Regular Expression

If we want to use **sed** instead of **grep** (or **egrep**) to find lines that do not match a regular expression (activated in **grep** with the -v option), we again use the print command, but this time we complement the address (!) in **sed.** Because we are again controlling the printing, we must use the no output option (-n). The following example demonstrates how the code is written:

```
grep -v 'regular expression'    file1
sed  -n  '/regular expression/!p' file1
```

Session 11.40 demonstrates how we can find all lines that do not start and end with an uppercase letter using either **grep** or **sed.**

SESSION 11.40   *Using **grep** or **sed** Example 2*

grep:
```
$ grep -v '^[A-Z].*[A-Z]$' file1.dat
```

Input:	Output:
abcdefghijklm	abcdefghijklm
NopqrstuvwxY	Z abcdefghijk
Z abcdefghijk	1MnopqrstursT

Continued

SESSION 11.40 *Using **grep** or **sed** Example 2*

```
1MnopqrstursT
UVwxyz AbcdeF
```

sed:

```
$ sed -n '/^[A-Z].*[A-Z]$/!p' file1.dat
```

Input:	Output:
abcdefghijklm	abcdefghijklm
NopqrstuvwxY	Z abcdefghijk
Z abcdefghijk	1MnopqrstursT
1MnopqrstursT	
UVwxyz AbcdeF	

11.7 Key Terms

hold space	one-to-one relationship	set-of-line address
instruction	pattern space	single-line address
nested address	range address	stream editor
one-to-many relationship	script	

11.8 Tips

1. The -e option defines that the script is inline.
2. The -f option defines that the script is in-file.
3. If the script is inline, it should be enclosed in quotes.
4. If the script is in-file, the name of the file should appear after the -f option.
5. Distinguish between a script file and an input file.
6. The script file should be created and saved before using the **sed** command.
7. There should be no space between the address and a command in an instruction.
8. A comment in a script is a line that starts with a pound sign (#).
9. If the address is missing, it means all the lines in the input file.
10. The insert (i) and the append (a) commands cannot be used with a range address.
11. The modify commands (i, a, c, d, and D) are applied to the whole line or lines; they can't be used to change part of a line or delete part of a line or add text to the line.
12. The flags (n, g, p, w) can be used only with the substitute command (s), not with other commands.
13. The substitute command (s), by default, replaces the first occurrence of the pattern with the replacement string. To replace other occurrences, use the number flag (n). To replace all occurrences use the global flag (g).
14. A single substitute command (s) does not allow the replacement of multiple patterns; to do so, you should use multiple commands.
15. Distinguish between the p flag (part of the s command) and the p command.
16. Distinguish between the w flag (part of the s command) and the w command.
17. The replacement string in the substitute command is each line, not a regular expression. The only metacharacters allowed are the back reference and the ampersand (&).

11.9 Commands

The **sed** command was discussed in this chapter. For more details, see Appendix F and the corresponding page shown in the following table.

Command	Description	Options	Page
sed	*Synopsis: sed [-options] script [file-list]* Edits specified lines in the input files and processes them.	n, e, f	373

The **sed** command, as a filter, uses a script file made of instructions. Each instruction consists of an address, the optional complement token (!), and one or more commands.

Table 11.2 lists four types of addresses.

TABLE 11.2 **sed** *Addresses*

Category	Examples		Page
Single-line	35 $	(line 35) (last line)	378
Set- of- line	/^A.*B$/ nothing	start at A and end at B every line	379
Range	35,70 32,/^A/ /^A/,/^B/ /^A/,35 1,$	 all lines	380

Nested address	30,50{
	    /^$/
	    }
			381

Table 11.3 lists the 24 **sed** commands.

TABLE 11.3 **sed** *Commands*

Category	Command	Description	Page
Line Number	=	Writes the line number.	381
Modify	i	Inserts text.	383
	a	Appends text.	384
	c	Changes text.	385
	d	Deletes the pattern space.	386
	D	Deletes the first line of pattern space.	386
Substitute	s	Substitutes a pattern with a replacement string.	388
Transform	y	Transforms a set of characters to another set.	393

Continued

TABLE 11.3 *sed Commands*

Category	Command	Description	Page
Input/Output	n	Reads the next line into the pattern space.	394
	N	Appends the next line in the file to the contents of the pattern space.	395
	p	Sends the contents of the pattern space to the standard output.	397
	P	Sends only the first line of the pattern space to the standard output.	397
	l	Lists the contents of the pattern space with nonprinting characters represented by their ASCII codes.	398
Files	r	Reads the contents of a file and appends to the pattern space.	399
	w	Writes the contents of the pattern space to a file.	400
Branch	:	Labels a line to be used by branch (b) and test (t) commands.	401
	b	Branches unconditionally to the label.	401
	t	Branches on successful substitution.	403
Hold Space	h	Copies the contents of the pattern space to the hold space.	404
	H	Appends the contents of the pattern space to the hold space.	404
	g	Copies the contents of the hold space to the pattern space.	404
	G	Appends the contents of the hold space to the pattern space.	404
	x	Swaps the contents of the pattern space with the contents of the hold space.	404
Quit	q	Stops processing the input file.	405

11.10 Summary

- The address in an instruction determines which lines in the input file are to be processed by the instruction.
- Addresses in **sed** can be one of four types: single line, set of lines, range of lines, and nested.
- A single-line address specifies one and only one line in the input file. There are only two kinds of single-line address: a line number, which defines a specific line, or a dollar sign ($), which defines the last line.
- A set-of-lines address uses a regular expression that may match zero or more lines in the input file. The regular expression is written between two slashes.

- A range address defines one or more consecutive lines. The format is two single-line or set-of-line address separated by a comma (and no spaces between the comma and the two addresses).
- The relationship between commands and addresses can be one to one or one to many.
- In a one-to-one relationship, an address is associated with one command. If the address is matched, the corresponding command is executed.
- In a one-to-many relationship, an address is associated with several commands. If the address is matched, all of the corresponding commands are executed.
- A nested address is an address that is contained within an address range or a set of line addresses.
- There are 24 commands that can be used in an instruction.
- The line-number command (=) adds line numbers to the lines as they are printed.
- The modify commands (i, a, c, d, and D) allow us to modify the whole line or a group of lines.
- The substitute command (s) substitutes part of a line with each line. Substitution here means adding to, deleting, or replacing part of a line.
- The transform command (y) translates a set of characters into another set.
- The input/output commands (n, N, p, P, and l) change the normal flow of input and output.
- The file commands (r and w) read or write a file.
- The branch commands (:, b, and t) provide branching capability in the script.
- The hold space commands (h, H, g, G, and x) transfer text between the pattern space and hold space.
- The quit command (q) stops processing more lines in the input file.

11.11 Practice Set

Review Questions

1. Define the **sed** utility.
2. What does the name **sed** stand for?
3. Explain two formats of the **sed** command.
4. What is an inline script?
5. What is a script file?
6. How can we use comments in a **sed** script file?
7. How is a script file created?
8. What is the pattern space?
9. What is the hold space?
10. What is the format for an instruction in **sed**?
11. What is the address in an instruction?
12. How many types of addresses are defined for an instruction?

13. What is a single-line address?

14. Can a single-line address select more than one line?

15. Which of the following is a single-line address?
    a. 4
    b. /UNIX/
    c. 3,5
    d. $

16. Which of the following is a set-of-line address?
    a. 24
    b. /^A/,/B$/
    c. /^$/
    d. 22,56

17. Which of the following is a range address?
    a. 1,$
    b. /^A/,/B$/
    c. /[0-9]/
    d. 22,56

18. What is the difference between the following two scripts?
    a. 20, 25d
    b. 20d ; 25d

19. What is the difference between the following two scripts?
    a. 1,$d
    b. d

20. What is the difference between the following two scripts?
    a. 1,$ {
       /^A/d
       }
    b. /^A/d

21. Separate the address and the command in each of the following instructions.
    a. 25d
    b. d
    c. 20,50s/A/B/g
    d. 25,/^A.*A$/s/A//g

22. Find any error in each of the following **sed** instructions.
    a. 25d
    b. 30,50,70d
    c. 20,s/A/B/
    d. /^A/,50s/^$/

23. If no address is mentioned in the **sed** instruction, it applies to
    a. every line
    b. no line
    c. last line
    d. current line

24. If no address is followed by an exclamation mark (!), the command is applied to
    a. each line
    b. no line
    c. every line that matches the address
    d. every line that does not match the address

25. Does the **sed** command modify the original file?

26. Describe the similarities and differences between the n and d commands.

27. Describe the similarities and differences between the N and D commands.

28. Describe the difference between the n and N commands.

29. Describe the difference between the p and P commands.

30. Describe the difference between the d and D commands.

31. Describe the difference between the h and H commands.

32. Describe the difference between the g and G commands.

33. Compare commands in **sed** and **ex** using the following table format.

Description	ex	sed
Line number		
Insert		
Append		
Change		
Delete		
Substitute		
Translate		
Input next line		
Print		
List		
Read		
Write		
Label		
Branch		
Test and Branch		

Exercises

34. Show the result of the **sed** command

```
sed "s/bc.*/Z/"
```

on the following file:

```
aaabbbcccddd
aaaabcsssss
aaaaabc
aabbss
```

35. Show the result of the **sed** command

```
sed "s/bc*./Z/"
```

on the following file:

```
aaabbbcccddd
aaaabcsssss
aaaaabc
aabbss
```

36. Show the result of the **sed** command

    ```
    sed "s/^[a-z].../Z/"
    ```

    on the following file:

    ```
    abcdefg
    a:237efg
    AbcDefg
    afe
    ```

37. Show the result of the **sed** command

    ```
    sed "s/\..*\$/Z/"
    ```

    on the following file:

    ```
    rs.ef$tt
    abc.ab
    abc.$$$$
    abc
    ```

38. Show the result of the **sed** command

    ```
    sed "s/s:?s*/Z/"
    ```

    on the following file:

    ```
    efgs:sgfe
    sssssssss
    rsts
    abc
    ```

39. Show the result of the **sed** command

    ```
    sed "s/:?.?/Z/"
    ```

    on the following file:

    ```
    :a????????
    eeeeeefffff?hhhh
    aaa::??????
    :?.\?
    ```

40. Show the result of the **sed** command

    ```
    sed "s/[^$]$/Z/"
    ```

    on the following file:

```
$$$$$$aaaaaa
bcdef$
$
abc
```

41. Show the result of the **sed** command
    ```
    sed "s/^[^$]*$/Z/"
    ```
    on the following file:

```
$$$$$$aaaaaa
bcdef$
$
abc
```

42. Show the result of the **sed** command
    ```
    sed "s/\$[0-9]$/Z/"
    ```
    on the following file:

```
$$$$$$$
$10
abc$
$
```

43. Show the result of the **sed** command
    ```
    sed "s/^\$[0-9][0-9]$/Z/"
    ```
    on the following file:

```
$$$$$$$
$10
abc$
$
```

44. What is done by the following command?
    ```
    sed "s/the/a/g" file1
    ```
45. What is done by the following command?
    ```
    sed "s/[A-Z]/&/g" file1
    ```
46. What is done by the following command?
    ```
    sed "32,45s/[()]//g" file1
    ```
47. What is done by the following command?
    ```
    sed "/^$/d" file1
    ```
48. What is done by the following command?
    ```
    sed "\([0-9]\)-\([0-9]\)/\1\2/g" file1
    ```

49. What is done by the following command?

```
sed "80q" file1
```

50. What is done by the following command?

```
sed "9r payroll" file1
```

51. What is done by the following script?

```
h
G
G
```

52. What is done by the following script?

```
n
d
```

53. What is done by the following script?

```
n
n
d
```

54. What is done by the following script?

```
10h
11,15H
20G
```

55. What is done by the following script?

```
10h
11,15H
10,15d
20G
```

56. Write a **sed** command that deletes the first character in each line in a file.

57. Write a **sed** command that deletes the second character in each line in a file.

58. Write a **sed** command that deletes the last character in each line in a file.

59. Write a **sed** command that deletes the character before the last character in each line in a file.

60. Write a **sed** command that deletes the first word in each line in a file.

61. Write a **sed** command that deletes the second word in each line in a file.

62. Write a **sed** command that deletes the last word in each line in a file.

63. Write a **sed** command that deletes the word before the last word in each line in a file.

64. Write a **sed** command that swaps the first and the second character in each line in a file.

65. Write a **sed** command that swaps the first and the last character in each line in a file.

66. Write a **sed** command that swaps the first and the second words in each line in a file.

67. Write a **sed** command that deletes any integer in each line in a file.

68. Write a **sed** command that deletes all leading spaces at the beginning of each line.

69. Write a **sed** command that replaces all single spaces (only single spaces) at the beginning of each line with a tab.

70. Write a **sed** command to surround all capital letters with parentheses.
71. Write a **sed** script to print each line three times.
72. Write a **sed** script to delete every other line.
73. Write a **sed** script to continuously copy two lines and delete the third.
74. Write a **sed** script to copy lines 22 to 33 after line 56.
75. Write a **sed** script to move lines 22 to 33 after line 56.
76. Write a **sed** script to move lines 22 to 33 after line 9.
77. Write a **sed** command to delete all trailing spaces at the end of each line.
78. Write a **sed** command to extract the first word of each line.
79. Write a **sed** command that finds a date in the form of mm/dd/yy in a line and changes it to the form of yy/mm/dd.
80. Write a **sed** command that prints the first and the third word of a line.
81. Write a **sed** command that extracts the month from a date in the form of mm/dd/yy.
82. Write a **sed** command that extracts the day from a date in the form of mm/dd/yy.
83. Write a **sed** command that extracts the year from a date in the form of mm/dd/yy.
84. Write a **sed** command that, using an input file, creates an output file that contains only lines with no alphabetic characters (no uppercase and lowercase letters).
85. Write a **sed** command that, using an input file, creates an output file that contains only lines that have at least five digits. The digits can be consecutive (next to each other) or separated by other characters.
86. Write a **sed** command that, using an input file, creates an output file. Each line in the output file is the same as the corresponding line in the input file except that the first and the last words are swapped.
87. Write a **sed** command that, using an input file, creates an output file. Each line in the output file is the same as the corresponding line in the input file except that the second word is deleted.
88. Write a **sed** command that double-spaces a file.
89. Write a **sed** command to simulate the following command (if possible):

    ```
    cp file1 file2
    ```

90. Write a **sed** command to simulate the following command (if possible):

    ```
    cat file1
    ```

91. Write a **sed** command to simulate the following command (if possible):

    ```
    head -20 file1
    ```

92. Write a **sed** command to simulate the following command (if possible):

    ```
    tail +40 file1
    ```

93. Can we simulate the following command using only a **sed** command?

    ```
    tail -40 file1
    ```

11.12 Lab Sessions

Session I

1. Log into the system
2. Create and save the following file. Call it `Ch11S1F1`. Note that the fields are separated by one or more spaces (randomly). The first field is the first name, the second field is the last name, and the third field is the age.

```
John   Adams    55
George Bull 77
Anne  Blue     99
Janet   Blue 67
Ben Benjamin       78
Ted White 32
```

3. Use a one-line **sed** command to reorganize the file using the comma/tab pattern shown in the following file. Note that the last name is before the first name, and there is only one space between the names and a space before the numbers. Use the same name for the new file.

```
Adams, John 55
Bull, George 77
Blue, Anne 99
Blue, Janet 67
Benjamin, Ben 78
White, Ted 32
```

4. Sort the file first according to the last name and then according to the age. Watch out for the comma after the last name. Use the same name for the new file.
5. Log out of the system.

Session II

1. Log into the system.
2. Create and save the following file. Call it `Ch11S2F1`.

```
UNIX is as UNIX does.

And DOS is as DOS does.

But UNIX is not as DOS does.

Nor is DOS as UNIX does.


So, if UNIX was as DOS does,

Would UNIX be DOS

Or would DOS be UNIX?
```

Continued

Session II—*Continued*

```
Or to put the question another way:

Is an operating system by any other name

As beautiful as a UNIX operating system?
```

3. Use a **sed** script (Ch11S2.sed) and a **sed** command to put a set of five asterisks at the beginning and end of each line that contains the pattern UNIX. Call the new file Ch11S2F2.
4. Log out of the system.

Session III

1. Log into the system.
2. Create a file of fifty lines (each line can have only a word or two). Call the file Ch11S3F1.
3. Use the **cat** command to insert a line number at the beginning of each line in a file. This will help to check the result of the next steps.
4. Write a **sed** script (Ch11S3.sed) and a **sed** command to split the file into four files. The first file, called Ch11S3F2, contains lines 10 to 15. The second file, called Ch11S3F3, contains lines 20 to 30. The third file, called Ch11S3F4, contains lines 31 to 37. The fourth file, called Ch11S3F5, contains the rest of the file.
5. Print all of the files created in this session and verify the output.
6. Log out of the system.

Session IV

1. Log into the system.
2. Create the following file and call it Ch11S4F1. Each line in the file is an absolute pathname of a file.

```
/bin/date
/bin/programs/cal
/usr/bin/date
/usr/report/file1
/usr/report/letters/lett1
/spool/mails
```

3. Write a **sed** script (Ch11S4.sed) and a **sed** command to extract the lowest level directory and the name of the file from the path (separated by spaces) and store it in a file called Ch11S4F2. The file should look like the following (directory then file):

Continued

```
/bin    date

/bin/programs cal

/usr/bin date

/usr/report file1

/usr/report/letters lett1

/spool mails
```

4. Log out of the system.

Session V

1. Log into the system.
2. Create the following file and call it Ch11S6F1. The file is a C program that multiplies two numbers. It contains some comments, which begin with the two-character token (/*) and end with the two-character token (*/). In this program, comments can be on one line or can span more than a line.

```
/* The greeting program. This program demonstrates   */
/*      some of the components of a simple C program.*/
/*      Written by:  your name here                  */
/*      Date:        date program written            */
#include <stdio.h>

int main (void)
{
/*      Statements */

  printf("Hello World!\n");

  return 0;
} /* main */
```

3. Write a **sed** script (Ch11S5.sed) and a **sed** command to delete the comments from the file. Call the new file Ch11S5F2. You will need to pay special attention to the slashes and asterisks (they need to be quoted).
4. Log out of the system.

Session VI

1. Log into the system.
2. Create the following file and call it Ch11S6F1. The file is a C program that multiplies two numbers. It contains some comments, which begin with the two-character token (/*) and end with the two-character token (*/). In this program, comments can be on one line or can span more than a line.

```
/* This program reads two integer numbers from the
   keyboard and prints their product.
        Written by:
```

Continued

Session VI—*Continued*

```
          Date:
*/

/*      Statements */
  scanf ("%d", &number1);
  scanf ("%d", &number2);
  result = number1 * number2;
  printf ("%d", result);
  return 0;
} /* main */
```

3. Write a **sed** script (Ch11S6.sed) and a **sed** command to delete the comments from the file. Call the new file Ch11S6F2.

4. Log out of the system.

awk

The **awk** utility, which takes its name from the initials of its authors (Alfred V. Aho, Peter J. Weinberger, and Brian W. Kernighan), is a powerful programming language disguised as a utility. Its behavior is to some extent like **sed.** It reads the input file, line by line, and performs an action on a part of or on the entire line. Unlike **sed,** however, it does not print the line unless specifically told to print it. The **awk** concept is presented in Figure 12.1.

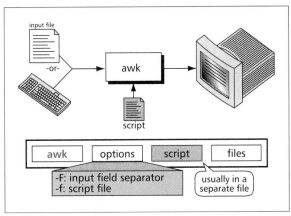

FIGURE 12.1 *The **awk** Concept*

There are only two UNIX options for the **awk** utility. The -F option specifies the input field separator. The -f option names the script file. When the script is contained in the command line, it should be quoted to protect it from the shell.

Multiple input files can be specified. If no file is given, the input is assumed to come from the keyboard. To provide input from the keyboard and one or more files, the keyboard is designated by a dash (-).

12.1 Execution

The **awk** utility is called like any other utility. In addition to input data, **awk** also requires one or more instructions that provide editing instructions. When there are only a few instructions, they may be entered at the command line from the keyboard. Most of the time, however, they are placed in a file known as an **awk** script (program). Each instruction in an **awk** script contains a pattern and an action. We will discuss patterns and actions later in this chapter. For now, let's look at how we call **awk.**

If the script is short and easily fits on one line, it can be coded directly in the command line. When coded on the command line, the script is enclosed in quotes. The format for the command-line script is:

```
$ awk 'pattern{action}' input-file
```

For longer scripts, or for scripts that are going to be executed repeatedly over time, a separate script file is preferred. To create the script, we use a text editor, such as **vi** or **emacs.** In this book, we suffix all **awk** scripts with `.awk`. This is not a requirement, but it does make it easier to identify executable scripts. Once the script has been created, we execute it using the file option (`-f`), which tells **awk** that the script is in a file. The following example shows how to execute an **awk** script:

```
$ awk -f scriptFile.awk input-file
```

12.2 Fields and Records

The **awk** utility views a file as a collection of fields and records. A **field** is a unit of data that has informational content. For example, in the UNIX list command (`ls`) output, there are several informational pieces of data, each of which is a field. Among list's output are the permissions, owner, date created, and filename. In **awk,** each field of information is separated from the other fields by one or more whitespace characters or other separators defined by the user.

Each line in **awk** is a **record.** A record is a collection of fields treated as a unit. In general, all of the data in a record should be related. Referring again to the list command output, we see that each record contains data about a file.

When a file is made up of data organized into records, we call it a **data file,** as contrasted with a **text file** made up of words, lines, and paragraphs. Let's look at an example of a data file with records and fields. Figure 12.2 shows an example of a file made of 10 records in which each record consists of four fields. The first two fields consist of first name and second name. The third field is the person's hourly pay rate in dollars. The last field shows how many hours the employee worked last week. With this description, it should be apparent that this file is part of a payroll system.

Although **awk** looks at a file as a set of records consisting of fields, it can also handle a text file. In this case, however, each text line is the record, and the words in the line are fields. Although the payroll file had four fixed fields per record, a text file would have a variable number of fields (words) per record. How we view the file depends on its content and how we intend to use it.

Buffers and Variables

The **awk** utility provides two types of buffers: record and field. A **buffer** is an area of memory that holds data while they are being processed (Figure 12.3).

Field Buffers

There are as many **field buffers** available as there are fields in the current record of the input file. Each field buffer has a name, which is the dollar sign ($) followed by the

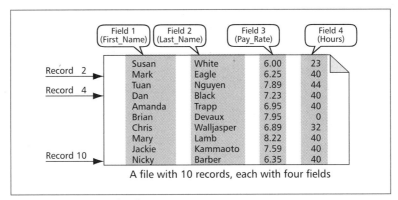

FIGURE 12.2 *A Data File*

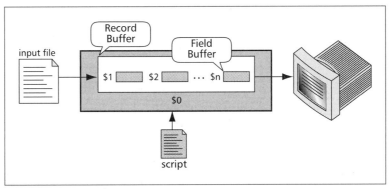

FIGURE 12.3 **awk** *Buffers*

field number in the current record. Field numbers begin with one, which gives us $1 (the first field buffer), $2 (the second field buffer), $3 (the third field buffer), and so on.

Record Buffer

There is only one record buffer available. Its name is $0. It holds the whole record. In other words, its content is the concatenation of all field buffers with one field separator character between each field.

As long as the contents of any of the fields are not changed, $0 holds exactly the same data as found in the input file. If any fields are changed, however, the contents of the $0, including the field separators, are changed. We will explore this more fully when we study **awk** actions later in the chapter.

> The record buffer ($0) contains the concatenation of all of the fields, which may be changed during script processing.

Variables

There are two different types of variables in **awk:** system variables and user-defined variables.

System Variables

There are more than twelve **system variables** used by **awk;** we discuss some of them in this section. Their names and function are defined by **awk.** Four of them are totally controlled by **awk.** The others have standard defaults that can be changed through a script. The system variables are defined in Table 12.1.

TABLE 12.1   *System Variables*

Variable	Function	Default
FS	Input field separator	space or tab
RS	Input record separator	newline
OFS	Output field separator	space or tab
ORS	Output record separator	newline
NF[a]	Number of nonempty fields in current record	
NR[a]	Number of records read from all files	
FNR[a]	File number of records read—record number in current file	
FILENAME[a]	Name of the current file	
ARGC	Number of command-line arguments	
ARGV	Command-line argument array	
RLENGTH	Length of string matched by a built-in string function	
RSTART	Start of string matched by a built-in string function	

[a]Totally controlled by **awk.**

User-Defined Variables

We can define any number of **user-defined variables** within an **awk** script. They can be numbers, strings, or arrays. Variable names start with a letter and can be followed by any sequence of letters, digits, and underscores. They do not need to be declared; they simply come into existence the first time they are referenced. All variables are initially created as strings and initialized to a null string ("").

12.3   Scripts

For years, data processing programs have followed a simple design: preprocessing or initialization, data processing, and postprocessing or end of job. In a similar manner, all **awk** scripts are divided into three parts: begin, body, and end (Figure 12.4). In this section, we discuss these three basic data processing concepts.

Initialization Processing (BEGIN)

The initialization processing is done only once, before **awk** starts reading the file. It is identified by the keyword, BEGIN, and the instructions are enclosed in a set of braces.

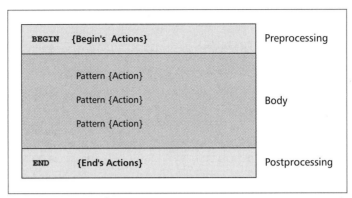

FIGURE 12.4 **awk** *Script Design*

The beginning instructions are used to initialize variables, create report headings, and perform other processing that must be completed before the file processing starts.

Body Processing

The **body** is a loop that processes the data in a file. The body starts when **awk** reads the first record or line from the file. It then processes the data through the body instructions, applying them as appropriate. When the end of the body instructions is reached, **awk** repeats the process by reading the next record or line and processing it against the body instructions. In this way, the **awk** utility processes each record or line in the file, one after the other, through the instructions in the body.

This means that if a file contains 50 records, the body will normally be executed 50 times, once for each record. On the other hand, if there are no records in the file, the body will not be executed at all. One final point: Unlike other utilities, **awk** does not write or print a record unless there is an explicit instruction to do so in the file.

End Processing (END)

The end processing is executed after all input data have been read. At this time, information accumulated during the processing can be analyzed and printed or other end activities can be conducted.

12.4 Operation

Before discussing the details of patterns and actions, let's demonstrate a simple **awk** example. We use a small file of four records, each with three numbers. We then run a simple script that adds the three numbers and prints them followed by their sum. Session 12.1 contains a copy of the script and its execution.

SESSION 12.1 *Example 1 Execution*

```
$ awk -f total.awk total.dat
# Begin Processing
BEGIN {print "Print Totals"}
```

Continued

SESSION 12.1 *Example 1 Execution—Continued*

```
# Body Processing
{total = $1 + $2 + $3}
{print $1 " + " $2 " + " $3 " = "total}

# End Processing
END {print "End Totals"}
```

Input:	Output:
22 78 44	Print Totals
66 31 70	22 + 78 + 44 = 144
52 30 44	66 + 31 + 70 = 167
88 31 66	52 + 30 + 44 = 126
	88 + 31 + 66 = 185
	End Totals

Although we have not discussed how to write instructions, this code is easy to follow. In **awk,** $1 is the name of the first number in a line, $2 is the second number, and $3 is the last number. There is only one instruction in the initialization, two in the body, and one in the end of job. Figure 12.5 shows the script along with the input and output. We have not shown the initialization and end of job lines to save space.

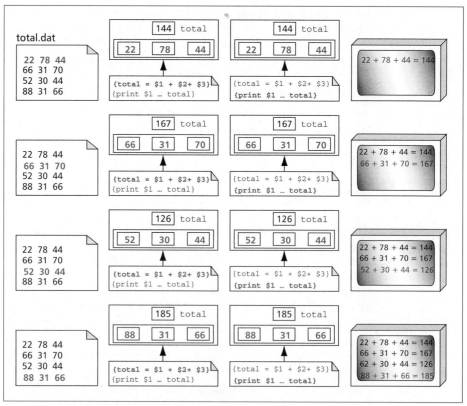

FIGURE 12.5 *Example 1 Execution*

Refer to Figure 12.5 as you follow the operation detailed in the following steps:

1. The begin instruction is executed once. It prints "Print Totals."
2. The body instruction is executed four times, once for each record.
   a. In the first iteration, the first body statement adds 22, 78, and 44, and the second instruction prints the three fields and the total, 144.
   b. In the second iteration, the first body statement adds 66, 31, and 70, and the second instruction prints the three fields and the total, 167.
   c. In the third iteration, the first body statement adds 52, 30, and 44, and the second instruction prints the three fields and the total, 126.
   d. In the fourth iteration, the first body statement adds 88, 31, and 66, and the second instruction prints the three fields and the total, 185.
3. After the last record is processed, end processing prints an end of script message, and the script ends.

These steps are shown in the script flowchart in Figure 12.6.

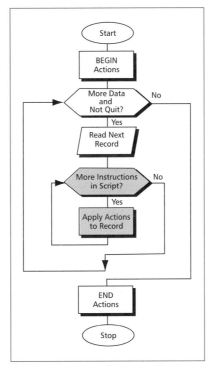

FIGURE 12.6 **awk** *Process Flow*

12.5 Patterns

As we have seen, the pattern identifies which records in the file are to receive an action. The **awk** utility can use several different types of patterns. As it executes a script, it evaluates the patterns against the records found in the file. If the pattern matches the record (that is, if it is true), the action is taken. If the pattern doesn't match the records (that is, if it is false), the action is skipped. A statement without a pattern is always true, and the action is always taken.

We divide **awk** patterns into two categories: simple and range (Figure 12.7).

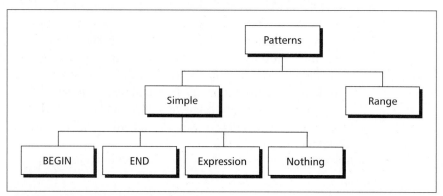

FIGURE 12.7 *Categories of Patterns*

Simple Patterns

A simple pattern matches one record. When a pattern matches a record, the result is true and the action statement is executed. As shown in Figure 12.7, there are four types of simple patterns: BEGIN, END, expression, and nothing (no expression).

BEGIN and END

BEGIN is true at the beginning of the file before the first record is read. It is used to initialize the script before processing any data; for example, it sets the field separators or other system variables. In Session 12.2, we set the field separator (FS) and the output field separator (OFS) to tabs.

SESSION 12.2 *Begin and End Patterns*

```
BEGIN
{
  FS  = "\t"
  OFS = "\t"
} # end BEGIN
  .
  .
  .
END
{
  print("Total Sales:", totalSales)
} # end END
```

END is used at the conclusion of the script. A typical use prints user-defined variables accumulated during the processing. The preceding session prints the total sales in the end processing.

Expressions

As shown in Figure 12.8, the **awk** utility supports four expressions: regular, arithmetic, relational, and logical.

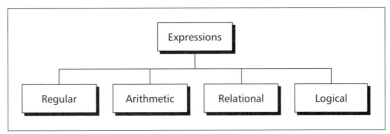

FIGURE 12.8 **awk** *Expressions*

Regular Expressions The **awk regular expressions** (regexp) are those defined in **egrep.** In addition to the expression, **awk** requires one of two operators: match (~) or not match (!~). When using a regular expression, remember that it must be enclosed in /slashes/. The match and not match operators are shown in Table 12.2.

TABLE 12.2 **awk** *Match and Not Match Operators*

Operator	Explanation
~	Regular expression must match text.
!~	Regular expression must not match text.

Session 12.3 demonstrates the use of regular expressions. Each example is commented with an explanation of its interpretation.[1]

SESSION 12.3 *Use of Regular Expressions*

```
$0 ~ /^A.*B$/        # Record must begin with 'A' and end with 'B'
$3 !~ /^ /           # Third field must not start with a space
$4 !~ /bird/         # Fourth field must not contain "bird"
```

In Session 12.4, we use a regular expression to print any line in "The Raven" that contains the word "bird." Note that the statement is quoted to protect it from the shell.

Arithmetic Expressions An arithmetic expression is the result of an arithmetic operation. When the expression is arithmetic, it matches the record when the value is nonzero, either plus or minus; it does not match the record when it is zero (false). Table 12.3 lists the operators used by **awk** in arithmetic expressions.

---

[1]A special case allows the first expression to be written without the match operator because it is testing the entire line ($0). However, the operator can never be omitted for a field test or for a does not match test. We recommend that you always use the operator.

SESSION 12.4 *Printing Lines with Regular Expressions*

```
$ awk "/bird/ {print}" TheRaven
```
Output:
```
Then this ebony bird beguiling my sad fancy into smiling,
Ever yet was blessed with seeing bird above his chamber door--
Then the bird said "Nevermore."
"Prophet!", said I, "thing of evil—profit still, if bird or devil!--
"Prophet!", said I, "thing of evil—profit still, if bird or devil!--
"Be that word our sign of parting, bird or fiend!" I shrieked, upstarting--
```

TABLE 12.3 **awk** *Arithmetic Expressions*

Operator	Example	Explanation
* / % ^	a^2	Variable a is raised to power 2 (a^2).
++	++a a++	Adds 1 to a.
--	--a a--	Subtracts 1 from a.
+ -	a + b, a - b	Adds or subtracts two values.
+	+a	Unary plus: Value is unchanged.
-	-a	Unary minus: Value is complemented.
=	a = 0	a is assigned the value 0.
*=	x *= y	The equivalent of $x = x * y$; x is assigned the product of $x * y$.
/=	x /= y	The equivalent of $x = x / y$; x is assigned the quotient of x / y.
%=	x %= y	The equivalent of $x = x \% y$ where '%' is the modulo operator; x is assigned the modulus of x / y.
+=	x += 5	The equivalent of $x = x + 5$; x is assigned the sum of x and 5.
-=	x -= 5	The equivalent of $x = x - 5$; x is assigned the difference ($x - 5$).

In the following example, two fields in a record are algebraically compared. If the result is nonzero, the line is printed.

```
$3 - $4 {print}
```

Relational Expressions Relational expressions compare two values and determine if the first is less than, equal to, or greater than the second. When the two values are numeric, an algebraic comparison is used; when they are strings, string comparison is used. If a string is compared to a number, the number is converted to a string and a string compare is used. Note, however, that we can force a string to be numeric by adding 0 to it; we can force a numeric to be a string by appending a null string (" ") to it. The relational expressions are listed in Table 12.4.

TABLE 12.4   *Relational Expressions*

Operator	Explanation
<	Less than
<=	Less than or equal
==	Equal
!=	Not equal
>	Greater than
>=	Greater than or equal

As an example, assume that we have a sales file for our local college bookstore. It has four departments: textbooks, computers, supplies, and clothing. Each record contains three fields: a quarter number, a department name, and total sales. If we need to see only our computer sales, we can compare the second field to the string shown in Session 12.5. In this example, the file has two records in which the department field contains `computers`.

SESSION 12.5   *Extract and Print Computers Sales*

```
$ awk '$2 == "computers" {print}' sales.dat
```

Input:			Output:		
1	clothing	3141	1	computers	9161
1	computers	9161	2	computers	12321
1	textbooks	21312			
2	clothing	3252			
2	computers	12321			
2	supplies	2242			
2	textbooks	15462			

Logical Expressions A **logical expression** uses logical operators to combine two or more expressions (Table 12.5).

TABLE 12.5   *Logical Operators*

Operator	Explanation
!expr	*Not* expression
expr$_1$ && expr$_2$	Expression 1 *and* expression 2
expr$_1$ || expr$_2$	Expression 1 *or* expression 2

The result of a logical *and* expression is true if and only if both expressions are true; it is false if either of the expressions is false. The result of a logical *or* expression is true if either of the expressions is true; it is false if and only if both expressions are false. The *not* operator complements the expression: If the expression is true, *not* makes it false; if it is false, *not* makes it true. These relationships are presented in Figure 12.9.

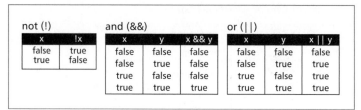

FIGURE 12.9 *Logical Expression Truth Table*

Using our sales file, the following compound expression reports all computer sales greater than $10,000. Note that in Session 12.6, computers is quoted to indicate that it is a string. In addition, because strings must be identified with double quotes, we use single quotes for the **awk** statement.

SESSION 12.6 *Extract and Print Computers Sales*

```
$ awk '$2 == "computers" && $3 > 10000 {print}' sales.dat
```

Input:			Output:		
1	clothing	3141	2	computers	12321
1	computers	9161			
1	textbooks	21312			
2	clothing	3252			
2	computers	12321			
2	supplies	2242			
2	textbooks	15462			

Nothing (No Pattern)

When no address pattern is entered, **awk** applies the action to every line in the input file. This is the easiest way to specify that all lines are to be processed.

Range Patterns

A range pattern is associated with a range of records or lines. It is made up of two simple patterns separated by a comma as shown here:

> **start-pattern, end-pattern**

The range starts with the record that matches the start pattern and ends with the next record that matches the end pattern. If the start and end patterns are the same, only one record is in the range.

Each simple pattern can be only one expression; the expression cannot be BEGIN or END. In Session 12.7, we print lines 8 through 13 of "The Raven," using simple expressions to identify the line number range.

If a range pattern matches more than one set of records in the file, then the action is taken for each set. However, the sets cannot overlap. Thus, if the start range occurs twice before the end range, there is only one matching set starting from the first start record through the matching end record. If there is no matching end range, the matching

SESSION 12.7   *Print Range*

```
$ awk 'NR == 8, NR == 13 {print NR, $0}' TheRaven
```

```
Output:
8 Ah, distinctly I remember it was in the bleak December;
9 And each separate dying ember wrought its ghost upon the floor.
10 Eagerly I wished the morrow; -- vainly I had sought to borrow
11 From my books surcease of sorrow -- sorrow for the lost Lenore
12 For the rare and radiant maiden whom the angels name Lenore
13 Nameless here for evermore.
```

set begins with the matching start record and ends with the last record in the file. These cases are in Figure 12.10.

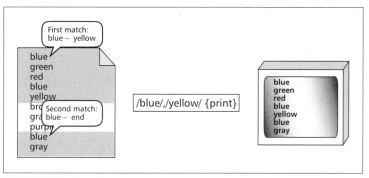

FIGURE 12.10   *Range Patterns*

For a more complex example, let's print lines 5, 6, and 7, 15, 16, and 17, 25, 26, and 27, and so forth through the whole file. We can do this using the modulo operator to select lines that end in 5, 6, and 7 as in Session 12.8. Note that we print only the first six lines of output.

SESSION 12.8   *Print Selected Subranges*

```
$ awk 'NR % 10 == 5, NR % 10 == 7 {print NR, $0}' TheRaven | head -6
```

```
Output:
5 "'Tis some visitor," I muttered, "tapping at my chamber door
6 Only this and nothing more."
7
15 And the silken, sad, uncertain rustling of each purple curtain
16 Thrilled me--filled me with fantastic terrors never felt before;
17 So that now, to still the beating of my heart, I stood repeating
```

Session 12.8 Analysis: Because we are creating a range, we need only calculate the beginning of the range (numbers ending in 5) and the end of the range (numbers ending in 7).

12.6 Actions

In programming languages, actions are known as instructions or statements. They are called **actions** in **awk** because they act when the pattern is true. Virtually all of the C language capabilities have been incorporated into **awk** and behave as they do in C. A word of caution, however; if you have not studied C, you should use them carefully and simply. In general, do not combine actions with other expressions.

In **awk,** an action is one or more statements associated with a pattern. There is a one-to-one relationship between an action and a pattern: One action is associated with only one pattern. The action statements must be enclosed in a set of braces; the braces are required even if there is only one statement. A set of braces containing pattern/ action pairs or statements is known as a **block.** When an action consists of several statements, they must be separated by a **statement separator.** In **awk,** the statement separators are a semicolon, a newline, or a set of braces (block).

> In **awk,** the end of a statement is designated by a newline, semicolon, or closing brace.

As we said in Scripts (page 428), an **awk** script can have only one optional pattern/ action pair at the beginning of the script, one optional pattern/action pair at the end of the script, and zero or more pattern/action pairs in the body of the script. This restriction is relaxed, however, because **awk** considers a block to be one statement.

Figure 12.11 demonstrates the syntactical rules for pattern/action pairs. As you study it, note that a block may contain only one statement (Figure 12.11a), multiple statements on one line separated by semicolons (Figure 12.11b), or multiple statements on separate lines (Figure 12.11c). When the statements are on separate lines, there is no need for the semicolon. A **nested block** is a block within a block. Some **awk** statements allow only one action statement. Once again, however, when multiple statements are enclosed in a block, they are considered one statement.

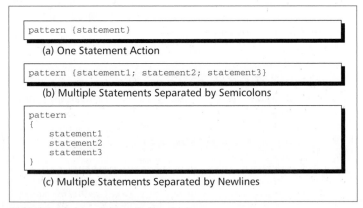

```
pattern {statement}
```
(a) One Statement Action

```
pattern {statement1; statement2; statement3}
```
(b) Multiple Statements Separated by Semicolons

```
pattern
{
    statement1
    statement2
    statement3
}
```
(c) Multiple Statements Separated by Newlines

FIGURE 12.11   *Pattern/Action Syntax*

The **awk** utility contains a rich set of statements that can solve virtually any programming requirement. The full set of statements is beyond the scope of this text;

however, we define the more important ones in the following sections. The ones we discuss are summarized in Figure 12.12.

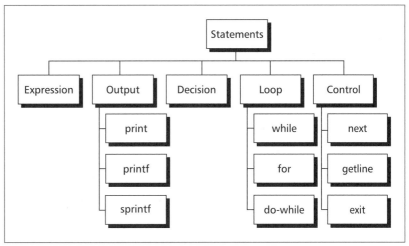

FIGURE 12.12 *Basic* **awk** *Statements*

Expression Statement

We introduced expressions in Patterns on page 431. An expression can be used in both the pattern and the action sections of an instruction.

When an expression is used in the pattern section, it has a value and sometimes an effect. The value, either true (nonzero) or false (zero), is used to select or skip a line for processing. The effect, if any, changes the contents of buffers or variables.

When an expression is used in the action section, it can also have a value and an effect. The value, however, is either a mathematical value or a logical value (true or false). The effect can change the value of a variable or a buffer ($1 to $9). When we use an expression only for its effect, discarding its value, the expression is an expression statement. For example,

```
{$2 = 6}
```

is an expression. Its value is 6. Its effect stores the value 6 in buffer $2. The value of the expression is discarded; the effect is the desired objective.

Expressions can become very complex. While simple expressions are intuitive and easily understood, we must carefully evaluate complex expressions as we create them. For example,

```
{total += ($6 + 4)}
```

is interpreted as

```
{total = (total + $6 + 4)}
```

The evaluation of the expression begins with the calculation of $6 + 4. It adds the result to total, which replaces the current value in total with the newly calculated value. The expression value is then discarded.

In Session 12.9, we add the sales field in each record and print it at the end of the file. The begin action is redundant in **awk** because it automatically initializes user-defined variables when they are created. However, the cost is minimal, and the resulting script is more readable.

SESSION 12.9   *Add and Print Sales Total*

```
$ awk -f totalSales.awk sales1.dat
```
```
# total Sales script
BEGIN {total = 0}
      {total += $3}
END   {print "Total Sales", total}
```

Input:			Output:
1	clothing	3141	Total Sales 66891
1	computers	9161	
1	textbooks	21312	
2	clothing	3252	
2	computers	12321	
2	supplies	2242	
2	textbooks	15462	

Session 12.9 Analysis: In this example, the BEGIN statement initializes the user-defined variable, total. The second action adds the third data value in each line to total. We use the compound sum and assignment action. Whenever an arithmetic calculation, such as add or multiply, is being performed on the receiving variable in the assignment action, it can be abbreviated. The expanded alternative action is:

$$total = total + \$3$$

Output Statements

There are three output actions in **awk.** The first is the simple print action that we have used throughout this chapter. The second is the C formatted print statement, printf. The third is sprintf.

Print

Print writes the specified data to the standard output file. Each print action writes a separate line. When multiple fields or variables are being written, they must be separated with commas. If no data are specified, the entire record (line) is printed. In Session 12.10, we use the whole line format. As each line is processed, it is copied to standard output. Because the entire line is being printed, the input line field separator (tab) is used, which aligns each field into columns.

In Session 12.11, we print another sales files, this time specifying the fields that we want printed. Because there are only three fields in the file, the same data are printed. But note the difference between the two printouts. When we print selected

SESSION 12.10 *Print Fields*

```
$ awk '{print}' sales2.dat
```

Output:		
1	clothing	3141
1	computers	9161
1	software	3141
1	supplies	2131
1	textbooks	21312
1	sporting	0
2	clothing	3252
2	computers	12321
2	software	3252
2	supplies	2242
2	textbooks	22452
2	sporting	2345
3	clothing	3363
3	computers	13431
3	software	3363
3	supplies	2353
3	textbooks	23553
3	sporting	4554

SESSION 12.11 *Print Selected Fields*

```
$ awk '{print $1, $2, $3}' sales2.dat | head -5
```

```
Output:
1 clothing 3141
1 computers 9161
1 software 3141
1 supplies 2131
1 textbooks 21312
```

fields, the output field separator is used. In this case, it was the default, a space. This time, we print only the first five fields by piping the output to the **head** utility.

When we print fields, if we want columns, we need to change the output field separator to a tab. Session 12.12 does that when **awk** begins. This time, the output is separated into columns. Again, we print only the first five lines.

SESSION 12.12 *Print Columns*

```
$ awk 'BEGIN {OFS = "\t"}; {print $1, $2, $3}' sales2.dat | head -5
```

Output:		
1	clothing	3141
1	computers	9161
1	software	3141
1	supplies	2131
1	textbooks	21312

Session 12.12 Analysis: The difference between this printout and the previous column output example is that the tabs were generated by **awk** rather than the ones contained in the input.

Formatted Print

The **awk** utility also contains the C formatted print statement, `printf`. Each `printf` action consists of a **format string,** enclosed in double quotes, and a list of zero or more values to be printed. The data formatting is described by a field specification, which begins with a percent sign and ends with a format code that defines the data type. Anything that is not a field specification is text that is to be printed.

Included in the field specification are three modifiers. The **width** is used to align data within print columns. Note, however, that when used, it specifies the *minimum* width. If the data require more space than specified in the column width specification, the data overflow into the following print areas.

The print width specifies the *minimum* width for output.

The **flag** controls the format of data with a column. Normally, data are printed right justified; that is, they are printed with the rightmost character in the data aligned at the right end of a column. Left justify, a minus sign, places text starting at the left of a print area. The sign flag specifies that numeric data are to be signed with a plus for positive values as well as the standard minus for negative numbers. The space flag prints positive numbers with a leading space instead of a plus sign. Finally, the zero flag formats a numeric value with leading zeros instead of spaces. This is important when the value being printed is a numeric identifier, such as a social security number, that we expect to see as a fixed number of digits.

The **precision** modifier specifies the number of decimal positions to be printed in a floating-point number. Its format is `.n`, where n specifies the number of digits of precision to be printed. When combined with a width specification, the format becomes `m.n`. For example, if a dollar value is being printed in a 10-position column, we would use a width-precision specification of 10.2. This code specifies seven leading digits, a decimal point, and two decimal places of precision.

At the end of the field specification is the **conversion code.** It describes the type of data being printed. While most of the conversion codes are self-explanatory, the floating-point formats require additional explanation. When a floating-point number is to be printed in a standard format, such as dollars and cents, the `f` conversion code is used. To print a number in scientific notation, such as $-1.23456e+07$, we use the `e` conversion code. The `g` conversion code is a combination of the other two. If the exponent (the two digits at the end of the number) is greater than -4 and less than the specified precision, standard notation is used; otherwise, scientific notation is used. The complete field specification format is in Figure 12.13.[2]

In Session 12.13, we use `printf` to format the data in our sales file. The month is printed in a two-character column followed by a space. The department is left-justified in a twelve-character column. The dollar sales are printed in a nine-character column with two decimal places. Only the first five records are printed.

---

[2]If you know C, you should note that a few of the standard C codes are missing.

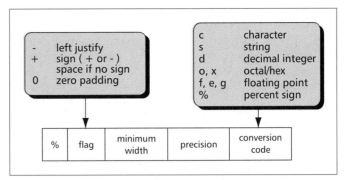

FIGURE 12.13 *Summary of* `printf` *Codes*

SESSION 12.13 *Formatting Output*

```
$ awk '{printf("%2d %-12s $%9.2f\n", $1, $2, $3)}' sales2.dat | head -5
```

```
Output:
 1 clothing     $  3141.00
 1 computers    $  9161.00
 1 software     $  3141.00
 1 supplies     $  2131.00
 1 textbooks    $ 21312.00
```

String Print

There is one more print command in **awk:** string print (`sprintf`). This command uses the formatted print concept to combine two or more fields into one string that can be used as a variable later in the script. As a simple demonstration, in Session 12.14, we combine the fields in the first record of our bookstore into one string and then print its length and contents.

SESSION 12.14 **sprintf** *Example*

```
$ awk -f sprintf.awk sales2.dat
```

```
# sprintf.awk script
# Demonstrate sprintf command
NR == 1 {
        str = sprintf("%2d %-12s $%9.2f\n", $1, $2, $3)
        len = length(str)
        print len " " str
        }
```

Input:			Output:
1	clothing	3141	27 1 clothing $ 3141.00
1	computers	9161	
1	textbooks	21312	
2	clothing	3252	
2	computers	12321	
2	supplies	2242	
2	textbooks	15462	

Decision Statements

Decision statements are about making decisions. We have been making decisions implicitly with pattern matching, but **awk** also provides action statements to make them explicitly. Regardless of how complex a decision is, however, all computer decisions must be reduced to a binary decision: An expression is true or it is false. When it is true, a true action is executed; when it is false, a false action is executed. The basic decision statement is the if-else statement.

The if-else Statement

The if-else action statement is common to all programming languages. In it, we evaluate an expression and take appropriate action. The true action is always required, although it can be a null statement (a semicolon with no action). The false action is optional but, if used, follows an else action statement. Any expression that reduces to true or false can be used, but the logical expressions are the most common. The basic decision format is in Figure 12.14.

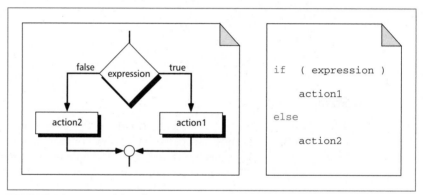

FIGURE 12.14   *Decision Flow*

When the action statement in an if-else is another if-else, we have what is known as **nested** if action statements. Great care must be taken with nested if statements to ensure that the else actions are properly associated with the correct if. Each else statement is matched with the closest unpaired if statement.

The rule is simple, but it is easy to code incorrectly. When it is incorrectly coded, we call it the *dangling* else problem.

Nested else Rule
Each else **action statement associates with the previous** *unassociated* if **statement.**

Figure 12.15 demonstrates the dangling else problem. The intent is that the nested if has no else statement; the else statement is properly associated with the first if action statement. Using **awk**'s association rules, however, action2 gets associated with the nested if (if expression2).

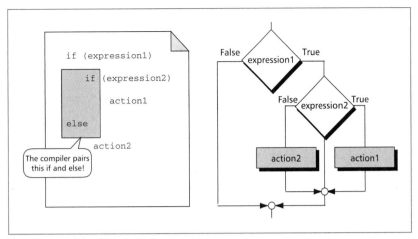

FIGURE 12.15 *Dangling* **else**

To fix the problem, we simply place the nested `if` in a compound statement (braces) as in Session 12.15.

SESSION 12.15 *Avoiding Dangling* **else** *Statements*

```
{
  if (expression1)
    {
      if (expression2)
          action1
    } # end of nested if
  else
      action2
} # end of outer if
```

Now let's write a session that computes the average sales for the computer department. If they are over our goal ($10,000), we print out a message that the sales are good. If they are below our goal, we print out a message that it's time for a peptalk. To test this script fully, we need to run it twice, first with a goal that prints the good sales message and then with a goal that prints the peptalk message. We show the good sales in Session 12.16.

SESSION 12.16 *Print Computer Department Averages*

```
$ awk -f compSalesAvg.awk sales1.dat
# compSalesAvg.awk
{
  if ($2 == "computers")
      {
        compSales += $3
        numMons++
      } # if computers true
} # end if
```

Continued

SESSION 12.16 *Print Computer Department Averages—Continued*

```
END {
    if (compSales / numMons > 10000)
        print "Good sales in computers: $", compSales
      else
        print "Time for a pep-talk: $", compSales
    } # END
```

Input:			Output:
1	clothing	3141	Good sales in computers: $ 21482
1	computers	9161	
1	textbooks	21312	
2	clothing	3252	
2	computers	12321	
2	supplies	2242	
2	textbooks	15462	

Control Actions

There are three statements that control the execution of the entire script: `next`, `getline`, and `exit`.

Next

The `next` statement terminates the processing of the current record and begins processing of the next one. If there are no more records to be processed, it transfers control to the end action if specified. This is the equivalent of going immediately to the end of the script and reading the next record; none of the actions or statements following `next` are executed.

In Session 12.17, which computes the sales average, we skip any record in which sales ($3) are zero.

SESSION 12.17 *Skip Zero Balances in Computer Sales*

```
$ awk -f averageSales.awk sales1.dat
# averageSales script
 $3 == 0 {next}
# Have non-zero sale
 {
   total += $3
   count++
 } # Non-zero sales
 END {avrg = total / count
      printf("Total sales     : $%9.2f\n", total)
      printf("Number of sales: %7d\n",    count)
      printf("Average sales   : $%9.2f\n", avrg)
     } # END
```

Input:			Output:
1	clothing	3141	Total sales : $66891.00
1	computers	9161	Number of sales: 7
1	textbooks	21312	Average sales : $ 9555.86

Continued

SESSION 12.17   *Skip Zero Balances in Computer Sales*

2	clothing	3252
2	computers	12321
2	supplies	2242
2	textbooks	15462

Get a Line

Like next, getline reads a record (line). Unlike next, it continues executing the script; it does not go back to the beginning of the body. The actions and statements following getline are applied to the new record just read. Its format is in the following example:

```
getline
```

While getline is used like a statement, it is actually a function. Being a function gives it three powerful capabilities:

1. The input can be directed to $0 (default) or to a separate variable.
2. getline returns a value that can be evaluated. The values are:
   a. 1: record successfully read
   b. 0: end of file
   c. −1: read error
3. The input can be read from another file.

The awk script must have one input, either standard input or a file passed as a parameter. This file can be automatically processed by the script or can be read using get-line. Regardless of how it is read, when it reaches end of file, **awk** passes control to the end section or, if there is no end section, terminates the execution.

The getline function can be used to read other files by using the redirection operator (<) as shown in the next example.

```
getline   variable   <   file
```

The variable is optional. If it is not provided, the fields are read into $0. Because getline does not automatically jump to the end processing at end of file when reading a file, you should test for a return of 0 and branch to the end processing when the rest of the statements are not to be processed.

Let's look at an example. Recall that in Chapter 11, we wrote Session 11.30, Exchange Lines in a File, (see page 444) to exchange every other line in a file. It had one problem, however; it could not handle an odd number of lines. When there was an odd line, it was repeated. Using **awk** and getline, we can solve the odd line problem. The code is shown in Session 12.18.

SESSION 12.18   *Exchange Lines in a File* (**awk**)

```
$ awk -f exchange.awk 5lines.dat
# exchange.awk script
# exchanges lines 2 by 2
{
```

Continued

SESSION 12.18 *Exchange Lines in a File (**awk**)—Continued*

```
  if ((getline evenLine) == 1)
     {
      print evenLine
      print $0
     } # if getline
  else
      print $0
}
```

Input:	Output:
line 1	line 2
line 2	line 1
line 3	line 4
line 4	line 3
line 5	line 5

Session 12.18 Analysis: This script demonstrates two of the `getline` capabilities. First, we read the even numbered lines into a variable, `evenLine`. Second, we use the return value to test for end of file. When `getline` returns successful read (1), we print `evenLine` and then print `$0`. When it doesn't return, we assume that we are at the end of the file and print just the odd line from `$0`. Technically, this is a potential bug because the result could be an error instead of end of file.

Exit

Whereas `next` skips to the end of the script and reads the next record, `exit` terminates the script. If an end pattern has been specified, it executes the end statements and then exits. If no end has been specified, it exits the script immediately. When `exit` is used in the end pattern, the script is immediately terminated without executing the rest of the end statements.

 `exit` should be reserved for error conditions. In Session 12.19, we guard against a zero divisor by testing the count for zero before dividing. Note that we use 100 as an attribute of the `exit` statement. This value can be used to communicate with the user. We will discuss this concept in more detail when we study shell scripting.

SESSION 12.19 *Using **exit** to Guard against Divide by Zero*

```
$ awk -f salesZeroDiv.awk zeroSales.dat
# salesZeroDiv.awk script
# with compare complemented for test

$3 == 0 {next}

{total += $3
 print $1 $2 $3
 count++
} # Not zero sales

END    {
        if (count == 0)
           {
```

Continued

SESSION 12.19 *Using **exit** to Guard against Divide by Zero*

```
              printf("No sales to average\n")
              exit 100
        }   # end if
    avrg = total / count
    printf("Total sales    : $%9.2f\n", total)
    printf("Number of sales: %7d\n",     count)
    printf("Average sales  : $%9.2f\n", avrg)
      }   # end END block
```

Input:			Output:
1	clothing	0	No sales to average
1	computers	0	
1	textbooks	0	

Loops

All three of the C language loops are available in **awk,** plus a special array processing loop that we discuss in the Associative Arrays (Section 12.7) section. Although the typical read file loop is not needed because **awk** controls the reading of data, there are still times when we need to loop through records to process data.

To explain loops, let's look at a typical example. Given a file in which the first field is a student id and the rest of the fields are scores, compute and print the average for each student. Such a typical file appears in Table 12.6.

TABLE 12.6 *A Student Average File*

ID	Score 1	Score 2	Score 3	Score 4
1234	87	83	91	89
2345	71	78	83	81
3456	93	97	89	91
4567	81	82	79	89
5678	78	86	81	79

Before solving this problem, let's look at how loops operate. Typically, there are four parts to a loop. Before the loop begins, it is often necessary to **initialize** variables that are used in the loop. For example, to calculate the average score for our students, we need to set the total accumulator to zero before the loop. While **awk** automatically initializes variables to zero the first time they are used, they are not initialized after the first loop. To ensure that they are initialized for each loop, therefore, we must initialize them ourselves.

The second component of a loop is the **limit test.** The limit test determines if another iteration of the loop is to be executed or if the loop is complete. To compute our students' averages, we need to loop until all of the scores have been totaled.

Within the loop itself, there are two actions. First, we need to process the data. In our example, this means add a score to the total score. When all data processing actions are complete, we then need to **update** the limit test variable. Without the update, the loop would not stop. In our student average example, the update adds one to the count variable.

While any of **awk**'s loops can be used to solve a problem, each of them has been designed to solve a particular class of problems. The `while` loop is designed to handle logic in which we don't know in advance how many iterations it will take to solve a problem. It loops until an event occurs that stops it. For this reason, it is also known as an **event control loop.** The `for` loop is designed to solve problems in which we know exactly how many times we will loop. It is usually based on a predetermined count of the number of items to be processed. For this reason, it is also known as a **count control loop.** The last loop, the `do-while`, is designed for problems in which we know in advance that there must always be at least one iteration of the loop.

The `while` *Loop*

Perhaps the most common of the loops, the `while` loop iterates as long as its expression is true. It is used whenever we don't know in advance how many times we need to iterate through a loop. Figure 12.16 contains a basic loop flowchart and its code.

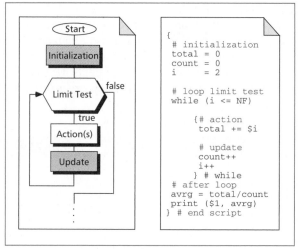

FIGURE 12.16 *The **while** Loop*

It is important to understand that this loop is a **pretest loop.** This means that the limit test is made before each iteration, *including the first.* So if the limit condition is false to begin with, there will be no loop action taken. In our example, this is helpful when there happened to be an empty line in the file. Since there are no fields in an empty line, the loop would be skipped. However, in this case, our session would fail because we did not guard it against a zero divide. The following example adds a divide by zero test. We could have coded it using the next action, but the code in Session 12.20 is a little more straightforward and easier to read.

SESSION 12.20 *Calculate Student Averages (**while** Loop)*

```
$ awk -f stuWhile.awk students.dat
# stuWhile.awk script
```

Continued

SESSION 12.20 *Calculate Student Averages (**while** Loop)*

```
{
 total = 0
 count = 0
 i    = 2

 while (i <= NF)
     {
       total += $i

       count++
       i++
     } # while

# test for zero divide
 if (count > 0)
     {
       avrg = total/count
       print ($1, avrg)
     } # zero divide test
} # body
```

Input:					Output:
1234	87	83	91	89	1234 87.5
2345	71	78	83	81	2345 78.25
3456	93	97	89	91	3456 92.5
4567	81	82	79	89	4567 82.75
5678	78	86	81	79	5678 81

Session 12.20 Analysis: Study the first line in the loop carefully. We reproduce it here for your convenience:

```
total += $i
```

We want to add fields $2, $3, $4, and $5; that is, we want to add the four student scores. When we are in the first loop, i is 2; the field $i is therefore $2. When we are in the second loop, i is 3; the field $i is therefore $3. The capability to determine the field number during execution makes this generalized logic possible.

The `for` Loop

Like the while loop, the for loop is also a pretest loop. It is most useful in those situations where we know exactly how many iterations of a loop we need to make.

The for loop is a self-contained loop: The loop initialization, limit test, and update are all contained within the loop itself. Its format is:

```
for (initialization; limit_test; update)
    statement
```

Often, as in our student average problem, there are multiple initialization or update actions required in each loop. Although the C language allows multiple expressions to be included in the initialization, limit test, and update statements, **awk** does not. The initialization and update are used only for the loop variant, i in our student average example. All other initialization and update actions must be coded as before. The for loop solution to the problem is in Session 12.21. The input and output are the same as in Session 12.20.

SESSION 12.21   *Calculate Student Averages (**for** Loop)*

```
# for loop example
{
 total = 0
 count = 0
 for (i = 2; i <= NF; i++)
    {
     total += $i
     count++
    } # for
} # end of student scores
# test for zero divide
count > 0 {
            avrg = total/count
            print ($1, avrg)
           } # zero divide test
# end
```

Session 12.21 Analysis: Note that in this session, we have coded all three parts of the for loop on one line. This is an **awk** requirement. If you need to write each on a separate line, you can do so by escaping the newline at the end as shown in the next example. Note that when we split the for statements, we align the second and third lines for readability.

```
 for (i = 2;\
     i <= NF;\
     i++)
```

The do-while Loop

The least useful of the loops is the do-while. In fact, it is not included in all **awk** implementations. To guarantee that the loop is executed at least once, the limit test is moved to the end of the loop. For this reason, it is sometimes known as a **posttest loop.** While we would never use it for a problem like our student averages, it can be done. Because we may have a student with no scores, we need to provide additional code to guard against division by zero. We do this by executing the loop only when there are at least two fields in a record (the first field is the student id). A flowchart and sample code are shown in Figure 12.17.

The code is in Session 12.22. Again, the input and output are the same as in Session 12.20.

SESSION 12.22   *Calculate Student Averages (**do-while** Loop)*

```
# do while example
{
 total = 0
 count = 0
```

Continued

SESSION 12.22 *Calculate Student Averages (**do-while** Loop)*

```
 i     = 2
} # initialization

 NF > 1 {
        do
           {
             total += $i
             count++
             i++
           } # do body
        while (i <= NF)

        avrg = total/count
        print ($1, avrg)
        } # NF > 1
# end script
```

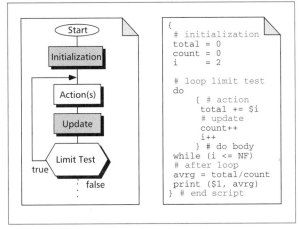

FIGURE 12.17   *The **do-while** Posttest Loop*

Session 12.22 Analysis: Some comments are in order for this code. First, note how we guard the `do-while` with the expression, `NF > 1`. If there aren't at least two fields in the record, the loop is not executed. Now study the `do-while` braces carefully. Note that the entire `do` action statement must be included in one set of braces. They are required because a `do-while` can have only one action statement. When multiple action statements are required, they must be enclosed in braces.

Because we test for at least two fields before the `do-while`, we don't need to repeat the test when we calculate the average. We therefore include the calculation of the average in the same compound action as the `do-while`.

12.7   Associative Arrays

An array is a collection of variables that can be referred to individually or as a collection. To refer to an individual element in the array, an index is used. To refer to the whole array (collection), the array name is used.

Most programming languages limit indexes to integers starting at either zero or one. On the other hand, **awk** uses strings for its indexes. Each index entry is a keyword or phrase that identifies data that are stored in an array element; that is, the index entry is associated with the array element. For this reason, **awk** arrays are known as associative arrays. It is important to remember, however, that although the index is associated with and identifies the element, the value of the element is different from the index.

To demonstrate the array concept, let's look at three different arrays. The first array associates name with ages. In this array, the names identify each person's age. The second array associates a department number with the sales for that department. The department number in this array identifies each department's sales, which is a floating-point value. We refer to the "department number" in this example, but it is not a number in the arithmetic sense. Because it is an index, it must be a string. Also, while historically department numbers may have been numeric, many organizations today use alphabetic characters in their department "numbers." The third example uses id's as the key to names. These examples are shown in Figure 12.18.

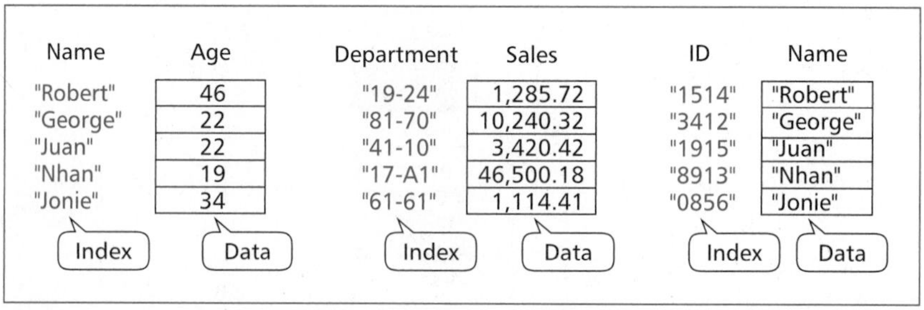

Name	Age	Department	Sales	ID	Name
"Robert"	46	"19-24"	1,285.72	"1514"	"Robert"
"George"	22	"81-70"	10,240.32	"3412"	"George"
"Juan"	22	"41-10"	3,420.42	"1915"	"Juan"
"Nhan"	19	"17-A1"	46,500.18	"8913"	"Nhan"
"Jonie"	34	"61-61"	1,114.41	"0856"	"Jonie"
Index	Data	Index	Data	Index	Data

FIGURE 12.18 *Associative Arrays*

The associative array structure has several design constraints that you must remember when you use them:

1. Indexes must be unique; that is, each index can be associated with an array value only once. This is seen in the name-age array.
2. Data values, on the other hand, may be duplicated: George and Juan are both 22.
3. The association of the index with its value is guaranteed. In the id-name array, **awk** guarantees that "1514" will be associated with "Robert."
4. There is no ordering imposed on the indexes. As a matter of fact, if you create an associative array and print it, there is no guarantee that the elements will be printed based on the ordering of the indexes or the order in which the array was created.
5. An array index cannot be sorted. The data values in the array can be sorted.

Processing Arrays

Now that we've seen the associative array structure, let's look at two examples that demonstrate how it can be processed. Before looking at the examples, however, we need to study the **awk** loop construct.

Array Loops: The `for...in` Loop

To process an associative array, **awk** provides a new format for looping: the `for...in` loop. The general format of the loop is:

```
for (index_variable in array_name)
```

The index variable can be data or simply a sequential number such as the line number as a file is read. The array is an associative array. Our first example reads a file of student data and prints it in reverse sequence (Figure 12.19).

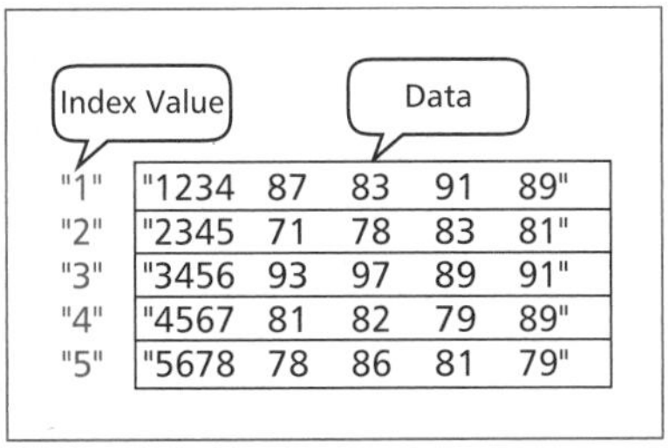

Index Value	Data
"1"	"1234 87 83 91 89"
"2"	"2345 71 78 83 81"
"3"	"3456 93 97 89 91"
"4"	"4567 81 82 79 89"
"5"	"5678 78 86 81 79"

FIGURE 12.19   *Associative Array of Students*

In this example, the index variable is the sequential record number as the file is read (NR). The first part of the script reads the file and puts it in an array. At the end of the file, we print the array backward starting at the last index entry. The code is in Session 12.23.

SESSION 12.23   *Print Student File Backward*

```
$ awk -f listStuBackward.awk students.dat

# listStuBackward.awk
{lines [NR] = $0}

END {
     for (i = NR; i > 0; i--)
          print lines[i]
     } # end END
```

Input					Output				
1234	87	83	91	89	5678	78	86	81	79
2345	71	78	83	81	4567	81	82	79	89
3456	93	97	89	91	3456	93	97	89	91
4567	81	82	79	89	2345	71	78	83	81
5678	78	86	81	79	1234	87	83	91	89

Session 12.23 Analysis: There is only one statement in the main routine of this session. It assigns the current record ($0) to an array named `lines`. We know `lines` is an array because it uses index brackets. NR is the **awk** system variable for the current record number (more specifically, the numbers of records read by the script).

When all data have been read, the session transfers to END. The `for` statement starts at the end of the array (NR) and moves toward the first entry, each time printing the line represented by `lines[i]`. Once again, remember that `i` is not a number; it is a string.

The array in the previous example looks just like any program array, although we know that there is a significant difference because it is an associative array. Let's write a loop that obviously uses an associative array. We would like to determine the total sales for each department using our college bookstore sales file. The names of the departments are strings: "clothing," "computers," "textbook," and "supplies." An associative array on departments ($2) is shown in Figure 12.20.

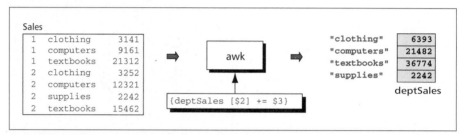

FIGURE 12.20 *An Associative Array on Departments*

The question is: How do we create the array? The answer is so simple that it is hard for many UNIX users to see it. An array element is created anytime we use the array operator (brackets) for the first time. For an array of departments, therefore, all we need to do is create a new variable and use brackets to identify it as an array element. If we want to index on the department, we use the department field number ($2). It's really as simple as the following example:

deptSales [$2]

Now that we have created an array, we simply use **awk** to add the sales to the array as shown in Session 12.24.

SESSION 12.24 *Sales by Department*

```
$ awk -f salesDeptLoop.awk sales1.dat
# salesDeptLoop.awk script
BEGIN    {OFS = "\t"}
{deptSales [$2] += $3}

END      {for (item in deptSales)
              {
                 print item, ":",  deptSales[item]
                 totalSales +=     deptSales[item]
              } # for
            print "Total Sales", ":", totalSales
} # END
```

Continued

SESSION 12.24   *Sales by Department*

Input:				Output:		
1	clothing	3141		computers	:	21482
1	computers	9161		supplies	:	2242
1	textbooks	21312		textbooks	:	36774
2	clothing	3252		clothing	:	6393
2	computers	12321		Total Sales	:	66891
2	supplies	2242				
2	textbooks	15462				

The first record creates an array entry for clothing and adds the sales to it. When we process the second record, **awk** determines that there is no index entry for computers, so it creates one and adds the sales to it. In a similar fashion, the third record creates an array entry for textbooks and adds the sales to it. Figure 12.21 traces these steps through Session 12.24. When we get to record four, **awk** finds that there is already a clothing entry in the array, so it just adds to it. Similarly, for record five, computers, there is already an index entry, so **awk** adds to it. Record six, supplies, is not in the array, so an entry is created and the sales added. The last record, textbooks, is already in the array, so **awk** adds its sales to the array entry.

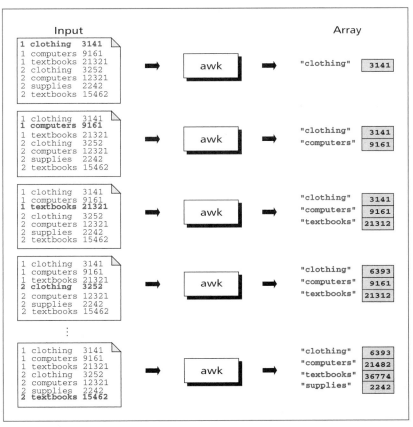

FIGURE 12.21   *Bookstore Sales*

Now that we've built the array, how do we print it out? In our first example, we knew what the index values were. In our sales example, however, the array entries are automatically created, and we don't know what they are. If a new department is created, the next run of the department sales script automatically adds it to the array. We don't have to change the script.

To print the array, we create an index variable and name it `item`. The array name, created in the main processing of the script, is `deptSales`. To print the array, we use the index variable and the array in a loop as shown in the next statement:

```
for (item in deptSales)
```

Each loop iteration prints the array index string and the array sales. After they are printed, it adds the sales to a sales total variable so that we can print the total sales at the end of the loop.

The index-in format can also be used to determine if an index value is already in the array. Given our department sales example, we could test any field using the following code:

```
if ("magazines" in deptSales)
```

This statement returns true if magazines is an index in the array and false if it isn't. The format can also be used with a variable. For example, to test if the current record's department is in the array, we could use the following statement:

```
if ($2 in deptSales)
```

As a final example, let's write a session to delete duplicate lines. Let's assume that we have previously created a file of words found in "The Raven," with each word on a line by itself. Using the words as the index, we can create an array that counts the number of times the word appears in the file. Session 12.25 contains the code and the results after we run it against the words in the first verse. Only the first and last couple of lines appear in the results.

SESSION 12.25 *Count Words in "The Raven"*

```
$ awk -f countWords.awk countWords.dat

# countWords.awk
# This script eliminates the duplicate words
# from a file of words and then prints them
# with their count.

# First create associative array of counts
{words[$0]++}

# Now print results
END{
    for (wrd in words)
```

Continued

SESSION 12.25 *Count Words in "The Raven"*

```
        print (words[wrd], "\t", wrd)
    } # END
```

Input:	Output:	
Once	2	my
upon	2	tapping
...	...	
nothing	1	there
more	3	a

Delete Array Entry

The **delete** function deletes an element from an array. Its format is:

> **delete array_name [index]**

The index must match an index (associative array) entry. If the array was built using integers, as in our student average example, the integer is automatically converted to a string. If it was built using strings, as in our sales example, then it is a string. If the index doesn't match an entry in the array, no action is taken and the script continues. In Session 12.26, we delete the supplies entry before we print the index.

SESSION 12.26 *Delete Supplies*

```
$ awk -f salesDltEntry.awk sales.dat
# salesDltEntry.awk
BEGIN   {OFS = "\t"}
{deptSales [$2] += $3}

END     {print "Deleting \"supplies\" index entry"
         delete deptSales["supplies"]
         for (item in deptSales)
            { print item, ":", deptSales[item]
              totalSales +=      deptSales[item]
            } # for
          print "Total Sales", ":", totalSales
         } # END
```

Input:			Output:		
1	clothing	3141	Deleting "supplies" index entry		
1	computers	9161	computers	:	21482
1	textbooks	21312	textbooks	:	36774
2	clothing	3252	clothing	:	6393
2	computers	12321	Total Sales	:	64649
2	supplies	2242			
2	textbooks	15462			

12.8 String Functions

The **awk** utility contains a rich set of string functions. Although we could write our own functions for any of them, it is easier to use the built-in functions. At the same time, it is reasonable to expect that the built-in functions are more efficient than any we could create because they can be tailored to the hardware on which the system is running.

Length

The **length** function has the format

```
length (string)
```

Length returns the number of characters in the string parameter. As an example of how it could be used, let's count the total number of characters in "The Raven." For simplicity, our count includes whitespace characters (excluding newlines), although it is possible to write a similar script to count only text characters. The solution is in Session 12.27.

SESSION 12.27 *String Length*

```
$ awk -f countChar.awk TheRavenV1
# countChar.awk
# This script counts the number of characters in each line.
# At the end, it prints the total characters in the file.

{
 print len = length($0), "\t", $0
 cntChar += len
}

END {print cntChar " Total characters in", FILENAME}
```

```
Output:
62      Once upon a midnight dreary, while I pondered, weak and weary,
55      Over many a quaint and curious volume of forgotten lore
62      While I nodded, nearly napping, suddenly there came a tapping,
57      As of someone gently rapping, rapping at my chamber door.
60      "'Tis some visitor," I muttered, "tapping at my chamber door
28      Only this and nothing more."
35      Perched, and sat, and nothing more.
359 Total characters in TheRavenV1
```

Index

The **index** function returns the first position of a substring within a string. Its format is:

```
index (string, substring)
```

The substring can be a string constant or variable. If the substring is not found, it returns zero. In Session 12.28, we print the location of four substrings in a file that contains only one field, MISSISSIPPI.

SESSION 12.28 *String Index*

```
$ awk -f stringIndex.awk
# stringIndex.awk
 BEGIN {print "Key MISSISSIPPI--At End key ^d"}

{locn = index ($0, "IS")
 print "'IS'  is found at...", locn, " in ", $0

 locn = index ($0, "SI")
 print "'SI'  is found at...", locn, " in ", $0

 locn = index ($0, "SIS")
 print "'SIS'  is found at...", locn, " in ", $0

 locn = index ($0, "IPPI")
 print "'IPPI' is found at...", locn, " in ", $0

 locn = index ($0, "MO")
 print "'MO'  is found at...", locn, " in ", $0
}
```

```
Script Execution:
Key MISSISSIPPI--At End key ^d
MISSISSIPPI
'IS'  is found at... 2  in  MISSISSIPPI
'SI'  is found at... 4  in  MISSISSIPPI
'SIS' is found at... 4  in  MISSISSIPPI
'IPPI' is found at... 8  in  MISSISSIPPI
'MO'  is found at... 0  in  MISSISSIPPI
^d
```

There are two concepts to study in this session. Because the input is coming from the keyboard, we prompt the user to enter the word MISSISSIPPI. The prompt must be done in BEGIN so that it is printed before the session begins looking at the data.

Now examine the output. Note that both 'SI' and 'SIS' start at index location 4. With a little reflection, however, it should be apparent that this is the correct answer. Also note that 'MO' is not found, so an index of zero is returned.

Substring

While the index will return the beginning location of a substring, the **substr** function extracts a substring from a string. It has two formats:

```
substr (string, position)
substr (string, position, length)
```

The only difference between the two functions is the length of the data to be returned. Both return the substring from string starting at position. If a length is specified, it returns up to length characters. If no length is specified, it returns everything to the end of the string.

In Session 12.29, we locate 'SIS' in MISSISSIPPI and then print it with a length of three and with no length. The first example prints it from the function return value, and the second stores it in a variable and then prints the variable. Once again, the input comes from the keyboard.

SESSION 12.29 *String Substring*

```
$ awk -f stringSubstr.awk
```

```
# stringSubstr.awk
 BEGIN {print "Key MISSISSIPPI--At End Key ^d"}
{
 locn = index ($0, "SIS")

 # print substr return value
 print "substr ($0, locn, 3) contains: ", substr ($0, locn, 3)

 # store return value and then print
 stringVar = substr ($0, locn)
 print "Variable contains                : ", stringVar
} # end stringSubstr
```

```
Script Execution:
Key MISSISSIPPI--At End Key ^d
MISSISSIPPI
substr ($0, locn, 3) contains:  SIS
Variable contains                :  SISSIPPI
```

Now let's look at a more practical substring example, albeit one with a problem. Often a file will have lines that are too long to be easily displayed in the UNIX window. We can reformat a file with long lines using Session 12.30, which breaks each line into 40-character substrings and prints them. For each input line, the session determines the line length with a length function and then uses a `for` loop to break the input into 40-character lines.

SESSION 12.30 *Break Up Long Lines*

```
$ awk -f stringLine40.awk TheRavenV1
```

```
# stringLine40.awk
{len = length($0)
 if (len <= 40)
     print $0
 else
   { for (i = 1; len > 40; i += 40)
         { print substr ($0, i, 40)
             len -= 40
         } # for
     print substr ($0, i)
   } # else
} # stringLine40.awk
```

```
Output:
Once upon a midnight dreary, while I pon
dered, weak and weary,
Over many a quaint and curious volume of
 forgotten lore
```

Continued

SESSION 12.30 *Break Up Long Lines*

```
While I nodded, nearly napping, suddenly
 there came a tapping,
As of someone gently rapping, rapping at
 my chamber door.
"'Tis some visitor," I muttered, "tappin
g at my chamber door
Only this and nothing more."
Perched, and sat, and nothing more.
```

Session 12.30 Analysis: Do you see the problem? If not, study the output. What happens when the line splits in the middle of a word? Because we break each line into exactly 40 characters, we may split a word at the end of a line. With a little more work, this problem can be corrected.

Split

Like the substring function, **split** has two formats:

```
split (string, array)
split (string, array, field_separator)
```

In the first format, the fields in a string are copied into an array. The end of each field is identified by a field separator character as currently set in the system variable, FS. In the second format, the field separator is specified as the third parameter.

Let's use the split function to extract the first and last names from a field formatted as in the next example. To make it easy to sort the data, we list the last name first, followed by a comma and a space, and then the first name.

```
last_name, first_name
```

Given this format, we can use the second format of the split function to separate the name. The following action statement splits the input into an array that contains the last and first names:

```
split ($0, lastFirst, ",")
```

Putting the problem into a larger context, assume that we have a list of phone contacts as in Session 12.31. This phone book file contains names and phone numbers. In the name field, the last name is separated from the first with a comma as we saw earlier. Separating the name field from the phone number field is a tab.

We would like to print the phone numbers with the person's first name and then last name. This requires that we first split the name and phone fields using the first option of the split function. We can then further split the name field into two subfields using the split function with a comma separator. The code is in Session 12.31. Note that we have set the field separator to a tab with the BEGIN address.

SESSION 12.31 *Phone List*

```
$ awk -f phoneList.awk phoneBook.dat
# phoneList.awk
BEGIN {FS = "\t"}
     { split($0, namePhone)
       split(namePhone[1], lastFirst, ",")
       print namePhone[2], lastFirst[2], lastFirst[1]
     }
```

Input:		Output:	
Black, Mary	555-0583	555-0583	Mary Black
Devaux, Brian	555-3802	555-3802	Brian Devaux
Forouzan, Behrouz	555-0902	555-0902	Behrouz Forouzan
Gilberg, Dick	555-8616	555-8616	Dick Gilberg
Lam, Huong	555-6780	555-6780	Huong Lam
Trapp, Amanda	555-1212	555-1212	Amanda Trapp
Walljasper, Chris	555-0238	555-0238	Chris Walljasper

Substitution

Most text editor programs have a function to substitute one string value for another. The **awk** utility is no different. Its string **substitution** function is sub; its format is:

sub (regexp, replacement_string, in_string)

The sub function returns 1 (true) if the substitution was successful; it returns 0 (false) if the target string could not be found and the substitution was not made.

In Session 12.32, we replace the string "bird" in "The Raven" with the string "RAVEN." We then print the record number and the line for only those lines that were changed. The results are then piped to **head** to list only the first five lines.

SESSION 12.32 *Substitution*

```
$ awk -f stringSub.awk TheRaven | head -5
# stringSub.awk
 {success = sub (/bird/, "RAVEN", $0)}
 {if (success > 0)
     # if a substitution was made
     print NR, $0
 } # if
# end script
```

```
Output:
49 Then this ebony RAVEN beguiling my sad fancy into smiling,
59 Ever yet was blessed with seeing RAVEN above his chamber door--
68 Then the RAVEN said "Nevermore."
91 "Prophet", said I, "thing of evil—profit still if RAVEN or devil!--
98 "Prophet", said I, "thing of evil—profit still if RAVEN or devil!--
```

Because the second argument is a string, we can create it in different ways. For example, rather than substitute for the target string, we can insert it in quotes using the hold pattern (&). In Session 12.33, we repeat Session 12.32, this time quoting "bird."

SESSION 12.33 *Substitution for Replacement*

```
$ awk -f stringSub2.awk TheRaven | head -5
```

```
# stringSub2.awk
 {success = sub (/bird/, "\"&\"")
  if (success > 0)
      print NR, $0
 } # end script
```

```
Output:
49 Then this ebony "bird" beguiling my sad fancy into smiling,
59 Ever yet was blessed with seeing "bird" above his chamber door--
68 Then the "bird" said "Nevermore."
91 "Prophet", said I, "thing of evil-profit still if "bird" or devil!--
98 "Prophet", said I, "thing of evil-profit still if "bird" or devil!--
```

Session 12.33 Analysis: Note that we have used only one set of braces to write this script. A couple of points merit discussion. First, to place the quotes around bird, we had to use the escape metacharacter (\). Second, to print the line, all we needed to do was search for bird. Even though we changed it to be quoted, we can still find it inside the quotes.

> We can use the hold pattern (&) in the replacement string, but we cannot use back references such as \1 or \2.

Global Substitution

We can also change all occurrences of a value by using **global substitution** (gsub). The format for the global substitution function is identical to sub. The only difference is that it replaces all occurrences of the matching text. For example, we can write a script that changes all occurrences of "tapping" to "POUNDING" as shown in Session 12.34.

SESSION 12.34 *Global Substitution*

```
$ awk -f stringGSub.awk TheRaven
```

```
# stringGSub.awk
{gsub (/tapping/, "POUNDING", $0)}
{ if (index ($0, "POUNDING"))
      print NR, $0
} # if
# end script
```

```
Output:
3 While I nodded, nearly napping, suddenly there came a POUNDING,
5 "'Tis some visitor," I muttered, "POUNDING at my chamber door
24 And so faintly you came POUNDING, POUNDING at my chamber door,
36 Soon again I heard a POUNDING somewhat louder than before.
```

Session 12.34 Analysis: Global substitution has the same general format as the substitution. Also note how we wrote the if statement. We did not use a relational operator; if the string "POUNDING" is found in the line, the index expression is true because the index location is not zero.

Match

The **match** string function returns the starting position of the matching expression in the line. If there is no matching string, it returns 0. In addition, it sets two system variables: RSTART to the starting position and RLENGTH to the length of the matching text string. Its format is shown below.

```
startPos = match (string, regexp)
```

As an example, let's print all lines that contain strings that start a line and end in a comma. The regular expression for this string is /^.*,/. We use it in Session 12.35.

SESSION 12.35 *String Match*

```
$ awk -f stringMatch.awk TheRaven | head -5
# stringMatch.awk
{if (match ($0, /^.*,/) > 0)
    print NR, substr($0, RSTART, RLENGTH)
} # end script
```

```
Output:
1 Once upon a midnight dreary, while I pondered, weak and weary,
3 While I nodded, nearly napping, suddenly there came a tapping,
4 As of someone gently rapping,
5 "'Tis some visitor," I muttered,
8 Ah,
```

Session 12.35 Analysis: This short script, which contains only one if statement, is relatively difficult to understand. We begin with a match statement to determine if there is a clause that starts at the beginning of the line and ends in a comma. If there is, then match returns the starting position, which must be 1; therefore, we test for a value greater than 0. If it is not greater than 0, there is no clause.

To print the results, we use the substr function to isolate the beginning and end of the data to be printed. Note, however, that this script demonstrates the greedy aspects of regular expressions. Three of the first five lines contain more than one comma. The values printed therefore include all of the text up to and including the last comma. If we wanted only the first clause, we could use the split function with a comma delimiter and then print only the first entry in the array.

Toupper and Tolower

The last two functions we wish to discuss convert uppercase characters to their lowercase representation, and vice versa. The toupper function converts lowercase characters in a string to their uppercase values. Any nonlowercase characters are unchanged. Similarly, tolower converts uppercase characters to their corresponding lowercase values without changing nonuppercase characters.

Let's write a script that uses several of the concepts we have been discussing. It uses match, toupper, substitution, and regular expressions. We have a file in which UNIX is inconsistently written. Sometimes it's Unix and sometimes it's unix. We have decided to make it uppercase at all times. Our script, therefore, must find either format and change it to uppercase. The solution is in Session 12.36.

SESSION 12.36 *Correct Formatting of UNIX*

```
$ awk -f formatUnix.awk formatUnix.dat
```
```
# formatUnix.awk
# This script reformats all spellings of UNIX to uppercase.
{
 match ($0 , /[Uu]nix/)
 upr = toupper (substr($0, RSTART, RLENGTH))
 gsub (/[Uu]nix/, upr)
 print $0
}
```
```
Input:
This is the first line of the formatUnix file.
Unix is a great system.
Many universities require UNIX.
The new Mac OS/X uses a "unix" kernel.
Unix yesterday, unix today, UNIX tomorrow.
This is the last line of the file.
```
```
Output:
This is the first line of the formatUNIX file.
UNIX is a great system.
Many universities require UNIX.
The new Mac OS/X uses a "UNIX" kernel.
UNIX yesterday, UNIX today, UNIX tomorrow.
This is the last line of the file.
```

12.9 Mathematical Functions

Table 12.7 lists mathematical functions not covered in this book. For information on these functions, we suggest that you refer to a good C text.

TABLE 12.7 *Other **awk** Functions*

Function	Comments
int	Truncates floating-point value to integer.
rand()	Returns next random number in series; range $0 \ldots 1$.
srand(seed)	Seeds random number series. Seed should be a prime number.
cos(x)	Returns cosine.
exp(x)	Returns e^x.
log(x)	Returns natural logarithm (base e) of x.
sin(x)	Returns sine of x.
sqrt(x)	Returns square root of x.
atang2(y,x)	Returns arc tangent of y/x in range $-\pi$ to π.

12.10 User-Defined Functions

We can write our own functions in **awk** just like we can in C. The format requires a function header, a body, and optionally, a return statement. The basic format is shown in Figure 12.22.

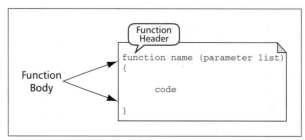

FIGURE 12.22 **awk** *Function Definition*

To demonstrate the concept, let's write a function that compares two values and returns the larger. We call the function larger, and another function is called smaller (Session 12.37).

SESSION 12.37 *User-Defined Functions*

```
$ awk -f larger.awk larger.dat
# larger.awk
{
 print larger($1, $2), " > ", smaller($1, $2)
}

# ======== larger =========
function larger(m, n)
{
 return m > n ? m : n
} # larger

# ======== smaller =========
function smaller(m, n)
{
 return m < n ? m : n
} # smaller
# end script
```

Input:		Output:	
123	321	321 > 123	
Juan	Tuan	Tuan > Juan	
Mary	June	Mary > June	
-123	123	123 > -123	

Although the concept resembles C, there are some syntactical differences that you need to be aware of:

1. There can be no space between the end of the function name and the opening parenthesis of the parameter list in the function call.
2. There can be no space between the end of the function name and the opening parenthesis in the function definition.
3. There are no semicolons at the end of the function statements.
4. As with all **awk** scripts, variables do not need to be declared before they are used.

12.11 Using System Commands in awk

System commands (utilities) can be used in an **awk** script in three ways: pipes, loops, and the system function.

Using Pipes

When the result of the utility is only one line, we code the utility as a string in double quotes and pipe the result back to the script. The pipe output is read with a `getline` command. Let's look at two examples: getting the date and searching a file.

Getting the Date

Recall that the date utility returns only one line, the date. To refresh yourself on the date command and its output, refer to Date (page 14). The concept is demonstrated in Session 12.38.

SESSION 12.38 *Getting the Date*

```
$ awk -f date.awk
# date.awk
BEGIN {
      "date" | getline
      print ($1, $4)      # Day of Week & time of day
      } # end of BEGIN

Output:
Sat 16:07:14
```

Session 12.38 Analysis: Although this script is very simple, its results are very unusual. First, we did not provide a file. Normally, this results in **awk** requesting input from the keyboard. It didn't ask for any input; furthermore, it executed immediately without waiting for input. Why?

To answer this question, first study the script carefully. Notice that it consists only of a `BEGIN` section; there are no body and no end sections. Because **awk** script input is read in the body section, no file was necessary. In a complete script, however, the date would be read before any input file because it is contained in the begin section.

Searching a File

In Chapter 11, we created a **sed** script to add a company letterhead and signature to a file (Session 11.26, page 438). The one thing we didn't do was automatically add a date to the letter. Using the same concept in **awk,** we can easily add the date.

To provide the maximum flexibility, we use global substitution to search for DATE and substitute the current date. The code is in Session 12.39. It begins by copying the letterhead data and then uses the **date** command to capture the month, day, and year. In the body of the script, it processes the letter file and checks to find any date that needs to be substituted before printing. The signature file is added in the end section.

SESSION 12.39   *Insert Date into File*

```
$ awk -f readFile.awk readLtrHead.dat readFile.dat readSignature.dat
# Script Name: readFile.awk
# This script inserts a letter-head and signature
# block in a file.
BEGIN {
       "date" | getline
       today = sprintf("%s. %s, %s",$2, $3, $6) # mmm. dd, yyyy
       } # end BEGIN

{      # Process header, letter, and signature files
       gsub (/DATE/,today)
       print ($0)
}      # End of body section
```

Input:	Output:
readLtrHead.dat	
`           UNIX Consultants Inc`	`           UNIX Consultants Inc`
`                P.O. Box 555`	`                P.O. Box 555`
`          Silicon Valley, CA 94555`	`          Silicon Valley, CA 94555`
readFile.dat	`Mar. 1, 2001`
DATE	
`John Doe`	`John Doe`
`Smart.com Inc.`	`Smart.com Inc.`
`1234 Success Way`	`1234 Success Way`
`Userville, CA 95555`	`Userville, CA 95555`
`.`	`.`
`.`	`.`
`.`	`.`
readSignature.dat	`Sincerely yours,`
`Sincerely yours,`	
	`Richard F. Gilberg`
`Richard F. Gilberg`	`UNIX Consultants Inc`
`UNIX Consultants Inc`	

Session 12.39 Analysis: Study the simplicity of this session. In the begin section, we get the date and save it in `today` for later reference. In the body section, we simply process all three files, identified as parameters in the execute **awk** command, changing any instance of DATE to the contents of the `today` field.

Loops

If there are multiple lines of output from the system command, they must be read with a loop. For example, if we need to copy who's on the system, we could use the script in Session 12.40. Note that we have also used the date command to add the time of the who list. Again, this is a BEGIN only script.

SESSION 12.40   *Creating a **who** File*

```
$ awk -f who.awk
# who.awk script
# creates a dated report of who was on the system
BEGIN {
        "date" | getline
        print ($1, $4)      # Day of Week & time of day

        while ("who" | getline)
            print($1, $2)
        } # end of BEGIN
```

```
Output:
Sat 21:32:22
nbx50783 ttyq2
kng47542 ttyq16
gilberg ttyq7
ttl38940 ttyq8
forouzan ttyq9
eo058879 ttyq11
```

Using the System Function

The **awk** utility contains a system function that executes a command passed to it as an argument. The command must return success (0) or failure (1), which is then passed back to the script. For example, when we write a script that modifies an existing file, we copy it as a backup file as a part of the script. Session 12.41 demonstrates the concept.

SESSION 12.41   *Execute a Shell Command*

```
$ awk -f sysCopy.awk
# sysCopy.awk
# copies file as backup (.bak)
BEGIN {
        if (system ("cp sysCopy.dat sysCopy.bak") != 0)
           {
            print ("Error copying sysCopy.dat")
            exit
           } # if cp
        print "sysCopy.dat copied"
        } # BEGIN & script
```

```
Output (Successful):
sysCopy.dat copied

Output (Unsuccessful):
sysCopy.dat - No such file or directory
Error copying sysCopy.dat
```

12.12 Applications

In this section, we discuss five applications that demonstrate solutions to common classes of problems.

Phone List

Given a file that contains names, addresses, and phone numbers as shown in the following example, extract only the name and phone number.

```
John Blue
2131 Main Street
Silicon Valley, CA 95555
(555) 555-0984
{Mandatory blank line except for last entry}
```

As you can see by the example, a person's entry is identified by a blank line after it. This design allows for one, two, or more address lines. Our **awk** script begins by setting the field separator (FS) and record separator (RS) in the begin section. This makes each line in the file a *field* and each group of lines a *record*. The **awk** utility then reads a complete address at one time, putting each line in a separate buffer. To print the name and address, we simply print the first *field* ($1) and the last *field* as designated by the number of fields ($NR). The resulting code is in Session 12.42.

SESSION 12.42 *Phone List*

```
$ wk -f phones.awk phones.dat
# phones.awk script
BEGIN {FS = "\n"; RS = ""}

# Body Section
{print ($1, "\t", $NF)}
```

Input:	Output:	
John Eagle	John Eagle	(123) 555-5523
2123 Old Wagon Road	Melissa Hiakawa	(455) 555-1837
Big Lake, WY 55545	Amanda Trapp	(408) 555-7147
(123) 555-5523		
Melissa Hiakawa		
1523 17th Avenue		
San Francisco, CA 95123		
(455) 555-1837		
Amanda Trapp		
9741 Oak Court		
Silicon Valley, CA 95222		
(408) 555-7147		

Session 12.42 Analysis: When you use this script, make sure that you code the field separator as a null string. There is no space between the two quotes. Also, to match the blank line in the file, the blank line can have no spaces.

Count Lines and Words

Now let's write an application to count the number of lines and words in a file. So that we can verify the output, we also display the line. The solution is in Session 12.43.

SESSION 12.43 *Count Lines and Words in a File*

```
$ awk -f countWdsLns.awk TheRavenV1
# countWdsLns.awk script
BEGIN {print "Record\tWords"}

# Body Section
{
 print (NR, ": \t", NF, $0)
 words += NF
} # Body Section

END    {
       print ("\nTotals:")
       print ("  Words:\t" words)
       print ("  Lines:\t" NR)
       } # End Script
```

```
Output:
Record  Words
1:      11 Once upon a midnight dreary, while I pondered, weak and weary,
2:      10 Over many a quaint and curious volume of forgotten lore
3:      10 While I nodded, nearly napping, suddenly there came a tapping,
4:      10 As of someone gently rapping, rapping at my chamber door.
5:      10 "'Tis some visitor," I muttered, "tapping at my chamber door
6:       5 Only this and nothing more."
7:       6 Perched, and sat, and nothing more.
Totals:
  Words:        62
  Lines:         7
```

Print Line Following a Blank Line

To print the line following a blank line, we need to use a flag. A flag is a variable that keeps track of a previous event. When the flag is true (1), we print a line and turn it off. When it is false (0), we do not print. To set the flag, we look for a line with nothing between the beginning and ending of the line ($^\$$). The solution is in Session 12.44.

SESSION 12.44 *Print Line After Blank Line*

```
$ awk -f blankLn.awk TheRaven | head -5
# blankLn.awk script
 flag == 1 {print $0; flag = 0}
 $0 ~/^$/ {flag = 1}
```

```
Output: (First five lines)
Ah, distinctly I remember it was in the bleak December;
And the silken, sad, uncertain rustling of each purple curtain
Presently my soul grew stronger; hesitating then no longer,
Deep into that darkness peering, long I stood there wondering, fearing,
Back into the chamber turning, all my soul within me burning,
```

Print Line Before a Blank Line

To print the line before a blank line, we must save the line in a variable. We will then have it when we find a blank line. The solution is in Session 12.45. Note that we guard against the first line in the file being blank using an *and* expression.

SESSION 12.45 *Print Line Before Blank Line*

```
$ awk -f afterBlkLn.awk TheRaven | head -5
# afterBlkLn.awk script
 $0 ~/^$/ && NR != 1 {print line}  # Print line
                     {line = $0}   # Save  line
```
```
Output: (First five lines)
Only this and nothing more."
Nameless here for evermore.
This it is and nothing more."
Darkness there and nothing more.
Merely this and nothing more.
```

Merge Files

For the last application, we merge two files. This application is shown in Session 12.46.

SESSION 12.46 *Merge Files*

```
$ awk -f merge.awk
# merge.awk script
# merge lines from two files
BEGIN {
      while ((getline first  < "5lines.dat") > 0\
          && (getline second < "7lines.dat") > 0)
             {
              print first
              print second
             } # while

      while ((getline first < "5lines.dat") > 0)
             { print first }

      while ((getline second < "7lines.dat") > 0)
             { print second }
      } # BEGIN -- End Of Script
```

Input: 5lines.dat	Input: 7lines.dat
line 1	line A
line 2	line B
line 3	line C
line 4	line D
line 5	line E
	line F
	line G

Continued

SESSION 12.46 *Merge Files*

```
Output:
line 1
line A
line 2
line B
line 3
line C
line 4
line D
line 5
line E
line F
line G
```

Session 12.46 Analysis: This is a relatively complex session. The first point to note is that all processing takes place in the begin section; there is no body section and no end section. Because all processing is in the begin section, no file parameters are required.

Because either file could end first, we must provide three loops. The first loop merges records until one of the input files is complete. At that point, we know that at least one file is at the end, but we don't know which one. So, we provide a loop that will read the first file (`5lines.dat`) until it has all been processed. Of course, because the `while` loop is a pretest loop, it will do nothing if the first file was the first to complete. Similarly, the third loop processes the second file until it is at the end. So, regardless of which one ends first, we process the other one until it ends. Note that to completely validate this script, we must also test it with the same number of records in both files and with the second file (`7lines.dat`) completing first.

12.13 awk and grep

As we saw in Chapter 10, the **grep** utility can be used to find (and print) the lines in a file that match (or do not match) a regular expression. The question that comes to mind is: If the **grep** utility is not available, can we use the **awk** utility to do the same job? The answer is yes. The **awk** utility is much more powerful than **grep**. Everything we can do in **grep,** we can do in **awk,** but the reverse is not true. However, we should be careful not to use **awk** instead of **grep** all of the time; **grep** is a much faster and more efficient utility. To give you the general idea of how to use **awk** instead of **grep**, we study two classifications of problems.

Find the Line That Matches a Regular Expression

If we want to use **awk** instead of **grep** (or **egrep**) to find the line that matches a regular expression, we use the print statement in **awk.** The following **grep** command can be simulated using the corresponding **awk** command that follows it:

```
grep 'regular expression' file1
awk  '$0 ~/regular expression/ {print $0}' file1
```

For example, Session 12.47 shows how we can find a line that starts and ends with an uppercase letter using **grep** or **awk**.

SESSION 12.47   *Simulate* **grep** *Expression That Matches Line*

grep	
`$ grep '^[A-Z].*[A-Z]$' file1.dat`	
Input:	**Output:**
`abcdefghijklm`	`NopqurstuvwxY`
`NopqurstuvwxY`	`UVwxyz AbcdeF`
`Z abcdefghijk`	
`1MnopqrstursT`	
`UVwxyz AbcdeF`	

awk	
`$ awk '$0 ~/^[A-Z].*[A-Z]$/ {print $0}' file1.dat`	
Input:	**Output:**
`abcdefghijklm`	`NopqurstuvwxY`
`NopqurstuvwxY`	`UVwxyz AbcdeF`
`Z abcdefghijk`	
`1MnopqrstursT`	
`UVwxyz AbcdeF`	

Find the Line That Does Not Match a Regular Expression

If we want to use **awk** instead of **grep** (or **egrep**) to find lines that do not match a regular expression (activated in **grep** with the –v option), we again use the print command, but this time, we complement the address (! ~) in **awk**. The following example demonstrates how the code is written:

```
grep   -v    'regular expression'  file1.dat
awk          '$0 !~/regular expression/ {print $0}' file1.dat
```

Session 12.48 demonstrates how we can find all lines that do not start and end with an uppercase letter using both **grep** and **awk**.

SESSION 12.48   *Using* **grep** *or* **awk** *Example 2*

grep	
`$ grep -v '^[A-Z].*[A-Z]$' file1.dat`	
Input:	**Output:**
`abcdefghijklm`	`abcdefghijklm`
`NopqurstuvwxY`	`Z abcdefghijk`
`Z abcdefghijk`	`1MnopqrstursT`
`1MnopqrstursT`	
`UVwxyz AbcdeF`	

awk	
`$ awk   '$0 !~ /^[A-Z].*[A-Z]$/ {print $0}' file1.dat`	
Input:	**Output:**
`abcdefghijklm`	`abcdefghijklm`
`NopqurstuvwxY`	`Z abcdefghijk`

Continued

SESSION 12.48   *Using **grep** or **awk** Example 2*

Z abcdefghijk 1MnopqrstursT UVwxyz AbcdeF	1MnopqrstursT

12.14 sed and awk

As we saw in Chapter 11, the **sed** utility can be used to extract desired information from a file. If **sed** is not available, can we use the **awk** utility to extract information? The answer is yes and no. The **awk** utility is much more powerful than **sed** in dealing with some problems and more lengthy when it comes to other kinds of problems.

To give you the general idea of how we can use **awk** instead of **sed,** we try to simulate some commands in **sed** using the **awk** utility.

Print Line Numbers

There is only one line number command (=) in **sed.** This command can be easily simulated in **awk** as follows:

```
sed '=' file1.dat
awk '{print NR ; print $0}' file1.dat
```

Session 12.49 demonstrates both commands.

SESSION 12.49   *Using **sed** and **awk** to Print Line Numbers*

sed	
$ sed '=' file1.dat	
Input: abcdefghijklm NopqrstuvwxY Z abcdefghijk 1MnopqrstursT UVwxyz AbcdeF	Output: 1 abcdefghijklm 2 NopqrstuvwxY 3 Z abcdefghijk 4 1MnopqrstursT 5 UVwxyz AbcdeF

awk	
$ awk '{print NR ; print $0}' file1.dat	
Input: abcdefghijklm NopqrstuvwxY Z abcdefghijk 1MnopqrstursT UVwxyz AbcdeF	Output: 1 abcdefghijklm 2 NopqrstuvwxY 3 Z abcdefghijk 4 1MnopqrstursT 5 UVwxyz AbcdeF

Modify a Line

As you remember, we had five modify commands in **sed** (i, a, c, d, D). We show how to simulate some of these commands in **awk** and leave the rest as exercises.

Insert Lines

The insert command (i) can be easily simulated using the print statement to print text before printing a specific line or set of lines. When the address is located, the action is executed and the lines are inserted. The code is in Session 12.50.

SESSION 12.50   *Insert Text with* **sed** *and* **awk**

```
sed
$ sed -f addLines.sed 5lines.dat
```
```
3i\
This is text\
to be added
```

Input:	Output:
line 1	line 1
line 2	line 2
line 3	This is text
line 4	to be added
line 5	line 3
	line 4
	line 5

```
awk
$ awk -f addLines.awk 5lines.dat
```
```
# addLines.awk
NR != 3 {print $0}
NR == 3 {print "This is text"; print "to be added" ; print $0}
```

Input:	Output:
line 1	line 1
line 2	line 2
line 3	This is text
line 4	to be added
line 5	line 3
	line 4
	line 5

Delete Lines

We can easily simulate **sed**'s delete command (d) using an **awk** script. Note that the logic for the **awk** script requires that we specify which lines we want to keep (print) rather than which ones we want to delete. The code is in Session 12.51.

SESSION 12.51   *Delete Text with* **sed** *and* **awk**

```
sed
$ sed '2,4d' 5lines.dat
```

Input:	Output:
line 1	line 1
line 2	line 5

Continued

SESSION 12.51 *Delete Text with* **sed** *and* **awk**

```
line 3
line 4
line 5
```

```
awk
$ awk 'NR < 2 || NR > 4 { print $0}' 5lines.dat
```

Input:	Output:
line 1	line 1
line 2	line 5
line 3	
line 4	
line 5	

Substitute

To substitute text, **sed** uses the substitute command (s) ; **awk** uses the sub the function. We can easily use the sub function in **awk** to do substitution. The concept is shown in Session 12.52

SESSION 12.52 *Substitute Text with* **sed** *and* **awk**

```
sed
$ sed '3s/line/order/' 5lines.dat
```

Input:	Output:
line 1	line 1
line 2	line 2
line 3	order 3
line 4	line 4
line 5	line 5

```
awk
$ awk -f sub.awk 5lines.dat
```

```
# sub.awk script
{
 if (NR == 3)
    sub (/line/, "order")
 print $0
}
```

Input:	Output:
line 1	line 1
line 2	line 2
line 3	order 3
line 4	line 4
line 5	line 5

Transform

The **sed** transform command (y) is not directly implemented in **awk.**

Input/Output

Next Commands

The **sed** next command (n) can be directly simulated using the `getline` action (see Next on page 446). The **sed** append next command (N) is not supported in **awk** because it does not support multiple-line buffers.

Print Commands

The **sed** print command (p) can be directly rewritten using the **awk** print command. The **sed** print first line command (P), however, cannot be directly simulated because **awk** does not support multiple-line buffers.

List Command

The list command (l) cannot be simulated by **awk.**

Files

Read Command

The **sed** read command (r) can be directly simulated using the **awk** `getline` action. Remember, however, that reading a file using `getline` reads only the next line from the file. To read more than one line, we must use a loop.

Write Command

The **sed** write command (w) can be directly simulated using the **awk** print command**.**

Branch

The **awk** utility has no commands that correspond to the **sed** branch (b, and t) and label (:) commands.

Quit

The **awk** equivalent of **sed**'s `quit` command is `exit`. Session 12.53 demonstrates how to stop a script in both utilities.

SESSION 12.53   *Quit in* **sed** *and Exit in* **awk**

```
sed
$ sed '4q' 7lines.dat
```

Input:	Output:
line A	line A
line B	line B
line C	line C
line D	line D
line E	
line F	
line G	

```
awk
$ awk '{ if (NR > 4) exit; else print $0}' 7lines.dat
```

Continued

SESSION 12.53 *Quit in* **sed** *and Exit in* **awk**

Input:	Output:
line A	line A
line B	line B
line C	line C
line D	line D
line E	
line F	
line G	

12.15 Key Terms

action	index function	relational expression
arithmetic expression	initialization processing	script
array	instruction	simple pattern
associative array	int function	split function
body processing	length function	sprintf
buffer	logical expression	srand function
decision statement	loop statement	string
do-while statement	match function	substitution function
end processing	next statement	substring
exit statement	output statement	substring function
expression statement	pattern	system function
field	print	system variable
field buffer	printf	tolower function
for statement	rand function	toupper function
function	range pattern	user-defined function
function-call statement	record	user-defined variable
getline function	record buffer	variable
global substitution function	regular expression	while statement

12.16 Tips

1. The **awk** utility sees a file made of fields and records, not as words and lines.
2. The name of the buffers in **awk** start with a dollar sign ($). The buffers are $0, $1, $2, and so on.
3. The variable names (system or user-defined) in **awk** do not start with a dollar sign.
4. NF is a system variable that holds the number of fields in each record. $NF defines the value of the last field.
5. Although we can directly access the value of the last field (using $NF), we cannot directly access the value of the field before the last field ($NF-1).
6. When a pattern is missing, it means every line.
7. When an action is missing, it means {print $0}.
8. Pattern matching can be done for individual fields or for the whole record.
9. A regular expression without a matching operator means that the expression should match the whole record. In other words, /RegExpr/ { . . .} means $0 ~/RegExpr/ {...}.

10. Relational operators can be used both with numbers and strings. Comparisons with numbers are based on the value of the numbers; comparisons with strings are based on the value of the individual characters.

11. A nonzero (positive or negative) number can be interpreted as a logical true value. A zero number can be interpreted as logical false value.

12. A range pattern uses two simple patterns separated by a comma. Neither of the simple patterns can be "nothing."

13. The `while` and `for` loops are pretest loops. Their body may never be executed. If you want your loop to be executed at least once, use a `do-while` loop.

14. Arrays in **awk** are associated arrays. The index is a string. Even if we use an integer as an index, it will be interpreted as a string by **awk.**

15. We can use `&` in the replace string of `sub` and `gsub` functions, but we cannot use back references (`\1`, `\2`, . . .).

16. The `getline` function does not need parentheses; it is used like any statement.

17. When `getline` is used to read a line from a file (other than the input file), the name of the file should be given as a string inside double quotes.

18. Each `getline` reads only one line. If you use `getline` in a loop, it reads one line the number of times it is excuted.

19. The line read by `getline` replaces the `$0` by default. If you want the line read to be stored in a variable, use the name of the variable as the argument to `getline`.

12.17 Commands

In this chapter, we covered only one command, **awk.**

Command	Description	Options	Page
awk	**Synopsis: awk** *[options] script [file-list]* Selects and processes specified lines in the input file.	-F, -f	425

The **awk** command, as a filter, uses a script file made of instructions. Each instruction is made of a pattern and an action. Table 12.8 lists different patterns.

TABLE 12.8   **awk** *Patterns*

Category	Types	Examples	Page
Simple	BEGIN	True before the first line is read; false everywhere else.	432
	END	True after the last line is read; false everywhere else.	432
	Expression	Arithmetic, Relational, Logical, Regular.	433
	No pattern	Nothing (which means every line).	436
Range		Two simple patterns (except nothing) separated by a comma.	436

12.18 Summary

- The **awk** utility takes its name from the initials of its authors (Alfred V. Aho, Peter J. Weinberger, and Brian W. Kernighan).
- The **awk** utility is a powerful programming language disguised as a utility.
- The **awk** utility reads the input file, line by line, and performs an action on a part of or on the entire line when the line is selected for processing.
- Unlike **sed, awk** does not print the line unless specifically told to do so.
- There are only two options for the **awk** utility: -F and -f.
- The **awk** utility sees a file as a collection of fields and records. It also can handle a text file. In this case, however, a word is a field and a line is a record.
- A field is a unit of data that has informational content.
- A record is a combination of related fields.
- The **awk** utility provides two types of buffers: field buffers and record buffers.
- The field buffers are designated as $1, $2, . . ., $n.
- The record buffer is designated as $0.
- There are two types of variables in **awk:** system variables and user-defined variables.
- An **awk** script is made of three sections: preprocessing, body, and postprocessing.
- The preprocessing section is executed only once (before the first line is read).
- The body can be executed as many times as there are lines in the input file.
- The postprocessing section is executed only once (after the last line has been read).
- The pattern identifies which records in the file are to receive an action.
- There are two categories of patterns: simple and range.
- A simple pattern acts on a single line or a set of lines.
- A range pattern acts on a range of lines.
- A simple pattern can be one of four kinds: BEGIN, END, expression, and nothing (lack of an address pattern).
- The BEGIN pattern is true before the first line of a file is read; it is false anywhere else.
- The END pattern is true after the last line is read; it is false anywhere else.
- An expression can be one of four kinds: regular expression, arithmetic expression, relational expression, and logical expression.
- If the pattern is missing, the action is applied to every line in the file.
- A range pattern is made of two simple patterns (except "nothing") separated by a comma.
- An action is one or more statements associated with a pattern.
- There are several types of statements in **awk,** some of which were covered in this chapter: expression statement, output statements (print and printf), decision statement (if-else), loop statements (while, for, do-while), control statements (next and exit), and function-call statements.

- An array is a collection of variables that can be referred to either individually or as a collection.
- Arrays in **awk** are called associative arrays because **awk** uses strings as array indexes.
- There are two types of functions in **awk:** predefined and user-defined.
- In this chapter, we covered some string functions: length, index, substring, split, substitution, global substitution, toupper, tolower.
- There are some other predefined functions: `int`, `rand`, `srand`, `sprintf`, `getline`, and `system`.
- A user-defined function is any function written by the user or the system administrator on behalf of the user.

12.19 Practice Set

Review Questions

1. What does the term **awk** stand for?
2. Can the **awk** command accept a regular expression?
3. Are all regular expression atoms supported by **awk**? If they are not all supported, which ones are missing? (Refer to Chapter 9, page 361, for a list of atoms.)
4. Are all regular expression operators supported by **awk**? If they are not all supported, which ones are missing? (Refer to Chapter 9, page 365, for a list of operators.)
5. Explain the two formats of the **awk** command.
6. What is an inline script?
7. What is a script file?
8. How can we use comments in an **awk** script file?
9. How is a script file created?
10. What is the format for an instruction in **awk**?
11. What is a pattern?
12. How many types of patterns are defined for **awk**?
13. What is a simple pattern?
14. What is a range pattern?
15. How many simple patterns are defined for **awk**?
16. When is the BEGIN pattern true? When is it false?
17. When is the END pattern true? When is it false?
18. How many types of pattern expressions are defined for **awk**?
19. What is the simple pattern that selects every line in the file?
20. Which of the following is a valid pattern?

    a. BEGIN   c. 3
    b. /UNIX/   d. 3 + 5

21. Which of the following is a valid pattern?

    a. NR == 5   c. 3,5
    b. !NR == 6   d. !(NR == 3, NR == 6)

22. Which of the following is a valid pattern?
    a. NR == 8 & NR == 11
    b. NR == 8 && NR == 11
    c. NR == 8 | NR == 11
    d. NR == 8 || NR == 11

23. What is the result of each of the following patterns if x is true and y is false?
    a. x && y
    b. x || y
    c. !(y && x)
    d. !(y || x)

24. What lines, if any, would be selected from the following pattern?
    NR == 8 && NR == 9

25. What lines, if any, would be selected from the following pattern?
    NR == 8 || NR == 9

26. What lines, if any, would be selected from the following pattern?
    $0 ~/UNIX/ && $0 ~/DOS/

27. What lines, if any, would be selected from the following pattern?
    $0 ~/UNIX/ || $0 ~/DOS/

28. If no pattern is mentioned in an **awk** command, the command applies to
    a. every line
    b. no line
    c. last line
    d. current line

29. Does the **awk** command modify the original file?

30. Describe the similarities and differences between the three loop statements in **awk** (while, for, and do-while).

31. Describe the similarities and differences between the next statement and the getline statement.

32. In the following table, provide the **awk** pattern that corresponds to the address in **sed.**

Address in sed	Pattern in awk
5	
$	
nothing	
5!	
13, 27	
13,27!	
/regexpr/	
/regexpr/,/regexpr/	
/regexpr/,/regexpr/!	

33. What is an action in **awk**?

34. Define an expression statement.

35. Compare and contrast three different **awk** output statements (print, printf, and sprintf).

36. How are the decisions made in **awk**?

37. Is the `for` loop a pretest loop?
38. Is the `while` loop a pretest loop?
39. Is the `do-while` loop a pretest loop?
40. Define an associative array.
41. Name the built-in string functions defined in this chapter.
42. Which of the following statements creates the dangling `else` problem?
    a. a nested `if` statement without a false section
    b. a nested `if` statement without a true section
    c. an `if` statement without a true or a false section
    d. any nested `if` section

Exercises

43. Simulate the following **sed** addresses (if possible) using **awk** patterns:
    a. 5   c. 5!
    b. $ d. $!

44. Simulate the following **sed** addresses (if possible) using **awk** patterns:
    a. /^A/   c. /^A/!
    b. no address (nothing)   d. /A$/

45. Simulate the following **sed** addresses (if possible) using **awk** patterns:
    a. 5,9   c. /UNIX/,/DOS/
    b. 5,9!   d. /UNIX/,10

46. Simulate the following **sed** script (if possible) using an **awk** script:
    ```
    /^A/i\
    This is the text to\
    be added'
    ```

47. Simulate the following **sed** script (if possible) using an **awk** script:
    ```
    /^A/a\
    This is the text to\
    be added
    ```

48. Simulate the following **sed** script (if possible) using an **awk** script:
    ```
    /^c/a\
    This is the text to\
    be added\
    ```

49. Simulate the following **sed** script (if possible) using an **awk** script:
    ```
    /^A/d
    ```

50. Simulate the following **sed** script (if possible) using an **awk** script:
    ```
    /^A/,/B$/s/[uU]nix/<&>/
    ```

51. Simulate the following **sed** script (if possible) using an **awk** script:
    ```
    /^A/,/B$/y/aeio/AEIO/
    ```

52. Simulate the following **sed** script (if possible) using an **awk** script:
    ```
    20r file1
    ```

53. Simulate the following **sed** script (if possible) using an **awk** script:
    ```
    20,60w file2
    ```

54. Simulate the following **sed** script (if possible) using an **awk** script:
    ```
    78q
    ```

55. Simulate the following **sed** script (if possible) using an **awk** script:
    ```
    /UNIX/q
    ```

56. Write an **awk** command that double-spaces a file.

57. Write an **awk** command to simulate the following shell command (if possible):
    ```
    cp file1 file2
    ```

58. Write an **awk** command to simulate the following shell command (if possible):
    ```
    cat file1
    ```

59. Write an **awk** command to simulate the following shell command (if possible):
    ```
    head -20 file1
    ```

60. Write an **awk** command to simulate the following shell command (if possible):
    ```
    tail +40 file1
    ```

61. Write an **awk** command to simulate the following shell command (if possible):
    ```
    tail -40 file1
    ```

62. Write a script that prints all input lines.

63. Write a script that prints the eighth line.

64. Write an **awk** command that prints the value of the first field of every input line.

65. Write an **awk** command that prints the total number of input lines.

66. Write an **awk** command that prints the number of fields in each line.

67. Write an **awk** command that prints the value of the last field in each line.

68. Write an **awk** command that prints the value of the last field of the last line.

69. Write an **awk** command that prints any input line that has more than four fields.

70. Write an **awk** command that prints lines in which the value of the last field is more than 4.

71. Write an **awk** command that prints the total number of fields in the file.

72. Write an **awk** command that prints the total number of lines that have more than five fields.

73. Write an **awk** command that prints the lines that contain UNIX.

74. Write an **awk** command that prints the second field of a line if its first field is greater than 9.

75. Write an **awk** command that prints all the lines. The order of fields must be field 4, field 3, field 2, and field 1.

76. Write an **awk** command that prints every line that has at least one field.

77. Write an **awk** command that prints the sum of all values in the third field.

78. Write an **awk** command that prints the number of blank lines.

79. Write an **awk** command that prints the lines in which the value of the third field is greater than 5.00 and the value of the fourth field is not zero.

80. Write an **awk** command that prints lines 5 to 56.

81. Write an **awk** command that adds one blank line after each line.

82. Write an **awk** command that adds the title "Document" at the top of the file.

83. Write an **awk** command that prints any line that follows a line whose first field is greater than 9. In other words, if the value of the first field in a line is greater than 9, the next line would be printed.

84. Write an **awk** command that prints any line that precedes a line whose first field is greater than 9. In other words, if the value of the first field in a line is greater than 9, the previous line would be printed.
85. Write an **awk** script to print each line three times.
86. Write an **awk** script to delete every other line.
87. Write an **awk** script to continuously copy two lines and delete the third.
88. Write an **awk** script to move lines 22 to 23 after line 56.
89. Write an **awk** script to copy lines 22 to 23 after line 56.
90. Write an **awk** command to extract the first word of each line.
91. Write an **awk** command that prints the first and the third word in each line.
92. If originally x = 4, what is the value of x after evaluation of the following expressions?

    a. x = 2   c. x += 4
    b. x *= 2   d. x /= x + 2

93. Evaluate the following expressions to true or false.

    a. !(3 + 3 >= 6)
    b. 1 + 6 == 7 || 3 + 2 == 1
    c. 1 > 5 || 6 < 50 && 2 < 5
    d. 14 != 55 && !(13 < 29) || 31 > 52

94. If x = 0, y = 5, z = 5, what is the value of x, y, and z for each of the following code fragments? (Assume that x, y, and z are their original values for each fragment.)

    a. if (z != 0)   c. if (x == 1)
          y = 295   {
       else   x = x - 3
          x = 10   z = z + 3
    b. if (y + z > 10)   }
          y = 99   else
          z = 8   y = 99
       x = ++z

95. Write an `if` statement that will assign the value 1 to the variable best if the integer variable score is 90 or greater.
96. Write an if statement that if the variable `flag` is true, read the integer variables a and b. Then calculate and print the sum and average of both inputs.
97. Write a function to find the smallest of 10 integers.

12.20 Lab Sessions

Session I

1. Log into the system.
2. Use a command to create and save the following file. Call it `Ch12S1F1`. Use tabs to separate the fields.

Continued

First Name	Last Name	Rate	Hours
George	White	18.00	23
Mark	Red	18.10	20
Mary	Blue	10.89	25
Dan	Black	12.00	0
Susan	Green	18.00	40
Nora	Brown	17.20	46
Bruce	Purple	12.20	52
John	Gray	11.00	39
Bob	Gold	15.00	45
Steve	Silver	14.67	25

3. Using file Ch12S1F1, write an **awk** command that prints the name (first and last) of the employees that did not work last week.

4. Using file Ch12S1F1, write an **awk** command that prints the whole record for employees whose rate is $15 or more.

5. Using file Ch12S1F1, write an **awk** command that prints the whole record of the employee(s) who worked the most hours. (Hint: Because there may be more than one, sort the data first.)

6. Using file Ch12S1F1, write an **awk** command that prints the whole record of the employee whose first name is Mary.

7. Using file Ch12S1F1, write an **awk** command that prints the number of hours worked for employees whose rate is more than $18.

8. Using file Ch12S1F1, write an **awk** command that prints the whole record of any employee whose rate is between $1 and $18.

9. Using file Ch12S1F1, write an **awk** command that prints the whole record of any employee who worked overtime (more than 40 hours).

10. Using file Ch12S1F1, write an **awk** command that prints the whole record of the employees who worked between 20 and 30 hours.

11. Log out of the system.

Session II

1. Log into the system.

2. Using the file created in Session I (Ch12S1F1), use an **awk** script and an **awk** command to create a report with five columns. Save the report in a file called Ch12S1R1.

   a. The report should have a general header "Weekly Report."

   b. Each column should have its own heading.

   c. A new (fifth) column should be added to show the total pay for each employee.

   d. For employees who worked overtime, calculate the overtime (more than 40 hours) at time and a half (150%).

Continued

Session II—*Continued*

   e. At the end of the report, show the total payroll cost with an appropriate caption.

   f. Print the report.

3. Log out of the system.

Session III

1. Log into the system.

2. Using an editor, create an inventory file for the following data (do not include the column heads, only the data). Call it Ch12S3F1.

Part No.	Price	Quantity on Hand	Reorder Point	Minimum Order
0123	1.23	23	20	20
0234	2.34	34	50	25
3456	34.56	56	50	10
4567	45.67	7	10	5
5678	6.78	75	75	25

3. Create a script to prepare an inventory report. The report is to contain the part number, price, quantity on hand, reorder point, minimum order, and order amount.

4. The order amount, calculated when the quantity on hand falls below the reorder point, is the sum of the reorder point and the minimum order less the quantity on hand.

5. Also provide a report heading, such as "Inventory Report," headings for each column, and an "End of Report" message at the end of the report.

6. Print the report.

7. Log out of the system.

Session IV

1. Log into the system.

2. Using an editor, create the following employee file. Call it Ch12S4F1. Do not include the column heads in the file.

Employee No.	Department	Pay Rate	Exempt	Hours Worked
0101	41	8.11	Y	49
0722	32	7.22	N	40
1273	23	5.43	Y	39
2584	14	6.74	N	45

Continued

3. Write a script to read the employee file and create a payroll register. Call it `Ch12S4.awk`. The register is to contain the following data.
   a. Employee number (print left-justified)
   b. Department
   c. Pay rate
   d. Exempt
   e. Hours worked
   f. Base pay (pay rate * hours worked)
   g. Overtime pay

   Overtime pay is calculated only for nonexempt employees. An employee is exempt if *Y* appears in the exempt column. Overtime is paid at time and one half for all hours worked over 40.

   h. Total pay
4. Print the report.
5. Log out of the system.

Session V

1. Log into the system.
2. Write a script to create the following file (`Ch12S5F1`) that contains data for a class of students. (Do not include the column heads.) The class may have up to 40 students. There are five quizzes during the term. Each student is identified by a four-digit student number.

Student	Quiz 1	Quiz 2	Quiz 3	Quiz 4	Quiz 5
1234	52	7	100	78	34
2134	90	36	90	77	30
3124	100	45	20	90	70
4532	11	17	81	32	77
5678	20	12	45	78	34
6134	34	80	55	78	45
7874	60	100	56	78	78
8026	70	10	66	78	56
9893	34	9	77	78	20
1947	45	40	88	78	55
2877	55	50	99	78	80
3189	22	70	100	78	77
4602	89	50	91	78	60
5405	11	11	0	78	10
6999	0	98	89	78	20

Continued

Session V—*Continued*

3. Create a second script to prepare a report in the following format:

Student	Quiz 1	Quiz 2	Quiz 3	Quiz 4	Quiz 5
1234	78	83	87	91	86
2134	67	77	84	82	79
3124	77	89	93	87	71
High Score	78	89	93	91	86
Low Score	67	77	84	82	71
Average	73.4	83.0	88.2	86.6	78.6

4. Log out of the system.

Session VI

1. Log into the system.
2. Use a command to create and save the following file. Call it Ch12S6F1. Use tabs to separate the fields. Do not type the column heads.

Month	Sales
January	124,567.89
February	234,567.78
March	349,123.77
April	112,248.00
May	107,345.22
June	180,670.23
July	122,457.03
August	345,789.99
September	234,567.80
October	145,890.95
November	245,789.76
December	111,890.22

3. Using file Ch12S6F1, create a total sales report for the year. This file presents a minor problem: We cannot add numbers, such as sales value, that have commas. Write an **awk** script to create the total sales using the following strategies:
   a. In the BEGIN section, initialize the total value to zero.
   b. Before adding each sales value to the total, call a function called RemoveCommas (that you write) to remove the commas from the sales value. Do not change the format in the file; the report is to contain commas.

Continued

c. In the END section, call a function called AddCommas (that you write) to add commas to the total before printing it.

4. Log out of the system.

Session VII

1. Log into the system.
2. Use a command to create and save the following file. Call it Ch12S7F1. Use tabs to separate the fields. Each column defines a time measured in the format hhmmss (hours, minutes, and seconds) from midnight in military format (1 o'clock pm is recorded as 13). Do not type the column heads.

Time 1	Time 2
034023	052030
051811	061150
061711	091050
071811	111150
031811	151150
091811	123412
060021	180042
123500	142832

3. Create a file called Ch12S7F2 with three columns using the following format:
   a. The format of the time in the first two columns should be hh:mm:ss (hours: minutes: seconds).
   b. The third column should show the difference between two times in the hh:mm:ss format.
      • Use the *substr* function to extract the hours, minutes, and seconds.
      • Convert each time to seconds (convert hours and minutes to seconds).
      • Find the difference.
      • Convert each column to the hh:mm:ss format.
   c. Each column should have the appropriate headings.
4. Use the following strategy to calculate the difference in time:
   a. Convert times to seconds.
   b. Subtract time2 from time1.
   c. Convert the difference to hours, minutes, and seconds.
5. Log out of the system.

Session VIII

1. Log into the system.
2. Use a command to create and save the following file. Call it Ch12S8F1. Use tabs to separate the fields.

Continued

Session VIII—*Continued*

```
Computer Science
Fall:            CIS14      CIS70      CIS32      CIS89
Winter:          CIS12      CIS70      CIS31      CIS99
Spring:          CIS14      CIS70      CIS22


Mathematics
Fall:            MAT10      MAT23      MAT56
Winter:          MAT11      MAT33      MAT56      MAT77
Spring:          MAT10      MAT23      MAT40


Biology
Fall:            BIO17      BIO22
Winter:          BIO14      BIO66      BIO23
Spring:          BIO18      BIO20      BIO56      BIO34


English
Fall:            ENG07      ENG10      ENG11
Winter:          ENG08      ENG12      ENG14      ENG21
Spring:          ENG07      ENG12      ENG34
```

3. We want to create three separate files for courses offered during fall, winter, and spring.

   a. The file for the fall quarter should be called Ch12S8Fall and should look like the following report:

```
Courses Offered for Fall Quarter

Department              Courses
----------              -------
Computer Science        CIS14
Computer Science        CIS70
Computer Science        CIS32
Computer Science        CIS89
Mathematics             MAT10
Mathematics             MAT23
Mathematics             MAT56
Biology                 BIO17
Biology                 BIO22
English                 ENG07
English                 ENG10
English                 ENG11
```

4. The file for the winter quarter should be called Ch12S8Winter and should have the same format as the one for the fall.

Continued

5. The file for the spring quarter should be called Ch12S8Spring and should have the same format as the one for the fall.

6. Use one or more **awk** scripts to create these files. The department name is identified because it is the only field on its line.

7. Log out of the system.

Session IX

1. Log into the system.

2. The **awk** utility can be used for data validation. For example, a superuser can use an **awk** script to validate the contents of the /etc/passwd file frequently. As we saw in Chapter 4, each line in this file is made of seven fields separated by colons. The file layout is shown in Figure 12.23.

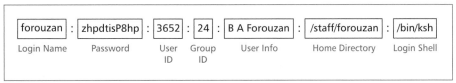

FIGURE 12.23 *File Layout for* /etc/passwd *(Session IX)*

3. Validation for this file is based on the following restrictions:

   a. The line must have seven fields.

   b. The first field can be alphanumeric.

   c. The second field should not be empty (if it is empty, anybody can access the system under that login name).

   d. The third and fourth fields should be numeric.

   e. No restriction on the fifth field.

   f. The sixth and seven fields should start with a slash (/).

4. Use a command to create and save the following file. Call it Ch12S9F1.

```
p1234:P7cryI:2286:Juan Paul:/staff/jp1234:/bin/ksh
frc5051:3G4z:5051:24:Bryan Devaux:/staff/frc5051:/bin/ksh
root:ghtrerty:44:AB:Behrouz Forouzan:\staff\forouzan:\bin\sh
gmh111:abc:13:George Right:\staff\accounting\right:\bin\ksh
gilberg:gI84o:3988:24:Richard Gilberg:/staff/rfg3988:/bin/ksh
phongvan:xjp8y:2140:24:Van Phong:/bin/ks
castroj:hDSI7:3855:24:Jorge Castro:/staff/castroj:/bin/ksh
rocker:gI84o:2566:24:Hal Rocker:/staff/rocker:/bin/ksh
sat8989:3G4z:5051:24:Sarah Trapp:/staff/sat8989:/bin/ksh
```

5. Write an **awk** script and an **awk** command to validate the foregoing criteria. The program should create a report called Ch12S9Report that appends any line that violates any of the criteria with the reason for violation.

6. Log out of the system.

The Shell Programming

In Part II we cover the concepts of shell programming, starting with basic user interaction without scripts and then script programming and advanced script programming. Because the Bash shell is virtually identical to the Korn shell, we do not provide a separate discussion for it. The differences are noted in Chapter 5 and Appendix 2.

## CHAPTER 13

Interactive Korn Shell

The Korn shell, developed by David Korn at the AT&T Labs, is a dual-purpose utility. It can be used interactively as an interpreter that reads, interprets, and executes user commands. It can also be used as a programming language to write shell scripts. In this chapter, we discuss how to use the Korn shell interactively. In the next two chapters, we use its programming language capability to create shell scripts.

13.1 Korn Shell Features

In this section, we discuss Korn shell features. Many of them were discussed previously in Chapter 5. New features are fully discussed in the following sections; those covered in Chapter 5 are summarized and cross-referenced.

Korn Shell Sessions

When we use the Korn shell interactively, we execute commands at the shell prompt. In Chapter 5, we discussed how to start a session, change shells, check the current shell, and terminate a session. The workflow is summarized in Figure 5.2 on page 144. We suggest that you review this material to make sure you remember how these commands work.

Standard Streams

In Section 5.2, Standard Streams on page 146, we defined the three standard streams—standard input (0), standard output (1), and standard error (2)—available in all shells. Figure 13.1 shows how the standard streams relate to a shell command.

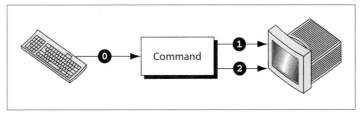

FIGURE 13.1   *Standard Streams*

Redirection

The standard streams can be redirected from and to files. In Section 5.3 (page 147), we discussed how to redirect standard streams. Stream redirection is summarized in Figure 13.2. As you study this figure, note that there is one operator (<) for redirecting standard input to a command and three operators for directing data to standard output or standard error (>, >|, and >>). If you don't remember the details, refer to Section 5.2 (page 146).

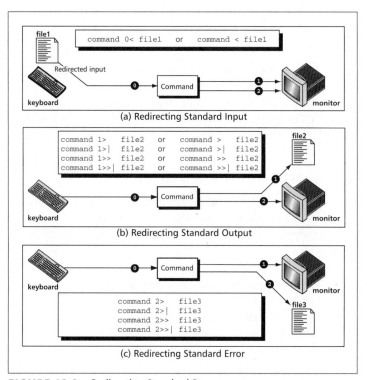

FIGURE 13.2   *Redirecting Standard Streams*

If we don't use redirection, standard output and standard error both go to the monitor. How do we write the redirection so that both go to the same file? This requires that we use and-redirection (see Redirecting to One File, page 150). We show how it is done in the next example.

```
command 1> file2  2>& 1
```

Pipes

The pipe operator temporarily saves the output from one command in a buffer that is being used at the same time as the input to the next command. Its operation is shown in Figure 13.3. Pipes are discussed in Section 5.4 on page 151.

tee Command

The **tee** command copies standard input to standard output and at the same time copies it to one or more files. If the stream is coming from another command, such as **who,** it can be piped to the **tee** command. For more information, refer to Section 5.5 on page 153.

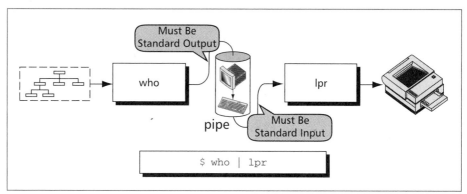

FIGURE 13.3 *Pipes*

Combining Commands

We can combine commands in four ways: sequenced commands, grouped commands, chained commands, and conditional commands. These command variations were discussed in Section 5.6 on page 154. The Korn shell supports all four.

Command-Line Editing

The Korn shell supports command-line editing as discussed in Chapter 5.

Quotes

In Section 5.8 on page 159, we discussed the three quote types: backslash, double quotes, and single quotes. The Korn shell supports all three. You may want to reread Section 5.8 to refresh your memory on their use.

Command Substitution

Command substitution is used to convert a command's output to a string that can be stored in another string or a variable. Although the Korn shell supports two constructs for command substitution [`'command'` and `$(command)`], we discuss only the dollar-sign-command format because we expect the quoted format to become deprecated in the future. The recommended form is shown in Figure 13.4.

FIGURE 13.4 *Korn Command Substitution*

Job Control

Job control is used to control how and where a job is executed in the foreground or background. It was discussed in Section 5.10. The Korn shell supports the features of job control discussed in Chapter 5.

Aliases

An **alias** is a means of creating a customized command by assigning a name or acronym to a command. If the name we use is one of the standard shell commands, such as **dir,** then the **alias** replaces the shell command. In the Korn shell, an alias is created by using the **alias** command. Its format is

```
alias name=command-definition
```

where **alias** is the command keyword, `name` is the name of the alias name being created, and `command-definition` is the code for the customized command. As we have seen, there can be no spaces before or after the assignment operator (=). Refer to Aliases on page 170 for examples of its use.

Listing Aliases

The Korn shell provides a method to list all aliases and to list a specific alias. Both use the **alias** command. To list all aliases, we use the **alias** command with no arguments. To list a specific command, we use the **alias** command with one argument, the name of the **alias** command. Both commands are in the next example:

```
$ alias                       # List all aliases (Output not shown)
$ alias dir                   # List only 'dir' alias (Output below)
dir='print¹ '\''Listing for Gilberg'\''; ls -l | more'
```

Removing Aliases

Aliases are removed by using the **unalias** command. It has one argument, a list of aliases to be removed. When it is used with the all option (-a), it deletes all aliases. You should be very careful, however, with this option: It deletes all aliases, even those defined by the system administrator. For this reason, some system administrators disable this option. The **unalias** command is discussed in Chapter 5 on page 173. The following example demonstrates its use:

```
$ unalias dir                 # Remove aliases for dir
$ unalias -a                  # Remove all aliases
```

13.2 Two Special Files

There are two special files in UNIX that can be used by any shell.

Trash File (`/dev/null`)

The trash file is a special file that is used for deleting data. Found under the device (dev) directory, it has a very special characteristic: Its contents are always emptied immediately after receiving data. In other words, no matter how much or how often data are written to it, they are immediately deleted. Physically, there is only one trash file in the system: It is owned by the superuser.

---

¹We introduce "print" later in the chapter.

> The /dev/null file is kept under the device directory, which is owned by the root. You can verify its ownership with the list command that follows. Note that it (the userid of the superuser) is a character special file ('c' as first byte) that can be read or written by any user.
>
> ```
> $ ls -l /dev/null
> crw-rw-rw-    1 root      sys         1,  2 Jan 22 17:04 /dev/null
> ```

Because it is a file, it can be used as both a source and a destination. However, when used as a source, the result is always end of file because it is always empty. While the following two commands are syntactically correct, the first has no effect because the string "Trash me," when sent to the trash file, is immediately deleted. The second has no effect because the file is always empty, which means that there is nothing to display.

```
$ print "Trash me" > /dev/null
$ cat  /dev/null
```

There are occasions when we need to know the exit status of a command without seeing the command output. For example, if we want to know if a key phrase is in a file without seeing the actual lines that contain it, we can send the standard output to trash. We then **print** the exit status to determine if we found the key phrase. This concept is shown in the next example:

```
$ grep '…' > /dev/null               # Send output to trash
$ print $?                           # Check if pattern found
```

Terminal File (/dev/tty)

Although each terminal in UNIX is a named file, such as /dev/tty13 and /dev/tty31, there is only one logical file, /dev/tty. This file is found under the device directory; it represents the terminal of each user. This means that someone using terminal /dev/tty13 can refer to the terminal using either the full terminal name (/dev/tty13) or the generic system name (/dev/tty). In fact, two different users can each refer to the terminal using the generic system name at the same time.

> The generic terminal file, /dev/tty, is owned by the root; everybody has permission to read and write it. It can be used as a source or a destination.
>
> ```
> $ ls -l /dev/tty
> crw-rw-rw-    1 root      sys         2,  0 Jan 22 16:18 /dev/tty
> ```

Both of the commands in the next example are syntactically correct:

```
$ cp file1 /dev/tty                  # Displays the contents of file1
$ cp /dev/tty file1                  # File1 is erased and becomes empty
```

Because the terminal file represents a terminal, it cannot store data. Thus, the contents of file1 in the previous example, when sent to the terminal file, are shown on the monitor but not saved. Because nothing is stored in a terminal file, the second command copies nothing to `file1`.

> The terminal file (`/dev/tty`) is a file under the device directory that belongs to the root. It represents the terminal assigned to each user.

By this time, you are probably wondering why UNIX has this capability when output automatically goes to the monitor already. The answer is that some commands, such as **tee**, require a file for output. If we want both to write to a file and at the same time pass the output to the monitor, we can use the `/dev/tty` file.

In Session 13.1, we want to send a complete list of all files to the monitor while saving a list of all scripts in a file. We do this by sending the list command results to a **tee** command that sends one copy of the file list to the `/dev/tty` file and the second copy to a pipe. The piped results are then fed into a **grep** command that redirects lines containing `.scr` to our file of data files. Because of the large output, the output lists are edited.

SESSION 13.1   *Sending Output to the* `tty` *File*

```
$ ls -l | tee /dev/tty | grep '\.scr$' > temp.file
total 146
-rw-r--r--    1 gilberg   staff         42 Jul 10   2000 ErrFile
-rwxr--r--    1 gilberg   staff        111 Jul 11   2000 IFS.scr
-rw-r--r--    1 gilberg   staff          0 Jun 11   2000 MidRaven
. . .
-rwxr--r--    1 gilberg   staff         36 Jul 31 13:42 who.scr.bak
-rwxr--r--    1 gilberg   staff         36 Jul 31 13:45 who.scrBak
-rwxr--r--    1 gilberg   staff        112 Jul  5   2000 xxforLoop.scr
$ cat temp.file
-rwxr--r--    1 gilberg   staff        111 Jul 11   2000 IFS.scr
-rwxr--r--    1 gilberg   staff        925 Jul 10   2000 addCol.scr
-rwxr--r--    1 gilberg   staff        129 Jul  7   2000 backup.scr
. . .
-rwxr--r--    1 gilberg   staff        225 Jun 18   2000 variableNum.scr
-rwxr--r--    1 gilberg   staff        171 Jul 29 14:12 whileRead.scr
-rwxr--r--    1 gilberg   staff         36 Jul  8   2000 who.scr
```

13.3 Variables

The Korn shell allows you to store values in variables (Figure 13.5). A shell variable is a location in memory where values can be stored. In the Korn shell, all data are stored as strings. There are two broad classifications of variables: user-defined and predefined.

User-Defined Variables

As implied by their name, user-defined variables are created by the user. Although the user may choose any name, it should not be the same as one of the predefined variables. Each variable must have a name. The name of a variable must start with an alphabetic or underscore (_) character. It then can be followed by zero or more alphanumeric or underscore characters. Figure 13.6 shows three variables.

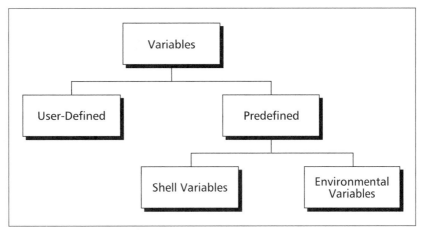

FIGURE 13.5 *Variables*

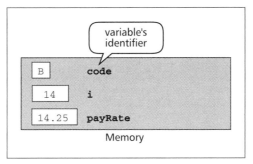

FIGURE 13.6 *Examples of Variables*

Predefined Variables

Predefined variables are either shell variables or environmental variables. The shell variables are used to configure the shell. For example, the internal field separator—the character that separates fields in a line—is normally a space or a tab, but it can be defined as any character. Because they are used mostly in shell scripts, they are discussed in the next chapter.

The environmental variables, discussed later in this chapter, are used to configure the environment. For example, a system variable determines which editor is used to edit the command history file.

Storing Values in Variables

There are several ways that we can store a value in a variable, but the easiest method is to use the assignment operator, =. The variable is coded first, on the left, followed by the assignment operator and then the value to be stored. There can be no spaces before and after the assignment operator; the variable, the operator, and the value must be coded in sequence immediately next to each other as in the following example:

```
varA=7
```

In this example, varA is the variable that receives the data, and 7 is the value being stored in it. While the receiving field must always be a variable, the value may be a constant, the value stored in another variable, or as we will see later, any expression that reduces to a single value. Table 13.1 shows some examples of storing values in variables.

TABLE 13.1 *Examples of Assignment Expressions*

Command	Result
x=2	x is "2"
x=Hello	x is "Hello"
x="Go Dons!"	x is "Go Dons!"

Note that although the first example in Table 13.1 contains a number, it is stored as a string of digits. That's why we show the results in double quote marks. The last two examples show how we store a character string. While we did not use quotes under the *Command* heading in the second example, we did in the last. The difference is that the last example contains spaces and special characters. Whenever a string contains spaces or special characters, it must be quoted. Figure 13.7 shows an example.

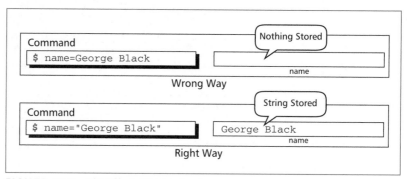

FIGURE 13.7 *The Effect of Using Quotes*

It helps to understand why the first example in Figure 13.7 stores nothing. When UNIX parses the line, it interprets it as a command to store the value George in the variable name. Then it finds the second argument, Black, which it interprets as a file. If the file doesn't exist, it displays a not found message. If there is a file named Black, it tries to execute it. At this point, it's hard to predict what will happen. The bottom line is that the value is not stored as we intended.

Accessing the Value of a Variable

To access the value of a variable, the name of the variable must be preceded by a dollar sign as shown in Session 13.2. The variable name dollar sign should not be confused with the system prompt $. The value in a variable can be used for many purposes. Values can be used anywhere in a string. For example, you can use the value of a variable at the beginning of the string, in the middle of a string, or at the end of a string. We demonstrate all three positions in Session 13.2.

SESSION 13.2   *Using Values in Strings*

```
$ count=7
$ print $count is the number after 6 and before 8
7 is the number after 6 and before 8

$ print The value of count is $count as expected.
The value of count is 7 as expected.

$ print My lucky number is $count.
My lucky number is 7.
```

The value of a variable can also be stored in another variable as in Session 13.3.

SESSION 13.3   *Assigning One Variable to Another*

```
$ count=5
$ number=$count
$ print count contains: $count; number contains: $number
count contains: 5; number contains: 5
```

The value of a variable can be used for other purposes. For example, imagine you want to frequently access a specific directory. To prevent errors and to save time when typing a long pathname for a directory, you can simply store the path in a variable (Session 13.4).

SESSION 13.4   *Storing a Path in a Variable*

```
$ newDir=~/report/letters
$ cd $newDir
$ pwd
/usr/forouzan/report/letters
```

Null Variables

If we access a variable that is not set (no value is stored in it), we receive what is called a null value (nothing). We can also explicitly store a null value in a variable by either assigning it a null string ("") or by assigning it nothing. In other words, the default value for any variable is null. Session 13.5 demonstrates the use of null variables.

SESSION 13.5   *Null Variables*

```
$ x=1                              #Good assignment
$ y=                              #Null assignment
$ z=""                            #Another null assignment
$ print "(x:" $x ") (y:" $y") (z:" $z")"
(x: 1) (y:) (z:)

$ x=""                            #Clear 'x' by setting to null
$ print "(x contains:" $x")"
(x contains: )

$ x=1
$ print "(x contains:" $x")"
(x contains: 1)
```

Unsetting a Variable

In Session 13.5, we demonstrated that we can clear a variable by assigning a null value to it. Although this method works, it is better to use the **unset** command (Session 13.6).

SESSION 13.6 *Unsetting Variables*

```
$ x=1
$ print "(x contains:" $x")"
(x contains: 1)

$ unset x                        #A better way to clear 'x'
$ print "(x contains:" $x")"
(x contains: )
```

Storing Filenames

We can also store a filename in a variable. We can even use wildcards. However, we should be aware of how wildcards are handled by the shell. The shell stores the filename including the wildcard in the variable without expanding it. When the value is used, the expansion takes place. Session 13.7 demonstrates how the script handles stored filenames containing wildcards.

SESSION 13.7 *Storing Filenames*

```
$ ls
file1      file2      file3.bak
$ filename="file*"
$ print "filename contains: $filename"          #show contents
filename contains: file*
$ print $filename
file1      file2      file3.bak

$ filename="file?"
$ print $filename
file1      file2
```

Session 13.7 Analysis: In the first example, we create a variable and store the asterisk wildcard value in it. We then print the variable value to prove that it contains the wildcard command. (Note that the variable name is included in the quoted string so it is not expanded.) When we used the variable with the **print** command, the wildcard is expanded by the shell to print the three matching files. In the second example, we used the question mark wildcard. In this case, only the first two files were listed because they had only five characters in their name. The third file had more than five characters and therefore didn't match the wildcard pattern.

Storing File Contents

We can also store the contents of a file in a variable for processing, such as parsing words. Two steps are required to store the file:

1. Create a copy of the file on standard output using the **cat** utility.
2. Using command substitution, convert the standard output contents to a string.

The string can now be stored in a variable. The entire process is done in one command line in Session 13.8.

SESSION 13.8 *Storing a File in a String*

```
$ cat storeAsVar.txt
This is      a              file
used to show
the result          of storing    a file in a            variable.
```
```
$ x=$(cat storeAsVar.txt)
$ print $x
This is a file used to show the result of storing a file in a variable.
```

Session 13.8 Analysis: We begin by showing the contents of a three-line file using **cat**. To demonstrate the full effect of storing a file in a variable, we used extra whitespace in the file. We then stored the file in a variable (x). Then to prove that the file was stored in the variable, we use **print** to write it to the monitor. In these three commands, we first showed the contents of a file, next converted the file to a string using command substitution, and then converted it back to a file (the monitor is actually a file, standard output) using the **print** command. This demonstrates that **print** and command substitution are the inverse of each other—one converts a file to a string and one converts a string to a file.

Now study the **print** output carefully. Note that the variable does not contain any of the extra whitespace found in the file. It contains the file as one string with words separated by a single space character. All nonspace whitespace characters are converted to a space, and all extra spaces are removed.

Storing Commands in a Variable

We can also store a command in a variable. For example, the list command can be stored in a variable. We can then use the variable at the command prompt to execute its contents as in Session 13.9.

SESSION 13.9 *Executing a Command Variable*

```
$ x="ls file*"
$ $x
file.scr       file2          file3.bak      file5          fileOut.rpt
file1          file2.bak      file4          file6          fileReport
file1bak       file3          file4.bak      fileList.dat
```

Storing commands in a variable works only with simple commands. If the command is complex (for example, piping the results of the list command to **more**), a command variable will not work. For a complex command, we need the **eval** command, which we discuss later in this chapter.

Read-Only Variables

Most programming languages provide a way for a programmer to define a named constant. A named constant defines a value that cannot be changed. Although the Korn shell does not have named constants, we can create the same effect by creating a variable, assigning it a value, and then fixing its value with the **readonly** command. The command format is:

`readonly variable-list`

Note that the command expects a variable list as its parameter. This means that we can make more than one value read-only at a time. In Session 13.10, we create two variables, make them read-only, and then try to change them. To prove that they weren't changed, we then **print** their values.

SESSION 13.10 *Creating **readonly** Constants*

```
$ cHello=Hello
$ cBye="Good Bye"
$ readonly cHello cBye

$ cHello=Howdy
cHello: is read only

$ cBye=TaTa
cBye: is read only

$ print $cHello "..." $cBye
Hello ... Good Bye
```

Exporting Variables

We noted in Chapter 5 that a shell can create another shell. The new shell is called a subshell, or a child shell. The process of creating another shell is known as **forking** a shell.

Figure 13.8 demonstrates the forking process. After executing a **date** command, we fork a new shell by entering **ksh.** This command creates a new subshell and waits for a command to be entered. At this point, we can enter any command. To leave the subshell, we enter **exit,** which deletes the subshell and takes us back to the parent.

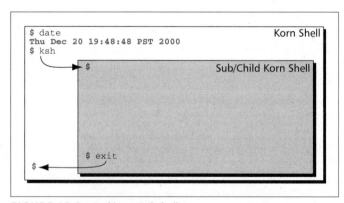

FIGURE 13.8 *Forking a Subshell*

The point we need to understand now is that shell variables are not automatically exported to subshells. This is demonstrated in Session 13.11.

SESSION 13.11 *Variables Are Not Automatically Exported*

```
$ name=George
$ print $name
George
$ ksh
$ print $name
$
```

If we want to make a variable available to a subshell, we must tell the current shell that we want it exported. The format of the **export** command is:

```
export variable-list
```

Note that once again we have a variable list. We can **export** multiple variables with one command. Once variables have been flagged as exportable, whenever a new shell is forked, the variable is automatically created in the subshell and initialized with the variable's current value. If another subshell is then created, the variable is again exported. Each shell's variable is a separate entity; if we change a subshell's variable value, it does not change the value in the parent shell. This process is demonstrated in Session 13.12.

SESSION 13.12 *Exporting Names*

```
$ name=George
$ print $name
George
$ export name
```
```
$ ksh                       # First subshell
$ print $name
George
```
```
$ ksh                       # Second subshell
$ print $name
George
```

To demonstrate that the variables are in fact separate, let's change the value in a subshell. Furthermore, to demonstrate that the subshell is deleted when we **exit,** we fork another subshell and show that the original value is exported; the changed value is indeed lost. These two situations are shown in Session 13.13.

SESSION 13.13 *Exported Variables Are Separate Entities*

```
$ name=George
$ print $name
George
$ export name
```
```
$ ksh                       # Subshell
$ print $name
George                      # name exported
```

Continued

SESSION 13.13 *Exported Variables Are Separate Entities—Continued*

`$ name=Jorge`	`# name changed`
`$ print $name`	
`Jorge`	
`$ exit`	`# Back to parent`
`$ print $name`	
`George`	`# name change lost`
`$ ksh`	`# New subshell`
`$ print $name`	
`George`	`# Original name exported to new shell`

Variable Attribute: The typeset Command

In the Korn shell, we can associate one or more attributes, such as character format and justification, with a variable with the **typeset** command. Once an attribute is associated with a variable, it controls the variable's contents and formatting. To associate an attribute with a variable, the attribute is passed to the **typeset** command as an attribute as shown in the next example:

```
$ typeset -attribute variable_name          # Set attribute
```

To remove an attribute from a variable, we use the following format:

```
$ typeset +attribute variable_name          # Remove attribute
```

Note, however, that the attributes have the effect of changing the physical format of a value in a variable. Thus, if a variable contains a lowercase string and we set its attribute to uppercase, the lowercase string becomes uppercase. Once a physical format has been changed, unsetting the attribute has no effect on the current contents. In the previous example, the string would remain uppercase until either the value is changed or until the lowercase attribute is applied to it. After it is unset, the next value will be stored as typed. Table 13.2 contains a list of variable attributes.

TABLE 13.2 *Variable Attributes*

Attribute	Characteristics
l	lowercase (ell character)
U	uppercase
i	integer
Rn	right-justify with a width of n characters (extra characters truncated)
Ln	left-justify with a width of n characters (extra characters truncated)
x	automatically export
r	read-only (cannot be changed)
RZn	right-justify with a width of n characters (extra characters truncated) and padded with zeros
LZn	removes leading zeros from a numeric variable

Session 13.14 demonstrates how we can use attributes to control the contents of a string variable.

SESSION 13.14   *Demonstrate Use of String Attributes*

```
$ str="HELLO WORLD!"
$ print $str
HELLO WORLD!
```
```
$ typeset -l str
$ print $str
hello world!                              # Verify typeset results
```
```
$ typeset +l str
$ print $str
hello world!                              # Verify result is permanent
```
```
$ typeset -L5 str
$ print $str
hello                                     # Verify left-justify results
```
```
$ typeset +L5 str
$ print $str
hello                                     # Verify result is permanent
```
```
$ str="hello world!"
$ typeset -R6 str
$ print $str
world!                                    # Verify right-justify results
```

Session 13.14 Analysis: We begin the session by storing a two-word string in a variable and verifying the results with a **print** command. After setting the type to lowercase, we verify that it was in fact changed. To prove that the type is permanently changed, we delete the lowercase typing and print the variable again. The lowercase results verify that the values were permanently changed by the **typeset** command.

In the next command, we use the justify-left command. The **print** command demonstrates that the string was truncated, with only the leftmost five characters remaining. After restoring the variable's contents, we demonstrate that justify-right truncates the variable to only the rightmost characters.

Now, let's look at what happens when we use integer types. Session 13.15 demonstrates the effect of setting the type on a numeric variable.

SESSION 13.15   *Demonstrate Use of Integer Types*

```
$ typeset -i num
$ print $num
                                          # Demonstrate numeric data - no data
```
```
$ num=124
$ print $num
124                                       # Demonstrate numeric data - data
```
```
$ num=abc
ksh: abc: bad number
$ print $?
1                                         # Demonstrate non numeric error
```

Continued

SESSION 13.15 *Demonstrate Use of Integer Types—Continued*

```
$ typeset -RZ10 num
$ print \"$num\"
"0000000124"                          # Demonstrate zero justified
```

```
$ typeset +RZ10 num
$ print \"$num\"
"0000000124"                          # Demonstrate permanent change
```

```
$ typeset -LZ10 num
$ print $num
124                                   # Demonstrate truncate leading zeros
```

Session 13.15 Analysis: We demonstrate three important concepts about the integer type here. First, note that when we type a field as numeric, it can accept only numeric data. If we try to assign it nonnumeric data, the assignment fails with an error code of 1.

Second, when we use zero fill, the full width is used. The primary use of adding zeros to a number is to make it a fixed length for networking or other operations that expect a fixed-size number.

In addition to the numeric operations shown in Session 13.15, we can also use the variable for arithmetic operations and binary, octal, and hexadecimal value displays (Session 13.16).

SESSION 13.16 *Demonstrate Use of Integer Arithmetic*

```
$ typeset -i x
$ x=12
$ x=$x+1
$ print $x
13                                    # Demonstrate arithmetic add

$ num=$x*7
$ print $num
91                                    # Demonstrate arithmetic multiply

$ typeset -i2 x
$ print $x
2#1101                                # Demonstrate binary format—13

$ typeset -i16 num
$ print $num
16#5b                                 # Demonstrate hexadecimal format—91
```

13.4 Output

The output statement in the Korn shell is the **print** command.[2] Although the Korn shell also supports the **echo** command (inherited from the Bourne shell), we use **print** because it is faster and because there is the possibility that **echo** may become deprecated in a future version of the Korn shell. The format of the **print** command is shown in Figure 13.9.

---

[2]We introduced **print** in some simple examples previously.

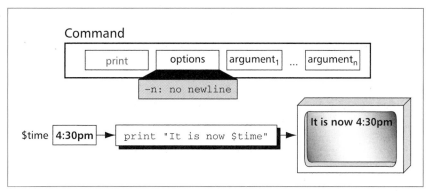

FIGURE 13.9 *The **print** Command*

The **print** command creates a file (in the standard output stream) from its arguments. Its arguments can be strings or variables. In Figure 13.9, we embedded a variable in a string. We could have produced the same results by putting the variable after the string. Note, however, that the quoting rules must be observed: The variable cannot be embedded in single quotes. Session 13.17 prints the time, first embedded in the string and then as a separate argument. The third example demonstrates that the variable is not expanded when we incorrectly use single quotes.

SESSION 13.17 *Using the **print** Command*

```
$ time=4:30pm
$ print "It is now $time"
It is now 4:30pm

$ print "It is now" $time
It is now 4:30pm

$ print 'It is now $time'
It is now $time                    # Error: $time not expanded
```

The **print** command automatically adds a terminating newline after the last argument. If for some reason we don't want a newline, we can use the −n option. To help format the output, there are nine C-like escape codes that can be used (Table 13.3). When using these codes, they must be enclosed in quotes.

TABLE 13.3 *C Character Codes for **print***

Code	Usage
\b	backspace
\c	no newline (same as −n)
\f	form feed
\n	newline
\r	carriage return

Continued

TABLE 13.3   *C Character Codes for* **print**—*Continued*

Code	Usage
\t	tab
\v	vertical tab
\\	print backslash
\0ddd	octal code for ASCII character to be printed

Session 13.18 demonstrates the interactive use of these codes.

SESSION 13.18   *Demonstrate Selected* **print** *Codes*

```
$ w1=Now
$ w2=Time
$ print $w1$w2
NowTime

$ print $w1'\b'$w2
NoTime

$ print $w1 "\t\t" $w2
Now                 Time

$ print $w1 '\012'$w2                    #\012 is octal for newline
Now
Time
```

13.5   Input

Reading data from a terminal or a file is done using the **read** command. The **read** command reads a line and stores the words in variables. It must be terminated by a return, and the input line must immediately follow the command. The **read** command format is shown in Figure 13.10.

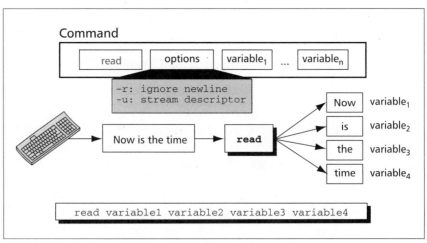

FIGURE 13.10   *Format of the* **read** *Command*

Reading Word by Word

When the **read** command is executed, the shell reads a line from the standard input (keyboard or redirected file) and stores it in variables word by word. Words are characters separated by spaces or tabs. The first word is stored in the first variable, the second is stored in the second variable, and so forth. Another way of saying this is that the **read** command parses the input string (line) into words.

If there are more words than there are variables, all the extra words are placed in the last variable. If there are fewer words than there are variables, the unmatched variables are set to a null value. Any value in them before the read is lost.

Session 13.19 demonstrates the use of the **read** command. The first example demonstrates what happens when not enough words are input. Note that word3 is null. In the second example, there are too many words. After the read, we print the variables and then just the third so that you can see exactly what happens. In each case, the first word is separated from the second word by a tab, and the rest of the words are separated by one or more spaces.

SESSION 13.19 *Demonstrate **read** Command*

```
$ read word1 word2 word3
Now      is
$ print $word1
Now
$ print $word2
is
$ print $word3


$ read word1 word2 word3
Now      is   the   time   for      all      good      students
$ print $word1 $word2
Now is
$ print $word3
the time for all good students

$ print $word1 $word2 $word3
Now is the time for all good students
```

Reading Line by Line

The design for handling extra words provides an easy technique for storing a whole line in one variable. We simply use the **read** command, giving it only one variable. When executed, the whole line is in the variable. This use of the **read** command is shown in Session 13.20.

SESSION 13.20 *Reading a Line into a Word*

```
$ read line
Now is the time                    for all good students
$ print $line
Now is the time for all good students
```

Session 13.20 Analysis: This session demonstrates that when we read a line into only one variable, the line is read as a string. Note that the extra spaces and tabs in the input line are replaced with a single space even when the entire line is placed in one variable.

One last point about the **read** command: It reads only the first line[3] from the keyboard or a redirected file; to read multiple lines or a file, we must use a loop as discussed in Chapter 14.

> The **read** command reads only the first line from the keyboard or a redirected file.

If you use redirection for the input, only the first line will be read. You cannot redirect a whole file without using a loop (see Section 14.4 on page 571). This limitation is demonstrated in Session 13.21.

SESSION 13.21 *Only the First Line Is Read*

```
$ read line1 < TheRaven
$ read line2 < TheRaven
$ print $line1
Once upon a midnight dreary, while I pondered, weak and weary,
$ print $line2
Once upon a midnight dreary, while I pondered, weak and weary,
```

Reading from a File

The Korn shell allows scripts to read from a user file. This is done with the stream-descriptor option (-u). A **stream descriptor** is a numeric designator for a file. We have seen that the standard streams are numbered 0, 1, and 2 for standard input, standard output, and standard error. In Chapter 15, we will discuss how to open a user file and associate it with a stream descriptor.

An example of a read from a user file is shown in the next example. Each **read** command reads the next line from the file. Note that there is no space between the option and the stream descriptor.

```
read -u4 variable_name
```

13.6 Exit Status of a Command

In the Korn shell, when a command is executed, it returns a value known as the **exit status** of the command. The exit status is stored in a shell variable with a name of (?). Like all named variables, the exit status is accessible by using its name ($?). If a command completes successfully, it returns a **zero** value, which is interpreted as **true;** if it does not complete successfully, it returns a **nonzero** value, which is interpreted as **false.** These concepts are shown in Figure 13.11.

---

[3]More specifically, it reads one string terminated in a newline character, regardless of its length.

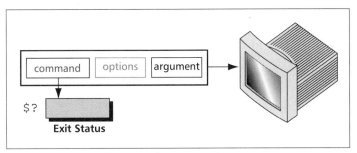

FIGURE 13.11 *Exit Status of a Command*

Let us look at two examples, one successful and one unsuccessful. In the first example, we list all files using the asterisk wildcard (file*). Then we repeat the command with a filename that doesn't match anything in the directory (Session 13.22).

SESSION 13.22 *Demonstrate Exit Status*

```
$ ls file*
file1       file2       file3.bak
$ print $?
0

$ ls none
Cannot access none: No such file or directory
$ print $?
2
```

13.7 eval Command

The **eval** command is used when the Korn shell needs to evaluate a command twice before executing it. To understand this, let's look at an example. To generalize a segment of code, we need to store the name of a variable in a second variable and then use the **print** command to display the value of the original variable. This permits us to reuse the code by placing a different variable in the second one, allowing us to change the variable that is being displayed.

Although the concept is simple, the direct approach doesn't work. Session 13.23 fails because the command is evaluated only once.

SESSION 13.23 *Wrong Way to Use a Variable in a Variable*

```
$ x=23
$ y=x                   # Store name of variable in y
$ print $y
x                       # Name of variable, not its value
```

As another example, we can try to prefix the value in the variable with a dollar sign to pick up its value. This concept doesn't work either as demonstrated by Session 13.24.

SESSION 13.24 *Another Wrong Way to Use a Variable in a Variable*

```
$ x=23
$ y=x                    # Store name of variable in y
$ print \$$y
$x                       # Still not x's value
```

The solution is to use the **eval** command so that the shell evaluates the command twice as in Session 13.25.

SESSION 13.25 *Correct Way to Use a Variable in a Variable*

```
$ x=23
$ y=x                    # Store name of variable in y
$ eval print \$$y
23
```

Session 13.25 Analysis: When the **eval** command is executed, it first evaluates $y, which generates the string value $x. The second evaluation then evaluates the variable $x, which produces the correct effect, the printing of the variable stored in y.

As a more complex example, let's store a command to print the file list and pipe its output to **head**. In Storing Commands in a Variable (page 509), we demonstrated how we could store a simple command in a variable and then execute the variable. At that time, we stated that the concept would not work with complex commands, such as combining the list (**ls**) and **more** commands in one variable. The reason complex commands don't work is because they require multiple evaluations. To prove that they don't work, we created Session 13.26 to demonstrate the error.

SESSION 13.26 *Variable Command Error*

```
$ list="ls -l | head -4"
$ $list
Cannot access |: No such file or directory
Cannot access head: No such file or directory
Cannot access -4: No such file or directory
```

In Session 13.27, we use the same two commands, but this time, we execute them with the **eval** command. The evaluate command first evaluates the contents of the variable, and then it executes the resulting command.

SESSION 13.27 *Evaluating a Multicommand Variable*

```
$ list="ls -l | head -4"
$ eval $list
total 155
-rw-r--r--      1 gilberg   staff            42 Jul 10   2000 ErrFile
-rwxr--r--      1 gilberg   staff           111 Jul 11   2000 IFS.scr
-rw-r--r--      1 gilberg   staff             0 Jun 11   2000 MidRaven
```

13.8 Environmental Variables

The environmental variables control the user environment. Table 13.4 lists the environmental variables. We discuss the commonly used ones in this section. Note that in the Korn shell, the environmental variables are in uppercase.

TABLE 13.4 *Environmental Variables*

Variable	Explanation
CDPATH	Contains the search path for **cd** command when the directory argument is a relative pathname.
COLUMNS	Defines the width, in characters, of your terminal. The default is 80.
EDITOR	Pathname of the command-line editor.
ENV	Pathname of the environment file.
HISTFILE	Pathname for the history file.
HISTSIZE	Maximum number of saved commands in the history file.
HOME	Pathname for the home directory.
LINES	Defines the height, in lines, of your terminal display. The default is 24.
LOGNAME	Contains the user's login name from the `/etc/passwd` file.
MAIL	Absolute pathname for the user's mailbox.
MAILCHECK	Interval between tests for new mail. The default is 600 seconds.
MAILPATH	List of files to be checked for incoming mail.
OLDPWD	Absolute pathname of the working directory before the last **cd** command.
PATH	Searches path for commands.
PS1	Primary prompt, such as $ and %.
PS2	Secondary prompt. Used when complete command not entered on first line. The default is >.
PS3	Select command prompt. Used only for **select** commands that we will discuss in Chapter 14. The default is #?.
PS4	Debug prompt. The default is plus (+).
PWD	Absolute pathname of the current directory.
RANDOM	Returns a random number each time it is called.
REPLY	Temporary buffer for **read** command.
SECONDS	Time in seconds since the shell was invoked.
SHELL	Pathname of the logging shell.
TERM	Terminal type.
TMOUT	Variable that determines how long a terminal may be idle before it is automatically logged out of the system. The default is 0, which means the session will never time out.
VISUAL	Same as EDITOR. However, VISUAL has precedence over EDITOR. If VISUAL is set, the system does not check the value of EDITOR.

Change Directory Path (CDPATH)

The CDPATH variable contains a list of pathnames separated by colons (:) as shown in the next example:

```
:$HOME:/bin/usr/files
```

There are three paths in the preceding example. Because the path starts with a colon, the first directory is the current working directory. The second directory is our home directory. The third directory is an absolute pathname to a directory of files.

The contents of CDPATH are used by the **cd** command with the following rules:

1. If CDPATH is not defined, the **cd** command searches the current directory to locate the requested directory. If the requested directory is found, **cd** moves to it. If it is not found, **cd** displays an error message.

2. If CDPATH is defined as in the previous example, the following actions are taken when this command is executed:

```
$ cd reports
```

   a. The **cd** command searches the current directory for the reports directory. If it is found, the current directory is changed to reports.

   b. If the reports directory is not found in the current directory, **cd** tries to find it in the home directory, which is the second entry in CDPATH. Note that the home directory may be the current directory. Again, if the reports directory is found in the home directory, it becomes the current directory.

   c. If the reports directory is not found in the home directory, **cd** tries to find it in /bin/usr/files, which is the third entry in CDPATH. If the reports directory is found in /bin/usr/files, it becomes the current directory.

   d. If the reports directory is not found in /bin/usr/files, **cd** displays an error message and terminates.

In Session 13.28, we set CDPATH to the path shown in the previous example and then print the path. Note that it begins with a colon, but HOME is replaced by its absolute path because we used $HOME.

SESSION 13.28 *Set* **CDPATH**

```
$ CDPATH=:$HOME:/bin/usr/files
$ print $CDPATH
:/mnt/diska/staff/gilberg:/bin/usr/files
```

History File Path (HISTFILE)

The history file stores commands that you have entered at the shell prompt; the HIST-FILE variable stores the pathname for the history file. Its size is set by the history size (HISTSIZE) environmental variable. Depending on a session's length, commands for more than one login session may be stored in the history file. For a complete discussion, see History File in Section 13.11 (page 532).

Home Path (HOME)

The HOME variable contains the path to your home directory. The default is your login directory. Some commands use the value of this variable when they need the path to your home directory. For example, when you use the **cd** command without any argument, the command uses the value of the home variable as the argument. You can change its value, but we do not recommend this because it will affect all the commands and scripts that use it. In Session 13.29, we demonstrate how it can be changed to the current working directory. Note that because **pwd** is a command, it must be enclosed in parentheses.

SESSION 13.29   *Demonstrate Change Home Directory*

```
$ print $HOME
/mnt/diska/staff/gilberg
$ oldHOME=$HOME
$ print $oldHOME
/mnt/diska/staff/gilberg
$ HOME=$(pwd)
$ print $HOME
/mnt/diska/staff/gilberg/unix16korn

$ HOME=$oldHOME
$ print $HOME
/mnt/diska/staff/gilberg
```

Login Name (LOGNAME)

The LOGNAME contains the login name of the user as found in the password file (etc/passwd). It can be used to display the user name (for example, on a report). Session 13.30 demonstrates its contents using a **print** command.

SESSION 13.30   *The* **LOGNAME** *Variable*

```
$ print $LOGNAME
gilberg
```

Mailbox Pathname (MAIL)

The MAIL variable contains the absolute pathname of the user's mailbox (file). As mail is received, the **mail** utility stores it in this file until the user is ready to read it. The file's name is the same as the user's login name. This variable is maintained by the shell, not the **mail** utility. Session 13.31 displays a typical MAIL value.

SESSION 13.31   *The* **MAIL** *Variable*

```
$ print $MAIL
/usr/mail/forouzan
```

Mail Check Interval (MAILCHECK)

The MAILCHECK variable contains the interval between tests for new mail. The default is 600 seconds. Session 13.32 displays the typical contents of the MAILCHECK variable.

SESSION 13.32 *The **MAILCHECK** Variable*

```
$ print $MAILCHECK
600
```

When you log in, the shell checks the mail file to determine if there is new mail. If there is, it displays a "You have mail" message. The shell then sets a timer to the value found in the MAILCHECK variable. When the timer goes off, it again checks the mail file to determine if there is new mail. You may ignore waiting mail or you may use the **mail** utility to read it. The shell will continue to test for new mail on the requested time cycle and report new mail if and when it arrives.

Incoming Mail Paths (MAILPATH)

The MAILPATH variable contains pathnames to files that can be checked for incoming mail. Normally, the Korn shell checks only the contents of the MAIL variable to find the path of the mailbox. However, some sophisticated mailers may allow the user to have several mailboxes. These mailers allow the user to sort the incoming mail according to some criteria (the sender name, for example). In this case, the MAILPATH variable is set to the list of files to be checked for the incoming file.

Directory Search Paths (PATH)

The PATH variable is used to search for a command directory. The entries in the PATH variable must be separated by colons.

PATH works just like CDPATH. When the shell encounters a command, it uses the entries in the PATH variable to search for the command under each directory in the PATH variable. The major difference is that for security reasons, such as a Trojan Horse virus, we should have the current directory last.

If we were to set the PATH variable as shown in the next example,

```
$ PATH=/bin:/usr/bin::
```

the shell would look for the **date** command by first searching the /bin directory, followed by the /usr/bin directory, and finally the current working directory.

Primary Prompt (PS1)

The primary prompt is set in the variable PS1. The shell uses the primary prompt when it expects a command. The default is the dollar sign ($) for the Korn shell. For a superuser, it is the pound sign (#).

We can change the value of the prompt as shown in Session 13.33. We begin by changing the primary prompt to reflect the shell we are working in. Because we have a blank at the end of the prompt, we must use quotes to set it. As soon as it is set, the new prompt is displayed. At the end, we change it back to the default.

SESSION 13.33   *Change the Primary Prompt*

```
$ PS1="Korn: "
Korn: print $PS1
Korn:
Korn: PS1="$ "
$
```

There are two built-in prompts that can be used: command number and directory.

Prompt Command Number (" ! :   ")

We can change the prompt to the command number in the history file. This option is very useful when using the history file, such as during the creation and debugging of a script. The bang (!) is required. It may be followed by any separation character desired. We prefer a colon and a space. Note that because it includes a space, it must be quoted. An example of a command number prompt is:

```
$ PS1="!: "
140: pwd
/mnt/diska/staff/gilberg/unix15korn
141:
```

To change the prompt to a bang, you must use double bangs (! !) as in the next example:

```
$ PS1="!! "
!
```

Directory Prompt (' $PWD ')

This prompt shows the current directory. It is useful for users who need to change their directory often. Its major disadvantage is that it can get very long. Note that we use single quotes. When the prompt is changed to the directory with a single quote, the directory is the current directory; it changes whenever we change directories. When the prompt is changed using double quotes, the prompt is changed to the current directory, but it does not change when we change directories. Because it is very confusing when the directory prompt does not change, we recommend that you always use single quotes. Session 13.34 demonstrates the use of the directory prompt.

SESSION 13.34   *Directory Prompts*

```
$ PS1='$PWD> '                          # Current Directory Prompt
/mnt/diska/staff/rfg3988> print $PWD
/mnt/diska/staff/rfg3988
/mnt/diska/staff/rfg3988> cd ../
/mnt/diska/staff> print $PWD
/mnt/diska/staff
/mnt/diska/staff> PS1="$PWD> "          # Constant prompt
/mnt/diska/staff> print $PWD
/mnt/diska/staff
/mnt/diska/staff> cd ~
```

Continued

SESSION 13.34   *Directory Prompts—Continued*

```
/mnt/diska/staff> print $PWD
/mnt/diska/staff/rfg3988
/mnt/diska/staff> cd unix15korn
/mnt/diska/staff> print $PWD
/mnt/diska/staff/rfg3988/unix15korn
/mnt/diska/staff> PS1="$ "
$
```

Secondary Prompt (PS2)

The secondary prompt (PS2) is used whenever a command is not completely coded on the first line. By default, it is a greater than character (>). The Korn shell uses it to prompt for the rest of the command. Session 13.35 contains an example in which we code the beginning of a print string on the first line and the rest of it on the following lines. Note that the newlines appear in the print output.

SESSION 13.35   *The Secondary Prompt (PS2)*

```
$ print "Now
> is
> the
> time"
```

```
Now
is
the
time
```

Third Prompt (PS3)

The shell uses the third prompt (PS3) to ask the user to enter data in a select loop (see Chapter 14). The default is #?, but we can change it when necessary.

Fourth Prompt (PS4)

Not actually a prompt, this variable is used to identify a debugging command (see Chapter 14) at the beginning of each expression. Its default is the plus sign (+).

> Make sure you add a space or other distinctive character, such as a greater than (>), to separate the prompt from your command.

User Input Default Variable (REPLY)

The shell uses REPLY when no specific input variable is specified for user input. It was specifically designed to be used with the read and select commands (see Chapter 14). Session 13.36 demonstrates one of its uses.

SESSION 13.36 *Demonstrate Use of* **REPLY** *Variable*

```
$ read
This is user input.
$ print $REPLY
This is user input.
```

Login Shell Path (SHELL)

The SHELL variable holds the path of your login shell. In Session 13.37, the login shell is the Korn shell as indicated by ksh.

SESSION 13.37 *The* **SHELL** *Variable*

```
$ print $SHELL
/bin/ksh
```

Terminal Description (TERM)

The TERM variable holds the description for the terminal you are using. The value of this variable can be used by interactive commands such as **vi** or **emacs**. You can test the value of this variable or reset it. Session 13.38 demonstrates typical TERM contents.

SESSION 13.38 *The* **TERM** *Variable*

```
$ print $TERM
vt100
```

Handling Environmental Variables

We need to set, unset, and display the environmental variables. Table 13.5 shows how this is done.

TABLE 13.5 *Setting and Unsetting Variables*

Operation	Command
Set	var=value
Unset	unset var
Display One	print $var
Display All	set

Set and Unset Variables

In the Korn shell, variables are set using the assignment operator as in the next example:

```
$ TERM=vt100
```

To unset a variable, we use the **unset** command. The following example shows how we can unset the TERM variable:

```
$ unset TERM
```

Display Variables

To display the value of an individual variable, we use the **print** command:

```
$ print $TERM
```

To display the variables that are currently set, we use the **set** command with no arguments:

```
$ set
```

13.9 Options

We use options in the Korn shell to control the way its commands are executed. The options are summarized in Table 13.6.

TABLE 13.6 *Korn Shell Options*

Option	Explanation
allexport	Sets all variable to be exported.
emacs	Use **emacs** for command-line editing and history file.
ignoreeof	Disallows ctrl+d to exit the shell.
noclobber	Does not allow redirection to clobber existing file.
noexec	Disables wildcard expansion.
noglob	Reads and syntactically checks commands in a script.
verbose	Prints commands before executing them.
vi	Uses **vi** for command-line editing and history file.
xtrace	Prints commands and arguments before executing them.

Export All (`allexport`)

When the allexport option is set, all variables are automatically flagged for exporting when they are assigned a value.

Command-Line Editor (`emacs` and `vi`)

To specify that the **emacs** editor is to be used in the Korn shell, we turn the emacs option on. To specify that the **vi** editor is to be used in the Korn shell, we turn the vi option on. Note that these options are valid only in the Korn shell.

Ignore End-of-File (`ignoreeof`)

Normally, if end of file (`ctrl+d`) is entered at the command line, the shell terminates. To disable this action, we can turn on the ignore end of file option, `ignoreeof`. With this option, end-of-file generates an error message rather than terminating the shell.

No Clobber in Redirection (`noclobber`)

When output or errors are directed to a file that already exists, the current file is deleted and replaced by a new file. To prevent this action, we set the `noclobber` option. To override the `noclobber` option, use a bar (`|`) after the redirection as in the next example:

```
wc >| file1
```

No Execute (`noexec`)

The `noexec` option must be set in a script (Chapter 14); it cannot be used interactively. We use it to check the syntax of a script before we run it. When it is the first command in a script, then the script interpreter simply reads the script and checks for syntax errors. If no errors are found, the command-line prompt is displayed. If it finds an error, it displays an error message and stops.

No Global (`noglob`)

The `noglob` option controls the expansion of wildcard tokens in a command. For example, when the no global option is off, the list file (**ls**) command uses wildcards to match the files in a directory. Thus, the following command lists all files that start with `file` followed by one character. Note the recursive nature of the list. When it sees `file?`, the filename acts as a wildcard command to list the files again.

SESSION 13.39   *No Global Option Off*

```
$ ls file?
file1   file2   file3   file4   file5   file6   file?
file1   file2   file3   file4   file5   file6
```

On the other hand, when the global option is on, wildcards become text characters and are not expanded. In this case, the preceding command would list only a file named `file?`.

SESSION 13.40   *No Global Option On*

```
$ set -o noglob
$ ls file?
file?
```

Verbosity (`verbose`)

The `verbose` option shows commands before they are executed by the shell. It is useful when debugging a script. We will show examples when we debug scripts in the next chapter.

Execute Trace (`xtrace`)

The `xtrace` option displays the command with a plus sign (+) and the evaluation of the expressions in each step of a command script. Like the `verbose` option, it is a debugging tool that we explain in the next chapter.

Handling Options

To customize our shell environment, we need to set, unset, and display options. Table 13.7 shows the appropriate commands for the Korn shell. They are discussed in the sections that follow.

TABLE 13.7   *Commands Used to Set, Unset, and Display Options*

Operation	Command
Set	`set -o option`
Unset	`set +o option`
Display All	`set -o`

Set and Unset Options

The Korn shell commands to set and unset options are shown in Table 13.7. The following example demonstrates how to set and unset the `noglob` option:

```
$ set -o noglob          # Turn noglob option on
$ set +o noglob          # Turn noglob option off
```

Display Options

To show all of the options (set or unset), we use the **set** command with an argument of `-o`. This option requests a list of all options names with their state, on or off.

```
$ set   -o               # lists all options
```

13.10 Startup Scripts

As we learned in Chapter 5, each shell uses one or more scripts to initialize the environment when a session is started. The Korn shell uses three startup files. They are shown in Figure 13.12 and described in the following section.

System Profile File

As you study Figure 13.12, note that there is one system-level profile file, which is stored in the `/etc` directory. Maintained by the system administrator, it contains general commands and variable settings that are applied to every user of the system at login time. The system profile file is generally quite large and contains many advanced commands.

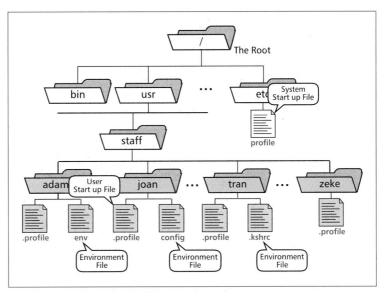

FIGURE 13.12 *Korn Shell Startup Files*

The system profile is a read-only file; its permissions are set so that only the system administrator can change it. We suggest that you locate and read it so that you will have an idea of what it contains. Session 13.41 shows a partial list of its contents.

SESSION 13.41 *Partial Listing of System Profile File*

```
$ cat /etc/profile
# /etc/profile - Default settings for all ksh users
#
...
# Ignore keyboard interrupts.
trap ""  QUIT INT
...
if [ "${TERM}" = "ansi" ]
then
        TERM=vt100
        export TERM
fi
```

Personal Profile File

The personal profile, `~/.profile`, contains commands that are used to customize the startup shell. It is an optional file that is run immediately after the system profile file. Although it is a user file, it is often created by the system administrator to customize a new user's shell. If you make changes to it, we highly recommend that you make a backup copy first so that it may be restored easily if necessary.

Environment File

The Korn shell allows users to create a command file containing commands that they want to be executed to personalize their environment. It is most useful when the Korn shell is started as a child of a non-Korn login shell. Because we can use any name for it, the absolute pathname of the environment file must be stored in the ENV variable. The shell then locates it by looking at the ENV variable. In Figure 13.12, we see three different environment files, each one with a different name.

Startup Process

Whenever a shell is started, UNIX uses these startup files. Which ones depend on whether the shell being started is a login shell or not. When a login shell is started, the system profile files are executed followed by the personal profile file. If a nonlogin shell is being forked, then only the environment file is executed. This process is shown in Figure 13.13.

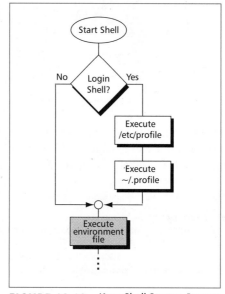

FIGURE 13.13   *Korn Shell Startup Process*

13.11 Command History

The Korn shell provides an extensive command history capability consisting of a combination of commands, environmental variables, and files. A major feature of the design is the ability to recall a command and reexecute it without typing it again.

History File

Every command that we type[4] is kept in a history file stored in our home directory. By default, the filename is ~/.sh_history. It can be renamed, provided that we store its pathname in the HISTFILE environmental variable. The size of the file (that is, the number of commands that it can store) is 128 unless changed. The HISTSIZE variable can be used to change it when we need to make it larger or smaller.

---

[4]Commands executed in a script are not included in the history file.

History Command

The formal command for listing, editing, and executing commands from the history file is the **fc** command. However, the Korn shell contains a preset alias, **history**, that is easier to use and more flexible.

Executed without any options, the **history** command lists the last 16 commands. A sample output is shown in Session 13.42. In the interest of space, we have deleted commands from the middle of the listing.

SESSION 13.42   *The* **history** *Command*

```
$ history
238      hold
239      history
...                                    # commands 240-250 deleted
251      cp mail_file mail_file.bak
252      pico mail_file
253      history
```

Note that each command is numbered for convenience in reuse. However, if we don't want the numbers, we can suppress them with the −n option as in Session 13.43.

SESSION 13.43   *The* **history** *Command without Numbers*

```
$ history -n
         history
         clear
...                                    # commands 241-251 deleted
         pico mail_file
         history
         history -n
```

We can change the number of commands listed by specifying the start number as a **history** command argument. If an invalid command number is provided, an error message is displayed. Session 13.44 demonstrates this capability.

SESSION 13.44   *Specify Start Line for the* **history** *Command*

```
$ history 251
251      cp mail_file mail_file.bak
252      pico mail_file
253      history
254      history -n
255      history 251
$ history 1
ksh: fc: bad number
```

To list the last *n* lines, we use the number of line as an option as shown in Session 13.45.

SESSION 13.45 *Specify Last n Lines for the **history** Command*

```
$ history -3
254     history -n
255     history -251
256     history 1
257     history -3
```

In all of the previous examples, the commands were listed earliest to latest. We can reverse the order by using the reverse option. In Session 13.46, we specify that we want the last four commands listed in reverse order. Note that when we combine options, they must each be listed separately.

SESSION 13.46 *Specify Reversed Output for the **history** Command*

```
$ history -4 -r
258     history -4 -r
257     history -3
256     history 1
255     history -251
254     history -n
```

Finally, we can specify a symbolic range. This is one of the more useful options because we don't need to know the history file command number. To specify a symbolic command, we specify the actual command as an argument. The **history** command then searches backward to find the most recent matching command. If no command matches, an error message is printed.

We can specify both a symbolic start and end command as arguments. In this case, **history** lists all of the commands starting with the first command and ending with the last command (Session 13.47).

SESSION 13.47 *Specify Symbolic Ranges for the **history** Command*

```
$ history ls history
240     ls
241     clear
242     rm mail_file.bak
243     history -10

$ history mkdir
ksh: mkdir:  not found
```

Table 13.8 summarizes the **history** commands discussed in this section.

TABLE 13.8 *Summary of **history** Command Options*

Command	Description
history	Lists last 16 commands.
history -n	Lists last 16 commands without command numbers.

Continued

TABLE 13.8 *Summary of* **history** *Command Options*

Command	Description
`history N`	Lists commands starting with number *N*.
`history -3`	Lists last 3 commands.
`history -r`	Lists commands in reverse order.
`history start`	Lists commands from most recent *start* command.
`history start end`	Lists commands from *start* to *end* command.

Redo Command (r)

Any command in the history file can be reexecuted using the redo command (**r**). We specify the command to be reexecuted by using its command number or symbolically by listing a command or a partial command. Session 13.48 demonstrates the use of a command number by reexecuting command 235.

SESSION 13.48 *The Redo Command*

```
$ history
235     ls f*
...                                   # history 236 - 241 deleted
242     vi file2
243     history

$ r 235
ls f*
file1           file2           file3
```

Rather than specifying the line number itself, we can specify a line number relative to the last command. To reexecute the command before the last one (two back), we use the format in Session 13.49. The output assumes that a command, such as clear, was executed after the redo command in Session 13.48.

SESSION 13.49 *The Relative Redo Command*

```
$ r -2
vi file2
# This command opens file2 in the vi editor.
```

An easier way to reexecute the **vi** command would be to use its name. We can reexecute it by symbolically typing enough of its name to make the command unique. When we reexecute a command symbolically, the shell searches the history file starting at the most recent entry until it finds a matching command. When the command is found, it is reexecuted.

SESSION 13.50 *Specify Symbolic Command for the Redo Command*

```
$ r v
vi file2
# Once again we are in the vi editor.
```

Substitution in Redo Command

When we redo a command, we can change part of the command. For example, assume that command 153 in the history file contains the following command:

```
cat file1 | head -50 | more | tail -10
```

To reexecute it, changing `file1` to `file2`, we would use the following command:

```
$ r 153 file1=file2
```

13.12 Command Execution Process

To understand the behavior of the shell, it helps to understand how Korn executes a command. Command execution is carried out in six sequential steps.

Execution Steps

The six execution steps are recursive. This means that when the shell performs the third step, command substitution, the six steps are followed for the command inside the dollar-parentheses.

Command Parsing

The shell first parses the command into words. In this step, it uses whitespaces as delimiters between the words. It also replaces sequences of two or more spaces or tabs with a single space.

Variable Evaluation

After completely parsing the command, the shell looks for variable names (unquoted words beginning with a dollar sign). When a variable name is found, its value replaces the variable name.

Command Substitution

The shell then looks for a command substitution. If found, the command is executed and its output string replaces the command, the dollar sign, and the parentheses.

Redirection

At this point, the shell checks the command for redirected files. Each redirected file is verified by opening it.

Wildcard Expansion

When filenames contain wildcards, the shell expands and replaces them with their matching filenames. This step creates a file list.

Path Determination

In this last step, the shell uses the PATH variable to locate the directory containing the command code. The command is now ready for execution.

Command Execution Example

To better understand the process, let's look at the **cat** command contained in the next example. To show the whitespace characters, we use ▲ to represent a space and → to represent a tab.

> $▲cat→→$var→→→report*▲1>▲▲file3→2>▲file4

1. In the first step, the shell parses words. It replaces all tabs and multiple spaces with a single space. The result is shown in the next example. Because all tabs and spaces have been parsed, we show a space in the normal fashion.

> $ cat $var report* 1> file3 2> file4

2. The second step replaces the variable ($var) with its value, file*. The result is:

> $ cat file* report* 1> file3 2> file4

3. The third step is skipped because there is no command substitution.
4. In the fourth step, the redirected files are handled: file3 is opened for output and file4 is opened for errors.
5. In the fifth step, the shell expands the wildcards. The command is now:

> $ cat fileA fileB fileC report1 report2 1> file3 2> file4

6. In the last step, the shell finds the /bin directory in the PATH variable. It completes the command as in the next example:

> $ /bin/cat fileA fileB fileC report1 report2 1> file3 2> file4

The **cat** utility is then called with five arguments and the names of the two files.

13.13 Key Terms

accessing a variable	export command	noclobber
allexport	exporting variable	noglob
assignment operator	HISTFILE	null variable
CDPATH	HISTSIZE	option
columns	HOME	output statement
command execution	ignoreeof	PATH
command parsing	input redirection	path determination
complex command	input statement	pipe
constant	interpreter	predefined variable
EDITOR	Korn shell	**print** command
emacs	LINES	PS1
ENV	LOGNAME	PS2
environmental variables	MAIL	PS3
eval command	MAILCHECK	PS4
exit status	MAILPATH	RANDOM

read command
read-only variable
redirecting error
input
redirecting output
redirection
REPLY
SECONDS
sequenced commands
session
setting a variable
SHELL
shell
shell program

shell script
shell session
shell variable
standard error
standard input
standard output
standard streams
startup files
startup scripts
stream
subshell
tee command
TERM
terminal file

TMOUT
trash file
unsetting a variable
user-defined variables
variable
variable evaluation
variable substitution
verbose
VISUAL
wildcard expansion
vi
xtrace

13.14 Tips

1. Understand the difference between the login shell and the current shell. (See also Chapter 5.)
2. Distinguish between the three standard streams. (See also Chapter 5.)
3. Distinguish between standard input, standard output, and standard error redirections. (See also Chapter 5.)
4. To understand pipes, you need to know where they can be used and where they cannot be used. (See also Chapter 5.)
5. Understand the use of the **tee** command. (See also Chapter 5.)
6. Understand the concept and use of command substitution. Note that the Korn shell uses the $(command) construct for command substitution.
7. Understand the concept of job control, foreground and background jobs, and how to execute a command in the background. (See also Chapter 5.)
8. Aliases are supported in the Korn shell.
9. Command-line editing is supported in the Korn shell.
10. Use only letters, digits, and underscore to name a user-defined variable. A hyphen may not be used.
11. The value of a variable is always a string of characters.
12. There is no limitation on the length of the string stored in a variable. This means that we can even store the whole contents of a file in a variable.
13. There can be no whitespace before or after the assignment operator.
14. If a variable is used before being assigned a value, the value of the variable is null.
15. Note that $ is not part of a user-defined variable name. So when you want to refer to the variable, do not use the $. The $ is used when you want to use the value of the variable.
16. The trash file in UNIX is /dev/null. Everything sent to this file is lost forever.

17. The terminal file in UNIX is /dev/tty. Everything sent to this file will be displayed on your terminal.
18. To force the Korn shell to evaluate a command twice before executing it, use the **eval** command.
19. To make a variable behave like a constant, make it read-only (using the **readonly** command).
20. To make a variable visible in subshells, you must export it.
21. While both work, in the Korn shell use the **print** command rather than **echo.**
22. The **read** command can read a line into only one variable or it can parse it into several variables. To read from a file rather than the keyboard, we use the -u option.
23. To check the success or failure of a command, test the value of the (?) variable.
24. Change the value of environmental variables discretely. Changes may affect your environment.
25. If you do not have a personal login file (~/.profile), create one. Add any command you want to be executed at login time to this file.
26. The Korn shell has a third startup file, the environment file.
27. Pay special attention to the order and the way the Korn shell executes a command.

13.15 Commands

The following commands were discussed in this chapter. For more details, see Appendix F and the corresponding pages shown in the following table.

Command	Description	Options	Page
eval	***Synopsis:*** *eval command –un* Evaluates the command two times before executing it.		519
read	***Synopsis:*** *read [options] variable-list* Reads values and stores them in variables.		516
readonly	***Synopsis:*** *readonly variable-list* Makes the variables read only.		509
export	***Synopsis:*** *export variable_list* Exports variables to subshells.		510
print	***Synopsis:*** *print argument list* Displays contents of a variable or a string.		528
typeset	***Synopsis:*** *typeset –attribute variable* *typeset +attribute variable* Associates (–) and unassociates (+) data attributes, such as numeric and justification, to a variable.		512
history	***Synopsis:*** *history -n	-r	command_name* Displays contents of the command history file.		533
r	***Synopsis:*** *r line	-line	command_name* Reexecutes (redo) specified command in history file.		535

13.16 Summary

- The Korn shell was developed by David Korn at the AT&T Labs.
- The Korn shell can be used either interactively to receive user commands and interpret them or as a programming language to create shell scripts.
- There are three standard streams: standard input (0), standard output (1), and standard error (2).
- The three standard streams are connected to the user terminal by default. They can be redirected to and from files.
- Commands can be chained using pipes.
- The **tee** command can split the output so that one copy is sent to the standard output and the other to a file.
- Complex commands can be formed using four constructs: sequencing, grouping, chaining, and combining with conditional operators.
- Quotes are used to change the meaning of characters in the Korn shell. The Korn shell supports three types of quotes: backslash, double quotes, and single quotes.
- Command substitution is supported by the Korn shell using $(command).
- Job control in the Korn shell is used to control how and where a job is executed.
- Two special files are available in UNIX: /dev/null and /dev/tty. The /dev/null is a trash file. The /dev/tty represents the user terminal.
- A variable in the Korn shell is used to store values.
- We can divide Korn shell variables into two broad categories: user-defined and predefined. The predefined variables can be further divided into two categories: shell variables and environmental variables.
- The name of user-defined variables should start with an alphabetic character or an underscore (_). It can be followed by zero or more alphanumeric or underscore characters.
- The assignment operator is used to store a value in a variable.
- To access the value of a variable, the name of the variable should be preceded by a dollar sign ($).
- A variable can be set or unset. When a variable is not set, its value is null.
- We can store any string in a variable including filenames, file contents, commands, and the names of other variables.
- We can create a constant out of the value of a variable by making it read-only.
- To make a variable available to a child shell, it must be exported.
- The output statement in the Korn shell is the **print** command.
- The input statement in the Korn shell is the **read** command.
- The exit status of a command is stored in a shell variable called (?).
- The **eval** command is used when the Korn shell needs to evaluate a command twice before executing it.
- The environmental variables control the user environment. They are automatically exported to subshells. The environmental variables in the Korn shell are all in uppercase.

- We defined 26 environmental variables in this chapter. They are summarized in Table 13.4 on page 521.
- Options in the Korn shell are used to control the way a command or a script is executed. We defined nine options in this chapter. They are summarized in Table 13.6 on page 528.
- The startup files in the Korn shell allow the user to customize the environment permanently (for every session). Three startup files are defined in the Korn shell: /etc/profile, ~/.profile, and the environment file.
- The Korn shell follows six distinct steps to execute a command: parsing, variable evaluation, command substitution, redirection, wildcard expansion, and path determination.

13.17 Practice Set

Review Questions

1. Explain the two purposes of the Korn shell.
2. Is the Korn shell the login shell in your system? How do you verify it? (See also Chapter 5.)
3. Is the login shell always the same as the current shell? How do you verify it? (See also Chapter 5.)
4. How do you find your current shell? (See Chapter 5.) How do you find your login shell? (See also Chapter 5.)
5. How can you create a child shell? (See Chapter 5.) How can you move to the parent shell after creating a child? (See also Chapter 5.)
6. What are the three standard streams?
7. What is the file descriptor that defines the standard input stream? The standard output stream? The standard error stream?
8. The standard input stream is normally associated with which physical device? (See Chapter 5.)
9. The standard output stream is normally associated with which physical device? (See Chapter 5.)
10. The standard error stream is normally associated with which physical device? (See Chapter 5.)
11. How can you redirect the standard input stream?
12. How can you redirect the standard output stream to a file?
13. How can you redirect the standard error stream to a file?
14. What is piping? What is the pipe operator?
15. Distinguish between a sequence of commands, a group of commands, and a chain of commands. (See Chapter 5.)
16. What are the two operators that make the execution of commands conditional? (See Chapter 5.)
17. What is quoting? What are the three sets of quoting tokens?
18. What is the difference between a backslash, a pair of double quotes, and a pair of single quotes? (See Chapter 5.)

19. What is command substitution? What is the token for command substitution in the Korn shell?

20. What is a job? Distinguish between a foreground and a background job. (See Chapter 5.)

21. Show how you can move a job from the background to the foreground, and vice versa. (See Chapter 5.)

22. List and explain the six different states of a job. (See Chapter 5.)

23. Define a variable and distinguish between a variable and a value.

24. Distinguish between a user-defined variable and a predefined variable.

25. Distinguish between a shell variable and an environmental variable. Which one is automatically exported to the subshells?

26. Identify the name of all environmental variables defined for the Korn shell in this chapter.

27. What is the exit status of a command? Where is it stored?

28. Which environmental variable holds the search path for your commands in the Korn shell? How do you display the value of this variable?

29. Which environmental variable holds the name of the login shell in the Korn shell? How do you display the value of this variable?

30. Which environmental variable holds the search path for the **cd** command in the Korn shell? How do you display the value of this variable?

31. Which environmental variable holds the primary prompt in the Korn shell? How do you display the value of this variable?

32. Which environmental variable holds the secondary prompt in the Korn shell? How do you display the value of this variable?

33. Which environmental variable holds the path of your home directory in the Korn shell? How do you display the value of this variable?

34. Which environmental variable holds the mail check interval in the Korn shell? How do you display the value of this variable?

35. Which environmental variable holds the path of your mailbox in the Korn shell? How do you display the value of this variable?

36. Which environmental variable holds the path of the default editor in the Korn shell? How do you display the value of this variable?

37. Which environmental variable holds your login name in the Korn shell? How do you display the value of this variable?

38. Which environmental variable holds the type of your terminal in the Korn shell? How do you display the value of this variable?

39. What is an option? List some options and their use.

40. What are the startup scripts (files) in the Korn shell?

Exercises

41. Which of the following commands show your login shell? (See Chapter 5.)
    a. `print $SHELL`   c. `print $shell`
    b. `print $0`   d. `print $login_shell`

42. Which of the following commands creates a Korn shell child? (See Chapter 5.)

    a. sh
    b. ksh
    c. csh
    d. none of the above

43. Which of the following is the descriptor of the input standard stream? Which one is the descriptor of the output stream? Which one is the descriptor of the error stream?

    a. 1
    b. 2
    c. 2
    d. 3

44. Identify at least two commands that cannot be used with input redirection.

45. Which of the following is a valid Korn shell variable?

    a. cat
    b. _first
    c. Var-1
    d. 2Var

46. If your current shell is Korn, what is the error (if any) in each of the following commands?

    a. a = 24
    b. set a=24
    c. a=$b
    d. set a=$b

47. If your current shell is Korn, what would be displayed from each of the following commands?

    a. a=44   ; print a ; print $a
    b. a=44   ; print $aa ; print a$a
    c. a=44   ; print "$a"a ; print aa

48. What will be displayed from the following commands?

    a. print " Hello the user of "UNIX" operating system"
    b. print " Hello the user of \"UNIX\" operating system"
    c. print " Hello the user of 'UNIX' operating system"
    d. print ' Hello the user of "UNIX" operating system'

49. Use a **grep** command and check its exit status. When is the result zero? When is the result nonzero? Check both cases.

50. Use a **sed** command and check its exit status. When is the result zero? When is the result nonzero? Check both cases.

51. Use an **awk** command and check its exit status. When is the result zero? When is the result nonzero? Check both cases.

52. Write the minimum number of commands to create three constants in the Korn shell. The first holds "Hello", the second "235", and the third "Dear Friend".

53. Use a command to show the value of all environmental variables in the Korn shell.

54. What will be displayed from the following sequence of commands? Explain the rationale for your answer.

```
$ x="Hello"
$ ksh
$ print $x
```

55. What will be displayed from the following sequence of commands? Explain the rationale for your answer.

```
$   x="Hello"
$   ksh
$   x="Bye"
$   print $x
$   exit
$   print $x
```

13.18 Lab Sessions

Session I

1. Log into the system.
2. What is your login shell? (See Chapter 5.)
3. If your login shell is not the Korn shell, create a Korn subshell.
4. Change the primary prompt of the Korn shell to "KSH:".
5. Change the secondary prompt of the Korn shell to ">>".
6. Create a new Korn subshell.
7. Check the primary prompt in this shell. Is it different from the parent shell? Explain your results.
8. Check the secondary prompt in this shell. Is is different from the parent shell? Explain your results.
9. Change the primary prompt to "KSH==>".
10. Change the secondary prompt to ">>>>".
11. Exit from the child shell and go to the Korn parent shell.
12. Check the primary prompt. Is it "KSH:" or "KSH==>"? Explain your results.
13. Check the second prompt. Is it ">>" or ">>>>"? Explain your results.
14. Log out of the system.

Session II

1. Log into the system.
2. Create a directory called SCRs under your home directory.
3. Use an editor and create a file called Ch13S2F1. Type the following two lines in this file:

   ```
   #!/bin/ksh
   ls -l
   ```

   This is called a shell script. We will learn about shell scripts in the next chapter. For the moment, save the file under the directory called SCRs, which you created under your home directory without moving from your home directory.
4. Use the **chmod** command and change the permission of the file to 700.
5. Be sure that you are at your home directory. At the prompt, type the name of the file (this means running the script). What do you get? Why?
6. Add the entry $HOME/SCR to your PATH variable.
7. Repeat step 5. What happens this time? Explain the difference.
8. Log out of the system.

Session III

1. Log into the system.
2. Create a directory A under your home directory.

Continued

3. Create a directory B under A (without moving from your home directory).
4. Create a directory C under B (without moving from your home directory).
5. While at your home directory, try the following command ($ is the prompt):
   ```
   $  cd C
   ```
   What happened? Can you explain the reason for error?
6. Add an entry to the value of your CDPATH environmental variable to be able to run the command in step 5 from your home directory.
7. Log out of the system.

Session IV

1. Log into the system.
2. Check the entry in the /etc/passwd file related to you to determine your login shell.
3. Confirm what you find using the value of the SHELL variable.
4. If your login shell is not the Korn shell, create a Korn subshell.
5. Display the contents of the /etc/profile file. Can you change the contents of this file? Explain the reason.
6. Make a list of all environmental variables that are set in this file.
7. If you do not have a ~/.profile file, create one.
8. Try to override one of the variables you found in the /etc/profile file with a new value in ~/.profile.
9. Display the value of the overridden variable. What did you get? Does it match the value in the /etc/profile or the value in ~/.profile? Explain the reason.
10. Log out of the system.

Session V

1. Log into the system.
2. Type the following command ($ is the prompt):
   ```
   $  >file1           ls            -l
   ```
   What happened?
3. You put the redirection at the beginning of the command and the shell recognized it. Why? What rule applies here?
4. Try the following two commands:
   ```
   $ x=$(ls -l | head -5 | tail +5 | awk '{print $NF}')
   $ cp $x file2
   ```
5. What did you accomplish in the previous step?
6. What are the contents of file2? Which file is copied to file2?
7. What is stored in variable x?
8. What is done first in the **cp** command, the variable evaluation or the command substitution? Explain what rules apply here.
9. Log out of the system.

## CHAPTER 14

Korn Shell Programming

In the previous chapter, we discussed the Korn shell features used in interactive sessions. Interactive sessions work well when the problems being solved are short and simple. As the problems become larger and more complex, especially if they need to be solved repetitively, we need to save the commands in a file. In this chapter, we discuss how to write and save commands as executable script files.

14.1 Basic Script Concepts

A **shell script** is a text file that contains executable commands. Although we can execute virtually any command at the shell prompt, long sets of commands that are going to be executed more than once should be executed using a script file. Figure 14.1 shows the flow of a script in UNIX.

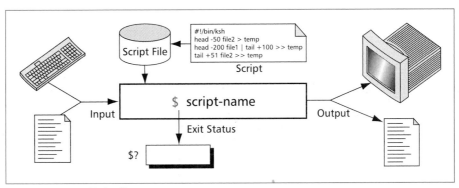

FIGURE 14.1   *Script Concept*

Script Components

Every script has three parts: the interpreter designator line, comments, and shell commands.

Interpreter Designator Line

One of the UNIX shells runs the script, reading it and calling the command specified by each line in turn. The first line of the script is the designator line; it tells UNIX the path to the appropriate shell interpreter. The designator line begins with a pound sign and a bang (# !).[1] If the designator line is omitted, UNIX will use the interpreter for the current

---

[1]Some texts refer to the pound sign as an octothorp. While correct, pound sign is much more common terminology.

shell, which may not be correct. We recommend, therefore, that you always use the designator line to ensure that the correct interpreter is used.

> The interpreter designator line must be the first line of the script file. There cannot even be a blank line before it. If it is not the first line, it is ignored and the current shell's default interpreter will be used.

The system name for the Korn shell is `ksh`. Check your system for the correct location. In most systems, it will be in one of the designators in the following example:

```
#!/bin/ksh          or          #!/usr/bin/ksh
```

Comments

Comments are documentation we add in a script to help us understand it. The interpreter doesn't use them at all; it simply skips over them.

Often, after we've used a script for a long time, we decide we want to improve it. Without comments, we may not remember why we chose the commands we used or what a complex pattern does. To help us remember, therefore, we write some comments.

Comments are identified with the pound sign token (#). The Korn shell supports only line comments. This means that we can only comment one line at a time; a comment cannot extend beyond the end of the line. When the pound sign is coded at the beginning of the line, the entire line is a comment. When it is coded after a command, then the command is processed by the interpreter, but the rest of the line starting with the pound sign is skipped.

We recommend that each script contain comments at the beginning to identify its name and purpose. The format we use throughout the text is shown in Script 14.1.

SCRIPT 14.1   *Recommended Minimum Documentation*

```
1 #!/bin/ksh                    # Korn shell path name
2 #   Script: doc.scr
3 #   This script demonstrates our recommended minimum documentation.
4
5 # Commands start here
```

Script 14.1 Analysis: Note that the name of the script ends in `.scr`. Although the shell does not need it, we use this extension for all shell scripts so that we can easily recognize them. You should also note that all comments are colored. We use color to separate the comments in the script from the commands. We also use color to separate the script output from the user input.

Commands

The most important part of a script is its commands. We can use any of the commands available in UNIX. However, they will not be executed until we execute the script;

they are not executed immediately as they are when we use them interactively. When the script is executed, each command is executed in order from the first to the last.[2]

Command Separators Commands in a script, as well as in an interactive session, should be separated from each other. Shells use two tokens to separate commands: semicolons and newlines. While we may use spaces to make the commands more readable, they are not separators. Shells skip over leading and trailing spaces automatically.

When a shell parses a script, it reads characters until it sees a command separator. It then executes the command, and the result is created. The following example contains three commands, two separated by a semicolon on the first line and one on the second line:

```
command1 ; command 2 <newline>command3
command3
```

Blank Lines Command separators can be repeated. When the script detects multiple separators, it considers them just one. This means that we can insert multiple blank lines in a script to make it more readable. The only place where we cannot put a blank line is before the shell interpreter designator line. As we said earlier, it must be the very first line of the script.

Combined Commands We can combine commands in a script just as we did in the interactive sessions. This means that we can chain commands using pipes, group commands, or conditional commands.

Making Scripts Executable

After creating a script, we must make it executable. As we learned in Chapter 4, this is done with the **chmod** command. We can make a script executable only by the user (ourselves), our group, or everybody. Because we have to test a new script, we always give ourselves execute permission. Whether or not we want others to execute it depends on many factors. Two of the more common commands used to set the execution privileges are shown in the following example (see Chapter 4, page 148, for the **chmod** command).

```
$ chmod 700 script.scr          #User rwx (none for group and others)
$ chmod 755 script.scr          #User rwx (group and others r-x)
```

Executing the Script

After the script has been made executable, it is a command and can be executed just like any other command. There are two specific methods of executing it: as an independent command or as an argument to a subshell command.

Independent Command

We do not need to be in the Korn shell to execute a Korn shell script as long as the interpreter designator line is included as the first line of the script. When it is, UNIX

---

[2]We will see later in the chapter that we can use flow control commands to change the sequential execution.

uses the appropriate interpreter as called out by the designator line. However, if the interpreter designator line is not included, the script will fail if it uses a command that the current shell doesn't recognize.

To execute the script as an independent command, we simply use its name as in the following example:

```
$ script_name
```

Child Shell Execution

To ensure that the script is properly executed, we can create a child shell and execute it in the new shell. This is done by specifying the shell before the script name as in the following example:

```
$ ksh script_name
```

In this case, the interpreter designator line is not needed, but the user needs to know which shell the script requires. Because this is a very user error-prone method, we recommend that all scripts include the interpreter designation, even if we pass it as an argument to a subshell.

Examples

To demonstrate how to create and execute a script, let's look at some simple examples.

Print File List: We use the command

```
ls -l | more
```

frequently and do not want to type the whole command each time. To make it easier to execute the command, let's create a shell script that contains these commands and execute it from the shell prompt. We name the script `dir.scr`. The script and an example of its execution are in Script 14.2.

SCRIPT 14.2   *The* **dir.scr** *Script*

```
1 #!/bin/ksh                      # The Script File
2 #  Script: dir.scr
3 #  A simple script
4
5 ls -l | more

$ dir.scr                       # Command Execution
Output:
total 8
-rw-r--r--    1 gilberg  staff         0 Jun  5 16:56 5
-rw-r--r--    1 gilberg  staff         0 Jun  6 14:10 =
```

Continued

SCRIPT 14.2 *The* **dir.scr** *Script*

```
-rw-------    1 gilberg  staff    5782 Jun  4 12:55 TheRaven
-rw-r--r--    1 gilberg  staff     330 Jun  4 13:04 TheRavenV1
-rwxr--r--    1 gilberg  staff      13 Jun 11 13:52 dirScript
-rw-r--r--    1 gilberg  staff       0 Jun 10 11:26 echo
-rw-r--r--    1 gilberg  staff     100 Jun  3 09:00 file1
-rw-r--r--    1 gilberg  staff     100 Jun  3 08:56 file2
```

Script 14.2 Analysis: Note that we do not show the **chmod** command in any of the scripts. We assume that the script permissions have been properly set.

Print Active Login Names: For another example, let's write a script to display the names of everyone logged into the system. We can use the **who** command. However, **who** lists one complete line for each user. What we want to see is only the names of the users. In this case, we could use the command

```
who | awk '{print $1}'
```

Script 14.3 contains the resulting script.

SCRIPT 14.3 *The* **who.scr** *Script*

```
1 #!/bin/ksh
2 #  Script: who.scr
3 #  Displays users currently logged in.
4
5 who | awk '{print $1}'
```

```
$ who.scr
```

```
Output:
st050019
gilberg
tran
srp50115
forouzan
nys26825
```

Extract Lines: While the command in the next script is considerably more complex in its concept, it is still easy to code. We want to extract one verse from the middle (lines 42 to 47) of our file, TheRaven, and create a new file that we will call MidRaven. The command for this extraction is

```
head -47 TheRaven | tail +42 > midRaven.txt
```

Figure 14.2 portrays the steps for this example. We first use the **head** utility to extract the first 47 lines of the poem and pipe them to the **tail** utility, which extracts what was lines 42 to 47, leaving us with only one verse (six lines). The results are then directed to the new file, midRaven.txt.

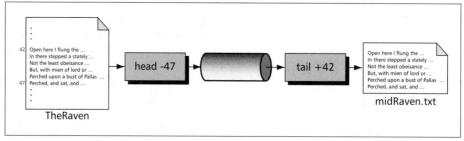

FIGURE 14.2 `midRaven.scr` *Design*

The code and execution of this script are in Script 14.4.

SCRIPT 14.4 *The* **midRaven.scr** *Script*

```
1  #!/bin/ksh
2  #   Script: midRaven.scr
3  #   Extracts one verse from middle of TheRaven file.
4
5  head -47 TheRaven | tail +42 > midRaven.txt
```

```
$ midRaven.scr
```

```
$ cat midRaven.txt
Open here I flung the shutter, when, with many a flirt and flutter
In there stepped a stately Raven of the saintly days of yore.
Not the least obeisance made he; not a minute stopped or stayed he;
But, with mien of lord or lady, perched above my chamber door--
Perched upon a bust of Pallas just above my chamber door--
Perched, and sat, and nothing more.
```

Insert Lines into Another File: All of the examples we have written so far are very trivial. They all can be done in one line. Now let us write a more complex example that requires several lines. We have been given an assignment to extract lines 3 through 5 of a file called `file3` and insert the extracted lines between lines 5 and 6 of another file called `file4`. The final result should be called `file5`.

This problem is complex enough that we need to design just how we are going to do it. After thinking about it for a while, we begin by sketching out a picture of what we need to do (Figure 14.3).

After assuring ourselves that the design is good, we sketch out the following English statements of what we want the script to do:[3]

1. Copy first 5 lines from `file4` to `file5`.
2. Extract lines 3 to 5 of `file3` and append to `file5`.
3. Copy line 6 to end of `file4` and append to `file5`.

It appears that these three steps will do the job, so it's time to write and test the script. The script and its results are in Script 14.5.

---

[3]An English-like description of the steps to accomplish a design is known as *tight English*. A more formal, codelike set of instructions is known as *pseudocode*.

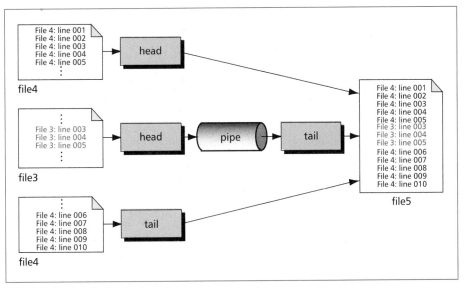

FIGURE 14.3 *Design for* **insert.scr**

SCRIPT 14.5   *The* **insert.scr** *Script*

```
1  #!/bin/ksh
2  #  Script: insert.scr
3  #  Inserts lines from one file into another
4
5  head -5 file4 > file5
6  head -5 file3 | tail +3 >> file5
7  tail +6 file4 >> file5
```

```
$ insert.scr
```

File3	File4	File5
File 3: line 001	File 4: line 001	File 4: line 001
File 3: line 002	File 4: line 002	File 4: line 002
File 3: line 003	File 4: line 003	File 4: line 003
File 3: line 004	File 4: line 004	File 4: line 004
File 3: line 005	File 4: line 005	File 4: line 005
File 3: line 006	File 4: line 006	File 3: line 003
File 3: line 007	File 4: line 007	File 3: line 004
File 3: line 008	File 4: line 008	File 3: line 005
File 3: line 009	File 4: line 009	File 4: line 006
File 3: line 010	File 4: line 010	File 4: line 007
		File 4: line 008
		File 4: line 009
		File 4: line 010

Script Termination (exit Command)

Occasionally, a script encounters a condition that does not allow it to continue processing. When that happens, it must stop. For these situations, UNIX provides an **exit** command.

The **exit** command terminates the script and sets the exit status. It can be used with a numeric argument or without an argument. When it is used with a number, the script's exit status is assigned the number. When it is used without an argument, the script's exit status is 0.

Arguments and Positional Parameters

The previous examples demonstrate the basic concept of shell scripting. However, shell scripts are more useful when they are generalized. A **generalized** script can be used in many different situations without change. For example, think of the extract lines problem (Extract Lines on page 551). It would be more useful if it worked with any input and output files and could extract any number of lines.

The Korn shell lets us generalize a script using arguments and positional parameters. Arguments are user-supplied data that follow the script name on the command line and are input to the script. Positional parameters are predefined memory variables (buffers) in the shell script. There are nine positional parameters,[4] labeled $1, $2, ..., $9, that are used to store the arguments that the user entered.

When the script is executed, the shell puts the first argument in the first positional parameter ($1), the second argument in the second positional parameter ($2), and so forth until all arguments have been stored. The script can then use them (properly prefixed by the dollar sign) anywhere a variable can be used. This concept is presented in Figure 14.4.

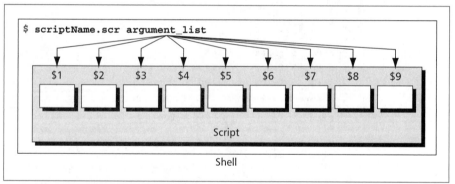

FIGURE 14.4   *Arguments and Positional Parameters*

Generalized Filenames: Let's repeat the Extract Lines example (see page 551), but instead of specific filenames, we will use positional parameters. In this case, we have four arguments and four positional parameters. The first argument is TheRaven. The fourth argument is midRaven.txt. The second and third arguments are the range of lines to be extracted. When the script is called, the value of argument 1 (TheRaven) is stored in $1. The value of argument 2 (42) is stored in parameter $2. With this mechanism, we can write a general script using the value of $1 through $4. The design is shown in Figure 14.5.

---

[4]We can have more than nine positional parameters, but we cannot access them directly. We must use the **shift** command to process them. These techniques are discussed later in the chapter.

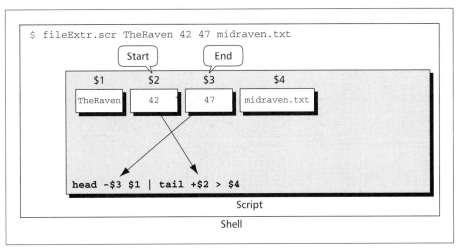

FIGURE 14.5 *Matching Arguments and Positional Parameters*

The advantage of using arguments and positional parameters is that we do not have to rewrite the extract script each time we want to extract lines from a different file or store the output in a different file. With a generalized script, we change the positional parameters simply by using different arguments (see Script 14.6).

SCRIPT 14.6   *The* **fileExtr.scr** *Script*

```
1  #!/bin/ksh
2  #  Script: fileExtr.scr
3  #  Extracts $2-$3 lines from $1 and places them in $4
4
5  head -$3 $1 | tail +$2 > $4
```
```
$ fileExtr.scr TheRaven 42 47 midRaven.txt
```
```
$ cat midRaven.txt
Open here I flung the shutter, when, with many a flirt and flutter
In there stepped a stately Raven of the saintly days of yore.
Not the least obeisance made he; not a minute stopped or stayed he;
But, with mien of lord or lady, perched above my chamber door--
Perched upon a bust of Pallas just above my chamber door--
Perched, and sat, and nothing more.
```

14.2 Expressions

Expressions are a sequence of operators and operands that reduces to a single value. The operators can be either mathematical operators, such as add and subtract, that compute a value; relational operators, such as greater than and less than, that determine a relationship between two values and return true or false; file test operators that report the status of a file; or logical operators that combine logical values and return true or false. We use mathematical expressions to compute a value and other expressions to make decisions. Figure 14.6 shows the four types of expressions.

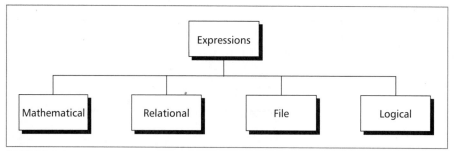

FIGURE 14.6 *Expression Forms*

Mathematical Expressions

Mathematical expressions in the Korn shell use integer operands and mathematical operators to calculate a value.

Mathematical Operators

Mathematical operators are used to compute a numeric value. The Korn shell supports the standard add, subtract, multiply, and divide operators plus a special operator for modulus. These operators are summarized in Table 14.1.

TABLE 14.1 *Mathematical Operators*

Operator	Description
+	Value is sum of two numbers.
−	Value is first value minus second value.
*	Value is product of two numbers.
/	Value is integral of first value divided by second value.
%	Value is remainder of first value divided by second.

From Table 14.1, we see that to use the expression operators, the data must be numeric values. As we discussed in Section 13.3 on page 557, however, the Korn shell stores all data as character strings. It cannot interpret numeric values. To better understand the problem created by storing numeric values as strings, let's see what happens when we add to a counter as in Session 14.1.

SESSION 14.1 *Adding to a String*

```
$ count=5
$ count=$count+2
$ print $count
5+2
```

We would expect the value of the variable count to be 7, but it is not. Its value is the string 5+2. This leads to the question: How can we evaluate numeric values in the Korn shell? The answer is that we must use either the **expr** or the **let** command.

let Command

The Korn shell uses either the **expr** command or the **let** command to evaluate expressions and store the result in another variable. The **expr** command is inherited from the Bourne shell; the **let** command is new. Because we expect the **expr** command to become deprecated, we discuss only the **let** command. A simple example follows:

```
$ let y=x+16
```

In this example, note that we don't use a dollar sign with the variables. The **let** command does not need the dollar sign; its syntax expects variables or constants.

The Korn shell has an alternate operator, a set of double parentheses, that may be used instead of the **let** command. The next example demonstrates this format. Once again, note that the variable dollar sign is not required with either the **let** command or the double-parentheses operator.

```
$ (( y = x + 16 ))
```

Session 14.2 contains an example of each expression operator.

SESSION 14.2 *Mathematical Expression Operators*

```
$ (( num = 15 * 6 ))
$ print $num
90

$ (( num = 15 / 6 ))
$ print $num
2

$ operand1=15
$ (( num = operand1 % 6 ))
$ print $num
3
$ operand2=6
$ (( num = 15 + operand2 ))
21
$ (( num = operand1 - operand2 ))
9
```

Relational Expressions

Relational expressions compare two values and return a logical value such as true or false. The logical value depends on the values being compared and the operator being used.

Relational Operators

The relational operators are listed in Table 14.2. The first column uses relational operators to compare numeric data. The third column uses relational operators to compare string data. Note that there is no operator to test whether one string is greater than or less than another string. We will write a string-compare script later in the chapter.

TABLE 14.2 *Logical Operators*

Numeric Interpretation	Meaning	String Interpretation
>	greater than	
>=	greater than or equal	
<	less than	
<=	less than or equal	
==	equal	=
!=	not equal	!=
	string length not zero	-n
	string length zero	-z

The string equal and not equal logical operators support patterns for the second (right) operand. The patterns supported are in Table 14.3.

TABLE 14.3 *Relational Patterns Supported by Korn Shell*

Pattern	Interpretation
string	Must exactly match the first operand.
?	Matches zero or one single character.
[...]	Matches one single character in the set.
*	Repeats pattern zero or more times.
?(pat1|pat2|...)	Matches zero or one of any of the patterns.
@(pat1|pat2|...)	Matches exactly one of the patterns.
*(pat1|pat2|...)	Matches zero or more of the patterns.
+(pat1|pat2|...)	Matches one or more of the patterns.
!(pat1|pat2|...)	Matches anything except any of the patterns.

Table 14.4 shows three examples of relational pattern use.

TABLE 14.4 *Examples of Relational Pattern Matching*

Pattern	Matches
?(Mr)	"Mr" or nothing.
?(Mr|Mrs)	"Mr," "Mrs," or nothing.
@(Mr|Mrs)	"Mr," "Mrs," but not nothing.

Relational Test Command

In the Korn shell, we can use either the test command inherited from the Bourne shell or one of two test operators, ((...)) or [[...]]. Because the test operators were designed for the Korn shell, we discuss only them.

Which operator is used depends on the data. Integer data require the double parentheses as shown in the next example:

```
(( x < y ))
```

For string expressions, the Korn shell requires the double bracket operator. Although the integer operator parentheses do not require the variable dollar sign, the double brackets operator does. The next example demonstrates this format:

```
[[ $x != $y ]]
```

In Session 14.3, we demonstrate each of the relational operators. Study the examples carefully until you understand each one.

SESSION 14.3   *Demonstrate Use of Relational Expression Operators*

# Numeric Expression Compares	# String Expression Compares
$ a=5	$ s="ab"
$ ((a == 5)) $ print $? 0 # true	$ [[$s = "ab "]] $ print $? 0 # true
$ ((a != 5)) $ print $? 1 # false	$ [[$s != "ab"]] $ print $? 1 # false
$ ((a > 4)) $ print $? 0 # true	
$ ((a >= 6)) $ print $? 1 # false	
$ ((a < 6)) $ print $? 0 # true	
$ ((a <= 4)) $ print $? 1 # false	
	$ [[-n $s]] $ print $? 0 # true
	$ [[-z ""]] # null string $ print $? 0 # true

File Expressions

File expressions use file operators and the test command to check the status of a file. A file's status includes characteristics such as open, readable, writable, or executable.

File Operators

There are several operators that can be used in a file test command to check a file's status. They are particularly useful in shell scripts when we need to know the type or status of a file. Table 14.5 lists the file operators and what file attributes they test.

TABLE 14.5 *File Status Operators*

Operator	Explanation
-r file	True if file exists and is readable.
-l file	True if file exists and is a symbolic link.
-w file	True if file exists and is writable.
-x file	True if file exists and is executable.
-f file	True if file exists and is a regular file.
-d file	True if file exists and is a directory.
-s file	True if file exists and has a size greater than zero.
file1 -nt file2	True if file1 is newer than file2.
file1 -ot file2	True if file1 is older than file2.

Test File Command

Although we could use the **test** command inherited from the Bourne shell, in the Korn shell we recommend the Korn shell double bracket operator to test the status of a file. Session 14.4 demonstrates the file status test format.

SESSION 14.4 *Test If File Exists*

```
$ ls -l file1 file2
-rw-r--r--    1 gilberg   staff        100 Mar 13 16:14 file1
-rw-r--r--    1 gilberg   staff       4405 Feb  3 12:11 file2
$ [[ -s file1 ]]
$ print $?
0                                       # true
```
```
$ [[ file1 -ot file2 ]]
$ print $?
1                                       # false
```

Session 14.4 Analysis: We begin with a long list of the file to verify its existence and size. The first test determines if the file exists and is not empty (file size greater than zero). When we test the return value, we see that the file does exist and contains data. The second test determines if file1 is older than file 2. The test verifies that it is not older.

Logical Expressions

Logical expressions evaluate to either true or false. They use a set of three logical operators.

Logical Operators

The Korn shell has three **logical operators**: *not* (!), *and* (&&), and *or* (| |). A common way to show logical relationships is in truth tables. Truth tables list the values that each operand can assume and the resulting value. Truth tables for *not, and,* and *or* are in Figure 14.7.

not			and				or		
x	! $x		x	y	$x && $y		x	y	$x || $y
false	true		false	false	false		false	false	false
true	false		false	true	false		false	true	true
			true	false	false		true	false	true
			true	true	true		true	true	true

FIGURE 14.7 *Logical Operators Truth Tables*

not The **not** operator (!) complements the value of an expression. It changes a true value to false and a false value to true.

and The **and** operator (&&) requires two expressions. For this reason, it is known as a binary operator. Because it is a binary operator, four distinct combinations of operand values in its evaluation are possible. The result is true only when both expressions are true; it is false in all other cases.

or The **or** operator (| |) also requires two expressions (binary operator). Again, because it is a binary operator, four distinct combinations of operand values are possible. The result is false only when both operands are false; it is true in all other cases.

Logical Test Command

Once again, we could use the old Bourne shell test command for logical tests. As we have consistently emphasized, however, it is better to use the new Korn bracket operators.

Session 14.5 demonstrates the use of logical expressions and their results. Most of the examples are easy to understand.

SESSION 14.5 *Logical Operators*

```
$ [[ 7 > 5 && 6 > 5 ]]
$ print $?
0                                       # true

$ [[ 7 > 5 && 6 > 7 ]]
$ print $?
1                                       # false

$ [[ 7 == 5 || 6 < 7 ]]
$ print $?
0                                       # true
```

Continued

SESSION 14.5 *Logical Operators—Continued*

```
$ [[ 5 > 7 || 6 > 7 ]]
$ print $?
1                                            # false
```
```
$ [[ "a" != "b" && 4 > 3 ]]
$ print $?
0                                            # true
```
```
$ [[ ! "a" = "b" ]]
$ print $?
0                                            # true
```
```
$ [[ ! 5 > 3 ]]
$ print $?
1                                            # false
```

Session 14.5 Analysis: The last two examples demonstrate how the *not* operator can be applied to the results of another logical expression. It is false that a is equal to b, but when the *not* operator is applied to the results of the logical expression (false), the result becomes true; that is, not false is true. Similarly, it is true that 5 is greater than 3, but when the *not* operator is applied to the results of the logical expression (true), the result becomes false; that is, not true is false.

Expression Type Summary

Table 14.6 summarizes the four expression types we discussed in this section along with an example of each format.

TABLE 14.6 *Expression Summary*

Expression	Numeric	String
Mathematical	((x + 16))	
Relational	((num == 2))	[["a" = $data]]
File	[[-s file1]]	
Logical	[[$a == 1 && $b != 2]]	

14.3 Decisions: Making Selections

In this section, we learn how to execute different sets of commands based on the exit status of a command or test expression. The Korn shell has two different statements that allow us to select between two or more alternatives. The first, the if-then-else statement, examines the data and chooses between two alternatives. For this reason, it is sometimes referred to as a two-way selection. The second, the **case** statement, selects one of several paths by matching patterns to different strings. These two statements are shown in Figure 14.8.

if-then-else

Every language has some variation of the if-then-else statement. The only difference between them is what keywords are required by the syntax. For example, the C language

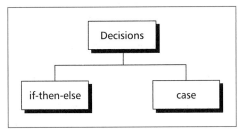

FIGURE 14.8 *Decisions*

does not use `then`. In fact, it is an error to use it. In all languages, however, something is tested. Most typically, data values are tested. In the Korn shell, the exit value from a command is used as the test.

In Figure 14.9, the flowchart shows a command being executed and its exit status being tested. On the right of the flowchart is the format for the Korn shell. The shell evaluates the exit status from the command following `if`. When the exit status is 0, the `then` set of commands is executed. When the exit status is 1, the `else` set of commands is executed.

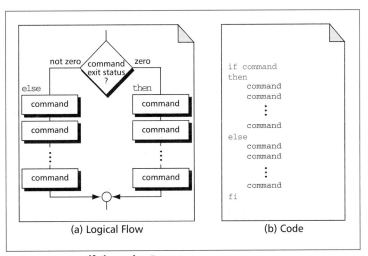

FIGURE 14.9 **if-then-else** *Format*

The Korn shell requires one more syntactical token. Each `if-then-else` statement ends with the keyword `fi`. This is the opposite of the keyword `if` that is used at the beginning of the statement. We will see this begin–end technique used again.

Exit Status

As we pointed out in the previous section, the condition being evaluated in the `if-then-else` statement must be the exit status of a command. This means that only another command can follow the keyword `if` in the `if-then-else` statement. The Korn shell then evaluates the exit status and executes either the `then` statement or the `else` statement as appropriate.

The commands in the if evaluation can be chained (piped); that is, there can be more than one command. When multiple commands are chained, the condition evaluated is the exit status of the last command in the chain.

Let's look at an example. We want to know if a user is currently logged on to UNIX. To answer this question, we use the **who** command and pipe the results to **grep** where we look for the person's login id. This is an example of a chained command ending in a **grep** search. Because the search is the last command, the Korn shell evaluates the search results to determine if the data were found. This code is in Script 14.7.

SCRIPT 14.7   *Using a Command*

```
 1  #!/bin/ksh
 2  #  Script: exit.scr
 3  #  Demonstrate use of exit status
 4  #  First parameter is user's login id
 5  if who | grep $1 > /dev/null              # put line in trash
 6  then
 7     print "$1 is logged in"
 8  else
 9     print "$1 is not logged in"
10  fi
```
```
$ exit.scr gilberg
```
```
Output:
gilberg is logged in
```

Script 14.7 Analysis: In the if statement (line 5), we redirect the output to the trash. If we didn't do this, the lines that match the argument would be printed by **grep.** Trash is identified as a null file in the device directory (/dev/null).

Test Command Evaluation

Recall that the expression in an if statement must be a command. The if statement then tests the exit status of the command to determine if it was successful or not. To use relational or logical operators to compare data, therefore, we must use the test command or equivalent operators—((...)) and [[...]]. The test command's exit status is true or false. If the result of a relational or logical operator is true, the exit status of the test command is success (true); alternately, if the result of the expression is false, the exit status of the test command is failure (false).

As an example of evaluating data, we look at the time of day and print an appropriate greeting, such as "good morning" or "good evening." This requires that we know what time it is. Fortunately, this information is available in the **date** command. In the output from the **date** command, the hour occupies characters 12 and 13. This means that we can simply execute the **date** command, pipe its output to **cut,** and then store the results in a variable we name hour. Once we have isolated the hour, we simply test it in an if-then-else statement. We demonstrate this example in Script 14.8. We will expand on this example when we discuss multiway selection later in this chapter.

SCRIPT 14.8   *Time of Day Greeting*

```
 1  #!/bin/ksh
 2  #   Script: gday.scr
 3  #   Demonstrate test command evaluation
 4  hour=$(date | cut -c 12-13)
 5  if (( hour <= 18 ))
 6      then
 7          print Good day, sir
 8      else
 9          print Good evening, sir
10  fi
    $ gday.scr
```

```
Output:
Good evening, sir
```

if *without* else

Often we make a test that requires action only if the test is true. No action is required if the test is false. In this case, we need a `then` statement without a matching `else`. When there is no false action, we simply omit the `else` (false) portion of the command as shown in Figure 14.10.

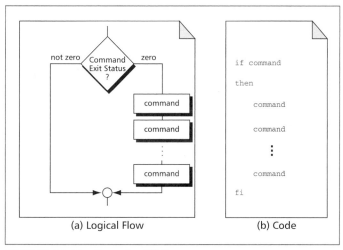

FIGURE 14.10   *Example of* **if-then**

As an example of a `then` without an `else`, consider the situation in which we need to print a file. If the file exists and contains data, we print it. If it doesn't, then we need do nothing. In Script 14.9, we use a test command to determine whether a file exists and is readable. If it is, we **cat** the file. If the file doesn't exist, we do nothing. There are no `else` commands because we are interested in taking action only if the file exists.

SCRIPT 14.9   *Example of* **if-then** *with* **No else**

```
 1 #!/bin/ksh
 2 #  Script: ifNoElse.scr
 3 #  Test existence of a file
 4 if [[ -r $1 ]]
 5 then
 6    cat $1
 7 fi
```

```
$ ifNoElse.scr file1
```

```
Output:
*******************
**               **
** This is file1 **
**               **
*******************
```

else *without* if: *Null Command*

Although we can have an if-then-else statement without an else action, we cannot have one without a then action. When there are no true actions in the if-then-else, we use what is called the null command for the true action. The null command is a colon (:). It does nothing but satisfy the requirement for a command in the then action. Script 14.10 shows the use of the null command.

SCRIPT 14.10   *Example of a Null* **if** *Command*

```
 1 #!/bin/ksh
 2 #  Script: ifNull.scr
 3 # Ensure argument 1 is valid file
 4 if [[ -r $1 ]]
 5 then
 6    :                        # null command
 7 else
 8    print $1 does not exist and cannot be opened
 9 fi
10 #  Rest of script here
```

```
$ ifNull.scr noFile
```

```
Output:
noFile does not exist and cannot be opened
```

Nested if *Statements*

Each branch in the if-then-else statement can be any command including another if-then-else statement. When an if-then-else statement is found in either the true or false branch of an if-then-else command, it is called a nested if. This type of nesting is so common that a compact format, in which the if and the else are combined into a word called elif, has been designed for it. While either the true or false action can be nested, it is more commonly the false action.

Let's use this format to solve a rather common academic problem: changing a numeric grade (between 0 and 100) to a letter grade (A, B, C, D, or F). We begin by designing the solution to the problem. The flowchart design is shown in Figure 14.11. Also shown in the figure is the code for the solution in both the regular and `elif` formats. As you study the two code examples, note that the regular format style is indented with each nested format but that the `elif` style is not. This change in the indentation style allows us to keep the code more compact.

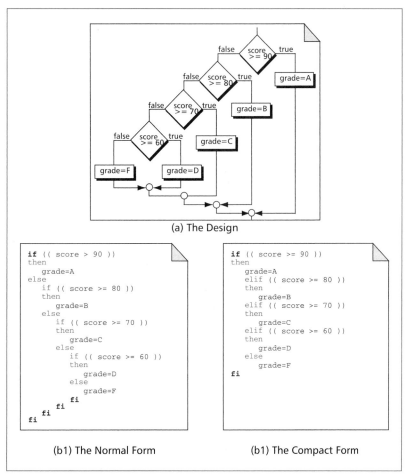

(a) The Design

```
if (( score > 90 ))
then
    grade=A
else
    if (( score >= 80 ))
    then
        grade=B
    else
        if (( score >= 70 ))
        then
            grade=C
        else
            if (( score >= 60 ))
            then
                grade=D
            else
                grade=F
            fi
        fi
    fi
fi
```

(b1) The Normal Form

```
if (( score >= 90 ))
then
    grade=A
elif (( score >= 80 ))
then
    grade=B
elif (( score >= 70 ))
then
    grade=C
elif (( score >= 60 ))
then
    grade=D
else
    grade=F
fi
```

(b1) The Compact Form

FIGURE 14.11 *Nested* **if-then-else**

Multiway Selection

The Korn shell implements multiway selection with the `case` statement. Given a string and a list of pattern alternatives, the `case` statement matches the string against each of the patterns in sequence. The first pattern that matches the string gets the action. If no patterns match, the `case` statement continues with the next command.

Case Syntax

The `case` statement contains the string that is evaluated. It ends with an end case token, which is `esac` (case spelled backward). Between the start and end case statements is the **pattern list.** For every pattern that needs to be tested, a separate pattern is defined in the pattern list. The pattern ends with a closing parenthesis. Associated with each pattern is one or more commands. The commands follow the normal rules for commands with the addition that the last command must end in two semicolons. The last action in the pattern list is usually the wildcard asterisk, making it the default if none of the other cases match. The decision logic flow for the multiway statement is shown in Figure 14.12.

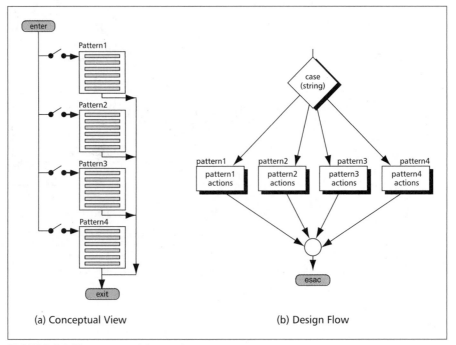

(a) Conceptual View (b) Design Flow

FIGURE 14.12   case *Decision Logic*

The `case` statement is a puzzle that must be solved carefully to avoid confusion. Think of it as a series of drawbridges (Figure 14.12a), one for each pattern. As a result of the pattern evaluation, a matching drawbridge is closed so that there will be a path for the script to follow. Once a drawbridge is closed, none of the patterns that follow it can be matched. After executing the matching commands from the closed drawbridge, the path flows to the exit. If none of the patterns match (that is, if none of the drawbridges are closed), the `case` statement continues with the next command. Figure 14.12(b) shows the design flow as it would be used in a flowchart.

As a simple example of a `case` statement, let's write a session that given a digit prints its textual spelling. The design appears in Figure 14.13.

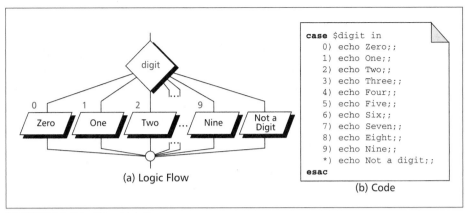

```
case $digit in
    0) echo Zero;;
    1) echo One;;
    2) echo Two;;
    3) echo Three;;
    4) echo Four;;
    5) echo Five;;
    6) echo Six;;
    7) echo Seven;;
    8) echo Eight;;
    9) echo Nine;;
    *) echo Not a digit;;
esac
```

(a) Logic Flow   (b) Code

FIGURE 14.13   *Print Digit Text*

The script to print the spelling of a digit and a sample execution are in Script 14.11.

SCRIPT 14.11   *Demonstrate the Case Statement*

```
 1  #!/bin/ksh
 2  #  Script: caseDigit.scr
 3  #  Demonstrate case statement
 4
 5  print "Enter a digit and I'll spell it for you: \c"
 6  read digit
 7  print "\nYou entered $digit. It is spelled: \c"
 8
 9  case $digit in
10      0) print Zero.;;
11      1) print One.;;
12      2) print Two.;;
13      3) print Three.;;
14      4) print Four.;;
15      5) print Five.;;
16      6) print Six.;;
17      7) print Seven.;;
18      8) print Eight.;;
19      9) print Nine.;;
20      *) print Not a digit.;;
21  esac
```

```
$ caseDigit.scr
```

```
Output: First run
Enter a digit and I'll spell it for you: 3

You entered 3. It is spelled: Three.
```

```
Output: Second run
Enter a digit and I'll spell it for you: x
You entered x. It is spelled: Not a digit.
```

Wildcard Characters

Note that the last pattern in Script 14.11 is a wildcard. Because each matching pattern ends the case, the wildcard default is selected only if none of the other patterns match. This allows us to print an error message, in this case, "Not a digit."

The matching pattern can be any of the patterns supported by the Korn shell. In Figure 14.13, the patterns were the single digits that were to be matched. If the user entered two digits, the pattern would not have been matched, and the default message would have been output.

Table 14.3 on page 558 contains the basic pattern formats supported by the Korn shell. All of these patterns can be used with the `case` statement. Note that the patterns used here are the same as the filename wildcards. They are not atoms or operators defined for regular expressions.

Wildcard patterns can be combined to form more complex patterns. In Table 14.7, we demonstrate several wildcard patterns. We suggest that you cover up the explanation and try to determine what the pattern matches before reading it.

TABLE 14.7 **case** *Pattern Examples*

Pattern	Explanation
hello	Matches only hello. Does not match jello, hallo, helo, and so forth.
[Hh]*	Matches any word beginning with upper- or lowercase H.
[Hh]?	Matches any two-character word beginning with upper- or lowercase H.
[Hh]	Matches any word containing an upper- or lowercase H.
H|h	Matches only one character: upper- or lowercase H.
[aeiouAEIOU]	Matches only one character: Must be a vowel (aeiou).
[0-9]	Matches one digit in range 0 to 9 inclusive.
[a-zA-Z]	Matches one alphabetic character.
?(Ms|Miss)	Matches Ms or Miss or nothing.
@(Mr|Ms)	Must match one of the two patterns.

For another **case** example, let's write a script that expands the time of day message in Script 14.8 to include good afternoon. We again use the **date** command, but this time, we **cut** the complete time (hh:mm). Then we test only the hour to determine the correct message. The script and a typical execution are in Script 14.12.

SCRIPT 14.12 *Time and Greeting Script*

```
1  #!/bin/ksh
2  #  Script: greeting.scr
3  #  Check hour to display proper greeting
4  hour=$(date | cut -c 12-16)
5  case $hour in
6    0?:??|1[01]:??) print "Good morning. It's $hour A.M.";;
```

Continued

SCRIPT 14.12   *Time and Greeting Script*

```
 7          1[2-7]:??) print "Good afternoon. It's $hour P.M.";;
 8    1[89]:??|2?:??) print "Good evening. It's $hour P.M.";;
 9              *) print "Sorry, I don't know the time";;
10 esac
```
```
$ greeting.scr
```
```
Output:
Good morning. It's 09:24 A.M.
```

14.4 Repetition

The real power of computers is their ability to repeat an operation or a series of operations many times. This repetition, known as looping, is one of the basic programming concepts. In this section, we discuss looping and introduce different looping constructs.

A **loop** is an action or a series of actions repeated under the control of loop criteria written by the programmer. Each loop tests the criteria. If the criteria tests valid, the loop continues; if it tests invalid, the loop terminates.

Command-Controlled and List-Controlled Loops

Loops in the Korn shell can be grouped into two general categories: command-controlled loops and list-controlled loops.

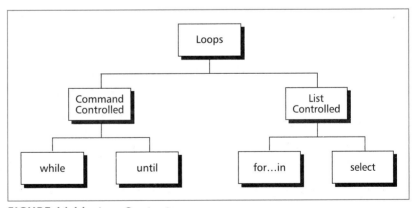

FIGURE 14.14   *Loop Constructs*

Command-Controlled Loops

In a **command-controlled loop,** the execution of a command determines whether the loop body executes or not. There are two command-controlled loops in the Korn shell: the `while` loop and the `until` loop.

The `while` *Loop*   The `while` loop is a basic command-controlled loop. It begins with `while`, which contains the loop command and loops as long as the command's exit status is true (zero). When the exit status becomes false (nonzero), the loop terminates. Figure 14.15 shows the format of the `while` loop.

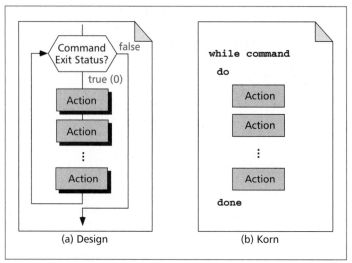

FIGURE 14.15 *The* **while** *Loop*

One of the most common loop applications in any language is reading data. Script 14.13 is a short example that demonstrates how to read data in a loop. We begin by writing a `while` loop that reads a line from the keyboard. As long as a line is successfully read (that is, as long as the exit status of the **read** command is true), it adds the number and iterates. When end of file (^d in UNIX) is entered, it prints the total and stops.

SCRIPT 14.13 *A Simple Read Loop*

```
 1 #!/bin/ksh
 2 #  Script: loopAdd.scr
 3 #  Demonstrate read file loop. Adds and prints total.
 4
 5 print "This utility adds numbers entered from the"
 6 print "keyboard. When all numbers have been entered,"
 7 print "key ^d (eof) to see the total.\n"
 8
 9 sum=0
10 print "Enter a number   :  \c"
11 while read data
12   do
13     (( sum = sum + data ))
14     print "Enter next number:  \c"
15   done
16 print "\n         Sum is: " $sum
```
```
$ loopAdd.scr
```
```
Output:
This utility adds numbers entered from the
keyboard. When all numbers have been entered,
key ^d (eof) to see the total.
```

Continued

SCRIPT 14.13   *A Simple Read Loop*

```
Enter a number   :   2
Enter next number:   4
Enter next number:   6
Enter next number:   ^D
            Sum is: 12
```

In Script 14.13, we read until the file was totally read. Another looping concept uses a sentinel to terminate the loop. A **sentinel** is a special data value that stops the loop. A common loop sentinel is -9999. Of course, the sentinel value cannot be a valid data value. Script 14.14 demonstrates the sentinel concept by using -9999 to indicate that a subtotal is to be displayed.

SCRIPT 14.14   *Using a Sentinel to Print Totals*

```
 1  #!/bin/ksh
 2  #   Script: loopSent.scr
 3  #   Demonstrate read file loop. Adds and prints total.
 4
 5  print This utility adds numbers entered from the
 6  print keyboard. When all numbers have been entered,
 7  print key -9999 to see the total.
 8  print
 9
10  sum=0
11  print "Enter a number   :   \c"
12  read data
13  while [[ $data != -9999 ]]
14    do
15       (( sum = sum + data ))
16       print "Enter next number:   \c"
17       read data
18    done
19
20  print "           Sum is: " $sum
```

```
$ loopSent.scr
```

```
Output:
This utility adds numbers entered from the
keyboard. When all numbers have been entered,
key -9999 to see the total.

Enter a number   :   2
Enter next number:   4
Enter next number:   6
Enter next number:   -9999
            Sum is: 12
```

The until *Loop* The *until* loop works just like the *while* loop, except that it loops as long as the exit status of the command is false. In this sense, it is the complement of the *while* loop. The syntax of the *until* loop is shown in Figure 14.16.

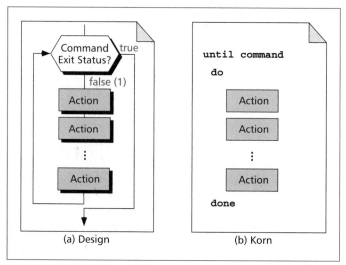

FIGURE 14.16 *The **until** Loop*

You may wonder why UNIX provides an until loop when the while loop is basically the same—the until is simply the complement of the while. The answer is that there are some loop situations in which we need the complement of the exit status. This is not easily done in a script. For example, if we need to process a file that is shared among all members of our group, we should guard against it being used by someone else when we need it. If someone else has it opened for writing, we cannot open it. Script 14.15 demonstrates a simple until loop that guards against this situation and loops until the file becomes available.

SCRIPT 14.15 *Demonstrate the **until** Loop*

```
 1  #!/bin/ksh
 2  #  Script: until.scr
 3  #  Demonstrate until command. Wait for a file to become available.
 4  #  File is passed as $1
 5
 6  #  Test if file is available.
 7  if [[ -r $1 ]]
 8  then
 9     :                           # File is available.
10  else
11     print "File $1 is not available. Waiting\c"
12     until [[ -r $1 ]]
13       do
14         sleep 5
```

Continued

SCRIPT 14.15   *Demonstrate the* **until** *Loop*

```
15            print ". \c"
16         done
17  fi
18
19  #  File is available. Continue processing.
20      print $1 is available for processing.
21
22  #  Rest of script follows here
```

List-Controlled Loops

In a list-controlled loop, there is a control list. The number of elements in the list controls the number of iterations. If the control list contains five elements, the body of the loop is executed five times; if the control list contains ten elements, the body of the loop is executed ten times.

The `for-in` Loop   The first list-controlled loop in the Korn shell is the `for-in` loop. The list can be any type of string; for example, it can be words, lines, sentences, or a file. Figure 14.17 shows the design and code of the `for-in` loop. In each iteration, the next element in `list` is moved to `variable` and processed.

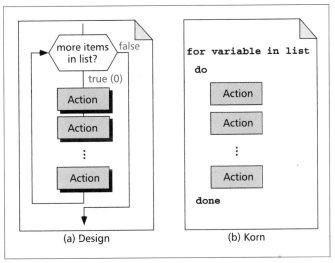

FIGURE 14.17   *The* **for-in** *Loop*

Let's write a very simple loop. In Script 14.16, we loop five times, each time displaying the loop control string (a digit) and the word "Hello."

SCRIPT 14.16   *A Simple* **for-in** *Loop*

```
1  #!/bin/ksh
2  #  Script: loopFor.scr
```
Continued

SCRIPT 14.16   *A Simple* **for-in** *Loop—Continued*

```
 3  #  Demonstrate a simple for...in loop
 4
 5  for i in 1 2 3 4 5
 6  do
 7      print $i Hello
 8  done
```
```
$ loopFor.scr
```
```
Output:
1 Hello
2 Hello
3 Hello
4 Hello
5 Hello
```

A list-controlled loop can be used to process a list of files. In the next example, we process a list of files in which each element in the control list is a filename. The file list is created as a separate UNIX file. The file is then used in a script to create the `for` loop list. This design makes it easy to use one script with different lists of files for each execution. To make it even more flexible, the file list is passed to the script as an argument.

In this example, we simply **cat** the file. The body of the loop first prints the filename and then the contents of the file. After the file is printed, we print a divider to separate it from the next file. The script and its output are in Script 14.17.

SCRIPT 14.17   *File Processing Loop*

```
 1  #!/bin/ksh
 2  #  Script: loopCatFiles.scr
 3  #  This script catenates files found in a control list
 4  #  The name of the control file is an argument ($1)
 5
 6  for filename in $(cat $1)
 7  do
 8      print $filename
 9      cat   $filename
10      print "========= End of $filename =========\n"
11  done
12
13  print      "********* End of File List *********"
```
```
$ loopCatFiles.scr loopCatFiles.dat
```
```
$cat loopCatFiles.dat
file1
file2
```
```
Output:
file1
******************
**              **
** This is file1 **
```

Continued

SCRIPT 14.17 *File Processing Loop*

```
      **              **
     ******************
     ========= End of file1 =========

     file2
     ******************
      **              **
     ** This is file2 **
      **              **
     ******************
     ========= End of file2 =========

     ********* End of File List *********
```

Script 14.17 Analysis: The simplicity of the code makes it very easy to understand what we are doing. But the simplicity also hides how the code works. The for statement creates a control list by using a **cat** statement to create the control list of the files in the argument ($1). Each element of the control list is a line containing the name of a file to be listed. The script then uses the control list first to display the name of the file being printed and then as the parameter to the **cat** statement in the loop body. When the control list has been completely processed, we exit the loop and display an end of script message.

select *Loop* The second Korn shell list-controlled loop is the select loop. The select loop is a special loop designed to create menus. A menu is a list of options displayed on the monitor. The user selects one of the menu options, which is then processed by the script. The format of the select loop is similar to the for-in loop. It begins with the keyword select followed by a variable and a list of strings:

```
$ select variable in list
```

Following the select command is the loop body. Script 14.18 demonstrates the most basic form of the loop.

SCRIPT 14.18 *Basic **select** Loop*

```
 1 #!/bin/ksh
 2 #  Script: selectOne.scr
 3 #  A simple demonstration of the select loop
 4
 5 clear
 6 select choice in month year quit
 7 do
 8    case $choice in
 9         month) cal;;
10         year)  yr=$(date "+%Y")
11                cal $yr;;
12         quit)  print "Hope you found your date"
13                exit;;
```

Continued

SCRIPT 14.18   *Basic* **select** *Loop—Continued*

```
14            *)        print "Sorry, I don't understand your answer."
15    esac
16 done
$ selectOne.scr
Output:
1) month
2) year
3) quit
#? 1
   March 2001
   S   M Tu  W Th  F  S
                  1  2  3
   4  5  6  7  8  9 10
  11 12 13 14 15 16 17
  18 19 20 21 22 23 24
  25 26 27 28 29 30 31
#? 4
Sorry, I don't understand your answer.
#? 3
Hope you found your date
```

Script 14.18 Analysis: There are four important points to note in this script. First, the prompt changes to prompt 3 (PS3) for the user response. In the next script, we will see how we can take advantage of this fact to improve the script.

Second, the interpreter generates a menu for us. Obviously, it would be a better menu if we also provided a line or two of explanation about the script.

Third, the user response is stored in two different forms. In the shell REPLY variable, the actual user response is stored. The list text that corresponds to the user's reply is stored in the variable in the select statement. In the script, the variable is choice, and depending on the user's response, it will contain either month or year. This is the form we used in this script.

Fourth, there is no way to get out of the loop; it never ends. To give the user a way out, therefore, we use a quit option. When the user selects quit, we print a message and exit the script.

> **The user's actual response is stored in the shell REPLY variable. The list text that corresponds to the user's response is stored in the variable specified in the select command.**

To improve the script, we can make two changes: one in the user interface and one in the script code. First, we improve the user interface by adding a short explanation of the script and a prompt. We display the explanation with one or more **print** commands before we start the loop. The prompt, however, can only be controlled by the loop. However, because it comes from the PS3 shell variable, we can tailor it by assigning our own message to the variable. The changes in the script code use a **case** command to control the selection and an option to quit when the user is done (Script 14.19).

SCRIPT 14.19 *Improved Select Script*

```
 1  #!/bin/ksh
 2  #   Script: selectTwo.scr
 3  #   An improved select loop
 4
 5  #   Display introduction message
 6  print "This script displays a message"
 7  print "in the language of your choice"
 8  PS3="Enter your selection: "
 9
10  #   Display menu and process response
11  select choice in English Spanish French Quit
12  do
13      case $choice in
14          English) print "Thank You";;
15          Spanish) print "Gracias";;
16          French)  print "Merci";;
17          Quit)    break;;
18          *)       print $REPLY is an invalid choice
19                   print Please try again;;
20      esac
21  done
```

```
$ selectTwo.scr
```

```
Output:
This script displays a message
in the language of your choice
1) English
2) Spanish
3) French
4) Quit
Enter your selection: 3
Merci
Enter your selection: 5
5 is an invalid choice
Please try again
Enter your selection: 4
```

Script 14.19 Analysis: This script has a much improved user interface. But it is not a very typical menu because all it does is process one of four sets of commands. A more typical loop would include much more code in the case selections. A common design would code the commands for each selection as a function and then call the appropriate function in each loop.

One point is not apparent from the script: What happens if the user doesn't enter anything? In that case, the loop repeats the menu and prompts the user again.

Background Loops

When a loop has many iterations, it should be executed in the background. For example, assume that we write a script to send out a monthly newsletter to members of a club. If there are a lot of members, it could take a long time to send the newsletter to all of them. In this case, we may want to put the loop in the background so that we can do other work.

To execute a loop in the background, we add an ampersand (&) at the end of the loop after the word done. We demonstrate background processing with a simple loop that creates a file of 500 numbers (Script 14.20). While the program was executing in the background, we used the **tail** command at three intervals to display the last three numbers generated.

SCRIPT 14.20   *Example of a Background Loop*

```
 1  #!/bin/ksh
 2  #  Script: loopBG.scr
 3  #  Loop in background
 4
 5  count=1
 6  until (( count == 500 ))
 7     do
 8         (( count = $count + 1 ))
 9         print $count >> bgLoop.out
10     done &
    $ loopBG.scr
```

```
Execution:
$ tail -3 bgLoop.out
103
104
105

$ tail -3 bgLoop.out
338
339
340

$ tail -3 bgLoop.out
498
499
500
```

Loop Redirection

Input from a file can be redirected to a loop, and the output from a loop can be redirected to a file.

Input Redirection

To redirect input from a file to a loop, we simply place the redirection at the end of the loop statement. As shown in Figure 14.18, only while and until loops support input redirection.

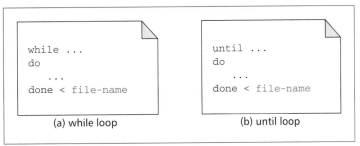

FIGURE 14.18 *Input File Redirection*

Script 14.21 demonstrates how to use redirection in a `while` loop to read from a file instead of the keyboard.

SCRIPT 14.21 *Input Redirection*

```
1  !/bin/ksh
2  #  Script: loopIPRedir.scr
3  #  Demonstrate input redirection in a loop
4
5  while read line
6    do
7       print $line
8    done < TheRavenV1
```

```
$ loopIPRedir.scr
```

```
Output
Once upon a midnight dreary, while I pondered, weak and weary,
Over many a quaint and curious volume of forgotten lore
While I nodded, nearly napping, suddenly there came a tapping,
As of someone gently rapping, rapping at my chamber door.
"'Tis some visitor," I muttered, "tapping at my chamber door
Only this and nothing more."
```

Output Redirection

The output from a loop can be redirected to a file by coding the redirection at the end of the loop. Only three loops can use output redirection. The output redirection code is shown in Figure 14.19.

For example, in Script 14.17 (File Processing Loop on page 576), if the files were large, we might want to redirect the output to a new file. Script 14.22 demonstrates the concept. In this session, we create a backup of each file by appending .out to the output created through redirection.

Compare the results of Script 14.22 with Script 14.17 to verify that the output from the first script matches the output from the **cat** statement in the second script.

Loop Piping

Loop input and output can also be piped. To pipe input to a loop, we place the pipe before the loop statement. To pipe output to another command, we place the pipe after the loop (Figure 14.20).

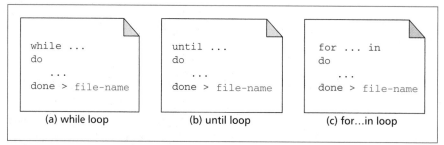

FIGURE 14.19 *Loop Output Redirection*

SCRIPT 14.22 *Redirection of Loop Output*

```
 1   #!/bin/ksh
 2   #   Script: loopRedir.scr
 3   #   This script catenates files found in a control list
 4   #   The name of the control file is an argument ($1)
 5   #   The output is redirected to a file (loopRedir.scr)
 6
 7   for filename in $(cat $1)
 8   do
 9      print $filename
10      cat    $filename
11      print "========= End of $filename =========\n"
12   done > loopRedir.out
13
14   print    "********* End of File List *********" > loopRedir.out
```

```
$ loopRedir.scr loopCatFiles.dat
```

```
$ cat loopCatFiles.dat
file1
file2
```

```
$ cat loopRedir.out
file1
*******************
**             **
** This is file1 **
**             **
*******************
========= End of file1 =========

file2
*******************
**             **
** This is file2 **
**             **
*******************
========= End of file2 =========

********* End of File List *********
```

> **Warning**
>
> Some old versions of the Korn shell create a subshell when a command script is redirected, either in or out. Variables created and changed in a subshell belong to the subshell, and the parent shell cannot see them. This means that if a variable is initialized or changed in a loop, the script cannot reference the variable after the loop is terminated. In this case, you should use redirection with the exec command as we demonstrate later. The newer version of the Korn shell does not create a subshell in this case.

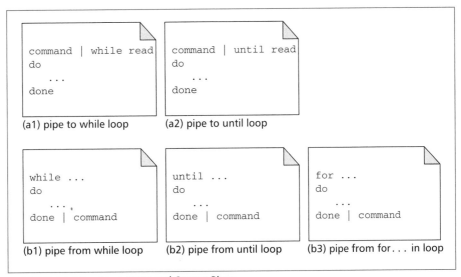

FIGURE 14.20 *Loop Input and Output Pipes*

Input Piping

Pipe input to a loop is shown in Figure 14.20(a). If our filenames are stored in a file, we can **cat** the file and pipe it to the loop as in Script 14.23.

SCRIPT 14.23 *Piping Data into a Loop*

```ksh
 1  #!/bin/ksh
 2  #   Script: loopInPipe.scr
 3  #   This script catenates files found in a file into a do loop
 4  #   The name of the file is an argument ($1)
 5
 6  cat $1 | while read filename
 7  do
 8      print $filename
 9      cat   $filename
10      print "========= End of $filename =========\n"
11  done
```

Continued

SCRIPT 14.23 *Piping Data into a Loop—Continued*

```
12
13 print      "********* End of File List *********"
```

```
$ loopInPipe.scr loopCatFiles.dat
```

```
$ cat loopCatFiles.dat
file1
file2
```

```
Output:
file1
*******************
**               **
** This is file1 **
**               **
*******************
========= End of file1 =========

file2
*******************
**               **
** This is file2 **
**               **
*******************
========= End of file2 =========

********* End of File List *********
```

Output Piping

To pipe the output from a loop to another command, we put the **pipe** command at the end of the loop. Output piping is shown in Figure 14.20(b).

Script 14.24 demonstrates this concept by passing the output to the count utility (**wc**) with the option set to count lines (-1).

SCRIPT 14.24 **Pipe** *Loop Output to* **wc** *Utility*

```
1 #!/bin/ksh
2 #   Script: loopOutPipe.scr
3 #   This script counts the number of lines in a file(s).
4 #   The file(s) to be counted are read from a file
5 #   passed as an argument ($1).
6
7 cat $1 | while read filename
8 do
9     cat $filename
10 done | wc -1
```

```
$ loopOutPipe.scr loopOutPipe.dat
```

```
Input File:
file1
file2
```

```
Output:
        10
```

Other Loop Control Statements

There are two other statements related to loops: **break** and **continue.**

break: The break statement immediately exits from the loop (but not from the script). Processing continues with the first command after the loop. The break statement is generally an action in a selection statement such as an if-then-else or a case.

continue: The continue statement causes the loop to ignore the rest of the body commands and immediately transfers control to the test command. If the loop is not complete, the next iteration begins. The break and continue actions are diagramed in Figure 14.21.

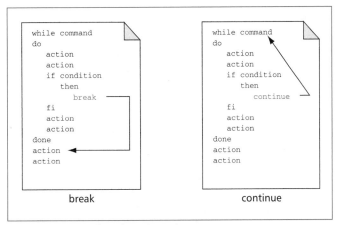

FIGURE 14.21   **break** *and* **continue**

14.5 Special Parameters and Variables

The Korn shell provides both special parameters and special variables for our use. We discuss them in this section.

Special Parameters

Besides having positional parameters numbered 1 to 9, the Korn shell script can have four other special parameters: one that contains the script filename, one that contains the number of arguments entered by the user, and two that combine all other parameters. The complete list of parameters is shown in Figure 14.22.

Script Name ($0)

The script name parameter ($0) holds the name of the script. This is often useful when a script calls other scripts. The script name parameter can be passed to the called script so that it knows who called it. As another use, when a script needs to issue an error message, it can include its name as part of the message. Having the script name in the message clearly identifies which script had a problem. The program name parameter, $0, is shown in Figure 14.22.

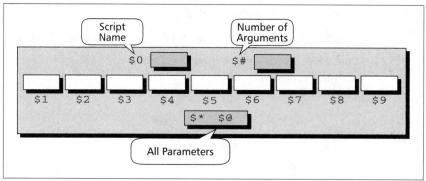

FIGURE 14.22 *Parameters in the Korn Shell*

Number of Arguments ($#)

A second special parameter holds the number of arguments passed to the script. Scripts can use this parameter, referred to as $#, programmatically in several ways. It is also shown in Figure 14.22. The script name and number of arguments are in Script 14.25.

SCRIPT 14.25   *Name and Number Arguments*

```
1  #!/bin/ksh
2  #  This script displays the $0 and $# special parameters
3  print "The program name is:" $0
4  print "Number of arguments:" $#
```
```
$ parmsNameNum.scr 1 2 3 4 5
```
```
Output:
The program name is: parmsNameNum.scr
Number of arguments: 5
```

All Parameters ($* and $@)

Two special parameters combine the nine positional parameters into one string. They can be used with or without quotes.

All Parameters without Quotes   When we use $* and $@ without quotes, they create a list of parameters. The number of elements in the list is the same as the number of arguments. To demonstrate the effect, let's write a simple loop that displays each parameter in turn. The script and its output are in Script 14.26.

SCRIPT 14.26   *Demonstrate All Parameters without Quotes*

```
1  #!/bin/ksh
2  #  Loops displaying parameter list one element at a time
3  for parm in $*
4  do
```

Continued

SCRIPT 14.26   *Demonstrate All Parameters without Quotes*

```
5    print $parm
6  done
```
```
$ parmLoop1.scr Anne "Don Juan" Tuan
```
```
Output:
Anne
Don
Juan
Tuan
```

Script 14.26 Analysis: Study the output. Note that the quoted argument, Don Juan, is treated as two separate words even though it is quoted.

Regardless of which all parameters parameter we use, we get the same results. To prove this, rewrite the script using $@ in line 3.

All Parameters with Quotes   When the all parameters tokens are used inside quotes, their behavior is different. The quoted string token ("$*") means combine all arguments into *one single string*. When used as a list, the list has only one member— a string containing all arguments. On the other hand, the quoted list token ("$@") creates a string list in which each argument is a separate string. The difference between the two is presented in Figure 14.23.

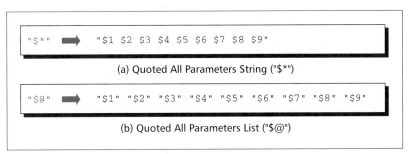

FIGURE 14.23   *Quoted All Parameters*

To further demonstrate the differences, let's write a script that takes a set of arguments and processes them first as a single string ($*) and then as a string list ($@). The script and its output are in Script 14.27.

SCRIPT 14.27   *String and List Special Parameters*

```
1  #!/bin/ksh
2  #  Demonstrate difference between $* and $@ special parameters
3
4  print "The program name is:" $0
5  print "Number of arguments:" $# "\n"
6
7  print 'Display arguments as a single string ($*): '
```
Continued

SCRIPT 14.27   *String and List Special Parameters—Continued*

```
 8  i=0
 9  for x in "$*"
10  do
11     (( i = i + 1 ))
12       print "Loop" i "is:" "$x"
13  done
14  print "At end of string loop: i is:" $i "\n"
15
16  print 'Display arguments as a list ($@): '
17  i=0
18  for x in "$@"
19  do
20     (( i = i + 1 ))
21       print "Loop" $i "is:" "$x"
22  done
23  print "At end of list loop: i is:" $i
```

```
$ parmLoop2.scr One Two "Buckle my shoe"
```

```
Output:
The program name is: parmLoop2.scr
Number of arguments: 3

Display arguments as a single string ($*):
Loop 1 is: One Two Buckle my shoe
At end of string loop: i is: 1

Display arguments as a list ($@):
Loop 1 is: One
Loop 2 is: Two
Loop 3 is: Buckle my shoe
At end of list loop: i is: 3
```

Script 14.27 Analysis: In Script 14.26, we noted that when the quoted argument was processed, the quotes were ignored; the quoted contents were treated as multiple arguments. In Script 14.27, we see the desired effect: The quoted argument is treated as one argument.

Special Variables

Internal Field Separator (IFS)

The internal field separator (IFS) variable holds the tokens used by the shell commands to parse a string into substrings such as words. The default tokens are the three whitespace tokens: the space, tab, and newline.

One common use of the internal field separators parses a **read** string into separate words (Script 14.28). It receives a login id as an argument and then searches the password file (/etc/passwd) for the matching id. When it finds it, it prints the login id and the user name.

Special Parameter and Variable Summary

The special variables are summarized in Table 14.8.

SCRIPT 14.28 *Demonstrate Use of Internal Field Separator (**IFS**)*

```
 1 #!/bin/ksh
 2 #  Script: IFS.scr
 3 #  Demonstrate IFS codes by printing search results.
 4 #  First argument is login id to be located
 5
 6 IFS=:                      # Set IFS for passwd
 7
 8 #  Read and process one line at a time. sk1 etc skip fields
 9 #  Find and print login ID and user name
10 while read id sk1 sk2 sk3 user sk4
11 do
12    if [[ $id = $1 ]]
13       then
14          print $id belongs to $user
15          exit 0
16    fi
17 done </etc/passwd             # redirect input
18
19 print $1 not found
20 exit 1
```

```
Execution:
$ IFS.scr gilberg
gilberg belongs to Richard F Gilberg
$ print $?
0
```

```
$ IFS.scr gilbert
gilbert not found
$ print $?
1
```

TABLE 14.8 *Special Parameter and Variable Summary*

Parameter or Variable	Description
$#	Number of arguments to a script
$0	Script name
$*	All parameters
$@	All parameters
$?	Exit status variable
IFS	Internal field separator

14.6 Changing Positional Parameters

The positional parameters can be changed within a script only by using the **set** command; values cannot be directly assigned to them. This means that to assign values to the script positional parameters, we must use **set.** The **set** command parses an input string and places each separate part of the string into a different positional parameter (up to nine). If the internal field separator (IFS, see page 588) is set to the default, **set** parses to words. We can set the IFS to any desired token and use **set** to parse the data accordingly.

Let's write a script to demonstrate how **set** can be used to store data in the positional parameters. The first part of the script stores one string containing two digits (note the quotes). Because there is only one string, it is stored in $1 as demonstrated by the **print** commands. We then store two numbers. Because we don't use quotes in the second example, each digit is assigned to a different positional parameter (Script 14.29).

SCRIPT 14.29   *Parse Strings Using the* **set** *Command*

```
 1 #!/bin/ksh
 2 #  Script: set.scr
 3 #  This script demonstrates the set command.
 4
 5 # Only one string: stored in $1
 6 print '$1 contains' $1
 7 print '$2 contains' $2 '\n'
 8
 9 set "1 2"
10 print After set there are $# parameters.
11 print '$1 contains:' $1
12 print '$2 contains:' $2
13 print
14
15 # Two strings: stored in $1-$2
16 set 1 2
17 print After set there are $# parameters.
18 print '$1 contains:' $1
19 print '$2 contains:' $2
20 print '$3 contains:' $3
```

```
$ set.scr Hello Dolly
```

```
Output:
$1 contains Hello
$2 contains Dolly

After set there are 1 parameters.
$1 contains: 1 2
$2 contains:

After set there are 2 parameters.
$1 contains: 1
$2 contains: 2
$3 contains:
```

Script 14.29 Analysis: We execute the script with two arguments and display them in the first command. Then, in line 9, we use the **set** command to assign the string "1 2" to $1. Because we quote 1 and 2, they form one string and are stored completely in $1. We verify this by displaying $1 and $2. Also note that the **set** command clears $2. Then, in line 16, we use the **set** command again, this time without quotes. This time, the 1 is placed in $1 and the 2 in $2. We verify the results by displaying $1 and $2.

As a more practical example, if you need to save the date to print a report, you can use **set** to assign the output from the **date** command to the positional parameters so that the date is available for printing. This concept is demonstrated in Script 14.30.

SCRIPT 14.30 *Saving Date for Future Using the* **set** *Command*

```
 1 #!/bin/ksh
 2 #  Script: getDate.scr
 3 set $(date)         # assigns date fields to parameters 1..6
 4                     # $1: alpha day (ddd)  $2: alpha month (mmm)
 5                     # $3: day of month     $4: time (hh:mm:ss)
 6                     # $5: time zone        $6: year (yyyy)
 7 print "Complete date is:" $*
 8 print
 9 today="$2 $3, $6"
10 print "Today's date is :" $today
```
```
$ getDate.scr
```
```
Output:
Complete date is: Thu Jun 16 21:31:09 PDT 2001

Today's date is : Jun 16, 2001
```

Script 14.30 Analysis: To convert the output from the **date** command to a string so that we can store it, we use command substitution (line 3). To display the output from the **date** command, we used the $* special processing parameter. If there were other parameters that we didn't want to display, we could have used the individual parameters for the date ($1...$6). Finally, note how we used comments to document the date format in each of the parameters. Next time we return to the script, we will not have to figure out the date format. It's all there in the documentation comments.

shift Command

One very useful command in shell scripting is the **shift** command. The shift command moves the values in the parameters toward the beginning of the parameter list. To understand the **shift** command, think of the parameters as a list rather than as individual variables. When we shift, we move each parameter to the left in the list. If we shift three positions, therefore, the fourth parameter will be in the first position, the fifth will be in the second position, and so forth until all parameters have been moved three positions to the left. The parameters at the end of the set become null. Note that while the special parameters do not participate in the shifting, their contents change as the shifting takes place. If **shift** does not have a parameter, it assumes **shift** 1. The **shift** operation is shown in Figure 14.24.

Recall that only the first nine parameters can be referenced by name ($1...$9). To process the rest of the parameters, we must use the **shift** command. Script 14.31 demonstrates the **shift** operator by using **shift** in a loop that prints only the first parameter ($1).

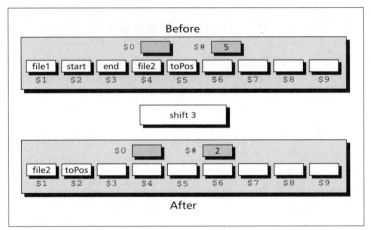

FIGURE 14.24 **shift** *Command*

Note that we use the number of parameters ($#) as the control for the loop. This also verifies that shifting reduces the parameter count by 1 for each parameter shifted out of the set.

SCRIPT 14.31 *Shift and Print All Parameters*

```
 1 #!/bin/ksh
 2 # Shift and print all parameters
 3 #
 4 print "There are" $# "parameters\n"
 5
 6 count=0
 7 while (( $# > 0 ))
 8 do
 9   (( count = count + 1 ))
10   print "$1 \c"
11   shift
12 done
13 print "\n"
14 print "There are now" $# "parameters"
15 print "End of script"
```

```
$ shiftAll.scr 1 2 3 4 5 6 7 8 9 10 11 12 13 14 15
```

```
Output:
There are 15 parameters

1 2 3 4 5 6 7 8 9 10 11 12 13 14 15

There are now 0 parameters
End of script
```

14.7 Argument Validation

Good programs are designed to be fail-safe. This means that anything that can be validated should be confirmed before it is used. In this section, we discuss techniques used to validate user-supplied arguments.

Number of Arguments Validation

The first code in a script that contains parameters should validate the number of arguments. Some scripts use a fixed number of arguments; other scripts use a variable number of arguments. Even when the number of arguments is variable, there is usually a minimum number that is required. Both fixed- and variable-numbered arguments are validated by using the number of arguments parameter ($#).

Fixed Number of Arguments

If the shell script expects a fixed number of arguments, we can easily make sure they are all there by checking the count parameter ($#). This script is in Script 14.32. Note that we test it twice, once with the correct number of arguments and once with too many arguments. To complete the testing, it should be run with no arguments and fewer than the correct number of arguments.

SCRIPT 14.32 *Validate Number of Parameters*

```
 1 #!/bin/ksh
 2 #  Script: arguFixed.scr
 3 #  Validate Number of Parameters
 4
 5 if (( $# != 3 ))
 6    then
 7       print "This script requires 3 arguments--not" $#"."
 8       print "Usage: arguFixed.scr argu1 argu2 argu3"
 9       exit 1
10    fi
11 print "Correct number of parameters"
12 # Rest of script follows here
```

```
Execution:
$ arguFixed.scr 1 2 3 4
This script requires 3 arguments--not 4.
Usage: arguFixed.scr argu1 argu2 argu3
```

```
$ arguFixed.scr 1 2 3
Correct number of parameters
```

Minimum Number of Arguments

When a script expects a variable number of arguments and there is a minimum number required, we should verify that the minimum number have been entered. This validation concept is in Script 14.33.

SCRIPT 14.33 *Validation for One or More Parameters*

```
 1  #!/bin/ksh
 2  #  Script: arguVar.scr
 3  #  Validate Minimum Number of Parameters
 4
 5  if (( $# < 1 ))
 6     then
 7        print "This script requires 1 or more arguments."
 8        print "Usage: arguVar.scr argu1 [argu2 ...arguN]"
 9        exit 1
10     fi
11  print $# "arguments received."
12  # Rest of script follows here
```

```
Execution:
$ arguVar.scr
This script requires 1 or more arguments.
Usage: arguVar.scr argu1 [argu2...arguN]
```

```
$ arguVar.scr one two three
3 arguments received.
```

Type of Argument Validation

After the exact or minimum number of arguments is validated, the script should verify that each argument's type is correct. While all arguments are passed as strings, the string contents can be a number, a filename, or any other verifiable type.

Numeric Validation

The value of numeric parameters is virtually unlimited; some scripts simply need a number. Scripts that extract a range of lines from a file are of this nature. Other scripts may require that the number be in a range; scripts that receive a date may require this type of validation. Let's write a script that uses both of these types of numeric validation. We first validate that an argument is numeric by using the **let** command to add to it. If we can successfully add to an argument, then it is numeric. Once we verify that the argument is numeric, we test to make sure that it is in the range 1 to 12. Both of these validations are in Script 14.34.

SCRIPT 14.34 *Validate Range*

```
 1  #!/bin/ksh
 2  #  Script: arguMonth.scr
 3  #  This script verifies that the first parameter is numeric and
 4  #  the second parameter is a month (1...12).
 5
 6  #  Test parameter 1 by adding. All output to trash
 7  let x=$1+1 2> /dev/null
 8  if [[ $? != 0 ]]                # if exit status is false
 9  then
```

Continued

SCRIPT 14.34 *Validate Range*

```
10      print $1 is not numeric
11      exit 1                      # exit command kills script
12  fi
13
14  # Test parameter 2 in range.
15  if (( $2 < 1 ))
16  then
17      print "Month $2 is less than 1: must be <1...12>"
18      exit 2                      # exit command kills script
19  fi
20
21  if (( $2 > 12 ))
22  then
23      print "Month $2 is greater than 12: must be <1...12>"
24      exit 3                      # exit command kills script
25  fi
26  # Rest of script follows here
```

```
Execution:
$ arguMonth.scr 2002 5

$ arguMonth.scr 2002 0
Month 0 is less than 1: must be <1...12>

$ arguMonth.scr 2002 13
Month 13 is greater than 12: must be <1...12>
```

File Type Validation

If an argument is an input file, we can verify that the file exists and that it has read permission. If the file is an output file, there is no need to verify it because UNIX will create it if it doesn't exist. Script 14.35 demonstrates how first to verify that a file exists and then to verify that it is readable.

SCRIPT 14.35 *Validate Input File*

```
 1  #!/bin/ksh
 2  #   Script: arguFile.scr
 3  #   Verify that a $1 is a valid input file.
 4  if [[ ! -s "$1" ]]
 5  then
 6      print "$1 does not exist or is empty"
 7      exit 1
 8  fi
 9
10  if [[ ! -r "$1" ]]
11  then
12      print "You do not have read permission for $1"
13      exit 2
14  fi
```

Continued

SCRIPT 14.35 *Validate Input File—Continued*

```
15  # Rest of script goes here

    $ arguFile.scr file1

    Output:
    $ arguFile.scr noFile
    noFile does not exist or is empty

    $ arguFile.scr agruNoPermFile
    You do not have read permission for noPermFile

    $ arguFile.scr file1
    $
```

Other Validations

Based on the script requirements, we may need to perform other validations. For
example, a script may require that the first argument be larger than the second argument. Script 14.36 demonstrates a script that serves as a model for these types of
requirements.

SCRIPT 14.36 *Validate Parameter Values*

```
 1  #!/bin/ksh
 2  #  Script:  argValOther.scr
 3  #  Validate Three Parameters -- File Num1 Num2 (Num1 < Num2)
 4
 5  if [[ $# != 3 ]]
 6     then
 7       print "This script requires three arguments."
 8       print "Usage: argValOther.scr file num1 num2 [num1 < num2]"
 9       exit 1
10     fi
11  if [[ ! -f "$1" ]]
12     then
13        print "Invalid file name."
14        print "Usage: argValOther.scr file num1 num2 [num1 < num2]"
15        exit 2
16     fi
17  if (( $2 >= $3 ))
18     then
19       print $2 "not less than" $3
20       print "Usage: argValOther.scr file num1 num2 [num1 < num2]"
21       exit 3
22     fi
23  # Rest of script follows here
```

```
    Execution:
    $ argValOther.scr nofilehere
    This script requires three arguments.
    Usage: argValOther.scr file num1 num2 [num1 < num2]

    $ argValOther.scr nofilehere 1 6
```

Continued

SCRIPT 14.36 *Validate Parameter Values*

```
    Invalid file name.
    Usage: argValOther.scr file num1 num2 [num1 < num2]
    $ argValOther.scr TheRaven 6 1
    6 not less than 1
    Usage: argValOther.scr file num1 num2 [num1 < num2]
```

14.8 Debugging Scripts

Whenever we write a script, we must test it. Often multiple tests are necessary. Sometimes the tests don't deliver the expected results. In these cases, we need to debug the script. There are two Korn shell options that we can use to help debug scripts: the verbosity (verbose) option and the execute trace (xtrace) option.

The verbose option prints each statement that is syntactically correct and displays an error message if it is wrong. Script output, if any, is generated.

The xtrace option prints each command, preceded by a plus (+) sign, before it is executed. It also replaces the value of each variable accessed in the statement. For example, in the statement y=$x, the $x is replaced with the actual variable value at the time the statement is executed. If the variable x contained 13, the display would be y=13. In a similar manner, expression values and test values are displayed. Combining the two options allows us to see the command first and then see it with a plus sign and all references to variables replaced by their values.

We can use these debug commands in two ways: include the options in the script and call the script with them.

Debug Options Included in the Script

Options are included in the script by using the **set** command. This method is demonstrated in Script 14.37.

SCRIPT 14.37 **verbose** *Debug Option*

```
 1 #!/bin/ksh
 2 #   Script: debugSetOptV.scr
 3 #   Demonstrate debug options set in script
 4
 5 set -o verbose
 6
 7 x=5
 8 (( y = x + 2 ))
 9
10 if (( y == 10 ))
11 then
12     print \$y contains 10
13 else
14     print \$y contains $y not 10
15 fi
16
```

Continued

SCRIPT 14.37 **verbose** *Debug Option—Continued*

```
17  while (( x != 0 ))
18  do
19      print Counting down: \$x is $x
20      (( x = x - 1 ))
21  done
```

```
$ debugSetOptV.scr
```

```
Output:
x=5
(( y = x + 2 ))

if (( y == 10 ))
then
    print \$y contains 10
else
    print \$y contains $y not 10
fi
$y contains 7 not 10

while (( x != 0 ))
do
    print Counting down: \$x is $x
    (( x = x - 1 ))
done
Counting down: $x is 5
Counting down: $x is 4
Counting down: $x is 3
Counting down: $x is 2
Counting down: $x is 1
```

Script 14.37 Analysis: This script is rather straightforward. In the output section, we have used black text for the displayed commands and color for the script output.

Note how we had to code the variable name to display it in the output. If we just used $x, we would have displayed the value. To display the variable name, we put a backslash before the dollar sign.

Debug Options on the Command Line

When the debug option is included in the script, we must edit it to remove the **set** command when we complete the debug sessions. We can avoid this extra step if we include the options on the command line. This requires that we invoke the Korn shell in the command as in Script 14.38. It is the same as Script 14.37 with the **set** option removed.

SCRIPT 14.38 *Execute* **xtrace** *Debug Option*

```
1  #!/bin/ksh
2  #  Script: debugOptions.scr
```

Continued

SCRIPT 14.38 *Execute **xtrace** Debug Option*

```
 3 | #  Script to demonstrate debug options
 4 |
 5 | x=5
 6 | (( y = x + 2 ))
 7 |
 8 | if (( y == 10 ))
 9 | then
10 |    print \$y contains 10
11 | else
12 |    print \$y contains $y not 10
13 | fi
14 |
15 | while (( x != 0 ))
16 | do
17 |    print Counting down: \$x is $x
18 |    (( x = x - 1 ))
19 | done
```

```
$ ksh -o xtrace debugOptions.scr
```

```
Output:
+ x=5
+ (( y = x + 2 ))
+ (( y == 10 ))
+ print $y contains 7 not 10
$y contains 7 not 10
+ (( x != 0 ))
+ print Counting down: $x is 5
Counting down: $x is 5
+ (( x = x - 1 ))
+ (( y != 0 ))
+ print Counting down: $x is 4
Counting down: $x is 4
+ (( x = x - 1 ))
+ (( x != 0 ))
+ print Counting down: $x is 3
Counting down: $x is 3
+ (( x = x - 1 ))
+ (( x != 0 ))
+ print Counting down: $x is 2
Counting down: $x is 2
+ (( x = x - 1 ))
+ (( x != 0 ))
+ print Counting down: $x is 1
Counting down: $x is 1
+ (( x = x - 1 ))
+ (( x != 0 ))
```

Script 14.38 Analysis: Study the output carefully. The script statements, shown in black, are all prefixed with a plus (+). The script output is shown in color.

As a final example, we repeat Script 14.38, this time using both options at once. The command line and output are shown in Script 14.39. Refer to Script 14.38 for the code.

SCRIPT 14.39   *Verbose and Trace Options Combined*

```
$ ksh -o xtrace -o verbose debugOptions.scr
Output:
x=5
+ x=5
(( y = x + 2 ))
+ (( y = x + 2 ))

if (( y == 10 ))
then
    print \$y contains 10
else
    print \$y contains $y not 10
fi
+ (( y == 10 ))
+ print $y contains 7 not 10
$y contains 7 not 10

while (( x != 0 ))
do
    print counting down: \$x is $x
    (( x = x -1 ))
done
+ (( x != 0 ))
+ print counting down: $x is 5
counting down: $x is 5
+ (( x = x -1 ))
+ (( x != 0 ))
+ print counting down: $x is 4
counting down: $x is 4
+ (( x = x -1 ))
+ (( x != 0 ))
+ print counting down: $x is 3
counting down: $x is 3
+ (( x = x -1 ))
+ (( x != 0 ))
+ print counting down: $x is 2
counting down: $x is 2
+ (( x = x -1 ))
+ (( x != 0 ))
+ print counting down: $x is 1
counting down: $x is 1
+ (( x = x -1 ))
+ (( x != 0 ))
```

Script 14.39 Analysis: Because both options are used, each statement is shown twice. The **xtrace** output lines start with a plus (+). The **verbose** lines are shown exactly as coded in the script; the **xtrace** lines are reformatted using the expression format and values rather than variable names.

14.9 Script Examples

In this section, we demonstrate some complete scripts applications. The applications were chosen to demonstrate different techniques we learned in the chapter. Each script begins with a set of documentation that we recommend for production scripts. (We have been using an abbreviated form of it in the scripts developed throughout the chapter.) This documentation includes the author's name, date, a synopsis of the script that is similar to the UNIX manual synopsis, a description of the code approach, and an explanation of the exit value. When the script is modified, we also recommend that you add the date and description of the modification after the original description.

Cat

The first script, `newCat.scr`, is a very simple version of the **cat** command. One point to study in this and the following script is the extensive argument validation. Production scripts must be as "bulletproof" as possible. A good script programmer tries to anticipate all possible errors a user could make and then guard against them.

SCRIPT 14.40   *Cat File Script*

```
 1 #!/bin/ksh
 2 #NAME:          newCat.scr
 3 #TASK:          Concatenate files in sequence
 4 #AUTHOR:
 5 #DATE WRITTEN:
 6 #SYNOPSIS:      newCat.scr file1 file2...
 7 #DESCRIPTION:   Reads files line by line and displays them
 8 #EXIT VALUE
 9 #              0       if successfully completed
10 #              1       if zero numbers of arguments
11 #              2       if one or more files do not exist
12 # =========================================================
13 print "\c" > errFile
14 exitStatus=0
15 if (( $# == 0 ))
16 then
17     print "At least one argument is needed" >> errFile
18     print "Usage: newCat.scr file1 [file2 ... fileN]" >> errFile
19     exitStatus=1
20 fi
21 for x in $*
22 do
23     if [[ ! -r "$1" ]]
24     then
25         print "Cannot read file $1" >> errFile
26         exitStatus=2
```

Continued

SCRIPT 14.40   *Cat File Script—Continued*

```
27      else
28          while read LINE
29          do
30              print "$LINE"
31          done < "$1"
32      fi
33      shift
34  done
35  while read errMsg
36  do
37      print "$errMsg"
38  done < errFile
39  exit $exitStatus
```

```
$ newCat.scr
At least one argument is needed
Usage: newCat.scr file1 [file2 ... fileN]
$ print $?
1
```

```
$ newCat.scr nofile
Cannot read file nofile
$ print $?
2
```

```
$ newCat.scr file1 file2
********************
**                **
** This is file1 **
**                **
********************
********************
**                **
** This is file2 **
**                **
********************
$ print $?
0
```

Script 14.40 Analysis: There is one new concept in this script. Because we are writing text to the monitor, we need to save any error messages that we encounter and then write them after all files have been displayed (see lines 13 and 17). We do this with a temporary file. We create the error file by initializing it to null by using just a cancellation character in line 13. This is necessary because we will append any errors to it. If it is not initialized, and if no error messages are written, the file will not be created. If the file does not exist, we will get an error message at the end of the job when we try to read it.

Production scripts require extensive error testing. As we write the script, we try to anticipate all possible errors. We then need to test them when the script is done. Although there are only two error conditions, you should run at least five tests. We have run the three obvious ones in Script 14.40. Because these scripts get rather long, we usually don't demonstrate all test cases. We recommend that you run a test with only one file, with one valid file and a nonexistent file, and with two good files and a nonexistent file between them.

Copy

In Script 14.41, we simulate the **copy** command. We begin by validating that we have the correct number of parameters and then that the input file exists and the output file doesn't. It would be a good idea to modify the script and ask the user if the output file should be overwritten. We leave this change for an exercise. After ensuring that everything is okay, we simply cat the input file and redirect it to the output file.

SCRIPT 14.41 *Copy Script File*

```
 1 #!/bin/ksh
 2 #NAME: newCopy.scr
 3 #TASK: Copy a file into another
 4 #AUTHOR:
 5 #DATE WRITTEN:
 6 #SYNOPSIS:     newCopy.scr file1 file2
 7 #DESCRIPTION: Copies files using the cat command
 8 #EXIT VALUE
 9 #          0       if successfully completed
10 #          1       if wrong number of arguments
11 #          2       if the source file does not exist
12 #          3       if the destination file already exists
13 # =======================================================
14 if (( $# != 2 ))
15     then
16         print "Requires two file arguments"
17         print "Usage: newCopy.scr from_file to_file"
18         exit 1
19 fi
20
21 if [[ ! -r $1 ]]
22     then
23         print "The first file cannot be read"
24         exit 2
25 fi
26
27 if [[ -f $2 ]]
28     then
29         print "The second file already exists"
30         exit 3
31 fi
32
   cat $1 > $2
```

```
$ newCopy.scr
Requires two file arguments
```

Continued

SCRIPT 14.41 *Copy Script File—Continued*

```
       Usage: newCopy.scr from_file to_file
       $ print $?
       1
       $ newCopy.scr noFile file1.bak
       The first file cannot be read
       $ print $?
       2
       $ newCopy.scr file1 file1.bak
       $ print $?
       0
       $ cat file1.bak
       ********************
       **                **
       ** This is file1 **
       **                **
       ********************
       $ newCopy.scr file1 file1.bak
       The second file already exists
       $ print $?
       3
```

Script 14.41 Analysis: Script 14.41 requires even more testing than Script 14.40. As you study the script and before you look at the test results, write a margin note for every situation that needs to be tested. Don't forget to look for combinations of errors. When you think you have discovered all the required test cases, compare your list with test results at the end of Script 14.41.

14.10 Key Terms

argument
argument validation
array
break statement
case statement
command
command-controlled loop
comment
compiler
continue command
debugging
executable script
exit command
expr command
expression
file expression
file operator

`for-in` statement
`if-then-else` statement
interpreter
interpreter designator line
Korn shell
let command
list-controlled loop
logical expression
logical operator
loop
loop piping
loop redirection
mathematical expression
mathematical operator
multiway selection
nested `if-then-else`
null command

operand
operator
parameter
positional parameter
relational expression
relational operator
repetition
`select` statement
set command
shell script
shift command
special parameter
special variables
test command
two-way selection
`until` statement
`while` statement

14.11 Tips

1. The interpreter designator line, such as #!/bin/ksh, must be the first line of a script.
2. Use the **chmod** command to make a script executable before executing it.
3. The Korn shell contains only nine accessible positional parameters.
4. Use the **let** command to evaluate a mathematical expression.
5. Only integral values can be used with the **let** command.
6. There is a difference between the divide (/) and modulus (%) operators. Divide calculates the quotient of a division; modulus calculates the remainder of a division.
7. The relational operators are different for integers and strings.
8. There are only two relational operators for strings: equal (=) and not equal (!=). The other relational operators (greater than, less than, and so on) must be simulated in a script.
9. In the Korn shell, the test command is replaced by two operators: ((...)) and [[...]].
10. The else clause of if-then-else can be eliminated, but the then clause cannot. Use the null command instead when the then is empty.
11. Wildcards, not regular expressions, can be used as part of the patterns in a case command.
12. A double semicolon (;;) is needed to terminate each section of a case command.
13. The while and the until loops need a command for their test expression.
14. The for-in and select loops need a list for their test expression.
15. The while, until, and for-in loops can be executed in the background by placing an ampersand (&) at the end of **done.** The select loop cannot be executed in the background.
16. Only while and until loops can use input redirection; the for-in and select loops cannot. Only the select loop does not allow output redirection.
17. Only while and until loops can use input piping; the for-in and select loops cannot. Only the select loop does not allow output piping.
18. Use the select loop only when you need to create and process menus.
19. There is a very big difference between $* and $@ special parameters when enclosed in double quotes. The first one creates one string; the second one creates a list of strings.
20. Wherever possible, validate arguments to your scripts. Validation should check the numbers to ensure that they are digits, types, ranges, and so forth.
21. Use the verbose and xtrace options to debug your script when testing does not generate the desired result.

14.12 Commands

The following commands were discussed in this chapter. For more details, see Appendix F and the corresponding pages shown in the following table.

Command	Description	Options	Page
`: (colon)`	*Synopsis:* *(Null Command)* Does nothing (a placeholder). The exit status is always true.		566
`break`	*Synopsis:* *break* Forces a loop to terminate.		585

`case`	*Synopsis:* *case string in*
	      pat) command (s);;
	      pat) command (s);;
	      ...
	      esac
	Creates a multiway selection.
			568

`continue`	*Synopsis:* *continue* Continues with the next iteration of the loop.		585
`exit`	*Synopsis:* *exit [status]* Sets the exit status and terminates the shell.		553
`expr`	*Synopsis:* *expr arguments* Evaluates a mathematical expression or manipulates a string.		557

`for-in`	*Synopsis:* *for variable in list*
	    do
	      body
	    done
	Executes loop body as long as there are items in the list.
			575

`if-then-else`	*Synopsis:* *if command*
	    then
	      ...
	    else
	      ...
	    fi
	Creates a two-way selection.
			562

`let`	*Synopsis:* *let variable=mathematical expression* Evaluates a mathematical expression.		557
`set`	*Synopsis:* *set expression* Sets the positional parameters.		589

`select`	*Synopsis:* *select variable in list*
	    do
	      ...
	    done
	Creates a menu environment.
			577

`shift`	*Synopsis:* *shift expression* Shifts the parameters to the left.		591
`test`	*Synopsis:* *test arguments* Evaluates a relational, logical, or file expression.		561

Command	Description	Options	Page
`until`	***Synopsis:*** *until command* *do* *body* *done* Repeats the body until the command is successful (exit status 0).		573
`while`	***Synopsis:*** *while command* *do* *body* *done* Repeats the body while the command is successful (exit status 0).		571

14.13 Summary

- A shell script is a text file that contains executable commands.
- We use a text editor, such as **vi,** to create the script.
- The script must be made executable (using the **chmod** command) before it can be executed.
- The first line of the script defines the path for the shell interpreter that reads and interprets the shell line by line.
- Arguments are user-supplied data that follow the script name on the command line and are input to the script.
- Positional parameters are predefined variables in the script. They are called $1, $2, $3, . . . , $9.
- The positional parameters receive their values from the command-line arguments.
- An expression is a sequence of operators and operands that reduces to a single value. The Korn shell supports four types of expressions: mathematical, relational, file, and logical.
- A mathematical expression uses integer operands and mathematical operators (+, −, *, /, and %) to create a value. The **let** command is used for mathematical expressions.
- A relational expression uses mathematical expressions and relational operators to create a true–false value. The test (**test**) command, the parenthetical operator, or the bracket operator is used to evaluate a relational expression.
- A file expression is used to test the status of a file. The **test** command or the bracket operator is used to evaluate a file expression.
- A logical expression is used to combine two relational expressions or to complement a relational expression. The **test** command or the bracket operator is used to evaluate a logical expression.
- The Korn shell has two different statements that allow us to select between two or more commands: `if-then-else` and `case`.
- The `if-then-else` statement uses the exit status of a command to make a decision. The exit status can be set by a **test** command, the parenthetical operator, or the bracket operator.

- The if-then-else statement can be used without the else clause but not without the then clause. In the latter case, a null command (a colon) is used to indicate that no action is to be taken when the exit status is 0.
- The case statement uses a string and patterns to make a decision about one of several choices. We can use wildcards in the patterns, but not regular expressions.
- The real power of computers is their ability to repeat an operation or a series of operations many times. The Korn shell supports four loop constructs: while, until, for-in, and select. The while and until loops are command-controlled loops; the for-in and select are list-controlled loops.
- The while loop is a basic command-controlled loop. It loops as long as the exit status of the testing command is zero.
- The until loop works just like the while loop, except that it loops as long as the exit status of command is not zero.
- The for-in command is a list-controlled command. The number of elements in the test list controls the number of iterations.
- The select statement is a list-controlled loop. It is used to create and process menus.
- All loops except the select can be executed in the background.
- We can use input redirection with while and until loops but not with the for-in or select loop. We can use output redirection with while, until, and for-in but not with the select loop.
- We can use input piping with while and until loops but not with the for-in or select loop. We can use output piping with while, until, and for-in but not with the select loop.
- The Korn shell uses five special parameters: $#, $0, $*, $@, and $?. It uses one special variable called IFS (input field separator).
- We can change the values of positional parameters using the **shift** command.
- Argument validation is necessary to make a script more robust. We should include several argument validations in our scripts: number of arguments, type of arguments, range of argument values, and so forth.
- To debug scripts, we use two Korn shell options: verbose and xtrace. The debugging options can be inserted in a script or applied at the command line when calling the script.

14.14 Practice Set

Review Questions

1. Can we use a goto statement in Korn shell?
2. Can a while loop be executed infinitely? Show an example.
3. Can an until loop be executed infinitely? Show an example.
4. Can a for-in loop be executed infinitely? Show an example.

5. Write each of the following expressions in the Korn shell:
   a. `3 + 4`
   b. `x * 14`
   c. `4 / x`
   d. `x % 5`

6. Write each of the following expressions in the Korn shell:
   a. `(3 + 4) * 8`
   b. `(x * 14) / y`
   c. `z = t * (4 / x) + 6`
   d. `x = x + y + z`

7. Write each of the following relational expressions in the Korn shell:
   a. `x > 9`
   b. `x < = y`
   c. `x != y`
   d. `x = = y`

8. Write each of the following logical expressions in the Korn shell:
   a. `(x == 5) && (y > 10)`
   b. `(x < = y) || (y > 10)`
   c. `(x != y) || (x > 7) && (y <= x)`
   d. `(x = = y) || (x > 5) || (y > 6)`

9. Write each of the following file expressions in the Korn shell:
   a. file1 is empty
   b. file2 is not readable

10. What is the exit status of each of the following commands?
    a. `(( 0 ))`
    b. `(( 5 ))`
    c. `(( -5 ))`
    d. `(( ))`

11. Show how to repeat a command 10 times using each of the following loops (if possible):
    a. a `while` loop
    b. an `until` loop
    c. a `for-in` loop
    d. a `select` loop

12. Devise a way to repeat a command 100 times using a `for-in` loop. What about 1000 times? Hint: One way is to use nested loops.

Exercises

13. If originally x=13 and y=5, what is the value of x and y after each of the following expressions (each expression is independent)?
    a. `(( x = x%2 ))`
    b. `(( x = x + 4 ))`
    c. `(( x = x * 3 ))`
    d. `(( x = x / y ))`

14. If originally x=13 and y=5.5, what is the value of x and y after each of the following expressions (each expression is independent)?
    a. `(( x / 2 ))`
    b. `(( x + y ))`
    c. `(( x * 4 ))`
    d. `(( x + 1.5 ))`

15. If originally x=13 and y=6, what is the value of each of the following expressions (each expression is independent)?
    a. `(( x < 12 ))`
    b. `(( y > 7 ))`
    c. `(( x < y ))`
    d. `(( y == x ))`

16. If originally x=13 and y=6, what is the value of each of the following expressions (each expression is independent)?
    a. `[[ $x < 12 && $y > 7 ]]`
    b. `[[ $y > 7 || $x < $x ]]`
    c. `[[ ! $y < 7 ] ]`
    d. `[[ !$x > 8 && !$x < 9 ]]`

17. What would be printed from the following loop?

```
while (( 10 ))
do
    print hello
done
```

18. What would be printed from the following loop?

```
while(( 0 ))
do
    print hello
done
```

19. What would be printed from the following loop?

```
while (( -10 ))
do
    print hello
done
```

20. What would be printed from the following loop?

```
while (( ))
do
    print hello
done
```

21. What would be printed from the following script segment? Explain why.

```
x=12

while (( x > 7 ))

  do

        print $x

done
```

22. What would be printed from the following script segment? Explain why.

```
x=12
while (( x > 7 ))
do
    print $x
    (( x = x - 1 ))
done
```

23. What would be printed from each of the following two loops? What is the difference?

    a.
```
while date
do
    print Hello
done
```
    b.
```
while $(date)
do
    print Hello
done
```

24. What would be printed from the following script segment? Explain why.

```
x=12
until (( x > 7 ))
```

```
do
    print $x
    (( x = x - 1 ))
done
```

25. What would be printed from the following script segment? Explain why.

```
for i in 12 11 10 8 7
do
    print $i
done
```

26. What would be printed from the following script segment? Explain why.

```
x="1 3 5"
for i in $x
do
    print Hello
done
```

27. What would be printed from the following script segment? Explain why.

```
x="1 3 5"
y="2 4 6 8"
for i in $x $y
do
    print Hello
done
```

28. What would be printed from the following script segment? Explain why.

```
x="This is a test"
for i in $x
do
    print Hello
done
```

29. What would be printed from the following script segment? Does it show the number of people who have logged in? Why or why not?

```
x=0
for i in $(who)
do
    (( x = x + 1 ))
    print $x
done
```

30. What would be printed from each of the following loops? What is the difference?

a.
```
for i in date
do
    print Hello
done
```

b.
```
for i in $(date)
do
    print Hello
done
```

31. What would be printed from the following script segment? Explain why.

```
for i in $(date)
do
    print $i
done | head -3
```

32. What would be printed from each of the following script segments if `file1` has 10 lines with each line containing only one word? What would be printed from each code if `file1` has 10 lines with each line containing three words?

    a.
    ```
    while read x
    do
            print $x
    done < file1
    ```

    b.
    ```
    while read x y z
    do
            print $x $y $z
    done < file1
    ```

33. What would be printed from the following script segment? Explain why.
    ```
    for i in 1 2 3 4 5
    do
            for j in 1 2 3 4 5
            do
                print -n $j
            done
            print
    done
    ```

34. What would be printed from the following script segment? Explain why.
    ```
    for i in 1 2 3 4 5 6 7 8 9 10
    do
            print $i
            (( i = i + 1 ))
    done
    ```

35. What would be printed from the following script segment? Explain why.
    ```
    for i in 1 2 3 4 5 6 7 8 9 10
    do
            (( i = i + 1 ))
            print $i
    done
    ```

36. What would be printed from the following script segment? Explain why.
    ```
    for i in 1 2 3 4 5 6 7 8 9
    do
            j=1
            while (( j <= i ))
                do
                    print -n $j
                    (( j = j + 1 ))
                done
            print
    done
    ```

37. What would be printed from the following script segment? Explain why.
    ```
    for j in 1 2 3 4 5 6 7 8 9
    do
            (( j = j * 2 ))
            (( j = j - 1 ))
            print $j
    done
    ```

38. What would be printed from the following script segment? Explain why.

```
for j in 1 2 3 4 5 6 7 8 9
do
    (( j = j * 2 ))
    (( j = j - 1 ))
    if (( j <= 9 ))
        then
    print $j
    fi
done
```

39. How do you simulate the following loop using a `for-in` loop?

```
while read line
do
    ...
done < file1
```

40. Show how you can use standard input, standard output, and standard error redirection with the `if-then-else` statement.

14.15 Lab Sessions

Each of the lab sessions in this chapter requires you to write a script, make it executable, and then execute it.

Session 1

Write a script to backup a list of files.

Preparation

1. Create a file and type in it the list of files (in your home directory) that you want to backup.
2. Create a directory in which you will store the backed-up files.

Script

- **Script Name:** `backup.scr`
- **Arguments:** A filename and a directory. The filename holds the list of the files that should be backed-up. The directory is where the backed-up files should be stored.
- **Validation:** The minimum validation requirements are:
    - Ensure that exactly two arguments are entered.
    - Check that the first argument is the name of a file that exists.
    - Check that the second argument is the name of the directory that exists.
- **Body Section:** Create backup files for all files listed in the first argument. The backup files should have the same name as the original file with the extension `.bak`. They should be copied to the directory given as the second argument.

Testing the Script

1. Test the script with no arguments.
2. Test the script with one argument.

Continued

Session I—*Continued*

3. Test the script with three arguments.
4. Test the script with two arguments in which the first one is not the name of a file.
5. Test the script with two arguments in which the second one is the name of a file rather than a directory.
6. Test the script with the name of the file and the name of the directory you created in the preparation section.

Testing the Effect of the Script

1. Check the contents of the directory to be sure that the files are copied.

Session II

Write a script that finds all soft links to a specific file.

Preparation

1. Create a file and type some junk in it.
2. Make at least five soft links to this file using completely arbitrary names.

Script

- **Script Name:** `softLinkFinder.scr`
- **Arguments:** A filename. The file for which we want to find the soft links.
- **Validation:** The minimum validation requirements are:
  - Ensure that exactly one argument is entered.
  - Check that the only argument is the name of a file and that the specified file exists.
- **Body Section:** Use the `ls -l` and **grep** commands to find all the soft links attached to `$1` positional parameter. Note that a file of type soft link is distinguished by lowercase `l`. Be sure to find the soft links to the file defined in `$1` and not other files.

Testing the Script

1. Test the script with no arguments.
2. Test the script with two arguments.
3. Test the script with one argument that is not a file.
4. Test the script with one valid argument.

Testing the Effect of the Script

1. Check to make sure all the soft links you created are included in the list of soft links.

Session III

Create a script that simulates the `ls -l` command but prints only three columns of our choice.

Continued

Preparation

None

Script

- **Script Name:** `ls.scr`
- **Arguments:** Three numeric arguments defining the column number of the `ls -l` output to be printed in the order we specify. For example, if we call the script with `ls.scr 4 2 1`, it means that we want to print columns 4, 2, and 1.
- **Validation:** The minimum validation requirements are:
  - Ensure that exactly three arguments are entered.
  - Ensure that all three arguments are numeric.
  - Ensure that each argument is less than or equal to the actual number of columns in the `ls -l` command output.
- **Body Section:** Creates a new command that shows the output of the `ls -l` command to be printed in three columns in the order we like.

Testing the Script

1. Test the script with no arguments.
2. Test the script with one argument.
3. Test the script with two arguments.
4. Test the script with three arguments, one of them nonnumeric.
5. Test the script with three arguments, two of them nonnumeric.
6. Test the script with three arguments, one of them too large.
7. Test the script with three arguments, 1 4 5.
8. Test the script with three arguments, 3 7 1.

Testing the Effect of the Script

None

Session IV

Create a script that sends the contents of a message file to everybody who has logged in.

Preparation

Create a file of a short friendly message and mention that this is a test message that should be discarded by the receiver.

Script

- **Script Name:** `message.scr`
- **Arguments:** One argument, a message file.
- **Validation:** The minimum validation requirements are:
  - Ensure that exactly one argument is entered.
  - Ensure that the argument is a readable filename.

Continued

Session IV—*Continued*

- **Body Section:** Create a script that uses **awk** to create a temporary file containing the usernames of those users who are logged into the system at this moment. Then send the message contained in the first argument to every logged-in user. Note that a user who has logged in more than once should receive only one message.

Testing the Script

1. Test the script with no arguments.
2. Test the script with two arguments.
3. Test the script with one argument that is not a readable file.
4. Test the script with one valid argument.

Testing the Effect of the Script

You should include yourself in the recipient list. Check to see if you have received the message.

Session V

Create a script that can be executed only from a specific terminal. This is done for security purposes. For example, a superuser may write scripts that can only be executed from his or her office and nowhere else.

Preparation

None

Script

- **Script Name:** `security.scr`
- **Arguments:** None
- **Validation:** The minimum validation requirement is:
  - Ensure that no argument is entered.
- **Body Section:** Create a script that prints a friendly message. However, the script can be executed only from one terminal. You can use the name of the terminal you are using when you write the script. If somebody uses the script from a terminal that is not authorized, the script is to exit immediately. Hint: Use the **tty** command to show your current terminal.

Testing the Script

1. Test the script with one argument.
2. Test the script from the right terminal.
3. Log into the system using another terminal and test the script.

Testing the Effect of the Script

None

## CHAPTER 15

Korn Shell Advanced Programming

In the previous chapter, we discussed basic Korn shell programming concepts. In this chapter, we extend those concepts. Topics include variable evaluation, string manipulation, script functions, signal processing, and other advanced concepts.

15.1 Variable Evaluation and Substitution

Variables have both a name and a value. If we consider a variable as a container that is used to store data, then when we use the variable name, we are referring to the container, not its contents. When we preface the variable name with a dollar sign, as in $var, we are referring to the contents of the container (that is, to its data). In this section, we discuss variable evaluation and a concept known as variable substitution.

Variable Evaluation

To evaluate a variable (that is, to use its contents), we have two different formats. The first, the dollar reference, has been used exclusively up to this point. The second, which we introduce here, uses braces to eliminate ambiguities. The two formats are:

```
$variable          ${variable}
```

The braced variable reference works everywhere. It is totally safe but not very convenient. We tend, therefore, to use the simpler format and use the brace format only when we need it to remove an ambiguity. As an example, consider the situation where we want to make a backup copy of a file. Traditionally, backup files have the same name as the original file except they end in .bak. Given that the filename is stored in the variable $file, the straightforward approach to copy and rename it would seem to be:

```
cp $file $file.bak                  # Doesn't work
```

This format doesn't work, however, because UNIX thinks the second operand references a variable named file.bak. When it can't find a variable, UNIX generates a usage error. Using braces, as shown in the next example, works at all times:

```
cp $file ${file}.bak
```

Variable Substitution

Variable substitution uses a variable or a positional parameter value to conditionally create a string. When we use variable substitution, we give the Korn shell two choices for the substitution. It can then examine the value of a variable and based on its value either use the variable value or the alternate value. The basic format is shown in Figure 15.1.

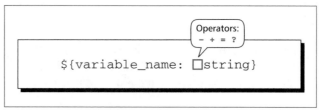

FIGURE 15.1   *Variable Substitution*

The four variable substitution operators are defined in Table 15.1.

TABLE 15.1   *Variable Substitution Operators*

Operator	Description
${variable: –string}	If variable is not null, use the value of variable; otherwise, use string. The value of variable is not changed.
${variable: +string}	If variable is not null, use string; otherwise, use the value of the variable (null).
${variable: =string}	If variable is not null, use the value of variable; otherwise, use the value of string and assign the string to variable.
${variable: ?string}	If variable is not null, use the value of variable; otherwise, print the value of string and exit.

Substitute If Variable Null (–)

The substitute if variable null operator is a minus (–). As shown in Figure 15.1, the operator is coded immediately after the variable's name and before the substitute value. The substitution takes place only when the variable is null; if the variable is not null, its value is used. There is no side effect. The concept appears in Figure 15.2.

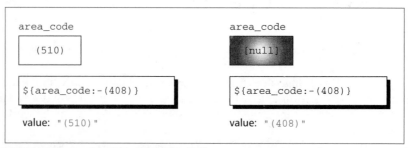

FIGURE 15.2   *Substitute If Variable Null*

This substitution is commonly used to provide a value when one is omitted by the user. For example, when users enter a telephone number, they often omit the area code. Script 15.1 demonstrates how we can substitute the local area code when the user does not enter one.

SCRIPT 15.1 *Substitute If Variable Null*

```
 1 #!/bin/ksh
 2 #  Script: condValid.scr
 3 #  Demonstrate Substitute If Variable Null(-)
 4
 5 print "Enter area code: \c"
 6 read  areaCode
 7
 8 areaCode=${areaCode:-(408)}
 9
10 print Area code is: $areaCode
11 #  Rest of script follows
   $ condValid.scr
```

```
Execution
Enter area code:
Area code is: (408)
```

Script 15.1 Analysis: This variable substitution form is very powerful. We are in area code 408. If the area code is missing for a phone number, then we want to default it to our local area code, which is exactly what happens when we use substitute if variable null.

Substitute If Variable Not Null (+)

This construct is the opposite of substitute if variable null. If the variable is not null, the substitute value is used. If it is null, the null value is used (nothing is substituted). The concept is presented in Figure 15.3.

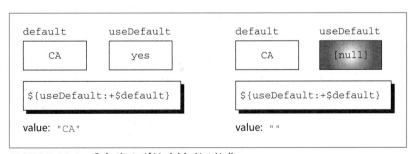

FIGURE 15.3 *Substitute If Variable Not Null*

Script 15.2 demonstrates a typical usage. In this example, we are going to delete a directory. Before deleting it, however, we want to verify that it is empty. If it is not, we display an error message.

SCRIPT 15.2 *Substitute If Variable Not Null*

```
 1  #!/bin/ksh
 2  #   Script: condNull.scr
 3  #   Demonstrate Substitute If Variable Not Null
 4  #   $1 is directory to be removed
 5
 6  dir=$(ls $1)
 7  print ${dir:+"Directory $1 not empty. Can't delete it"}
 8
 9  if [[ -z "$dir" ]]
10  then
11      rmdir $1
12      print $1 was removed
13  fi
```

```
Execution:
$ ls cond*                              # Verify directory status
condNull.scr    condValid.scr

condDirNull:                            # Directory is not empty
file1

$ condNull.scr condDirNull
Directory condDirNull not empty. Can't delete it

$ rm ./condDirNull/file1                # Delete only file
$ ls cond*
condNull.scr    condValid.scr

condDirNull:                            # Directory now empty
$ condNull.scr condDirNull
condDirNull was removed
```

Script 15.2 Analysis: Our approach is rather straightforward. We begin by listing the directory and storing the resulting list in a variable, dir (line 6). If dir is empty, the directory is empty and we can delete it. However, we want to display a message if dir is not null. This is the situation for substitute if not null. When dir is not null, the error message is displayed; when it is null, no message is displayed. Note that in this example, we are using a variable (dir) for the substitution. Because it is a variable, it must have the dollar sign.

Substitution Assignment (=)

With substitution assignment, if the variable is null, the string is used as the default. The difference between conditional substitution and substitution assignment is that the assignment has the side effect of assigning the default to the variable. The concept is shown in Figure 15.4.

One use of substitution assignment is to initialize a variable in a loop. Recall that variables are set to null before they are used. Therefore, if we use substitute assignment to initialize a variable in a loop, it will be initialized only the first time. We use a simple loop to demonstrate substitution assignment in Script 15.3.

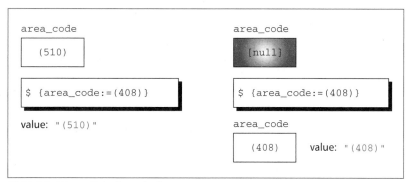

FIGURE 15.4 *Substitute Assignment*

SCRIPT 15.3 *Demonstrate Substitution Assignment*

```
 1 #!/bin/ksh
 2 #  Script: subAsgnmt.scr
 3 #  Demonstrate Substitution Assignment
 4
 5 print "count contains: $count\n"
 6
 7 while (( ${count:=1} < 10 ))
 8 do
 9    print  "$count \c"
10    (( count = count + 1 ))
11 done
12 print "\n"
```
```
$ subAsgnmt.scr
```
```
Output:
count contains:

1 2 3 4 5 6 7 8 9
```

Substitution Validation (?)

Substitution validation tests the variable. If the variable is not null, its value is used. If it is null, then the value in the string is written to standard error. If substitution validation is used in a script file and the test variable is null, the script terminates. The concept appears in Figure 15.5.

We can use substitution validation to verify that a required value is entered. If it is not, we quit the script. In Script 15.4, the script terminates if the user does not enter a value as requested.

SCRIPT 15.4 *Substitution Validation*

```
 1 #!/bin/ksh
 2 #  Script: subValid.scr
 3 #  This script verifies that the user entered a value
 4
```

Continued

SCRIPT 15.4 *Substitution Validation—Continued*

```
5 print "Enter a value \c"
6 read val
7 test=${val:?"You did not enter a value: Script terminates"}
8
9 print "Script continues"
```

```
Execution:
$ subValid.scr
Enter a value
subValid.scr[7]: val:  You did not enter a value: Script terminates
$ subValid.scr
Enter value 1
Script continues
```

Script 15.4 Analysis: This script is quite simple. However, it has one subtle point. Note that in line 7 we assign the results of the substitution to a variable named `test`. This is necessary because after the evaluation, the script thinks that the result ("1" in our test) is a command and should be executed. But there is no such command. This creates an error. The solution is to assign the substitution result to a variable, `test` in our script.

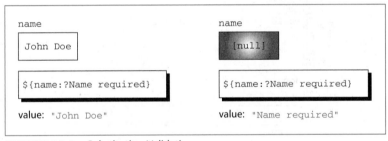

FIGURE 15.5 *Substitution Validation*

15.2 String Manipulation

When working with strings, it is often necessary to edit or process only a part of the string. The Korn shell allows a limited set of string manipulation operations: compress string, string length determination, substring extraction, and determination of a character in a string.

Compress Strings

A relatively common problem is extra spaces in a text file. Extra spaces occur for many reasons. Two very common ones are the deletion of words in the file and typing extra spaces when creating the file. Extra spaces can be easily removed by using the **print** command on a line of text as long as **print**'s argument is not quoted. Script 15.5 is a very simple script that takes the first input argument and prints it back to the monitor.

SCRIPT 15.5 *Compress String Argument*

```
1 #!/bin/ksh
2 #  Script: strDltSpaces.scr
```

Continued

SCRIPT 15.5   *Compress String Argument*

```
3 # This script used print to delete extra spaces in a string.
4 # $1 is text string
5 line=$1
6 print $line

$ strDltSpaces.scr "Too    many    spaces      here."

Output:
Too many spaces here.
```

The only problem with this script is that it compresses only one line. To make it truly useful, we need to put it in a loop. The production version is in Script 15.6.

SCRIPT 15.6   *Compress File*

```
1 #!/bin/ksh
2 #  Script: strComprFile.scr
3 #  Compress all lines in a file
4 #  $1 is file ID
5
6 cat $1 | while read line
7        do
8            print $line
9        done

$ strComprFile.scr spacy.dat

$ cat spacy.dat
Too    many     spaces in   this text.
Way  too     many spaces.
Our  compress        script will    delete the extra spaces.

Output:
Too many spaces in this text.
Way too many spaces.
Our compress script will delete the extra spaces.
```

String Length

To determine the length of a string in the Korn shell, we use the following code:

```
${#string_name}
```

In Script 15.7, we determine a string's length and then print it. This code can easily be incorporated into another script.

SCRIPT 15.7   *String Length*

```
1 #!/bin/ksh
2 # Returns length of a string
3 print "Enter a string: \c"
```

Continued

SCRIPT 15.7 *String Length—Continued*

```
4  read strIn
5  strlen=${#strIn}
6  print The string length is: $strlen

$ strlen.scr
```

```
Output:
Enter a string: Now is the time
The string length is: 15
```

Locating a Substring in a String

Locating a substring in a string is relatively easy with **egrep.** We demonstrate how in Script 15.8.

SCRIPT 15.8 *Use* **egrep** *to Find a Substring*

```
 1  #!/bin/ksh
 2  #  Script: strinstrGrep.scr
 3  #  Determine if substring is in a string using grep
 4  #  $1 is string; $2 is a substring
 5
 6  if (( $# != 2 ))
 7  then
 8     print Two parameters are required.
 9     print Usage: strinstrGrep.scr string substring
10     exit 2
11  fi
12
13  if print $1 | egrep "$2" > /dev/null/
14  then
15     print \"$2\" found in \"$1\"
16  else
17     print \"$2\" not in \"$1\"
18  fi
```

```
$ strinstrGrep.scr "Now is the time" "Now"
"Now" found in "Now is the time"
```

```
$ strinstrGrep.scr "The time is now" "is"
"is" found in "The time is now"
```

```
$ strinstrGrep.scr "The time is now" "it"
"it" not in "The time is now"
```

```
$ strinstrGrep.scr "The time is now"
Two parameters are required.
Usage: strinstrGrep.scr string substring
```

Script 15.8 Analysi s: Remember that **grep** does not accept a string as input; it processes files. Therefore, we need to turn the string into a one-line file so that **grep** can process it. This is done in line 13. The **print** command creates a file on standard output, which is then piped into the **egrep** command. Once it has the input line, **egrep** can test it for the substring.

Even though this is a test script, we included validation to ensure that there were two parameters. We also printed the arguments to make it easy to verify the results. We tested it three times. The first test locates a string at the beginning of the string; the second test locates a string in the middle. The third test used a substring that was not in the string. To complete the validation, we should test with a substring at the end of the string.

The last discussion point is the redirection (`> /dev/null/`) at the end of the expression statement. Because we don't need the output from the **egrep** command, we simply put it in the UNIX trash can.

Extract Substring

To extract a substring from a string, we use the string match command (**expr**). Its syntax is shown in Figure 15.6. There are three regular expressions after the colon. The first refers to characters before the substring we want to extract. The second is a regular expression for the substring to be matched. The third regular expression is for the characters after the substring. The first expression or the third expression or both can be null. For example, if we want to start at the beginning of a string (line), the first expression would be null. Likewise, if we wanted to include the last character in the string, the third expression would be null.

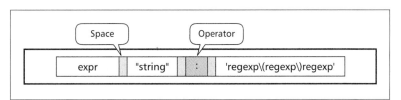

FIGURE 15.6 **expr** *String Match Command*

In Script 15.9, we extract the date by first storing the system date in a variable and then use the string match command to extract the hour and minute. The extraction expression general format appears in line 7.

SCRIPT 15.9 · *Extract Hour and Minutes from* **date**

```
1  #!/bin/ksh
2  #  Script: substr.scr
3  #  Extracts hh:mm from system date.
4
5  str=$(date)
6  print The date is $str
7  substr=$("$str" : '...........\(.....\).*')
8  print The time is \"$substr\"
```
```
$ substr.scr
```
```
Output:
The date is Mon Jul 10 11:08:54 PDT 2000
The time is "11:08"
```

Table 15.2 shows the script code for several substring extractions. Remember that each extraction requires three regular expressions. In several cases, the first and/or last expression is null. Study the patterns and make sure you clearly understand each.

TABLE 15.2 *Examples of Substring Extraction Expressions*

Command	Explanation
`expr "string" : '\(...\)'`	Extracts first three characters.
`expr "string" : '.*\(....\)'`	Extracts last four characters.
`expr "string" : '....\(...\)'`	Extracts characters 5, 6, and 7.
`expr "string" : '\(.*\)....'`	Extracts leading characters leaving last 4.
`expr "string" : '.*\([a].*[z]\)'`	Extracts string starting with a and ending with z.

Stripping Strings

There are times when we need to delete part of a string and leave the rest. This process is known as stripping the string. The Korn shell defines four string manipulation constructs to strip characters from the front or the rear of a string (Table 15.3).

TABLE 15.3 *Examples of Stripping Strings*

Command	Explanation
`${var#pattern}`	Starting at the beginning of the string, strips the shortest portion of the string that matches the pattern.
`${var##pattern}`	Starting at the beginning of the string, strips the longest (greedy) portion of the string that matches the pattern.
`${var%pattern}`	From the end of the string, strips the shortest portion of the string that matches the pattern.
`${var%%pattern}`	From the end of the string, strips the longest (greedy) portion of the string that matches the pattern.

Session 15.1 contains five string stripping examples.

SESSION 15.1 *Examples of Stripping Strings*

```
$ x=Hello
$ print ${x#???}         # Strip three characters from beginning
lo
$ print ${x%???}         # Strip three characters from end
He
$ path=/bin/usr/staff/file
$ print ${path##*/}      # Greedy strip from beginning
file
$ print ${path%/*}       # Strip from end
/bin/usr/staff
$ eName=forouzan@fhda.edu
$ print ${eName%@*}      # Strip from end
forouzan
```

Using Other Utilities

We are not limited to using the **expr** command and the **grep** family. We can also use **sed** or **awk** in those situations where they provide the better alternative. The syntax is basically the same. Regardless of which filter we use, however, there are several points that we must remember:

1. Each of these utilities needs a file as its input. If we want to apply them to a string, we must first change the string into a file using the **print** command. This turns a string into a one-line file that can be used as the input file.

2. Each of these utilities creates an output file. If the output must be a string, we use command substitution to change the output file into a string.

3. When we need to pass the value of a local variable to **sed,** we must use double quotes in the regular expression, not single quotes. When a variable, which is prefaced by a dollar sign, is used in double quotes, its value becomes part of the string; if it is enclosed in single quotes, the "$" and variable name such as "$var" are treated as a string.

4. There is a conflict between the usage of $1, $2, and so forth in **awk** and the Korn shell. The **awk** utility uses the dollar references as field designators; the Korn shell uses them as positional parameters. If we use $1 in an **awk** command, it thinks we are referring to the first field of its pattern space, not the first positional parameter. Depending on the situation, there are two solutions.

   a. If we want to use the value in a parameter (such as in $1) in a shell script, we can pass the value to **awk** by defining a local variable within **awk** and setting the **awk** variable to the parameter when we invoke **awk.** For example, to print only lines in which the first column matches the value in the $1 parameter, we would use the following code:

   ```
   awk '$1==value {print $0}' value=$1 filename
   ```

   Two important points: First, use only single quotes for the **awk** statement. Second, do not use a dollar sign with the **awk** variable, value, in the previous example.

   b. To pass a field designator to **awk,** we again create an **awk** local variable and assign the field designator to it when we invoke **awk.** This time, however, we must use the dollar sign with the parameter in the **awk** statement. For example, to print a specified field within a line, we would use the following code:

   ```
   awk '{print $field}' field=$1 filename
   ```

   In this case, the parameter $1 contains the field designator for the column that we want to print.

5. When the **sed** or **awk** instructions are longer than one line, we have two ways to code the command.

   a. We can use a separate **awk** or **sed** script file and include the instructions there; the name of the **awk** or **sed** script file is then used in the Korn script we are writing. The problem with this approach is that the Korn script is not independent; it always needs to be able to access the **awk** or **sed** script.

   b. To include the multiline instruction in the Korn script, we can use the backslash (\) at the end of each line except the last. This technique negates the return at the end of the line and continues the command on the next line. As an alternative to backslashes before the return, we can use a single quote at the beginning of the **awk** or **sed** command and close it at the end. This technique makes the separate lines part of one long quote. Its disadvantage is that we cannot use single quotes in the **awk** or **sed** instructions. The advantage to both of these techniques is that the Korn script becomes independent.

15.3 Here Document

As we have seen, we can read data into a script. There are times, however, when we want to include the text in the script itself rather than read it from a file. This is done with the here document operator (<<).[1] Script 15.10 demonstrates how we might write a script to email a note to everyone who is on our project. The document in line 6 contains the email addresses of members of the project, one address per line.

SCRIPT 15.10   *Using Text in the Script*

```
 1  #!/bin/ksh
 2  #  Script: hereDoc.scr
 3  #  This script uses a message contained in the document itself
 4  #  To send a meeting notice to all project members.
 5
 6  list=$(cat hereDocTeam.mail)
 7
 8  for i in $list
 9  do
10     mail $i << MSG
11        The next project meeting is scheduled for next Friday.
12        LOCATION: Conf Room 12
13        TIME:       9am
14        AGENDA:     Please be prepared to discuss project schedule.
15                    We have been asked to complete 3 months early.
16
17        Anne
18  MSG
19
20  done
    $ funHereDoc.scr
```

Script 15.10 Analysis: There is one point in this script that is not obvious. Note the word `MSG` in lines 10 and 18. This word marks the text that is included in the script. You can use any marker as long as it is matched at the beginning and end of the message. The end of message marker must be on the left margin. Within the markers, the text can be formatted appropriately for the message. For example, we included a blank line. The output from this script is input to the mail system. You can verify that it went okay by including yourself in the mail list document.

---

[1]It is called the *here document* operator because it gets its text from here in the script itself.

15.4 Functions

The Korn shell supports functions. A function is a named section of code that can be executed from within the body of a script. To execute a function, the script makes a **function call.** When the function executes, it is said to be called. The function format is in Script 15.11.

SCRIPT 15.11 *Function Format*

```
 1 function_name ( )       # Name the function
 2 {                       # Opening brace is required
 3   statement
 4   statement
 5   .
 6   .
 7   .
 8   statement
 9
10   return value          # value is optional
11 }                       # Closing brace is required
```

A function consists of two parts: the function body and the function arguments. The function body consists of all of the code between the opening and closing braces. The function arguments use the positional parameters to receive data. When the function terminates, it may optionally return a value.

Writing Functions

When a function is written in a script, it must be placed at the beginning of the file. Because UNIX interprets and executes the script line by line, it must know that the function exists before it encounters a command that calls the function. As the interpreter parses the script, it stores the line number of the script so it will know where the function is located.

A script passes data to a function through an argument list following the function name. This is the same format we use when we pass data to the script from the command line. Just as the data at the command are arguments, so the names after the function call are arguments. The function receives them as positional parameters; $1 refers to the first parameter, $2 refers to the second parameter, and so forth.

To demonstrate the concept, Script 15.12 contains a simple function that lists specified files and pipes them to **more.** Obviously, we would never use this function in a real script, but its simplicity makes the concept clear.

SCRIPT 15.12 *Script with a Simple Function*

```
 1 #!/bin/ksh
 2 #  Script: funList.scr
 3 #  This script demonstrates the script concept
 4
 5 # List Function
```
Continued

SCRIPT 15.12   *Script with a Simple Function—Continued*

```
 6│list( )
 7│{
 8│  ls -l $1 | more
 9│}
10│
11│# Script Body
12│
13│# Call List Three Times
14│list file1
15│list file2
16│list
```

```
$ funList.scr
```

```
Output:
-rw-r--r--      1 gilberg    staff        100 Jan 21 15:20 file1
-rw-r--r--      1 gilberg    staff        100 Jan 21 10:39 file2
total 154
-rwxr--r--      1 gilberg    staff        111 Jan 20 09:47 IFS.scr
-rw-r--r--      1 gilberg    staff       1425 Jan 25 17:50 MidRaven.bak
...
-rwxr--r--      1 gilberg    staff         36 Jan 20 09:47 who.scr.bak
-rwxr--r--      1 gilberg    staff         36 Jan 20 09:47 who.scrBak
```

Script 15.12 Analysis: Let's look at the code carefully. We begin by naming the function, in this case `list`. Note the parentheses after the name. They are required to tell the script that `list` is a function. Without them, it will think `list` is a variable. However, unlike other languages, there will never be anything in the parentheses.

The body of the function (that is, the code between the braces) contains only one statement: a long list (**ls**) of a file passed as an argument ($1). The output is then piped to the **more** command.

Now look at the function calls in lines 14, 15, and 16. Each call can pass the function one or more arguments. The first two calls pass the name of a file to be listed. The last call has no argument.

It is not apparent from the output, but there is a **more** pause after each of the first two lines. Each call to the function is separate. As it executes, its output is piped to **more**. Because there is only one line of output for `file1` and `file2`, **more** pauses. For the third call, there are 154 lines of output. We show only the first and last two. For this list, **more** pauses at the end of each full screen.

> Because shell programming uses interpreters rather than compilers, function code must be placed before the function is called.

As another example, let's write a function that verifies that its argument is valid. In Script 15.13, we use the **let** command to verify that the argument is numeric. If it is not, we print an error message.

SCRIPT 15.13   *Script with a Validate Function*

```
 1  #!/bin/ksh
 2  #   Script: funValid.scr
 3  #   This script contains a function to validate numeric arguments.
 4
 5  # Valid Function
 6  valid( )
 7  {
 8  #   Test parameter 1 by adding. All output to trash
 9   let x=$1+1 >/dev/null 2>&1
10   if (( $? != 0 ))                   # if exit status is false
11   then
12      print "$1 is not numeric"
13      exit 1                         # exit command kills script
14   fi
15   return
16  }
17  #   Script Body
18   valid $1
19   valid $2
```

```
Execution:
$ funValid.scr 23 44
```

```
$ funValid.scr 23 b
b is not numeric
```

```
$ funValid.scr a b
a is not numeric
```

Script 15.13 Analysis: The first time we executed this script, we used two valid numbers, so there was no output. In the second test, the first argument was valid, but the second one wasn't, so there is an error message. The third test has two invalid arguments, but note that only one of these errors is reported because we exit the script in line 13 when we detect an error. Note that in this script, we used a return statement even though it doesn't do anything. In this case, it serves as documentation that we are at the end of the function.

Returning Values

In Script 15.13, we used a null return. We can also use a function to return a single value. The value is stored in exit status ($?). To demonstrate how a value is returned, let's write a small script that adds two numbers and returns their value. The code is in Script 15.14.

SCRIPT 15.14   *A Function That Returns a Value*

```
 1  #!/bin/ksh
 2  #   Script: funAdd.scr
 3  #   This script contains a function that adds two arguments.
 4  # Add Function
```

Continued

SCRIPT 15.14 *A Function That Returns a Value—Continued*

```
 5  add( )
 6  {
 7   # Add parameters $1 and $2
 8   (( res = $1 + $2 ))
 9   return $res
10  }
11  # Script Body
12   add 4 5
13   print " 4 +  5 is" $?
14
15   add 42 96
16   print "42 + 96 is" $?
17  # End script
```

```
$ funAdd.scr
```

```
Output:
  4 +  5 is 9
 42 + 96 is 138
```

Comparing Strings

The Korn shell has no operator to test if one string is greater than or less than another string. It can only test if they are equal. Because testing greater and less than is required so often, we create a compare function.

The approach is really quite easy. We begin the function by testing for equal strings using the built-in comparison operator (=). If they are equal, we return 0. If the strings are not equal, we put them in a temporary two-line file and sort it. We then assign the smaller (first one in the file) to a variable named smaller. If smaller is equal to the first parameter ($1), then the first argument is smaller and we return 1; if it is not, the second argument is smaller and we return 2 (Script 15.15).

SCRIPT 15.15 *Compare Strings Function*

```
 1  #!/bin/ksh
 2  #   Script: funStrCmp.scr
 3  #   Function to compare two strings
 4  #      Returns 0 if $1 = $2
 5  #             1 if $1 < $2
 6  #             2 if $1 > $2
 7
 8  strcmp( )
 9  {
10      if [[ $1 = $2 ]]
11      then
12         res=0
13      else
14        ( print "$1" ; print "$2" ) > temp     # creating a two-line file
15          smaller=$(sort temp | head -1)        # sort and store smaller
```
                                                                    Continued

SCRIPT 15.15   *Compare Strings Function*

```
16              if [[ $smaller = "$1" ]]
17              then
18                   res=1
19              else
20                   res=2
21          fi   # if smaller
22      fi       # if equal
23      return $res
24  }   # End of strcmp function
25
26  # Script Body
27      strcmp $1 $2
28      res=$?                                    # Save compare result
29
30      if (( $res == 0 ))
31        then
32            print "$1 = $2"
33      else
34        if (( $res == 1 ))
35            then
36                print "$1 < $2 :"
37            else
38                print "$1 > $2 :"
39        fi   # $? == 1
40      fi # strcmp
```

```
Execution:
$ funStrCmp.scr Hello Hello
Hello = Hello
```

```
$ funStrCmp.scr Hello Bye
Hello > Bye
```

```
$ funStrCmp.scr Hello "So Long"
Hello < So Long
```

Functions in Files

In addition to placing functions at the beginning of a script, we can put them in files.

Functions in the Profile File

When a function is added to the profile file (~/.profile), it becomes a command that can be executed at the command line. For example, we have added the compare function to our profile file. Session 15.2 demonstrates how it can be used at the command line.

SESSION 15.2   *Demonstrate Profile File Command*

```
$ strcmp hello hello
$ print $?
0
```

Continued

SESSION 15.2 *Demonstrate Profile File Command—Continued*

```
$ strcmp hello "so long"
$ print $?
1
```

```
$ strcmp hello bye
$ print $?
2
```

Functions in a Library File

We can also create a separate library file for our functions. The functions can then be made available to the shell by executing the library file. To execute the function file, we simply use the dot command (page 641) as in the following example:

```
$ . functions.scr
```

In Script 15.16, we create a function file and place string compare in it. We then create a test script that parallels Script 15.15. To demonstrate that the function's file string compare is executing and not the profile string compare, we changed its name to fun_strcmp.

SCRIPT 15.16 *Demonstrate Function File*

```
 1  #!/bin/ksh
 2  #  funTest.scr
 3  #  Test Function Library--fun_strcmp
 4     . functions.scr                      # Activate Function Library
 5     fun_strcmp $1 $2
 6     res=$?                               # Save compare result
 7
 8     if (( $res == 0 ))
 9        then
10           print "$1 = $2"
11     else
12        if (( $res == 1 ))
13           then
14              print "$1 < $2"
15           else
16              print "$1 > $2"
17        fi # $? == 1
18     fi # strcmp
```

```
Execution:
$ funTest.scr hello hello
hello = hello
```

```
$ funTest.scr hello "so long"
hello < so long
```

```
$ funTest.scr hello bye
hello > bye
```

15.5 Arrays

An **array** is a sequenced collection of elements that has one name. Given the name of an array, we can refer to individual elements of the array using indexes. An **index** in an integral value that identifies an element in the array. When referencing an element in an array, the index is enclosed in a set of brackets. These concepts are presented in Figure 15.7.

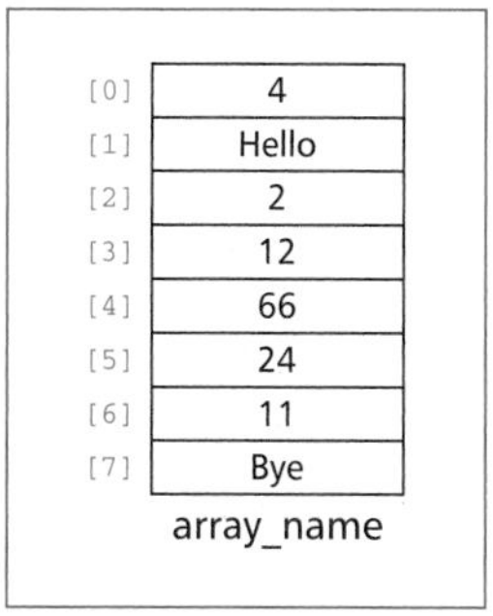

[0]	4
[1]	Hello
[2]	2
[3]	12
[4]	66
[5]	24
[6]	11
[7]	Bye

array_name

FIGURE 15.7 *An Array*

The array in Figure 15.7 is known as a one-dimensional array or a vector because it has only one direction. As we drew it, it has only one column. If we laid it on its side, it would have only one row. Korn supports only one-dimensional arrays. Other languages support multidimensional arrays.

The first thing to notice in Figure 15.7 is that the indexes start at zero; that is, the first index of the array is [0]. To refer to the number 4 in Figure 15.7, we use the index [0]; to refer to the number 24 in the array, we use the index [5]. To access an array, we use the following format:

$${array_name[index]}$$

If the array name is month, to refer to the first element, we would use ${month[0]}; to refer to the fourth element, we would use ${month[3]}. Note that because the first index is [0], the value of the index is always 1 less that its ordinal position in the array. Thus, the fifth element of the array is ${month[4]}, and the sixth element is ${month[5]}.

To assign a set of values to an array, we use the **set** command with an option of –A followed by the values. For example, if we needed an array that contained the three-character names of the months of the year, we could create it as shown in Session 15.3.

SESSION 15.3 *Create Months Array*

```
$ set -A months Jan Feb Mar Apr May Jun Jul Aug Sep Oct Nov Dec
$ print ${months[1]}
Feb
```

We have a problem with our array, however. Month 1 is supposed to be Jan, not Feb. Can you figure out why? The answer is that the array indexes start at 0; therefore, index 1 is the second month, not the first. To fix the problem, we use an extra entry at the beginning of the array so that Jan starts in the second element. The code is in Session 15.4.

SESSION 15.4 *Create Months Array Revisited*

```
$ set -A months 0 Jan Feb Mar Apr May Jun Jul Aug Sep Oct Nov Dec
$ print ${months[1]}
Jan
```

In the previous examples, we have used a constant for the index. The index can also be a variable. In fact, it is more often a variable than a constant. In Session 15.5, we create a variable named index and assign it the value 5, representing May.

SESSION 15.5 *Create Months Array Revisited Again*

```
$ set -A month 0 Jan Feb Mar Apr May Jun Jul Aug Sep Oct Nov Dec
$ index=5
$ print ${months[$index]}
May
```

15.6 Signals

Signals are interrupts that are generated by the kernel or other processes. One of the simplest is the user action to cancel a running script. In this section, we discuss signals and how they can be handled in a script. When a signal is generated that can be handled by a script, the script traps or intercepts it. Once a signal is trapped, the script assumes control over the action that will be taken. Not all signals can be trapped by a script.

A signal is a message sent to a process (such as a running script) on one of two occasions:

1. It is sent by another process to send a message to the receiving process. For example, a child process may send a signal to the parent process that it has been terminated.
2. It is sent by the operating system (kernel) to inform the receiving process of some interruption or error.

Signal Types

A signal is represented by an integer and a name which defines the event. Because some of the integers are system dependent, it is recommended to use the names for portability to other systems or shells. The names are in uppercase and start with SIG (Table 15.4).

TABLE 15.4 *Interrupt Signals*

Number	Name	Function
1	SIGHUP	Hangup
2	SIGINT	Interrupt
3	SIGQUIT	Quit
9	SIGKILL	Definite kill
15	SIGTERM	Software termination (default kill)
24	SIGTSTP	Suspension

SIGHUP The hang-up signal is sent to the process when there is hang up. For example, a modem may be disconnected or a terminal turned off.

SIGINT The interrupt signal is sent to the process when there is an interrupt from the terminal. The terminal interrupt is normally associated with the cancel command (ctrl + c).

SIGQUIT The quit signal is sent to the process when there is a quit message from the terminal. The terminal quit is normally associated with the quit command (ctrl + \).

SIGKILL The kill signal is sent to the process when it is necessary to kill the process. This signal, as we will see, cannot be trapped.

SIGTERM The software termination signal is sent to the process by the kill command.

SIGTSTP The suspension signal, sent by the user (ctrl+z), suspends a background command.

Response to Signals

A shell script (or any process) can respond to a received signal in one of three ways:

Accept the Default

In this case, the process does nothing. It lets the signal do its default action, which is normally to kill the process.

Ignore the Signal

In this case, the process ignores the signal. The process continues executing its code as though nothing has happened. Note that some signals, such as SIGKILL, cannot be ignored.

Catch the Signal

In this case, the process catches the signal and holds it until it can take an action. Although the process may still be terminated, it can prepare itself for termination; this might include backup activities or garbage collection.

trap Command

The **trap** command can be used to respond to the signals. The format of the trap command is:

```
trap "command or commands" signal-numbers (or names)
```

Note that the command or commands should be enclosed in quotes. More than one signal number or name can be separated by space(s).

1. If the trap command is missing, it means that the script accepts the default action of the signal.
2. If the command argument of the trap signal is an empty string, it means that the script wants to ignore those signals. For example, the following trap command ignores signals 2 and 3:

```
trap "" 2 3
```

Note that some signals cannot be ignored (number 9, for example). In this case, the signal takes its own action even if it is ignored.

3. If the command argument of the trap signal includes a command or commands, it means that the script wants to catch the signal and hold it for a while to perform some action before the signal takes its own action. The following is an example of catching a signal:

```
trap "cp file1 ~/backup/file1" 2 3 15
```

trap Example Script 15.17 is an example of using both signal 2 and 24 in a script. If you use `ctrl+z` to stop, it is ignored; if you use `ctrl+c`, it will stop after completing the current display. You will not see a shell prompt until you key Return.

SCRIPT 15.17 *Demonstrate Signal Traps*

```
 1  #!/bin/ksh
 2  #   Script: signal.scr
 3  #   Demonstrate use of signal traps
 4
 5  (( i = 1 ))
 6  while (( $i < 1000 ))
 7  do
 8      print $i
 9
10      trap "" 24                              # Ignore trap 24
11      trap "print Cancelled by user.; exit 3" 2
12
13      (( i = i + 1 ))
14  done
```

Continued

SCRIPT 15.17 *Demonstrate Signal Traps*

```
$ signal.scr
Output:
1
2
3
...                                  # Lines 4...92 manually deleted
93
94
Cancelled by user.
```

Script 15.17 Analysis: When we ran the script, we first pressed `ctrl+z`. It did not stop the script. We then immediately pressed `ctrl+c`, which stopped the script after it completed printing `94`. You must be quick, however, because it doesn't take long to complete the display of all 1000 numbers.

15.7 Built-in Commands

Shell scripts can use any command or utility in UNIX. This includes user-created utilities (scripts). Many of the standard commands and utilities are so common that they are built into the shell itself. This means that they are immediately available; the shell does not need to search the libraries to find and execute the commands. These commands are summarized in Table 15.5.

TABLE 15.5 *Built-in Commands*

Command	Description
:	Null statement. Does nothing (a placeholder).
.	As a command, dot causes the command or utility that follows it to be executed in the current shell rather than a child shell.
break	Forces a loop or a case statement to terminate.
case	Specifies commands to be executed for matching value.
cd	Changes the current directory.
continue	Continues with the next iteration of the loop.
eval	Reads its argument and executes the resulting command.
exec	Executes the command in another shell.
exit	Sets the exit status and exits the shell.
export	Flags variables listed as arguments as exportable.
expr	Evaluates mathematical operators in an expression.
for	Processes data in a list.
if	Standard two-way selection command.
print	Displays argument on standard output. Can also be used to compress strings.

Continued

TABLE 15.5 *Built-in Commands—Continued*

Command	Description
pwd	Displays the current directory.
read	Reads a line or part of a line from the standard input.
readonly	Makes its arguments read-only.
return	Returns to the calling command.
select	Menu loop.
set	Sets specified variables.
shift	Shifts positional parameters to the left.
test	Evaluates a relational, logical, or file expression.
trap	Runs a command when a signal is received.
type	Interprets how the shell will use a command.
ulimit	Displays or sets resources available to the user.
umask	Displays or sets default file creation modes.
unset	Unsets a variable or function.
until	Loops until variable is true.
wait	Waits until a child process finishes.
while	Loops while variable is true.

Most of these commands have been discussed already. We present two more built-in commands next.

sleep Command

The **sleep** command requires one argument: the number of seconds to pause (sleep). When executed, the shell suspends script execution for the specified duration. It is often executed in a background script.

The **sleep** command can be used to monitor status. For example, if we need to contact another user who is not currently logged in, we can create a script to monitor who is currently on the system. When it finds that the user has logged in, it then sends a message. This concept is demonstrated in Script 15.18. Note that we start the job in the background by coding an ampersand (&) immediately after the user login id.

SCRIPT 15.18 *Demonstrate* **sleep** *Command*

```
1  #!/bin/ksh
2  #  Script: sleep.scr
3
4  #  Monitors who is logged in and sends call me message
5
```

Continued

SCRIPT 15.18 *Demonstrate* **sleep** *Command*

```
 6 | #  Check every minute to see if $1 is logged in
 7 |
 8 | until who | grep "$1" >/dev/null
 9 |    do
10 |       sleep 60
11 |    done                            # Run in background
12 |
13 | #  User is now logged in
14 | write $1 << MSG
15 |    Urgent we talk.
16 |    Please call me A.S.A.P!
17 |
18 |    Gilberg
19 | MSG
     $ sleep.scr forouzan&
```

Dot Command

The **dot command** is used to designate the current shell. When a command is executed, it generally forks a subshell for the execution. We can direct that the command be executed in the current shell by using the dot command before the script name as in the next example:

```
$ . script.scr
```

Do not confuse the dot command with the pathname dot. When dot is used in a pathname, it means the current directory. In this case, it is not a command.

Beware: Because the dot command forces the command to be executed in the current shell, any environmental changes made by the command are permanent (see Section 15.9, page 655).

15.8 Scripting Techniques

In this section, we show some techniques that can be used in shell scripting. Many of them require that we process strings rather than words or values. Before demonstrating the scripts, therefore, let's discuss what happens when we pass strings as arguments or when we read strings in a script.

Reading Strings

When a string is passed as an argument, its format determines how it is parsed into the script parameters. If it is enclosed in quotes, it is placed in one parameter. If it is passed without quotes, each word is a separate parameter.

Script 15.19 demonstrates this concept. We begin by printing the complete argument list ($*) and then the four positional parameters individually.

SCRIPT 15.19 *Demonstrate String Parameters*

```
1  #!/bin/ksh -f
2  #  Script: strArguments.scr
3  #  Demonstrate how string argument format affects read
4
5  print All Arguments: $*
6  print Parm1 is: $1
7  print Parm2 is: $2
8  print Parm3 is: $3
9  print Parm4 is: $4
```

```
Execution:
$ strArguments.str Now is the time
All Arguments: Now is the time
Parm1 is: Now
Parm2 is: is
Parm3 is: the
Parm4 is: time
```

```
$ strArguments.str "Now is the time"
All Arguments: Now is the time
Parm1 is: Now is the time
Parm2 is:
Parm3 is:
Parm4 is:
```

User Interaction

Although many scripts run by themselves, others require interactive input. This means that the user must receive a prompt and the shell must receive an answer. In this section, we demonstrate how to make a shell script interactive. Several of these techniques have been demonstrated in previous scripts.

Creating a Prompt

A prompt is a line of output that does not end in a newline and that requires a response from the user. We typically end the prompt with a colon and a space. The user's response is typed at the end of the prompt after the colon. Script 15.20 demonstrates a prompt that asks for a filename. We print the input for verification. Typically, prompts do not repeat in response. As you study the script, note that the prompt is enclosed in quotes. Quotes are required because of the cancel newline command at the end of the string. We could have put the quotes around only the cancel command.

SCRIPT 15.20 *Prompt Script*

```
1  #!/bin/ksh
2  #  Script: prompt.scr
3  #  Demonstrate a typical user prompt
4
```

Continued

SCRIPT 15.20 *Prompt Script*

```
5 print "Enter file name: \c"
6 read fileName
7 print You entered $fileName
```

```
$ prompt.scr
```

```
Output:
Enter file name: payroll.dat
You entered payroll.dat
```

Question Prompt

Often interactive script processing must ask the user a question. The most common question is: Do you want to continue? The next script asks the question and sets a flag based on the answer. Depending on the nature of the script, a flag may be set or the script may end with an **exit** command. Script 15.21 shows how we can ask questions using a prompt.

SCRIPT 15.21 *Question Script*

```
 1 #!/bin/ksh
 2 #  Script question.scr
 3 #  Demonstrate question prompt
 4 contFlag=2
 5 while (( contFlag == 2 ))
 6 do
 7    print "Do you want to continue [y/n]: \c"
 8    read answer
 9    case $answer in
10       y|Y) contFlag=1;;
11       n|N) contFlag=0;;
12         *) print Invalid response.
13             print Usage: \'y\' or \'n\'.
14    esac
15 done
16
17 if (( contFlag == 1 ))
18 then
19    print script Continues
20 else
21    print script will stop; exit 1
22 fi
23 #  rest of script here
```

```
Execution:
$ question.scr
Do you want to continue [y/n]: z
Invalid response.
Usage: 'y' or 'n'.
Do you want to continue [y/n]: y
script Continues
```

Continued

SCRIPT 15.21   *Question Script—Continued*

```
$ question.scr
Do you want to continue [y/n]: N
script will stop
```

Script 15.21 Analysis: There is a very important point to study in this script. Many scriptwriters make the mistake of testing for one answer, such as yes, and then defaulting to the no answer. This is an unforgiving technique. If the user accidentally enters the wrong answer, the default is always taken. We have tested for both answers. Only if the user enters a completely wrong answer does the default come into play. Because we enclosed the question in a loop, we can display an error message and give the user another chance to enter a valid response.

We have also added code so that we can verify the user response. The testing is not complete. We have not tested for all valid responses; that is, we have not tested for both upper- and lowercase responses for yes and no. We suggest that you code and run this script and verify that it works for all possible responses.

Parsing Options

Most built-in utilities in UNIX allow users to define options when they execute the utilities. For example, the list (**ls**) command is a utility that can accept several options, one by one or in groups. For example, we can type `ls` or `ls -l` or `ls -dl`.

When we write a script, we may also need to include some options in it. The script will behave differently depending on which options are set or not set. Options must be validated. One validation approach requires that the script parse the options, validate them, and then adjust its execution based on them. In this design, they should be treated separately from any arguments.

A better method is to use the **getopts** command. This command reads the command line and, if there are options, takes each option, one by one, validates it, and then handles it. This command is complex, so we need to study it carefully.

Options with No Values

The simplest case is when we allow only options without any value. An example of an option without a value is the long list command (`ls -l`).

Options with no values are defined by a minus sign[2] and a letter—nothing else. The options can be separated or combined with each other. For options with no values, we use a very simple format of the **getopts** command:

```
getopts  xyz variable              # x, y, and z are the allowed options
```

Each use of the **getopts** command gets the next option from the command line and stores the option (without the minus sign) in its variable. If we want to get all options, we must use a loop. The **getopts** exit status is true when there are more options; it is false when all options have been processed. This means that **getopts** can be used as the

---

[2]The **getopts** command cannot handle plus sign options.

command in the `while` loop. As long as there are options, the loop is repeated. If **getopts** should find an option that is not in its argument list, it displays an error message and continues. Script 15.22 demonstrates a simple script that does not use option values.

SCRIPT 15.22   *Options with No Values*

```
 1  #!/bin/ksh
 2  #   Script: optNoVal.scr
 3  #   Demonstrate options with no values
 4
 5  while getopts xy variable
 6  do
 7      case $variable in
 8         x) print "processing x option here" ;;
 9         y) print "processing y option here" ;;
10      esac
11  done
```

```
Execution:
$ optNoVal.scr                                    # No options entered

$ optNoVal.scr -x                                 # Only one option
processing x option here

$ optNoVal.scr -xy                                # Both options combined
processing x option here
processing y option here

$ optNoVal.scr -x -y                              # Options separated
processing x option here
processing y option here

$ optNoVal.scr -xy Hello                          # With argument
processing x option here
processing y option here

$ optNoVal.scr -xz                                # Invalid option
processing x option here
optNoVal.scr[3]: getopts: z bad option(s)         # getopts message
```

Script 15.22 Analysis: The only allowed options are x and y, as indicated by the first argument to **getopts** (line 5). The script is executed several times to demonstrate different combinations.

We can improve Script 15.22 in two ways:

1. The **getopts** command stores a question mark (?) in its variable if the option is not in the list of valid options (argument 1). We can use this value to detect invalid options and exit if the user enters a wrong option.

2. With this design, we should redirect the **getopts** error message to the trash.

The improved version is in Script 15.23: Note that we used a backslash (\) to prevent the shell from interpreting the question mark.

SCRIPT 15.23   *Detecting Invalid Options*

```
 1│#!/bin/ksh
 2│#  Script: optNoVal2.scr
 3│#  Demonstrate options with no values
 4│
 5│while getopts xy variable 2> /dev/null
 6│do
 7│    case $variable in
 8│      x)  print "processing x option here" ;;
 9│      y)  print "processing y option here" ;;
10│      \?) print "Invalid option: Quitting" ; exit 1 ;;
11│    esac
12│done
```

```
Execution:
$ optNoVal2.scr -xy                     # Both options combined
processing x option here
processing y option here

$ optNoVal2.scr -xw                     # Invalid option
processing x option here
Invalid option: Quitting
```

Options with Values

A script may need an option that should have a value (sometimes called option argument). For example, if we want to write a script that accepts a delimiter different from the default, we need to pass the delimiter to the script. The **getopts** command provides a predefined variable called OPTARG. This variable holds the value for the option. In the **getopts** command, if an option needs a value, it must be followed by a colon (:).

SCRIPT 15.24   *Options with Values*

```
 1│#!/bin/ksh
 2│#  Script: optWithVal.scr
 3│#  Demonstrate option arguments with values
 4│
 5│while getopts x:y: variable 2>/dev/null   # Both x & y have arguments
 6│do
 7│    case $variable in
 8│      x)  print "Processing x option here"
 9│          print "Value of the x option is $OPTARG" ;;
10│      y)  print "Processing y option here"
11│          print "Value of the y option is $OPTARG" ;;
12│      \?) print "Invalid option: Quitting" ; exit 1 ;;
13│    esac
14│done
15│
16│print Processing in body: Parameters contain $1 $2 $3 $4
```

```
$ optWithVal.scr -x XXX -y YYY Hello
```

Continued

SCRIPT 15.24 *Options with Values*

```
Output:
Processing x option here
Value of the x option is XXX
Processing y option here
Value of the y option is YYY
Processing in body: Parameters contain -x XXX -y YYY
```

Script 15.24 Analysis: Note that although we use the **getopts** command, the option values are not lost. The first option is stored in $1, and its value is stored in $2. The second option is stored in $3, and its value is stored in $4.

The **getopts** command uses another built-in variable, OPTIND, which provides the number of the first argument after the options in the command line. It can be used to shift the options out of the positional parameters so that the first parameter ($1) holds the first actual argument. Script 15.25 demonstrates the use of OPTIND.

SCRIPT 15.25 *Shifting Options with* OPTIND

```
 1  #!/bin/ksh
 2  #   Script: optWithVal2.scr
 3  #   Demonstrate use of OPTIND
 4
 5  while getopts xy: variable 2>/dev/null          # y has value
 6  do
 7      case $variable in
 8        x)  print "Processing x option here" ;;
 9        y)  print "Processing y option here"
10            print "Value of the y option is $OPTARG" ;;
11        \?) print "Invalid option: Quitting" ; exit 1 ;;
12      esac
13
14  done
15
16  print Processing in body:
17  print OPTIND contains: $OPTIND
18  shift (( $OPTIND-1 ))
19  print \$1 contains $1
20  print \$2 contains $2
```

```
$ optWithVal2.scr -xy YYY Hello Good-bye
```

```
Output
Processing x option here
Processing y option here
Value of the y option is YYY
Processing in body:
OPTIND contains: 3
$1 contains Hello
$2 contains Good-bye
```

Script 15.25 Analysis: This script demonstrates why we should use the **getopts** command. If this script were repeated without it, we would find the combined options (-xy) in the first positional parameter and yyy in the second positional parameter. With **getopts**, the two options are separated automatically for our processing.

Parsing Pathnames

When working with UNIX files, the pathnames can become quite long, especially when they are absolute paths (see Chapter 3, Absolute Pathnames, page 71). Pathnames, whether absolute or relative, can be divided into two parts: the *directory name* and the *base name*. These two parts are separated by the last slash (/) in the pathname.

The base name can be the name of a directory or a file. The directory name is always the pathname of a directory. If the base name is a file, the directory name is the pathname of the file's directory; if the base name is a directory, the directory name is the pathname of its parent directory. Table 15.6 shows examples of parsing pathnames.

TABLE 15.6   *Examples of Parsing Pathnames*

Pathname	Directory Name	Base Name
/usr/gilberg/file1	/usr/gilberg	file1
/usr/gilberg/A	/usr/gilberg	A
gilberg/file1	gilberg	file1
file1	.	file1

In the last example in Table 15.6, the pathname is just one name. In this case, the directory name is the current directory as represented by the dot.

Pathname Commands

In the Korn shell, we can use the **dirname** and **basename** commands inherited from the Bourne shell to extract different parts of a pathname. While these commands work in the Korn shell, the stripping patterns described on page 626 are much easier to use. For completeness, we include a description of these commands here.

dirname   The **dirname** command, when used with only a pathname as an argument, extracts the directory name from the pathname (Figure 15.8). The result can then be stored in a variable and manipulated as needed.

basename   The **basename** command extracts the base name from the pathname. Again, the result can be stored in a variable. This concept is also shown in Figure 15.8.

These commands are demonstrated in Script 15.26. Note that we have executed the script twice, first with a directory name and then without one. The dot in the second execution represents the current directory.

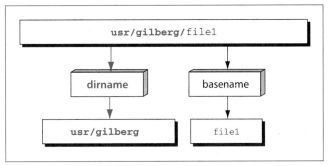

FIGURE I5.8   *Using* **dirname** *and* **basename**

SCRIPT 15.26   *Separate Filenames and Pathnames*

```
1  #!/bin/ksh
2  #  Script: file.scr
3  #  Uses dirname and basename to separate path from name
4  #  $1 is filename with path
5
6  dir=$(dirname $1)
7  base=$(basename $1)
8
9  print "Complete pathname     :" $1
10 print "Directory portion only :" $dir
11 print "Base portion only      :" $base
```

```
Execution:
$ file.scr gilberg/scripts/file.scr
Complete pathname       : gilberg/scripts/file.scr
Directory portion only : gilberg/scripts
Base portion only       : file.scr
```

```
$ file.scr file.scr
Complete pathname       : file.scr
Directory portion only : .
Base portion only       : file.scr
```

Separating Filename from Extension

The base name command can also be used to separate a filename from its extension. This version of the command requires a string (filename) and a second argument, which is the string to be stripped. For example, given a filename of file1.dat, we can strip off the extension by using the base name command with the filename and the extension as follows:

```
$ basename file1.dat .dat
```

As another example, to strip off everything except file, the second argument contains 1.ext.

Extending the concept further, we could use the base name command to change the extensions of a list of files. For example, we could change all files in a directory from `filename.ren` to `filename.zzz`. The first solution that comes to mind is to use the move (**mv**) command with wildcards:

```
$ mv *.ren *.zzz                        # Doesn't work
```

This solution doesn't work, however, because wildcards cannot be used in the destination of a move command. To solve the problem, we must use the base name command in a loop (Script 15.28).

SCRIPT 15.27 *Rename File Family*

```
 1  #!/bin/ksh
 2  #  Script: renameFiles.scr
 3  #  Renames a file family by changing only the extensions.
 4  #  $1 is from file type; $2 is to file type
 5
 6  if [[ $# != 2 ]]
 7     then
 8         print "Requires two file type arguments"
 9         print "Usage: $0 from_type to_type"
10         exit 1
11  fi
12
13  for name in *.$1
14  do
15     first=$(basename $name $1)
16     mv $name ${first}$2
17  done
```

```
Input:
$ ls rename?.*
rename1.ren   rename2.ren   rename3.ren   rename4.ren   rename5.ren
```
```
Execution
$ renameFiles.scr ren zzz
```
```
Output:
$ ls rename?.*
rename1.zzz   rename2.zzz   rename3.zzz   rename4.zzz   rename5.zzz
```

Script 15.27 Analysis: This script is rather straightforward except for line 13. Recall that UNIX expands wildcards wherever they are encountered. In line 13, we use the wildcard `*.$1`, which is expanded to `rename1.ren`, `rename2.ren`, and so forth. The `for` loop then processes each filename, one by one, and changes the extension from `ren` to `zzz`.

Separating Filename from Extension: Another Way

The stripping pattern shown in the following example can also be used to separate a filename from its extension. For example, given a variable containing a filename with the format `file1.dat`, we can strip off the extension by using the strip-from-end pattern as in the next example:

```
$ {variable%.*}                        # Strip dot and everything after it
```

The code is in Script 15.28.

SCRIPT 15.28   *Rename File Family*

```
 1  #!/bin/ksh
 2  #   Script: renameFiles.scr
 3  #   Renames a file family by changing only the extensions.
 4  #   $1 is from file type; $2 is to file type
 5
 6  if(( $# != 2 ))
 7  then
 8      print "Requires two file type arguments"
 9      print "Usage: $0 from_type to_type"
10      exit 1
11  fi
12
13  for name in *.$1
14  do
15      first=${name%.*}
16      mv $name ${first}.$2
17  done
```

```
Input:
$ ls rename?.*
rename1.ren   rename2.ren   rename3.ren
```
```
Execution
$ renameFiles.scr ren zzz
```
```
Output:
$ ls rename?.*
rename1.zzz   rename2.zzz   rename3.zzz
```

Opening and Closing Files

The scripts to this point have all used input or output redirection to get data into or out of a script. As we have said before, however, redirection can cause problems in some versions of the Korn shell. In these systems, redirection causes the loop to be executed in a subshell. This means that variables in the main body of the script cannot be referenced in the loop, and variables in the loop are not available after the loop completes. One solution to this problem is to use an execute command (**exec**) to open and close files in the script.

Opening Files

To open a file, a script needs to know the filename. The **exec** command then opens the file as in the following examples:

```
exec 0< inFileName              # open for input
exec 1> outFileName             # open for output
exec 2> errFileName             # open for error
```

The concept is similar to the one used to identify the standard files for redirection. A file stream descriptor is created to represent each file. For the standard files, the file descriptors are 0 (standard input), 1 (standard output), and 2 (standard error).

To designate that a file is input, we use an input redirection token (<). To designate that a file is output or error, we use an output redirection token (>).

When we open a file as input, we redirect it to standard input (0). Once opened, we can use the **read** command in a loop to read the specified file one line at a time. Similarly, when we open a file as output, we can redirect standard output to it. As we write to standard output, the output is redirected to our specified file.

To demonstrate how we open and process files, let's write a small script that copies a file. We specify the input and output files as parameters in the script. It begins by opening the files and then uses a read loop to copy the first file to the second file. Script 15.29 uses this script to make a copy of TheRavenV1. We name it TheRavenV1.bak.

SCRIPT 15.29 *Copy File Script*

```
 1  #!/bin/ksh
 2  # This script copies the contents of the first file ($1) to
 3  # the file specified in the second argument ($2).
 4
 5  # Open the files
 6  exec 0< $1
 7  exec 1> $2
 8
 9  # Read and copy in loop
10  while read line
11  do
12      print $line
13  done
```

```
$ openCopy.scr TheRavenV1 TheRavenV1.bak
```

```
TheRavenV1.bak
Once upon a midnight dreary, while I pondered, weak and weary,
Over many a quaint and curious volume of forgotten lore
While I nodded, nearly napping, suddenly there came a tapping,
As of someone gently rapping, rapping at my chamber door.
"'Tis some visitor," I muttered, "tapping at my chamber door
Only this and nothing more."
```

Script 15.29 Analysis: As you study this script, make sure you understand the open commands (lines 6 and 7). Line 6 opens the file specified in the first parameter ($1) and associates it with standard input (0). Whenever the script reads the standard input, therefore, it is actually reading our file. Line 7, on the other hand, opens our output file ($2) and associates it with standard output. Whenever the script writes a line to standard output, therefore, the line is actually written to our file. Now study the body of the loop. All it does is print the line read in line 10 to the standard output file.

Closing Files

You may have noticed that we did not close the files in Script 15.29. If the files do not need to be reused, they do not need to be closed, although it is a good idea to close them anyway. The end of the script automatically closes all open files.

For those occasions, however, in which we need to write a file in the first part of a script and read it in the second part, we need to close and then reopen it. The close commands are:

```
exec 0<&-                                    exec 1>&-
```

The first example closes an input file; the second closes an output file. For example, to close an output file and then open it as input, we use the redirection substitution operators to first close the output $(4>\&-)^3$ and then open it as input $(4<\&)$. The number indicates which stream descriptor is being closed. The minus is the close command's syntax.

Open Multiple Input or Output Files

In Script 15.29, we used only one input and one output file. With the execute command, we can open multiple input and output files. To demonstrate working with multiple files, we return to our bookstore example that we introduced in Chapter 12. It contains data for three terms (Table 15.7).

TABLE 15.7 *Data for Script 15.30*

Term	Department	Sales
1	clothing	3141
1	computers	9161
1	supplies	2563
1	textbooks	21312
2	clothing	3252
2	computers	12321
2	supplies	2242
2	textbooks	15462
3	clothing	2845
3	supplies	1805
3	computers	10262
3	textbooks	20754

In Script 15.30, we read the bookstore file and write it to four files, one for each department.

---

[3]See Redirecting to One File on page 150.

SCRIPT 15.30 *Split Bookstore Files*

```
 1 #!/bin/ksh
 2 #  Script: splitFile.scr
 3 #  Split bookstore file by departments into four files
 4 #  The files are passed as arguments
 5
 6 # Open files
 7 exec 0<$1                        # Input file
 8 exec 3>$2                        # Clothing
 9 exec 4>$3                        # Computers
10 exec 5>$4                        # Supplies
11 exec 6>$5                        # Texts
12
13 while read line
14 do
15     print $line | egrep 'clothing'   1>& 3
16     print $line | egrep 'computers'  1>& 4
17     print $line | egrep 'supplies'   1>& 5
18     print $line | egrep 'textbooks'  1>& 6
19 done
20
21 # Close files
22 exec 0<&-
23 exec 3>&-
24 exec 4>&-
25 exec 5>&-
26 exec 6>&-
27
28 print File processing complete.
```

```
$ splitFile.scr bookstore.dat clot.dat comp.dat supp.dat text.dat
```

```
Output:
File processing complete.
```

```
$ cat clot.dat
1 clothing 3141
2 clothing 3252
3 clothing 2845
```

```
$ cat comp.dat
1 computers 9161
2 computers 12321
3 computers 10262
```

```
$ cat supp.dat
1 supplies 2563
2 supplies 2242
3 supplies 1805
```

```
$ cat text.dat
1 textbooks 21312
2 textbooks 15462
3 textbooks 20754
```

Script 15.30 Analysis: This script merits some discussion. First, carefully study the open file commands. We must relate the input file, parameter $1, to standard input because we are using the **read** command, which requires that it get its input from standard input. The rest of the files are assigned to file stream descriptors starting with 3. To be able to remember them, we add a comment identifying the department to each line.

There are several different solutions to this problem. We chose an **egrep** solution because it uses standard expressions. However, it would be very inefficient if we directly used the **egrep** statements in the test because each one would pass the entire file in turn. To make the script efficient, therefore, we printed the current line and piped it to **egrep.** Using this design, each **egrep** statement sees only one line at a time. This means that the first file line is processed by each **egrep** statement in turn, then the second line, and so forth until the file has been completely processed.

At the end of the script, we print an end message. This is a good technique that confirms to the user that the script completed normally. The output of each file is displayed using **cat** so that we can verify that the script worked correctly.

15.9 Shell Environment and Script

A script, after it is made executable, becomes a command for the shell. Like any command, the script is executed in a child shell. The child shell inherits its environment from its parent. As it executes, it may modify its environment, but any changes are lost when it terminates and control returns to the parent shell. In other words, a script may modify its environment, but it cannot modify its parent environment. To demonstrate how environmental changes are made, we wrote Script 15.31.

SCRIPT 15.31 *Child Shells: Temporary Environmental Changes*

```
1 #!/bin/ksh
2 #   Script: childScript.scr
3 #   Modify environment by changing pwd
4
5 print "Current directory was:    " $(pwd)
6 cd ../
7 print "Current directory is now: " $(pwd)
```

```
Execution:
$ pwd                                    # Before executing script
/mnt/diska/staff/gilberg/unix14Korn

$ childScript.scr
Current directory was:     /mnt/diska/staff/gilberg/unix14Korn
Current directory is now:  /mnt/diska/staff/gilberg

$ pwd                                    # After executing script
/mnt/diska/staff/gilberg/unix14Korn
```

Script 15.31 Analysis: The script itself is very simple. The only complexity is that we used command substitution to execute the **pwd** command from within the script. The script execution is of importance. We begin by displaying the current working directory. We then execute the script, which displays the current directory, changes it, and then displays it to prove that it was changed. When the script completes, we again display the current directory to prove that the change made by the child shell has in fact been lost.

Having demonstrated that the changes made by a child command are temporary, we now show you how to make them permanent. We accomplish this with the dot command. Because the script is then executed in the current shell, any environmental changes made are permanent. To demonstrate running the script in the current shell, we reexecute Script 15.31 in Script 15.32. Note that the dot is a command, and there must be a space between it and the argument.

SCRIPT 15.32 *Child Shells: Permanent Environmental Changes*

```
$ pwd                              # Before executing script
/mnt/diska/staff/gilberg/unix14Korn

$ . childScript.scr
Current directory was:      /mnt/diska/staff/gilberg/unix14Korn
Current directory is now:   /mnt/diska/staff/gilberg

$ pwd                              # After executing script
/mnt/diska/staff/gilberg
```

15.10 Script Examples

In this section, we demonstrate some complete scripts applications. The applications were chosen to demonstrate different techniques presented in the chapter. We use the same documentation format discussed in the previous chapter.

Calculate

Script 15.33 is a small calculator that adds, subtracts, multiplies, and divides only two integers. There are two division options; one returns the quotient and one returns the remainder. The script requires three arguments: the operation to be used and two integer numbers. The options are add (-a), subtract (-s), multiply (-m), quotient (-q), and remainder (-r).

SCRIPT 15.33 *Calculate Script File*

```
 1  #!/bin/ksh
 2  #NAME:          calc.scr
 3  #TASK:          Adds, subtracts, multiplies, and divides integers
 4  #AUTHOR:
 5  #DATE WRITTEN:
 6  #SYNOPSIS:      calculate option num1 num2
 7  #                   options: -a: add       -s: subtract
 8  #                            -m: multiply -q: quotient  -r: remainder
 9  #DESCRIPTION:   Adds, subtracts, multiplies or divides two integers
10  #                   based on argument 1.
11  #EXIT VALUE
```

Continued

SCRIPT 15.33 *Calculate Script File*

```
12 #                 0       if successfully completed
13 #                 1       if wrong number of arguments
14 #                 2       if wrong option
15 # ========================================================
16
17 # Load Korn shell user functions (contains numeric())
18 . functions.scr
19
20 if (( $# != 3 ))
21 then
22     print "Exactly one option and two integers needed"
23     print "Usage: $0 -option integer integer"
24     exit 1
25 fi
26
27 getopts asmqr opt 2> /dev/null          # System messages to trash
28 case $opt in
29     a) opr=+                 ;;
30     s) opr=-                 ;;
31     m) opr=\*                ;;
32     q) opr=/                 ;;
33     r) opr=%                 ;;
34    \?) print "Invalid option"   ;
35        print "Usage: $0 -{asmqr} integer integer" ;
36        exit 2                 ;;
37 esac
38
39 shift
40
41 # Use numeric() to validate $1 and $2
42 valid $1
43 valid $2
44
45 ((res = $1 $opr $2 ))
46
47 print "$1 $opr $2 is $res"
48 exit 0
```

```
Execution:
$ calc.scr -a a 3
a is not numeric
```

```
$ calc.scr -a 2 b
b is not numeric
```

```
$ calc.scr -a 2 3
2 + 3 is 5
```

```
$ calc.scr -s 2 3
2 - 3 is -1
```

```
$ calc.scr -m 2 3
2 * 3 is 6
```

```
$ calc.scr -q 7 3
```

Continued

SCRIPT 15.33   *Calculate Script File—Continued*

```
    7 / 3 is 2
    $ calc.scr -r 7 3
    7 % 3 is 1
    $ calc.scr -r 7
    Exactly one option and two integers needed
    Usage: calc.scr -option integer integer
    $ calc.scr -x 7 3
    Invalid option
    Usage: calc.scr -{asmqr} integer integer
```

Script 15.33 Analysis: As you might imagine, this little script requires lots of testing. In Script 15.13, we developed a validate function to verify that a value is numeric. That function has been placed in our function file (functions.scr) and we use it in this script to validate the numeric arguments. The function library is loaded by the dot command in line 18.

We validate the options using the **getopts** command in line 27. The last test demonstrates its output. We must have five tests just to test the five math operations. Then we must test for no arguments, not enough arguments, and too many arguments. To test the numeric arguments, we call valid( ) in lines 42 and 43. There is one more test that we didn't do. Looking at the script, can you see what it is?[4]

Reverse

To reverse a string, we start at the left end and extract the first character. We put it in a new string called rev. We then loop and extract the second character and put it in on the front of rev. We continue looping until all characters have been extracted and assigned to the new string. (Script 15.34).

SCRIPT 15.34   *Reverse a String Script File*

```
 1 #!/bin/ksh
 2 #NAME:         strrev.scr
 3 #TASK:         Reverse a string received as an argument.
 4 #AUTHOR
 5 #DATE WRITTEN:
 6 #SYNOPSIS:     strrev.str string
 7 #          or strrev.str "aa bbb cccc"
 8 #DESCRIPTION: Reverses a string using a loop. If string contains
 9 #             white space, it must be enclosed in quotes.
10 #EXIT VALUE
11 #             0    if successfully completed
12 #             1    if wrong number of arguments
13 # =========================================================
```
Continued

---

[4]We didn't test for a zero divisor. If a user enters a zero divisor, the system will display an error message, but it would be better to have the script do it. We leave this problem for an exercise.

SCRIPT 15.34   *Reverse a String Script File*

```
14  if (( $# != 1 ))
15     then
16         print "This script requires one argument."
17         print "Usage: $0 string"
18         exit 1
19  fi
20
21  org=$1
22  rev=""
23  len=${#1}
24
25  while (( $len > 0 ))
26  do
27     left=$(expr "$org" : '\(.\).*')
28     org=$(expr  "$org" : '.\(.*\)')
29     rev=$left$rev
30     (( len = len - 1 ))
31  done
32
33  print $rev
34  exit $0
```

```
Execution:
$ strrev.scr
This script requires one argument.
Usage: strrev.scr string
```

```
$ strrev.scr string
gnirts
```

```
$ strrev.scr strings are very useful
This script requires one argument.
Usage: strrev.scr string
```

```
$ strrev.scr 'strings are very useful'
lufesu yrev era sgnirts
```

Script 15.34 Analysis: Testing for Script 15.34 is relatively easy. The only error is the wrong number of arguments. We therefore test it with no arguments and with more than one argument. For valid tests, we need at least two: one with no whitespace and one with whitespace in the string. Note that the documentation at the beginning of the script tells the user that strings with whitespace must be enclosed in quotes.

Add Column

This script demonstrates some of the power we have in UNIX. With a very simple script, we are able to read a file and calculate and print the sum of a column. We demonstrate this capability in Script 15.35.

SCRIPT 15.35   *Add Column Script*

```
1  #!/bin/ksh
2  #NAME:        addCol.scr
```
Continued

SCRIPT 15.35   *Add Column Script—Continued*

```
 3  #TASK:          Add the values in a specific column in a file
 4  #AUTHOR:
 5  #DATE WRITTEN:
 6  #SYNOPSIS:      addCol.scr file column_num
 7  #DESCRIPTION:   Uses awk to determine column.
 8  #               File must be in columns separated by whitespace
 9  #                    1       2       3
10  #                    11      22      33
11  #                    111     222     333
12  #EXIT VALUE
13  #               0       if successfully completed
14  #               1       if wrong number of arguments
15  #               2       if the second argument is not numeric
16  #
17  # =======================================================
18  # Validate Numeric Function
19  numeric( )
20  {
21   # Test parameter 1 by adding.
22   # If error, display error and quit.
23   # All output to trash.
24   let x=$1+1 1>/dev/null 2>&1
25   if (( $? != 0 ))                  # if exit status is false
26   then
27      print $1 is not numeric
28      exit 1                         # exit command kills script
29   fi
30   return
31  } #End of Function
32
33  # Script body
34  if (( $# != 2 ))
35  then
36      print "Exactly two arguments required"
37      print "Usage: $0 file_name column_number"
38      exit 1
39  fi
40
41  #Test for numeric column number
42  numeric $2
43
44  filename=$1
45  awk '{total += $colNum} END {print total}' colNum=$2 $filename
46  exit 0
```

```
Input File: add.dat
              1       2       3
              11      22      33
              111     222     333
```

Continued

SCRIPT 15.35 *Add Column Script*

```
Execution:
$ addCol.scr                                # No arguments
Exactly two arguments required
Usage: addCol.scr file_name column_number

$ addCol.scr 1 add.dat                      # Arguments reversed
add.dat is not numeric
Usage: addCol.scr file_name column_number

$ addCol.scr add.dat 1
123

$ addCol.scr add.dat 3
369
```

Script 15.35 Analysis: To test for a numeric column, we generalized Script 15.13. Study it to see how we passed the number to be validated.

Study line 45 carefully; it contains a key concept. We cannot pass a positional parameter to **awk** because it uses the dollar arguments (such as $2) as field designations (see item 4 on page 627). To pass a positional parameter to **awk**, therefore, we assign it to a variable.

To test the script, we use a file that contains the three columns described in the script documentation. Two additional tests are required to verify that the validation tests work.

15.11   Key Terms

accepting signal	function call	signal
basename command	**getopts** command	signal type
built-in command	here document	**sleep** command
catching signal	ignoring signal	string comparison
dirname command	opening and closing files	string compression
dot command	parsing option	string length
exec command	parsing pathname	trap command
finding substrings	prompt	variable evaluation
function	return command	variable substitution
function body	shell environment	

15.12   Tips

1. Use ${...} if you want to evaluate a variable and concatenate the result with another string.

2. Use the **expr** command to extract a substring from a string.

3. The **grep, sed,** and **awk** utilities need an input file and create an output file. If you want to manipulate a string using these commands, you should first change the string to a one-line file (using the **print** command). The result of the **grep** command is also a file. If you want to change the result back to a string, you should use command substitution (backquotes) with the **grep** command.

4. To use a variable in **grep, sed,** or **awk,** enclose it in double quotes, not single quotes.

5. To use a positional parameter with **awk,** first assign it to another variable and then use the new variable inside the **awk** script.

6. Place the ending token of a here document at the beginning of a line.

7. In a script, a function must be placed before it is called.

8. A function can return a value only through its exit status.

9. Functions can be put in the `.profile` file. Because the profile file is executed at login, these functions will always be available. However, before using newly created functions, the `.profile` file must be executed with the dot command to activate them.

10. Functions can also be put in a library file. However, before using functions in a library file, they must be activated by executing it with the dot command.

11. Use a **trap** command if you do not want a script to respond to a signal using a default action.

12. Use the dot command to execute a command in the current shell rather than a subshell.

13. If you want to change the environment of the current shell using a command, execute the command in the current shell by using the dot command.

14. To consider a string containing whitespaces as one single argument, enclose it in double quotes.

15. If you use options, the shell interprets each option as one argument. To separate options from real arguments, use the **getopts** command to handle the options and then use the **shift** command to discard the options and position the first argument in $1.

16. Use **dirname** and **basename** commands to extract the directory name and a base name from a pathname.

17. Use **basename** with two arguments to extract the filenames from the file extension. Use it in a loop to change the extensions of a set of files.

18. Use the **exec** command to open and close files inside the script.

15.13 Commands

The following commands were discussed in this chapter. For more details, see Appendix F and the corresponding pages shown in the following table.

Command	Description	Options	Page
. (dot)	*Synopsis: . command* Reads files from the current shell.		641
basename	*Synopsis: basename pathname [argument]* Extracts base name or extension of a pathname.		648
dirname	*Synopsis: dirname pathname* Extracts the directory name of a pathname.		648
exec	*Synopsis: exec ...* Opens and closes files.		651

Continued

Command	Description	Options	Page
`getopts`	***Synopsis:*** *getopts options variable* Parses options.		644
`return`	***Synopsis:*** *return [expression]* Returns from function.		631
`sleep`	***Synopsis:*** *sleep seconds* Sleeps for a number of seconds.		640
`trap`	***Synopsis:*** *trap "action" signals* Runs a command when a signal is received.		638

15.14 Summary

- To evaluate a variable (that is, to use its contents), we can use one of two formats: `$variable` or `${variable}`. The second format should be used when we want to concatenate a variable value with a string.
- Variable substitution uses a variable or a positional parameter value to conditionally create a string. The Korn shell supports four types of substitution: substitute if variable null (–), substitute if variable not null (+), substitution assignment (=), and substitution validation (?).
- We can use several types of string manipulation in the Korn shell: compress string, string length, locate a substring in a string, and extract a substring.
- The here document token (<<) allows us to insert text after a command instead of reading it from a file.
- The Korn shell allows the use of functions in a script. The function must be before the call to the function. Normally, functions are placed at the beginning of the script, just after the documentation.
- The function starts with the function name and a pair of parentheses. The function body should be enclosed between two braces.
- We can place functions in a file. The most commonly used file for a function is the profile file. The second file choice is a library file; library files must be executed using the dot command before the function is used.
- A signal is a message sent to a process, such as a running script, by either another process or the operating system (kernel).
- There are several signal types defined in the Korn shell. The most common are SIGHUP, SIGINT, SIGQUIT, SIGKILL, SIGTERM, and SIGTSTP.
- A process (script) can respond to a signal in one of three ways: accept the default, ignore the signal, and catch the signal.
- The **trap** command is used to catch and process a signal.
- The built-in commands are those commands that are included in the Korn shell interpreter. Because they are part of the interpreter, they don't need to be loaded and can therefore be executed faster than general UNIX commands.
- The **sleep** command allows the script to sleep for a number of seconds. It is used to wait for an event to happen.

- The dot command allows the execution of a command in the current shell instead of in a subshell.
- Scripts can be enhanced using several scripting techniques discussed in the chapter.
- We can read a string, including whitespaces, as one single argument if we use double quotes around the string.
- We can create prompts using the **print** command.
- We can parse script options using the **getopts** command.
- We can parse a pathname using the **dirname** and **basename** commands. We can also use the **basename** command to separate a filename and an extension.
- We can open and close files using a version of the **exec** command.

15.15 Practice Set

Review Questions

1. What would be printed from the following commands?
   ```
   x=24
   print ${x:-30}
   ```
2. What would be printed from the following command assuming y is null?
   ```
   print ${y:-30}
   ```
3. What would be printed from the following commands?
   ```
   x=Hello
   print ${x:+40}
   ```
4. What would be printed from the following commands?
   ```
   x=Hello
   print ${x:=40}
   print $x
   ```
5. What would be printed from the following commands?
   ```
   x=Hello
   print ${x:?40}
   print $x
   ```
6. What would be printed from the following commands?
   ```
   print ${x:?40}
   ```
7. What is the result of the following command?
   ```
   print "This is the              world of              UNIX"
   ```
8. What are the results of the following commands?
   ```
   a. expr "Hello World"  :  '\(..\).*'
   b. expr "Hello World"  :  '...\(..\).*'
   c. expr "Hello World"  :  '.*\(..\)'
   ```
9. Demonstrate how to use the **sed** command to simulate the following **expr** command:
   ```
   expr "Hello World"  :  '\(..\).*'
   ```
10. Demonstrate how to use the **sed** command to simulate the following **expr** command:
    ```
    expr "Hello World"  :     '...\(..\).*'
    ```

11. Demonstrate how to use the **sed** command to simulate the following **expr** command:

```
expr "Hello World"  :    '.*\(..\)'
```

12. Demonstrate how to trap a SIGHUP signal.

13. Demonstrate how a script can ignore a SIGHUP signal.

14. Demonstrate how a script can trap either a SIGINT or SIGTSTP signal. The script should copy a file before allowing either of the signals to terminate the script.

15. Demonstrate how to use **getopts** to capture two options, a and b, when the first one can have a value and the second one does not.

Exercises

16. Write a short script that, given a string as the only command-line argument, uses **grep** to determine whether the first and last character of the string are the same.

17. Repeat Exercise 16 using a **sed** command in the script.

18. Write a short script that, given a string as the only command-line argument, exchanges the first three characters of the string with the last three characters.

19. Write a short script that, given the name of the file as an argument, reads the file and creates a new file containing only lines consisting of one word.

20. Write a short script that changes the name of files passed as arguments to lowercase.

21. Write a short script that, given a filename as the argument, deletes all even lines (lines 2, 4, 6, . . . , n) in the file.

22. Write a short script that, given a filename as the argument, deletes all odd lines (lines 1, 3, 5, . . . , n) in the file.

23. Write a short script that, given a filename as the argument, combines odd and even lines together. In other words, lines 1 and 2 become line 1, lines 3 and 4 become line 2, and so on.

24. Write a short script that changes the first three letters of the name of all files (passed as arguments) to lowercase.

25. Write a short script that, given two file names as arguments, prints the name of the file that is newer.

26. If a script is run as pgm.scr -a -b file[345], what is the value of $#? What is the value of $*?

27. What is the exit status of the following script?

```
#!/bin/ksh
## end
```

28. What is the exit status of a **grep** command when it finds a pattern? What is the exit status of a **grep** command when it does not find a pattern? Write a one-line script that verifies your answers.

29. What is the exit status of a **sed** command when it finds a pattern? What is the exit status of a **sed** command when it does not find a pattern? Write a one-line script that verifies your answers.

30. What is the exit status of an **awk** command when it finds a pattern? What is the exit status of an **awk** command when it does not find a pattern? Write a one-line script that verifies your answers.

31. A script uses up to four options and exactly three arguments. The options are called s, t, u, and v. Use the necessary commands to store the first argument in $1 using the **getopts** command.

15.16 Lab Sessions

Each of the lab sessions in this chapter requires you to write a script, make it executable, and then execute it.

Session 1

Create a script that finds each line in a file that contains a specified string.

Preparation

Create a file of at least 20 lines and insert a double quoted string, such as "hello," in several lines.

Script

- **Script Name:** search.scr
- **Arguments:** Two arguments. The first is the string to be found; the second is the name of the file.
- **Validation:** The minimum validation requirements are:
  - Ensure that exactly two arguments are entered.
  - Ensure that the second argument is the name of the file that exists and is not empty.
- **Body Section:** Create a script that uses **grep** and loops to find the line numbers in which the string is found. Note that **grep** should be applied to each line, not the whole file. The script should print the result in the following format:
  ```
  Line Number: [Line contents]
  ```

Testing the Script

1. Test the script with no arguments.
2. Test the script with one argument.
3. Test the script with two arguments but the second one is not a file.
4. Test the script with two correct arguments.

Testing the Effect of the Script

Compare the results of your script with a printout of the file.

Session II

Modify the script written in Session I to search for multiple occurrences of the specified string in each line. Print the result in the following format:

```
Line Number: Count: [Occurrences] [Line contents]
...

Line Number: Count: [The line contents]


        Total Count: [Total Occurrences]
```

Change the original file to include two or three occurrences of the string in some lines. Follow the same requirements as Session I.

Session III

Create a script that compiles all C source files in your home directory and creates executable files.

Preparation

Create at least five C source files in your home directory. The files do not have to be real C source files; at a minimum, they should contain a comment line that contains a unique program name such as the following example:

```
/* ........ file1.c ........*/
```

The name of the files should have a C source file extension (.c), such as file1.c.

Script

- **Script Name:** compile.scr
- **Arguments:** None
- **Validation:** The minimum validation requirement is:
    - Ensure that there is no argument.
- **Body Section:** Create a script that finds all files with extension (.c) under your directory and compiles them one by one. Each executable file should have the same name as the source file except that the extension should be (.exe). For example, if the source filename is file1.c, the executable filename should be file1.exe. Use the following command to compile a file:

```
cc -o executable_filename source_filename
```

Testing the Script

1. Test the script with one or two arguments.
2. Test the script with no arguments.

Testing the Effect of the Script

Verify that executable files were created under your home directory.

Session IV

In a C program, there is only one comment format. All comments must start with an open comment token, /*, and end with a close comment token, */. C++ programs

Continued

Session IV—*Continued*

use the C tokens for comments that span several lines. Single-line comments start with two slashes (//). In either case, the start token can be anywhere on the line.

Write a script to change every single-line comment in a C++ source file that uses C program start and end comment tokens to a single-line comment starting with a C++ single-line token. The comment itself is to be unchanged.

Preparation

Create at least five C++ source files in your home directory. The files do not have to be real C++ source files; they can contain only a few lines of comments, some with C program tokens and some with C++ single-line tokens. Each program should have at least one multiline comment and at least one single-line comment that uses the C program tokens. Use one or more blank lines between comments. The name of the files should have a C++ extension (.c++), such as `file1.c++`.

Script

- **Script Name:** `commentType.scr`
- **Arguments:** None
- **Validation:** The minimum validation requirement is:
    - Ensure that there is no argument.
- **Body Section:** Create a script that finds all files with extension (.c++) under your directory and change only the lines with comments. The name of the files should be preserved. If a file has the name `file1.c++`, the name still should be `file1.c++` after the change.

Testing the Script

1. Test the script with one or two arguments.
2. Test the script with no arguments.

Testing the Effect of the Script

Check to see if the comments are changed in the files.

Session V

Write a script that creates a file out of the `/etc/passwd` file.

Preparation

None

Script

- **Script Name:** `newEtcPasswd.scr`
- **Arguments:** One. The name of the file.
- **Validation:** The minimum validation requirement is:
    - Ensure that there is only one argument.
- **Body Section:** Create a script that makes a file out of the information in the `/etc/passwd` file using the following format:

Continued

User Name	User ID	Group ID	Home Director
---------	-------	--------	-------------
John	234	23	/etc/usr/staff/john
...	...	...	...

Testing the Script

1. Test the script with two or more arguments.
2. Test the script with no arguments.
3. Test the script with one argument that is not the name of a file.
4. Test the script with one argument that is the name of the file.

Testing the Effect of the Script

Verify the file was created and contains the correct information and format.

Session VI

Create a script that, given a user name, finds the home directory of the user using the `/etc/passwd` file.

Preparation

None

Script

- **Script Name:** `findHomeDirectory.scr`
- **Arguments:** One. The user name.
- **Validation:** The minimum validation requirement is:
  - Ensure that there is only one argument.
- **Body Section:** Create a script that, given the name of a user (as the only argument), prints the absolute pathname of the user's home directory.

Testing the Script

1. Test the script with two or more arguments.
2. Test the script with no arguments.
3. Test the script with one argument.

Testing the Effect of the Script

Verify the script by using your user name.

Session VII

Create a script that finds all files in subdirectories that have the same filename.

Preparation

Make several directories, at different levels, under your home directory. For example, make ~/A, ~/B, ~/C, ~/A/AA, ~/A/BB, ~/A/AA/AAA, and so on until you have at

Continued

Session VII—*Continued*

least 15 directories. Copy a small junk file named `file1` under some of these directories; do not change its name. Copy another small junk file named `file2` under some other directories. Copy a third junk file under several directories. Be sure that some directories get a combination of `file1` and `file2` or `file1` and `file3`. In at least three of the directories, create a junk file with a unique name.

Script

- **Script Name:** `duplicateName.scr`
- **Arguments:** None
- **Validation:** The minimum validation requirement is:
  - Ensure that there is no argument.
- **Body Section:** Create a script that uses **find** and **awk** commands to create a list of files that are duplicated; use the full pathname for the duplicated filenames. Hint: Use a **basename** command and an array in **awk**. The output should look like the following example:

```
file1: ~/A/file1      ~/A/AA/file1      ~/A/B/BB/BBB/file1
file2: ~/B/file2      ~/C/file2
...
file3: ~/BB/BBB/BBBB
```

Testing the Script

1. Test the script with one argument.
2. Test the script with no arguments.

Testing the Effect of the Script

Use a recursive long list command to list the complete contents of your home directory. Verify the output of your script against the list command output.

## CHAPTER 16

Interactive C Shell

The C shell was developed by William Joy at the University of California, Berkeley. Like other UNIX shells, the C shell is a dual-purpose utility. It can be used interactively as an interpreter that reads, interprets, and executes user commands. It can also be used as a programming language to write shell scripts. In this chapter, we discuss how to use the C shell interactively. In the next two chapters, we use its programming language capability to create shell scripts.

16.1 C Shell Features

In this section, we discuss C shell features. Many of them were discussed previously in Chapter 5. New features are fully discussed in the following sections; those covered in Chapter 5 are summarized and cross-referenced.

C Shell Sessions

When we use the C shell interactively, we execute commands at the shell prompt. In Chapter 5, we discussed how to start a session, change shells, check the current shell, and terminate a session. The workflow is summarized in Figure 5.2 on page 144. We suggest that you review this material to make sure you remember how these commands work.

Standard Streams

In Section 5.2, Standard Streams on page 146, we defined the three standard streams—standard input (0), standard output (1), and standard error (2)—available in all shells. Figure 16.1 shows how the standard streams relate to a shell command.

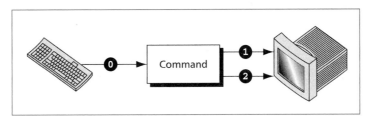

FIGURE 16.1   *Standard Streams*

Redirection

The standard streams can be redirected from and to files. In Section 5.3 on page 147, we discussed how to redirect standard streams. Stream redirection is summarized in Figure 16.2. As you study this figure, note that there is one operator (<) for redirecting standard input to a command and four operators for directing data to standard output or standard error (>, >!, >>, and >>!). If you don't remember the details, refer to page 147.

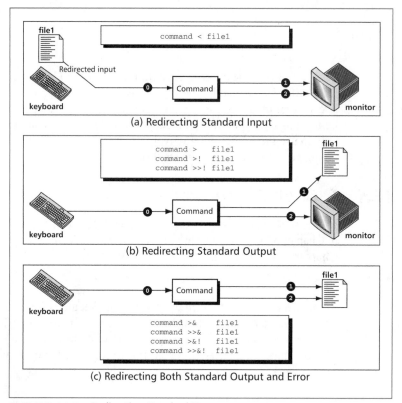

FIGURE 16.2 *Redirecting Standard Streams*

If we don't use redirection, standard output and standard error both go to the monitor. How do we write the redirection so that both go to the same file? This requires that we use and-redirection (see Redirecting to One File on page 150). We show how it is done in the next example.

```
command >& file1
```

Pipes

The pipe operator temporarily saves the output from one command in a buffer that is being used at the same time as the input to the next command. Its operation is shown in Figure 16.3. Pipes are discussed in Section 5.4 on page 151.

tee Command

The **tee** command copies standard input to standard output and at the same time copies it to one or more files. If the stream is coming from another command, such as

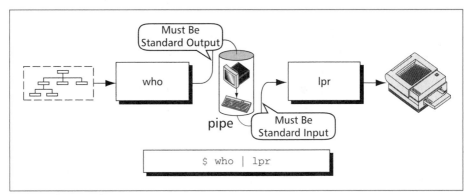

FIGURE 16.3 *Pipes*

who, it can be piped to the **tee** command. For more information, refer to Section 5.5 on page 153.

Combining Commands

We can combine commands in four ways: sequenced commands, grouped commands, chained commands, and conditional commands. These command variations were discussed in Section 5.6 on page 154. The C shell supports all four.

Command-Line Editing

The C shell does not support command-line editing. It is possible, however, to edit commands using **history** commands.

Quotes

In Section 5.8 on page 159, we discussed the three quote types: backslash, double quotes, and single quotes. The C shell supports all three. You may want to reread Section 5.8 to refresh your memory on their use.

Command Substitution

Command substitution is used to convert a command's output to a string that can be stored in another string or a variable. We discussed its use in Section 5.9 on page 164. The C shell supports command substitution using backquotes (the parenthetical construct is not supported) as shown in Figure 16.4.

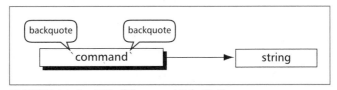

FIGURE 16.4 *C Shell Command Substitution*

Session 16.1 demonstrates command substitution in the C shell.

SESSION 16.1   *Command Substitution*

```
$ echo The date and time are: `date`
The date and time are: Mon Aug 6  8:27:25 PDT 2001
```

Job Control

Job control is used to control how and where a job is executed in the foreground or background. It was discussed in Section 5.10, Job Control. The C shell supports the features of job control discussed in Chapter 5.

Aliases in the C Shell

An **alias** is a means of creating a customized command by assigning a name or acronym to a command. If the name we use is one of the standard shell commands, such as **dir,** then the **alias** replaces the shell command. In the C shell, an alias is created by using the **alias** command. The basic format is:

```
alias name definition
```

In this code, **alias** is the command keyword, `name` is the name of the alias name being created, and `definition` is the command or command combination to be renamed. As a simple example, let's create a new directory list. The new command is shown in Session 16.2.

SESSION 16.2   *Alias Definition in C Shell*

```
% alias dir "echo Gilberg Directory List; ls -l | more"
% dir
Gilberg's Directory List
total 30
-rw-------    1 gilberg  staff      5782 Sep 10 16:19 TheRaven
...
-rw-r--r--    1 gilberg  staff       149 Apr 18  2000 teeOut1
-rw-r--r--    1 gilberg  staff       149 Apr 18  2000 teeOut2
```

Arguments to Alias Commands

The C shell **alias** command has a powerful set of features, especially for argument definition.Whereas the Korn shell positions arguments only at the end of the generated command, the C shells allows us to define where the arguments are located. Table 16.1 lists the position designators used for alias arguments.

TABLE 16.1   *C Shell Argument Designators*

Designator	Meaning
\ ! *	Position of only argument.
\ ! ^	Position of first argument.

Continued

TABLE 16.1 *C Shell Argument Designators*

Designator	Meaning
$\backslash!\$$	Position of last argument.
$\backslash!:n$	Position of nth argument.

In Session 16.3, we rewrite the list command using only one argument. We run the command twice, once with an argument and once with no argument. The no-argument output is abbreviated, with only the first and last line shown.

SESSION 16.3 *Only Argument Position Example*

```
% alias fl 'ls -l \!* | more'
% fl TheRavenV1
-rw-------   1 gilberg  staff       366 Sep  9 19:56 TheRavenV1

% fl
total 30
-rw-------   1 gilberg  staff      5782 Sep 10 16:19 TheRaven
...
-rw-r--r--   1 gilberg  staff       149 Apr 18  2000 teeOut2
```

Session 16.3 Analysis: Note that the quotes are placed around the **alias** command, including the only argument designator ($\backslash!*$), which placed it in the middle of the command exactly where it belongs. Note also that when no argument is provided, the full list is generated.

For a more complex example, let's write a command that copies one file and renames it. We need two parameters: one for the original filename and one for the copy name. The code is in Session 16.4.

SESSION 16.4 **alias** *Command with Two Arguments*

```
% ls ~/delete.me
No such file or directory

% alias cpto 'cp \!:1 \!:$'
alias cpto '\$:1 \$:2'

% cpto file1 ~/delete.me
% ls -/delete.me
/mnt/diska/staff/gilberg/delete.me
```

Session 16.4 Analysis: We start this script with a list command to prove that the file doesn't exist. We then create the copy-to command and execute it copying `file1` from the current directory to the home directory ($\sim/$) and renaming it `delete.me`. After the copy, we run the list command again to prove that the file was copied.

Listing Aliases

The C shell provides a method to list all aliases or to list a specified alias. Both use the **alias** command. To list all aliases, we use the **alias** command with no arguments. To list a specific command, we use the **alias** command with one argument, the name of the **alias** command. Session 16.5 contains an alias list of all our **alias** commands.

SESSION 16.5   *List Alias Example*

```
% alias
cpto    (cp cpto ~/cp cpto /mnt/diska/staff/gilberg/cp)
dir     echo "Gilberg Directory List; ls -l | more"
fl      ls -l !* | more
```

Removing Aliases

Aliases are removed by using the **unalias** command. It has one argument, a list of aliases to be removed. When it is used with the all option (-a), it deletes all aliases. You should be very careful, however, with this option: It deletes all aliases, even those defined by the system administrator. For this reason, some system administrators disable this option. The **unalias** command is discussed in Chapter 5 on page 173. Session 16.6 demonstrates the **unalias** command.

SESSION 16.6   *Removing Aliases in C Shell*

```
% unalias fl
% alias
cpto    (cp cpto ~/cp cpto /mnt/diska/staff/gilberg/cp)
dir     echo "Gilberg Directory List; ls -l | more"
```

Alias Summary

Table 16.2 Summarizes the **alias** Command.

TABLE 16.2   *Alias Summary*

Feature	Command Summary
Define	% alias x command
Argument	Anywhere
List	% alias
Remove	% unalias x, y, z
Remove All	% unalias -a

16.2   Two Special Files

There are two special files in UNIX that can be used by any shell.

Trash File (`/dev/null`)

The trash file is a special file that is used for deleting data. Found under the device (`/dev`) directory, it has a very special characteristic: Its contents are always emptied immediately after receiving data. In other words, no matter how much or how often data are written to it, they are immediately deleted. Physically, there is only one trash file in the system: It is owned by the superuser.

The `/dev/null` file is kept under the device directory, which is owned by the root. You can verify its ownership with the list command that follows. Note that it is a character special file ('c' as first byte) that can be read or written by any user.

```
% ls -l /dev/null
crw-rw-rw-    1 root       sys        1,  2 Jan 22 17:04 /dev/null
```

Because it is a file, it can be used as both a source and a destination. However, when used as a source, the result is always end of file because it is always empty. While the following two commands are syntactically correct, the first has no effect because the string "Trash me," when sent to the trash file, is immediately deleted. The second has no effect because the file is always empty, which means that there is nothing to display.

```
% echo "Trash me" > /dev/null
% cat /dev/null
%
```

There are occasions when we need to know the exit status of a command without seeing the command output. For example, if we want to know if a key phrase is in a file without seeing the actual lines that contain it, we can send the standard output to trash. We then echo the exit status ($status) to determine if we found the key phrase. This concept is shown in the next example:

```
% grep '…' > /dev/null          # Send output to trash
% echo $status                  # Check if pattern found
```

Terminal File (`/dev/tty`)

Although each terminal in UNIX is a named file, such as `/dev/tty13` and `/dev/tty31`, there is only one physical file, `/dev/tty`. This file is found under the device directory; it represents the terminal of each user. This means that someone using terminal `/dev/tty13` can refer to the terminal using either the full terminal name (`/dev/tty13`) or the generic system name (`/dev/tty`). In fact, two different users can each refer to the terminal using the generic system name at the same time.

The generic terminal file, `/dev/tty`, is owned by the root; everybody has permission to read and write it. It can be used as a source or a destination.

```
% ls -l /dev/tty
crw-rw-rw-    1 root       sys        2,  0 Jan 22 16:18 /dev/tty
```

Both of the commands in the next example are syntactically correct:

```
% cp file1 /dev/tty          # Displays the contents of file1
% cp /dev/tty file1          # File1 is erased and becomes empty
```

Because the terminal file represents a terminal, it cannot store data. Thus, the contents of `file1` in the previous example, when sent to the terminal file, are shown on the monitor but not saved. Because nothing is stored in a terminal file, the second command copies nothing to `file1`.

> The terminal file (`/dev/tty`) is a file under the device directory that belongs to the root. It represents the terminal assigned to each user.

By this time, you are probably wondering why UNIX has this capability when output automatically goes to the monitor already. The answer is that some commands, such as **tee**, require a file for output. If we want both to write to a file and at the same time pass the output to the monitor, we can use the `/dev/tty` file.

In Session 16.7, we want to send a complete list of all files to the monitor while saving a list of all scripts in a file. We do this by sending the list command results to a **tee** command that sends one copy of the file list to the `/dev/tty` file and the second copy to a pipe. The piped results are then fed into a **grep** command that redirects lines containing `.scr` to `temp.file`. Because of the large amount of output, the output lists are edited.

SESSION 16.7   *Sending Output to the **tty** Monitor*

```
% ls -l | tee /dev/tty | grep '\.scr$' > temp.file
total 146
-rw-r--r--    1 gilberg   staff         42 Jul 10   2000 ErrFile
-rwxr--r--    1 gilberg   staff        111 Jul 11   2000 IFS.scr
-rw-r--r--    1 gilberg   staff          0 Jun 11   2000 MidRaven
   .
   .
   .
-rwxr--r--    1 gilberg   staff         36 Jul 31 13:42 who.scr.bak
-rwxr--r--    1 gilberg   staff         36 Jul 31 13:45 who.scrBak
-rwxr--r--    1 gilberg   staff        112 Jul  5   2000 xxforLoop.scr
% cat temp.file
-rwxr--r--    1 gilberg   staff        111 Jul 11   2000 IFS.scr
-rwxr--r--    1 gilberg   staff        925 Jul 10   2000 addCol.scr
-rwxr--r--    1 gilberg   staff        129 Jul  7   2000 backup.scr
   .
   .
   .
-rwxr--r--    1 gilberg   staff        225 Jun 18   2000 variableNum.scr
-rwxr--r--    1 gilberg   staff        171 Jul 29 14:12 whileRead.scr
-rwxr--r--    1 gilberg   staff         36 Jul  8   2000 who.scr
```

16.3 Variables

The C shell allows you to store values in variables (Figure 16.5). A shell variable is a location in memory where values can be stored. There are two broad classifications of variables: user-defined and predefined.

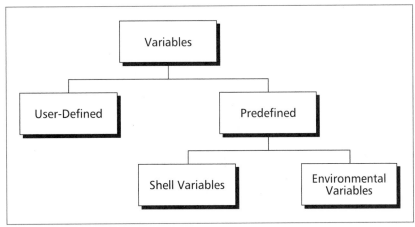

FIGURE 16.5   *Variables*

User-Defined Variables

As implied by their name, user-defined variables are created by the user. Although the user may choose any name, it should not be the same as one of the predefined variables. Each variable must have a name. The name of a variable must start with an alphabetic or underscore (_) character. It then can be followed by zero or more alphanumeric or underscore characters. Figure 16.6 shows three variables.

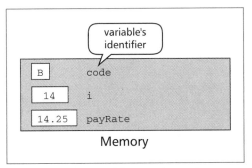

FIGURE 16.6   *Variable Examples*

Predefined Variables

Predefined variables are either shell variables or environmental variables. The shell variables are used to configure the shell. For example, the internal field separator—the character that separates fields in a line—is normally a space or a tab, but it can be defined as any character. Because they are used mostly in shell scripts, they are discussed in the next chapter.

The environmental variables, discussed later in this chapter, are used to configure the shell environment. For example, the term *environmental variable* determines the user's terminal settings.

Storing Values in Variables

The C shell uses the **set** command to store a value in a variable. The format is the **set** command followed by the variable, assign token (=), and value. Note that spaces are permitted before and after the assign token as in the following example:

```
set varA = 7
```

In this example, `varA` is the variable that receives the data, and `7` is the value being stored in it. While the receiving field must always be a variable, the value may be a constant, the value stored in another variable, or as we will see later, any expression that reduces to a single value. Table 16.3 shows some examples of storing values in variables.

TABLE 16.3 *Examples of Assignment Expressions*

Command	Result
set x = 123	x is "123"
set x = Hello	x is "Hello"
set x = "Go Dons!"	x is "Go Dons!"

Note that although the first example in Table 16.3 contains a number, it is stored as a string of digits. That's why we show the results in double quote marks. The last two examples show how we store a character string. While we did not use quotes under the *Command* heading in the second example, we did in the last. The difference is that the last example contains spaces and special characters. Whenever a string contains spaces or special characters, it must be quoted. Figure 16.7 shows an example.

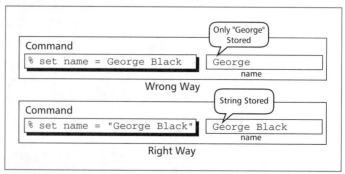

FIGURE 16.7 *The Effect of Using Quotes*

Accessing the Value of a Variable

To access the value of a variable, the name of the variable must be preceded by a dollar sign as shown in Session 16.8. The variable name dollar sign should not be confused with the system prompt $. The value in a variable can be used for many purposes. Values can be used anywhere in a string. For example, you can use the value of a variable at the beginning of the string, in the middle of a string, or at the end of a string. We demonstrate all three positions in Session 16.8.

SESSION 16.8   *Using Values in Strings*

```
% set count = 7
% echo $count is the number after 6 and before 8
7 is the number after 6 and before 8

% echo The value of count is $count as expected.
The value of count is 7 as expected.

% echo My lucky number is $count.
My lucky number is 7.
```

The value of a variable can also be stored in another variable as in Session 16.9.

SESSION 16.9   *Assigning One Variable to Another*

```
% set count = 5
% set number = $count
% echo count contains: $count; number contains: $number
count contains: 5; number contains: 5
```

The value of a variable can be used for other purposes. For example, imagine you want to frequently access a specific directory. To prevent errors and to save time when typing a long pathname for a directory, you can simply store the path in a variable (Session 16.10).

SESSION 16.10   *Storing a Path in a Variable*

```
% set newDir = ~/report/letters
% cd $newDir
% pwd
/usr/forouzan/report/letters
```

Null Variables

If we access a variable that is not set (no value is stored in it), we receive what is called a null value (nothing). We can also explicitly store a null value in a variable by either assigning it a null string ("") or by assigning it nothing. In other words, the default value for any variable is null. Session 16.11 demonstrates the use of null variables.

SESSION 16.11   *Null Variables*

```
% set x = 1                        #Good assignment
% set y =                          #Null assignment
```

Continued

SESSION 16.11 *Null Variables—Continued*

```
% set z = ""                                #Another null assignment
% echo "(x:" $x ") (y:" $y") (z:" $z")"
(x: 1) (y:) (z:)
```

```
% set x= ""                                 #Clear 'x' by setting to null
% echo "(x contains:" $x")"
(x contains: )
```

```
% set x = 1
% echo "(x contains:" $x")"
(x contains: 1)
```

Unsetting a Variable

In Session 16.11, we demonstrated that we can clear a variable by assigning a null value to it. Although this method works, it is better to use the **unset** command (Session 16.12).

SESSION 16.12 *Unsetting Variables*

```
% set x = 1
% echo "(x contains:" $x")"
(x contains: 1)
```

```
% unset x                        #A better way to clear 'x'
% echo "(x contains:" $x")"
x - Undefined variable
```

There is a subtle difference between using **unset** and a null assignment. Both set the variable to a null value. The **unset,** however, also removes the variable name from the list of active variables. If you try to echo a variable after it is **unset,** you will get the error message "Undefined variable."

Storing Filenames

We can also store a filename in a variable. We can even use wildcards. However, we should be aware of how wildcards are handled by the shell. The shell stores the filename including the wildcard in the variable without expanding it. When the value is used, the expansion takes place. Session 16.13 demonstrates how the script handles stored filenames containing wildcards.

SESSION 16.13 *Storing Filenames*

```
% ls
file1       file2       file3.bak
% set filename = "file*"
% echo "filename contains: $filename"           #show contents
filename contains: file*
% echo $filename
file1       file2       file3.bak
```

```
% set filename = "file?"
% echo $filename
file1       file2
```

Session 16.13 Analysis: In the first example, we create a variable and store the aster-isk wildcard value in it. We then print the variable value to prove that it contains the wild-card command. (Note that the variable name is included in the quoted string so it is not expanded.) When we used the variable with the **echo** command, the wildcard is expanded by the shell to print the three matching files. In the second example, we used the question mark wildcard. In this case, only the first two files were listed because they had only five characters in their name. The third file had more than five characters and therefore didn't match the wildcard pattern.

Storing File Contents

We can also store the contents of a file in a variable for processing, such as parsing words. Two steps are required to store the file:

1. Create a copy of the file on standard output using the **cat** utility.
2. Using command substitution (backquotes), convert the standard output contents to a string.

The string can now be stored in a variable. The entire process is done in one command line in Session 16.14.

SESSION 16.14 *Storing a File in a String*

```
% cat storeAsVar.txt
This is       a              file
used to show
the result         of storing    a file in a          variable.
% set x = `cat storeAsVar.txt`
% echo $x
This is a file used to show the result of storing a file in a variable.
```

Session 16.14 Analysis: We begin by showing a three-line file using **cat**. To demon-strate the full effect of storing a file in a variable, we used extra whitespace in the file. We then stored the file in a variable (x). Then, to prove that the file was stored in the variable, we use **echo** to write it to the monitor. In these three commands, we first showed the contents of a file, next converted the file to a string using command substi-tution, and then converted it back to a file (the monitor is actually a file, standard out-put) using the **echo** command. This demonstrates that **echo** and command substitution are the inverse of each other—one converts a file to a string and one converts a string to a file.

Now study the **echo** output carefully. Note that the variable does not contain any of the extra whitespace found in the file. It contains the file as one string with words sepa-rated by a single space character. All nonspace whitespace characters are converted to a space, and all extra spaces are removed.

Storing Commands in a Variable

We can also store a command in a variable. For example, the list command can be stored in a variable. We can then use the variable at the command to execute its con-tents as in Session 16.15.

SESSION 16.15   *Executing a Command Variable*

```
% set x = "ls file*"
% $x
file.scr        file2           file3.bak       file5           fileOut.rpt
file1           file2.bak       file4           file6           fileReport
file1bak        file3           file4.bak       fileList.dat
```

Storing commands in a variable works only with simple commands. If the command is complex (for example, piping the results of the list command to **more**) a command variable will not work. For complex commands, we need the **eval** command, which we discuss later in this chapter.

Exporting Variables

We noted in Chapter 5 that a shell can create another shell. The new shell is called a subshell, or a child shell. The process of creating another shell is known as **forking** a shell.

Figure 16.8 demonstrates the forking process. After executing a **date** command, we fork a new shell by entering `csh`. This command creates a new subshell and waits for a command to be entered. At this point, we can enter any command. To leave the subshell, we key `exit`, which deletes the subshell and takes us back to the parent.

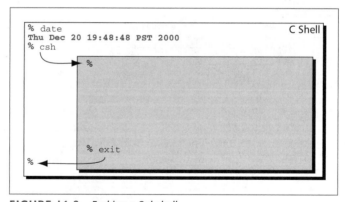

FIGURE 16.8   *Forking a Subshell*

The point we need to understand now is that shell variables are not automatically exported to subshells. This is demonstrated in Session 16.16.

SESSION 16.16   *Variables Are Not Automatically Exported*

```
% set name = George
% echo $name
George
% csh
% echo $name                       # In child shell
% name - Undefined variable
```

If we want to make a variable available to a subshell, we must tell the current shell that we want it exported. Exportable variables are maintained separately from non-exportable variables in the C shell. Exportable variables are created with the **setenv** command; nonexportable variables are created with the **set** command. The format of the **setenv** command follows. Note that only one variable can be declared exportable at a time.

```
setenv variable value
```

Once an exportable variable has been created, whenever a new shell is forked, the variable is automatically created in the subshell and initialized with the variable's current value. If another subshell is then created, the variable is again exported. Each shell's variable is a separate entity; if we change a subshell's variable value, it does not change the value in the parent shell. This process is demonstrated in Session 16.17.

SESSION 16.17 *Exporting Variables*

```
% setenv name George              # Create exportable variable
% echo $name
George

% csh                             # First subshell
% echo $name
George

% csh                             # Second subshell
% echo $name
George
```

To demonstrate that the variables are in fact separate, let's change the value in a subshell. Furthermore, to demonstrate that the subshell is deleted when we exit, we fork another subshell and show that the original value is exported; the changed value is indeed lost. These two situations are shown in Session 16.18.

SESSION 16.18 *Exported Variables Are Separate Entities*

```
% setenv name George              # Create exportable variable
% echo $name
George

% csh                             # Subshell
% echo $name
George                            # name exported

% setenv name Jorge               # name changed
% echo $name
Jorge

% exit                            # Back to parent
% echo $name
George                            # name change lost

% csh                             # Back to subshell
% echo $name
George                            # Original name exported to new shell
```

As has been stated, the nonexportable and exportable variables are maintained separately. This is true even to the point that they can have the same name. However, if both are set, the nonexportable version overrides the exportable version in the current shell. We demonstrate this in Session 16.19.

SESSION 16.19   *Exportable and Nonexportable Variables*

```
% setenv name Ming
% echo $name
Ming                        # Exportable variable
% set name = Margo
% echo $name
Margo                       # Non-exportable variable
% csh                       # Create and move to subshell
% echo $name
Ming                        # Exportable variable
% exit                      # Return to parent
% echo $name
Margo                       # Non-exportable variable active
%
```

> Although technically possible, do not create an exportable and a nonexportable variable with the same name. Duplicate names cause comfusion and eventually errors.

16.4 Output

The output statement in the C shell is the **echo** command.[1] Its format is shown in Figure 16.9.

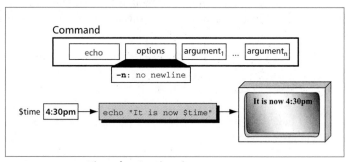

FIGURE 16.9   *The **echo** Command*

The **echo** command creates a file (in the standard output stream) from its arguments. Its arguments can be strings or variables. In Figure 16.9, we embedded a variable in a string. We could have produced the same results by putting the variable after the string. Note, however, that the quoting rules must be observed: The variable cannot be

---

[1]We introduced **echo** in some simple examples previously.

embedded in single quotes. Session 16.20 prints the time, first embedded in the string and then as a separate argument. The third example demonstrates that the variable is not expanded when we incorrectly use single quotes.

SESSION 16.20   *Using the* **echo** *Command*

```
% set time = 4:30pm
% echo "It is now $time"
It is now 4:30pm

% echo "It is now" $time
It is now 4:30pm

% echo 'It is now $time'
It is now $time                        # Error: $time not expanded
```

The **echo** command automatically adds a terminating newline after the last argument. If for some reason we don't want a newline, we can use the -n option. To help format the output, there are nine C-like escape codes that can be used (Table 16.4). When using these codes, they must be enclosed in quotes.

TABLE 16.4   *C Shell Character Codes for* **echo**

Code	Usage
\b	backspace
\c	no newline (same as -n)
\f	form feed
\n	newline
\r	carriage return
\t	tab
\v	vertical tab
\\	print backslash
\0ddd	octal code for ASCII character to be printed

Session 16.21 demonstrates the interactive use of these codes.

SESSION 16.21   *Demonstrate Selected* **echo** *Codes*

```
% set w1 = Now
% set w2 = Time
% echo $w1$w2
NowTime

% echo $w1'\b'$w2
NoTime

% echo $w1 "\t\t" $w2
Now     Time
% echo $w1 '\012'$w2                    #\012 is octal for newline
Now
Time
```

16.5 Input

In the C shell, data are read from a terminal or a file using its read construct ($<).

Reading Line by Line

The C shell allows data to be read using its read construct as shown in Session 16.22.

SESSION 16.22   *Interactive Read*

```
% set x = $<
This is a line.
% echo $x
This is a line.
```

Reading Word by Word

The C shell reads only lines. We can effectively read word by word by using an array. We show how to use the array to read words in Chapter 17.

16.6 Exit Status of a Command

In the C shell, when a command is executed, it returns a value known as the **exit status** of the command. The exit status is stored in the **status** shell variable. Like all named variables, the exit status is accessible by using its name ($status). If a command completes successfully, it returns a **zero** value, which is interpreted as **true**; if it does not complete successfully, it returns a **nonzero** value, which is interpreted as **false.** These concepts are shown in Figure 16.10.

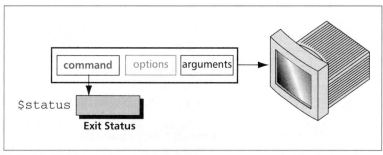

FIGURE 16.10   *Exit Status of a Command*

Let us look at two examples, one successful and one unsuccessful. In the first example, we list all files using the asterisk wildcard (file*). Then we repeat the command with a filename that doesn't match anything in the directory (Session 16.23).

SESSION 16.23   *Demonstrate Exit Status*

```
% ls file*
file1       file2       file3.bak
```

Continued

SESSION 16.23 *Demonstrate Exit Status*

```
% echo $status
0
```
```
% ls none
Cannot access none: No such file or directory
% echo $status
2
```

16.7 eval Command

The **eval** command is used when the C shell needs to evaluate a command twice before executing it. To understand this, let's look at an example. To generalize a segment of code, we need to store the name of a variable in a second variable and then use the **echo** command to display the value of the original variable. This permits us to reuse the code by placing a different variable in the second one, allowing us to change the variable that is being displayed.

Although the concept is simple, the direct approach doesn't work. Session 16.24 fails because the command is evaluated only once.

SESSION 16.24 *Wrong Way to Use a Variable in a Variable*

```
% set x = 23
% set y = x              # Store name of variable in y
% echo $y
x                        # Name of variable, not its value
```

As another example, we can try to prefix the value in the variable with a dollar sign to pick up its value. This concept doesn't work either as demonstrated by Session 16.25.

SESSION 16.25 *Another Wrong Way to Use a Variable in a Variable*

```
% set x = 23
% set y = x              # Store name of variable in y
% echo \$$y
$x                       # Still not x's value
```

The solution is to use the **eval** command so that the shell evaluates the command twice as in Session 16.26.

SESSION 16.26 *Correct Way to Use a Variable in a Variable*

```
% set x = 23
% set y = x              # Store name of variable in y
% eval echo \$$y
23
```

Session 16.26 Analysis: When the **eval** command is executed, it first evaluates y, which generates the string value $x. The second evaluation then evaluates the variable $x, which produces the correct effect, the printing of the variable stored in y.

As a more complex example, let's store a command to print the file list and pipe its output to **head.** In Storing Commands in a Variable on page 683, we demonstrated how we could store a simple command in a variable and then execute the variable. At that time, we stated that the concept would not work with complex commands, such as combining the list (**ls**) and **more** commands in one variable. The reason complex commands don't work is because they require multiple evaluations. To prove that they don't work, we created Session 16.27 to demonstrate the error.

SESSION 16.27   *Variable Command Error*

```
% set list = "ls -l | head -4"
% $list
Cannot access |: No such file or directory
Cannot access head: No such file or directory
Cannot access -4: No such file or directory
```

In Session 16.28, we use the same two commands, but this time, we execute them with the **eval** command. The evaluate command first evaluates the contents of the variable, and then it executes the resulting command.

SESSION 16.28   *Evaluating a Multicommand Variable*

```
% set list = "ls -l | head -4"
% eval $list
```

Output:
total 155
-rw-r--r--   1 gilberg   staff   42 Jul 10   2000 ErrFile
-rwxr--r--   1 gilberg   staff   111 Jul 11   2000 IFS.scr
-rw-r--r--   1 gilberg   staff   0 Jun 11   2000 MidRaven

16.8   Environmental Variables

The environmental variables control the user environment. In the C shell, there are two types of environmental variables: uppercase and lowercase. By tradition, the uppercase variables are set to be exportable and the lowercase variables are not. However, this is not a rule enforced by the C shell.[2] Table 16.5 lists the common environmental variables that we discuss in this section.

TABLE 16.5   *Environmental Variables*

Variable		Explanation
CDPATH	cdpath	Contains the search path for **cd** command when the directory argument is a relative pathname.
HOME	home	Pathname for home directory.

Continued

---

[2]In some implementations, if you change the contents of a lowercase variable, the system changes the contents of its uppercase version also.

TABLE 16.5 *Environmental Variables*

Variable		Explanation
	mail	Absolute pathname for the user's mailbox.
PATH	path	Searches path for commands.
PROMPT	prompt	Primary prompt, such as default %.
SHELL	shell	Pathname of the logging shell.
TERM	term	Terminal type.
USER	user	Contains the user's login name from the /etc/passwd file.

Change Directory Path (CDPATH/cdpath)

The CDPATH variable contains a list of pathnames separated by spaces as shown in the next example:

```
" $home /bin/usr/files"
```

There are three paths in the preceding example. Because the path starts with a space, the first directory is the current working directory. The second directory is our home directory. The third directory is an absolute pathname to a directory of files.

The contents of CDPATH are used by the **cd** command with the following rules:

1. If CDPATH is not defined, the **cd** command searches the current directory to locate the requested directory. If the requested directory is found, **cd** moves to it. If it is not found, **cd** displays an error message.

2. If CDPATH is defined as shown in the previous example, the following actions are taken when this command is executed:

```
% cd reports
```

   a. Because CDPATH starts with a space, the **cd** command searches the current directory for the reports directory. If it is found, the current directory is changed to reports.

   b. If the reports directory is not found in the current directory, **cd** tries to find it in the home directory, which is the second entry in CDPATH. Note that the home directory may be the current directory. Again, if the reports directory is found in the home directory, it becomes the current directory.

   c. If the reports directory is not found in the home directory, **cd** tries to find it in /bin/usr/files, which is the third entry in CDPATH. If the reports directory is found in /bin/usr/files, it becomes the current directory.

   d. If the reports directory is not found in /bin/usr/files, **cd** displays an error message and terminates.

In Session 16.29, we set CDPATH to " $home /bin/usr/files" and then echo the path. HOME is replaced by its absolute path because we used $HOME.

SESSION 16.29   *Set* **CDPATH**

```
% echo $CDPATH
CDPATH - Undefined variable
% setenv CDPATH " $HOME /bin/usr/files"
% echo $CDPATH
 /mnt/diska/staff/gilberg /bin/usr/files
```

Session 16.29 Analysis: The **setenv** command assigns the path in the string to the variable and makes the variable exportable. It is covered fully on page 694.

Home Directory (HOME/home)

The HOME variable contains the path to your home directory. The default is your login directory. Some commands use the value of this variable when they need the path to your home directory. For example, when you use the **cd** command without any argument, the command uses the value of the home variable as the argument. You can change its value, but we do not recommended you change it because this will affect all the commands and scripts that use it. In Session 16.30, we demonstrate how it can be changed to the current working directory. Note that because **pwd** is a command, it must be enclosed in backquotes.

SESSION 16.30   *Demonstrate Change Home Directory*

```
% echo $HOME
/mnt/diska/staff/gilberg
% set oldHOME=$HOME
% echo $oldHOME
/mnt/diska/staff/gilberg
% setenv HOME `pwd`
% echo $HOME
/mnt/diska/staff/gilberg/unix20csh
% setenv HOME $oldHOME
% echo $HOME
/mnt/diska/staff/gilberg
```

User Login Name (USER/user)

The USER variable contains the login name of the user as found in the password file (/etc/passwd). It can be used to display the user name (for example, on a report). Session 16.31 demonstrates its contents using an **echo** command.

SESSION 16.31   *The* **USER** *Variable*

```
% echo $USER
gilberg
```

Location of Mailbox (mail)

The mail variable contains the absolute pathname of the user's mailbox (file). As mail is received, the mail utility stores it in this file until the user is ready to read it. The file's name is the same as the user's login name. This variable is maintained by the shell, not the `mail` utility. Note that there is no uppercase version of the `mail` variable. Session 16.32 displays a typical value for the `mail` variable.

SESSION 16.32   *The **mail** Variable*

```
% echo $mail
/usr/mail/forouzan
```

There is no separate mail check variable in the C shell. Rather, setting the time interval between mail checks is done with the **mail** command as shown in the next example:

```
set mail = (time mail_file)
```

The time is set in seconds. The mail file is the file that is used to store the incoming mail. To check the mail every half hour, we would use the command in the next example:

```
% set mail = (1800 /usr/mail/forouzan)
```

Path Variable (`PATH/path`)

The `PATH` variable is used to search for a command directory. The entries in the `PATH` variable must be separated by colons.

PATH works just like `CDPATH`. When the shell encounters a command, it uses the entries in the `PATH` variable to search for the command under each directory in the `PATH` variable. The major difference is that for security reasons, such as a Trojan horse virus, we should have the current directory last.

If we were to set the `PATH` variable as shown in the next example,

```
% setenv PATH /bin:/usr/bin::
```

the shell would look for the **date** command by first searching the `/bin` directory, followed by the `/usr/bin` directory, and finally the current working directory.

Primary Prompt (`prompt`)

The primary prompt is set in the variable `prompt`. The shell uses the primary prompt when it expects a command. The default is the percent sign (`%`) for the C shell.

We can change the value of the prompt as shown in Session 16.33. We begin by changing the primary prompt to reflect the shell we are working in. Because we have a blank at the end of the prompt, we must use quotes to set it. As soon as it is set, the new prompt is displayed. At the end, we change it back to the default.

SESSION 16.33   *Change the Primary Prompt*

```
% set prompt = "C: "
C: echo $prompt
C:
C: set prompt = "% "
%
```

Secondary Prompt

The secondary prompt is used whenever a command is not completely coded on the first line. By default, it is a question mark (?). It has no variable and cannot be changed. Session 16.34 contains an example in which we code the beginning of a **echo** string on the first line and the rest of it on the following lines. Note that the new-lines appear in the **echo** output.

SESSION 16.34   *The Secondary Prompt*

```
$ echo "Now
? is
? the
? time"

Now
is
the
time
```

Login Shell (SHELL)

The SHELL variable holds the path of your login shell. In Session 16.35, the login shell is the C shell as indicated by csh.

SESSION 16.35   *The **SHELL** Variable*

```
% echo $SHELL
/bin/csh
```

Terminal (TERM)

The TERM variable holds the description for the terminal you are using. The value of this variable can be used by interactive commands such as **vi** or **emacs.** You can test the value of this variable or reset it. Session 16.36 demonstrates typical TERM contents.

SESSION 16.36   *The **TERM** Variable*

```
% echo $TERM
vt100
```

Handling Environmental Variables

As mentioned earlier, the C shell has two sets of environmental variables: exportable and nonexportable. With the exception of **echo,** each type has its own commands to set, unset, and display the environmental variables. Table 16.6 shows how this is done.

Set and Unset Variables

By convention, the uppercase variables are set to be exportable and the lowercase variables are nonexportable. As mentioned previously, however, this is a convention and not a C shell rule.

TABLE 16.6 *Setting and Unsetting Variables*

Operation	Exportable	Not Exportable
Set	`setenv variable value`	`set variable = value`
Unset	`unsetenv variable`	`unset var`
Display One	`echo $variable`	`echo $var`
Display All	`setenv`	`set`

To make a variable exportable, it is set using the **setenv** command. When a variable is set as exportable, we highly recommend that its name be uppercase. To make a variable nonexportable, it is set using the **set** command. Again, we highly recommend that nonexportable variables be lowercase. Both commands are shown in the next example:

```
% setenv TERM vt100            % set term = vt100
```

Similarly, to unset an exportable variable, we use the **unsetenv** command; to unset a nonexportable variable, we use the **unset** command. The following example shows how we can unset the terminal variables:

```
% unsetenv TERM                % unset term
```

Display Variables

To display the value of an individual variable, we use the **echo** command for both exportable and nonexportable:

```
% echo $TERM                   % echo $term
```

To display the variables that are currently set, we use the **set** command with no arguments:

```
% setenv                       % set
```

16.9 On-Off Variables

The C shell uses on-off variables that can be set and unset. It uses these on-off variables to control the way its commands are executed.[3] The on-off variables are summarized in Table 16.7.

No Global (`noglob`)

The no global variable (`noglob`) controls the expansion of wildcard tokens in a command. For example, when the no global variable is off, the list file (**ls**) command uses

---

[3]If you have studied the corresponding Korn shell chapter (Chapter 13), you will recognize that the C shell on-off variables are equivalent to their corresponding Korn shell variables.

TABLE 16.7 *C Shell Options*

Option	Explanation
`noglob`	Disables wildcard expansion (no global).
`verbose`	Prints commands before executing them (verbose).
`noclobber`	Does not allow redirection to clobber existing file.
`ignoreeof`	Disallows `ctrl+d` to exit the shell.

wildcards to match the files in a directory. Thus, the following command lists all files that start with `file` followed by one character.

SESSION 16.37 *No Global Option Off*

```
% ls file?
file1  file2  file3  file4  file5  file6  file?
```

On the other hand, when the global option is on, wildcards become text characters and are not expanded. In this case, the preceding command would list only a file named `file?`.

SESSION 16.38 *No Global Option On*

```
% ls file?
file?
```

Verbosity (`verbose`)

The `verbose` option shows commands before they are executed by the shell. It is useful when debugging a script. We will show examples when we debug scripts in the next chapter.

No Clobber in Redirection (`noclobber`)

When output or errors are directed to a file that already exists, the current file is deleted and replaced by a new file. To prevent this action, we set the `noclobber` option. To override the `noclobber` option when it is set, we use an exclamation mark (`!`) after the redirection as in the next example:

```
wc >! file1
```

Ignore End of File (`ignoreeof`)

Normally, if end of file (`ctrl+d`) is entered at the command line, the shell terminates. To disable this action, we can turn on the ignore end of file option, `ignoreeof`. With this option, end of file generates an error message rather than terminating the shell.

Handling On-Off Variables

To customize our shell environment, we need to set, unset, and display on-off variables. Table 16.8 shows the appropriate commands for the C shell. They are discussed in the sections that follow.

TABLE 16.8   *Commands Used to Set, Unset, and Display Options*

Operation	Example
Set	`set noglob`
Unset	`unset noglob`
Display All	`set`

Set and Unset On-Off Variables

In the C shell, on-off variables are set using the **set** command. Similarly, they are unset using the **unset** command. The following example demonstrates how to set and unset the verbose option in C shell:

```
% set    verbose
% unset verbose
```

Display Options

To display which on-off variables are set, we use the **set** command without an argument. However, the C shell displays the setting of all variables including the on-off variables. The on-off variables can be recognized because there is no value assigned to them: Only their names are listed. The next example shows how to display the on-off variables:

```
% set                    # C shell format: lists all variables
```

16.10 Startup and Shutdown Scripts

As we learned in Chapter 5, each shell uses one or more scripts to initialize the environment when a session is started. The C shell provides two sets of startup files: one systemwide set created by the system administrator that establishes the basic shell configuration for all users and one personal set that tailors the shell for our individual use. Each set consists of one file used for the basic configuration and one for environmental and user variables. In addition, there are two shutdown files: one created by the system administrator for all users and one personal file we can create for our needs.

These four startup and two shutdown files are shown in Figure 16.11 and described in the following sections.

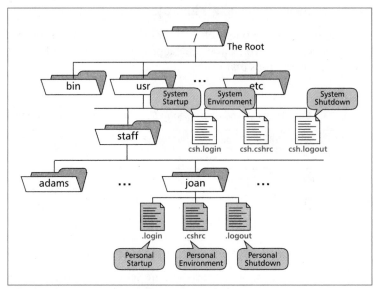

FIGURE 16.11   *C Shell Startup and Shutdown Files*

System Startup Files

As you study Figure 16.11, note that there are two system startup files, one for the shell and one for the environment. These system startup files are read-only files; their permissions are set so that only the system administrator can change them. They contain the initial configuration for all users on the system. We suggest that you locate and read them so that you will have an idea of what they contain.

Personal Startup Files

The C shell provides two personal startup files: one for the shell and one for the environment (Figure 16.11). The personal startup file, ~/.login, can be used to provide any commands that apply to the whole session. Typical commands used in this file are **setenv** to set the TERM or PROMPT system variables and **stty** to configure a terminal. The startup personal environment file, ~/.cshrc, is used to set environmental or user variables to personalize the environment.

Startup Process

Whenever a shell is started, UNIX uses these startup files. Which ones depend on whether the shell being started is a login shell or not. When a login shell is started, the system startup files are executed followed by the personal startup files. If a nonlogin shell is being forked, then only the personal startup files are executed. This process is shown in Figure 16.12.

Shutdown Files

The C shell provides two shutdown files: one for the system and one personal. They are executed, first the personal and then the system file, when a session is terminated from a C shell. The personal shutdown file, ~/.logout, is used for operations such as critical file backup.

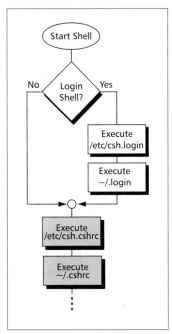

FIGURE 16.12 *Startup Process*

16.11 Command History

The C shell provides an extensive command history capability consisting of a combination of commands, environmental variables, and files. A major feature of the design is the ability to recall a command and reexecute it without typing it again.

History File

Every command that we type[4] is kept in a history file stored in our home directory. By default, the filename is ~/.history. It can be renamed, provided that we store its pathname in the HISTFILE environmental variable. The size of the file is controlled by two system variables: history, which controls the maximum number of commands stored in a session, and savehist, which controls the number of commands that will be retained from session to session (that is, between logins).

History Command

The command for listing, editing, and executing commands from the history file is **history.** Executed without any options, the **history** command lists the last 16 commands. A sample output is shown in Session 16.39. In the interest of space, we have deleted commands from the middle of the listing.

---

[4]Commands executed in a script are not included in the history file.

SESSION 16.39   *The **history** Command*

```
% history
238      hold
239      history
  .

  .

  .
251      cp mail_file mail_file.bak
252      pico mail_file
253      history
```

We can control the number of commands listed by providing a number as a **history** command argument. If an invalid command number is provided, an error message is displayed. Session 16.40 demonstrates this capability. In this example, the last five commands are listed.

SESSION 16.40   *Specify Start Line for the **history** Command*

```
$ history 5
251      cp mail_file mail_file.bak
252      pico mail_file
253      history
254      history -n
255      history 5
```

Reexecuting Previous Commands

Commands in the history file can be reexecuted. The command to reexecute a previous command is the bang character (!). The specific command to be reexecuted can be specified in four ways: two consecutive bangs—the second indicates the previous command; a positive number, which specifies the command number in the history file; a negative number, which specifies the command relative to the current command; or a string, which is used to match a part of the command to be executed. The **history** command that is executed is displayed before it is executed. For example, to reexecute the previous command, we use the following code:

```
% ls -l ErrFile
-rw-r--r--    1 gilberg   staff          42 Jul 10  2000 ErrFile
% !!
% ls -l ErrFile
-rw-r--r--    1 gilberg   staff          42 Jul 10  2000 ErrFile
```

If command 8 is a change directory command in the history file, it would be reexecuted using the positive-number method as shown in the following example:

```
% !8
% cd ~
%
```

To reexecute command 2 before the last command, we would use a –3 (three back relative to the current command) as shown in the following example:

```
% !-3
% date
Sun Aug 5 18:27:25 PDT 2001
```

The **date** command in the previous command could have been reexecuted by using only the beginning of the word "date." When the argument is a string, the history file is searched, starting with the most recent command, until a command that starts with a matching string is found. This format is:

```
% !da
% date
Sun Aug 5 18:27:27 PDT 2001
```

If the string is not at the beginning of a command, such as a command argument, it is enclosed in question marks as shown in the next example:

```
% !?File?
% ls -l ErrFile
-rw-r--r--   1 gilberg  staff         42 Jul 10  2000 ErrFile
```

Substitute and Reexecute

We can make changes to a command before we reexecute it. The changes are specified as a substitute pattern:

$$s/.../.../$$

The substitute pattern immediately follows the reexecute command and is separated from it by a colon (:). In the following example, we reexecute the list command from the previous example, but this time listing `TheRaven`:

```
% !ls:s/ErrFile/TheRave1
% ls -l TheRaven
-rw-------   1 gilberg  staff       5782 Sep 10 16:19 TheRaven
```

The previous example executed the most recent list command in the history file after making the substitution for the first matching string. To change all occurrences of a matching pattern, we would specify global substitution by coding a g before the substitution pattern as shown in the following format:

$$!find:gs/txt/bak/$$

This example would reexecute the most recent **find** command in the history file after changing all `txt` extensions to `bak` as specified in the substitution pattern.

Using Arguments from Previous Command

It is possible to use any or all arguments from the previous command. To specify that the last argument is to be used, we code the new command followed by the history previous command (!) and a dollar sign. For example, the following commands create a new directory and then change to it:

```
% mkdir projectA25
% cd !$
% cd projectA25
```

To specify that all arguments are to be used, we use an asterisk in the **history** command as shown in the next example:

```
% cp file1 file2
% lpr !*
% lpr file1 file2
```

History Modifier

The previous history applications can be used with only the most recent command. We can also use the argument and/or verb of any previous command. For example, if the following command is the most recent,

```
% ls file1 file2 file3 file4 file5
```

to use the first argument in a new command, we would use !:1; to specify the third argument, we would use !:3. As an alternate to the first argument, we could also use a caret (^). The following example shows four ways to reference an argument in the previous command:

```
cat !:1                        # use file1
cat !:3                        # use file3
cat !:^                        # use file1 (first argument)
cat !:$                        # use file5 (last argument)
```

If the **history** command to be used is not the most recent, the desired command must be specified between the bang and the colon as shown in the next example:

```
% ls file1 file2 file3 file4 file5
% cat !:1                      # use file1 of previous command
% cat !-2:3                    # use file3 of second previous command
% cat !ls:4                    # use file4 of most recent ls command
```

A very interesting extension of the modifier concept is that we can use the verb from one command and the arguments from another. The verb is designated by a zero (0) and the arguments are coded as shown in the previous examples. For example, to use the verb from the most recent command and the first argument from the third most previous command, we would code the command as follows:

```
% !:0 !-3:^
```

We can also combine arguments from different commands as shown in the next example, which specifies the command from the second most previous command; the third, fourth, and fifth arguments from the command number 4; and the last argument from the sixth most previous command.

```
% !-2:0 !4:3-5 !-6:1
```

Pathname Modifier

The pathname modifier uses a path or part of a path from a command in the history file. There are three parts to a path: the head, which is everything from the beginning of the path up to the last slash in the path; the tail, which is the last directory or file in the path; and the root, which is a filename without an extension—such as theRaven in theRaven.txt.

The pathname modifier is a single character following the colon—an h for head, a t for tail, and an r for root. Session 16.41 demonstrates each format.

SESSION 16.41   *Using the Pathname Modifiers*

```
% ls /usr/staff/joan/files/file1.txt
-rw-------     1 joan       staff         5782 Jul 21 19:23 file1.txt
% cd !$:h                                 # use head from previous command
% cd /usr/staff/joan/files
% ls !-2:t                                # use tail from second previous
% ls file1.txt
-rw-------     1 joan       staff         5782 Jul 21 19:23 file1.txt
% ls !$:r.bak                             # use root from previous command
% ls file1.bak
-rw-------     1 joan       staff         5782 Jun 30 15:05 file1.bak
```

Session 16.41 Analysis: In the first command, Joan uses a pathname to list a file. She then moves to the directory of the file she just listed using the **cd** command with the head pathname modifier. Now in /usr/staff/joan/files, she uses the tail modifier to relist the file and then uses the root modifier to list the file's backup.

History Command Summary

Table 16.9 summarizes the **history** command codes discussed in this section.

TABLE 16.9   **history** *Command Codes*

Code	Description	Example
!!	Reexecutes the previous command.	% !!
!n	Reexecutes command n in history file.	% !52

Continued

TABLE 16.9 **history** *Command Codes—Continued*

Code	Description	Example
`!-n`	Reexecutes command n relative to current command.	`% !-5`
`!string`	Reexecutes latest command beginning with string.	`% !date`
`!?string?`	Reexecutes latest command containing string.	`% !?file1?`
`!n:s/s1/s2/`	Reexecutes command n substituting s2 for s1.	`% !n:s/file1/file2/`
`!s1:gs/s2/s3/`	Reexecutes latest commands starting with s1 substituting s3 for s2.	`% !rm:gs/file1/file*/`
`command !$`	Executes command using last argument from previous command.	`% cd !$`
`command !*`	Executes command using all arguments from previous command.	`% lpr !*`
`command !n`	Executes command using argument n from previous command.	`% cat !:3`
`command !^`	Executes command using first argument from previous command.	`% cat !:^`
`command !$:h`	Executes previous command using argument head.	`% cat !$:h`
`command !$:t`	Executes previous command using argument tail.	`% cat !$:t`
`command !$:r`	Executes previous command using argument root.	`% cat !$:r`

16.12 Command Execution Scripts

To understand the behavior of the shell, it helps to understand how the C shell executes a command. Command execution is carried out in six sequential steps.

Execution Steps

The six execution steps are recursive. This means that when the shell performs the third step, command substitution, the six steps are followed for the command inside the backquotes.

Command Parsing

The shell first parses the command into words. In this step, it uses whitespaces as delimiters between the words. It also replaces sequences of two or more spaces or tabs with a single space.

Variable Evaluation

After completely parsing the command, the shell looks for variable names (unquoted words beginning with a dollar sign). When a variable name is found, its value replaces the variable name.

Command Substitution

The shell then looks for a command contained in a set of backquotes. If found, the command is executed and its output string replaces the command and its backquotes.

Redirection

At this point, the shell checks the command for redirected files. Each redirected file is verified by opening it.

Wildcard Expansion

When filenames contain wildcards, the shell expands and replaces them with their matching filenames. This step creates a file list.

Path Determination

In this last step, the shell uses the PATH variable to locate the directory containing the command code. The command is now ready for execution.

Command Execution Example

To better understand the process, let's look at the **cat** command contained in the next example. To show the whitespace characters, we use ▲ to represent a space and → to represent a tab.

```
$▲cat→→$var→→→report*▲1>&▲▲file3
```

1. In the first step, the shell parses words. It replaces all tabs and multiple spaces with a single space. The result is shown in the next example. Because all tabs and spaces have been parsed, we show a space in the normal fashion.

```
% cat $var report* >& file3
```

2. The second step replaces the variable ($var) with its value, file*. The result is:

```
% cat file* report* >& file3
```

3. The third step is skipped because there is no command substitution.
4. In the fourth step, the redirected files are handled: file3 is opened for output and errors.
5. In the fifth step, the shell expands the wildcards. The command is now:

```
% cat fileA fileB fileC report1 report2 >& file3
```

6. In the last step, the shell finds the /bin directory in the PATH variable. It completes the command as in the next example:

```
% /bin/cat fileA fileB fileC report1 report2 >& file3
```

The **cat** utility is then called with five arguments and the names of the file.

16.13 Key Terms

accessing a variable
alias
assignment operator
backgroud job
C shell
CDPATH/cdpath
chained commands
command execution
command-line editing
command parsing
command substitution
complex command
conditional commands
constant
echo command
environmental variables
eval command
exit status
exporting variable
foreground job
group commands
HOME/home
input redirection
input statement

ignoreeof
job control
mail
noclobber
noglob
null statement
null variable
on-off variable
option
output statement
PATH/path
path determination
pipe
predefined variable
PROMPT/prompt
quoting
redirecting error
redirecting input
redirecting output
redirection
sequenced commands
session
setting a variable
SHELL/shell

shell program
shell script
shell session
shell variable
standard error
standard input
standard output
standard streams
startup files
startup scripts
stream
subshell
tee command
TERM/term
trash file
unsetting a variable
user-defined variables
USER/user
variable
variable evaluation
variable substitution
verbose
wildcard expansion

16.14 Tips

1. Understand the difference between the login shell and the current shell. (See also Chapter 5.)

2. Distinguish between the three standard streams. (See also Chapter 5.)

3. Distinguish between standard input, standard output, and standard error redirections. (See also Chapter 5.)

4. To understand pipes, you need to know where they can be used and where they cannot be used. (See also Chapter 5.)

5. Understand the use of the **tee** command. (See also Chapter 5.)

6. Understand the concept and use of command substitution. Note that the C shell uses backquotes for command substitution. (See also Chapter 5.)

7. Understand the concept of job control, foreground and background jobs, and how to execute a command in the background. (See also Chapter 5.)

8. Aliases are supported in the C shell.

9. Command-line editing is not supported in the C shell.

10. Use only letters, digits, and underscores to name a user-defined variable. A hyphen may not be used.

11. The value of a variable is always a string of characters.

12. There is no limitation on the length of the string stored in a variable. This means that we can even store the whole contents of a file in a variable.

13. If a variable is used before being assigned a value, the value of the variable is null.

14. Note that $ is not part of a user-defined variable name. So when you want to refer to the variable, do not use the $. The $ is used when you want to use the value of the variable.

15. The trash file in UNIX is /dev/null. Everything sent to this file is lost forever.

16. The terminal file in UNIX is /dev/tty. Everything sent to this file will be displayed on your terminal.

17. To force the C shell to evaluate a command twice before executing it, use the **eval** command.

18. The $< construct can read a line into only one variable, or it can parse it into several variables.

19. To check the success or failure of a command, test the value of the exit status ($status) variable.

20. Change the value of environmental variables discretely. Changes may affect your environment.

21. If you do not have a personal login file ($HOME/.login), create one. Add any command you want to be executed at the login time to this file.

22. Pay special attention to the order and the way the C shell executes a command.

16.15 Commands

The following commands were discussed in this chapter. For more details, see Appendix F and the corresponding pages shown in the following table.

Command	Description	Options	Page
alias	**Synopsis:** *alias name definition* Defines an alias for a command.		674
eval	**Synopsis:** *eval command* Evaluates the command two times before executing it.		689
setenv	**Synopsis:** *setenv variable value* Defines an exportable variable.		685

16.16 Summary

- The C shell was developed by William Joy at the University of California, Berkeley.
- The C shell can be used either interactively to receive user commands and interpret them or as a programming language to create shell scripts.
- There are three standard streams: standard input (0), standard output (1), and standard error (2).
- The three standard streams are connected to the user terminal by default. They can be redirected to and from files.

- Commands can be chained using pipes.
- The **tee** command can split the output so that one copy is sent to the standard output and the other to a file.
- Complex commands can be formed using four constructs: sequencing, grouping, chaining, and combining with conditional operators.
- Quotes are used to change the meaning of characters in the C shell. The C shell supports three types of quotes: backslash, double quotes, and single quotes.
- Command substitution is supported by the C shell using backquotes.
- Job control in the C shell is used to control how and where a job is executed.
- Two special files are available in UNIX: /dev/null and /dev/tty. The /dev/null is a trash file. The /dev/tty represents the user terminal.
- A variable in the C shell is used to store values.
- We can divide C shell variables into two broad categories: user-defined and predefined. The predefined variables can be further divided into two categories: shell variables and environmental variables.
- The name of user-defined variables should start with an alphabetic character or an underscore (_). It can be followed by zero or more alphanumeric or underscore characters.
- The **set** and **setenv** commands are used to store a value in a variable.
- To access the value of a variable, the name of the variable should be preceded by a dollar sign ($).
- A variable can be set or unset. When a variable is not set, its value is null.
- We can store any string in a variable including filenames, file contents, commands, and the names of other variables.
- To make a variable available to a child shell, it must be exported.
- The output statement in the C shell is the **echo** command.
- The input statement in the C shell is the &< construct.
- The exit status of a command is stored in a shell variable called **status**.
- The **eval** command is used when the C shell needs to evaluate a command twice before executing it.
- The environmental variables control the user environment. There are two distinct versions of the environmental variables in the C shell: uppercase and lowercase. The uppercase variables are automatically exported to subshells; the lowercase variables are not.
- We defined eight environmental variables in this chapter: CDPATH/cdpath, HOME/home, mail, PATH/path, PROMPT/prompt, SHELL/shell, TERM/term, and USER/user.
- On-off variables in the C shell are used to control the way a command or a script is executed. We defined four on-off variables: noglob, verbose, noclobber, and ignoreeof.
- The startup files in the C shell allow the user to customize the environment permanently (for every session). Two startup files are defined in the C shell: $home/.login and $HOME/.cshrc.

- The C shell uses the ~/.logout file to cleanup the environment when the user logs out.
- The C shell follows six distinct steps to execute a command: parsing, variable evaluation, command substitution, redirection, wildcard expansion, and path determination.

16.17 Practice Set

Review Questions

1. Explain the two purposes of the C shell.
2. Is the C shell the login shell in your system? How do you verify it? (See also Chapter 5.)
3. Is the login shell always the same as the current shell? How do you verify it? (See also Chapter 5.)
4. How do you find your current shell? (See Chapter 5.) How do you find your login shell? (See also Chapter 5.)
5. How do you exit from a child shell and return to the parent shell? (See Chapter 5.)
6. How can you create a child shell? (See Chapter 5.) How can you move to the parent shell after creating a child? (See also Chapter 5.)
7. What are the three standard streams?
8. The standard input stream is normally associated with which physical device? (See Chapter 5.)
9. The standard output stream is normally associated with which physical device? (See Chapter 5).
10. The standard error stream is normally associated with which physical device? (See Chapter 5).
11. How can you redirect the standard input stream to a file?
12. How can you redirect the standard output stream to a file?
13. How can you redirect the standard error stream to the same file as the output is redirected?
14. What is piping? What is the pipe operator?
15. Distinguish between a sequence of commands, a group of commands, and a chain of commands. (See Chapter 5.)
16. What are the two operators that make the execution of commands conditional? (See Chapter 5.)
17. What is quoting? What are the three sets of quoting tokens?
18. What is the difference between a backslash, a pair of double quotes, and a pair of single quotes? (See Chapter 5.)
19. What is command substitution? What is the token for command substitution in the C shell?

20. What is a job? Distinguish between a foreground and a background job. (See Chapter 5.)

21. Show how you can move a job from the background to the foreground, and vice versa. (See Chapter 5.)

22. List and explain the six different states of a job. (See Chapter 5.)

23. Define a variable and distinguish between a variable and a value.

24. Distinguish between a user-defined variable and a predefined variable.

25. Distinguish between a shell variable and an environmental variable.

26. Identify the names of all environmental variables defined for the C shell in this chapter.

27. What is the exit status of a command? Where is it stored?

28. Which environmental variable holds the search path for your commands in the C shell? How do you display the value of this variable?

29. Which environmental variable holds the name of the login shell in the C shell? How do you display the value of this variable?

30. Which environmental variable holds the search path for the **cd** command in the C shell? How do you display the value of this variable?

31. Which environmental variable holds the primary prompt in the C shell? How do you display the value of this variable?

32. Which environmental variable holds the path of your home directory in the C shell? How do you display the value of this variable?

33. Which environmental variable holds the interval checking of your mail in the C shell? How do you display the value of this variable?

34. Which environmental variable holds your login name in the C shell? How do you display the value of this variable?

35. Which environmental variable holds the type of your terminal in the C shell? How do you display the value of this variable?

36. What is an on-off variable? List some of these variables and their use.

37. What are the startup scripts in the C shell?

38. What is the shutdown script in the C shell?

Exercises

39. Which of the following commands show your login shell? (See Chapter 5.)
    a. `echo $SHELL`　　　　　　　　c. `echo $shell`
    b. `echo $0`　　　　　　　　　　d. `echo $login_shell`

40. Which of the following commands creates a C shell child? (See Chapter 5.)
    a. `sh`　　　　　　　　　　　　c. `csh`
    b. `ksh`　　　　　　　　　　　d. none of the above

41. Identify at least five commands that cannot be used with input redirection.

42. If your current shell is C, what is the error (if any) in each of the following commands?
    a. `a = 24`　　　　　　　　　　c. `a=$b`
    b. `set a=24`　　　　　　　　　d. `set a=$b`

43. If your current shell is C, what would be displayed from each of the following commands?

```
a. set a = 44   ; echo a ; echo $a
b. set a = 44   ; echo $aa ; echo a$a
c. set a = 44   ; echo "$a"a ; echo $a$a
```

44. What will be displayed from the following commands?

```
a. echo " Hello the user of "UNIX" operating system"
b. echo " Hello the user of \"UNIX\" operating system"
c. echo " Hello the user of 'UNIX' operating system"
d. echo ' Hello the user of "UNIX" operating system'
```

45. Use a **grep** command and check its exit status. When is the result zero? When is the result nonzero? Check both cases.

46. Use a **sed** command and check its exit status. When is the result zero? When is the result nonzero? Check both cases.

47. Use an **awk** command and check its exit status. When is the result zero? When is the result nonzero? Check both cases.

48. Use a command to show the value of all environmental variables in the C shell.

16.18 Lab Sessions

These sessions are designed to be run in the C shell. If your login shell is not the C shell, create a C subshell for them.

Session I

1. Log into the system.
2. What is your login shell? (See Chapter 5.)
3. Change the primary prompt of the C shell to "CSH:".
4. Create a new C subshell.
5. Check the prompt in this shell. Is it different from the parent shell? Explain your results.
6. Change the prompt to "CSH==>".
7. Exit from the child shell and go to the C parent shell.
8. Check the prompt. Is it "CSH:" or "CSH==>"? Explain your results.
9. Log out of the system.

Session II

1. Log into the system.
2. Create a directory called SCRs under your home directory.
3. Use an editor and create a file called Ch16S2F1. Type the following two lines in this file:

```
#!/bin/csh
ls -l
```

Continued

Session II—*Continued*

This is called a shell script. We will learn about C shell scripts in the next chapter. For the moment, save the file under the directory called SCRs, which you created under your home directory without moving from your home directory.

4. Use the **chmod** command and change the permission of the file to 700.
5. Be sure that you are at your home directory. At the prompt, type the name of the file (this means running the script). What do you get? Why?
6. Add the entry $HOME/SCR to your PATH variable.
7. Repeat step 5 What happens this time? Explain the difference.
8. Log out of the system.

Session III

1. Log into the system.
2. Create a directory A under your home directory.
3. Create a directory B under A (without moving from your home directory).
4. Create a directory C under B (without moving from your home directory).
5. While at your home directory, try the following command (% is the prompt):
   ```
   %  cd C
   ```
   What happened? Can you explain the reason for error?
6. Add an entry to the value of your CDPATH environmental variable to be able to run the command in step 5 from your home directory.
7. Log out of the system.

Session IV

1. Log into the system.
2. Check the entry in the /etc/passwd file related to you to determine your login shell.
3. Confirm what you find using the value of the SHELL variable.
4. If you do not have a ~/.login file, create one.
5. Add values for some of the uppercase environmental variables in this file.
6. Add values for some of the lowercase environmental variables in this file.
7. Create a subshell.
8. Check the values of the uppercase variables you set in step 5
9. Check the values of the lowercase variables you set in step 6
10. Repeat steps 5 to 9 for the ~/.cshrc file. Compare the results and explain any differences between the two files.
11. Log out of the system.

Session V

1. Log into the system.
2. Type the following command (% is the prompt):

   ```
   %  >file1          ls            -l
   ```

   What happened?
3. You put the redirection at the beginning of the command and the shell recognized it. Why? What rule applies here?
4. Try the following two commands:

   ```
   % set x = `ls -l | head -5 | tail +5 | awk '{print $NF}'`
   % cp $x file2
   ```

5. What did you accomplish in the previous step?
6. What are the contents of `file2`? Which file is copied to `file2`?
7. What is stored in variable x?
8. What is done first in the **cp** command: the variable evaluation or the command substitution? Explain what rules apply here.
9. Log out of the system.

## CHAPTER 17

C Shell Programming

In the previous chapter, we discussed the C shell features used in interactive sessions. Interactive sessions work well when the problems being solved are short and simple. As the problems become larger and more complex, especially if they need to be solved repetitively, we need to save the commands in a file. In this chapter, we discuss how to write and save commands as executable script files.

17.1 Basic Script Concepts

A **shell script** is a text file that contains executable commands. Although we can execute virtually any command at the shell prompt, long sets of commands that are going to be executed more than once should be executed using a script file. Figure 17.1 shows the flow of a script in UNIX.

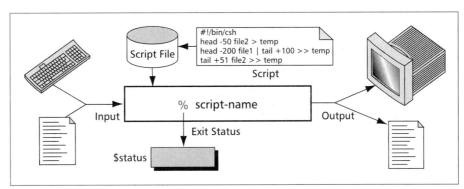

FIGURE 17.1   *Script Concept*

Script Components

Every script has three parts: the interpreter designator line, comments, and shell commands.

Interpreter Designator Line

One of the UNIX shells runs the script, reading it and calling the command specified by each line in turn. The first line of the script is the designator line; it tells UNIX the path to the appropriate shell interpreter. The designator line begins with a pound sign and a bang (#!).[1] If the designator line is omitted, UNIX will use the interpreter for the current

---

[1]Some texts refer to the pound sign as an octothorp. While correct, pound sign is much more common terminology.

shell, which may not be correct. We recommend, therefore, that you always use the designator line to ensure that the correct interpreter is used.

> The interpreter designator line must be the first line of the script file. There cannot even be a blank line before it. If it is not the first line, it is ignored and the current shell's default interpreter will be used.

The system name for the C shell is `csh`. Check your system for the correct location. In most systems, it can be in one of the designators in the following example:

```
#!/bin/csh          or          #!/usr/bin/csh
```

Comments

Comments are documentation we add in a script to help us understand it. The interpreter doesn't use them at all; it simply skips over them.

Often, after we've used a script for a long time, we decide we want to improve it. Without comments, we may not remember why we chose the commands we used or what a complex pattern does. To help us remember, therefore, we write some comments.

Comments are identified with the pound sign token (#). The C shell supports only line comments. This means that we can only comment one line at a time; a comment cannot extend beyond the end of the line. When the pound sign is coded at the beginning of the line, the entire line is a comment. When it is coded after a command, then the command is processed by the interpreter, but the rest of the line starting with the pound sign is skipped.

We recommend that each script contain comments at the beginning to identify its name and purpose. The format we use throughout the text is shown in Script 17.1.

SCRIPT 17.1   *Recommended Minimum Documentation*

```
1  #!/bin/csh                    # C shell path name
2  #  Script: doc.scr
3  #  This script demonstrates our recommended minimum documentation.
4
5  # Commands start here
```

Script 17.1 Analysis: Note that the name of the script ends in `.scr`. Although the shell does not need it, we use this extension for all shell scripts so that we can easily recognize them. You should also note that all comments are colored. We use color to separate the comments in the script from the commands. We also use color to separate the script output from the user input.

Commands

The most important part of a script is its commands. We can use any of the commands available in UNIX. However, they will not be executed until we execute the script;

they are not executed immediately as they are when we use them interactively. When the script is executed, each command is executed in order from the first to the last.[2]

Command Separators Commands in a script, as well as in an interactive session, should be separated from each other. Shells use two tokens to separate commands: semicolons and newlines. While we may use spaces to make the commands more readable, they are not separators. Shells skip over leading and trailing spaces automatically.

When a shell parses a script, it reads characters until it sees a command separator. It then executes the command, and the result is created. The following example contains three commands, two separated by a semicolon on the first line and one on the second line:

```
command1 ; command 2 <newline>
command3
```

Blank Lines Command separators can be repeated. When the script detects multiple separators, it considers them just one. This means that we can insert multiple blank lines in a script to make it more readable. The only place where we cannot put a blank line is before the shell interpreter designator line. As we said earlier, it must be the very first line of the script.

Combined Commands We can combine commands in a script just as we did in the interactive sessions. This means that we can chain commands using pipes, group commands, or use conditional commands.

Making Scripts Executable

After creating a script, we must make it executable. As we learned in Chapter 4, this is done with the **chmod** command. We can make a command executable only by the user (ourselves), our group, or everybody. Because we have to test a new script, we always give ourselves execute permission. Whether or not we want others to execute it depends on many factors. Two of the more common commands used to set the execution privileges are shown in the following example:

```
$ chmod 700 script.scr          #User rwx (none for group and others)
$ chmod 755 script.scr          #User rwx (group and others r-x)
```

Executing the Script

After the script has been made executable, it is a command and can be executed just like any other command. There are two specific methods of executing it: as an independent command or as an argument to a subshell command.

Independent Command

We do not need to be in the C shell to execute a C shell script as long as the interpreter designator line is included as the first line of the script. When it is, UNIX uses the appropriate interpreter as called out by the designator line. However, if the interpreter

---

[2]We will see later in the chapter that we can use flow control commands to change the sequential execution.

designator line is not included, the script will fail if it uses a command that the current shell doesn't recognize.

To execute the script as an independent command, we simply use its name as in the following example:

```
% script_name
```

Child Shell Execution

To ensure that the script is properly executed, we can create a child shell and execute it in the new shell. This is done by specifying the shell before the script name as shown in the following example:

```
% csh script_name
```

In this case, the interpreter designator line is not needed, but the user needs to know which shell the script requires. Because this is a very user error-prone method, we recommend that all scripts include the interpreter designation, even if we pass it as an argument to a subshell.

Examples

To demonstrate how to create and execute a script, let's look at some simple examples.

Print File List: We use the command

```
ls -l | more
```

frequently and do not want to type the whole command each time. To make it easier to execute the command, let's create a shell script that contains these commands and execute it from the shell prompt. We name the script dir.scr. The script and an example of its execution are in Script 17.2.

SCRIPT 17.2 *The* **dir.scr** *Script*

```
1  #!/bin/csh
2  #   Script: dir.scr
3  #   A simple script
4
5  ls -l | more
```
```
% dir.scr                          # Command Execution
```
```
Output:
total 8
-rw-r--r--    1 gilberg  staff         0 Jun  5 16:56 5
-rw-r--r--    1 gilberg  staff         0 Jun  6 14:10 =
-rw-------    1 gilberg  staff      5782 Jun  4 12:55 TheRaven
-rw-r--r--    1 gilberg  staff       330 Jun  4 13:04 TheRavenV1
```
Continued

SCRIPT 17.2   *The **dir.scr** Script*

```
-rwxr--r--   1 gilberg   staff         13 Jun 11 13:52 dirScript
-rw-r--r--   1 gilberg   staff          0 Jun 10 11:26 echo
-rw-r--r--   1 gilberg   staff        100 Jun  3 09:00 file1
-rw-r--r--   1 gilberg   staff        100 Jun  3 08:56 file2
```

Script 17.2 Analysis: Note that we do not show the **chmod** command in any of the scripts. We assume that the script permissions have been properly set.

Print Active Login Names: For another example, let's write a script to display the names of everyone logged into the system. We can use the **who** command. However, **who** lists one complete line for each user. What we want to see is only the names of the users. In this case, we could use the command

```
who | awk '{print $argv[1]}'
```

Script 17.3 contains the resulting script.

SCRIPT 17.3   *The **who.scr** Script*

```
1  #!/bin/csh
2  #  Script: who.scr
3  #  Displays users currently logged in.
4
5  who | awk '{print $argv[1]}'
```

```
% who.scr
```

```
Output:
st050019
gilberg
tran
srp50115
forouzan
nys26825
```

Extract Lines: While the command in the next script is considerably more complex in its concept, it is still easy to code. We want to extract one verse from the middle (lines 42 to 47) of our file, TheRaven, and create a new file that we will call MidRaven. The command for this extraction is

```
head -47 TheRaven | tail +42 > midRaven.txt
```

Figure 17.2 portrays the steps for this example. We first use the **head** utility to extract the first 47 lines of the poem and pipe them to the **tail** utility, which extracts lines 42 to 47, leaving us with only one verse (six lines). The results are then directed to the new file, midRaven.txt.

The code and execution of this script are in Script 17.4.

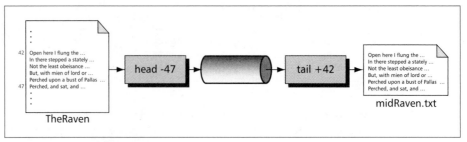

FIGURE 17.2 **midRaven.scr** *Design*

SCRIPT 17.4 *The* **midRaven.scr** *Script*

```
1  #!/bin/csh
2  #  Script: midRaven.scr
3  #  Extracts one verse from middle of TheRaven file.
4
5  head -47 TheRaven | tail +42 > midRaven.txt
```
```
% midRaven.scr
```
```
% cat midRaven.txt
Open here I flung the shutter, when, with many a flirt and flutter
In there stepped a stately Raven of the saintly days of yore.
Not the least obeisance made he; not a minute stopped or stayed he;
But, with mien of lord or lady, perched above my chamber door--
Perched upon a bust of Pallas just above my chamber door--
Perched, and sat, and nothing more.
```

Insert Lines Into Another File: All of the examples we have written so far are very trivial. They all can be done in one line. Now let us write a more complex example that requires several lines. We have been given an assignment to extract lines 3 through 5 of a file called file3 and insert the extracted lines between lines 5 and 6 of another file called file4. The final result should be called file5.

This problem is complex enough that we need to design just how we are going to do it. After thinking about it for a while, we begin by sketching out a picture of what we need to do (Figure 17.3).

After assuring ourselves that the design is good, we sketch out the following English statements of what we want the script to do.[3]

1. Copy first 5 lines from file4 to file5.
2. Extract lines 3 to 5 of file3 and append to file5.
3. Copy line 6 to end of file4 and append to file5.

It appears that these three steps will do the job, so it's time to write and test the script. The script and its results are in Script 17.5.

---

[3]An English-like description of the steps to accomplish a design is known as *tight English*. A more formal, codelike set of instructions is known as *pseudocode*.

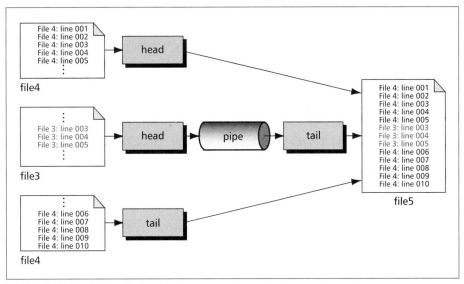

FIGURE 17.3 *Design for* **insert.scr**

SCRIPT 17.5 *The* **insert.scr** *Script*

```
1   #!/bin/csh
2   #   Script: insert.scr
3   #   Inserts lines from one file into another
4
5   head -5 file4 > file5
6   head -5 file3 | tail +3 >> file5
7   tail +6 file4 >> file5
```

```
% insert.scr
```

File3	File4	File5
File 3: line 001	File 4: line 001	File 4: line 001
File 3: line 002	File 4: line 002	File 4: line 002
File 3: line 003	File 4: line 003	File 4: line 003
File 3: line 004	File 4: line 004	File 4: line 004
File 3: line 005	File 4: line 005	File 4: line 005
File 3: line 006	File 4: line 006	File 3: line 003
File 3: line 007	File 4: line 007	File 3: line 004
File 3: line 008	File 4: line 008	File 3: line 005
File 3: line 009	File 4: line 009	File 4: line 006
File 3: line 010	File 4: line 010	File 4: line 007
		File 4: line 008
		File 4: line 009
		File 4: line 010

Script Termination (exit Command)

Occasionally, a script encounters a condition that does not allow it to continue processing. When that happens, it must stop. For these situations, UNIX provides an **exit** command.

The **exit** command terminates the script and sets the exit status. It can be used with a numeric argument or without an argument. When it is used with a number, the script's exit status is assigned the number. When it is used without an argument, the script's exit status is 0.

Arguments and Positional Parameters

The previous examples demonstrate the basic concept of shell scripting. However, shell scripts are more useful when they are generalized. A **generalized** script can be used in many different situations without change. For example, think of the extract lines problem (Extract Lines on page 719). It would be more useful if it worked with any input and output file and could extract any number of lines.

The C shell lets us generalize a script using arguments and positional parameters. Arguments are user-supplied data that follow the script name on the command line and are input to the script. Positional parameters are predefined memory variables (buffers) in the shell script. There are nine positional parameters,[4] labeled $argv[1], $argv[2],..., $argv[9], that are used to store the arguments that the user entered.

When the script is executed, the shell puts the first argument in the first positional parameter ($argv[1]), the second argument in the second positional parameter ($argv[2]), and so forth until all arguments have been stored. The script can then use them (properly prefixed by the dollar sign) anywhere a variable can be used. This concept is presented in Figure 17.4.

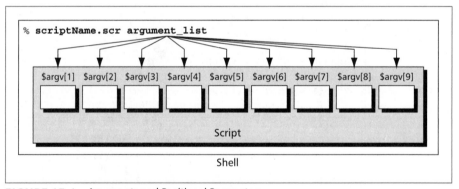

FIGURE 17.4 *Arguments and Positional Parameters*

Generalized Filenames Let's repeat the Extract Lines example (see page 719), but instead of specific filenames, we will use positional parameters. In this case, we have four arguments and four positional parameters. The first argument is TheRaven. The fourth argument is midRaven.txt. The second and third arguments are the range of lines to be extracted. When the script is called, the value of argument 1 (TheRaven) is stored in $argv[4]. The value of argument 4 (midRaven.txt) is stored in parameter $argv[2]. With this mechanism, we can write a general script using the value of $argv[1] through $argv[4]. The design is shown in Figure 17.5.

---

[4]We can have more than nine positional parameters, but we cannot access them directly. We must use the **shift** command to process them. These techniques are discussed later in the chapter.

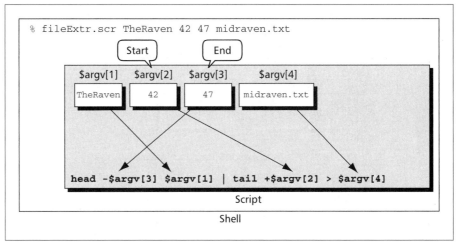

FIGURE 17.5 *Matching Arguments and Positional Parameters*

The advantage of using arguments and positional parameters is that we do not have to rewrite the extract script each time we want to extract lines from a different file or store the output in a different file. With a generalized script, we change the positional parameters simply by using different arguments (Script 17.6).

SCRIPT 17.6   *The **fileExtr.scr** Script*

```
1  #!/bin/csh
2  #   Script: fileExtr.scr
3  #   Extracts $argv[2]-$argv[3] lines from $argv[1]
4  #   and places them in $argv[4]
5
6  head -$argv[3] $argv[1] | tail +$argv[2] > $argv[4]
```
```
% fileExtr.scr TheRaven 42 47 midRaven.txt
```
```
% cat midRaven.txt
Open here I flung the shutter, when, with many a flirt and flutter
In there stepped a stately Raven of the saintly days of yore.
Not the least obeisance made he; not a minute stopped or stayed he;
But, with mien of lord or lady, perched above my chamber door--
Perched upon a bust of Pallas just above my chamber door--
Perched, and sat, and nothing more.
```

17.2 Expressions

Expressions are a sequence of operators and operands that reduces to a single value. The operators can be either mathematical operators, such as add and subtract, that compute a value; relational operators, such as greater than and less than, that determine a relationship between two values and return true or false; file test operators that report the status of a file; or logical operators that combine logical values and return true or false. We use mathematical expressions to compute a value and other expressions to make decisions. Figure 17.6 shows the four types of expressions.

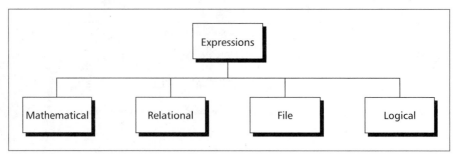

FIGURE 17.6 *Expression Forms and Operators*

Mathematical Expressions

Mathematical expressions in the C shell use integer operands and mathematical operators to calculate a value.

Mathematical Operators

Mathematical operators are used to compute a numeric value. The C shell supports the standard add, subtract, multiply, and divide operators plus several other operators found in the C language. These operators are summarized in Table 17.1.

TABLE 17.1 *Mathematical Operators*

Operator	Description
+	Value is sum of two numbers.
–	Value is first value minus second value.
*	Value is product of two numbers.
/	Value is integral of first value divided by second value.
%	Value is remainder of first value divided by second.
++	Add one to variable.
– –	Subtract one from variable.
=	Assignment.
+= -= *= /= %=	Expand mathematical expression (a op= b) to (a = a op b), Perform arithmetic operation (op) and store result in a.

From Table 17.1, we see that to use the expression operators, the data must be numeric values. As we discussed in Section 13.3 on page 504, however, the C shell stores all data as character strings. It cannot interpret numeric values. To better understand the problem created by storing numeric values as strings, let's see what happens when we add to a counter as in Session 17.1.

We would expect the value of the variable count to be 7, but it is not. Its value is the string 5+2. This leads to the question: How can we evaluate numeric values in the C shell? The answer is that we must use the arithmetic (@) command.

SESSION 17.1 *Adding to a String*

```
% set count = 5
% set count=$count+2
% echo $count
5+2
```

Arithmetic (@) Command

As shown in Table 17.1, the C shell provides a full set of arithmetic operators. However, they must be used with the arithmetic (@) command. The arithmetic command works only with integers; it cannot handle a floating-point value. Figure 17.7 depicts the arithmetic command syntax.

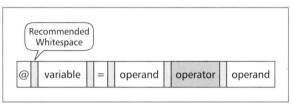

FIGURE 17.7 *Format of the @ Command*

As you study Figure 17.7, note that the spaces are not required, but we highly recommend that you use them. The operator can be any of the arithmetic operators previously discussed. Session 17.2 contains an example of a multiply operator in the arithmetic command.

SESSION 17.2 *Mathematical Expression Operators*

```
% set operand1 = 15
% set operand2 = 6
% @ result = $operand1 * $operand2
% echo $result
90
```

We are now ready to solve our original problem of adding to a variable. At the beginning of this section, we demonstrated in Session 17.1 that it couldn't be done using what would be considered the intuitive approach. Rather, we must use an expression to do the addition or any other mathematical operation. This code is in Session 17.3.

SESSION 17.3 *Using an Expression to Add*

```
% set count = 5
% @ count += 2
% echo $count
7
```

Relational Expressions

Relational expressions compare two values and return a logical value such as true or false. The logical value depends on the values being compared and the operator being used.

Relational Operators

The relational operators are listed in Table 17.2. The second column shows the relational operators to compare numeric data. The third column shows the relational operators to compare string data. The fourth column shows the pattern matching operators. Note that there is no operator to test whether one string is greater than or less than another string.

TABLE 17.2   *Logical String Operators*

Meaning	Numeric	String	Patterns
greater than	>		
greater than or equal	>=		
less than	<		
less than or equal	<=		
equal	==	==	
not equal	!=	!=	
pattern matches			=~
pattern does not match			!~

Using Relational Operators

The C shell allows the use of relational expressions whenever we need a logical value in a command, such as in the selection and looping commands. We develop their use as the chapter progresses.

File Expressions

File expressions use file operators to check the status of a file. A file's status includes characteristics such as open, readable, writable, or executable.

File Operators

There are several operators that can be used in a file test command to check a file's status. They are particularly useful in shell scripts when we need to know the type or status of a file. Table 17.3 lists the file operators and what file attributes they test.

TABLE 17.3   *File Status Operators*

Operator	Explanation
`-e file`	True if file exists.
`-r file`	True if file is readable.
`-l file`	True if file exists and is a symbolic link.
`-w file`	True if file exists and is writable.
`-x file`	True if file exists and is executable.

Continued

TABLE 17.3 *File Status Operators*

Operator	Explanation
`-o file`	True if the user owns it.
`-f file`	True if file exists and is a regular file.
`-d file`	True if file exists and is a directory.
`-s file`	True if file exists and has a size greater than zero.
`-z file`	True if file length is zero (empty).

Using File Expressions

The C shell allows the use of file expressions whenever we need a logical value in a command, such as in the selection and looping commands. We develop their use as the chapter progresses.

Logical Expressions

Logical expressions evaluate to either true or false. They use a set of three logical operators and a third variation of the test command.

Logical Operators

The C shell has three **logical operators**: *not* (!), *and* (&&), and *or* (||). These operators can be used only with relational or file expressions; they cannot be used with variables.

A common way to show logical relationships is in truth tables. Truth tables list the values that each operand can assume and the resulting value. Truth tables for *not, and,* and *or* are in Figure 17.8.

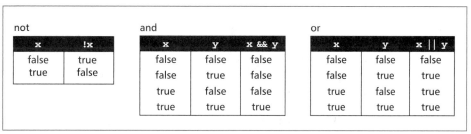

FIGURE 17.8 *Logical Operators Truth Table*

not The **not** operator (!) complements the value of an expression. It changes a true value to false and a false value to true.

and The **and** operator (&&) requires two expressions. For this reason, it is known as a binary operator. Because it is a binary operator, four distinct combinations of operand values in its evaluation are possible. The result is true only when both expressions are true; it is false in all other cases.

or The **or** operator (||) also requires two expressions (binary operator). Again, because it is a binary operator, four distinct combinations of operand values are possible. The result is false only when both operands are false; it is true in all other cases.

Using Logical Expressions

The C shell allows the use of logical expressions whenever we need a logical value in a command, such as in the selection and looping commands. We develop their use as the chapter progresses.

17.3 Decisions: Making Selections

In this section, we learn how to execute different sets of commands based on the value of an expression. The C shell has two different commands that allow us to select between two or more alternatives. The first, the `if-then-else` statement, examines the data and chooses between two alternatives. For this reason, it is sometimes referred to as a two-way selection. The second, the `switch` statement, selects one of several paths by matching patterns to different strings. These two statements are shown in Figure 17.9.

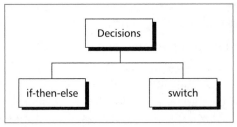

FIGURE 17.9 *Decisions*

if-then-else

Every language has some variation of the `if-then-else` statement. The only difference between them is what keywords are required by the syntax. For example, the C language does not use `then`. In fact, it is an error to use it. In all languages, however, something is tested. Most typically, data values are tested. In the C shell, the value of an expression is tested.

In Figure 17.10, the flowchart shows an expression being evaluated. On the right of the flowchart is the format for the C shell. The shell evaluates the expression. When the value is true (nonzero), the `then` set of commands is executed. When the value is false (0), the `else` set of commands is executed. Note that the C shell requires one more syntactical token: Each `if-then-else` statement must end with the keyword `endif`.

As an example of evaluating data, we look at the time of day and print an appropriate greeting, such as "good morning" or "good afternoon." This requires that we know what time it is. Fortunately, this information is available in the **date** command. In the output from the **date** command, the hour occupies characters 12 and 13. This means that we can simply execute the **date** command, pipe its output to **cut**, and then store the results in a variable we name `hour`. Once we have isolated the hour, we simply test it in an `if-then-else` statement. We demonstrate this example in

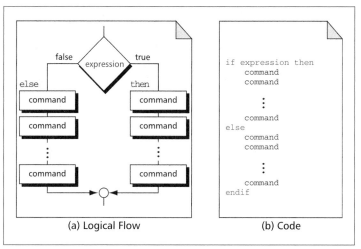

FIGURE 17.10 **if-then-else** *Format*

SCRIPT 17.7 *Time of Day Greeting*

```
1   #!/bin/csh
2   #   Script: gday.scr
3   #   Demonstrate test command evaluation
4   set hour = `date | cut -c 12-13`
5   if ($hour <= 18) then
6       echo Good day, sir
7   else
8       echo Good evening, sir
9   endif
% gday.scr

Output:
Good day, sir
```

Script 17.7. We will expand on this example when we discuss multiway selection later in this chapter.

Using Commands as Expressions

We can also use a command and its exit status as the value of the expression. However, the command must be enclosed in braces. The syntax is shown in the following example:

```
{ command }
```

If the command is successful, the exit status (0) is interpreted as true; if it is not successful, the exit status (nonzero) is interpreted as false. If we want to negate the command results, we use the *not* operator (!) in front of the braces as shown in the next example:

```
!{ command }
```

The previous example does not work with complex commands. When a command is complex, we must first execute it and then test the exit status with a separate command. Let's look at an example that uses a complex command. We want to know if a user is currently logged on to UNIX. To answer this question, we use the **who** command and pipe the results to **grep** where we look for the person's login id. This is an example of a chained command ending in a **grep** search. Because the search is the last command, the C shell evaluates the search results to determine if the data were found. This code is in Script 17.8.

SCRIPT 17.8   *Using a Command*

```
 1  #!/bin/csh
 2  #   Script: exit.scr
 3  #   Demonstrate use of exit status
 4  #   First parameter is user's login id
 5  who | grep $argv[1] > /dev/null              # puts line in trash
 6  if ($status == 0) then
 7      echo $argv[1] 'is logged in'
 8  else
 9      echo $argv[1] 'is not logged in'
10  endif
```

```
% exit.scr gilberg
```

```
Output:
gilberg is logged in
```

Script 17.8 Analysis: In the `who | grep` statement (line 5), we redirect the output to the trash. If we didn't do this, the lines that match the argument would be printed by **grep.** Trash is identified as a null file in the device directory (`/dev/null`).

if *without* else

Often we make a test that requires action only if the test is true. No action is required if the test is false. In this case, we need a `then` statement without a matching `else`. When there is no false action, we simply omit the `else` (false) portion of the command as shown in Figure 17.11.

As an example of a `then` without an `else`, consider the situation in which we need to print a file. If the file exists and contains data, we print it. If it doesn't, then we need do nothing. In Script 17.9, we use a test command to determine whether a file exists and is readable. If it is, we **cat** the file. If the file doesn't exist, we do nothing. There are no `else` statements because we are interested in taking action only if the file exists.

else *without* if: *Null Command*

Although we can have an `if-then-else` statement without an `else` action, we cannot have one without a `then` action. When there are no true actions in the `if-then-else`, we use what is called the null command for the true action. The null command is a colon: It does nothing but satisfy the requirement for a command in the `then` action. Script 17.10 shows the use of the null command.

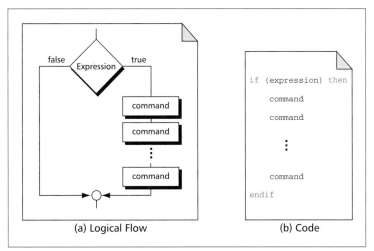

FIGURE 17.11   *Example of* **if-then**

SCRIPT 17.9   *Example of* **if-then** *with* **No else**

```
1  #!/bin/csh
2  #   Script: ifNoElse.scr
3  #   Test existence of a file
4  if (-e $argv[1]) then
5      cat $argv[1]
6  endif
```
```
% ifNoElse.scr file1
```
```
Output:
********************
**                **
** This is file1 **
**                **
********************
```

SCRIPT 17.10   *Example of a Null* **if** *Command*

```
1  #!/bin/csh
2  #   Script: ifNull.scr
3  # Ensure argument 1 is valid file
4  if (-e $argv[1]) then
5      :
6  else
7      echo $argv[1] does not exist and cannot be opened
8  endif
9  #   Rest of script here
```
```
$ ifNull.scr noFile
```
```
Output:
noFile does not exist and cannot be opened
```

Nested `if` Statements

Each branch in the `if-then-else` statement can be any command including another `if-then-else` statement. When an `if-then-else` statement is found in either the true or false branch of an `if-then-else` statement, it is called a nested `if`. This design is shown in Figure 17.12.

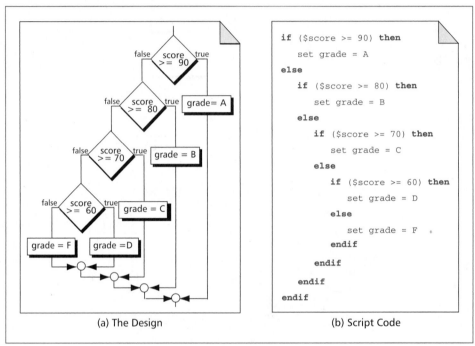

(a) The Design

(b) Script Code

FIGURE 17.12   *Nested* **if-then-else**

Let's use this format to solve a rather common academic problem: changing a numeric grade (between 0 and 100) to a letter grade (A, B, C, D, or F). We begin by designing the solution to the problem. The flowchart design is shown in Figure 17.12. Also shown in the figure is the code for the solution. As you study the code examples, note that the script code is indented with each nested format.

Multiway Selection

The C shell implements multiway selection with the `switch` statement. Given a string and a list of pattern alternatives, the `switch` statement matches the string against each of the patterns in sequence. The first pattern that matches the string gets the action. If no patterns match, the `switch` statement continues with the next command. The decision logic for the multiway statement is shown in Figure 17.13 along with a design flowchart.

`switch` *Syntax*

The `switch` syntax format is shown in Figure 17.14. The command starts with the string, enclosed in parentheses, that is to be evaluated. It ends with an end switch token, **endsw.** Between the start and end switch is the **pattern list.**

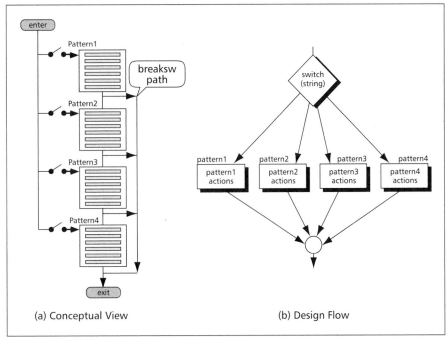

FIGURE 17.13 **switch** *Decision Logic*

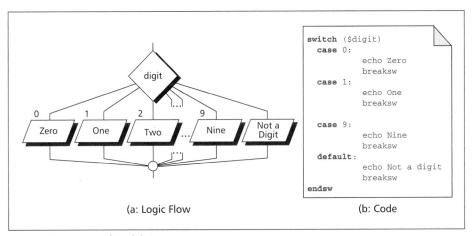

FIGURE 17.14 *Echo Digit Text*

case *Syntax*

For every pattern that needs to be tested, a separate pattern is defined in the pattern list. The patterns are identified by the keyword, case, followed by the pattern and terminated by a colon. The case syntax is:

```
case string_constant:
```

Associated with each pattern is one or more commands. The commands, which must be on a separate line following the case statement, follow the normal rules for commands. Generally, they are coded one command to a line. The last action in the pattern list is usually the default commands to be executed if none of the other cases match.

The switch statement is a puzzle that must be solved carefully to avoid confusion. Think of it as a series of drawbridges, one for each pattern. As a result of the pattern evaluation, the first matching drawbridge is closed so that there will be a path for the script to follow. Once a drawbridge is closed, none of the patterns that follow it can be matched. After executing the matching commands from the closed drawbridge, the path flows to the exit. If none of the patterns match (that is, if none of the drawbridges are closed), the switch statement continues with the next command. The switch flow appears in Figure 17.14.

To see the continuous flow from one statement to the next, examine the code in Script 17.11.

SCRIPT 17.11 *Demonstrate **switch** Flow*

```
 1  #!/bin/csh/
 2  #   Script: default.scr
 3  #   Demonstrate case default operation.
 4  echo "Enter a character:   \c"
 5  set char = $<
 6
 7  switch ($char)
 8     case A:
 9             echo You entered $char
10     case B:
11             echo You entered $char
12     default:
13             echo You did not enter A or B.
14  endsw
```
```
% default.scr
```
```
Output:
Enter a character:   A
You entered A
You entered A
You did not enter A or B.
```

Script 17.11 Analysis: When we ran the script, we entered A, which matched the first case pattern. After executing the **echo** command, however, the control flow followed to the second case. Because the flow is continuous, the input did not have to match the second case pattern or the default. All three statements were executed.

breaksw *Syntax*

Once a case statement is entered, the command flow continues until either a break switch command or the end of the switch is encountered. The break switch (breaksw) statement interrupts the flow and transfers to the next statement after the end of the **switch** command. Because of this unconditional flow transfer, there should *not* be statements after a break switch command.

As a more typical example of a switch statement, let's write a session that, given a digit, echoes its text spelling. The script and a sample execution are in Script 17.12.

SCRIPT 17.12 *Demonstrate the* **switch** *Statement*

```
 1 #!/bin/csh
 2 #  Script: switchDigit.scr
 3 #  Demonstrate switch statement
 4
 5 echo -n "Enter a digit and I'll spell it for you: "
 6
 7 set digit = $<
 8 echo -n "\nYou entered $digit. It is spelled "
 9
10 switch ($digit)
11    case 0:
12            echo Zero.
13            breaksw
14    case 1:
15            echo One.
16            breaksw
17    case 2:
18            echo Two.
19            breaksw
20    case 3:
21            echo Three.
22            breaksw
23    case 4:
24            echo Four.
25            breaksw
26    case 5:
27            echo Five.
28            breaksw
29    case 6:
30            echo Six.
31            breaksw
32    case 7:
33            echo Seven.
34            breaksw
35    case 8:
36            echo Eight.
37            breaksw
38    case 9:
39            echo Nine.
40            breaksw
41    default:
```

Continued

SCRIPT 17.12 *Demonstrate the **switch** Statement—Continued*

```
42            echo Not a digit.
43            breaksw
44 endsw
```

```
$ switchDigit.scr
```

```
Output:
Enter a digit and I'll spell it for you: 1

You entered 1. It is spelled One.
```

17.4 Repetition

The real power of computers is their ability to repeat an operation or a series of operations many times. This repetition, known as looping or iteration, is one of the basic programming concepts. In this section, we discuss looping and introduce different looping constructs.

A **loop** is an action or a series of actions repeated under the control of loop criteria written by the programmer. Each loop tests the criteria. If the criteria tests true, the loop continues; if it tests false, the loop terminates.

C Shell Loops

As shown in Figure 17.15, there are three loops in the C shell: the `while` loop, the `foreach` loop, and the `repeat` loop.

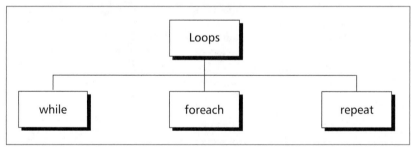

FIGURE 17.15 *Loop Constructs*

The `while` *Loop*

The **while** loop is an expression-controlled loop. In an expression-controlled loop, the loop body is repeated as long as the expression is true. The loop begins with *while,* which contains the loop expression and loops as long as the expression is true. That is to say, it loops "while" the expression is true. When the expression becomes false, the loop terminates. Figure 17.16 shows the format of the `while` loop.

One of the most common loop applications in any language is reading data. Script 17.13 is a short example that demonstrates how to read data in a loop. We begin by writing a `while` loop that reads data a line at a time from the keyboard. As long as there is input, it adds the number and iterates. When there is no input, either because

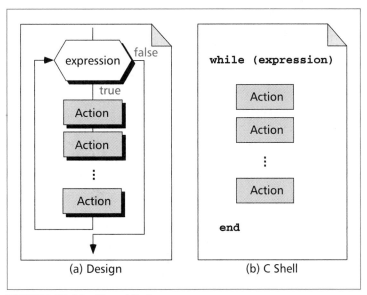

FIGURE 17.16   The **while** Loop

the user keys Return without data or enters end of file (^d in UNIX), the script prints the total and stops. In Script 17.13, we entered end of file.

SCRIPT 17.13   *A Simple Read Loop*

```
 1  #!/bin/csh
 2  #  loopAdd.scr
 3  #  Loops adding data until end
 4
 5  echo This script adds numbers. Enter your numbers at the prompt.
 6  echo When you are done, key return without a value or key ^d
 7
 8  set sum = 0
 9
10  echo -n "Enter a number:          "
11  set num = $<
12
13  while ($num != "")
14       @ sum += $num
15       echo -n "Enter the next number: "
16       set num = $<
17  end
18
19  echo "\nThe sum of the numbers is: $sum"
```

```
% loopAdd.scr
```

```
Output:
This script adds numbers. Enter your numbers at the prompt.
When you are done, key return without a value or key ^d
```

Continued

SCRIPT 17.13   *A Simple Read Loop—Continued*

```
Enter a number:        2
Enter the next number: 4
Enter the next number: 6
Enter the next number: ^D

The sum of the numbers is: 12
```

Script 17.13 Analysis: There is one potential problem with this script. It works as long as there is not a blank line in the input. If there is a blank line, the `while` expression becomes false, and the loop stops.

In Script 17.13, we read until end of file is read. Another looping concept uses a sentinel to terminate the looping. A **sentinel** is a special data value that stops the loop. A common loop sentinel is -9999. Of course, the sentinel value cannot be a valid value. Script 17.14 demonstrates the sentinel concept by using -9999 to indicate that the script is done and the total is to be displayed.

SCRIPT 17.14   *Using a Sentinel to Print Sum*

```
 1 #!/bin/csh -f
 2 #  Script: loopSent.scr
 3 #  Demonstrates read file with sentinel
 4
 5 echo This script adds numbers. Enter your numbers at the prompt.
 6 echo When you are done, key -9999
 7
 8 set sum = 0
 9
10 echo -n "Enter a number:        "
11 set num = $<
12
13 while ($num != -9999)
14     @ sum += $num
15     echo -n "Enter the next number: "
16     set num = $<
17 end
18
19 echo "The sum of the numbers is: $sum"
```
```
% loopSent.scr
```
```
Output:
This script adds numbers. Enter your numbers at the prompt.
When you are done, key -9999
Enter a number:        2
Enter the next number: 4
Enter the next number: 6
Enter the next number: -9999
The sum of the numbers is: 12
```

The `foreach` Loop

The `foreach` statement is a list-controlled loop. In a list-controlled loop, there is a control list. The number of elements in the list controls the number of iterations. If the control list contains five elements, the body of the loop is executed five times; if the control list contains ten elements, the body of the loop is executed ten times. Note that the list must be enclosed in parentheses.

There is only one list-controlled loop in the C shell: the `foreach` loop. The list can be any type of string; for example, it can be words, lines, sentences, or a file. Figure 17.17 shows the design and code of the `foreach` loop. In each iteration, the next element in `list` is moved to `variable` and processed.

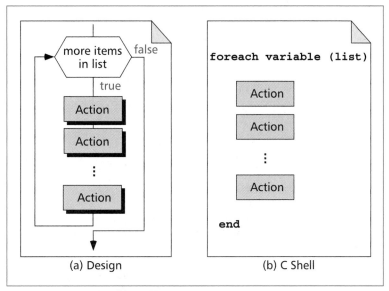

(a) Design   (b) C Shell

FIGURE 17.17   *The* **foreach** *Command*

Let's write a very simple loop. In Script 17.15, we loop five times, each time displaying the loop control string (a digit) and the word "Hello."

SCRIPT 17.15   *A Simple* **foreach** *Loop*

```
1  #!/bin/csh
2  #   Script: loopForeach.scr
3  #   Demonstrate a simple foreach loop
4
5  foreach i (1 2 3 4 5)
6      echo $i Hello
7  end
```
```
% loopForeach.scr
```
Continued

SCRIPT 17.15 *A Simple* **foreach** *Loop—Continued*

```
Output:
1 Hello
2 Hello
3 Hello
4 Hello
5 Hello
```

List of Files In this example, we process a list of files; that is, each element in the control list is a filename. The file list is created as a separate UNIX file. The file is then used in a script to create the foreach loop list. This design makes it easy to use one script with different lists of files for each execution. To make it even more flexible, the file list is passed to the script as an argument.

To get the data, we simply **cat** the file. The body of the loop first prints the filename and then the contents of the file. After the file is printed, we print a divider to separate it from the next file. The script and its output are in Script 17.16.

SCRIPT 17.16 *File Processing Loop*

```
 1  #!/bin/csh
 2  #   Script: loopCatFiles.scr
 3  #   This script catenates files found in a control list
 4  #   The name of the control file is an argument ($argv[1])
 5
 6  foreach filename (`cat $argv[1]`)
 7      echo $filename
 8      cat  $filename
 9      echo "========= End of $filename =========\n"
10  end
11
12  echo      "********* End of File List *********"
```

```
% loopCatFiles.scr loopCatFiles.dat
```

```
cat loopCatFiles.dat
file1
file2
```

```
Output:
file1
******************
**              **
** This is file1 **
**              **
******************
========= End of file1 =========

file2
******************
**              **
** This is file2 **
**              **
```

Continued

SCRIPT 17.16   *File Processing Loop*

```
*******************
========= End of file2 =========

********* End of File List *********
```

Script 17.16 Analysis: The simplicity of the code makes it very easy to understand what we are doing. But the simplicity also hides how the code works. The `foreach` statement creates a control list by using a **cat** command to create the control list of the files in the argument (`$argv[1]`). Each element of the control list is a line containing the name of a file to be listed. The script then uses the control list first to display the name of the file being printed and then as the parameter to the **cat** command in the loop body. When the control list has been completely processed, we exit the loop and display an end of script message.

Now study the first statement (line 6) carefully. Because the list must be enclosed in parentheses, we place them around the **cat** command and its backquotes.

repeat *Loop*

The `repeat` loop is a very simple loop that executes one command a specified number of times. It requires two parameters: the number of times to loop and a single command to be executed. The command must be simple; that is, it cannot have a pipe or other complex construct. Script 17.17 contains a very simple example of a `repeat` statement.

SCRIPT 17.17   *Demonstrate* **repeat** *Command*

```
1  #!/bin/csh/ -f
2  #  Script: loopRepeat.scr
3  #  Demonstrate repeat command
4  set looper = 5
5
6  repeat $looper echo Hello
```
```
% loopRepeat.scr
```
```
Output:
Hello
Hello
Hello
Hello
Hello
```

Other Loop Control Commands

There are three other commands related to loops: `break`, `continue`, and `goto`. These commands are diagrammed in Figure 17.18.

break: The `break` statement immediately exits from the loop (but not from the script). Processing continues with the first command after the loop. The `break` statement is generally an action in a selection command such as an `if-then-else` or a `case` statement.

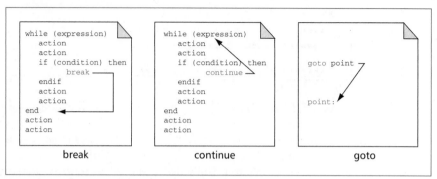

FIGURE 17.18 **break**, **continue**, *and* **goto**

continue: The continue statement causes the loop to ignore the rest of the body commands and immediately transfers control to the test command. If the loop is not complete, the next iteration begins.

goto: Although highly discouraged, the goto command can be used in the C shell. The goto requires a named location in the script as a target. A named point is created by a name immediately followed by a colon. While most often used in a loop, the goto can be used anywhere in a script. We demonstrate it in Script 17.18.

SCRIPT 17.18 *Demonstrate* **goto** *Command*

```
 1  #!/bin/csh
 2  #  Script: goto.scr
 3  #  Demonstrate the goto command
 4  #  We recommend that the goto not be used.
 5
 6  echo Start of demonstration.
 7  goto point
 8
 9  echo Not executed.
10
11  point: echo Now at point.
```
```
% goto.scr
```
```
Output:
Start of demonstration.
Now at point.
```

17.5 Special Parameters

Besides having positional parameters numbered $argv[1] to $argv[9], the C shell script can have three other special parameters: one that contains the script filename, one that contains the number of arguments entered by the user, and one that combines all of the positional parameters. The complete list of parameters is shown in Figure 17.19.

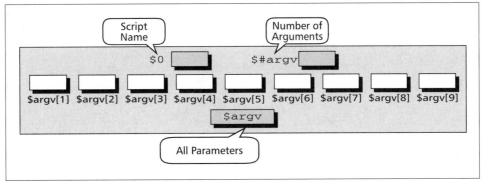

FIGURE 17.19 *Parameters in the C Shell*

Script Name ($0)

The script name parameter ($0) holds the name of the script. This is often useful when a script calls other scripts. The script name parameter can be passed to the called script so that it knows who called it. As another use, when a script needs to issue an error message, it can include its name as part of the message. Having the script name in the message clearly identifies which script had a problem. The script name parameter, $0, is shown in Figure 17.19.

Number of Arguments ($#argv)

A second special parameter holds the number of arguments passed to the script. Scripts can use this parameter, referred to as $#argv, programmatically in several ways. It is also shown in Figure 17.19. The script name and number of arguments are in Script 17.19.

SCRIPT 17.19 *Name and Number of Arguments*

```
1  #!/bin/csh
2  #   Script: parmsNameNum.scr
3  #   This script displays the $0 and $# special parameters
4  echo "The program name is:" $0
5  echo "Number of arguments:" $#argv
```
```
% parmsNameNum.scr 1 2 3 4 5
```
```
Output:
The program name is: parmsNameNum.scr
Number of arguments: 5
```

All Parameters ($argv)

The all parameters variable ($argv) creates a list of parameters. The number of elements in the list is the same as the number of arguments. To demonstrate how it works, let's write a simple loop that displays each parameter in turn. The script and its output are in Script 17.20.

SCRIPT 17.20   *Demonstrate All Parameters without Quotes*

```
1  #!/bin/csh
2  #   Script: parmLoop1.scr
3  #   Loops displaying parameter list one element at a time
4  foreach parm in ($argv)
5     echo $parm
6  end
```

```
% parmLoop1.scr Anne "Don Juan" Tuan
```

```
Output:
Anne
Don
Juan
Tuan
```

Script 17.20 Analysis: Study the output. Note that the quoted argument, `Don Juan`, is treated as two separate words even though it is quoted.

Special Parameter Summary

The special parameters are summarized in Table 17.4.

TABLE 17.4   *Special Parameter Summary*

Parameter	Description
$0	Script name
$#	Number of arguments to a script
$argv	All parameters

17.6 Changing Positional Parameters

The positional parameters can be changed within a script only by using the **set** command; values cannot be directly assigned to them. This means that to assign values to the script positional parameters, we must use **set.** The **set** command parses an input string and places each separate part of the string into a different positional parameter (up to nine). The format of the assignment is shown in the following example. Note that the parentheses are required.

```
% set argv = (argument1, argument2, …, argumentN)
```

Let's write a script to demonstrate how **set** can be used to store data in the positional parameters. The first part of the script stores one string containing two digits (note the quotes). Because there is only one string, it is stored in $argv[1] as demonstrated by the **echo** commands. We then store two numbers. Because we don't use quotes in the second example, each digit is assigned to a different positional parameter (Script 17.21).

SCRIPT 17.21 *Parse Strings Using the **set** Command*

```
 1 #!/bin/csh
 2 #  Script: set.scr
 3 #  This script demonstrates the set command.
 4
 5 # Only one string: stored in $argv[1]
 6 echo '$argv[1] contains' $argv[1]
 7 echo '$argv[2] contains' $argv[2] '\n'
 8
 9 set argv = ("1 2")
10 echo After set there are $#argv parameters.
11 echo '$argv[1] contains:' $argv[1]
12 echo
13
14 # Two strings: stored in $argv[1]-$argv[2]
15 set argv = (1 2)
16 echo After set there are $#argv parameters.
17 echo '$argv[1] contains:' $argv[1]
18 echo '$argv[2] contains:' $argv[2]
```

```
% set.scr Hello Dolly
```

```
Output:
$argv[1] contains Hello
$argv[2] contains Dolly

After set there are 1 parameters.
$argv[1] contains: 1 2

After set there are 2 parameters.
$argv[1] contains: 1
$argv[2] contains: 2
```

Script 17.21 Analysis: We execute the script with two arguments and display them in the first command. Then, in line 9, we use the **set** command to assign the string "1 2" to argv. Because we quote 1 and 2, they form one string and are stored completely in $argv[1]. We verify this by displaying $argv[1]. We cannot display $argv[2] because it doesn't exist, and the script interpreter raises an error when an empty argument is accessed. Because the **set** command clears $argv[2], it no longer exists. Then, in line 15, we use the **set** command again, this time without quotes. This time, the 1 is placed in $argv[1] and the 2 in $argv[2]. We verify the results by displaying $argv[1] and $argv[2].

As a more practical example, if you need to save the date to print a report, you can use **set** to assign the output from the **date** command to the positional parameters so that the date is available for printing. This concept is demonstrated in Script 17.22.

SCRIPT 17.22 *Saving Date for Future Using the* **set** *Command*

```
 1 #!/bin/csh
 2 #  Script: getDate.scr
 3 #  assigns date fields to parameters 1..6
 4 set argv = (`date`)
 5      # $argv[1]: alpha day (ddd)   $argv[2]: alpha month (mmm)
 6      # $argv[3]: day of month      $argv[4]: time (hh:mm:ss)
 7      # $argv[5]: time zone         $argv[6]: year (yyyy)
 8 echo "Complete date is:" $argv
 9 echo
10 set today = "$argv[2] $argv[3], $argv[6]"
11 echo "Today's date is :" $today
```

```
% getDate.scr
```

```
Output:
Complete date is: Thu Jun 16 21:31:09 PDT 2001

Today's date is : Jun 16, 2001
```

Script 17.22 Analysis: To convert the output from the **date** command to a string so that we can store it, we use command substitution (backquotes). To display the output from the **date** command, we used the $argv special processing parameter. If there were other parameters that we didn't want to display, we could have used the individual parameters for the date ($argv[1]...$argv[6]). Finally, note how we used comments to document the date format in each of the parameters. Next time we return to the script, we will not have to figure out the date format. It's all there in the documentation comments.

shift Command

One very useful command in shell scripting is the **shift** command. The **shift** command moves the values in the parameters toward the beginning of the parameter list. To understand the **shift** command, think of the parameters as a list rather than as individual variables. When we shift, we move each parameter to the left in the list. If we shift three positions, therefore, the fourth parameter will be in the first position, the fifth will be in the second position, and so forth until all parameters have been moved three positions to the left. The parameters at the end of the set become null. Note that while the special parameters do not participate in the shifting, their contents change as the shifting takes place. If **shift** does not have a parameter, it assumes **shift** 1. The **shift** operation is shown in Figure 17.20.

Recall that only the first nine parameters can be referenced by name ($argv[1]...$argv[9]). To process the rest of the parameters, we must use the **shift** command. Script 17.23 demonstrates the **shift** operator by using **shift** in a loop that prints only the first parameter ($argv[1]). Note that we use the number of parameters ($#argv) as the control for the loop. This also verifies that shifting reduces the parameter count by 1 for each parameter shifted out of the set.

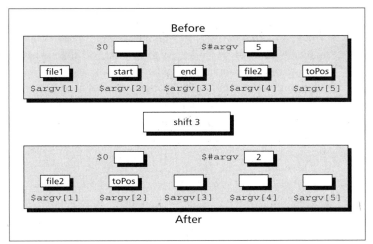

FIGURE 17.20   *The* **shift** *Command*

SCRIPT 17.23   *Shift and Print All Parameters*

```
 1  #!/bin/csh -f
 2  #  Script: shiftAll.scr
 3  #  Shift and print all parameters
 4  echo "There are" $#argv "parameters\n"
 5
 6
 7
 8  while ($#argv > 0)
 9
10      echo -n "$argv[1] "
11      shift
12  end
13
14  echo "\n"
15  echo "There are now" $#argv "parameters"
16  echo "End of script"
```
```
%  shiftAll.scr 1 2 3 4 5 6 7 8 9 10 11 12 13 14 15
```
```
Output:
There are 15 parameters

1 2 3 4 5 6 7 8 9 10 11 12 13 14 15

There are now 0 parameters
End of script
```

17.7 Argument Validation

Good programs are designed to be fail-safe. This means that anything that can be validated should be confirmed before it is used. In this section, we discuss techniques used to validate user-supplied arguments.

Number of Arguments Validation

The first code in a script that contains parameters should validate the number of arguments. Some scripts use a fixed number of arguments; other scripts use a variable number of arguments. Even when the number of arguments is variable, there is usually a minimum number that is required. Both fixed- and variable-numbered arguments are validated by using the number of arguments parameter ($#argv).

Fixed Number of Arguments

If the shell script expects a fixed number of arguments, we can easily make sure they are all there by checking the count parameter ($#argv). This script is in Script 17.24. Note that we test it twice, once with the correct number of arguments and once with too many arguments. To complete the testing, it should be run with no arguments and fewer than the correct number of arguments.

SCRIPT 17.24 *Validate Number of Parameters*

```
 1 #!/bin/csh
 2 #  Script: arguFixed.scr
 3 #  Validate Number of Parameters
 4
 5 if ($#argv != 3) then
 6     echo "This script requires 3 arguments--not" $#argv"."
 7     echo "Usage: $0 argv1 argv2 argv3"
 8     exit 1
 9 endif
10 echo "Correct number of parameters"
11 # Rest of script follows here
```

```
Execution:
% arguFixed.scr 1 2 3 4
This script requires 3 arguments--not 4.
Usage: argvFixed.scr argv1 argv2 argv3
```

```
% arguFixed.scr 1 2 3
Correct number of parameters
```

Minimum Number of Arguments

When a script expects a variable number of arguments and there is a minimum number required, we should verify that the minimum number have been entered. This validation concept is in Script 17.25.

SCRIPT 17.25 *Validation for One or More Parameters*

```
 1 #!/bin/csh
 2 #  Script: arguVar.scr
 3 #  Validate Minimum Number of Parameters
 4
 5 if ($#argv < 1) then
```

Continued

SCRIPT 17.25 *Validation for One or More Parameters*

```
 6        echo "This script requires 1 or more arguments."
 7        echo "Usage: $0 argu1 [argu2 ...arguN]"
 8        exit 1
 9  endif
10  echo $#argv "arguments received."
11  # Rest of script follows here
```

```
Execution:
% arguVar.scr
This script requires 1 or more arguments.
Usage: arguVar.scr argu1 [argu2...arguN]
```

```
% arguVar.scr one two three
3 arguments received.
```

Type of Argument Validation

After the exact or minimum number of arguments is validated, the script should verify that each argument's type is correct. While all arguments are passed as strings, the string contents can be numeric, a filename, or any other verifiable type.

Numeric Validation

The values in numeric parameters are virtually unlimited. Some scripts simply need a number; scripts that extract a range of lines from a file are of this nature. Other scripts may require that the number be in a range; scripts that receive a date may require this type of validation. Let's write a script that uses both of these types of numeric validation. We first validate that an argument is numeric by using **grep.** Once we verify that the argument is numeric, we test to make sure that it is in the range 1 to 12. Both of these validations are in Script 17.26.

SCRIPT 17.26 *Validate Range*

```
 1  #!/bin/csh
 2  #   Script: arguMonth.scr
 3  #   This scripts verifies that the second argument is
 4  #   numeric and is between 1 and 12 (a month)
 5
 6  # Exit values
 7  #      0    Success
 8  #      1    Not Numeric
 9  #      2    Less than 1
10  #      3    Greater than 12
11
12  echo $argv[2] > temp
13  grep '^[0-9]*$' temp > /dev/null
14
15  if ( $status != 0 ) then
16      echo "Month argument is not numeric"
```

Continued

SCRIPT 17.26 *Validate Range—Continued*

```
17    exit 1
18  endif
19
20  if ( $argv[2] < 1 ) then
21      echo "Month argument is less than 1: must be <1...12>"
22      exit 2
23  endif
24
25  if ( $argv[2] > 12 ) then
26      echo "Month argument is greater than 12: must be <1...12>"
27      exit 3
28  endif
29  echo "Validation is OK. We continue."
```

```
Execution:
% arguMonth.scr 2002 8
Validation is OK. We continue.

% arguMonth.scr 2002 May
Month argument is not numeric

% arguMonth.scr 2002 0
Month argument is less than 1: must be <1...12>

% arguMonth.scr 2002 13
Month argument is greater than 12: must be <1...12>
```

File Type Validation

If an argument is an input file, we can verify that the file exists and that it has a read permission. If the file is an output file, there is no need to verify it because UNIX will create it if it doesn't exist. Script 17.27 demonstrates how first to verify that a file exists and then to verify that it is readable.

SCRIPT 17.27 *Validate Input File*

```
 1  #!/bin/csh
 2  #  Script: arguFile.scr
 3  #  Verify that a $argv[1] is a valid input file.
 4  if (! -s "$argv[1]") then
 5      echo "$argv[1] does not exist or is empty"
 6      exit 1
 7  endif
 8
 9  if (! -r "$argv[1]") then
10      echo "You do not have read permission for $argv[1]"
11      exit 2
12  endif
```

Continued

SCRIPT 17.27 *Validate Input File*

```
Execution:
% arguFile.scr noFile
noFile does not exist or is empty
```
```
% arguFile.scr noPermFile
You do not have read permission for noPermFile
```
```
% arguFile.scr file1
%
```

Other Validations

Based on the script requirements, we may need to perform other validations. For example, a script may require that the first argument be larger than the second argument. Script 17.28 demonstrates a script that serves as a model for these types of requirements.

SCRIPT 17.28 *Validate Parameter Values*

```
 1 #!/bin/csh
 2 #  Script:  argValOther.scr
 3 #  Validate Three Parameters -- File Num1 Num2 (Num1 < Num2)
 4
 5 if ($#argv != 3) then
 6     echo "This script requires three arguments."
 7     echo "Usage: $0 file num1 num2 [num1 < num2]"
 8     exit 1
 9 endif
10 if (! -f "$argv[1]") then
11     echo "Invalid file name."
12     echo "Usage: $0 file num1 num2 [num1 < num2]"
13     exit 2
14 endif
15 if ($argv[2] >= $argv[3])
16 then
17    echo $argv[2] "not less than" $argv[3]
18    echo "Usage: $0 file num1 num2 [num1 < num2]"
19    exit 3
20 endif
21 # Rest of script follows here
```
```
Execution:
% argValOther.scr nofilehere
This script requires three arguments.
Usage: argValOther.scr file num1 num2 [num1 < num2]
```
```
% argValOther.scr nofilehere 1 6
Invalid file name.
Usage: argValOther.scr file num1 num2 [num1 < num2]
```
```
% argValOther.scr TheRaven 6 1
6 not less than 1
Usage: argValOther.scr file num1 num2 [num1 < num2]
```

17.8 Debugging Scripts

Whenever we write a script, we must test it. Often multiple tests are necessary. Sometimes the tests don't deliver the expected results. In these cases, we need to debug the script. There are two C shell options that we can use to help debug scripts: the verbose option and the execute trace option.

The verbosity option (verbose) echoes each statement that is syntactically correct and displays an error message if it is wrong. Script output, if any, is generated.

The execute trace option (xtrace) echoes each command, preceded by a plus (+) sign, before it is executed. It also replaces the value of each variable accessed in the statement. For example, in the statement

```
set y = $x
```

the $x is replaced with the actual variable value at the time the statement is executed. If the variable x contained 13, the display would be x = 13. In a similar manner, expression values and test values are displayed. Combining the two options as shown in the next statement

```
set verbose; set xtrace
```

allows us to see the command first and then see it with a plus sign and all references to variables replaced by their values. We can use these debug commands in two ways: include the options in the script and call the script with them.

Debug Options Included in the Script

Options are included in the script by using the **set** command. This method is demonstrated in Script 17.29.

SCRIPT 17.29   **verbose** Debug Option

```
 1 #!/bin/csh
 2 #   Script: debugSetOptV.scr
 3 #   Demonstrate debug options set in script
 4
 5 set verbose
 6
 7 set x = 5
 8 @ y = $x + 2
 9
10 if ($y == 10) then
11     echo \$y contains 10
12 else
13     echo \$y contains $y not 10
14 endif
```

Continued

SCRIPT 17.29 **verbose** *Debug Option*

```
15
16 while ($x != 0)
17    echo Counting down: \$x is $x
18    @ x = $x - 1
19 end
```

```
% debugSetOptV.scr
```

```
Output:
set x = 5
@ y = $x + 2

if ( $y == 10 ) then

echo \$y contains $y not 10
$y contains 7 not 10
endif

while ( $x != 0 )
echo Counting down: \$x is $x
Counting down: $x is 5
@ x = $x - 1
end

# iterations 2, 3, 4 not shown

while ( $x != 0 )
echo Counting down: \$x is $x
Counting down: $x is 1
@ x = $x - 1
end
while ( $x != 0 )
```

Script 17.29 Analysis: This script is rather straightforward. In the output section, we have used black text for the displayed commands and color for the script output. Because of the length of the output, we have also deleted the second, third, and fourth iterations of the loop; only the first and last are shown.

Note how we had to code the variable name to display it in the output. If we just used $x, we would have displayed the value. To display the variable name, we put a backslash before the dollar sign.

Debug Options on the Command Line

When the debug option is included in the script, we must edit it to remove the **set verbose** command when we complete the debug sessions. We can avoid this extra step if we include the options on the command line. This requires that we invoke the C shell in the command as in Script 17.30. It is the same as Script 17.29 with the **set** option removed.

SCRIPT 17.30   *Execute extrace Debug Option*

```
 1  #!/bin/csh
 2  #   Script: debugOptions.scr
 3  #   Script to demonstrate debug options
 4
 5  set x = 5
 6  @ y = $x + 2
 7
 8  if ($y == 10) then
 9      echo \$y contains 10
10  else
11      echo \$y contains $y not 10
12  endif
13
14  while ($x != 0)
15      echo Counting down: \$x is $x
16      @ x = $x - 1
17  end
```

```
% csh -x debugOptions.scr
```

```
Output:
set x = 5
@ y = 5 + 2
if ( 7 == 10) then
echo $y contains 7 not 10
$y contains 7 not 10
endif
while ( 5 != 0 )
echo Counting down: $x is 5
Counting down: $x is 5
@ x = 5 - 1
end
while ( 4 != 0 )
echo Counting down: $x is 4
Counting down: $x is 4
@ x = 4 - 1
end
while ( 3 != 0 )
echo Counting down: $x is 3
Counting down: $x is 3
@ x = 3 - 1
end
while ( 2 != 0 )
echo Counting down: $x is 2
Counting down: $x is 2
@ x = 2 - 1
end
while ( 1 != 0)
echo Counting down: $x is 1
Counting down: $x is 1
@ x = 1 - 1
```

Continued

SCRIPT 17.30 *Execute extrace Debug Option*

```
end
while ( 0 != 0 )
```

Script 17.30 Analysis: To help you trace the script execution, we again use black text for the statements and colored text for the script output.

As a final example, we repeat Script 17.30, this time using both commands at once. The command line and output are shown in Script 17.31. Refer to Script 17.30 for the code.

SCRIPT 17.31 **verbose** *and* **xtrace** *Options Combined*

```
% csh -x -v debugOptions.scr
set x = 5
set x = 5
@ y = $x + 2
@ y = 5 + 2

if ( $y == 10 ) then
if ( 7 == 10 ) then

echo \$y contains $y not 10
echo $y contains 7 not 10
$y contains 7 not 10
endif
endif

while ( $x != 0 )
while ( 5 != 0 )
echo Counting down: \$x is $x
echo Counting down: $x is 5
Counting down: $x is 5
@ x = $x - 1
@ x = 5 - 1
end
end
while ( $x != 0 )
while ( 4 != 0 )
echo Counting down: \$x is $x
echo Counting down: $x is 4
Counting down: $x is 4
@ x = $x - 1
@ x = 4 - 1
end
end
while ( $x != 0 )
while ( 3 != 0 )
echo Counting down: \$x is $x
echo Counting down: $x is 3
Counting down: $x is 3
```

Continued

SCRIPT 17.31 **verbose** and **xtrace** Options Combined—*Continued*

```
@ x = $x - 1
@ x = 3 - 1
end
end
while ( $x != 0 )
while ( 2 != 0 )
echo Counting down: \$x is $x
echo Counting down: $x is 2
Counting down: $x is 2
@ x = $x - 1
@ x = 2 - 1
end
end
while ( $x != 0 )
while ( 1 != 0 )
echo Counting down: \$x is $x
echo Counting down: $x is 1
Counting down: $x is 1
@ x = $x - 1
@ x = 1 - 1
end
end
while ( $x != 0 )
while ( 0 != 0 )
```

Script 17.31 Analysis: Once again, script statements are black and the script output is colored. Note that for each statement, it is first shown as coded, then repeated with values replacing the variable names.

17.9 Script Examples

In this section, we demonstrate a complete script. The application was chosen to demonstrate some of the techniques we learned in the chapter. It begins with a set of documentation that we recommend for production scripts. (We have been using an abbreviated form of it in the scripts developed throughout the chapter.) This documentation includes the author's name, date, a synopsis of the script that is similar to the UNIX manual synopsis, a description of the code approach, and an explanation of the exit value. When the script is modified, we also recommend that you add the date and description of the modification after the original description.

Copy

In Script 17.32, we simulate the copy command. We begin by validating that we have the correct number of parameters and then that the input file exists and the output file doesn't. It would be a good idea to modify the script and ask the user if the output file should be overwritten. We leave this change for an exercise at the end of the chapter. After ensuring that everything is okay, we simply cat the input file and redirect it to the output file.

SCRIPT 17.32 *Copy Script File*

```
 1  #!/bin/csh
 2  #NAME: newCopy.scr
 3  #TASK: Copy a file into another
 4  #AUTHOR:
 5  #DATE WRITTEN:
 6  #SYNOPSIS:    newCopy.scr file1 file2
 7  #DESCRIPTION: Copies files using the cat command
 8  #EXIT VALUE
 9  #        0       if successfully completed
10  #        1       if wrong number of arguments
11  #        2       if the source file does not exist
12  #        3       if the destination file already exists
13  # =======================================================
14  if ($#argv != 2) then
15        echo "Requires two file arguments"
16        echo "Usage: $0 from_file to_file"
17        exit 1
18  endif
19
20  if (! -r $argv[1]) then
21        echo "The first file cannot be read"
22        exit 2
23  endif
24
25  if (-f $argv[2]) then
26        echo "The second file already exists"
27        exit 3
28  endif
29
30  cat $argv[1] > $argv[2]
```

```
% newCopy.scr
Requires two file arguments
Usage: newCopy.scr from_file to_file
% echo $status
1
```

```
% newCopy.scr noFile file1.bak
The first file cannot be read
% echo $status
2
```

```
% newCopy.scr file1 file1.bak
% echo $status
0

% cat file1.bak
*******************
**               **
** This is file1 **
**               **
*******************
```

```
% newCopy.scr file1 file1.bak
```

Continued

SCRIPT 17.32 *Copy Script File—Continued*

```
    The second file already exists
% echo $status
    3
```

Script 17.32 Analysis: As you study the script and before you look at the test results, write a margin note for every situation that needs to be tested. Don't forget to look for combinations of errors. When you think you have discovered all the required test cases, compare your list with test results at the end of Script 17.32.

17.10 Key Terms

argument	file operator	parameter
argument validation	`foreach` statement	positional parameter
`breaksw` statement	`if-then-else` statement	relational expression
C shell	interpreter	relational operator
case command	interpreter designator line	repeat statement
comment	list-controlled loop	repetition
continue statement	logical expression	**set** command
debugging	logical operator	shell script
`else`	loop	**shift** command
`end`	mathematical expression	special parameter
`endif`	mathematical operator	special variables
`endsw`	multiway selection	switch statement
executable script	nested `if-then-else`	`then`
exit command	null command	two-way selection
expression	operand	`while` statement
file expression	operator	

17.11 Tips

1. The interpreter designator line, such as `#!/bin/csh`, must be the first line of a script.
2. Use the **chmod** command to make a script executable before executing it.
3. The C shell contains only nine accessible positional parameters.
4. Use the @ command to evaluate a mathematical expression.
5. Only integral values can be used with the @ command.
6. The @ command requires arguments that must be separated from each other and from the command by at least one space.
7. There is a difference between the divide (/) and modulus (%) operators. Divide calculates the quotient of a division; modulus calculates the remainder of a division.
8. The relational operators are different for integers and strings.
9. There are only two relational operators for strings: equal (==) and not equal (!=). The other relational operators (greater than, less than, and so on) must be simulated in a script.
10. There are two relational operators (=~ and !~) that determine if a pattern is matched in a string.

11. The `else` clause of `if-then-else` can be eliminated, but the `then` clause cannot.

12. A `breaksw` is needed to terminate each section of a `switch` statement.

13. The `while` loop needs an expression.

14. The `foreach` loop needs a list for its test expression.

15. Wherever possible, validate arguments to your scripts. Validation should check the numbers to ensure that they are digits, types, ranges, and so forth.

16. Use `-v` and `-x` at the command line to debug your script when testing does not generate the desired result.

17.12 Commands

The following commands were discussed in this chapter. For more details, see Appendix F and the corresponding pages shown in the following table.

Command	Description	Options	Page
break	**Synopsis:** *break* Forces a loop to terminate.		741
breaksw	**Synopsis:** *breaksw* Terminates execution of case commands.		734
continue	**Synopsis:** *continue* Continues with the next iteration of the loop.		742
exit	**Synopsis:** *exit [status]* Sets the exit status and terminates the shell.		721
foreach	**Synopsis:** *foreach variable (list)* *body* *end* Executes loop body as long as there are items in the list.		739

if-then-else	**Synopsis:** *if expression then*
	    ...
	  else
	    ...
	  endif
	Creates a two-way selection.
			728

shift	**Synopsis:** *shift expression* Shifts the parameters to the left.		746
switch	**Synopsis:** *switch (expression)* Selects among alternatives.		732
while	**Synopsis:** *while (expression)* *body* *end* Repeats the body while the expression is successful (exit status 0).		736

17.13 Summary

- A shell script is a text file that contains executable commands.
- We use a text editor, such as **vi,** to create the script.
- The script must be made executable (using the **chmod** command) before it can be executed.
- The first line of the script defines the path for the shell interpreter that reads and interprets the shell line by line.
- Arguments are user-supplied data that follow the script name on the command line and are input to the script.
- Positional parameters are predefined variables in the script. They are called $argv[1], $argv[2], $argv[3],..., $argv[9].
- The positional parameters receive their values from the command-line arguments.
- An expression is a sequence of operators and operands that reduces to a single value. The C shell supports four types of expressions: mathematical, relational, file, and logical.
- A mathematical expression uses integer operands and mathematical operators (+, -, *, /, %, =, +=, *=, /=, %=, ++, and --) to create a value. The @ command is used for mathematical expressions.
- A relational expression uses mathematical expressions and relational operators to create a true-false value.
- A file expression is used to test the status of a file.
- A logical expression is used to combine two relational expressions.
- The C shell has two different commands that allow us to select between two or more commands: if-then-else and switch.
- The if-then-else statement uses the exit status of a command to make a decision.
- The if-then-else statement can be used without the else clause but not without the then clause.
- The switch statement uses a string and patterns to make a decision about one of several choices.
- The real power of computers is their ability to repeat an operation or a series of operations many times. The C shell supports three loop constructs: while, foreach, and repeat.
- The while statement loops as long as the expression is true.
- The foreach statement iterates as long as there are elements in the list.
- The repeat statement loops a specified number of times.
- The C shell uses four special parameters: $0, $#argv, $argv, and $status.
- We can change the values of positional parameters using the **shift** command.
- Argument validation is necessary to make a script more robust. We should include several argument validations in our scripts: number of arguments, type of arguments, range of argument values, and so forth.
- To debug scripts, we use two C shell options: verbose and xtrace. The debugging options can be inserted in a script or applied at the command line when calling the script.

17.14 Practice Set

Review Questions

1. Can we use a `goto` statement in the C shell?
2. Can a `while` loop be executed infinitely? Show an example.
3. Can a `foreach` loop be executed infinitely? Show an example.
4. Write each of the following expressions in the C shell:
   - a. `3 + 4`
   - b. `x * 14`
   - c. `4 / x`
   - d. `x % 5`
5. Write each of the following expressions in the C shell:
   - a. `(3 + 4) * 8`
   - b. `(x * 14) / y`
   - c. `z = t * (4 / x) + 6`
   - d. `x = x + y + z`
6. Write each of the following relational expressions in the C shell:
   - a. `x > 9`
   - b. `x < =`
   - c. `x != y`
   - d. `x = = y`
7. Write each of the following logical expressions in the C shell:
   - a. `(x == 5) && (y > 10)`
   - b. `(x < = y) || (y > 10)`
   - c. `(x != y) || (x > 7) && (y <= x)`
   - d. `(x = = y) || (x > 5) || (y > 6)`
8. Write each of the following file expressions in the C shell:
   - a. file1 is empty
   - b. file2 is not readable
9. Show how to repeat a command 10 times using each of the following loops:
   - a. a `while` loop
   - b. a `foreach` loop
   - c. a `repeat` loop
10. Devise a way to repeat a command 100 times using a `foreach` loop. What about 1000 times? Hint: One way is to use nested loops.

Exercises

11. If originally `x=13` and `y=5`, what is the value of `x` and `y` after each of the following expressions (each expression is independent)?
    - a. `@ x %= 2`
    - b. `@ x += 4`
    - c. `@ x *= 3`
    - d. `@ x += $`
12. If originally `x=13` and `y=6`, what is the value of each of the following expressions (each expression is independent)?
    - a. `( $x < 12  )`
    - b. `( $y > 7  )`
    - c. `( $x < $y )`
    - d. `( $y == $x )`
13. If originally `x=13` and `y=6`, what is the value of each of the following expressions (each expression is independent)?
    - a. `( $x < 12 && $y > 7  )`
    - b. `( $y > 7 || $x < $x )`
    - c. `( ! $y < 7 )`
    - d. `( ! $x >= 8 && ! $x <  9 )`

14. What would be printed from the following loop?

```
while ( 10 )
        echo hello
end
```

15. What would be printed from the following loop?

```
while ( 0 )
        echo hello
end
```

16. What would be printed from the following loop?

```
while ( -10 )
        echo hello
end
```

17. What would be printed from the following loop?

```
while ( )
        echo hello
end
```

18. What would be printed from the following loop?

```
foreach i ( 5 < 6 )
        echo hello
end
```

19. What would be printed from the following loop?

```
foreach i ( 5 < 6 )
     echo $i
end
```

20. What would be printed from the following script segment? Explain why.

```
@ x = 12
while ( $x > 7 )
     echo $x
end
```

21. What would be printed from the following script segment? Explain why.

```
@ x = 12
while ( $x > 7 )
     echo $x
     @ x--
end
```

22. What would be printed from the following script segment? Explain why.

```
foreach i (12 11 10 8 7)
     echo $i
end
```

23. What would be printed from the following script segment? Explain why.

```
setx="1 3 5"
foreach i ($x)
     echo Hello
end
```

24. What would be printed from the following script segment? Explain why.

```
set x = "1 3 5"
set y = "2 4 6 8"
foreach i ($x $y)
     echo Hello
end
```

25. What would be printed from the following script segment? Explain why.

```
set x = "This is a test"
foreach i ($x)
    echo Hello
end
```

26. What would be printed from the following script segment? Does it show the number of people who have logged in? Why or why not?

```
set x = 0
foreach i ('who')
    @ x++
    echo $x
end
```

27. What would be printed from each of the following loops? What is the difference?

a.
```
foreach i (date)
    echo Hello
end
```

b.
```
foreach i ('date')
    echo Hello
end
```

28. What would be printed from the following script segment? Explain why.

```
foreach i (1 2 3 4 5)
    foreach j (1 2 3 4 5)
        echo -n $j
    end
    echo
end
```

29. What would be printed from the following script segment? Explain why.

```
foreach i (1 2 3 4 5 6 7 8 9 10)
    echo $i
    @ i++
end
```

30. What would be printed from the following script segment? Explain why.

```
foreach i (1 2 3 4 5 6 7 8 9 10)
    @ i--
    echo $i
end
```

31. What would be printed from the following script segment? Explain why.

```
foreach i (1 2 3 4 5 6 7 8 9)
    set j = 1
    while ( $ <= $i )
            echo -n $j
            @ j++
        end
    echo
end
```

32. What would be printed from the following script segment? Explain why.

```
foreach i (1 2 3 4 5 6 7 8 9)
    @ i *= 2
    @ i -= 1
    echo $i
end
```

33. What would be printed from the following script segment? Explain why.

```
foreach i (1 2 3 4 5 6 7 8 9)
    @ i *= 2
    @ i -= 1
    if ( $i <= 9 ) then
    echo $i
    endif
end
```

17.15 Lab Sessions

Each of the lab sessions in this chapter requires you to write a script, make it execut-able, and then execute it.

Session I

Write a script to backup a list of files.

Preparation

1. Create a file and type in it the list of files (in your home directory) that you want to backup.
2. Create a directory in which you will store the backed-up files.

Script

- **Script Name:** `backup.scr`
- **Arguments:** A filename and a directory. The filename holds the list of the files that should be backed-up. The directory is where the backed-up files should be stored.
- **Validation:** The minimum validation requirements are:
  - Ensure that exactly two arguments are entered.
  - Check that the first argument is the name of a file that exists.
  - Check that the second argument is the name of the directory that exists.
- **Body Section:** Create backup files for all files listed in the first argument. The backup files should have the same name as the original file with the extension `.bak`. They should be copied to the directory given as the second argument.

Testing the Script

1. Test the script with no arguments.
2. Test the script with one argument.
3. Test the script with three arguments.
4. Test the script with two arguments in which the first one is not the name of a file.
5. Test the script with two arguments in which the second one is the name of a file rather than a directory.
6. Test the script with the name of the file and the name of the directory you created in the preparation section.

Testing the Effect of the Script

1. Check the contents of the directory to be sure that the files are copied.

Session II

Write a script that finds all soft links to a specific file.

Preparation

1. Create a file and type some junk in it.
2. Make at least five soft links to this file using completely arbitrary names.

Script

- **Script Name:** softLinkFinder.scr
- **Arguments:** A filename. The files for which we want to find the soft links.
- **Validation:** The minimum validation requirements are:
  - Ensure that exactly one argument is entered.
  - Check that the only argument is the name of a file and that it exists.
- **Body Section:** Use the ls -l and **grep** command to find all the soft links attached to $argv[1] positional parameter. Note that a file of type softlink is distinguished by lowercase l. Be sure to find the soft links to the file defined in $argv[1] and not other files.

Testing the Script

1. Test the script with no arguments.
2. Test the script with two arguments.
3. Test the script with one argument that is not a file.
4. Test the script with one valid argument.

Testing the Effect of the Script

1. Check to make sure all the soft links you created are included in the list of soft links.

Session III

Create a script that simulates the ls -l command but prints only three columns of our choice.

Preparation

None

Script

- **Script Name:** ls.scr
- **Arguments:** Three numeric arguments defining the column number of the ls -l output to be printed in the order we specify. For example, if we call the script with ls.scr 4 2 1, it means that we want to print columns 4, 2, and 1.
- **Validation:** The minimum validation requirements are:
  - Ensure that exactly three arguments are entered.
  - Ensure that all three arguments are numeric.

Continued

Session III—*Continued*

- • Ensure that each argument is less than or equal to the actual number of columns in the `ls -l` command output.
- **Body Section:** Creates a new command that shows the output of the `ls -l` command to be printed in three columns in the order we like.

Testing the Script

1. Test the script with no arguments.
2. Test the script with one argument.
3. Test the script with two arguments.
4. Test the script with three arguments, one of them nonnumeric.
5. Test the script with three arguments, two of them nonnumeric.
6. Test the script with three arguments, one of them too large.
7. Test the script with three arguments, 1 4 5.
8. Test the script with three arguments, 3 7 1.

Testing the Effect of the Script

None

Session IV

Create a script that sends the contents of a message file to everybody who has logged in.

Preparation

Create a file of a short friendly message and mention that this is a test message that should be discarded by the receiver.

Script

- **Script Name:** `message.scr`
- **Arguments:** One argument, a message file.
- **Validation:** The minimum validation requirements are:
  - • Ensure that exactly one argument is entered.
  - • Ensure that the argument is a readable filename.
- **Body Section:** Create a script that uses **awk** to create a temporary file containing the usernames of those users who are logged into the system at this moment. Then send the message contained in the first argument to every logged-in user. Note that a user who has logged in more than once should receive only one message.

Testing the Script

1. Test the script with no arguments.
2. Test the script with two arguments.
3. Test the script with one argument that is not a readable file.
4. Test the script with one valid argument.

Continued

Testing the Effect of the Script

You should include yourself in the recipient list. Check to see if you have received the message.

Session V

Create a script that can be executed only from a specific terminal. This is done for security purposes. For example, a superuser may write scripts that can only be executed from his or her office and nowhere else.

Preparation

None

Script

- **Script Name:** `security.scr`
- **Arguments:** None
- **Validation:** The minimum validation requirement is:
  - Ensure that no arguments are entered.
- **Body Section:** Create a script that prints a friendly message. However, the script can be executed only from one terminal. You can use the name of the terminal you are using when you write the script. If somebody uses the script from a terminal that is not authorized, the script is to exit immediately. Hint: Use the **tty** command to show your current terminal.

Testing the Script

1. Test the script with one argument.
2. Test the script from the right terminal.
3. Log into the system using another terminal and test the script.

Testing the Effect of the Script

None

## CHAPTER 18

C Shell Advanced Programming

In the previous chapter, we discussed basic C shell programming concepts. In this chapter, we extend those concepts. Topics include variable evaluation, string manipulation, script functions, signal processing, and other advanced concepts.

18.1 Variable Evaluation

Variables have both a name and a value. If we consider a variable as a container that is used to store data, then when we use the variable name, we are referring to the container, not its contents. When we preface the variable name with a dollar sign, as in $var, we are referring to the contents of the container (that is, to its data). In this section, we discuss variable evaluation.

To evaluate a variable (that is, to use its contents), we have two different formats. The first, the dollar reference, has been used exclusively up to this point. The second, which we introduce here, uses braces to eliminate ambiguities. The two formats are:

```
$variable       ${variable}
```

The braced variable reference works everywhere. It is totally safe, but not very convenient. We tend, therefore, to use the simpler format and use the brace format only when we need it to remove an ambiguity. As an example, consider the situation where we want to make a backup copy of a file. Traditionally, backup files have the same name as the original file except they end in .bak. Given that the filename is stored in the variable $file, the straightforward approach to copy and rename it would seem to be:

```
% cp $file $file.bak              # Does not work
```

This format doesn't work, however, because UNIX thinks the second operand references a variable named file.bak. When it can't find a variable, UNIX generates a usage error. Using braces, as shown in the next example, works at all times.

```
cp $file ${file}.bak
```

18.2 String Manipulation

When working with strings, it is often necessary to edit or process only a part of the string. The C shell allows a limited set of string manipulation operations: compress string, string length determination, substring extraction, and determination of a character in a string.

Compress Strings

A relatively common problem is extra spaces in a text file. Extra spaces occur for many reasons. Two very common ones are the deletion of words in the file and typing extra spaces when creating the file. Extra spaces can be easily removed by using the **echo** command on a line of text as long as **echo**'s argument is not quoted. Script 18.1 is a very simple script that takes the first input argument and echoes it back to the monitor.

SCRIPT 18.1 *Compress String Argument*

```
 1  #!/bin/csh
 2  #  Script: strDltSpaces.scr
 3  #  This script used echo to delete extra spaces in a string.
 4  #  $1 is text string
 5  set line = "$argv"
 6  echo $line
```
```
% strDltSpaces.scr "Too    many    spaces    here."
```
```
Output:
Too many spaces here.
```

The only problem with this script is that it compresses only one line. To make it truly useful, we need to put it in a loop. The production version is in Script 18.2. Note that we redirect the file into the script.

SCRIPT 18.2 *Compress File*

```
 1  #!/bin/csh
 2  #  Script: strComprFile.scr
 3  #  Compress all lines in a file
 4  #  $argv[1] is file ID
 5  set line = $<
 6
 7  while ( "$line"  != "" )
 8     echo $line
 9     set line = $<
10  end
```
```
% strComprFile.scr <spacy.dat
```
```
% cat spacy.dat
Too    many      spaces in   this text.
Way   too     many spaces.
Our   compress         script will    delete the extra spaces.
```
Continued

SCRIPT 18.2 *Compress File*

```
Output:
Too many spaces in this text.
Way too many spaces.
Our compress script will delete the extra spaces.
```

Script 18.2 Analysis: There is one potential problem with this script. It works as long as there is not a blank line in the input. If there is a blank line, then the `while` expression becomes false and the loop stops.

Using Other Utilities

Most of the string processing in the C shell should be done using utilities such as **sed** and **awk:**

1. Each of these utilities needs a file as its input. If we want to apply them to a string, we must first change the string into a file using the **echo** command. This turns a string into a one-line file that can be used as the input file.

2. Each of these utilities creates an output file. If the output must be a string, we use backquotes to change the output file into a string.

3. When we need to pass the value of a local variable to **sed,** we must use double quotes in the regular expression, not single quotes. When a variable, which is prefaced by a dollar sign, is used in double quotes, its value becomes part of the string; if it is enclosed in single quotes, the name of the variable, such as `$var`, is left in the string.

4. Using positional parameters, such as `$argv[1]`, in **awk** must be handled with care. Depending on the situation, there are two ways to handle them.

   a. If we want to use the value in a parameter (such as in `#argv[1]`) in a shell script, we can pass the value to **awk** by defining a local variable within **awk** and setting the **awk** variable to the parameter when we invoke **awk.** For example, to print only lines in which the first column matches the value in the `$argv[1]` parameter, we would use the following code.

   ```
   awk '$1==value {print $0}' value=$argv[1] filename
   ```

   Two important points: First, use only single quotes for the **awk** statement. Second, do not use a dollar sign with the **awk** variable, `value`, in the foregoing example.

   b. To pass a field designator to **awk,** we again create an **awk** local variable and assign the field designator to it when we invoke **awk.** This time, however, we must use the dollar sign with the parameter in the **awk** statement. For example, to print a specified field within a line, we would use the following code:

   ```
   awk '{print $field}' field=$argv[1] filename
   ```

   In this case, the parameter `$argv[1]` contains the field designator for the column that we want to print.

5. When the **sed** or **awk** instructions are longer than one line, we have two ways to code the command.

   a. We can use a separate **awk** or **sed** script file and include the instructions there; the name of the **awk** or **sed** script file is then used in the C script we are writing. The problem with this approach is that the C script is not independent; it always needs to be able to access the **awk** or **sed** script.

   b. To include the multiline instruction in the C script, we can use the backslash (\) at the end of each line except the last. This technique negates the return at the end of the line and continues the command on the next line. As an alternative to a backslash before the return, we can use a single quote at the beginning of the **awk** or **sed** command and close it at the end. This technique makes the separate lines part of one long quote. Its disadvantage is that we cannot use single quotes in the **awk** or **sed** instructions. The advantage to both of these techniques is that the C script becomes independent.

18.3   Here Document

As we have seen, we can read data into a script. There are times, however, when we want to include the text in the script itself rather than read it from a file. This is done with the here document operator (<<).[1] Script 18.3 demonstrates how we might write a script to email a note to everyone who is on our project. The document in line 6 contains the email addresses of members of the project, one address per line.

SCRIPT 18.3   *Using Text in the Script*

```
 1  #!/bin/csh
 2  #  Script: hereDoc.scr
 3  #  This script uses a message contained in the document itself
 4  #  To send a meeting notice to all project members.
 5
 6  set list = `cat hereDocTeam.mail`
 7
 8  foreach i ($list)
 9      mail $i << MSG
10      The next project meeting is scheduled for next Friday.
11      LOCATION: Conf Room 12
12      TIME:      9am
13      AGENDA:   Please be prepared to discuss project schedule.
14                We have been asked to complete 3 months early.
15
16      Anne
17  MSG
18  echo mail sent to $i
19  end
```
```
% hereDoc.scr
```

---

[1]It is called the *here document* operator because it gets its text from here in the script itself.

Script 18.3 Analysis: There is one point in this script that is not obvious. Note the word MSG in lines 9 and 17. This word marks the text that is included in the script. You can use any marker as long as it is matched at the beginning and end of the message. The end of message marker must be on the left margin. Within the markers, the text can be formatted appropriately for the message. For example, we included a blank line. The output from this script is input to the mail system. You can verify that it went okay by including yourself in the mail list document.

18.4 Signals

A signal is a message sent to a process (such as a running script) on one of two occasions:

1. It is sent by another process to send a message to the receiving process. For example, a child process may send a signal to the parent process that it has been terminated.
2. It is sent by the operating system (kernel) to inform the receiving process of some interruption or error.

Signal Types

A signal is represented by an integer and a name which defines the event. Because some of the integers are system dependent, it is recommended to use the names for portability to other systems or shells. The names are in uppercase and start with SIG (Table 18.1). Note, however, that only SIGINT is usable by the C shell.

TABLE 18.1 *Interrupt Signals*

Number	Name	Function
1	SIGHUP	Hang up
2	SIGINT	Interrupt
3	SIGQUIT	Quit
9	SIGKILL	Definite kill
15	SIGTERM	Software termination (default kill)
24	SIGTSTP	Suspension

SIGHUP The hang-up signal is sent to the process when there is hang up. For example, a modem may be disconnected or a terminal turned off.

SIGINT The interrupt signal is sent to the process when there is an interrupt from the terminal. The terminal interrupt is normally associated with the cancel command (ctrl + c).

SIGQUIT The quit signal is sent to the process when there is a quit message from the terminal. The terminal quit is normally associated with the quit command (ctrl + \).

SIGKILL The kill signal is sent to the process when it is necessary to kill the process.

SIGTERM The software termination signal is sent to the process by the kill command.

SIGTSTP The suspension signal, sent by the user (`ctrl+z`), suspends a background command.

Response to Signals

A shell script (or any process) can respond to a received signal in one of three ways:

Accept the Default

In this case, the process does nothing. It lets the signal do its default action, which is normally to kill the process.

Ignore the Signal

In this case, the process ignores the signal. The process continues executing its code as though nothing has happened. Note that some signals, such as `SIGKILL`, cannot be ignored.

Catch the Signal

In this case, the process catches the signal and holds it until it can take an action. Although the process may still be terminated, it can prepare itself for termination; this might include backup activities or garbage collection.

On Interrupt Command

As stated previously, the C shell does not have the capability to handle all of the interrupts. It can handle only keyboard interrupts (cancel). To catch and handle a keyboard interrupt, the C shell uses the on interrupt (**onintr**) command. The command has three forms, all of which can only be used in a script.

On Interrupt (onintr) without Options

The no-option version of the on interrupt command is the default. Without it, the shell interpreter terminates the script on a keyboard interrupt. With it, the action is the same: The script is terminated on a keyboard interrupt.

On Interrupt (onintr) with Option

When the on interrupt command is entered with only a dash (–), the keyboard interrupt is disabled. If it is put at the beginning of the script, keyboard interrupts are disabled for the entire script. If it is put anywhere else in the script, keyboard interrupts are disabled from that point to the end of the script. The format of the disable interrupt option is

```
onintr -
```

On Interrupt (onintr) with Label

This is the most useful version. With it, we write our own commands to determine what is to happen when a keyboard interrupt is trapped.

A label is a named point in the script. When the **onintr** command contains a label, the script will jump to the label when a keyboard interrupt is detected. The format of the disable interrupt option with label is

```
onintr label
```

In Script 18.4, we demonstrate this version of the command. In this demonstration, we continue the loop; that is, we notify the user that we don't want to be interrupted and continue. We could just as easily have executed an **exit** command and terminated the script.

SCRIPT 18.4 *Demonstrate Interrupt Handling*

```
 1  #!/bin/csh/ -f
 2  #  Script: onintr.scr
 3  #  This script demonstrates interrupt handling in the C shell
 4
 5  echo Test interrupt trap commands.
 6  set count = 0
 7  while ($count < 10000)
 8      onintr catch          # set interrupt catch
 9      @ count++
10      continue              # Interrupt handler follows
11
12      catch:
13      echo "Count is: $count\nCannot interrupt at this time"
14  end
```
```
% onintr.scr
```
```
Output:
Test interrupt trap commands.
Count is: 1715
Cannot interrupt at this time
Count is: 7337
Cannot interrupt at this time
```

18.5 Built-in Commands

Shell scripts can use any command or utility in UNIX. This includes user-created utilities (scripts). Many of the standard commands and utilities are so common that they are built into the shell itself. This means that they are immediately available; the shell does not need to search the libraries to find and execute the commands. These commands are summarized in Table 18.2.

TABLE 18.2 *Built-in Commands*

Command	Description
break	Forces a loop statement to terminate.
breaksw	Forces a switch statement to terminate.

Continued

TABLE 18.2 *Built-in Commands—Continued*

Command	Description
case	Specifies commands to be executed for matching value.
cd	Changes the current directory.
continue	Continues with the next iteration of the loop.
echo	Displays argument on standard output. Can also be used to compress strings.
eval	Reads its argument and executes the resulting command.
exec	Executes the command in another shell.
exit	Sets the exit status and exits the shell.
foreach	Processes data in a list.
if	Standard two-way selection command.
onintr	Prevents keyboard interrupts or provides commands to handle them.
pwd	Displays the current directory.
return	Returns to the calling command.
set	Sets specified variables.
setenv	Sets exportable variables.
shift	Shifts positional parameters to the left.
source	Causes the command or utility that follows it to be executed in the current shell rather than a child shell.
switch	Selects among several case patterns.
test	Evaluates a relational, logical, or file expression.
type	Interprets how the shell will use a command.
ulimit	Displays or sets resources available to the user.
umask	Displays or sets default file creation modes.
unset	Unsets a variable or function.
wait	Waits until a child process finishes.
while	Loops while variable is true.

Most of these commands have been discussed already. We present two more built-in commands next.

sleep Command

The **sleep** command requires one argument: the number of seconds to pause (sleep). When executed, the shell suspends script execution for the specified duration. It is often executed as a background script.

The **sleep** command can be used to monitor status. For example, if we need to contact another user who is not currently logged in, we can create a script to monitor who is currently on the system. When it finds that the user has logged in, it then sends a message. This concept is demonstrated in Script 18.5. Note that we start the job in the background by coding an ampersand (&) immediately after the user login id.

SCRIPT 18.5 *Demonstrate* **sleep** *Command*

```
 1 #!/bin/csh
 2 #  Script: sleep.scr
 3 #  Monitors who is logged in and sends call me message
 4
 5 #  Check every minute to see if $1 is logged in
 6 who | grep "$argv[1]" >/dev/null
 7 set st = $status
 8 while ($st !=0)
 9    sleep 60
10    who | grep "$argv[1]" >/dev/null     # Run in background
11    set st = $status
12 end
13 #  User is now logged in
14 write $argv[1] << MSG
15    Urgent we talk.
16    Please call me A.S.A.P!
17
18
19    Gilberg
20 MSG
   $ sleep.scr forouzan&                   # Running in the background
```

Source Command

The **source** command is used to designate the current shell. When a command is executed, it generally forks a subshell for the execution. We can direct that the command be executed in the current shell by using the source command before the script name as in the next example:

```
$ source script.scr
```

Beware: Because the **source** command forces the following command to be executed in the current shell, any environmental changes made by the command are permanent (see Section 18.7 on page 780).

18.6 Scripting Techniques

In this section, we show some techniques that can be used in shell scripting. Many of them require that we process strings rather than words or values. Before demonstrating the scripts, therefore, let's discuss what happens when we pass strings as arguments or when we read strings in a script.

Reading Strings

When a string is passed as an argument, its format determines how it is parsed into the script parameters. If it is enclosed in quotes, it is placed in one parameter. If it is passed without quotes, each word is a separate parameter.

Script 18.6 demonstrates this concept. We begin by printing the complete argument list ($argv) and then the four positional parameters individually.

SCRIPT 18.6 *Demonstrate String Parameters*

```
 1  #!/bin/csh
 2  #  Script: strArguments.scr
 3  #  Demonstrate how string argument format affects read
 4
 5  echo All Arguments: $argv
 6  echo Parm1 is: $argv[1]
 7  echo Parm2 is: $argv[2]
 8  echo Parm3 is: $argv[3]
 9  echo Parm4 is: $argv[4]
```
```
    Execution:
    % strArguments.str Now is the time
    All Arguments: Now is the time
    Parm1 is: Now
    Parm2 is: is
    Parm3 is: the
    Parm4 is: time
```
```
    % strArguments.str "Now is the time"
    All Arguments: Now is the time
    Parm1 is: Now is the time
    Subscript out of range
```

Script 18.6 Analysis: Study the second example. It demonstrates what happens when a nonexistent argument is encountered in a script. Because we quoted the argument, there is only one. It displays completely with the first **echo.** But when the second **echo** is executed, the script fails because there is no $argv[2].

User Interaction

Although many scripts run by themselves, others require interactive input. This means that the user must receive a prompt and the shell must receive an answer. In this section, we demonstrate how to make a shell script interactive. Several of these techniques have been demonstrated in previous scripts.

Creating a Prompt

A prompt is a line of output that does not end in a newline and that requires a response from the user. We typically end the prompt with a colon and a space. The user's response is typed at the end of the prompt after the colon. Script 18.7 demonstrates a prompt that asks for a filename. We print the input for verification. Typically, prompts do not repeat in response. As you study the script, note that the prompt is enclosed in quotes. Quotes are required because of the cancel newline command at the end of the string. We could have put the quotes around only the cancel command. We demonstrate that technique in the next script.

SCRIPT 18.7   *Prompt Script*

```
1  #!/bin/csh
2  #  Script: prompt.scr
3  #  Demonstrate a typical user prompt
4
5  echo "Enter file name: \c"
6  set fileName = $<
7  echo You entered $fileName
```

```
% prompt.scr
```

```
Output:
Enter file name: payroll.dat
You entered payroll.dat
```

Parsing Pathnames

When working with UNIX files, the pathnames can become quite long, especially when they are absolute paths (see Chapter 3, Absolute Pathnames on page 78). Pathnames, whether absolute or relative, can be divided into two parts: the directory name and the base name. These two parts are separated by the last slash (/) in the pathname.

The base name can be the name of a directory or a file. The directory name is always the pathname of a directory. If the base name is a file, the directory name is the pathname of the file's directory; if the base name is a directory, the directory name is the pathname of its parent directory. Table 18.3 shows examples of parsing pathnames.

TABLE 18.3   *Examples of Parsing Pathnames*

Pathname	Directory Name	Base Name
/usr/gilberg/file1	/usr/gilberg	file1
/usr/gilberg/A	/usr/gilberg	A
gilberg/file1	gilberg	file1
file1	.	file1

In the last example in Table 18.3, the pathname is just one name. In this case, the directory name is the current directory as represented by the dot.

The **dirname** and **basename** commands are available in the C shell. However, in the C shell, we can use pathname modifiers. They are more flexible and easier to use. There are four modifiers. They all follow the same format as shown in the next example:

```
$variable:modifier
```

The modifiers are listed in Table 18.4.

TABLE 18.4 *Pathname Modifiers*

Modifier	Meaning	Explanation
:r	root	The path without extensions.
:e	extension	Only the extension (after the dot).
:h	head	Only the directory name.
:t	tail	Only the base name.

Script 18.8 demonstrates each of the modifiers. While we simply echo the results, they can also be assigned to a variable for further processing.

SCRIPT 18.8 *Demonstrate Pathname Modifiers*

```
 1 #!/bin/csh
 2 #  Script: pathMod.scr
 3 #  Demonstrates four variable modifier options.
 4 set name = "/usr/staff/gilberg/pgm1.c++"
 5
 6 echo "Complete path:         $name"
 7 echo "Path without extension: $name:r"
 8 echo "Only the extension:    $name:e"
 9 echo "Only the basename:     $name:t"
10 echo "Only the directory:    $name:h"
```

```
pathMod.scr
```

```
Output:
Complete path:          /usr/staff/gilberg/pgm1.c++
Path without extension: /usr/staff/gilberg/pgm1
Only the extension:     c++
Only the basename:      pgm1.c++
Only the directory:     /usr/staff/gilberg
```

18.7 Shell Environment and Script

A script, after it is made executable, becomes a command for the shell. Like any command, the script is executed in a child shell. The child shell inherits its environment from its parent. As it executes, it may modify its environment, but any changes are lost when it terminates and control returns to the parent shell. In other words, a script may modify its environment, but it cannot modify its parent environment. To demonstrate how environmental changes are made, we wrote Script 18.9.

SCRIPT 18.9 *Child Shells: Temporary Environmental Changes*

```
 1 #!/bin/csh
 2 #  Script: childScript.scr
```

Continued

SCRIPT 18.9   *Child Shells: Temporary Environmental Changes*

```
3  #   Modify environment by changing pwd
4
5  echo "Current directory was:      " `pwd`
6  cd ../
7  echo "Current directory is now: " `pwd`
```

```
Execution:
% pwd                                    # Before executing script
/mnt/diska/staff/gilberg/unix20csh

% childScript.scr
Current directory was:      /mnt/diska/staff/gilberg/unix20csh
Current directory is now:   /mnt/diska/staff/gilberg

% pwd                                    # After executing script
/mnt/diska/staff/gilberg/unix20csh
```

Script 18.9 Analysis: The script itself is very simple. The only complexity is that we used backquotes to execute the **pwd** command from within the script. The script execution is what you need to study. We begin by displaying the current working directory. We then execute the script, which displays the current directory, changes it, and then displays it to prove that it was changed. When the script completes, we again display the current directory to prove that the change made by the child shell has in fact been lost.

Having demonstrated that the changes made by a child command are temporary, we now show you how to make them permanent. We accomplish this with the source command. Because the script is then executed in the current shell, any environmental changes made are permanent. To demonstrate running the script in the current shell, we reexecute Script 18.9 in Script 18.10.

SCRIPT 18.10   *Child Shells: Permanent Environmental Changes*

```
% pwd                                    # Before executing script
/mnt/diska/staff/gilberg/unix20csh

% source childScript.scr
Current directory was:      /mnt/diska/staff/gilberg/unix20csh
Current directory is now:   /mnt/diska/staff/gilberg

% pwd                                    # After executing script
/mnt/diska/staff/gilberg
```

18.8   Arrays

The C shell supports array processing. An array is a sequenced list of strings (words) separated by spaces or tabs. Arrays are addressed by indexes, which are integral values enclosed in brackets. The first array element is located at index 1, the second element is at index 2, and the last element is located at index $#arrayname.

> In the C shell, an array is a sequenced list of words accessed with indexes starting at 1.

Creating an Array

We can create an array in three ways: assignment, command substitution, and string conversion.

Creating an Array with Assignment

To create an array by assigning values to it, we use the **set** command. Because we want a list of values to be assigned at the same time, we enclose the values in parentheses. Script 18.11 demonstrates the concept. Note that the index can be a constant or a variable. When it is a variable, however, it must contain an integral value in the array's range. If it is not in the range, the script will fail.

SCRIPT 18.11 *Creating an Array: Assignment*

```
1  #!/bin/csh
2  #  Script: aryAsgn.scr
3  #  Demonstrate creating an array by assignment
4  set ary = (one two three four five)
5
6  echo "The whole array:        $ary"
7  echo "The number of elements: $#ary"
8  echo "The first element:      $ary[1]"
9  echo "The last element:       $ary[$#ary]"
```
```
% aryAsgn.scr
```
```
Output
The whole array:        one two three four five
The number of elements: 5
The first element:      one
The last element:       five
```

Creating an Array with Command Substitution

Another way to create an array is with command substitution. This method is especially useful when the contents of the array are in a file. We demonstrate it in Script 18.12.

SCRIPT 18.12 *Creating an Array: Command Substitution*

```
1  #!/bin/csh
2  #  Script: aryCmdSub.scr
3  #  Demonstrate creating an array by command substitution
4  set ary = `cat ary.dat`
5
6  echo "The whole array:        $ary"
7  echo "The number of elements: $#ary"
8  echo "The first element:      $ary[1]"
9  echo "The last element:       $ary[$#ary]"
```
```
% aryCmdSub.scr
```

Continued

SCRIPT 18.12   *Creating an Array: Command Substitution*

```
Input:
one
two
three four five
Output
The whole array:       one two three four five
The number of elements: 5
The first element:     one
The last element:      five
```

Creating an Array with String Conversion

The third method of creating an array is to assign it a string of words. To convert a string into a list, we enclose it in parentheses. We demonstrate this method in Script 18.13. In this script, we pass the string to the script as argument one.

SCRIPT 18.13   *Creating an Array: String Conversion*

```
 1  #!/bin/csh
 2  #   Script: aryString.scr
 3  #   Demonstrate creating an array by string conversion
 4  #   String is in argv[1]
 5  set ary = ($argv[1])
 6
 7  echo "The whole array:       $ary"
 8  echo "The number of elements: $#ary"
 9  echo "The first element:     $ary[1]"
10  echo "The last element:      $ary[$#ary]"
```
```
% aryString.scr "one two three four five"
```
```
Output
The whole array:       one two three four five
The number of elements: 5
The first element:     one
The last element:      five
```

Parsing Input

Parsing requires that we break a string into its component parts so that we can analyze them. We can use array processing to parse any string for processing. As a simple example, let's count the number of words in a file. Script 18.14 demonstrates the concept by counting the words in the first verse of "The Raven."

SCRIPT 18.14   *Count Words in a File*

```
 1  #!/bin/csh
 2  #   Script: aryString.scr
 3  #   Demonstrate creating an array through a string
```
Continued

SCRIPT 18.14   *Count Words in a File—Continued*

```
 4│# String is in argv[1]
 5│
 6│set totalWords = 0
 7│set line = $<
 8│
 9│while ("$line" != "")
10│   set words = ($line)
11│   @ totalWords += $#words
12│   set line = $<
13│end
14│
15│echo Total Words: $totalWords
```

```
% aryParse.scr <TheRavenV1
```

```
Output:
Total Words: 56
```

Script 18.14 Analysis: As we saw in Script 18.2, there is a potential problem with this script. It works as long as there is not a blank line in the input. If there is a blank line, the while expression becomes false and the loop stops.

18.9 Script Examples

In this section, we demonstrate some complete scripts applications. The applications were chosen to demonstrate different techniques presented in the chapter. We use the same documentation format discussed in the previous chapter.

Simulate find Command

We are always searching for something. This script enhances the **find** command by adding error messages that explain why the command failed. You may find it helpful to refresh your memory on the **find** command by referring to "Find (**find**) File Command" on page 108.

Our find.scr script requires one or two arguments. If only one argument is entered, it is the file to be located, starting with our home directory. If two arguments are entered, the first is the start directory and the second is the file. The solution is in Script 18.15.

SCRIPT 18.15   *Find Files*

```
 1│#!/bin/csh -f
 2│# NAME:          find.scr
 3│# TASK:          Find the pathname of a file
 4│# AUTHOR:
 5│# DATE WRITTEN:
 6│# SYNOPSIS:      find.scr searchpath file or find.scr file
 7│# DESCRIPTION:   It finds the pathname of a file
```

Continued

SCRIPT 18.15 *Find Files*

```
 8 │ #                    argv[1] is file name
 9 │ #              or argv[1] is path and argv[2] is file name
10 │ # Exit value
11 │ #    0    if successful
12 │ #    1    if wrong number of arguments
13 │ #    2    if the search-path is not a directory
14 │ #    3    if the file is not found
15 │
16 │ set noglob
17 │ if ( $#argv < 1 || $#argv > 2 ) then
18 │     echo "$0 needs one or two arguments"
19 │     exit 1
20 │ endif
21 │
22 │ if ( $#argv == 2 ) then
23 │     set srchPath = $argv[1]
24 │     shift
25 │     if ( ! -d $srchPath ) then
26 │         echo "$srchPath is not a directory"
27 │         exit 2
28 │     endif
29 │ else
30 │     set srchPath = $HOME
31 │ endif
32 │
33 │ if ( ! -d $srchPath ) then
34 │     echo "$srchPath is not a directory"
35 │     exit 2
36 │ endif
37 │ set temp = ./t.temp
38 │
39 │ find $srchPath -name $argv[1] -print | tee $temp
40 │
41 │ if (-z $temp) then                  # Test for empty output file
42 │     echo "Cannot find file $argv[1]"
43 │     exit 3
44 │ endif
45 │
46 │ rm $temp                            # Delete temporary file
47 │ exit 0
```

Execution:
```
% find.scr
find.scr needs one or two arguments
```

```
% find.scr x y
x is not a directory
```

```
% find.scr file5
/mnt/diska/staff/gilberg/unix13bourne/file5
/mnt/diska/staff/gilberg/unix14bourne/file5
```

Continued

SCRIPT 18.15   *Find Files—Continued*

```
    /mnt/diska/staff/gilberg/unix20csh/file5
    /mnt/diska/staff/gilberg/unix3files/delRecDir.bak/DirB/file5
    /mnt/diska/staff/gilberg/unix17korn/file5
  % find.scr . file5
    ./file5
```

Script 18.15 Analysis: This script is relatively simple. The most difficult part is determining whether or not the **find** command was successful. Our solution is to pipe the output through a **tee** to a temporary file (see line 39). If the file is empty, then there is no output. After executing the **find** command, we test for an empty file on line 41.

General Ledger System

A large system, such as a general ledger system, requires many scripts. Large systems are also generally driven by a menu system that is active until the system is turned off at the end of the day. In this application, we demonstrate the basic concepts necessary to create such a system. It is not a complete system; rather, it is just a skeleton with stubs for the major components.[2] The basic design of the system is shown in Figure 18.1.

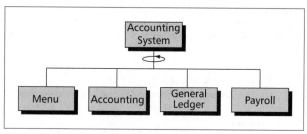

FIGURE 18.1   *Accounting System Design*

As you study the accounting script, note that it is conceptually very simple. We use **cat** to display a menu and then use a **switch** command to execute the requested application. Each application could in turn use the same design to run its application. Script 18.16 contains the application main script. The called scripts are in Script 18.17 (menu), Script 18.18 (accounting), Script 18.19 (general ledger), and Script 18.20 (payroll).

SCRIPT 18.16   *Large System Design: Main Script*

```
1  #!/bin/csh
2
3  # NAME:             acctMain.scr
4  # TASK:             Runs different accounting programs
5  # AUTHOR:
6  # DATE WRITTEN:
                                                              Continued
```

---

[2]A stub is an empty script that temporarily represents the application until it can be developed. In this application, the stubs simply echo a message that they were executed.

SCRIPT 18.16 *Large System Design: Main Script*

```
 7 # SYNOPSIS:        acctMain.scr
 8 # DESCRIPTION:     Uses a menu
 9
10 # Exit value
11 #    0    if successful
12
13 clear
14 set menu = ./acctMenu.scr
15 set acc  = ./
16
17 while (1)
18    cat $menu
19    echo -n "Choose an option: "
20    set answ = $<
21    switch ($answ)
22
23       case [aA] :
24                  ${acc}/acctAcct.scr
25                  breaksw
26       case [gG] :
27                  ${acc}/acctGL.scr
28                  breaksw
29       case [pP] :
30                  ${acc}/acctPay.scr
31                  breaksw
32       case [qQ] :
33                  echo "\n\nThank you for using Accounting"
34                  exit 0
35                  breaksw
36       default   :
37                  echo " $answ is invalid. Enter <AGPQ>"
38                  breaksw
39    endsw
40 end
```

```
% acctMain.scr
```

```
Output:
********* MENU *********
**                   **
**  A. Accounting    **
**  G. General Ledger **
**  P. Payroll       **
**  Q. Quit          **
**                   **
***********************
Choose an option: x
 x is invalid. Enter <AGPQ>


********* MENU *********
**                   **
```

Continued

SCRIPT 18.16 *Large System Design: Main Script—Continued*

```
     **  A. Accounting     **
     **  G. General Ledger **
     **  P. Payroll        **
     **  Q. Quit           **
     **                    **
     ************************
     Choose an option: g

     This is the general ledger program

     ********* MENU *********
     **                    **
     **  A. Accounting     **
     **  G. General Ledger **
     **  P. Payroll        **
     **  Q. Quit           **
     **                    **
     ************************
     Choose an option: q


     Thank you for using Accounting
```

SCRIPT 18.17 *Large System Design: Menu*

```
1  ********* MENU *********
2  **                    **
3  **  A. Accounting     **
4  **  G. General Ledger **
5  **  P. Payroll        **
6  **  Q. Quit           **
7  **                    **
8  ************************
9
```

SCRIPT 18.18 *Large System Design: Accounting*

```
1  #!/bin/csh
2  #  Script: acctAcct.scr
3  #  This is a stub for the accounting program.
4
5  echo "\nThis is the basic accounting program"
```

SCRIPT 18.19 *Large System Design: General Ledger*

```
1  #!/bin/csh
2  #  Script: acctGL.scr
3  #  This is a stub for general ledger.
4
5  echo "\nThis is the general ledger program"
```

SCRIPT 18.20 *Large System Design: Payroll*

```
1  #!/bin/csh
2  #  Script: acctPay.scr
3  #  This is a stub for payroll.
4
5  echo "\nThis is the payroll program"
```

Eliminate Duplicates

We often need to reduce a set of elements to its unique items by deleting any duplicates in the set. This is easily done in a script. We begin by building an array that contains all elements in the set. Then, one by one, we compare the next element to the elements already in the array. If the next element is unique, we insert it into the new element array. At the end of the processing, we write the new array to a file. This design is demonstrated in Script 18.21.

SCRIPT 18.21 *Remove Duplicates*

```
 1  # NAME:           rmDups.scr
 2  # TASK:           Removes duplicate words from a list/file
 3  # AUTHOR:
 4  # DATE WRITTEN:
 5  # SYNOPSIS:       rmDups.scr input_list output_list
 6  # DESCRIPTION:  Uses a flag to remove duplicates
 7  #                    argv[1] is input list
 8  #                    argv[2] is output list
 9  # Exit value
10  #    0    if successful
11  #    1    if wrong number of arguments
12
13  if ( $#argv != 2 ) then
14          echo "$0 requires two arguments"
15          echo "$0 infile outfile"
16          exit 1
17  endif
18
19  set newlist
20  set oldlist = `cat $argv[1]`
21
22  foreach element ($oldlist)
23     set flag = "on"
24
25     # Test each word in newlist to see if newElement is dupe
26     foreach newElement ($newlist)
27        if ($newElement == $element ) then
28           set flag = "off"
29           break                       # Found dupe. Get out.
30        endif
```

Continued

SCRIPT 18.21   *Remove Duplicates—Continued*

```
31    end # foreach newElement
32
33    if ($flag == "on") then
34        set newlist = ($newlist $element)
35    endif
36 end # foreach element
37
38 # Newlist complete. Write it to argv[2]
39 echo $newlist > $argv[2]
40 exit 0
```

```
% rmDups.scr rmDups.dat outfile
```

Input:	Output:
`% cat rmDups.dat`	`% cat outfile`
one	one two three four
two	
two	
three	
three	
three	
one four	

18.10 Key Terms

accepting signal	**onintr** command	**sleep** command
built-in command	parsing pathname	**source** command
catching signal	prompt	string compression
here document	shell environment	variable evaluation
ignoring signal	signal	variable substitution

18.11 Tips

1. Use ${...} if you want to evaluate a variable and concatenate the result with another string.

2. The **grep, sed,** and **awk** utilities need an input file and create an output file. If you want to manipulate a string using these commands, you should first change the string to a one-line file (using the **echo** command). The result of the **grep** command is also a file. If you want to change the result back to a string, you should use command substitution (backquotes) with the **grep** command.

3. To use a variable in **grep, sed,** or **awk,** enclose it in double quotes, not single quotes.

4. To use a positional parameter with **awk,** first assign it to another variable and then use the new variable inside the **awk** script.

5. Place the ending token of a here document at the beginning of a line.

6. Use the **onintr** command if you do not want a script to respond to a signal using a default action.

7. Use the **source** command to execute a command in the current shell rather than a subshell.

8. If you want to change the environment of the current shell using a command, execute the command in the current shell by using the **source** command.

9. To consider a string containing whitespaces as one single argument, enclose it in double quotes.

18.12 Commands

The following commands were discussed in this chapter. For more details, see Appendix F and the corresponding pages shown in the following table.

Command	Description	Options	Page
onintr	***Synopsis:*** *onintr [label]* Runs a command when a signal is received.		774
sleep	***Synopsis:*** *sleep seconds* Sleeps for a number of seconds.		776
source	***Synopsis:*** *source command* Executes command in current shell.		777

18.13 Summary

- To evaluate a variable (that is, to use its contents), we can use one of two formats: `$variable` or `${variable}`. The second format should be used when we want to concatenate a variable value with a string.
- We can compress strings using quotes.
- The here document token (<<) allows us to insert text after a command instead of reading it from a file.
- A signal is a message sent to a process, such as a running script, by either another process or the operating system (kernel).
- A process (script) can respond to a signal in one of three ways: accept the default, ignore the signal, or catch the signal.
- The **onintr** command is used to catch and process an interrupt signal.
- The built-in commands are those commands that are included in the C shell interpreter. Because they are part of the interpreter, they don't need to be loaded and can therefore be executed faster than general UNIX commands.
- The **sleep** command allows the script to sleep for a number of seconds. It is used to wait for an event to happen.
- The **source** command allows the execution of a command in the current shell instead of in a subshell.
- Scripts can be enhanced using several scripting techniques discussed in the chapter.
- We can read a string, including whitespaces, as one single argument if we use double quotes around the argument.
- We can create prompts using the **echo** command.

18.14 Practice Set

Review Questions

1. What is the result of the following command?

```
echo "This is the                          world of                UNIX"
```

2. Demonstrate how to catch an interrupt signal. The signal should be kept until the script sends the message "I will quit."

3. Given the following command, what is the number of elements in the array, `ary`, if `file1` has nine words?

```
set ary = `cat file1`
```

4. Given the following command, what is the number of elements in the array, `ary`, if `file1` has nine lines and there are five words in each line?

```
set ary = `cat file1`
```

5. What is printed from the following code?

```
set ary = (44 66 77)
foreach i($ary)
    echo $ary[$i]
end
```

6. What is printed from the following code?

```
set ary = (44 66 77)
foreach i($ary)
    echo $ary[1]
    echo $ary[2]
    echo $ary[3]
end
```

7. What is printed from the following code?

```
set ary = (44 66 77)
set n = 1
foreach i($ary)
    echo $ary[$n]
    @ n++
end
```

8. Show how you can use the loop in Question 7 to print the words in a file that has each word on a separate line.

9. What is printed from the following code?

```
set ary = `cat file1`
echo $#ary
```

Exercises

10. Write a short script that, given the name of the file as an argument, reads the file and creates a new file containing only lines consisting of one word.

11. Write a short script that changes the name of files passed as arguments to lowercase.

12. Write a short script that, given a filename as the argument, deletes all even lines (lines 2, 4, 6, . . . , n) in the file.

13. Write a short script that, given a filename as the argument, deletes all odd lines (lines 1, 3, 5, . . . , n) in the file.

14. Write a short script that, given a filename as the argument, combines odd and even lines together. In other words, lines 1 and 2 become line1, lines 3 and 4 become line 2, and so on.

15. Write a short script that changes the first three letters of the name of all files (passed as arguments) to lowercase.

16. If a script is run as `pgm.scr -a -b file[345]`, what is the value of `$#argv`? What is the value of `$argv`?

17. What is the exit status of the following script?

```
#!/bin/csh
## end
```

18. What is the exit status of a **grep** command when it finds a pattern? What is the exit status of a **grep** command when it does not find a pattern? Write a one-line script that verifies your answers.

19. What is the exit status of a **sed** command when it finds a pattern? What is the exit status of a **sed** command when it does not find a pattern? Write a one-line script that verifies your answers.

20. What is the exit status of an **awk** command when it finds a pattern? What is the exit status of an **awk** command when it does not find a pattern? Write a one-line script that verifies your answers.

18.15 Lab Sessions

Each of the lab sessions in this chapter requires you to write a script, make it executable, and then execute it.

Session 1

Create a script that finds each line in a file that contains a specified string.

Preparation

Create a file of at least 20 lines and insert a double-quoted string, such as "hello," in several lines.

Script

- **Script Name:** `search.scr`
- **Arguments:** Two arguments. The first is the string to be found; the second is the name of the file.
- **Validation:** The minimum validation requirements are:
  - Ensure that exactly two arguments are entered.
  - Ensure that the second argument is the name of the file that exists and is not empty.

Continued

Session I—*Continued*

- **Body Section:** Create a script that uses **grep** and loops to find the line numbers in which the string is found. Note that **grep** should be applied to each line, not the whole file. The script should print the result in the following format:
  ```
  Line Number: [Line contents]
  ```

Testing the Script

1. Test the script with no arguments.
2. Test the script with one argument.
3. Test the script with two arguments but the second one is not a file.
4. Test the script with two correct arguments.

Testing the Effect of the Script

Compare the results of your script with a printout of the file.

Session II

Modify the script written in Session I to search for multiple occurrences of the substring in each line. Print the result in the following format:

```
Line Number: Count: [Occurrences] [Line contents]
...
Line Number: Count: [Occurrences] [Line contents]

       Total Count: [Total Occurrences]
```

Change the original file to include two or three occurrences of the string in some lines. Follow the same requirements as Session I.

Session III

Create a script that compiles all C source files in your home directory and creates executable files.

Preparation

Create at least five C source files in your home directory. The files do not have to be real C source files; at a minimum, they should contain a comment line that contains a unique program name such as the following example:

```
/* ........ file1.c ........*/
```

The name of the files should have a C source file extension (.c), such as file1.c.

Script

- **Script Name:** compile.scr
- **Arguments:** None
- **Validation:** The minimum validation requirement is:
  - Ensure that there is no argument.
- **Body Section:** Create a script that finds all files with extension (.c) under your directory and compiles them one by one. Each executable file should have the same name as the source file except that the extension should be (.exe). For

Continued

example, if the source filename is `file1.c`, the executable filename should be `file1.exe`. Use the following command to compile a file:

```
cc -o executable_filename source_filename
```

Testing the Script

1. Test the script with one or two arguments.
2. Test the script with no arguments.

Testing the Effect of the Script

Verify that executable files were created under your home directory.

Session IV

In a C program, there is only one comment format. All comments must start with an open comment token, `/*`, and end with a close comment token, `*/`. C++ programs use the C tokens for comments that span several lines. Single-line comments start with two slashes (`//`). In either case, the start token can be anywhere on the line.

Write a script to change every single-line comment in a C++ source file that uses C program start and end comment tokens to a single-line comment starting with a C++ single-line token. The comment itself is to be unchanged.

Preparation

Create at least five C++ source files in your home directory. The files do not have to be real C++ source files; they can contain only a few lines of comments, some with C program tokens and some with C++ single-line tokens. Each program should have at least one multiline comment and at least one single-line comment that uses the C program tokens. Use one or more blank lines between comments. The name of the files should have a C++ extension (`.c++`), such as `file1.c++`.

Script

- **Script Name:** `commentType.scr`
- **Arguments:** None
- **Validation:** The minimum validation requirement is:
  - Ensure that there is no argument.
- **Body Section:** Create a script that finds all files with extension (`.c++`) under your directory and change only the lines with comments. The name of the files should be preserved. If a file has the name `file1.c++`, the name still should be `file1.c++` after the change.

Testing the Script

1. Test the script with one or two arguments.
2. Test the script with no arguments.

Testing the Effect of the Script

Check to see if the comments are changed in the files.

Session V

Write a script that creates a file out of the /etc/passwd file.

Preparation

None

Script

- **Script Name:** newEtcPasswd.scr
- **Arguments:** One. The name of the file.
- **Validation:** The minimum validation requirement is:
    - Ensure that there is only one argument.
- **Body Section:** Create a script that makes a file out of the information in the /etc/passwd file using the following format:

User Name	User ID	Group ID	Home Directory
John	234	23	/etc/usr/staff/john
...	...	...	...

Testing the Script

1. Test the script with two or more arguments.
2. Test the script with no arguments.
3. Test the script with one argument that is not the name of a file.
4. Test the script with one argument that is the name of the file.

Testing the Effect of the Script

Verify the file was created and contains the correct information and format.

Session VI

Create a script that, given a user name, finds the home directory of the user using the /etc/passwd file.

Preparation

None

Script

- **Script Name:** findHomeDirectory.scr
- **Arguments:** One. The user name.
- **Validation:** The minimum validation requirement is:
    - Ensure that there is only one argument.
- **Body Section:** Create a script that, given the name of a user (as the only argument), prints the absolute pathname of the user's home directory.

Continued

Testing the Script

1. Test the script with two or more arguments.
2. Test the script with no arguments.
3. Test the script with one argument.

Testing the Effect of the Script

Verify the script by using your user name.

Session VII

Create a script that finds all files in subdirectories that have the same filename.

Preparation

Make several directories, at different levels, under your home directory. For example, make ~/A, ~/B, ~/C, ~/A/AA, ~/A/BB, ~/A/AA/AAA, and so on until you have at least 15 directories. Copy a small junk file named `file1` under some of these directories; do not change its name. Copy another small junk file named `file2` under some other directories. Copy a third junk file under several directories. Be sure that some directories get a combination of `file1` and `file2` or `file1` and `file3`. In at least three of the directories, create a junk file with a unique name.

Script

- **Script Name:** `duplicateName.scr`
- **Arguments:** None
- **Validation:** The minimum validation requirement is:
  - Ensure that there is no argument.
- **Body Section:** Create a script that uses **find** and **awk** commands to create a list of files that are duplicated; use the full pathname for the duplicated filenames. Hint: Use a **basename** command and an array in **awk**. The output should look like the following example:

```
file1: ~/A/file1      ~/A/AA/file1      ~/A/B/BB/BBB/file1
file2: ~/B/file2      ~/C/file2
...
file3: ~/BB/BBB/BBBB
```

Testing the Script

1. Test the script with one argument.
2. Test the script with no arguments.

Testing the Effect of the Script

Use a recursive long list command to list the complete contents of your home directory. Verify the output of your script against the list command output.

ASCII Table

The American Standard Code for Information Interchange (ASCII) is described in this appendix. Table A.1 indicates the decimal, hexadecimal, octal, and graphical codes with an English interpretation, if appropriate. As you study the table, look for the following patterns:

- The decimal value of each character determines its ordering (position) within the ASCII sequence. For example, the character A has a decimal value of 65; the character B has a decimal value of 66. Because 65 is less than 66, the character A comes before the character B in ascending sort sequence.
- Control (nonprintable) characters occupy the first 32 characters (0–31).
- The smallest printable character is the space (blank) with a decimal value of 32.
- The digits (0–9) occupy positions 48 through 57. This means that they are less than the alphabetic characters.
- The uppercase letters are less than the lowercase letters. The uppercase letters have values from 65 through 90; the lowercase letters have values from 97 through 122. This means that uppercase Z sorts before lowercase a.
- The punctuation characters are spread throughout the sequence—between the space and the digits, between the digits and the uppercase alphabetic characters, between the uppercase and lowercase alphabetic characters, and after the last alphabetic character.

Figure A.1 summarizes these points in a visual format.

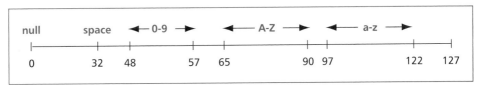

FIGURE A.1   *A Graphical Representation of ASCII*

TABLE A.1   *ASCII Codes*

Decimal	Hex	Octal	Symbol	Interpretation
0	00	00	null	NULL value
1	01	01	SOH	ctrl + a
2	02	02	STX	ctrl + b
3	03	03	ETX	ctrl + c

Continued

TABLE A.1   *ASCII Codes—Continued*

Decimal	Hex	Octal	Symbol	Interpretation
4	04	04	EOT	ctrl + d
5	05	05	ENQ	ctrl + e
6	06	06	ACK	ctrl + f
7	07	07	BEL	ctrl + g
8	08	10	BS	ctrl + h
9	09	11	HT	ctrl + i
10	0A	12	LF	ctrl + j
11	0B	13	VT	ctrl + k
12	0C	14	FF	ctrl + l
13	0D	15	CR	ctrl + m
14	0E	16	SO	ctrl + n
15	0F	17	SI	ctrl + o
16	10	20	DLE	ctrl + p
17	11	21	DC1	ctrl + q
18	12	22	DC2	ctrl + r
19	13	23	DC3	ctrl + s
20	14	24	DC4	ctrl + t
21	15	25	NAK	ctrl + u
22	16	26	SYN	ctrl + v
23	17	27	ETB	ctrl + w
24	18	30	CAN	ctrl + x
25	19	31	EM	ctrl + y
26	1A	32	SUB	ctrl + z
27	1B	33	ESC	ctrl + [
28	1C	34	FS	ctrl + \
29	1D	35	GS	ctrl +]
30	1E	36	RS	ctrl + ^
31	1F	37	US	ctrl + _
32	20	40	SP	Space
33	21	41	!	
34	22	42	"	Double quote
35	23	43	#	
36	24	44	$	
37	25	45	%	

Continued

TABLE A.1 *ASCII Codes*

Decimal	Hex	Octal	Symbol	Interpretation
38	26	46	&	
39	27	47	'	Apostrophe
40	28	50	(	
41	29	51	)	
42	2A	52	*	
43	2B	53	+	
44	2C	54	,	Comma
45	2D	55	–	Minus
46	2E	56	.	
47	2F	57	/	
48	30	60	0	
49	31	61	1	
50	32	62	2	
51	33	63	3	
52	34	64	4	
53	35	65	5	
54	36	66	6	
55	37	67	7	
56	38	70	8	
57	39	71	9	
58	3A	72	:	Colon
59	3B	73	;	Semicolon
60	3C	74	<	
61	3D	75	=	
62	3E	76	>	
63	3F	77	?	
64	40	100	@	
65	41	101	A	
66	42	102	B	
67	43	103	C	
68	44	104	D	
69	45	105	E	
70	46	106	F	
71	47	107	G	

Continued

TABLE A.1 *ASCII Codes—Continued*

Decimal	Hex	Octal	Symbol	Interpretation
72	48	110	H	
73	49	111	I	
74	4A	112	J	
75	4B	113	K	
76	4C	114	L	
77	4D	115	M	
78	4E	116	N	
79	4F	117	O	
80	50	120	P	
81	51	121	Q	
82	52	122	R	
83	53	123	S	
84	54	124	T	
85	55	125	U	
86	56	126	V	
87	57	127	W	
88	58	130	X	
89	59	131	Y	
90	5A	132	Z	
91	5B	133	[	Open bracket
92	5C	134	\	Backslash
93	5D	135	]	Close bracket
94	5E	136	^	Caret
95	5F	137	_	Underscore
96	60	140	`	Grave accent
97	61	141	a	
98	62	142	b	
99	63	143	c	
100	64	144	d	
101	65	145	e	
102	66	146	f	
103	67	147	g	
104	68	150	h	
105	69	151	i	

Continued

TABLE A.1   *ASCII Codes*

Decimal	Hex	Octal	Symbol	Interpretation
106	6A	152	j	
107	6B	153	k	
108	6C	154.	l	
109	6D	155	m	
110	6E	156	n	
111	6F	157	o	
112	70	160	p	
113	71	161	q	
114	72	162	r	
115	73	163	s	
116	74	164	t	
117	75	165	u	
118	76	166	v	
119	77	167	w	
120	78	170	x	
121	79	171	y	
122	7A	172	z	
123	7B	173	{	Open brace
124	7C	174	|	Bar
125	7D	175	}	Close brace
126	7E	176	~	Tilde
127	7F	177	DEL	Delete

A Short History

The history of UNIX can be roughly divided into two distinct periods: the early years and the modern era. Much of the information for the early years was obtained from the WWW.

B.1 The Early Years

The roots of UNIX are found in the early multiuser operating system of the 1960s. In 1965, the AT&T Bell Telephone Laboratories, General Electric, and MIT joined in a project to develop the Multics (**Mult**iplexed **I**nformation and **C**omputing **S**ervice) operating system. Its primary goals were to provide remote access to the computer and shared access to data.

In 1969, Ken Thompson, unhappy with Multics, created the **Un**iplexed **I**nformation and **C**omputing **S**ystem[1] on a PDP-7 to support his project at the Bell Labs. Joined by Dennis Ritchie in 1971, the system was renamed UNIX and moved to the PDP 11/20. Written in assembly language, this system was designated as Version 1 (V1) and was the start of several version improvements that were to last 7 years. During this period, all of the work was done by the Bell Labs and used only within the labs.

V1 was documented in a manual that became the *First Edition of the UNIX Programmer's Manual*. It became a tradition that different UNIX versions are referred to by the different editions of the manual. Some of the significant releases were:

- V1. The "original" release of UNIX.
- V3. The first version with programs written in C. (1973)
- V4. Completely rewritten in C, the system was now portable to other hardware platforms with a minimal effort. (1973)
- V5. First version released for use in universities. (1974)
- V7. This release included the Bourne shell and was the last of the original UNIX series. (1979)

Figure B.1 traces the evolution of UNIX.

B.2 The Modern Era

In 1979, UNIX development split into two camps. The Bell Labs continued their work with what eventually became known as UNIX System V, which was released in 1984. At the same time, the University of California at Berkeley began the development of a different UNIX system that became known as BSD (Berkeley Software Distribution)

---

[1]The name Unics was created as a pun on Multics.

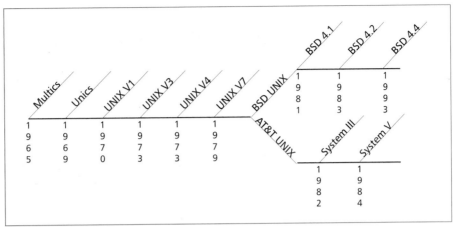

FIGURE B.1   *History of UNIX*

UNIX. As should be expected, with two different development teams working on similar projects, the two systems diverged into separate implementations.

AT&T UNIX

After the release of the seventh edition, AT&T of Bell Labs started to create a commercial version of UNIX. Their first commercial system, System III, was released in 1982. In 1984, they released System V, which is now maintained by AT&T and UNIX System Laboratories. It is the basis of many commercially available UNIX systems.

BSD UNIX

BSD UNIX began as a vehicle to teach operating system concepts at the university and was originally developed for DEC VAX systems. The first commercial release was BSD 4.2 in 1983. While Berkeley has dropped support for BSD UNIX, it has become the foundation of many commercial releases, most notably Sun®OS.

B.3   Descendants of System V and BSD4

Today, there are many different variations of UNIX, all of which have either System V, or BSD4, or both as the parent(s). Many of them are hardware-specific releases. They are summarized in Table B.1.

TABLE B.1   *Descendants of System V and BSD4*

Name	Creator	Parent	Comments
AIX	IBM	AT&T	Also supports some features of BSD.
Digital Unix	Digital Equipment	Both	Replaces DEC's ULTRIX, which has been discontinued.
HP_UX	Hewlett Packard	AT&T	

Continued

TABLE B.1 *Descendants of System V and BSD4—Continued*

Name	Creator	Parent	Comments
IRIX	Silicon Graphics	Both	Originally BSD but later enhanced with some AT&T features.
Linux[a]	Linus Tovalds		Public domain (free) version of UNIX that has been ported to many platforms.
Solaris	Sun Microsystems	AT&T	
SunOS	Sun Microsystems	BSD	First to include Network File System (NFS).

[a]The name Linux, pronounced both *lynn*-ex or *line*-ex, is a contraction of **Lin**us and **UNIX**.

B.4 POSIX

The IEEE has developed a set of UNIX standards called Portable Operating System Interface (POSIX). These standards define interfaces to the application programs, a shell standard, and Internet interfaces. When POSIX is fully implemented, UNIX will become a totally portable operating system, and applications written in one system should run on another system without modification.

emacs

emacs is an acronym for **e**diting **mac**ros. A **macro** is a named set of one or more commands that replaces a command in a command stream. Like **vi**, **emacs** is a screen editor.

When you start **emacs**, the contents of a file are loaded into its buffer. As you change the text on the screen, the text in the buffer is changed. When you are through, the buffer contents may be written back to the file using either the original filename or a new one or discarded.

In this appendix, we discuss the more common **emacs** operations. Not all commands are discussed.

C.1 Loading the File

To edit a file, you must load it into the editor. Like all UNIX operations, this requires that we execute a command, in this case, the **emacs** command (Figure C.1). While there are some options for **emacs**, they are not necessary for its basic operation and will not be discussed here.

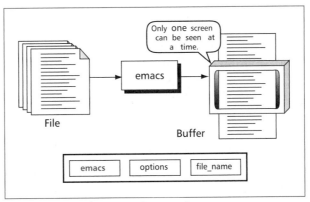

Only one screen can be seen at a time.

File

Buffer

| emacs | options | file_name |

FIGURE C.1   *The* **emacs** *Command*

emacs opens in either the text mode or the tutorial mode. If you provide a filename attribute, it opens in the text mode ready to begin editing. If no filename is provided, it opens in the tutorial mode.

Text Mode

Assuming that the file already exists, when you load it, it is displayed in the buffer window with the first line of text at the top of the window. If the file doesn't exist, an empty buffer is loaded and a new file message appears just below the status message. Figure C.2 shows the **emacs** window for a file called *time*.

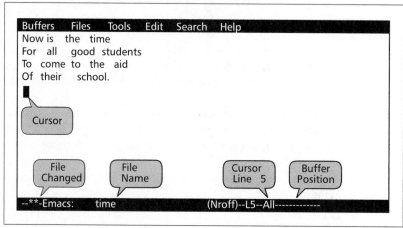

FIGURE C.2   *The **emacs** Window*

Note that there are two inverse text[1] bars in the window. The text at the top of the screen simply lists the options that are available. It is not a menu and cannot be accessed with a mouse or otherwise used. For that matter, your mouse does not function in **emacs** except to copy and paste data.

At the bottom of the window is the **status bar**. It contains several important items. Reading from the left, we see the file status and name, the current cursor position, and the position of the current window of text within the buffer. The **file-changed** indicator is two asterisk characters[2] near the left of the status bar. The asterisk characters indicate that the data in the file have been changed. If there have been no changes to the file, you will see hyphens rather than asterisks. The **filename** is simply that, the name of the file on your disk. The **cursor position** indicator is constantly changing as you work through the document. In the example, the cursor is on line 5. It appears as a black rectangle the size of one character and is seen in the figure just below the last line of the text. Finally, the **buffer position** shows the relative position of the buffer to the window. As you move through the file, it takes on one of four values. In Figure C.2, all of the text is visible in the window, so the buffer position is **All**. With a larger document, it would be **Top** if the first line of the file is visible, **Bot** if the last line of the file is visible, and **nn%** if the middle portion of the document is currently in the window.

Tutorial Mode

If you start **emacs** without specifying a file document, you are in the tutorial mode. Rather than a filename appearing in the status line, `*scratch*` is shown. If you type any text, the text is lost when you close **emacs**, although you can save it before you

---

[1]Inverse text is white text on a black background.

[2]UNIX programmers refer to the asterisk as a splat. The explanation for this name is left to your imagination.

exit. Note, however, that if you forget to save it, the text is lost forever. You will get no warning that the document was changed as you do when you exit from a text-mode file—that is, one that was opened with a filename specified. When you save a document opened in the tutorial mode, the buffer reverts to the text mode.

C.2 Editing the Text

Once the file has been opened, we can begin entering or editing text. If you have used any other text editors, you are familiar with the basic operations that we need to perform. Besides entering and deleting text data, we need to position the cursor, copy and paste text, and search the file for specified text.

Entering text simply requires that we type the data on the keyboard while we are in the text mode. To delete data, we can use the delete key to move the cursor backward. More often than not, however, the cursor is not at the right position to enter or delete data. This means that we must move it. (Remember, you cannot use the mouse.)

To position the cursor, we need to use an **emacs** command and that's where the fun begins. If your keyboard is properly configured, you can use the arrow keys to move data. If you don't have arrow keys, however, you can use **emacs** commands. To distinguish commands from text, **emacs** uses command keys. There are actually two Command keys: the control character and the metacharacter. The **control character** is usually the Control (sometimes abbreviated `ctrl`) key on your keyboard; the **metakey** is usually the Escape (`esc`) key, although it may also be the `alt` key on some keyboards. When you use a Command key, **emacs** recognizes it and interprets the next key as a command rather than text. In other words, the Command key puts the editor in the command mode rather than the text mode. This concept is seen in Figure C.3.

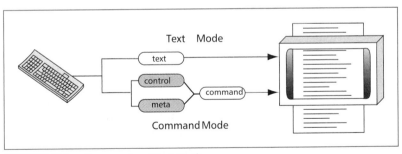

FIGURE C.3 *Command and Text Mode*

Before we can discuss **emacs** commands, there are two more points that we need to clarify. Control key commands are issued by holding down the Control key and at the same time keying the Command key. This is usually indicated by `ctrl+key`. Meta-commands are issued by first keying the metakey and then keying the Command key. In other words, control commands are keyed by pressing the Command key at the same time that we are pressing the Control key, whereas metacommands are keyed by first pressing the metakey, releasing it, and then pressing the Command key.

810 • APPENDIX C • emacs

Positioning the Cursor

There is an extensive set of **emacs** commands to move the cursor. In addition, depending on your keyboard configuration, you may also be able to move the cursor using the arrow keys.

Keyboard Move Commands

You can move the cursor as little as one character or as much as a whole buffer. To be more specific, you can move the cursor by characters, words, lines, sentences, screens, or by the whole buffer, top or bottom. With one exception, the character and line commands are Control key combinations. The word, sentence, screen, and buffer commands are metasequences. All of the keyboard positioning commands are shown in Table C.1.

TABLE C.1   **emacs** *Move Cursor Commands*

	Keys	Direction	Keys	
Characters	ctrl + b	back	meta b	Word
	ctrl + f	forward	meta f	
Line	ctrl + a	beginning	meta a	Sentence
	ctrl + e	end	meta e	
	ctrl + p	previous		
	ctrl + n	next		
Screen	ctrl + v	backward top	meta <	Buffer
	ctrl + l	center		
	meta v	forward end	meta >	

Some definitions are in order here. A **word** is a series of characters separated by spaces. A **sentence** is a series of characters ending in period and two spaces. A **line**, on the other hand, is a series of characters ending in a return character. This means that a line may contain multiple sentences, which is not what you would expect. While **vi** also provides for a paragraph, **emacs** does not.

The direction of the move is relative to the text, not to the monitor. This means that when we move forward, we are moving toward the end of the document. Likewise, when we move backward, we are moving the cursor toward the beginning of the document.

Finally, a screen is generally set at 22 physical lines, each 80 characters wide, on the monitor. The screen line should not be confused with the logical line definition used by **emacs**.

Screen and Buffer Moves   When we scroll the screen forward (meta v—think of the v as an arrow pointing toward the end of the document), the text scrolls forward with new text appearing at the bottom of the monitor. The actual screen scroll is two lines less than a full screen; the last two lines from the previous screen are now at the top as a frame of reference. When we scroll backward, we move up the text (ctrl+v), toward the beginning. The screen center command (ctrl+l—the character is an el, not a one) refreshes the screen display and moves the cursor to the middle of the screen.

When we scroll the buffer up (meta <), we move to the top of the buffer. When we scroll the buffer down (meta >), we move to the end of the buffer. There is no equivalent to scroll screen center.

Line and Sentence Moves When we move the cursor up, we are moving the text toward the beginning of the text. Moving the cursor to the beginning of the line (ctrl+a) or beginning of the sentence (meta a), and moving it to the previous line (ctrl+a), all move toward the beginning of the text with the cursor at the beginning of the line or sentence. If the cursor is in the first line of text, moving to the previous line or sentence moves the cursor to the beginning of the first line. Moving the cursor to the end of the line (ctrl+e) or to the end of the sentence (meta e) moves it toward the end of the text. After the command, the cursor is at the end of the current line.

Character and Word Moves For character moves, the cursor moves one character to the left (ctrl+b) or one character to the right (ctrl+f). For words, the cursor is moved to the beginning of the current word (meta b) or to the end of the current word (meta f).

Inserting Text

When inserting text, we need to understand how an editor handles the text. In a **line editor**, when we get to the end of the line, we can enter no more text. The **vi** editor is like that. Furthermore, if the line is larger than the screen, long lines must be horizontally scrolled to read all of the text. In other words, in addition to having a limit on the size of the line, line editors don't word wrap.

Most **screen editors**, and **emacs** is a screen editor, allow an unlimited number of characters to a line and perform some form of word wrap when we type a paragraph. While **emacs** does line wrap, it does not word wrap. If you enter more than 80 characters, it inserts a backslash (\) character at the end of the line and continues on the next line. If you happen to split a word, so be it. This backslash is just there as a visual guide, however. It is not actually stored in the file, and when you print the file, you will not see it.

To actually insert text, therefore, all you need to do is position the cursor at the insertion location and begin typing. One word of caution, however; be sure to put a return character at the end of the last line in the file. The return character is generated by the Return or Enter key on your keyboard.

Erasing Text

There are two ways to erase text: deleting it and killing it. When we **delete text**, it is permanently destroyed.[3] When we kill text, as it is deleted, it is copied to a kill[4] ring

---

[3]We will shortly discuss the undo command, which allows you to recover some deleted text.

[4]Obviously, UNIX was written when we were less sensitive about the terms we created.

that allows us to retrieve the data. The **kill ring** is a circular storage structure that has enough space for 30 entries. We can therefore recover data back 30 deletions. Whether you delete or kill depends on the size of the data. Characters and words are deleted; anything larger, such as a sentence or a line, is killed.

Deleting Data

To delete a character, you need to determine if you want to delete the character before the cursor or the character that the cursor is currently on. To delete the character before the cursor, you use the **Backspace key**. Repeatedly depressing it deletes a series of characters, one at a time. To delete the current character, you need to use the delete command, `ctrl+d`.

TABLE C.2   emacs *Delete Commands*

	Keys		Keys		
Character: Previous	bksp		meta	bksp	Word: Previous
Character: Current	ctrl	+ d	meta	d	Word: Next

To delete a word, you use a metacommand. Assuming that the cursor is on a space between two words, `meta backspace` deletes the word in front of the cursor (that is, the previous word); `meta d` deletes the current word.

You might be wondering what happens if the cursor is in the middle of a word. In this case, `meta backspace` deletes the part of the word in front of the cursor, but not the letter under the cursor. If you use `meta d`, then the characters starting with the character under the cursor to the end of the word are deleted. Punctuation at the end of the word, like a comma or period, is not deleted.

Killing Data

As we said earlier, if you delete more than a word, the deleted text is copied to the kill ring as it is erased. There are two commands that use the kill ring: kill line and kill region.

The **kill ring** contains the last 30 killed items. It is called a ring because of its operation; to insert text, the ring is first rotated one position and then the new text is copied into the ring. If the ring is full, the oldest text in the ring is replaced when, after rotation, the new text is copied into the current position overlaying the original text (Figure C.4).

Kill Line

The **kill line** command is `ctrl+k`. This command removes all text from the cursor to the end of the line. It does not remove the return character at the end of the line unless it is the only character in the line. To kill the entire line, we use a move to beginning of line (`ctrl+a`) followed immediately by the kill command. At this point, we have a blank line in the document. We can either enter new text on the line, or if we want to com-

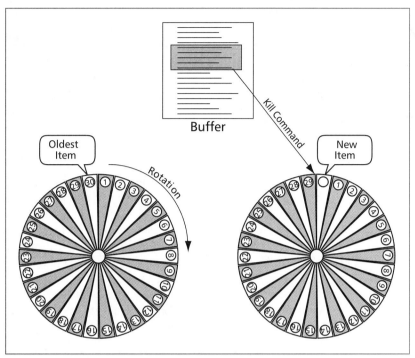

FIGURE C.4   *The Kill Ring*

pletely delete the line, enter a second kill command. Note that the second kill command does not place anything in the kill ring. The following example shows the commands to completely remove a line.

```
$ ctrl+a ctrl+k ctrl+k
```

Kill Region

A region is the text buffer area starting with the buffer and moving either forward or backward to a position identified by a mark. The **mark** is a position in the text set with the mark command, ctrl+@.

When you set a mark, it is pushed onto a **mark ring** that operates just like the kill ring described previously. The mark ring holds up to 16 marks. Unlike the cursor, the mark is not movable; it can only be reset, at which time the mark ring is rotated and the new mark becomes the current mark.

To set a mark, position the cursor at the beginning of a region. Remember that the region can be set either forward or backward. Enter the mark command (ctrl+@). Then using an appropriate move command, move the cursor to the end of the region you want to create. The region is not set from the current cursor to the mark.

Once the region has been set, you can use any of the region commands shown in Table C.3.

TABLE C.3 **emacs** *Region Commands*

Command	Explanation
`ctrl` + `w`	Kill region and insert into kill ring.
`meta` `W`	Copy region to kill ring—leave text in text buffer.

Retrieving Text: The Yank Commands

The beauty of the kill ring is that it allows you to retrieve any of the text in the ring by rotating it to the desired position and then retrieving the text.

Text is copied from the kill ring to the text buffer with the **yank** command, `ctrl+y`. Note that the yank command leaves the text in the ring. The only time that text is erased from the ring is when a kill command is executed and the ring is already full.

The yank command always operates on the last item inserted into the kill ring, the item at location 1 in Figure C.4. To retrieve any of the other items, we must turn the ring. To turn the ring, we first issue a yank command and then use the **rotate** command, `meta y`, to rotate the ring and retrieve the text at the previous position. The yank and rotate command effects are seen in Figure C.5.

For example, assume that the kill ring has its full 30 pieces of text, represented by the numbers 1 to 30 in Figure C.5. The last item inserted, the current item, is in position 1. If we yank the ring, the text at location 1 is inserted into the document at the current cursor location. At this point, if we move the cursor, enter text, or issue any command other than a rotate, the text is left in the buffer; that is, the rotation is complete.

On the other hand, if the yank is *immediately* followed by a rotate, then the text at position 2 *replaces* the text yanked from position 1 and the text buffer now contains position 2's text. The text from position 1 is still in the kill ring, but it is not in the buffer.

Once again, any operation other than a rotation leaves the text in the document. To retrieve the text in the fifth ring location, therefore, we would execute the following set of commands:

1. Yank (`ctrl+y`) position 1 and place its text in the document buffer.
2. Rotate (`meta y`) to position 2, replacing text from position 1.
3. Rotate (`meta y`) to position 3, replacing text from position 2.
4. Rotate (`meta y`) to position 4, replacing text from position 3.
5. Rotate (`meta y`) to position 5, replacing text from position 4.
6. Use any other command or enter text to leave the text from position 5 in the buffer.

Moving Text

The kill and yank commands are used to move text from one place in a document to somewhere else, or as it is generally known, to **cut and paste**. In a cut and paste operation, the text is first killed and placed into the kill ring. The cursor is then positioned in the document where the text is to be moved and the ring yanked. This takes three steps.

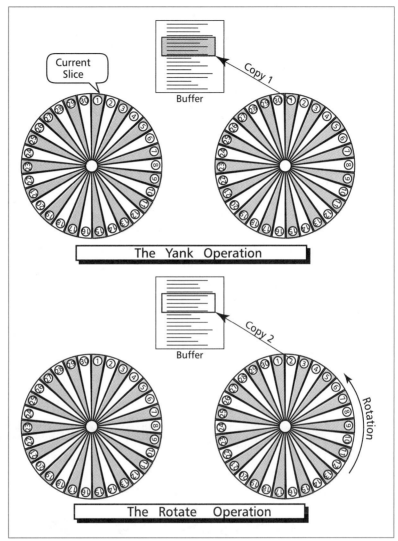

FIGURE C.5   *The Yank and Rotate Commands*

1. Kill the text to be moved.
2. Reposition the cursor at the text destination location.
3. Yank the kill ring.

Copying Text

Those familiar with standard text editing concepts know the kill and yank operation as cut and paste. Another familiar and useful command is **copy and paste**, in which text is first copied and then pasted elsewhere in a document. There is no copy and paste command in **emacs**, but we can easily simulate it with the kill and yank commands. This operation takes four steps.

1. Kill the text to be copied.
2. Immediately yank the text to replace it in the document.
3. Move the cursor to the insert position.
4. Yank the kill ring positioning a copy of the text in the document.

C.3 Saving and Leaving emacs

When you are working with a text document, you should occasionally save your work to ensure that it is not lost if the system should fail. In UNIX, there are three components that can fail: your terminal (or client computer), the communications link, or the server. With so many different fail points, it is even more important that you save often.

Most UNIX systems install **emacs** with an autosave feature. This means that the system is automatically saving a copy of your work occasionally. Nevertheless, we recommend that you get in the habit of saving your work yourself. Whenever you switch from UNIX to another application on your personal computer, save; whenever you need to leave your computer, save; when the phone rings, save before you answer it; when you need to organize your thoughts before you proceed, save; when you haven't saved in 15 minutes, save. The **emacs save command** is very simple—just two commands issued in sequence. First, key ctrl+x and then ctrl+s (for save).

When you leave **emacs**, you are given a chance to save your work if you changed it since the last time you saved. To save your work and leave **emacs**, you use two commands: ctrl+x and ctrl+c (for close). Assuming that the file has been changed, you will see an action request similar to Figure C.6.

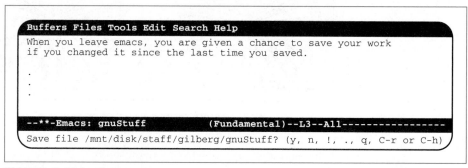

FIGURE C.6 *Leaving* **emacs**

Note the text in the message line below the status. It is asking if you want to save your work and then gives the options that are available. You should reply y for yes. If you reply n, you will be asked to confirm that you don't want to save the changes. The confirmation message is:

```
Modified buffers exist; exit anyway? (yes or no)
```

You must spell out your answer to the confirmation message: yes to delete the changes and exit, no to return to **emacs** and select another option.

The meaning of the other options is shown in Table C.4.

TABLE C.4   *Save Changed File Options*

Code	Explanation
!	Bang: same as y. Saves file and exits.
.	Period: same as y. Saves file and exits.
q	Quit: same as n. Asks for confirmation.
ctrl+r	Return to editing. Do not exit.
ctrl+h	Help. Displays options available.

Table C.5 summarizes the **emacs** exit commands.

TABLE C.5   **emacs** *Exit Command Summary*

Command		Explanation
ctrl + x	ctrl + s	Saves file and remains in edit mode.
ctrl + x	ctrl + w	Saves to a different file.
ctrl + x	ctrl + c	Quits. You will be prompted for file disposition if changed.

C.4 Miscellaneous Command

In this section, we describe seven commands that you will find helpful.

Suspend Editing

While editing a document, you receive a message that requires you to immediately send a note to someone. You could close **emacs**, send your note, and then restart **emacs**. It is much simpler, however, to temporarily suspend **emacs** and then resume when your other business has been taken care of. To suspend **emacs**, key ctrl+z. This places **emacs** in a suspended mode in the background and returns you to the UNIX command line. At this point, you may execute any UNIX command you need. To restart **emacs**, you key the UNIX foreground command, fg. You are immediately back in **emacs** at the exact point where to left.

Undo

One of the most powerful **emacs** commands is undo. Every keystroke you make is recorded in a special undo activity record. While there is a limit to the number of key-strokes and commands that are maintained, it is so large[5] that you will never be able to use it all.

---

[5]On the order of 15,000 characters.

The undo command is a sequence of two keys, `ctrl+x` and `u`. When you key the undo command, the last command you executed is reversed (that is, it is undone and removed from the activity record). If you key undo again, the next command (going in reverse) is undone. If you keep it up, you could eventually undo everything. It is easier, however, simply to close and not save the buffer.

Let's assume that your are killing a large number of lines and accidentally go too far. While you could use the kill ring to restore up to 30 lines, it is rather awkward to use. It is much easier to use undo. By holding down the control and shift keys while tapping the underscore, you can quickly restore as many lines as you need.

Repeat

There are two repeat commands: digit argument and universal command.

Digit Argument

The digit argument uses the metakey and a number. The number specifies how many times the command is to be repeated. For example, to delete five characters, you would use the metakey followed by 5 and then the delete character command.

```
[meta 5][ctrl+d]
```

Universal Command

The second way to repeat a command is with the universal command, `ctrl+u`. This command can be optionally followed by a number. If the number is missing, the command is repeated four times; if the number is present, the command is repeated the number of times specified by the number. Its format is:

```
ctrl+u [ number ] command
```

For example, if you knew exactly how many actions you needed to undo, you could use the repeat command. To kill five lines, you would enter

```
ctrl+u 5 ctrl+k                          # kill 5 lines
```

Repeating the universal command without specifying a repeat number has a multiplicative effect. Two universal commands mean square the default (4). The next example would kill 16 lines (4^2)

```
ctrl+u ctrl+u ctrl+k                      # kill 4 * 4 lines
```

and three universal commands would repeat the command 64 (4^3) times.

```
ctrl+u ctrl+u ctrl+u ctrl+k              # kill 4 * 4 * 4 lines
```

Abort

Sometimes **emacs** seems to get lost in its own thoughts and simply won't respond to anything. When this happens, first try to recenter the screen. If that doesn't work, try the abort command, `ctrl+g`. Ideally, you have saved the buffer recently, so not too much work is lost. You may also find the abort command helpful when you start to enter a control command and want to cancel it, although it is safer simply to key meta twice.

Split Screen

Have you ever found yourself reading a textbook with your fingers marking two or three different places so you could quickly switch back and forth among them? You can do the same thing in **emacs** with split screen. While you can have more than two screen windows open at a time, remember that all you have are 22 lines to work with.

To create a second screen, enter the split screen command as in the following example:

```
ctrl+x  screen_option
```

The screen options are shown in Table C.6.

TABLE C.6   *Split Screen Window Options*

Option	Action
2	Splits screen into two windows, one above the other.
3	Splits screen into two windows, side by side.
4 f	Loads file in new window.
4 r	Loads file in new window in read-only mode.

Screen option 2 splits the window into two evenly divided windows, one over the other, and screen option 3 splits it into two side-by-side windows. Windows created with options 2 and 3 both contain the same document. Option 4 f splits the screen and loads it with a new document. Option 4 r splits the screen also, but in this case, the loaded document is in read-only mode. This protects it so that you cannot accidentally change it.

By far the most useful split-window operation is to view two parts of the same document. Figure C.7 shows TheRaven split into two windows. The top window is set to line 1 of the document (note the line position and "top" in its status bar in the center of the screen). The second window shows the last line of the first verse and the second verse of the poem. It is on line 8 (6%). To move from one window to the next, you use the other window command, `ctrl+x`, followed by o (the letter oh). If there are multiple windows open, it cycles between them in rotation. Unless the windows are in read-only mode, changes made in one window are reflected in the other. In other words, there is only one buffer, although there are two windows.

When working with one document in two windows, there is only one kill ring, regardless of how many different documents are in open windows. This allows us to copy text from one window or document to the other.

Search String

Although **emacs** can search using regular expressions, by far the easier and more useful search for an editor is simply to search for a string. The **emacs** text searches can be

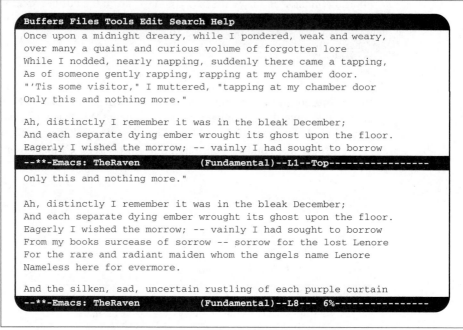

FIGURE C.7 *Split Screen in* **emacs**

either incremental or full string. In an incremental search, **emacs** starts the search as soon as the first character is entered. As each additional character is entered, the search continues until the complete match is found. The full string search prompts for the search string and doesn't start the search until the string is entered. Both searches wrap the buffer. That is, if when searching forward the matching string is not found by the end of the buffer, the search continues from the front of the buffer.

There are two text search commands for each search type. Both start with the search command, either forward or backward. In the incremental search, the search starts with the first character entered immediately after the search command. To use the full string search, we must key Escape after the command. At that point, we are prompted for the text string.

The search command for a forward search is `ctrl+S`; the command for a backward search is `ctrl+R`. These commands are summarized in Table C.7.

TABLE C.7 **emacs** *Text Search Commands*

Command	Explanation
[ctrl] + [S]	Incremental search forward.
[ctrl] + [R]	Incremental search backward.
[ctrl] + [S] [meta]	Full text search forward.
[ctrl] + [R] [meta]	Full text search backward.

Numbering Systems

Today, the whole world uses the decimal number system developed by Arabian mathematicians in the eighth century. We acknowledge their contribution to numbers when we refer to our decimal system as using Arabic numerals. But decimal numbers were not always commonly used. The first to use a decimal numbering system were the ancient Egyptians. The Babylonians improved on the Egyptian system by making the positions in the numbering systems meaningful.

But the Babylonians also used a sexagesimal (base 60) numbering system. Whereas our decimal system has 10 values in its graphic representations, a sexagesimal system has 60. We still see remnants of the Babylonians' sexagesimal system in time, which is based on 60 minutes to an hour, and in the division of circles, which contain $360°$.

D.1 Computer Numbering Systems

There are four different numbering systems used in computers today. The computer itself uses a binary system. In a binary system, there are only two values for each number position: 0 and 1. Programmers use two different shorthand notations to represent binary numbers: octal and hexadecimal. And of course, programmers also use the decimal system. Since all these systems are used in UNIX, you will need to have a basic understanding of each to fully understand the language.

Decimal Numbers

We all readily understand the decimal numbering system. In fact, we have used it so much that it is basically intuitive. But do you really understand why the second position in the decimal system is tens and the third position is hundreds? The answer lies in the powers of the base to the system, which in decimal is 10. Thus, the first position is 10 raised to the power zero, the second position is 10 raised to the power one, and the third position is 10 raised to the power two. Figure D.1 shows the relationship between the powers and the number 243.

Binary Numbers

Whereas the decimal system is based on 10, the binary system is based on 2. There are only two digits in binary: 0 and 1. Binary digits are known as bits, which is an acronym created from **b**inary dig**it**.

Figure D.2 shows the powers table for a binary system and the value 243 in binary. In the position table, each position is double the previous position. Again, this is because the base of the system is 2. You will need to memorize the binary powers to at least 2^{10}.

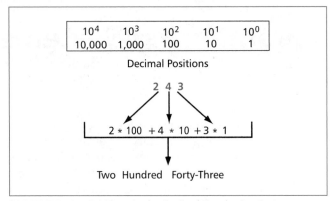

FIGURE D.1 *Positions in the Decimal Numbering System*

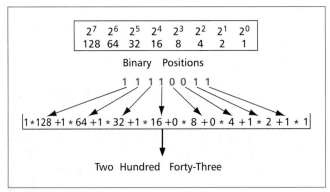

FIGURE D.2 *Positions in the Binary Numbering System*

Octal Numbers

The base of the octal system is 8. This means that there are eight different symbols: 0, 1, 2, 3, 4, 5, 6, and 7. Although octal is not commonly used in modern computer systems, it is still supported by UNIX and needs to be understood. The octal numbering system is shown in Figure D.3. Again, the number represented is 243.

Hexadecimal Numbers

The hexadecimal system is based on 16 (*hexadec* is Greek for 16). This means that there are 16 symbols: 0, 1, 2, 3, 4, 5, 6, 7, 8, 9, A, B, C, D, E, and F. Since the base is 16, each positional value is 16 times the previous one (Figure D.4).

Look carefully at the decimal, binary, octal, and hexadecimal numbering systems in Table D.1. Do you see that some of the values are duplicated? This is because octal and hexadecimal are simply shorthand notations for binary. Rather than represent a number as a large string of 0s and 1s, it is therefore possible to use either octal or hexadecimal.

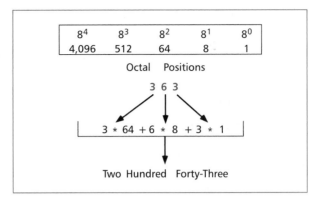

FIGURE D.3 *Positions in the Octal Numbering System*

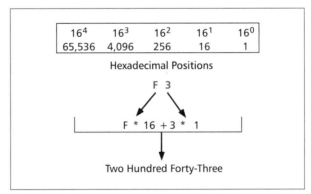

FIGURE D.4 *Positions in the Hexadecimal Numbering System*

TABLE D.I *Decimal, Binary, Octal, and Hexadecimal Table*

Decimal	Binary	Octal	Hexadecimal
0	0000	0	0
1	0001	1	1
2	0010	2	2
3	0011	3	3
4	0100	4	4
5	0101	5	5
6	0110	6	6
7	0111	7	7
8	1000	10	8
9	1001	11	9
10	1010	12	A
11	1011	13	B
12	1100	14	C
13	1101	15	D
14	1110	16	E
15	1111	17	F
16	10000	20	10

D.2 Integer Transformations

Since you are going to be working in all four numbering systems, you will need to learn how to convert to and from binary to the other formats. If you understand the concepts shown in the previous section, you will find it easy to do the conversions.

Binary to Decimal

Let's start by converting a number from binary to decimal. Refer to Figure D.5 for this discussion. To convert from binary to decimal, you start with the binary number and multiply each binary digit by its value from the binary positions table in Figure D.2 on page 900. Since each binary bit can be only 0 or 1, the result will be either 0 or the value of the position. After multiplying all the digits, add the results.

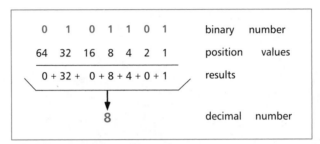

FIGURE D.5   *Binary to Decimal Conversion*

Decimal to Binary

To convert from decimal to binary, you use repetitive division. The original number, 45 in the example, is divided by 2. The remainder (1) becomes the first binary digit, and the second digit is determined by dividing the quotient (22) by 2. Again the remainder (0) becomes the binary digit, and the quotient is divided by 2 to determine the next position. This process continues until the quotient is 0. This conversion is shown in Figure D.6.

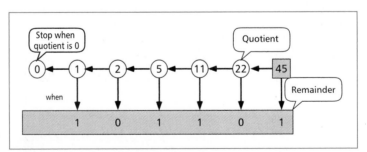

FIGURE D.6   *Decimal to Binary Conversion*

Binary to Octal or Hexadecimal

The previous section showed a mathematical way to convert from binary to decimal. Converting from binary to octal and hexadecimal is done by grouping binary digits into groups of three for octal and groups of four for hexadecimal. Do you see why we use these groupings? Table D.1 shows the bit configurations for the binary, octal, hexadecimal, and decimal representations of the numbers 1 to 16.

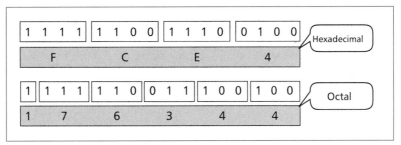

FIGURE D.7 *Converting a Large Binary Number*

Now if we have a large binary number, we can easily change it to a hexadecimal using the foregoing information. We divide the number into 4-bit sections (from the right). Then to each section, we assign the appropriate hexadecimal digit. This concept is shown in Figure D.7.

If we have a large binary number, we can easily change it to an octal number using the same concept. Divide the number into 3-bit sections (from the right). Then to each section, assign the appropriate octal digit. This is also shown in Figure D.7.

Predefined Variables

This appendix contains a table of the shell built-in variables in different shells. The Korn and Bash shells use only uppercase identifiers. The C shell uses both lower- and uppercase. Not all of the variables are available in all shells. Refer to the corresponding chapters for details.

Variable	Meaning
CDPATH	List of directories to be searched by the **cd** command.
COLUMNS	Width of monitor display in characters.
EDITOR	Path to the visual editor.
ENV	Name of the environment file.
ERRNO	Error number of last command that failed.
FCEDIT	Default editor for **fc** command.
HISTFILE	In Korn shell, the name of the history file.
history	In C shell, the name of the history file.
HISTSIZE	Minimum number of commands in history file.
HOME	Full pathname of home directory.
IFS	Internal field separator.
LINENO	Line number in function or script.
LINES	Height of monitor display in lines.
LOGNAME	User login name.
MAIL	Full pathname of user mail file.
MAILCHECK	How often to check for mail (in seconds).
MAILPATH	List of filenames to be checked for new mail (if MAIL undefined).
OLDPWD	Previous working directory.
OPTARG	Argument to options being processed by **getopts**.
OPTIND	Number of first argument after options.
PATH	Search path for commands.
PPID	Process ID (PID) of parent process.
prompt	In C shell, the environmental variable that holds the primary prompt value.
PS1, PS2, PS3, PS4	In Korn shell, the environmental variables that hold the various prompt values.

Continued

Variable	Meaning
PWD	Current working directory.
RANDOM	Random number between 0 and 32,767 inclusive.
REPLY	User response to select command. Also result of **read** command.
SECONDS	Number of seconds since shell was invoked.
SHELL	Full pathname of shell.
TERM	Terminal type.
TMOUT	Seconds after which idle shell terminates.
USER	User id.
VISUAL	Path to the visual editor (same as EDITOR).

UNIX Commands

This appendix contains a summary of all commands discussed in the text. It uses the same format found at the end of each chapter.

Command	Description	Options	Page
. (dot)	**Synopsis:** *. command* Reads files from the current shell.		641
: (colon)	**Synopsis:** *(Null Command)* Does nothing (a placeholder). The exit status is always true.		566

alias	**Synopsis:** *alias name definition*
	    alias [name=definition] #Korn and Bash
	    alias [name definition] #C shell
	Lists exiting aliases or creates a new alias for a command.
			170, 674

awk	**Synopsis:** **awk** *[options] script [file-list]* Selects and processes specified lines in the input file.	-F, -f	425
basename	**Synopsis:** *basename pathname [argument]* Extracts base name or extension of a pathname.		648
bash	**Synopsis:** *bash* Creates a new Bash shell.		144
bc	**Synopsis:** *bc* Calculator.		29
bg	**Synopsis:** bg *[job_number]* Moves a suspended job to the background.		168
break	**Synopsis:** *break* Forces a loop to terminate.		585, 741
breaksw	**Synopsis:** *breaksw* Terminates execution of case commands.		734
cal	**Synopsis:** *cal [[month] year]* Displays the calendar for a month or a year.		17

case	**Synopsis:** *case string in*
	            pat) command (s);;
	            pat) command (s);;
	            ...
	        esac
	Creates a multiway selection.
			568

Command	Description	Options	Page
`cat`	**Synopsis:** *cat [-options] [file-list]* Concatenates files. It may also be used to display files or create new files.	e, n, s, t, u, v	202
`cd`	**Synopsis:** *cd [directory]* Changes the current directory to the directory defined by the pathname. If the pathname is missing, the home directory becomes the working directory.		88
`chgrp`	**Synopsis:** *chgrp [-option] group list* Changes a group associated with a list of files or directories.	R	133
`chmod`	**Synopsis:** *chmod [-option] mode list* Sets or changes the permission of a list of files or directories.	R	126
`chown`	**Synopsis:** *chown [-option] owner [:group] list* Changes the owner (and the group associated to) a list of files or directories.	R	133
`clear`	**Synopsis:** *clear* Clears monitor screen.		25
`cmp`	**Synopsis:** *cmp [-options] file1 file2* Determines if files are identical.	l, s	238
`comm`	**Synopsis:** *comm file1 file2* Displays common lines in two files.		243
`continue`	**Synopsis:** *continue* Continues with the next iteration of the loop.		585, 742
`cp`	**Synopsis:** *cp [-options] source destination* Copies files or directories from source to the destination.	p, i, r	93
`csh`	**Synopsis:** *csh* Creates a new C shell.		144
`ctrl+c`	Terminates (aborts) a foreground job.		166
`ctrl+z`	Stops (suspends) a foreground job.		166
`cut`	**Synopsis:** *cut [-options] [file-list]* Splits files into columns.	c, d, f, s	210
`date`	**Synopsis:** *date [-options] [+format]* Displays the time and date.	u	15

`diff`	**Synopsis:** *diff [-options] file1 file2*
	        diff [-options] file1 dir
	        diff [-options] dir file2
	        diff [-options] dir1 dir2
	Identifies differences between two files.
		b, w, i	240

`dirname`	**Synopsis:** *dirname pathname* Extracts the directory name of a pathname.		648

Command	Description	Options	Page
echo	**Synopsis:** *echo [message]* Displays its argument.	n	21
egrep	**Synopsis:** *egrep [-options] 'regexpr' [file-list]* Selects lines that match the regular expression.	b, c, i, l, n, s, v, x, f	356
eval	**Synopsis:** *eval command –un* Evaluates the command two times before executing it.		519, 689
ex	**Synopsis:** *ex [-option] [file-name]* Creates a new file or edits an existing file.	R	311
exec	**Synopsis:** *exec ...* Opens and closes files.		651
exit	**Synopsis:** *exit [status]* Sets the exit status and terminates the shell. Moves the user from a subshell to the parent shell.		146, 553, 721
export	**Synopsis:** *export variable_list* Exports variables to subshells.		510
expr	**Synopsis:** *expr arguments* Evaluates a mathematical expression or manipulates a string.		557
fg	**Synopsis:** *fg [job_number]* Moves a suspended job to the foreground.		165
fgrep	**Synopsis:** *fgrep [-options] 'string' [file-list]* Selects lines that match the string.	b, c, i, l, n, s, v, x, f	356
find	**Synopsis:** *find pathname criteria* Finds a file or a directory based on the criteria.		108

foreach	**Synopsis:** *foreach variable (list)*
	      body
	      end
	 Executes loop body as long as there are items in the list.
			739

for-in	**Synopsis:** *for variable in list*
	      do
	        body
	      done
	 Executes loop body as long as there are items in the list.
			575

ftp	**Synopsis:** *ftp domain_name* Transfers files to and from the remote computer defined by the argument (domain_name).		279
getopts	**Synopsis:** *getopts options variable* Parses options.		644

Command	Description	Options	Page
`grep`	***Synopsis:*** *grep [-options] 'regexpr' [file-list]* Selects lines that match the regular expression.	b, c, i, l, n, s, v, x, f	355
`groups`	***Synopsis:*** *groups [user id]* Displays the user's group.		121
`head`	***Synopsis:*** *head [-options] [file-list]* Displays lines at the beginning of a file (default is 10 lines).	-N	207
`history`	***Synopsis:*** *history -n	-r	command_name* Displays contents of the command history file.		533
`if-then-else`	***Synopsis:*** *if command* *then* *…* *else* *…* *fi* Creates a two-way selection.		562, 728
`jobs`	***Synopsis:*** *jobs* Displays the list of active jobs.		168
`kill`	***Synopsis:*** *kill [job_number]* Kills a job.		166
`ksh`	***Synopsis:*** *ksh* Creates a new Korn shell.		144
`let`	***Synopsis:*** *let variable=mathematical expression* Evaluates a mathematical expression.		557
`ln`	***Synopsis:*** *ln [-options] source link* Links the source to the destination.	s, i, f	102
`lpr`	***Synopsis:*** *lpr [-options] [file-list]* Prints the file list.	P	23, 92
`ls`	***Synopsis:*** *ls [-options] [pathname]* Lists the contents of a directory.	l, d, n, r, t, u, c, p, R, 1, i	81
`mail`	***Synopsis:*** *mail [receiver-list]* Used to read or send email. When it is used without argument, it is in the read mode. When an argument is used, it is in the send mode.		265
`man`	***Synopsis:*** *man command-name* Displays online documentation for the command.		22
`mkdir`	***Synopsis:*** *mkdir [-options] directory-list* Creates one or more directories.	p, m	86

Command	Description	Options	Page
more	*Synopsis:* *more [-options] [file-list]* Displays the contents of a file one screenful at a time.	c, d, f, l, r, s, u, w, lines, +nmbr, +/ptrn	90
mv	*Synopsis:* *mv [-options] source destination* Moves a file or directory from source to destination or renames a file or directory.	f, i	100
onintr	*Synopsis:* *onintr [label]* Runs a command when a signal is received.		774
passwd	*Synopsis:* *passwd* Changes the user password.		20
paste	*Synopsis:* *paste [-options] [file-list]* Combines lines of files into one single line.	d	214
print	*Synopsis:* *print argument list* Displays contents of a variable or a string.		528
ps	*Synopsis:* *ps* Displays information about the active processes.		170
pwd	*Synopsis:* *pwd* Displays the absolute pathname of the current (working) directory.		80
r	*Synopsis:* *r line	-line	command_name* *Reexecutes (redo) specified command in history file.*		535
read	*Synopsis:* *read [options] variable-list* Reads values and stores them in variables.		516
readonly	*Synopsis:* *readonly variable-list* Makes the variables read only.		509
return	*Synopsis:* *return [expression]* Returns from function.		631
rm	*Synopsis:* *rm [-options] list* Removes (deletes) files or directories.	f, i, r	106
rmdir	*Synopsis:* *rmdir directory-list* Removes (deletes) directories.		89
script	*Synopsis:* *script [filename]* Records interactive session.	a	27
sed	*Synopsis:* *sed [-options] script [file-list]* Edits specified lines in the input files and processes them.	n, e, f	373

Command	Description	Options	Page
select	***Synopsis:*** *select variable in list* *do* *...* *done* Creates a menu environment.		577
set	***Synopsis:*** *set expression* *set var=value* #C shell *set -o option* #Korn and Bash *set +o option* #Korn and Bash Sets a value for a variable or sets an option. Also unsets an option in the Korn shell when used with plus option. Sets the positional parameters.		178, 589
setenv	***Synopsis:*** *setenv var = value* *setenv variable value* Defines an exportable variable. In C shell, sets a value for an environmental variable.		182, 685
shift	***Synopsis:*** *shift expression* Shifts the parameters to the left.		591, 746
sleep	***Synopsis:*** *sleep seconds* Sleeps for a number of seconds.		640, 776
sort	***Synopsis:*** *sort [-options] [field-specifiers] [file-list]* Sorts or merges files.	b, c, d, f, m, n, r, t, u	217
source	***Synopsis:*** *source command* Executes command in current shell.		777
stop	***Synopsis:*** *stop [job_number]* Stops (suspends) a background job.		167
stty	***Synopsis:*** *stty* Sets or unsets selected terminal input/output options.	a, g	25
switch	***Synopsis:*** *switch (expression)* Selects among alternatives.		732
tail	***Synopsis:*** *tail [-options] [file]* Displays lines at the end of a file (default is 10 lines).	-N, +N, b, c, l, r	208
talk	***Synopsis:*** *talk user-id [terminal]* Used to create a chatting environment between two users that are logged into the same or a different system.		257
tee	***Synopsis:*** *tee [-option] file-list* Copies standard input to standard output and at the same time copies to one or more files.	a	153

Command	Description	Options	Page
telnet	**Synopsis:** *telnet* Connects the user to the remote computer defined by the argument (domain_name).		276
test	**Synopsis:** *test arguments* Evaluates a relational, logical, or file expression.		561
tr	**Synopsis:** *tr [-options] [string1] [string2]* Translates (replaces) a set of characters (string1) with another set (string2).	c, d, s	230
trap	**Synopsis:** *trap "action"signals* Runs a command when a signal is received.		638
tty	**Synopsis:** *tty* Displays name of terminal.		24
typeset	**Synopsis:** *typeset –attribute variable* *typeset +attribute variable* Associates (–) and unassociates (+) data attributes, such as numeric and justification, to a variable.		512
umask	**Synopsis:** *umask [mask]* Displays or sets the default permission for newly created files or directories.		132
unalias	**Synopsis:** *unalias alias-list* Removes some or all aliases.	a (Korn and Bash)	173
uname	**Synopsis:** *uname* Displays system data.	a, n, r, s, sr	28
uniq	**Synopsis:** *unique [-options] [input_file]* Displays the unique lines in a file.	u, c, d	233
unset	**Synopsis:** *unset variable* *unset option* #C shell Unsets the value of a variable or unsets an option.		182
unsetenv	**Synopsis:** *unsetenv variable* In C shell, unsets the value of an environmental variable.		182

until	**Synopsis:** *until command*
	        do
	            body
	        done
	Repeats the body until the command is successful (exit status 0).
			573

vi	**Synopsis:** *vi [-options] [file-name]* Used to create a new file or edit an existing file.	R	42, 292

Command	Description	Options	Page
wc	***Synopsis:*** *wc [-options] [file-list]* Displays the number of lines, words, and characters in a file.	c, l, w	237
while	***Synopsis:*** *while (expression)* *body* *end* Repeats the body while the expression is successful (exit status 0).		571, 736
who	***Synopsis:*** *who [-options] [am i]* Displays all users currently logged into the system.	H, u	18
whoami	***Synopsis:*** *whoami* Displays the id of the user.		20
write	***Synopsis:*** *write user-id [terminal]* Used to send a message to a receiver logged into the same or a different system from the sender.		260

Shell Metacharacters

The shells use a selected set of metacharacters in commands. Metacharacters are associated with a special interpretation. This appendix contains a list of the more common metacharacters.

Character	Meaning
* ? [ ] ^	Wildcards
$	Variable reference and command substitution
|	Pipe
< > >> >&	Redirection
! ^	History reference
! wildcard	Complements wildcard evaluation
&	Background execution
;	Command separator
space	Word separator
`...`	Command substitution (backquote or grave accent)
\	Escape next character
'...'	Single quotes
"..."	Double quotes
~	Home directory

Korn and C Shell Differences

This appendix highlights the differences between the Korn shell and the C shell. We have shown only the most important features of the shells that are normally confused by users.

H.1 Variables

Both shells support variables as summarized in Table H.1.

TABLE H.1 *Variables*

Feature	Korn	C
Storing (setting)	`variable=value`	`set variable = value`
Accessing	`$variable` or `${variable}`	`$variable` or `${variable}`
Unsetting	`unset variable`	`unset variable`
Readonly	`readonly variable`	
Exporting	`export variable-list`	`setenv variable value`
Attributes (setting and unsetting)	`typeset -attribute variable` `typeset +attribute variable`	

H.2 Command-Line Editing

Command-line editing is summarized in Table H.2.

TABLE H.2 *Command-Line Editing*

Feature	Korn	C
Setting	`set -o vi`[a]	
Unsetting	`set +o vi`[a]	

[a]or **emacs**

H.3 Command Substitution

Command substitution is summarized in Table H.3.

TABLE H.3 *Command Substitution*

Feature	Korn	C
Command substitution	`$(command)`	`` `command` ``

H.4 Aliases

Aliases are summarized in Table H.4.

TABLE H.4 *Aliases*

Feature	Korn	C
Defining	`alias name=command`	`alias name definition`
Parameters		`anywhere`
Listing one	`alias name`	`alias name`
Listing all	`alias`	`alias`
Removing one	`unalias name`	`unalias name`
Removing all	`unalias -a`	`unalias *`

H.5 Input/Output

Input/output commands are summarized in Table H.5.

TABLE H.5 *Input/Output Commands*

Feature	Korn	C
Input	`read [-ru] variable`	`set variable = $<`
Output	`print [-n] string`	`echo $variable`

H.6 Environmental Variables

Environmental variables are summarized in Table H.6.

TABLE H.6 *Environmental Variables*

Feature	Korn	C
List of variables	See Chapter 13, page 575	See Chapter 16, Page 839
Set	`set variable=value`	`set variable=value`
Unset	`unset variable`	`unset variable`
Display one	`print $variable`	`echo $variable`
Display all	`set`	`set`

H.7 Startup Files

Startup files are summarized in Table H.7.

TABLE H.7 *Startup Files*

Feature	Korn	C
System (Shell)	`/etc/profile`	`/etc/csh.login`
System (Env.)		`/etc/csh.cshrc`
User (Shell)	`$HOME/.profile`	`$HOME/.login`
User (Env.)	`Path stored in $ENV`	`$HOME/.cshrc`

H.8 Shutdown Files

Shutdown files are summarized in Table H.8.

TABLE H.8 *Shutdown Files*

Feature	Korn	C
System		`/etc/ch.logout`
User		`$HOME/.logout`

H.9 Options and On-Off Variables

Options and on-off variables are summarized in Table H.9. Note that in the C shell, the on-off variables serve as options.

TABLE H.9 *Options and On-Off Variables*

Feature	Korn	C (on-off variables)
List of options	See Chapter 13, page 583	See Chapter 16, Page 840
Set	`set -o option`	`set variable`
Unset	`set +o option`	`unset variable`
Display one		`echo $variable`
Display all	`set -o`	`set`

H.10 History

History is summarized in Table H.10.

TABLE H.10 *History Commands*

Feature	Korn	C
Listing commands	`history`	`history`
Reexecuting	`r cmd-num`	`! cmd-num`
Substituting	`r cmd-num str1=str2`	`! cmd-num: s/ .../ .../`
History modifier		`! cmd-num: argument`
Path modifier		`! cmd-num: path(h, t, or r)`

H.11 Parameters

Parameters are summarized in Table H.11.

TABLE H.11 *Parameters*

Feature	Korn	C
Positional	`$1, $2, ..., $9`	`$argv[1], $argv[2], ..., $argv[9]`
Special	`$0, $#, $*, $@`	`$0, $argv#, $argv`

H.12 Special Variables

Special variables are summarized in Table H.12.

TABLE H.12 *Special Variables*

Feature	Korn	C
Exit status	$?	$status
Input file separator	IFS	IFS

H.13 Expressions

Expressions are summarized in Table H.13.

TABLE H.13 *Expressions*

Feature	Korn	C
Mathematical	`(( ... ))` or **let** command	`@ command`

Relational	`(( ... ))`
	`for integers`
	`[[ ... ]]`
	`for strings`
		`( ... )`

File	`[[ ... ]]`	`( ... )`
Logical	`[[ ... ]]`	`( ... )`

H.14 Selection

Selection is summarized in Table H.14.

TABLE H.14 *Selection*

Feature	Korn	C

Two-way	`if command`
	   `then`
	     `...`
	   `else`
	     `...`
	`fi`
		`if condition then`
		     `...`
		`else`
		     `...`
		`endif`

Continued

TABLE H.14 *Selection—Continued*

Feature	Korn	C
| Multiway selection | ```
case $string in
    pat1 )   ... ;;
    pat2 )   ... ;;
    ...
    ...
    patN)    ... ;;
esac
``` | ```
switch ($string)
    case value1 :  ...
        breaksw
    case value1 :  ...
        breaksw
    ...
    default :      ...
    breaksw
endsw
``` |

H.15 Repetition

Repetition is summarized in Table H.15.

TABLE H.15 *Repetition*

Feature	Korn	C
| while loop | ```
while command
do
    ...
done
``` | ```
while    (expression)
    ...
    ...
end
``` |
| until loop | ```
until command
do
    ...
done
``` | |
| for loop | ```
for variable in list
do
    ...
done
``` | ```
foreach variable (list)
    ...
    ...
end
``` |
| select loop | ```
select variable in
list
do
    ...
done
``` | |
| repeat loop | | ```
repeat number command
``` |
```

H.16 Arrays

Arrays are summarized in Table H.16.

TABLE H.16 *Arrays*

Feature	Korn	C

Initialize	`name[0]=value`
	`name[1]=value`
	`...`
	`name[N - 1]=value`
		set `name = (A B ...N)`
		set `name[2] = "A"`
		set `name = `ls``

Access	`{name[0]}`
	`{name[1]}`
	`...`
	`{[name[*]}`
	`{#name[*]}`
		`$name[1]`
		`$name[2]`

H.17 Functions

The Korn shell supports functions; the C shell does not. Functions are summarized in Table H.17.

TABLE H.17 *Functions*

Feature	Korn	C

Definition	**function** `name ()`
	`{`
	  `...`
	`}`	

Call	`name (arguments)`	

Glossary

A

absolute pathname any UNIX pathname that begins with a slash (/) indicating that path starts from the root. Contrast with *relative pathname*.

action in **awk**, one or more statements associated with a pattern.

algorithm the logical steps necessary to solve a problem in a computer.

alias a means of creating customized commands by assigning an alternate name or acronym to a command.

alternation operator used to define one or more alternatives in a regular expression.

anchor atom a regular expression atom showing the position of a pattern within a string. The anchors are: beginning of line, end of line, beginning of word, and end of word.

and operator (&&) a binary logical operator with the property that the expression is true if and only if both operands are true.

application software computer software developed to support a specific user requirement. Contrast with *system software*.

application-specific software any application software that can be used for only one purpose, such as an accounting system.

argument the values, such as an option or a filename, following a command.

argument validation a process that edits (validates) the number and the type of arguments in a script.

arithmetic expression an expression containing only arithmetic operators such as +, − , *, /, and %.

array a fixed-sized, sequenced collection of elements of the same data type that can be referred to individually or as a collection.

ascending sequence a list/sort order in which each element in the list has data greater than or equal to its predecessors.

ASCII the American Standard Code for Information Interchange. An encoding scheme that defines control characters and graphical characters for the first 128 values in a byte.

assignment expression an expression containing the assignment operator (=) that results in the value of the expression being placed into the variable on the left of the assignment operator.

assignment operator the equal sign (=). See *assignment expression*.

associative array an array in which the indexes are strings instead of integers.

atom that part of a regular expression that specifies what text is to be matched and where it is to be found.

auxiliary storage any storage device outside main memory; permanent data storage; external storage.

B

background job See *background processing*.

background processing a running program or utility that is capable of running without user interaction and that has been given a low priority by the user; that is, that has been moved to the background. Multiple programs can run concurrently in the background. Contrast with *foreground processing*.

back-reference atom an atom that refers back to previous saved atoms in a regular expression. Only nine back-reference atoms are available \1, \2, . . . , \9.

bang UNIX name for exclamation point (!).

basename the portion of the pathname after the last slash; it may be a directory or a file.

basename command the command that extracts a basename from a pathname.

Bash Bourne Again Shell. The new Bourne shell used in Linux.

binary file a collection of data stored in the internal format of the computer. Contrast with *text file*.

bit acronym for **b**inary dig**it**. The basic storage unit in a computer with the capability of storing only the values 0 or 1.

block in **awk** and shell functions, a group of commands enclosed in a set of braces; in physical storage, a set of records or data items read or written as a unit.

block special file a file representing a physical device, such as a disk, that reads or write data a block at a time.

body of loop the code executed during each iteration of a loop.

boot block the physical location on a disk that contains the boot program.

boot program the program used to initially load an operating system into memory; the program that starts the operating system when a computer is turned on.

Bourne shell the first UNIX shell; developed by Steve Bourne at AT&T Labs.

braces the { and } symbols.

break command a statement that causes a `switch` or loop statement to terminate.

built-in command the commands that are included in a shell and run faster than general utilities.

buffer (1) hardware, usually memory, used to synchronize the transfer of data to and from main memory. (2) memory used to hold data that have been read before they are processed, or data that are waiting to be written.

buffered input/output input or output that is temporarily stored in intermediate memory while being read or written.

bug a colloquial term used for any error in a piece of software.

byte a unit of storage, usually 8 bits.

C

C Shell the shell developed at Berkeley by Bill Joy.

called function in a function call, the function to which control is passed.

calling function in a function call, the function that invokes the call.

case command a command in the Korn shell that allows decisions among alternatives.

case label in the C shell, the entry point for a value in a `switch` statement.

case statement each statement used in a switch command in the C shell.

catching signal an action that allows a process to handle a signal.

CDPATH an environmental variable that holds the path used by the **cd** command.

central processing unit (CPU) the part of a computer that interprets and executes instructions. In a personal computer, a microchip containing a control unit and an arithmetic-logical unit.

chained commands a combination of UNIX commands in which the output of the first command becomes the input to the second command; the output of the second command then becomes the input to the third command; and so forth until the last command is complete.

character a member of the set of values that are used to represent data or control operations. See *ASCII*.

character set the set of values in a computer's alphabet, usually ASCII.

character special file a file that represents a physical device, such as a terminal, that reads or writes one character at a time.

class atom a single-character atom in a regular expression that matches a set of characters.

client in a client/server network, the computer that provides the basic application computing; the computer residing in the user's physical area.

client/server   a computer system design in which two separate computers control the processing of the application, one providing the basic application computing (the client) and the other providing auxiliary services, such as database access (the server).

client/server environment   an environment in which the interaction between application programs is based on client/server relationship. The client access the servers for services; the server responds to the client.

command   an action request given to the UNIX shell for execution.

command control loop   a loop in which a command is executed and the loop is iterated based on the exit status of the command. The `while` and `until` loops in the Korn shell are command control loops.

command-line arguments   the arguments (data) that a command needs to carry out the execution.

command-line editing   using an editor, such as **vi** or **emacs**, to recall and execute previous commands.

command mode   one of two modes in the **vi** editor. When **vi** is in the command mode, everything typed is interpreted as command. Contrast with *text mode*.

command parsing   breaking a command into separate words and interpreting them.

command substitution   the UNIX facility that converts the result of a command to a string.

comment   in a UNIX script, any line that starts with a pound sign (#).

compiler   a program that translates a high-level language into machine language.

complex command   a command made of several chained simple commands.

compound statement   a sequence of statements enclosed in braces. See also *block*.

computer language   any of the syntactical languages used to write programs for computers, such as machine language, assembly language, C, COBOL, and FORTRAN.

computer system   the set of computer components required for a complete system, consisting of at least an input device, an output device, a monitor, and a central processing unit.

conditional command   a command that combines several commands using `&&` and `||` operators.

conditional expression   an expression that evaluates to true or false.

concatenation   the joining of one string to the end of another to form a new string.

constant   a data value that cannot change during the execution of the program. Contrast with *variable*.

continue command   in **awk**, a statement that causes remaining code in a loop iteration to be skipped.

control character   a nonprintable character value whose function is to perform some operation, such as form feed, or that is used to indicate status, such as the start of a transmission.

conversion code   in **awk**, the code in the format specification that identifies the data type.

counter-controlled loop   in **awk**, a looping technique in which the number of iterations is controlled by a count. Contrast with *event-controlled loop*.

country domain address   an email address in which the last label is an abbreviation for the corresponding country.

CPU   See *central processing unit.*

current character   in an editor, the character at the cursor.

current directory   the working directory. The directory that a user is in at the present time.

current line   in an editor, the line that contains the cursor.

D

dangling else   a code sequence in a nested `if` statement in which there is no `else` statement for one of the `if` statements.

data block   in a UNIX file system, the block containing user data, directory files, symbolic link files, FIFO files, character block files, special files, and sockets.

data name an identifier given to data in a program.

data validation the process of verifying and validating data read from an external source.

debugging removing errors (bugs) from a program or a script.

decision statement a statement that tests a condition or the exit status of a command and based on the result selects one of the two sets of commands for execution.

default the entry point to the code that is to be executed if none of the case values match the `switch` expression.

descending sequence a sequence in decreasing order. Contrast with *ascending sequence.*

directory a file that contains the names and inodes of other files. A folder for grouping files.

directory level permission permission that allows users to access a directory.

dirname command a command that extracts the parent directory out of a path name.

disk an auxiliary storage medium used to store data and programs required for a computer.

distribution list a special mail file that is used to create substitute mail addresses for one or more addressees.

domain name address the part of an email address that defines the email server. In `forouzan@fhda.edu`, the domain name address is `fhda.edu`.

dot atom a single-character atom in a regular expression that matches any character.

dot command the command that allows the execution of a command in the current shell instead of creating a subshell.

do-while statement in **awk**, a loop in which the testing is done after each iteration.

drive an auxiliary storage device that can write and read data, such as the internal hard disk, a floppy disk, or a tape unit.

E

echo command the command that displays a string argument on standard output.

editing the process of creating and modifying a document.

editor a utility that allows the user to change the contents of a document. Two common UNIX editors are **vi** and **emacs**.

else-if a style (as opposed to syntax) convention used to implement a multiway selection for a nonintegral expression. Each expression in the series must evaluate the same variable.

end of file the condition that occurs when a read operation attempts to read after it has processed the last piece of data.

environment the setting for a process.

environment customization modification of a user's environment using environment files.

environment file a shell file that holds environmental variables that are to be exported to subshells and programs that run under the shell.

environmental variable a variable that determines the nature of the environment for a process.

EOF end of file. A flag set to indicate that a file is at the end.

error redirection the process by which the user specifies that errors are to be written to a file rather than standard error.

error stream the stream of characters that contains errors generated by a command.

escape character in UNIX, the backslash (\) character used to identify a special interpretation for the character that follows it.

eval command the command that evaluates another command twice, with the results of the first evaluation being used in the second.

event-controlled loop a loop whose termination is predicated upon the occurrence of a specified event. Contrast with *counter-controlled loop.*

ex mode the line-editing mode of the **vi/ex** editor.

exec command   the command that can be used to open files in a shell script.

executable file   a file that contains program code in its executable form.

executable script   See *executable file*.

execute permission   the permission of a file that changes the file to a command.

execute trace option (x)   an option that allows the debugging of a script.

exit command   the command that terminates a script.

exit status   the condition that shows if a command is executed successfully or not. If the exit status of a command script is 0, the command executed successfully.

export command   the command that allows the value of variables to be visible in subshells.

expr command   the command that evaluates a mathematical expression in a shell.

expression   a sequence of operators and operands that reduces to a single value.

expression statement   in **awk**, the use of an expression only to change a variable or a buffer; the value is discarded.

extended global regular expression print (egrep)   a version of the **grep** command in which more regular expression metacharacters are allowed.

F

false   the logical value used to indicate that an expression is not true.

fast global regular expression print (fgrep)   a version of the **grep** command that is faster than **grep** but does not allow the use of regular expressions.

field   the smallest unit of data that has meaning in describing information.

field specifier   in sort, a set of two numbers that together identify the first and last field in a sort domain.

field width   the number of characters in a field.

FIFO   First In, First Out. A waiting list mechanism in which the first entered in the list is

the first that is served. Contrast with *LIFO*.

FIFO file   a file that is used for interprocess communication. Also known as a named pipe.

file   a named collection of related data stored on an auxiliary storage device; in UNIX, the concept of files is extended to include system input (usually the keyboard) and system output (usually the monitor).

file expression   an expression that tests the status and attributes of a file.

file level permission   the permission that allows access to a file.

file operator   an operator used in a file expression.

file state   the operating condition of a file: read state, write, or error state.

file system   in UNIX, a disk or a portion of a disk structured to store data. A file system contains at least four sets of blocks: boot block, super block, inode block, and data blocks.

filename   the operating system name of a file on an auxiliary storage device.

filter   any command that gets its input from standard input stream, manipulates the data, and then sends them to standard output.

float   a single-precision floating-point type.

floating-point number   a number that contains both an integral and a fraction.

flowchart   a program design tool in which standard graphical symbols are used to represent the logical flow of data through a function.

for statement   in **awk**, a counter-controlled loop.

for-in statement   a list-controlled loop in the Korn shell.

for-in command   See *for-in statement*.

foreach command   a list-controlled loop in the C shell.

foreground job   a job that is executing in the foreground and controlling the standard input/output. See *foreground processing*.

foreground processing   a program or utility that is running under the control of the user.

Only one foreground program can run at a time. Contrast with *background processing.*

fork the facility by which the currently executing process (the parent) creates a new process (the child).

format string in **awk**, the first parameter in a formatted input or output function used to describe the data to be read or written.

formatted input/output in **awk**, any of the standard library functions that can reformat data to and from text while they are being read or written.

forwarding mail the process that sends received mail to someone else.

function a named block of code that performs a task within a program.

function body the code within a function that is contained in the function's definition and statement sections.

function call a statement that invokes another function.

function header in a function definition, that part of the function that supplies the return type, function identifier, and in some cases, formal parameters. Contrast with *function body.*

G

generic domain address the type of email address in which the last label defines the nature of the organization. The addresses ended in com, edu, and so on are generic domain addresses.

getline function the command in **awk** that gets the next line in the file, overriding the normal flow of the process.

getopts command the command in the Korn shells that handles options.

global regular expression print (grep) a powerful utility that is used to search a file using regular expressions.

global substitute function a function in **awk** that substitutes all occurrences of a string with another string.

greedy pattern matching the pattern matching deployed by a regular expression.

In greedy matching, a pattern matches as many characters as it can.

group a named collection of users sharing resources in a system.

group id the unique number that defines a group of users in a system.

groups command a command that changes the group association of a file.

H

hard copy any computer output that is written to paper or other readable media such as microfiche. Contrast with *soft copy.*

hard link a file attribute that allows a file to be referred by more than one name in a file system.

hardware any of the physical components of a computer system, such as a keyboard or a printer.

here document a form of standard input with double brackets (<<) that allows the input to the command to be part of the command itself.

hexadecimal a numbering system with base 16. Its digits are 0 1 2 3 4 5 6 7 8 9 A B C D E F.

history command the command that allows the reexecution of previous commands.

history file a special UNIX file that contains a list of commands used during a session.

hold space a **sed** buffer that allows the temporary storage of the contents of the pattern space. See *pattern space.*

HOME/home the shell or environmental variable that holds the pathname of the home directory.

home directory the directory that a user is in when he or she first logs into the system.

hot key a keyboard command that is effective immediately; that is, it is effective without an Enter or Return being keyed.

I

identifier the name of an object. In UNIX, identifiers can consist only of digits, letters, and the underscore.

index function the function that finds the

position of a substring in a string.

infinite loop   a loop that does not terminate.

initialization   the process of assigning values to a variable at the beginning of a program or a function.

inode   a structure in a disk that holds the attributes and address of files.

inode block   in a UNIX file system, the block containing information about each file on the disk.

input device   a device that provides data to be read by a program.

input redirection   the process by which the user specifies that input is to be read from a file rather than standard input. See also *output redirection*.

input statement   the statement that allows a script to read data from the terminal or a file.

instruction   a command or a statement.

interpreter designator line   the line that starts with #! and the pathname of the shell interpreter. It should be the first line of any shell script.

integer   an integral number; a number without a fractional part.

interrupt   an event that causes the kernel to transfer control to an error processing function in the currently executing program or to terminate its execution if no handler is provided.

IP   Internet Protocol. Together with TCP forms the standard Internet protocols.

iteration   a single execution of the statements in a loop.

J

job   a line of commands.

job control   a feature that allows moving jobs between background and foreground.

job number   a number given to a job by a system.

K

kernel   the heart of the UNIX system, containing the two most basic parts of the operating system, process control and resource

management.

key   one or more fields that are used to identify a record (structure).

keyboard   an input device used for text or control data that consists of alphanumeric keys and function keys.

keyboard file   See *standard input stream*.

keyword   a UNIX identifier that has been defined by a system and cannot be used by users for named objects.

Korn shell   the shell created by David Korn at the AT&T Labs.

L

leading characters   the characters at the beginning of a string.

leading fields   the fields at the beginning of a record or line.

left justification   the orientation of variable-length data in an output format such that the first data character is at the left end of the print area. Contrast with *right justification*.

length function   the function in **awk** that finds the length of a string.

let command   the Korn shell command that accepts integers and mathematical operators as arguments and performs mathematical calculations.

LIFO   Last In, First Out. A waiting list mechanism in which the last entered in the list is the first that is served. Contrast with *FIFO*.

line   in **vi**, all of the text beginning with the first character after a newline to the next newline.

line editor   an editor that modifies a file a line at a time. The **ex** editor is an example of a line editor.

link   a logical relationship between an inode and a file that relates the name of a file to its physical location.

list-controlled loop   a loop that iterates as long as there is an item in a list. The `for-in` and `foreach` loops are list-controlled loops.

literal   an unnamed constant coded in an expression.

local address   the part of the email address that defines the user name in the computer.

local host   a computer connected to the user terminal without going through the Internet.

local login   a login to a local computer. Contrast with *remote login.*

logical data   data whose values can be only true or false.

logical expression   an expression containing logical operators.

logical operator   one of the three operators (&&, ||, and !) used in a logical expression.

login   the process that, if successful, allows the user to access the system resources.

login name   the name used by a user to access a system. The list of authorized login name is held in /etc/passwd file. See *user ID.*

login shell   the shell that the user is in after logging into the system.

LOGNAME   a shell or environmental variable that holds the login name of a user.

logout   the process that disconnects the user from the system.

loop   repeating a set of commands.

loop control expression   the expression in a loop statement that is used to determine if the body of the loop is to be executed.

loop piping   receiving the input to a loop from the output of a command.

loop redirection   redirecting the result of a loop to a file.

loop statement   the statement that repeats a set of commands.

loop update   the code within a loop statement or body that changes the environment such that the loop will eventually terminate.

M

mail command   the command that allows the reading and sending of mail.

MAIL/mail   a shell or environmental variable that stores the pathname of the mailbox for the user.

mailbox   a text file that holds the incoming mail for the user.

main memory   See *memory.*

mask   an octal code that defines the default permissions of a file or directory.

mathematical expression   a combination of mathematical operators and operands.

mathematical operator   one of the operators such as +, -, *, /, and % that allows manipulation of numbers.

memory   the main memory of a computer consisting of random access memory (RAM) and read-only memory (ROM); used to store data and program instructions.

merge   to combine two or more sequential files into one sequential file based on a common key and structure format.

monitor   the visual display unit of a computer system, usually a video display device.

multiprocessing   an operating system facility that allows multiple programs to execute concurrently.

multiuser system   a system that allows more than one user to access a system at the same time.

multiway selection   a selection statement that is capable of evaluating more than two alternatives. In the C shell, the switch statement. Contrast with *two-way selection.*

N

natural language   any spoken language.

nested address   an address inside another address.

nested if statement   an if statement coded as either the true or false statement within another if.

nested if-then-else   See *nested if statement.*

nested loop   a loop contained within another loop.

networking   connecting computers together for the purpose of sharing hardware and software resources.

next statement   the statement in **awk** that ignores the rest of the code in a script and reads the next record for processing.

noclobber option the option that does not allow the destroying (clobbering) of an existing file in redirection unless it is overridden by the | operator in the Korn shell or the ! operator in the C shell.

noglob option an option that does not allow wildcard expansion.

null command the command that does nothing. It is only a placeholder.

null else the absence of a false statement in an if statement.

O

object designator in **vi**, a mark or a token that indicates the type of object and the direction of the endpoint.

octal a numbering system with a base of 8. The octal digits are 0 1 2 3 4 5 6 7.

octal code permission codes in the octal number system. An octal code is made of three octal digits such as 777 or 751.

one-dimensional array an array with only one level of indexing.

onintr command the command in the C shell that handles interrupts.

open operating system an operating system whose interface specifications are published and freely available to the computing community.

operand the object in a statement on which an operation is performed. Contrast with *operator*.

operating system the software that controls the computing environment and provides an interface to the user.

operator the syntactical token representing an action on data (the operand). Contrast with *operand*.

option a string starting with a – or + sign that changes the default behavior of a command.

or operator (||) a binary logical operator with the property that if any of the operands are true, the expression is true.

ordered list a list in which the elements are arranged so that the key values are placed in ascending or descending sequence.

ordinary file See *regular file*.

output device a device that can be written but not read in the current state of a file.

output redirection the process by which the user specifies that output is to be written to a file rather than standard output. See also *input redirection*.

output statement any shell command that writes to the monitor or a file.

P

paragraph in **vi**, a range of text starting with the first character in the file buffer or the first character after a blank line (a line consisting only of a newline) to the next blank line or the end of the buffer.

parameter a value passed to a command when it is executed from the shell command line.

parent directory the directory above the current directory or the referred directory in the directory hierarchy.

parse a process that breaks a string into its component parts according to a predefined syntax.

parsing pathname breaking a pathname to a dirname and a basename.

password a secret code needed for accessing a system during the login process.

password file a file containing information including the encrypted password about each user.

PATH/path a shell or environmental variable that contains a list of directories that the shell uses to find a command.

pattern a set of characters to be matched.

pattern space a buffer in the **sed** utility that holds a line of text while it is being processed.

permission code a combination of characters or digits defining the access permission to a file or directory.

personal computer (PC) a computer designed for individual use.

personal environment an environment involved with only one personal computer.

personal profile file   the Korn startup file in a user's home directory that contains commands and variable settings that are used to configure the shell. It is run after the *system profile file* at startup time.

pipe   a UNIX utility that joins two utilities by connecting the output of the first to the input of the second.

portability   a software attribute that addresses the ease with which a system can be moved to other hardware environments.

positional parameter   a parameter whose usage is determined only by its position in an argument list.

POSIX   Portable Operating System Interface. A standard based on UNIX.

posttest loop   a loop in which the terminating condition is tested only after the execution of the loop statements. Contrast with *pretest loop*.

predefined variable   a variable whose name is already defined by the system.

pretest loop   a loop in which the terminating condition is tested before the execution of the loop statements. Contrast with *post-test loop*.

primary storage   See *memory*.

print command   the output command in the Korn shell.

printable character   a character value that is associated with a printable graphic.

printer   an output device that displays the output on paper.

printf   the formatted output command used in **awk**.

process   a running program.

process id   a unique integer defining a process.

processing unit   See *central processing unit*.

profile file   a file that contains commands and variable settings that are used to configure a shell.

prompt   a token displayed by the shell to tell the user that it is ready to accept a command; in the C shell, the variable that holds the primary prompt. The default is a percent (%).

PS1   in the Korn shell, the variable that holds

the primary prompt. The default is a dollar sign ($).

PS2   in the Korn shell, the variable that holds the second prompt in a shell. The default is a greater than sign (>).

PS3   in the Korn shell, the variable that holds the third prompt in a shell.

PS4   in the Korn shell, the variable that holds the fourth prompt.

pseudoterminal driver   a piece of software that simulates the characteristics of a terminal on the remote host.

Q

quoting   the process of using one of the quotes characters (backslash, single quotes, or double quotes) to remove the special meaning of a single character or a group of characters.

R

range pattern   in **awk**, a pattern that selects a range of lines.

read command   the command in the Korn shell that inputs data from the keyboard or a file.

read permission   in files, the permission that allows the user to read or copy a file. In directories, the permission that allows the user to use the list command or copy a file from the directory.

read-only variable   a variable whose contents cannot be changed.

realtime   processing in which updating takes place at the time the event occurs.

recursion   a feature of some UNIX commands that starts processing from a directory and successively applies the processing to all directories under the start directory.

redirecting error   See *error redirection*.

redirecting input   See *input redirection*.

redirecting output   See *output redirection*.

redirection   the process by which the user specifies that one or more files are to be used rather than the standard input or output files. See also *input redirection* and *output redirection*.

regular expression a pattern consisting of a sequence of characters to be matched against text.

regular file a file containing user data that needs to be available for future processing. Also known as an ordinary file.

relational expression an expression that compares two values and returns a logical value.

relational operator one of the operators, such as greater than or less than, used to compare two numbers or two strings.

relative pathname the pathname relative to the current directory. A relative pathname should not be started with a slash (/). Contrast with *absolute pathname*.

remote host the host accessed through the Internet. Contrast with *local host*.

remote login a login to a computer via the Internet. Contrast with *local login*.

repeat command the **vi** or **emacs** command used to specify how many times a command is to be executed.

repetition operator a regular expression operator that repeats the previous atom or atoms. \{m, n\}, *, ?, and + are examples of repetition operators.

reserved words the set of words in UNIX that has a predetermined interpretation and cannot be used in the definition of an object.

return the **awk** or Korn shell statement that causes the execution of a function to terminate.

return code the value sent back to the calling function by a called function.

right justification the orientation of variable length data in an output format such that leading null values are inserted and the last data character is at the right end of the print area. Contrast with *left justification*.

root the superuser login name.

root directory the top-most directory in a file system. It is defined by a slash (/).

S

save operator a regular expression operator that saves text for later backward reference.

screen editor an editor that uses the cursor to edit text on the screen. Contrast with *line editor*.

script an executable file that contains shell commands that perform a useful function.

scrolling moving a part of the text down or up relative to its position on the screen.

search the process that examines a list to locate one or more elements containing a designated value known as a search argument.

secondary storage See *auxiliary storage*.

security the quality factor that addresses the ease or difficulty with which an unauthorized user can access data.

selection statement a statement that chooses between two or more alternatives. In shell programming, the if. . .else or switch statements.

sendmail the common implementation of email in UNIX.

sentence in **vi**, a range of text that ends in a period followed by two spaces or a newline.

sequence operator in a regular expression, the operator that combines two or more atoms in sequence. The sequence operator is "nothing," which means that the lack of an operator between any two atoms is interpreted as a sequence operator.

sequenced commands a combination of two or more commands separated by a semicolon.

sequential file a file structure in which data must be processed serially from the first entry in the file.

server in a client/server system, the computer that provides services to the clients.

session the lapse of time between a login and logout.

set command the command that (1) sets options in all shells and (2) stores values in variables in the C shell.

set-of-line address in **sed** and **awk**, an address that defines every line that matches a pattern.

setting a variable storing a value in a variable.

shell the UNIX utility that also receives and interprets user commands.

SHELL the environmental variable that holds the pathname of the login shell.

shell environment the configuration of a shell as determined by environmental variables.

shell program See *script.*

shell script See *script.*

shift command the command that deletes one or more positional parameters at the beginning of the parameter list and moves the remaining parameters forward to fill the deleted values.

shutdown files shell scripts that are executed at logout time.

signal a flag sent from the kernel to an executing process to notify it that some external event has occurred and must be processed.

single-character atom an atom that can match only one character.

single-line address an address that can select only one line for execution.

sleep command the command that allows a script to wait.

snail mail the U.S. Post Office or any of the value-added carriers that deliver mail non-electronically.

socket a special file that is used for network communication.

soft copy computer output written to a non-permanent display such as a monitor. Contrast with *hard copy.*

soft link a file attribute that allows a file to be referenced by more than one name in one or different file systems.

software the application and system programs, including their documentation and any required procedures, necessary to accomplish a task.

sort the process that orders a list or file.

sort key the data that control the sequence of the list.

sort pass a process by which the sort command sorts a file based on the contents of a specific field.

source command in the C shell, the command that allows the execution of another command in the current shell. Compare with *dot command* in the Korn shell.

special parameter any of the parameters, such as $0, $#, and $*, predefined in a shell script.

splat a term for an asterisk (*).

square brackets the [and] symbols.

squeeze to replace a set of identical consecutive characters by only one of them.

standard error stream the stream that is generated by a command because of an error condition.

standard input stream the stream that feeds characters to a command.

standard output stream the stream that contains the characters generated by a command.

standard streams the input, output, and error streams.

startup files the files that are executed automatically when a shell starts.

startup scripts See *startup files.*

statement in UNIX, synonymous with command.

stream the sequence of characters in time.

stream editor a line editor.

string a sequence of characters.

string comparison the process by which two strings are evaluated for equality or inequality.

string length the number of characters in a string.

subshell a shell created by another shell using the fork function.

substitute function in **awk**, a function that allows the substitution of part of a string with another substring.

substring part of a string.

substring function in **awk**, a function that allows the extraction of part of a string.

super block in a UNIX file system, the block containing information about the file system itself.

superuser any user with system administration permission in UNIX. The home directory of a superuser is the root directory.

switch command See *switch statement*.

switch statement a statement in a C shell that allows the choice between different command sequences based of the value of a string.

symbolic code the use of codes in the **chmod** command that allows the user to set or change the file or directory permission. Contrast with *octal code*.

symbolic link file a file that contains the pathname of another file.

syntax the "grammatical" rules of a language. In shell programming, the set of keywords and formatting rules that must be followed when writing a script.

system profile file a Korn startup file located in the /etc directory that contains commands and variable settings that are used to configure the shell. It is run at startup time before the *personal profile file*.

system security the security level that allows access to the system.

system software any software whose primary purpose is to support the operation of the computing environment. Contrast with *application software*.

system variable in **awk**, one of 14 variables that is used to control the operation of the utility. Contrast with *user-defined variable*.

T

tape storage an auxiliary storage medium that stores data as a sequential file on a magnetic recording surface.

TCP Transmission Control Protocol. An Internet protocol. See also *IP*.

TCP/IP the standard Internet protocol. See *IP* and *TCP*.

tee a command that creates two separate outputs, one on the screen and one in a file.

TERM the environmental variable that holds the type of the user terminal.

terminal driver the software that controls the terminal.

terminal file a file that represents the user terminal.

text editor software, such as a word processor or a source program editor, that maintains text files.

text file a file in which all data are stored as characters. Contrast with *binary file*.

text mode one of two modes in the **vi** editor. When **vi** is in the text mode, everything typed is interpreted as text. Contrast with *command mode*.

text object a section of text between two points, one of which must be the cursor.

time-sharing environment an operating system concept in which more than one user has access to a computer at the same time.

token a syntactical construct, often a single character, that represents an entity (such as a directory), operation (such as equal), or flag (such as an option).

trap command the command that handles an interrupt.

trash file a file that is used to delete the result of a command. Its name is /dev/null.

two-way selection a selection statement that is capable of evaluating only two alternatives. The if. . .else statement. Contrast with *multiway selection*.

U

uniform resource locator a symbolic Internet address. Also known as URL.

unsetting a variable the process of setting a variable to a null state.

until command a command-controlled loop in the Korn shell that executes a command and, if the exit status of the command is nonzero, then executes the body of the loop.

URL See *uniform resource locator*.

user/USER the C shell variable that holds the name of the user.

user-defined function any function written by the programmer, as opposed to a standard library function.

user-defined variable in **awk**, any of an unlimited number of variables used in a script. Contrast with *system variable*.

user id a unique integer defining each user in the system.

user mask the set of permission codes that determines the default permissions for a file or directory when it is created.

user prompts monitor messages to a user that request the user to input one or more values.

utility a standard UNIX program that provides a support process for users.

V

value the contents of a variable.

variable a memory storage object whose value can be changed during the execution of a program. Contrast with *constant*.

variable access the process of reading a value stored in a variable; the result is an expression value that is the same as the stored value.

variable substitution the use of a parameter or variable value to create a string to be used in another command.

verb the part of a command that defines the action to be taken. A command is made of a verb, options, and arguments.

verbose option the option that causes each statement in a script to be printed before it is executed.

W

while command See *while statement*.

while statement in **awk**, a pretest loop. In the Korn shell, a command-controlled loop. In the C shell, an expression-controlled loop.

whitespace a collective term for the space, vertical and horizontal tabs, newline, and form-feed characters.

wildcard a special character used by a shell to match a group of filenames with a single expression. The commonly used wildcards are * and ?.

wildcard expansion the process by which multiple filenames are matched by a single expression that contains wildcards.

word in **vi**, a series of non-whitespace characters terminated by a whitespace character.

working directory See *current directory*.

write permission in a file, the permission to change the contents of the file. In a directory, the permission to copy or create a file under that directory.